TATTOOS
TATOUAGES
TÄTOWIERUNGEN
TATOEAGES

© 2010 **booQs**publishers bvba
Godefriduskaai 22
2000 Antwerp
Belgium
Tel: 00 32 3 226 66 73
Fax: 00 32 3 226 53 65
www.booqs.be
info@booqs.be

ISBN: 978-94-60650-369
WD: D/2010/11978/037
(Q055)

Editor & texts: Paz Diman
Art direction: Mireia Casanovas Soley
Design and layout coordination:
Emma Termes Parera
Layout: Esperanza Escudero
Cover art: SANTANA XIII TATUAJES "NACIDO Y
CRIADO EN EL SUR"
Translation: Cillero & de Motta

Editorial project:

maomao publications
Via Laietana, 32, 4.º, of. 104
08003 Barcelona, Spain
Tel.: +34 932 688 088
Fax: +34 933 174 208
maomao@maomaopublications.com
www.maomaopublications.com

Printed in China

TATTOOS
TATOUAGES
TÄTOWIERUNGEN
TATOEAGES

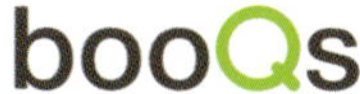

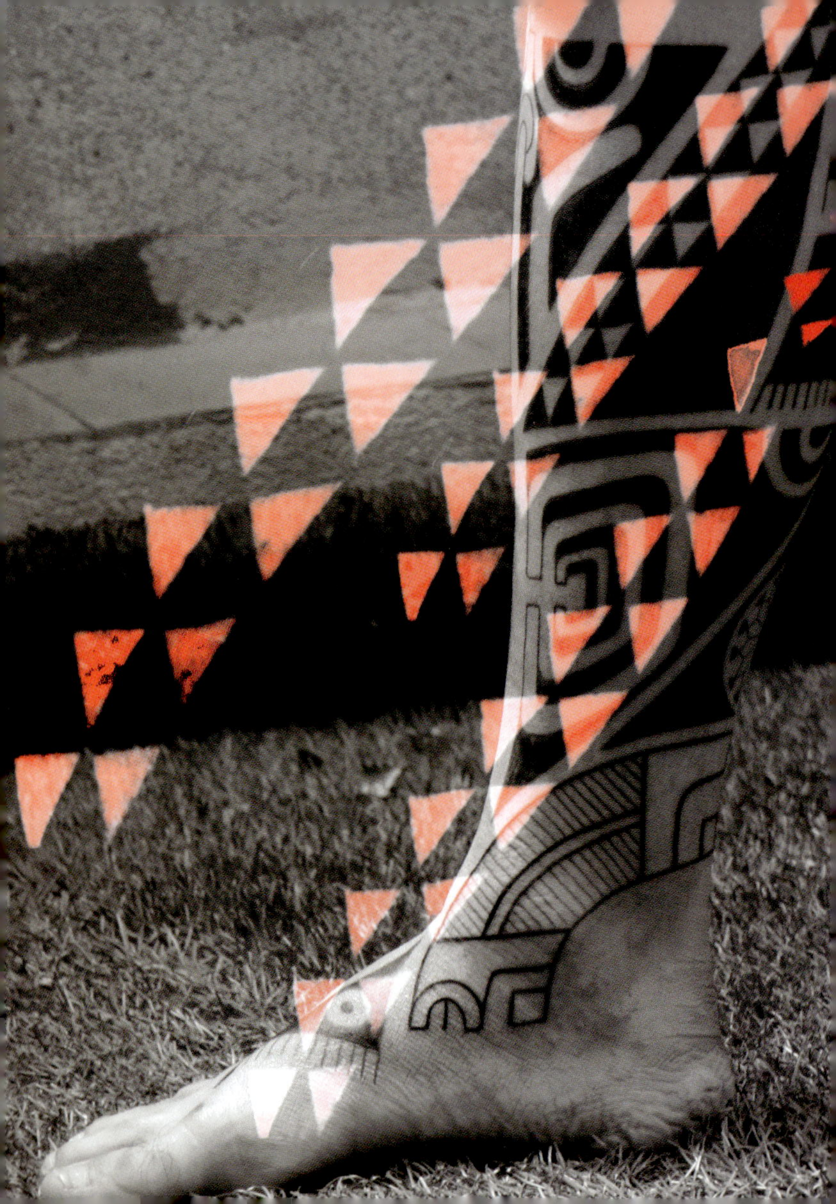

CONTENTS

The history of tattoos dates back 5000 years. In ancient Egypt the tradition of decorating the skin was already being practiced. The process was slow and painful and was generally performed on females. It is possible that the first tattoos had a mystical or magical significance since they appear to have only have been performed on priestesses. In fact, the most famous tattooed mummy is the priestess Amunet, who had several dots and lines on her body.

In some tribal cultures that created their designs by cutting the skin and smearing the wound with ash or ink, tattoos represented courage and maturity. Among the natives of Central America, body drawings of images of gods were common and for early American cultures, tattoos were a unique mark that would help the soul overcome the obstacles on the road towards death.

The Japanese tattoo, which arrived to the western world when trade routes were opened around the year 1000, was reserved to mark those who had committed serious crimes. The punishment was so severe, that individuals with tattoos were rejected by their families. The emperor Matsuhito, who tried to give the impression of a "modern" society, banned the practice as he associated with "savagery."

Navigation also shed new light on the art forms that the inhabitants of Borneo and Java had marked on their skin In the eighteenth century, sailors led by the legendary Captain Cook returned from their travels covered with this ancient art form, and thus, creating the classic association between sailors and tattoos. This also strengthened the connection between tattoos and crime, as those who embarked for long periods often did so to escape the law.

Today almost 150 years after the establishment of the first tattoo studio in New York and 120 years after the invention of the first tattoo machine, drawings on the skin are becoming more accepted by contemporary society. Alternative cultures gave the impetus to their popularity, and today, tattoos are not only linked to personal stories, but also the artistic skill of those who perform them. The book is a collection of the most recent work of these new artists who transform the tradition of marking the skin and, without doubt, elevate it to the status of art.

L'histoire du tatouage remonte à plus de 5000 ans. Au temps de l'ancienne Égypte, la tradition de décorer la peau existait déjà. Le processus était lent, très douloureux et généralement pratiqué par les femmes. Il est possible que ces premiers tatouages aient été liés à une signification mystique ou magique car ils semblent avoir été réservés aux prêtresses. D'ailleurs, la momie tatouée la plus célèbre est celle de la prêtresse Amunet, plusieurs points et lignes ayant été observés marquant son corps.

Au sein de certaines cultures tribales qui créaient leurs dessins en coupant la peau et en oignant la blessure avec de la cendre ou de l'encre, les tatouages représentaient le courage et la maturité. Pour les habitants natifs d'Amérique centrale, les dessins sur le corps d'images de dieux étaient habituels et pour les premières cultures nord-américaines, les tatouages étaient une marque unique qui aiderait l'âme à franchir les obstacles dans son chemin vers la mort.

Le tatouage japonais, qui est entré au sein du monde occidental à partir de l'ouverture de routes commerciales autour de l'an 1 000, était réservé pour marquer les personnes qui avaient commis un délit grave. Le châtiment était considéré si terrible que les individus portant des tatouages étaient rejetés par leurs familles. Tentant de donner l'impression d'une société

« moderne », l'empereur Mutsuhito a interdit cette pratique en l'associant à de la « sauvagerie ».

La navigation permit également de découvrir les formes artistiques que les habitants de Bornéo et de Java portaient sur leur peau. Au XVIII siècles, les marins avec à leur tête le mythique Capitaine Cook revinrent de leurs voyages couverts par cet art millénaire et c'est ainsi qu'est née l'association classique entre marins et tatouages. Cela a également renforcé le lien entre les tatouages et la délinquance, car ceux qui s'embarquaient pendant aussi longtemps le faisaient souvent pour fuir la justice.

Aujourd'hui, quasiment 150 ans après l'établissement du premier studio de tatouage à New York et 120 ans après l'invention de la première machine de tatouage, les dessins sur la peau sont de plus en plus acceptés par la société contemporaine. Les cultures alternatives ont donné l'impulsion nécessaire à leur popularisation et à ce jour, les tatouages sont non seulement liés à des histoires personnelles mais également à l'adresse artistique de la personne les réalisant. Ce livre est une collection des travaux les plus récents de ces nouveaux artistes qui transforment la tradition de marquer la peau et qui l'élèvent sans aucun doute à la catégorie d'art.

Die Geschichte der Tätowierung geht auf mehr als 5.000 Jahre zurück. Bereits im antiken Ägypten praktizierte man die Tradition der Hautverschönerung. Der Prozess war langwierig und äußerst schmerzhaft und wurde im Allgemeinen von Frauen ausgeführt. Möglich ist, dass diese ersten Tätowierungen an eine mystische oder magische Bedeutung geknüpft waren, denn scheinbar waren sie allein Priesterinnen vorbehalten. In der Tat ist die bekannteste tätowierte Mumie die der Priesterin Amunet, an der man verschiedene Punkte und Striche, die ihren Körper markierten, erkennen kann.

In einigen Stammeskulturen, die durch Einschnitte in die Haut und Auftragen von Asche oder Tinte auf die Wunden Zeichnungen kreierten, waren Tätowierungen Symbole für Mut und Reife. Unter den Ureinwohnern Mittelamerikas waren Körperbemalungen von Göttern weit verbreitet und für die ersten nordamerikanischen Kulturen stellten Tätowierungen eine nicht zu wiederholende Markierung dar, die ihrer Seele helfen sollte, die Hindernisse auf dem Weg zum Tod zu überwinden.

Die japanischen Tätowierungen, die mit der Öffnung der Handelsrouten um das Jahr 1000 auch ihren Einzug in die westliche Welt hielt, waren für das Brandmarken derjenigen vorbehalten, die schwere Straftaten begangen hatten. So fürchterlich schien diese Bestrafung, dass Personen mit Tätowierungen von ihren Familien verstoßen wurden. Kaiser Matsuhito trachtete danach, der Gesellschaft einen „modernen" Eindruck zu verleihen und verbot diesen Brauchtum, das er mit der „Barbarei" verband.

Auch die Schifffahrt hat den künstlerischen Formen, die Bewohner von Borneo und Java auf ihrer Haut trugen, ihren Stempel aufgedrückt. Im 18. Jahrhundert kamen die Seeleute unter der Anführung des berühmt-berüchtigten Kapitän Cook von ihren Reisen voller jahrtausendealter Motive zurück, und so begann die klassische Assoziierung zwischen Seemännern und Tätowierungen. Dies verstärkte noch die gedankliche Verbindung zwischen Tätowierungen und der Unterwelt, denn viele, die damals lange Zeit auf See fuhren, taten dies, um von der Justiz zu flüchten.

Heute beinahe 150 Jahre nachdem das erste Tattoo-Studie in New York eröffnete und 120 Jahre nach Erfindung der ersten Tätowiermaschine finden die Hautzeichnungen immer größere Akzeptanz innerhalb der modernen Mainstream-Gesellschaft. Die Alternativkulturen gaben den notwendigen Anstoß zu ihrer Popularisierung und heutzutage weisen Tätowierungen nicht nur eine Verbindung zu persönlichen Geschichten auf, sondern sagen viel über die künstlerische Geschicklichkeit der Tätowierer. Dieses Buch ist eine Sammlung von jüngsten Werken dieser neuen Künstler, die die Tradition des Brandmarkens der Haut verwandelt und zweifelsohne in die Kategorie der Kunst erhoben haben.

De geschiedenis van de tatoeage gaat terug tot meer dan 5.000 jaar geleden. Al in het Oude Egypte werd de traditie van het versieren van de huid beoefend. Het proces was langzaam en erg pijnlijk en werd over het algemeen uitgevoerd door vrouwen. Het is mogelijk dat deze eerste tatoeages een mystieke of magische betekenis hadden, aangezien ze voorbehouden leken te zijn aan priesteressen. De bekendste getatoeëerde mummie is dan ook die van priesteres Amunet, wier lichaam wordt gemarkeerd door verschillende punten.

In sommige tribale culturen, die hun ontwerpen creëerden door in de huid te snijden en de wond met as of inkt in te smeren, stonden tatoeages voor moed en volwassenheid. Onder de inboorlingen van Midden-Amerika waren de tekeningen op het lichaam veelal afbeeldingen van goden en voor de eerste Noord-Amerikaanse culturen vormden tatoeages een uniek merkteken, dat de geest hielp om de hindernissen op weg naar de dood te overwinnen.

De Japanse tatoeage, die in de westerse wereld zijn entree deed sinds het onstaan van de handelsroutes rond het jaar 1.000, was gereserveerd om degenen die ernstige delicten hadden gepleegd, te merken. Deze straf was blijkbaar zo erg, dat personen met tatoeages door hun families werden verstoten. In een poging om de indruk van een "moderne" samenleving te creëren, verbood Keizer Matsuhito deze praktijken, omdat die volgens hem gelijk stonden aan "barbaarsheid".

Ook de zeevaart liet een nieuw licht schijnen op de kunstvormen die de inwoners van Borneo en Java op hun huid gemarkeerd hadden. In de 18de eeuw kwamen zeelieden, onder leiding van de mythische Kapitein Cook, van hun reizen terug vol met deze eeuwenoude kunst. Zo onstond de klassieke associatie tussen zeelieden en tatoeages. Dit versterkte tevens het verband tussen tatoeages en criminaliteit, aangezien personen die voor lange tijd aan boord gingen, dat meestal deden omdat ze op de vlucht waren voor justitie.

Thans is het bijna 150 jaar geleden dat de eerste tatoeagestudio in New York werd opgericht en 120 jaar dat de eerste tatoeagemachine werd uitgevonden. Vandaag de dag zijn tekeningen op de huid steeds meer door de maatschappij geaccepteerd. De alternatieve culturen gaven de nodige impuls voor de popularisering daarvan en tegenwoordig zijn tatoeages niet alleen meer verbonden aan persoonlijke geschiedenissen, maar ook aan de artistieke vaardigheid van degenen die ze maken. Dit boek bevat een collectie van de meest recente werken van deze nieuwe artiesten, die de traditie van het merken van de huid transformeren en deze ongetwijfeld verheffen tot de categorie kunst.

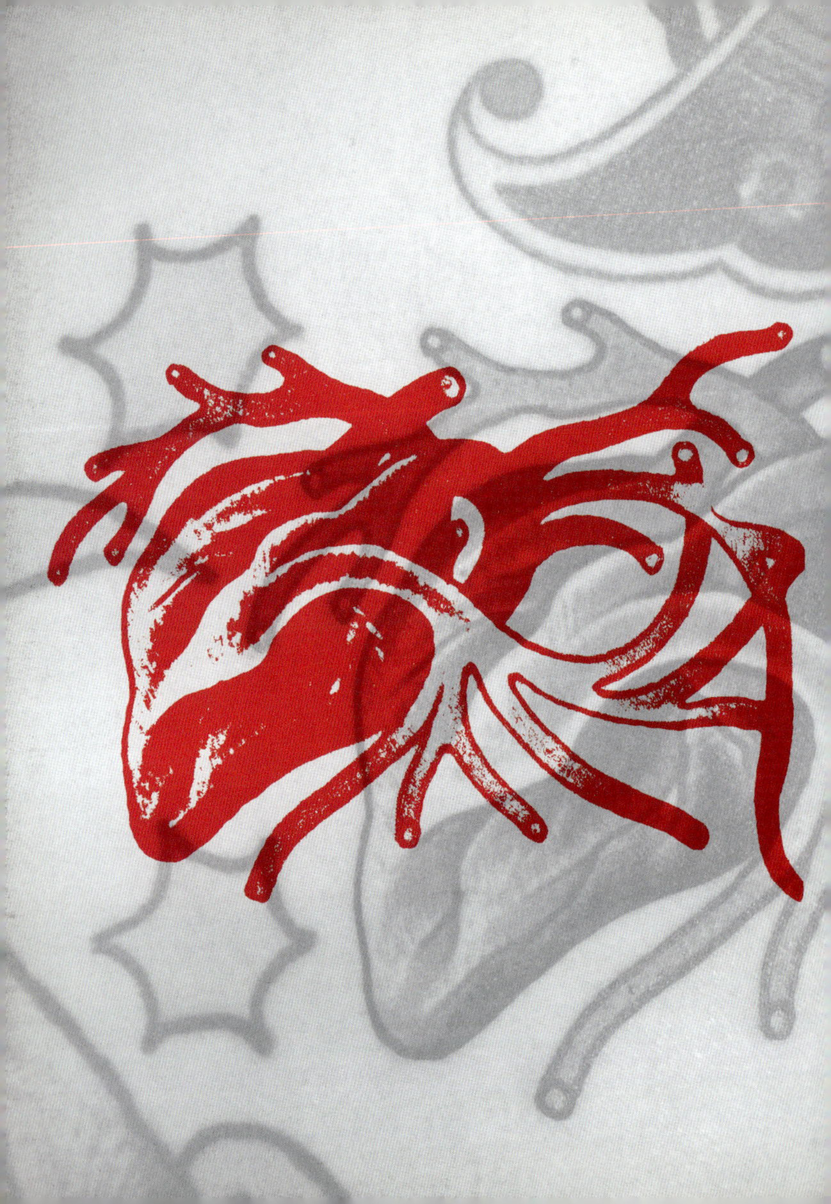

Traditional American

Traditionnel américain

Traditionell amerikanisch

Traditioneel Amerikaans

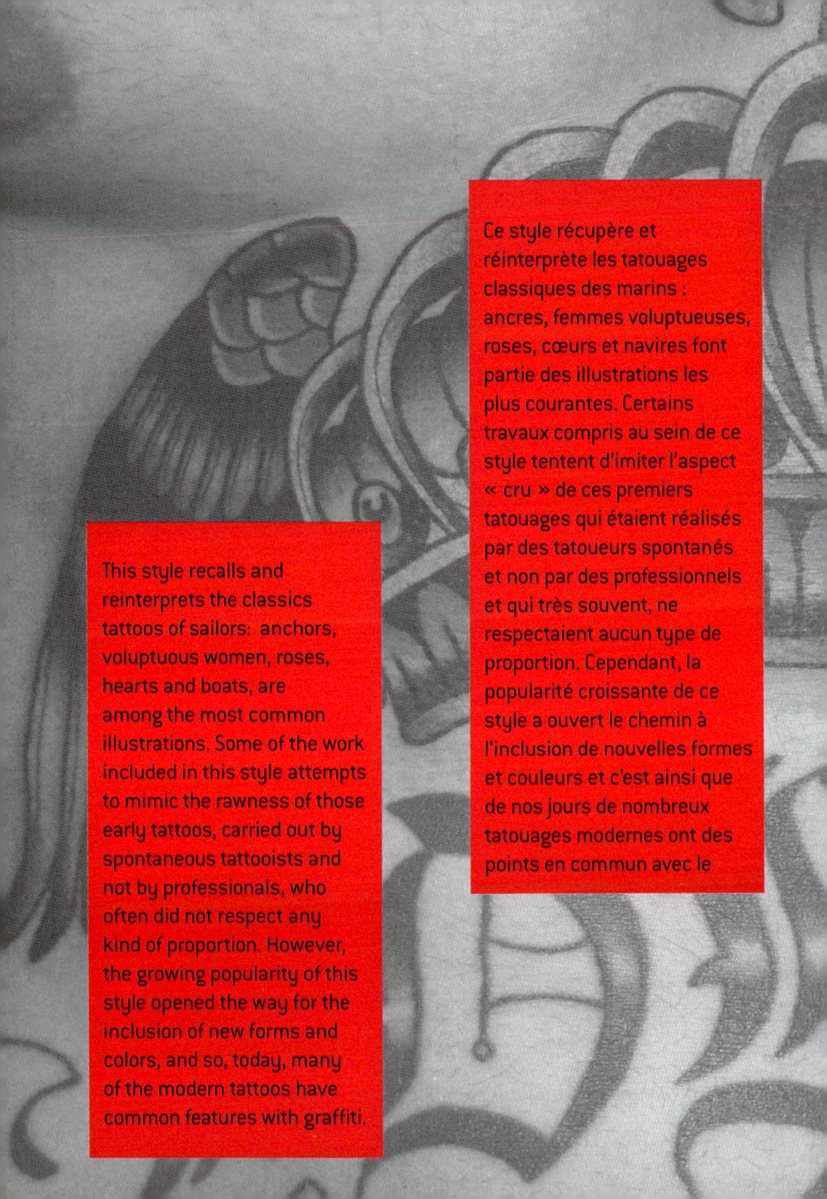

This style recalls and reinterprets the classics tattoos of sailors: anchors, voluptuous women, roses, hearts and boats, are among the most common illustrations. Some of the work included in this style attempts to mimic the rawness of those early tattoos, carried out by spontaneous tattooists and not by professionals, who often did not respect any kind of proportion. However, the growing popularity of this style opened the way for the inclusion of new forms and colors, and so, today, many of the modern tattoos have common features with graffiti.

Ce style récupère et réinterprète les tatouages classiques des marins : ancres, femmes voluptueuses, roses, cœurs et navires font partie des illustrations les plus courantes. Certains travaux compris au sein de ce style tentent d'imiter l'aspect « cru » de ces premiers tatouages qui étaient réalisés par des tatoueurs spontanés et non par des professionnels et qui très souvent, ne respectaient aucun type de proportion. Cependant, la popularité croissante de ce style a ouvert le chemin à l'inclusion de nouvelles formes et couleurs et c'est ainsi que de nos jours de nombreux tatouages modernes ont des points en commun avec le

Diese Stilrichtung holt die klassischen Tätowierungen der Seeleute wieder zum Vorschein und interpretiert diese neu: Anker, Frauen mit Kurven, Rosen, Herzen und Schiffe sind einige der häufigsten Motive. Verschiedene der hier gezeigten Arbeiten dieses Stils versuchen, die Rauheit dieser ersten Tätowierungen nachzuahmen, die durch selbst ernannte und nicht professionelle Tätowierer ausgeführt wurden und häufig keinerlei Proportionen wahrten. Die immer größere Beliebtheit dieses Stils hat aber auch dazu geführt, dass nun der Weg zum Einsatz neuer Formen und Farben geebnet wurde, und so haben heute viele moderne Tattoos nicht wenige Gemeinsamkeiten mit Graffitis.

Deze stijl haalt de klassieke zeemanstatoeages terug en herinterpreteert ze: ankers, wulpse vrouwen, rozen, harten en boten zijn enkele van de meest voorkomende afbeeldingen. Enkele van de werken die onder deze stijl vallen proberen de rauwheid te immiteren van deze eerste tatoeages, die spontaan werden gezet door onprofessionele tatoeëerders, waarbij de proporties vaak helemaal niet werden gerespecteerd. De groeiende populariteit van deze stijl maakte echter de weg vrij voor de opkomst van nieuwe vormen en kleuren, en zo komt het dat veel van de moderne tatoeages punten gemeen hebben met de graffiti.

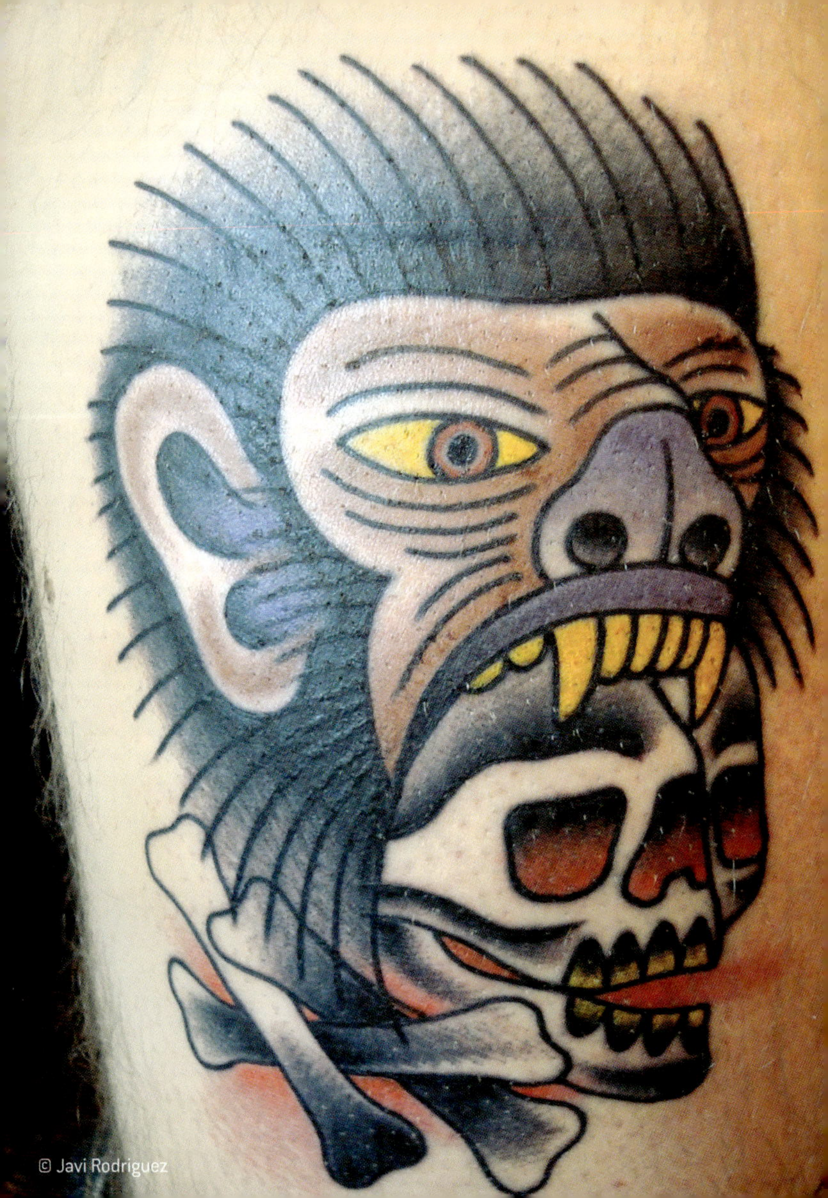

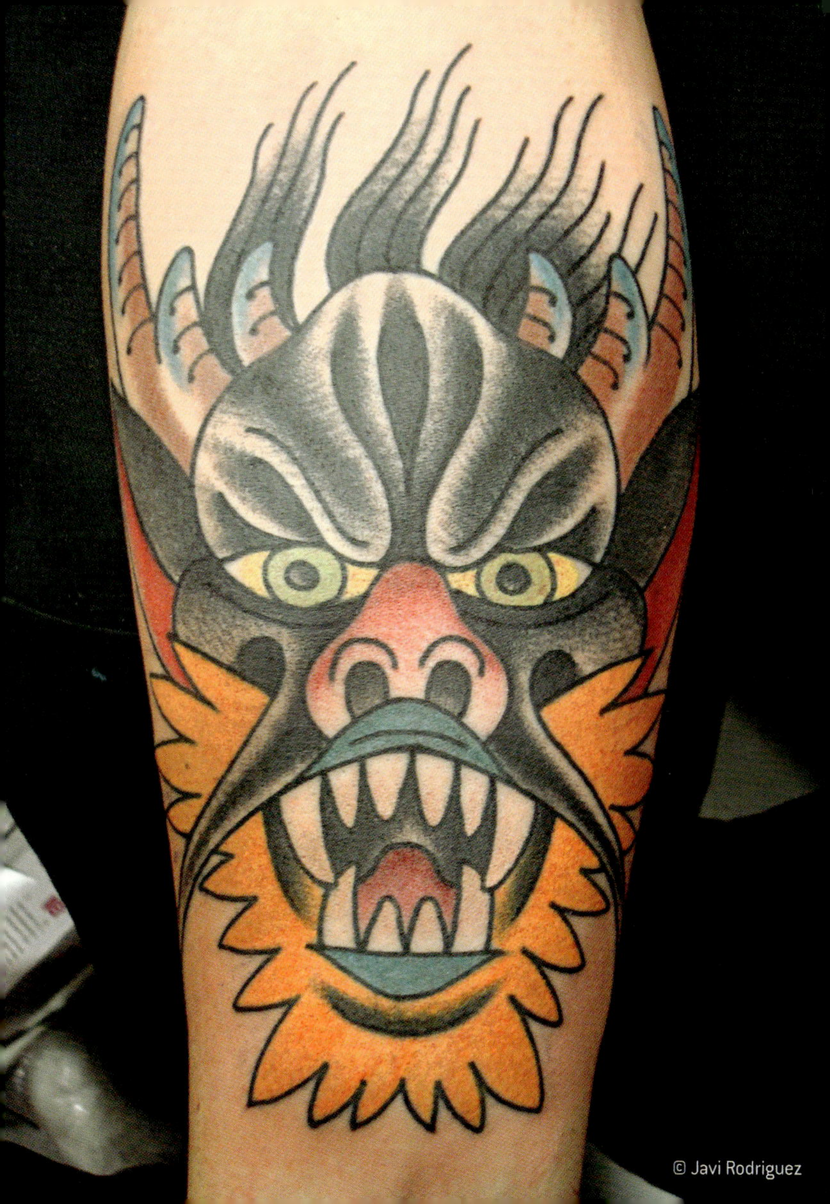
© Javi Rodriguez

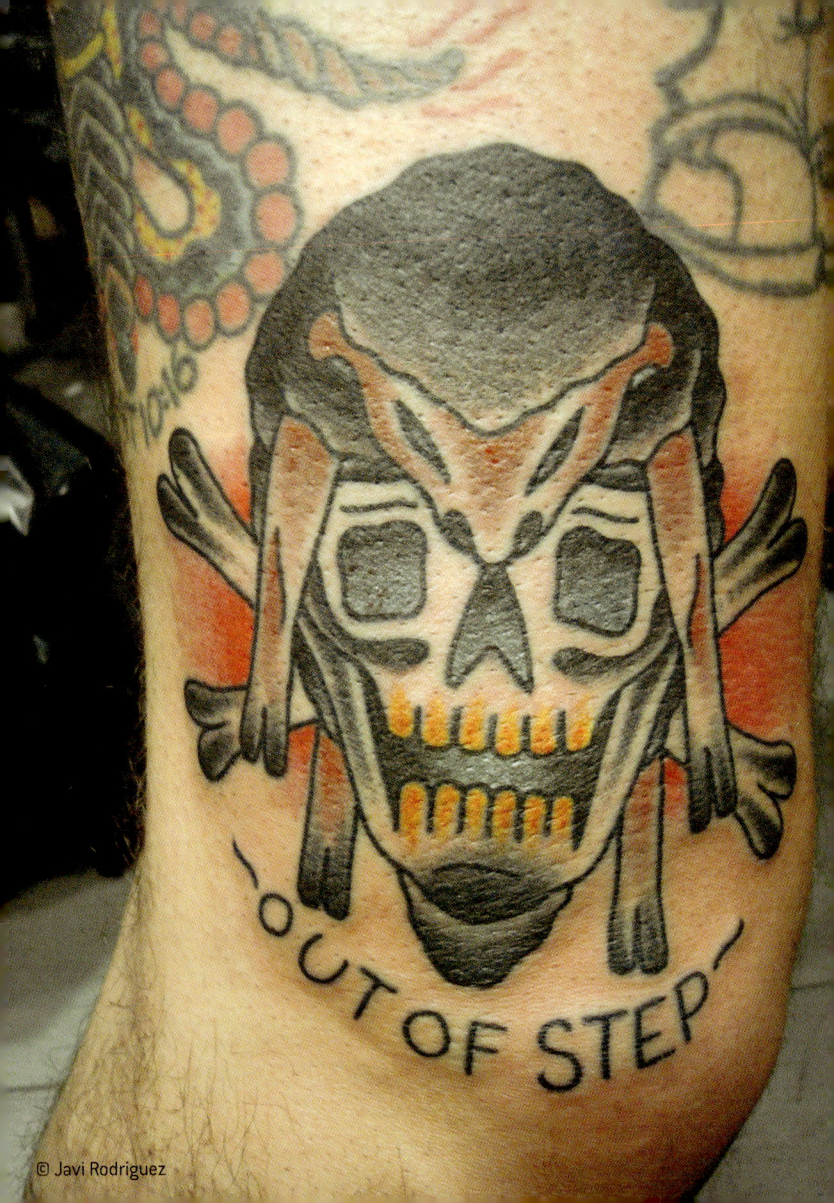
OUT OF STEP

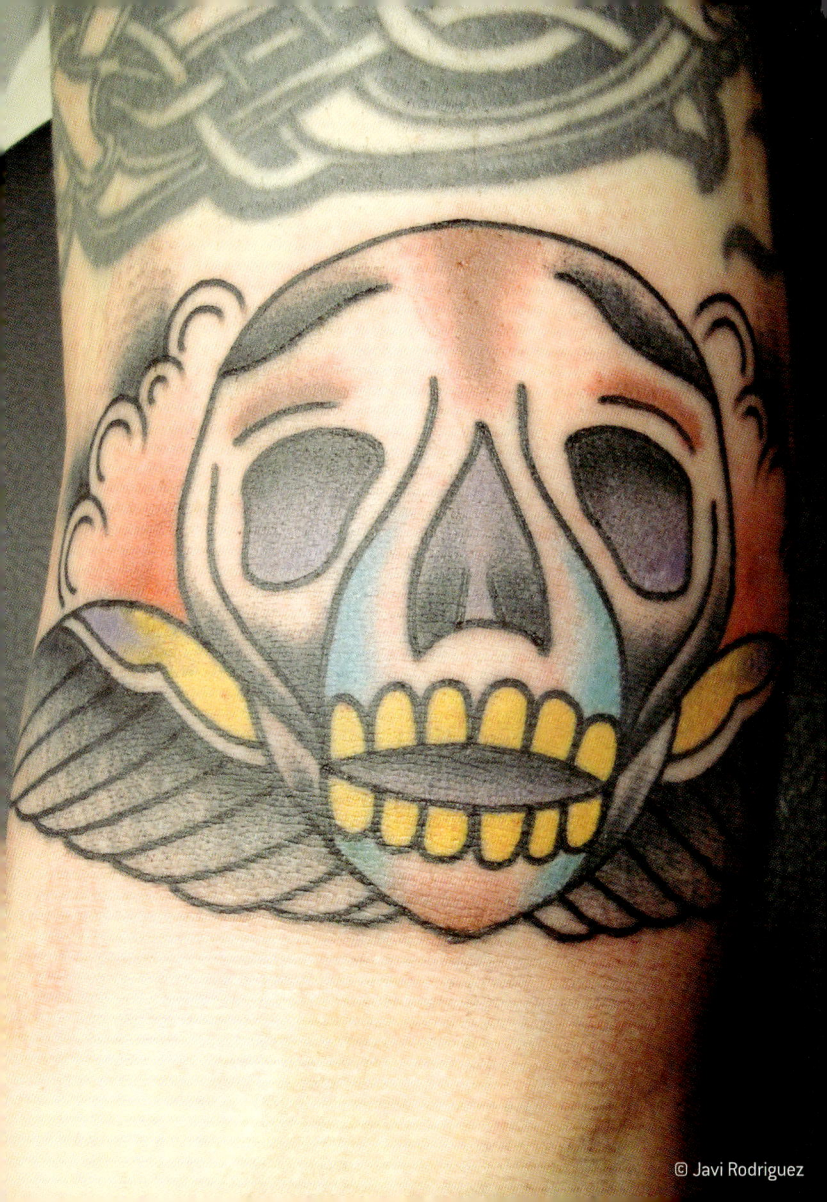
© Javi Rodriguez

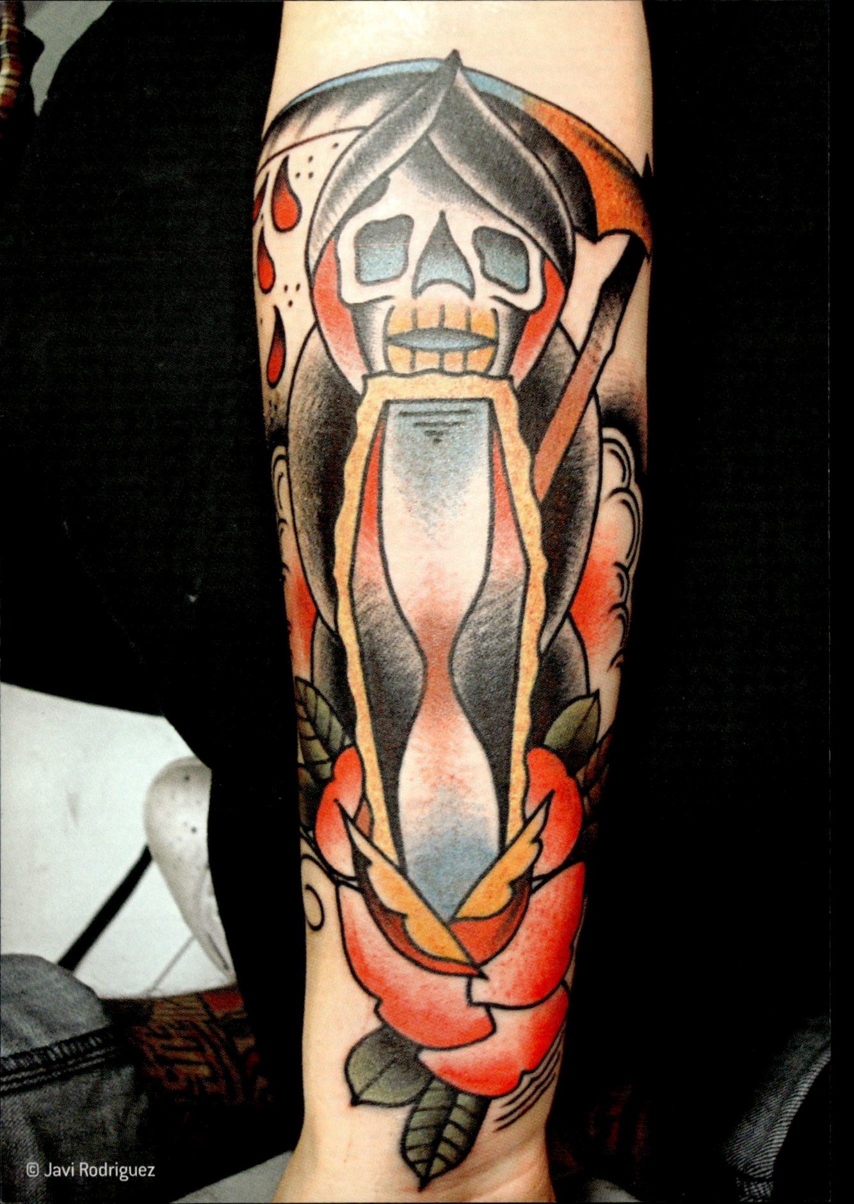

© Javi Rodriguez

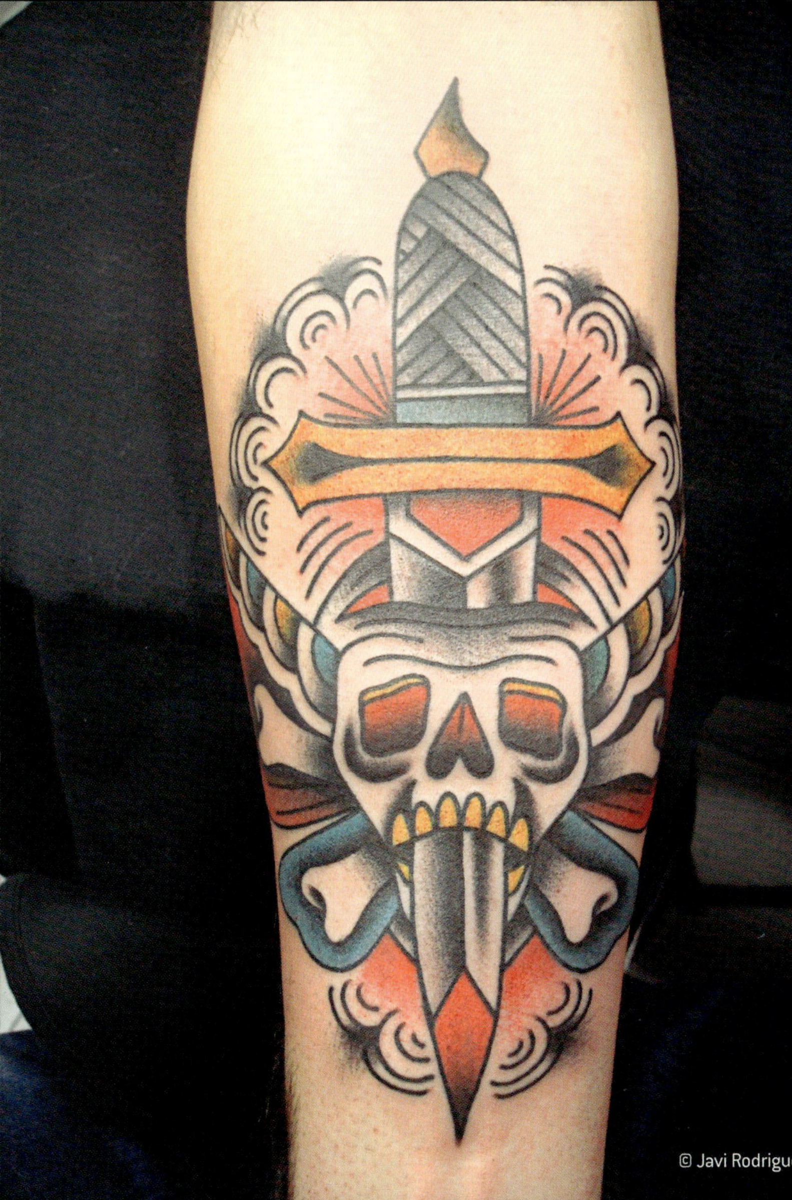
© Javi Rodrigu

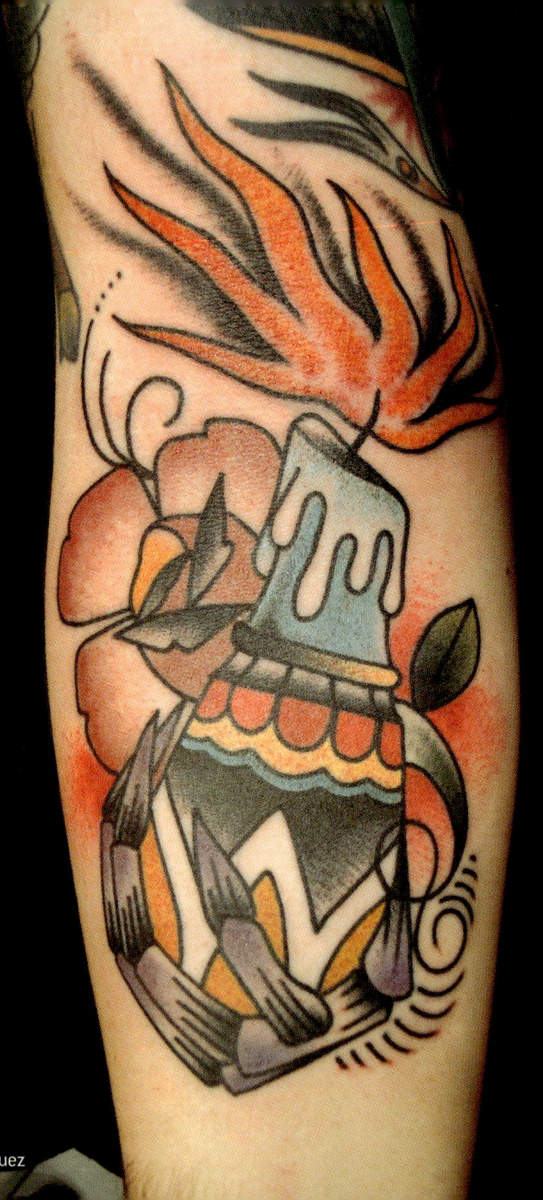

© Javi Rodriguez

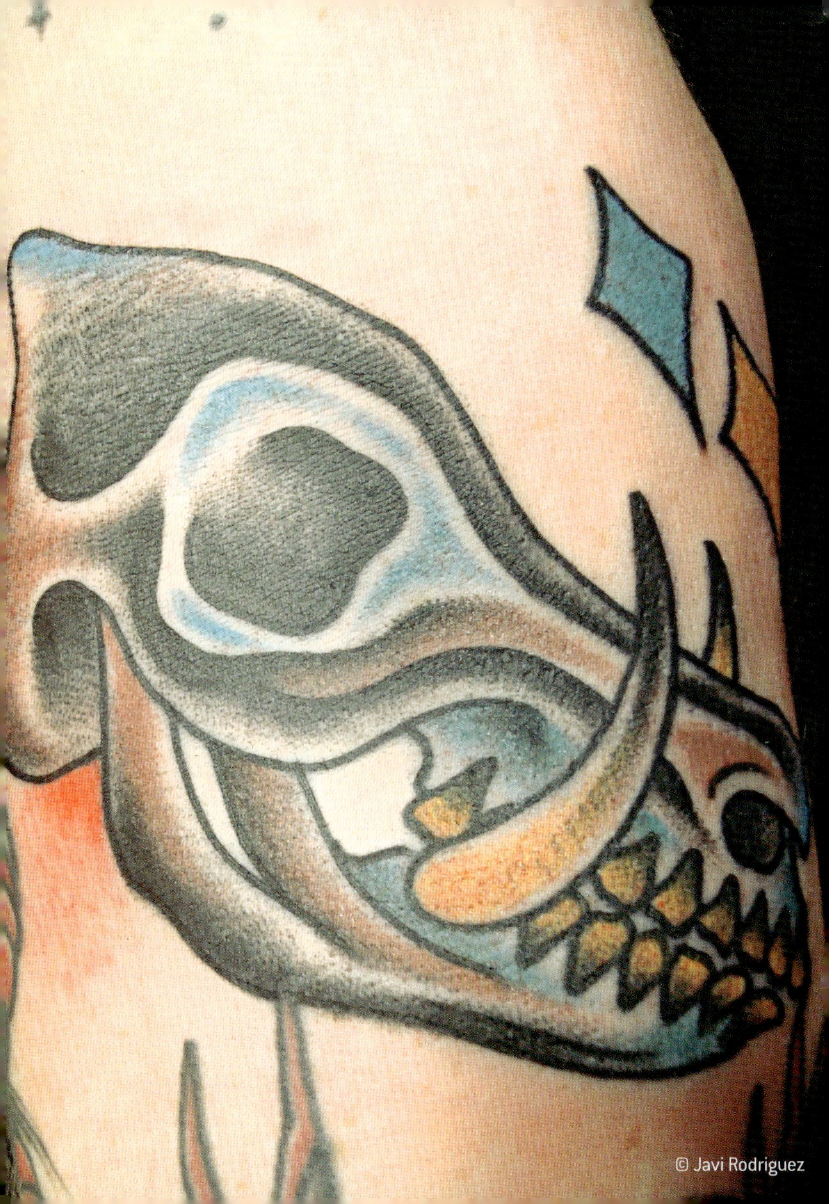
© Javi Rodriguez

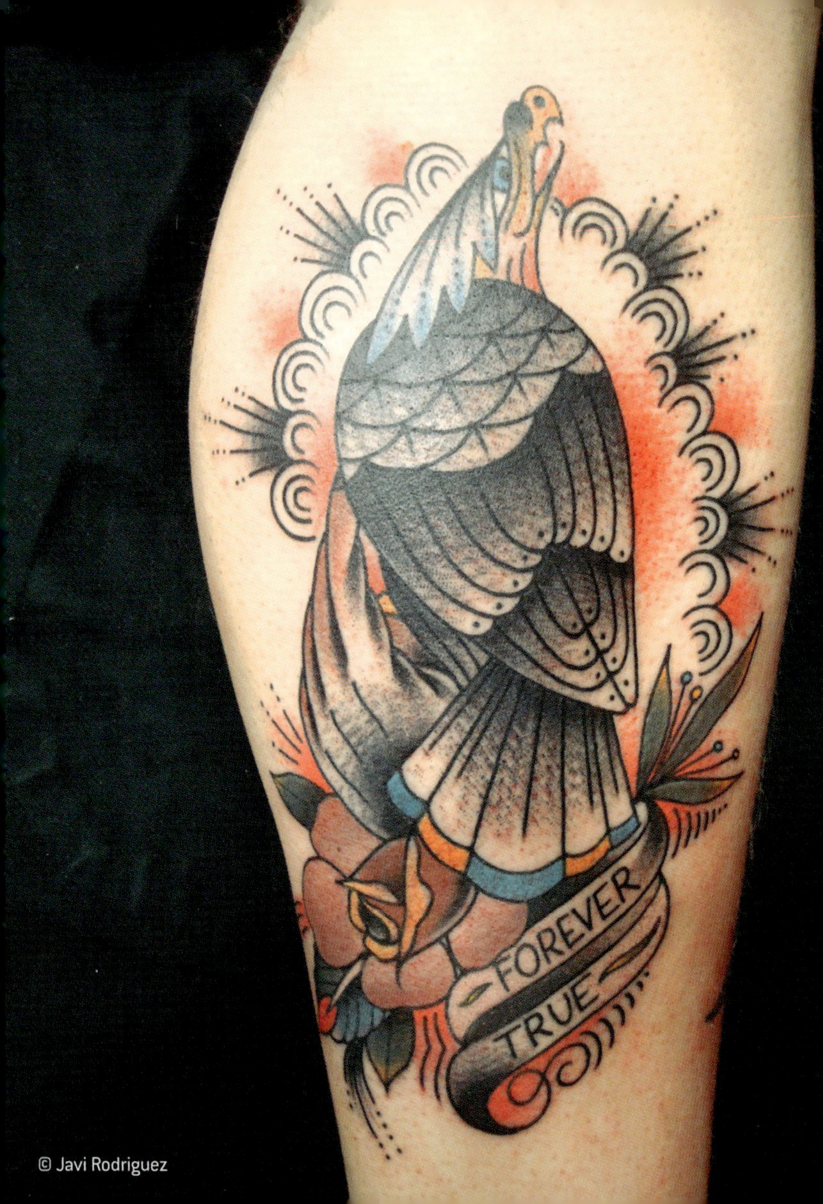

FOREVER
TRUE

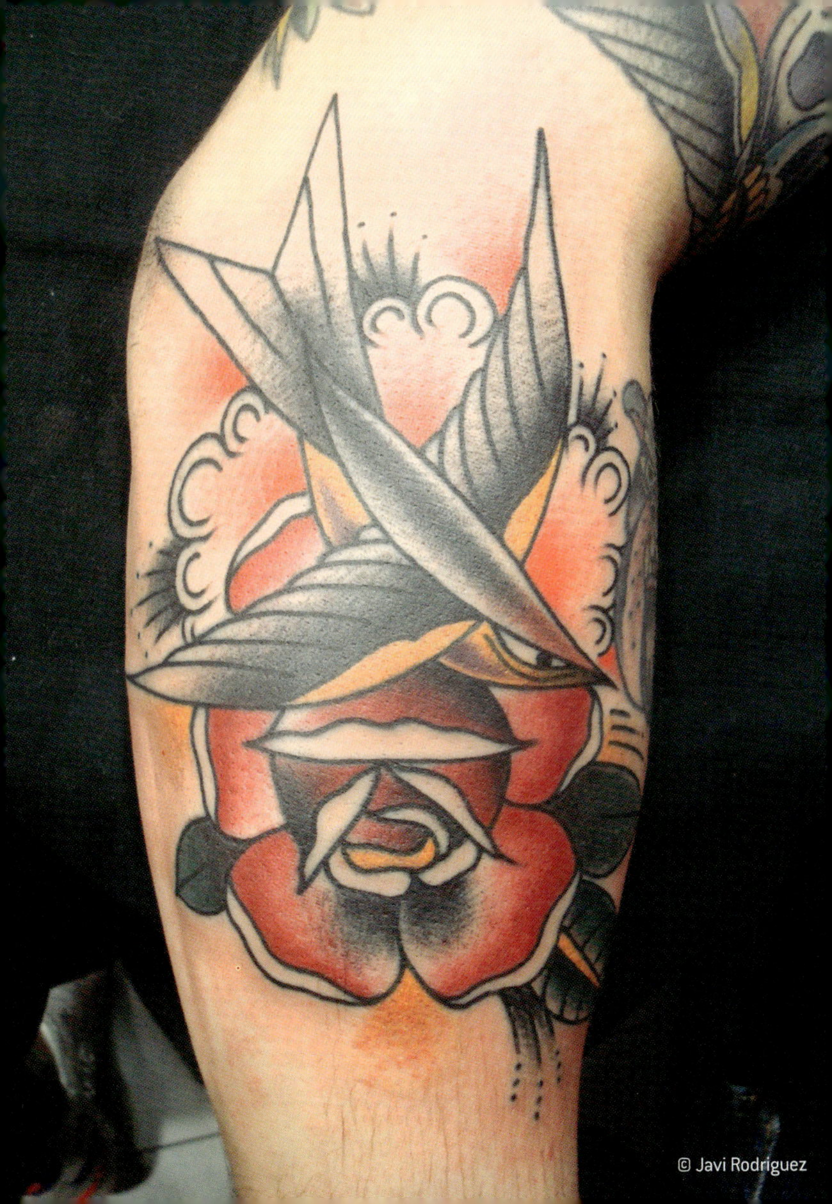
© Javi Rodriguez

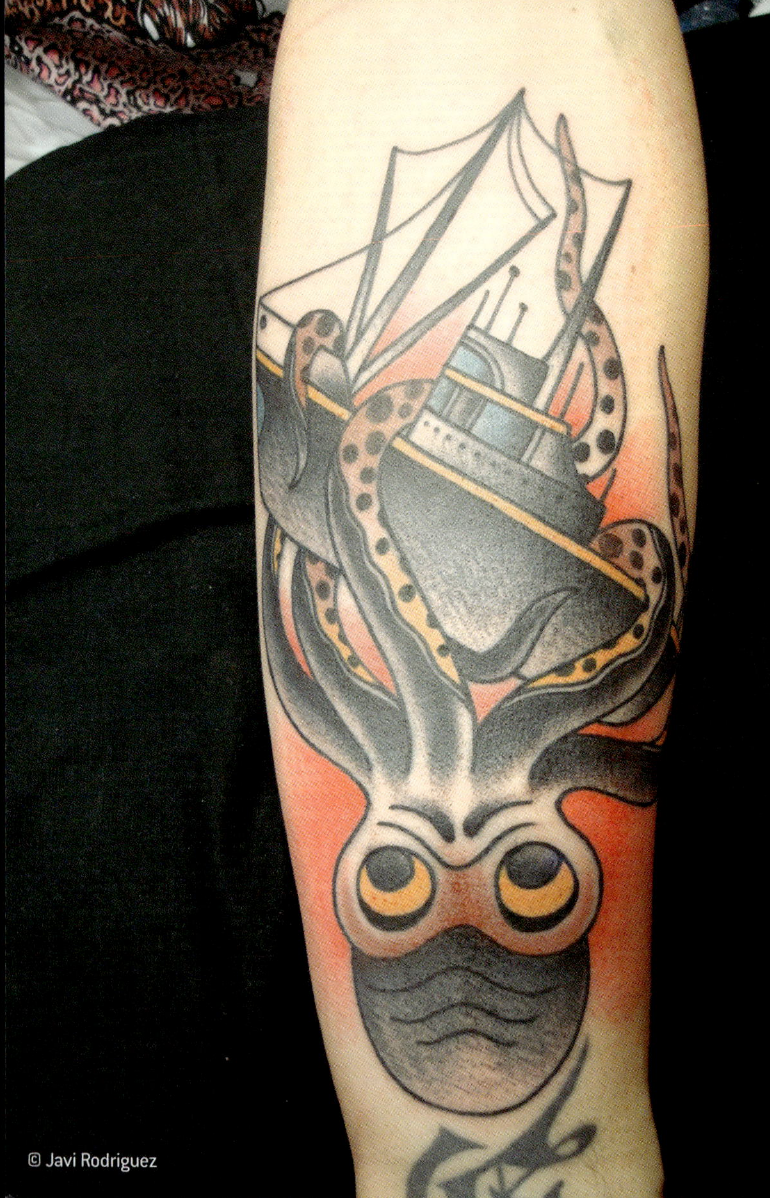

© Javi Rodriguez

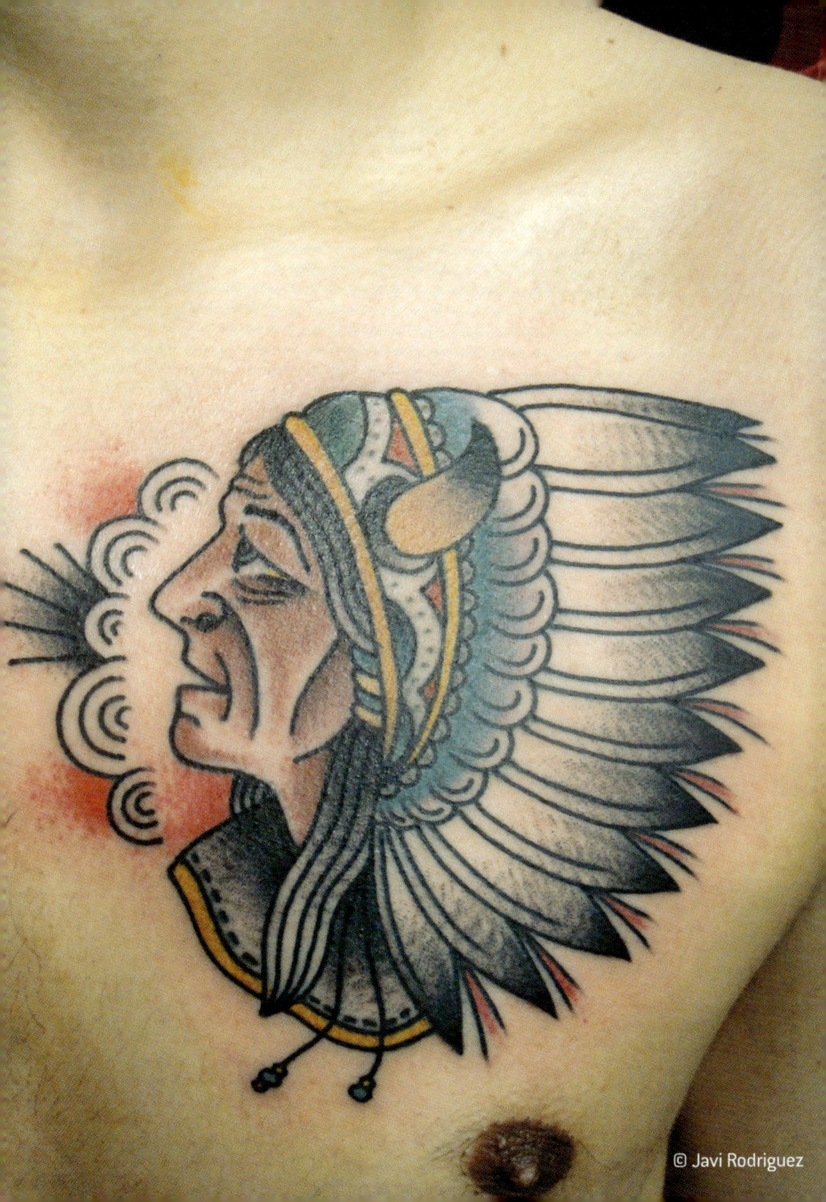
© Javi Rodriguez

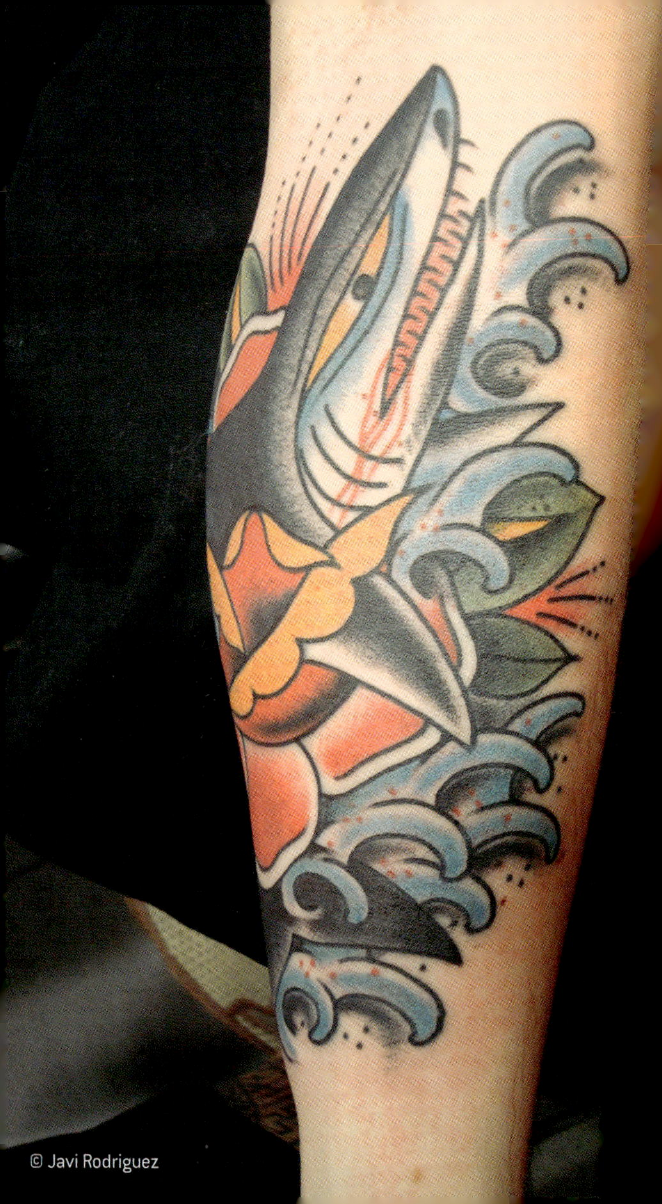

© Javi Rodriguez

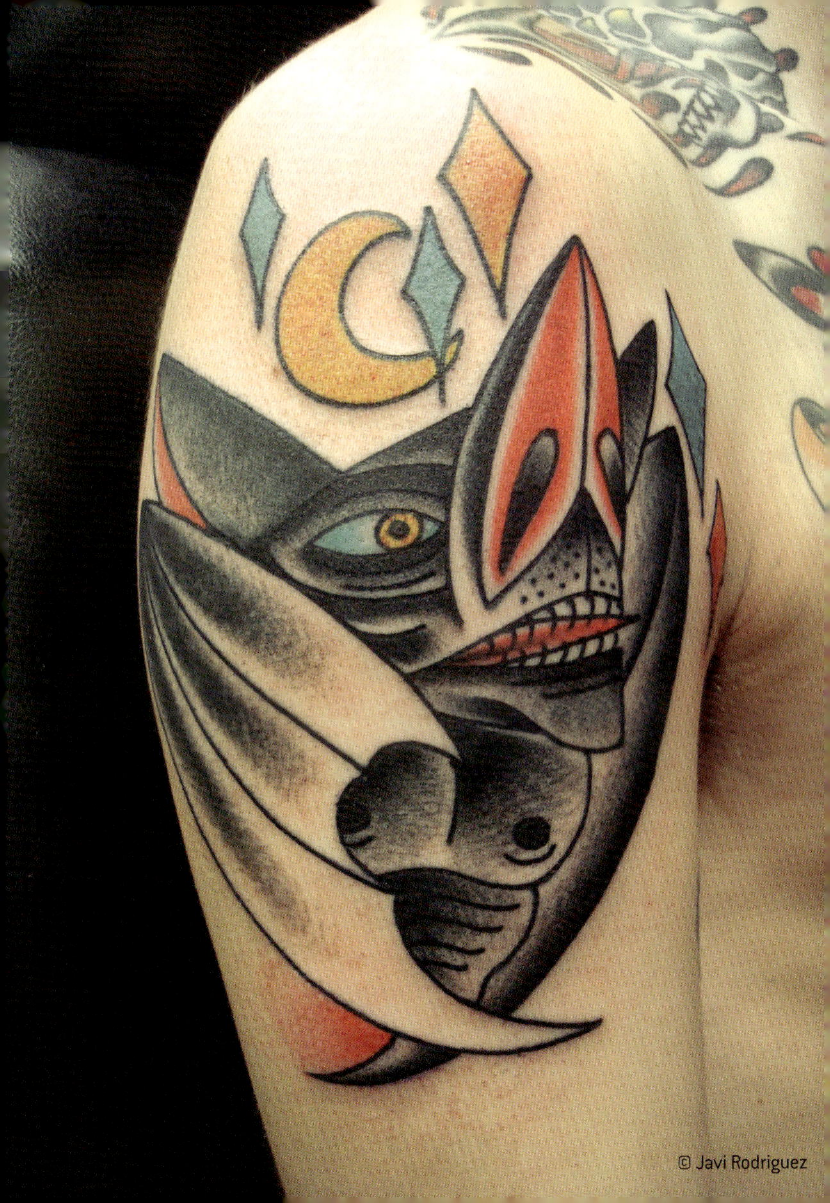

© Javi Rodriguez

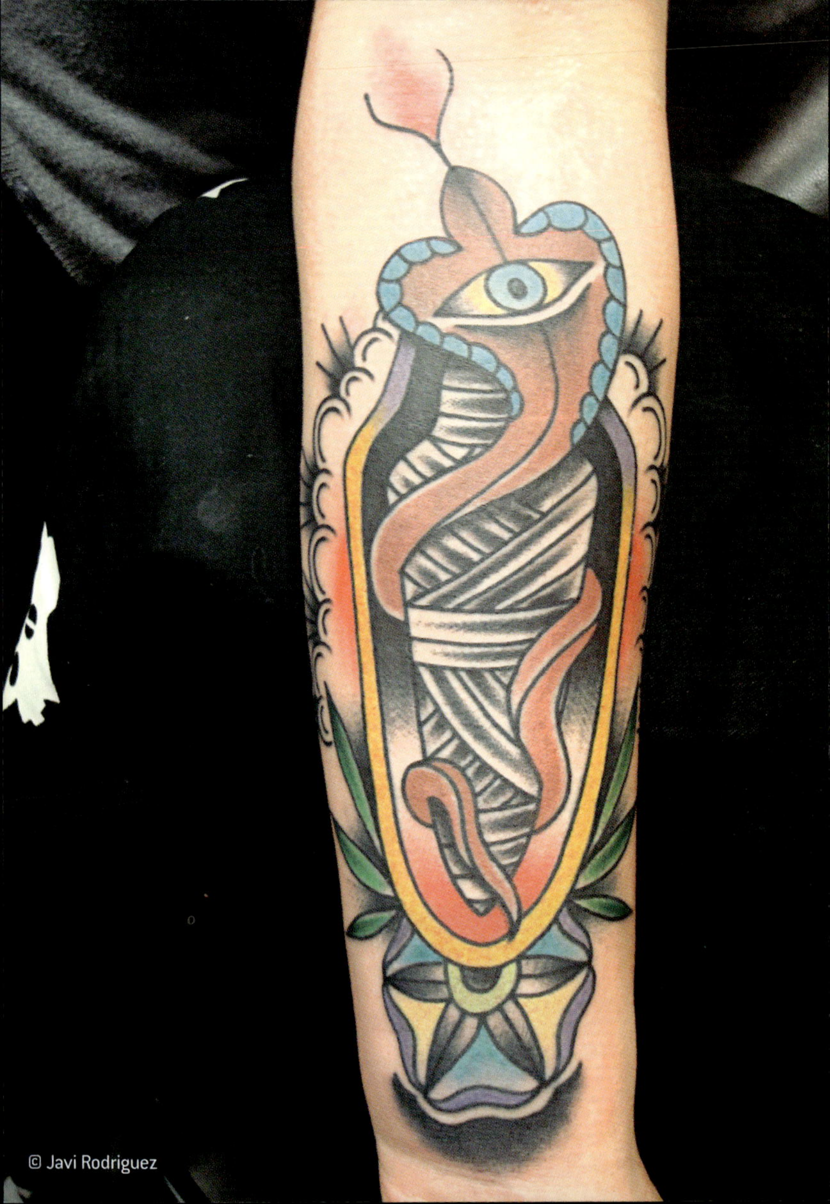

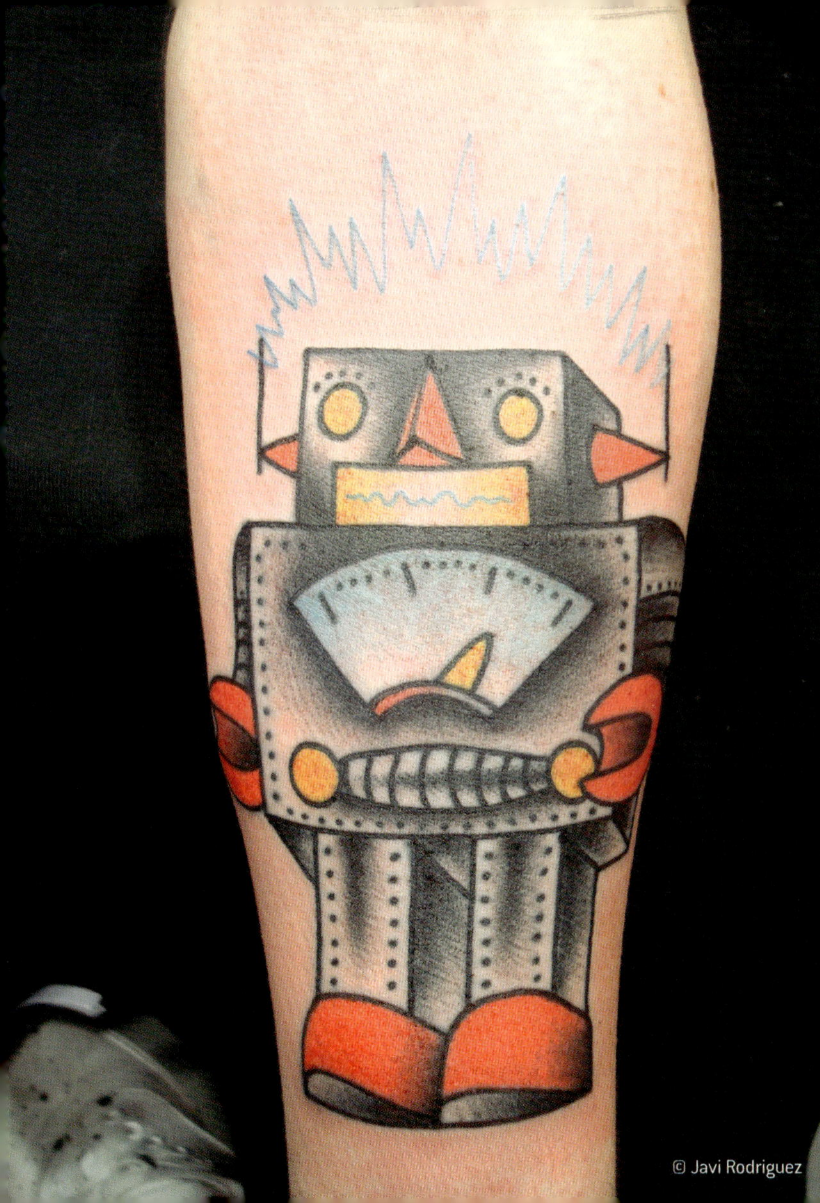

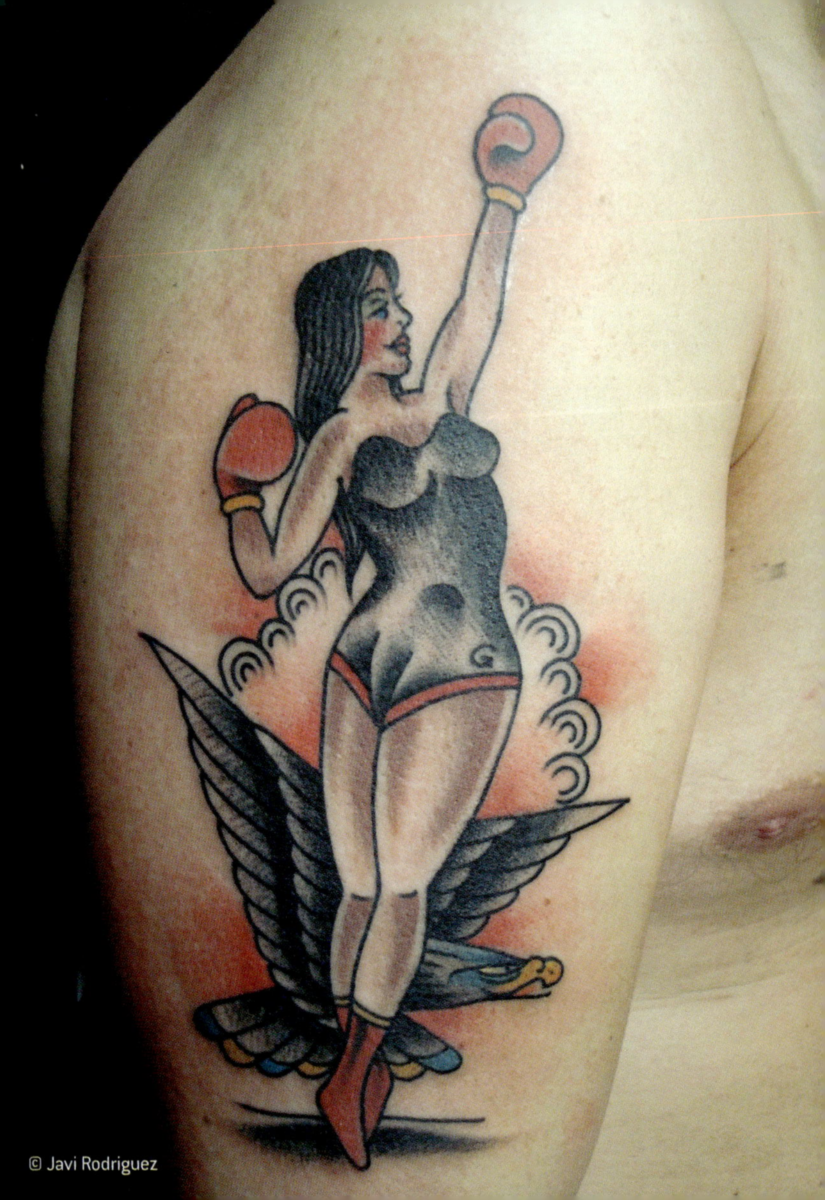
© Javi Rodriguez

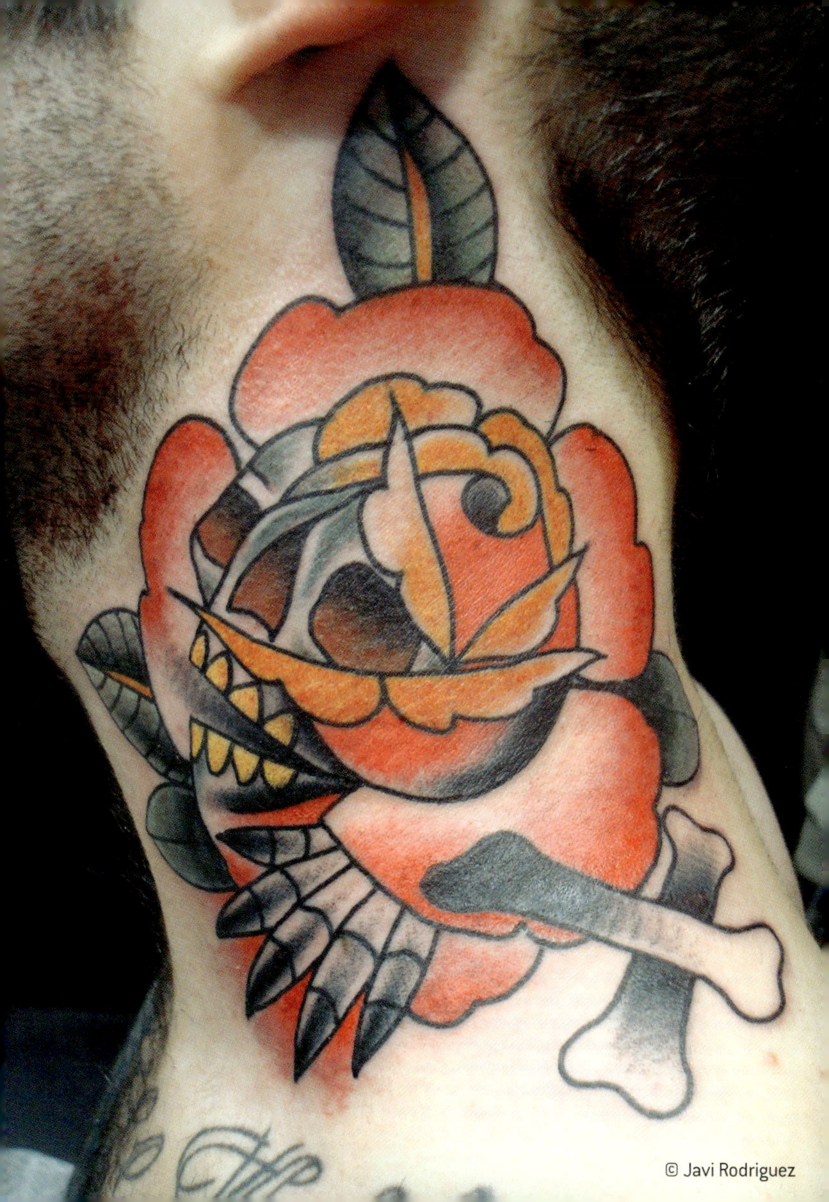
© Javi Rodriguez

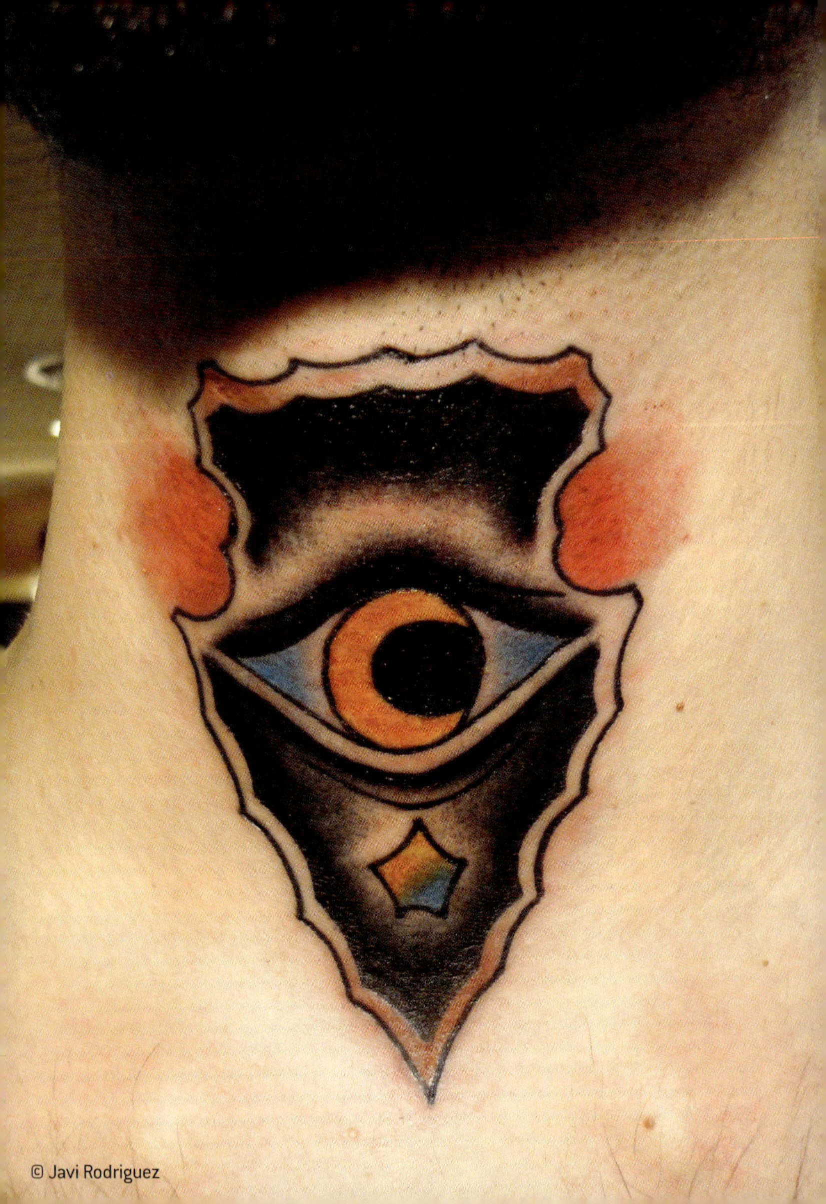

© Javi Rodriguez

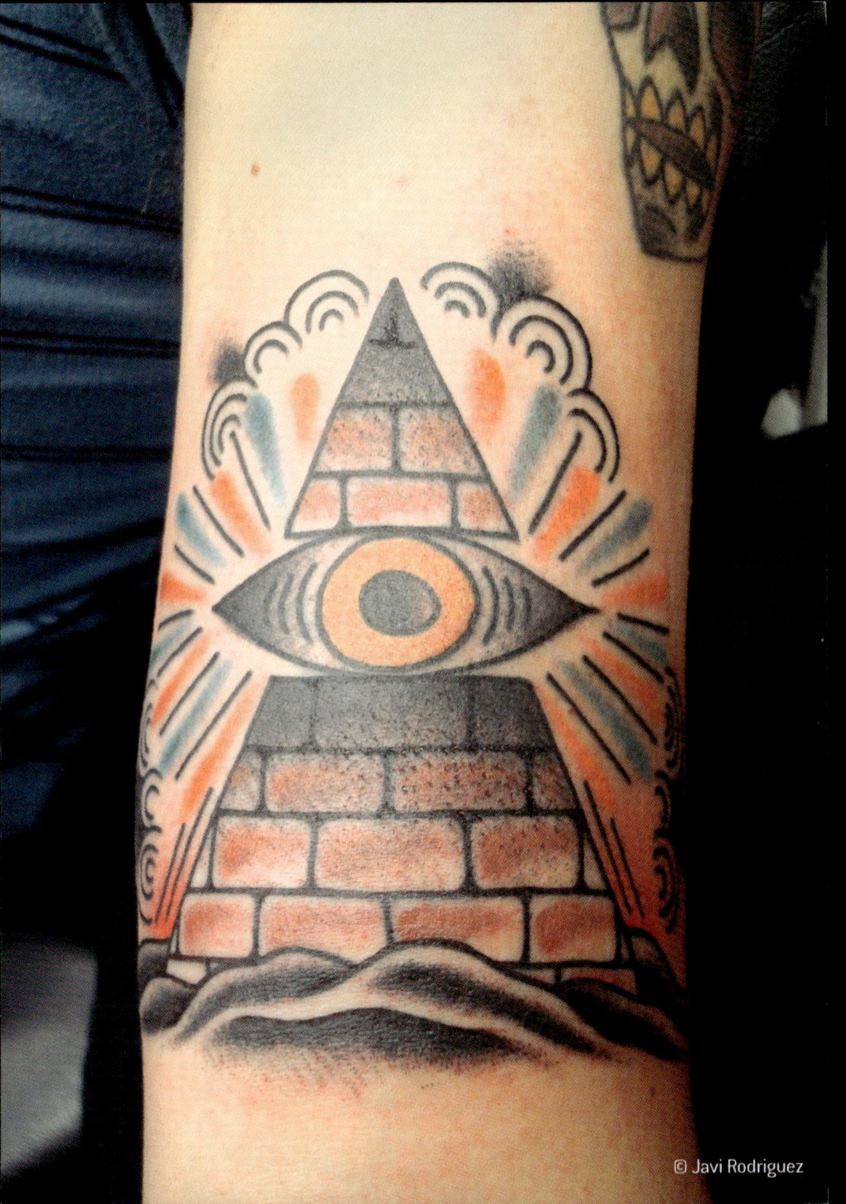

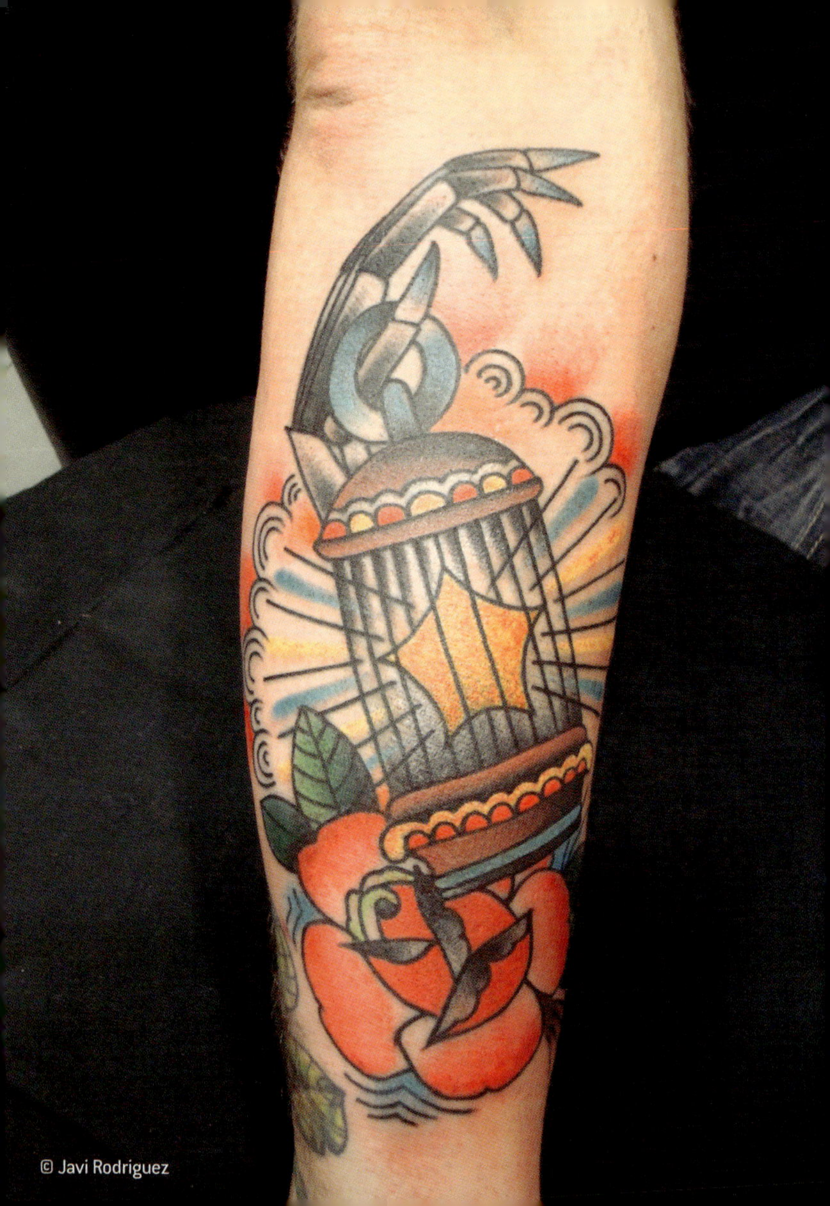

© Javi Rodriguez

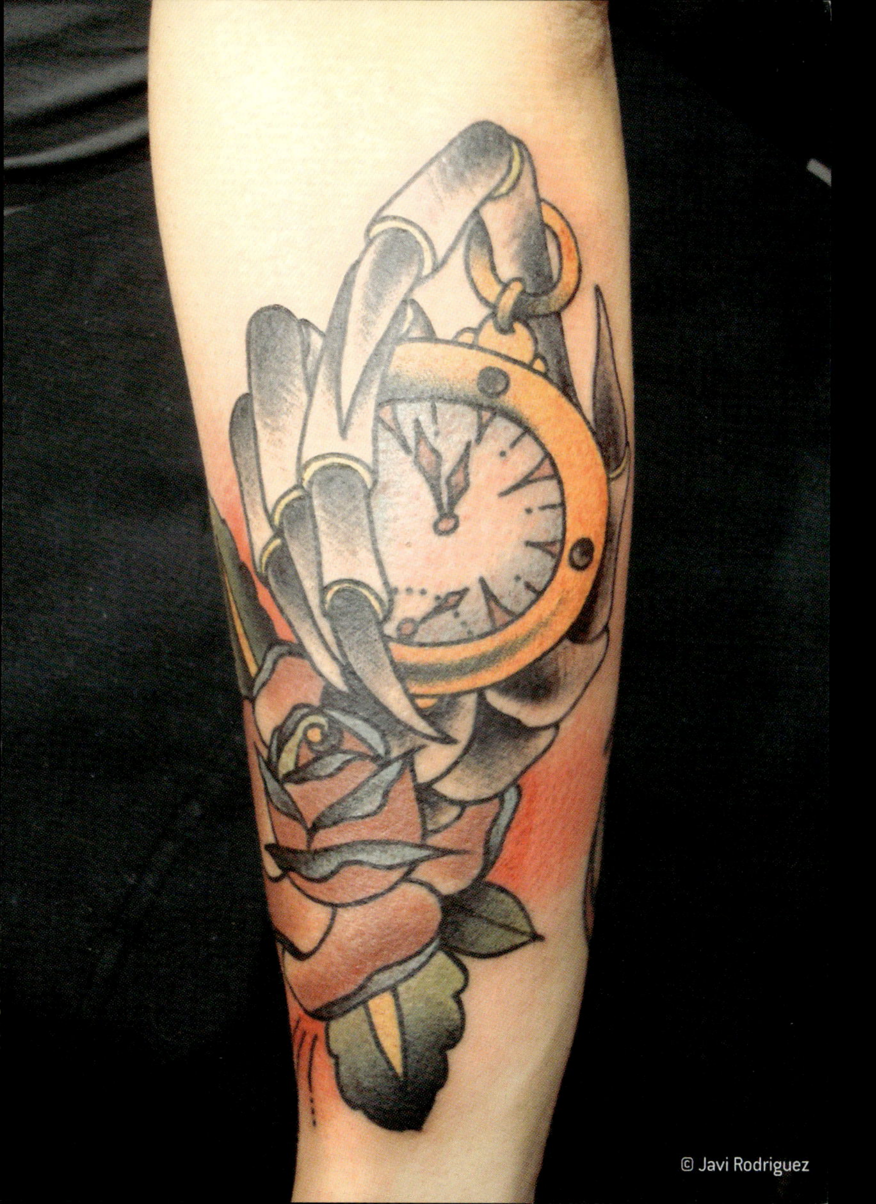

© Javi Rodriguez

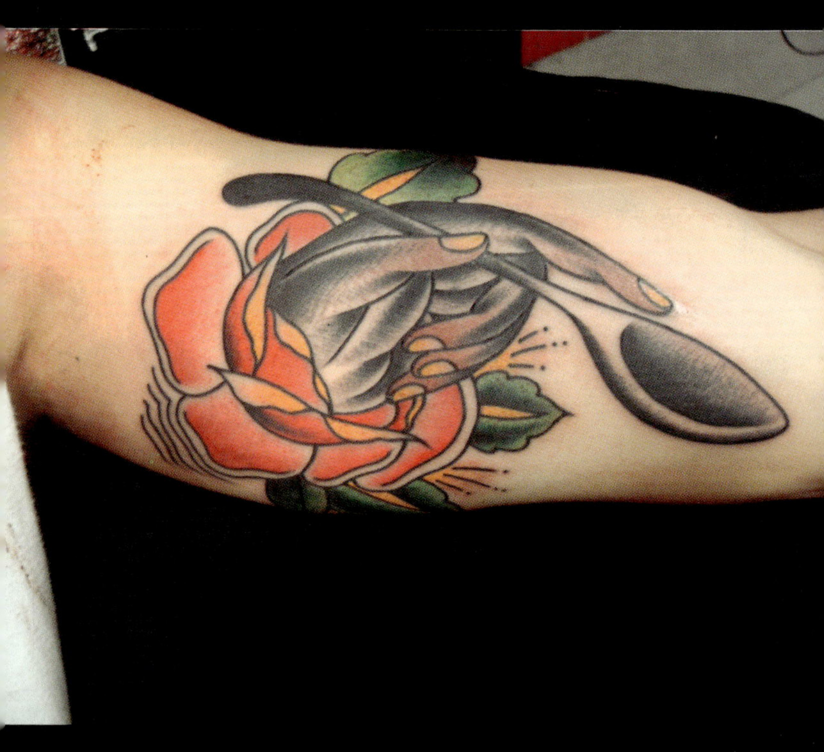

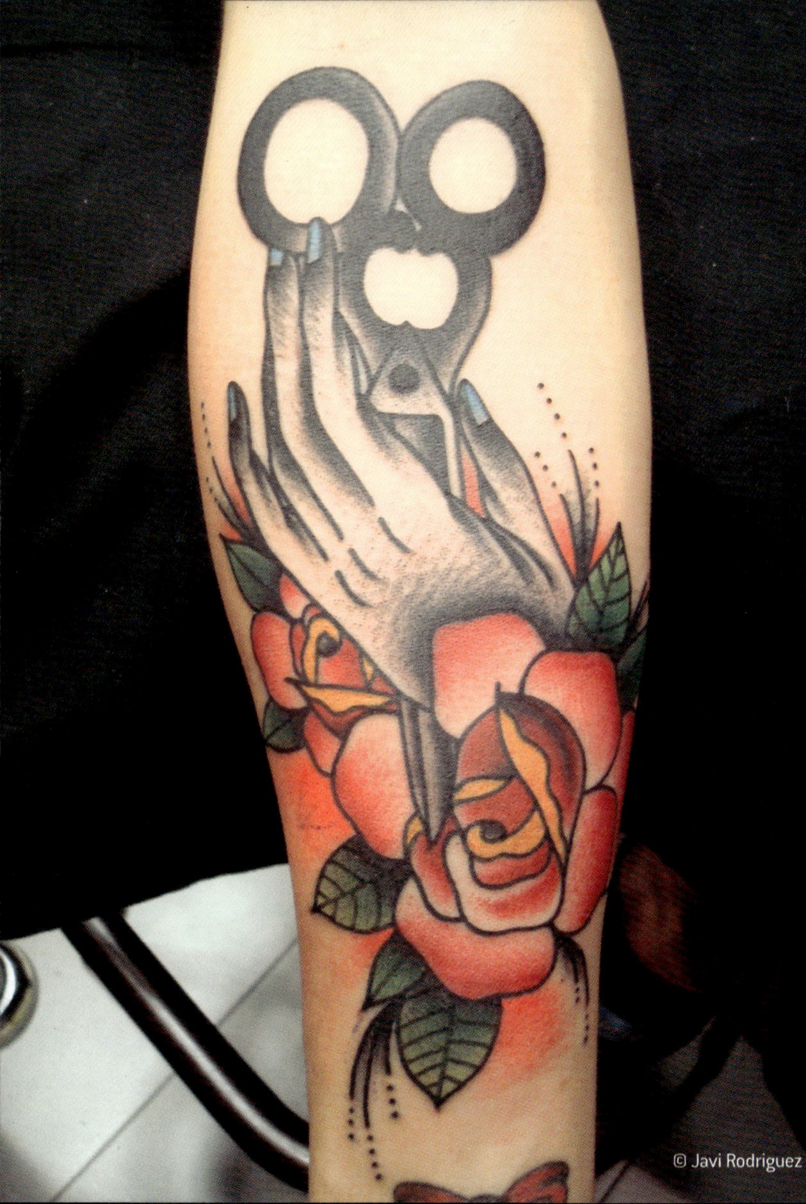
© Javi Rodriguez

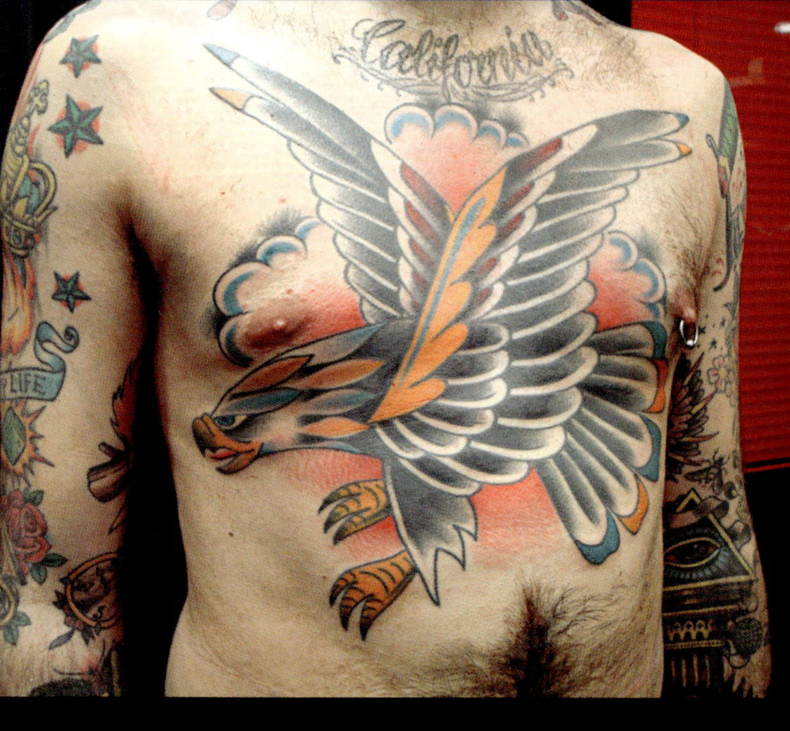

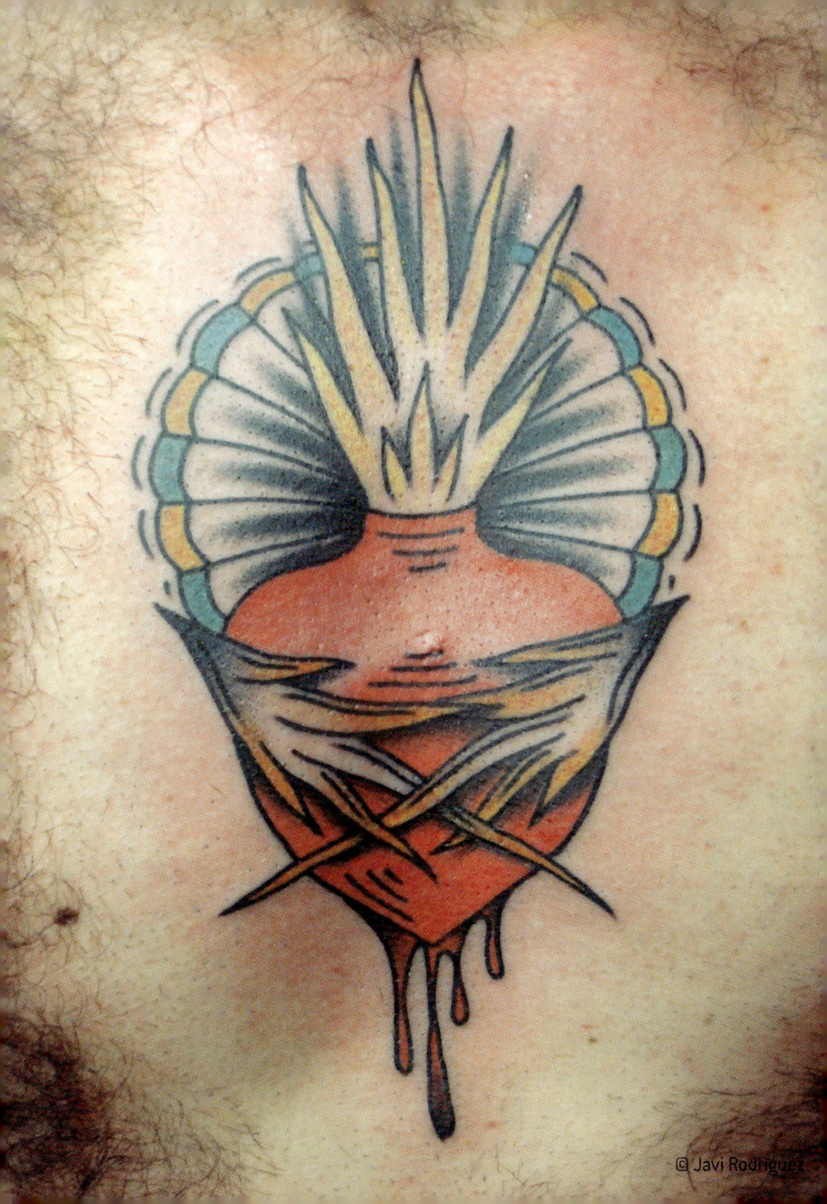

© Javi Rodriguez

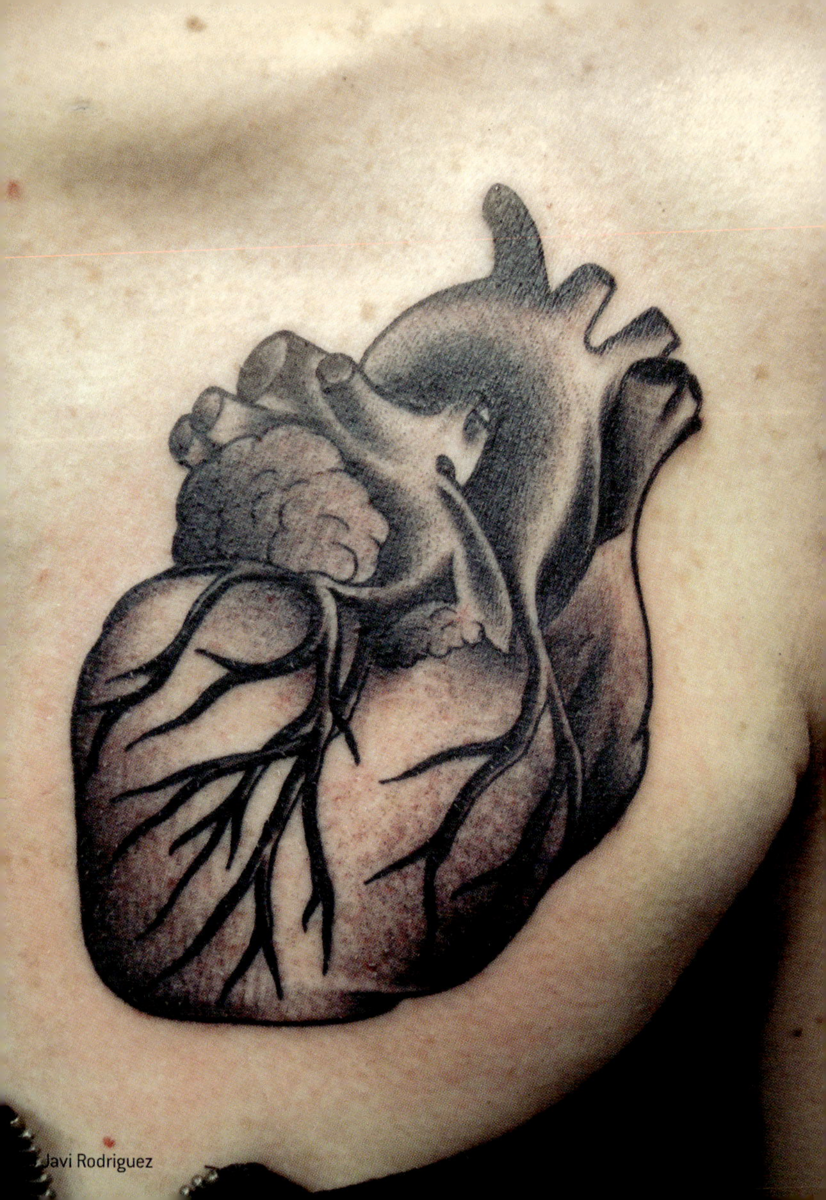

Javi Rodriguez

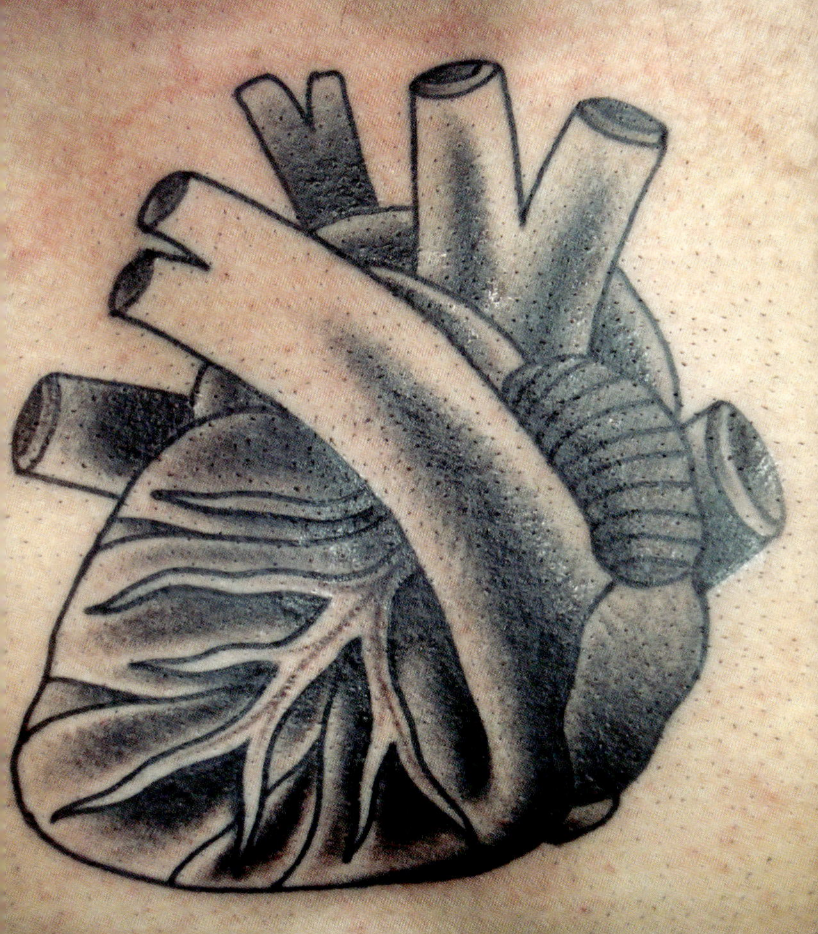

© Javi Rodriguez

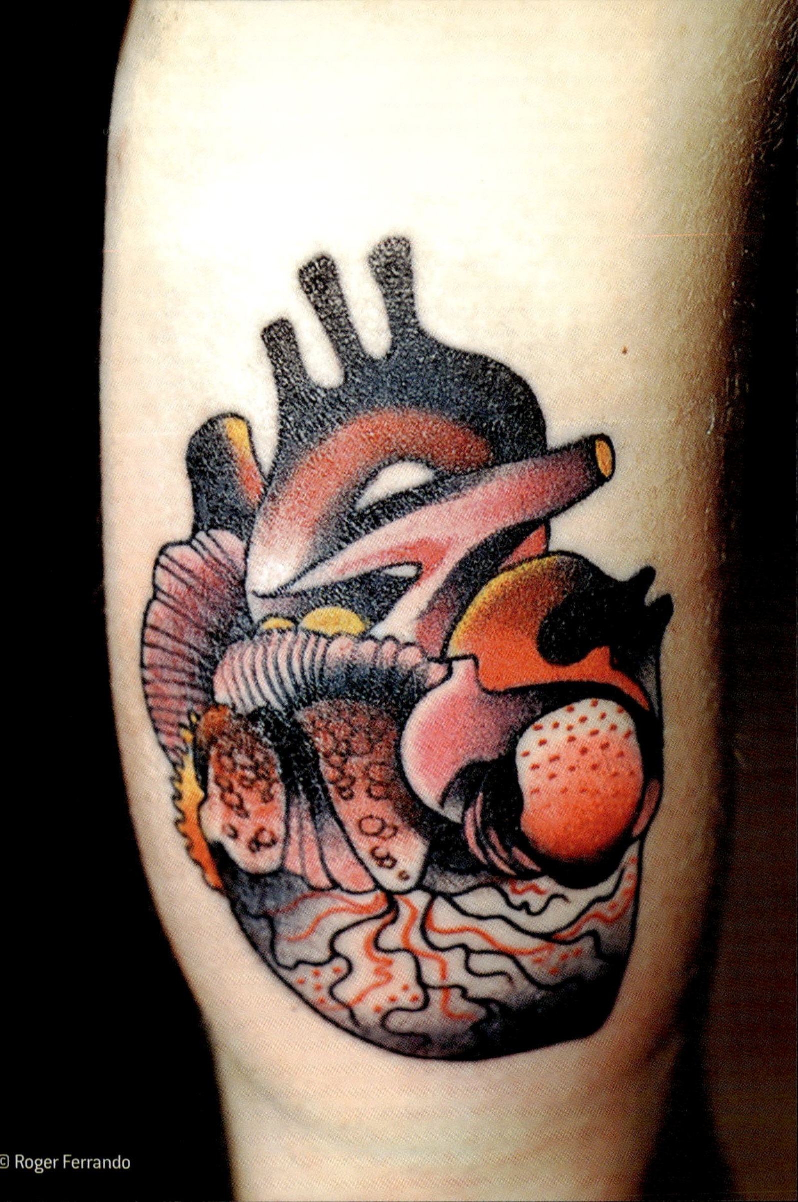

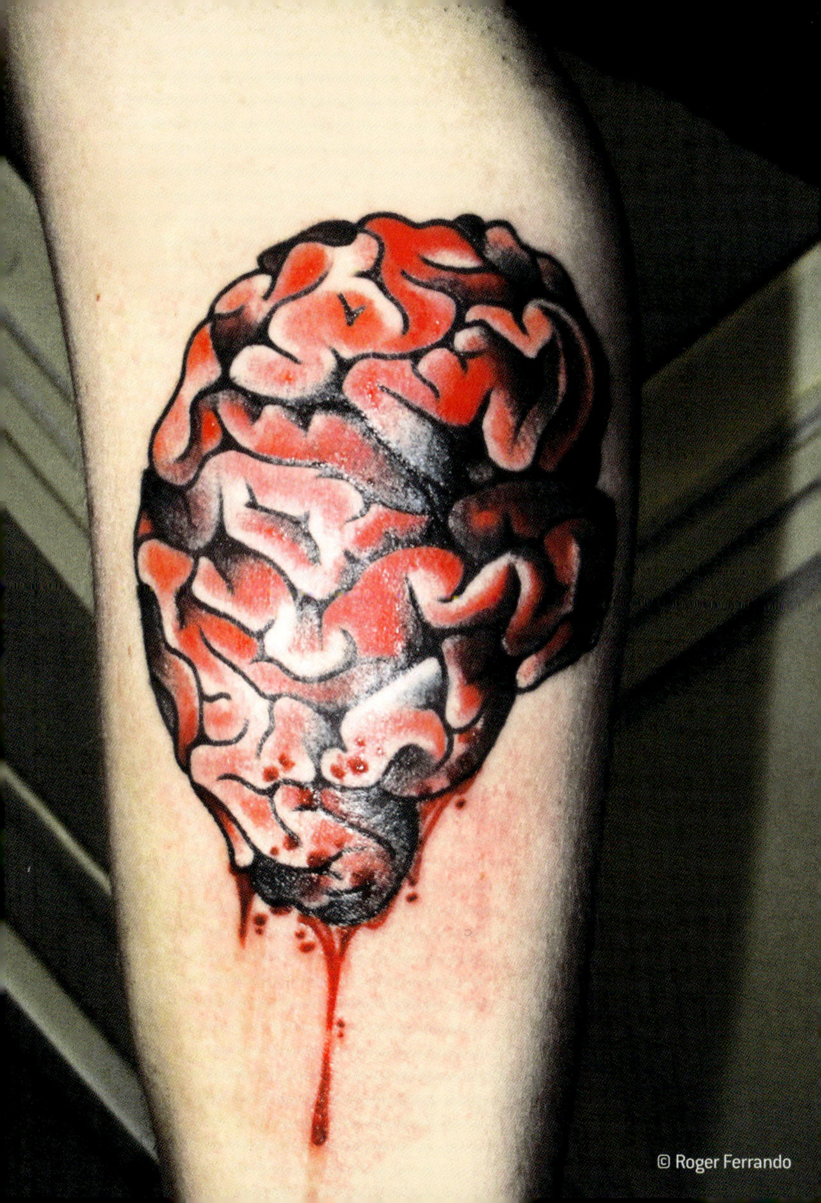

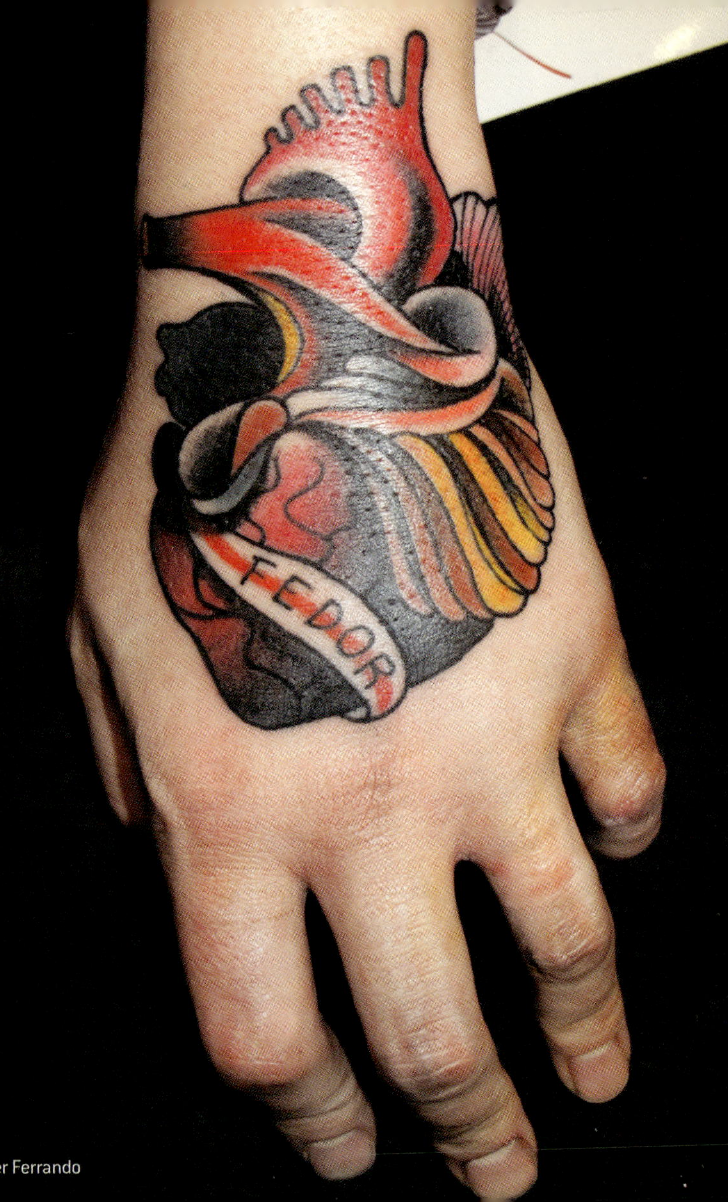

FEDOR

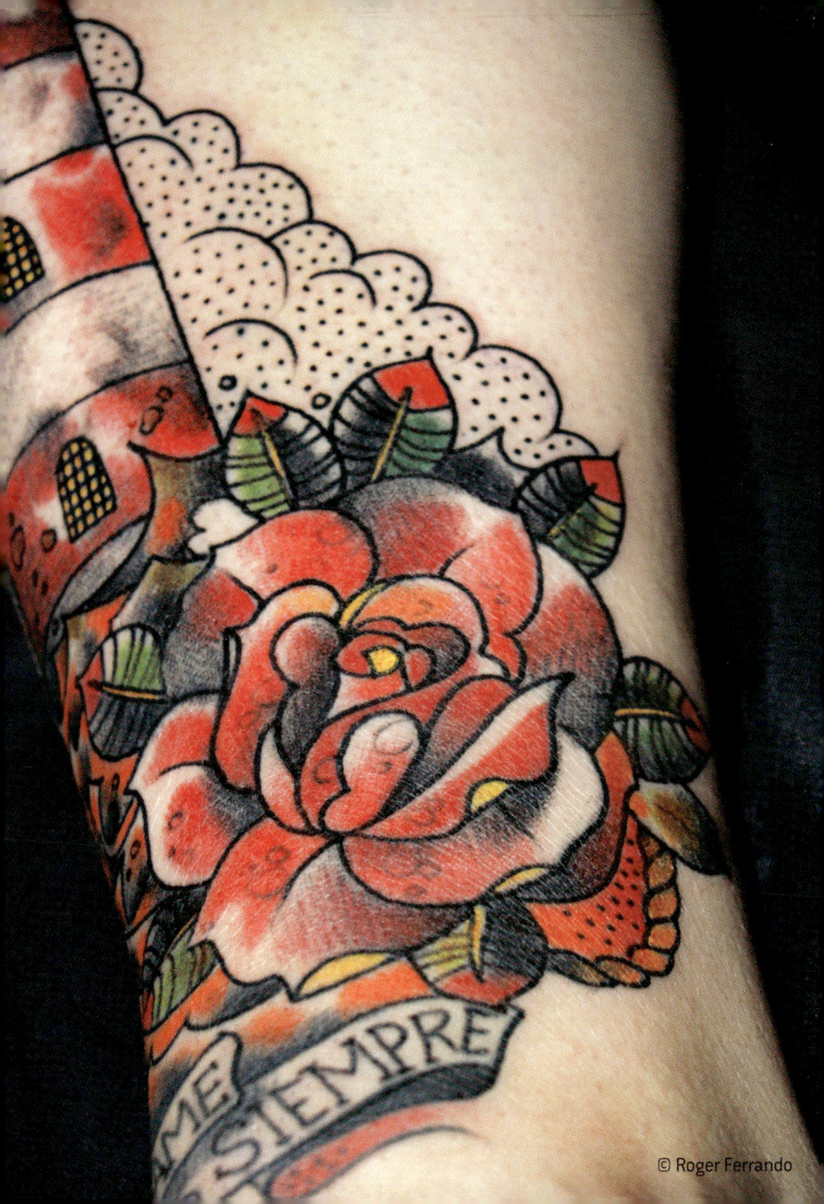
ME SIEMPRE

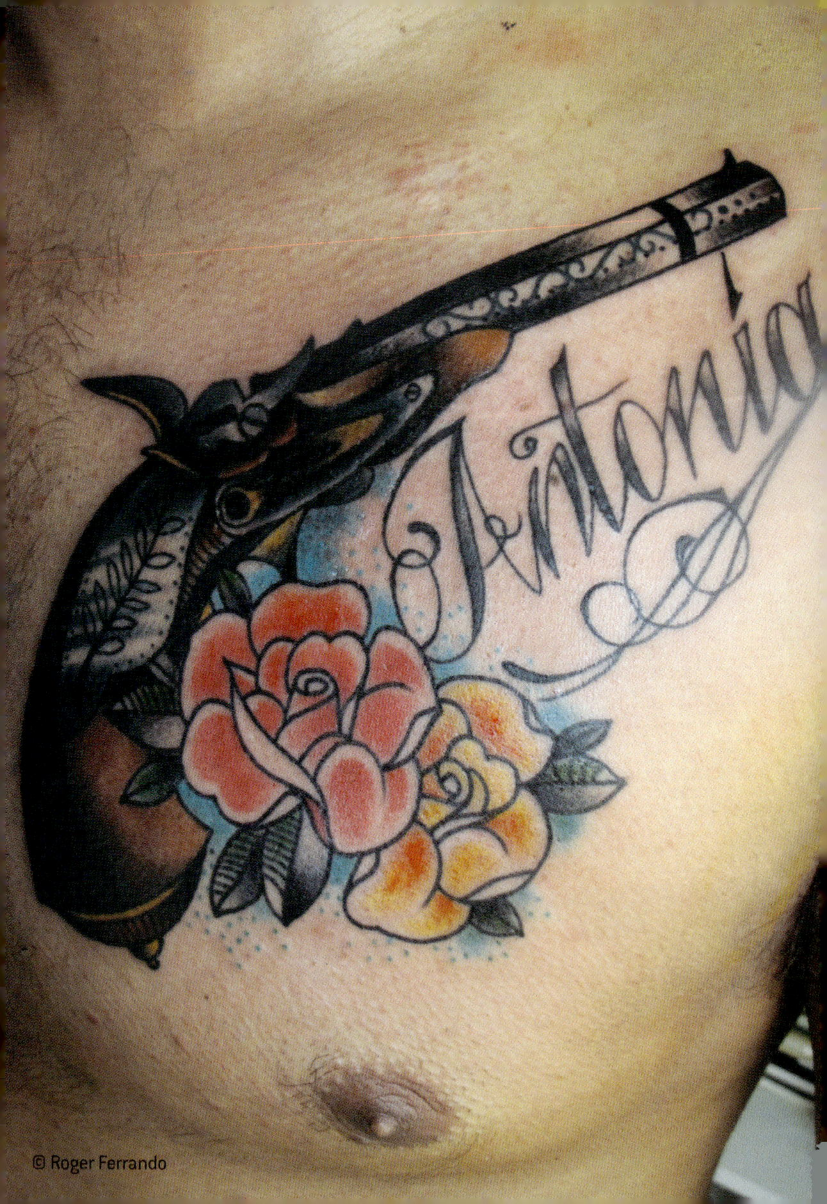

Antonia

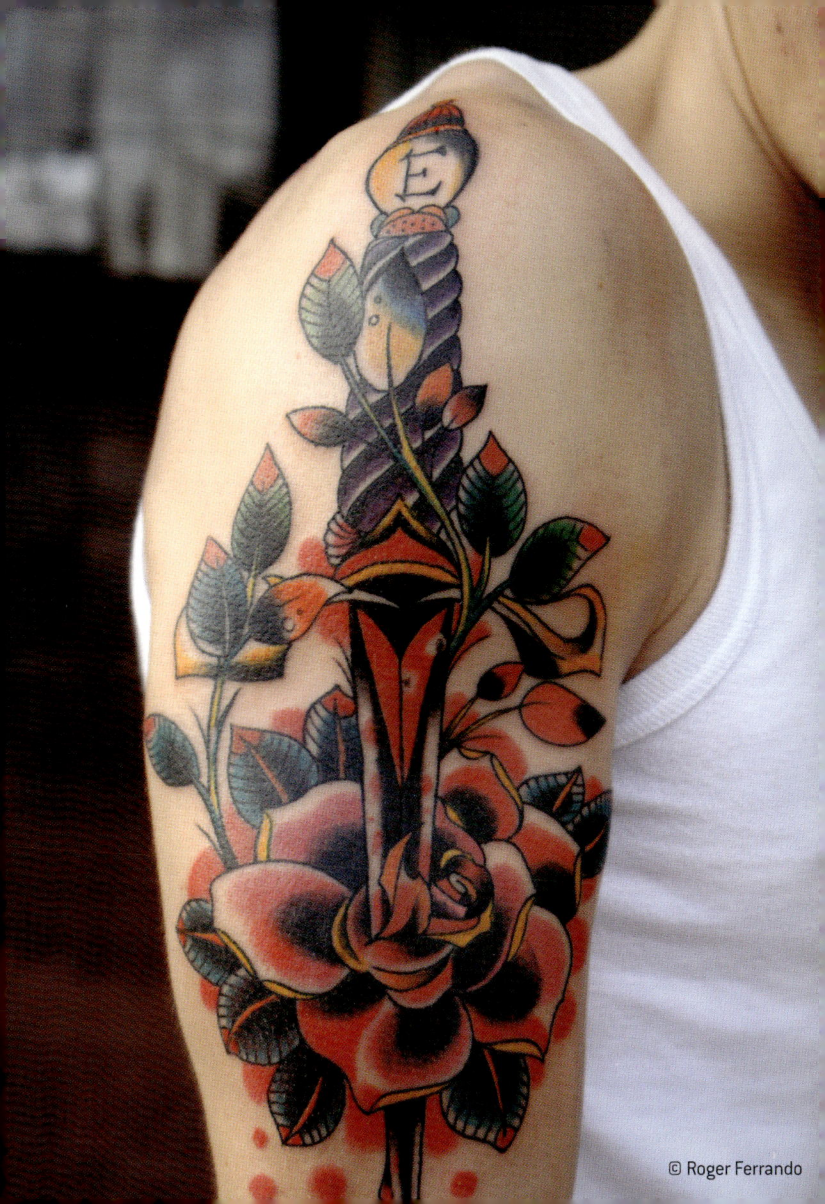

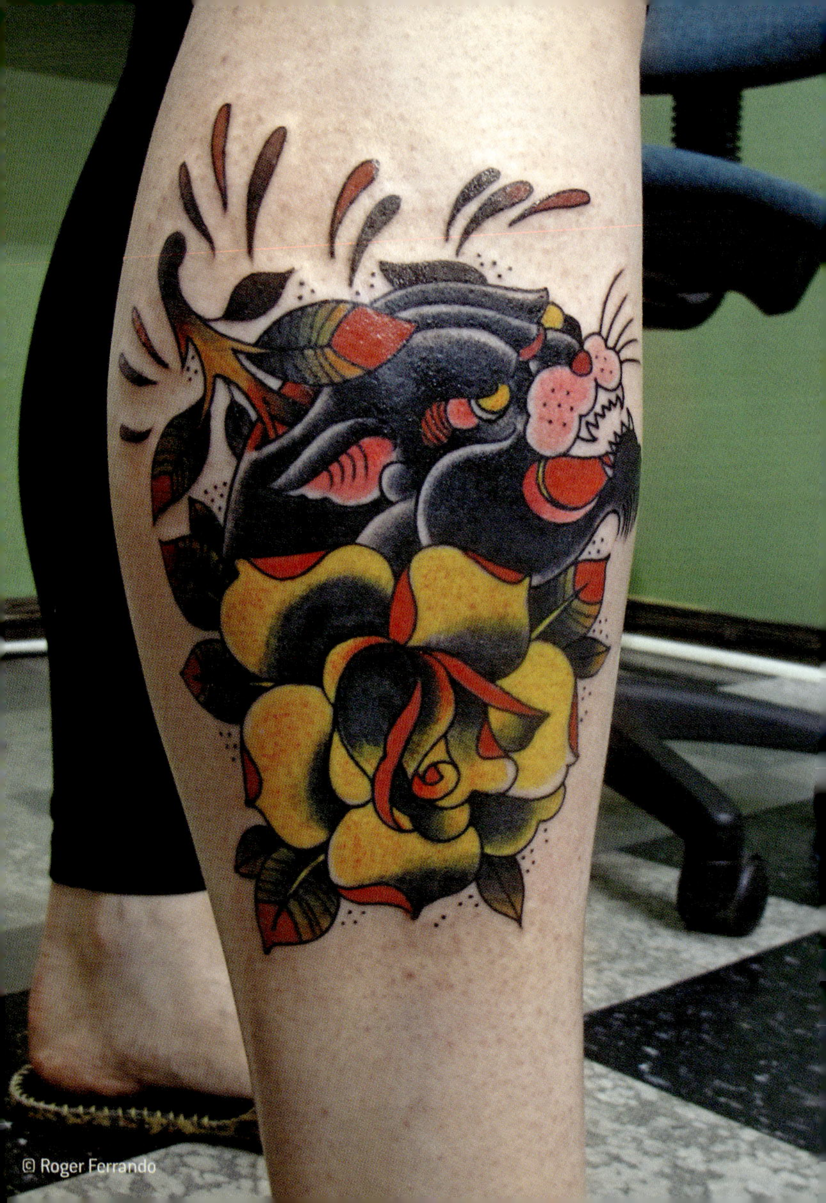

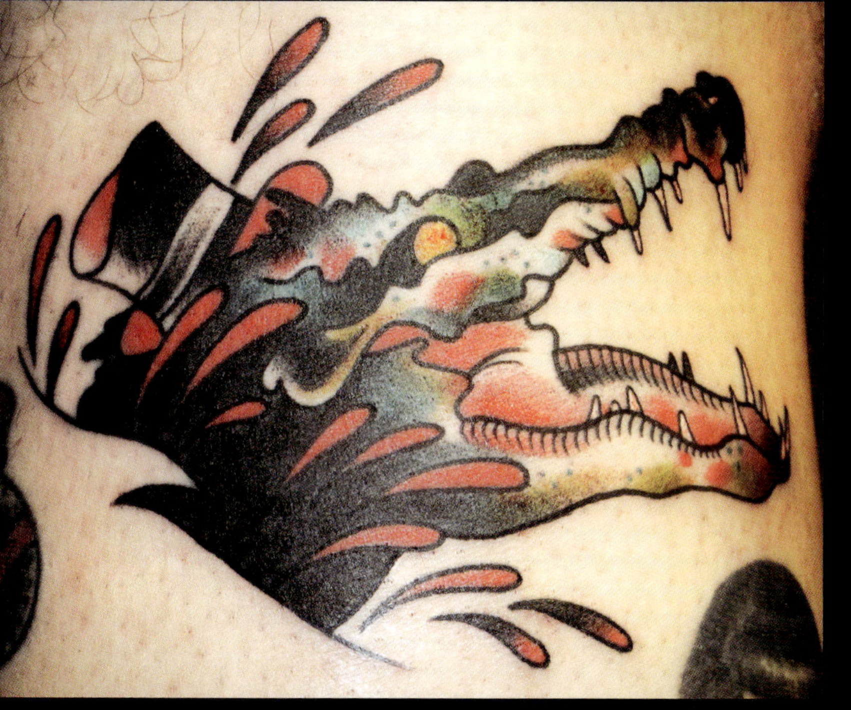

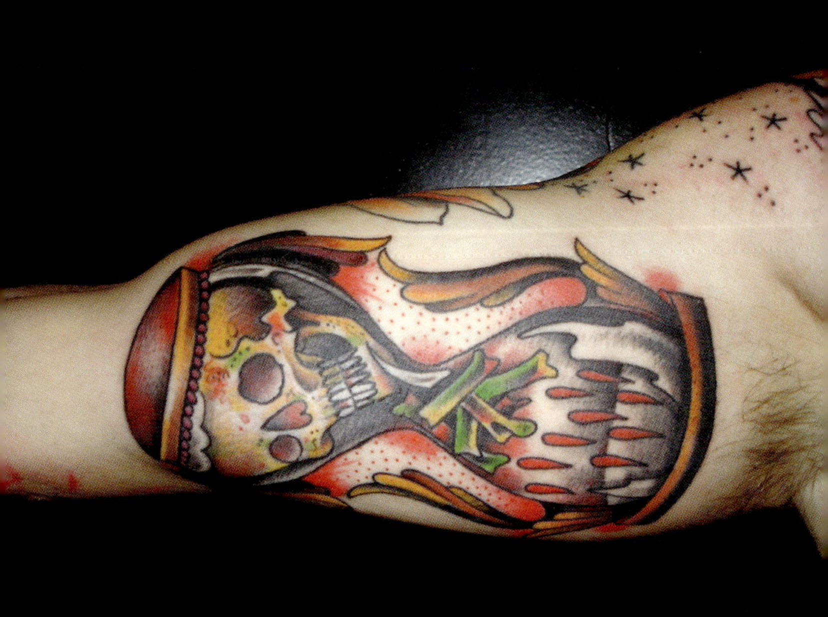

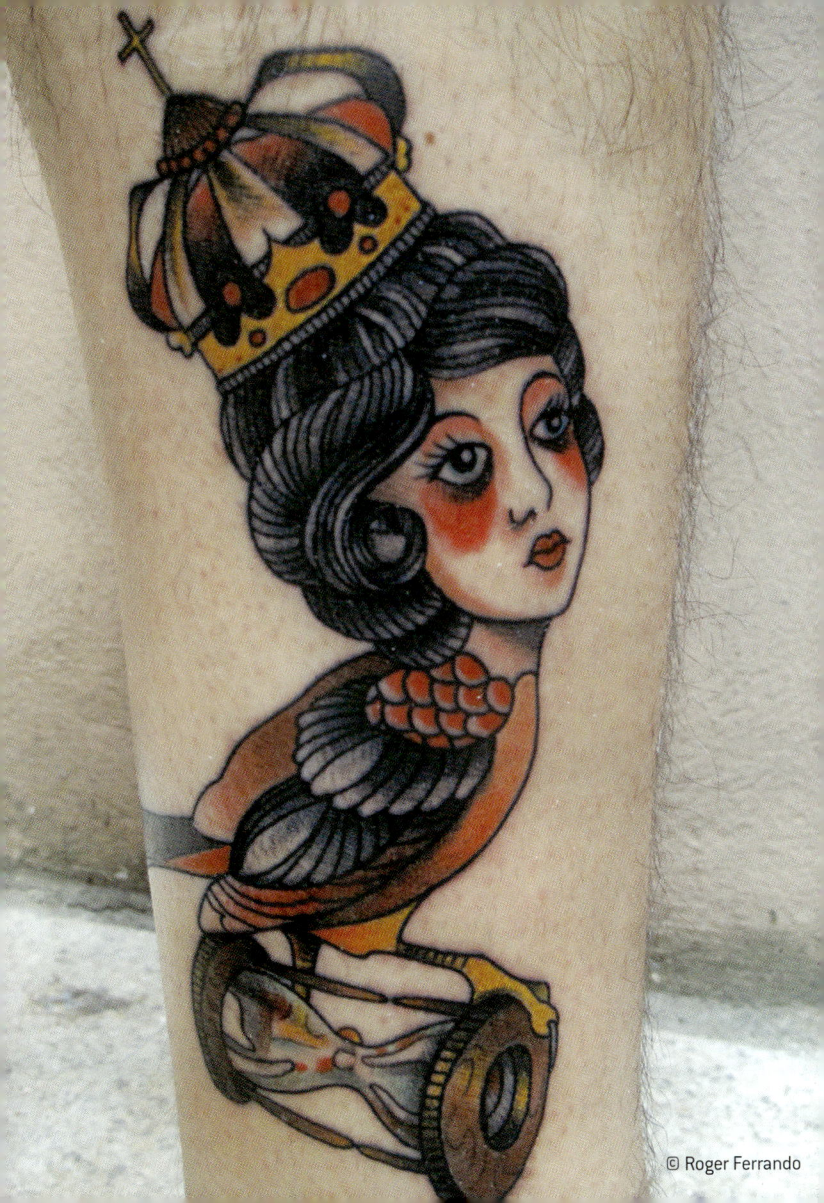

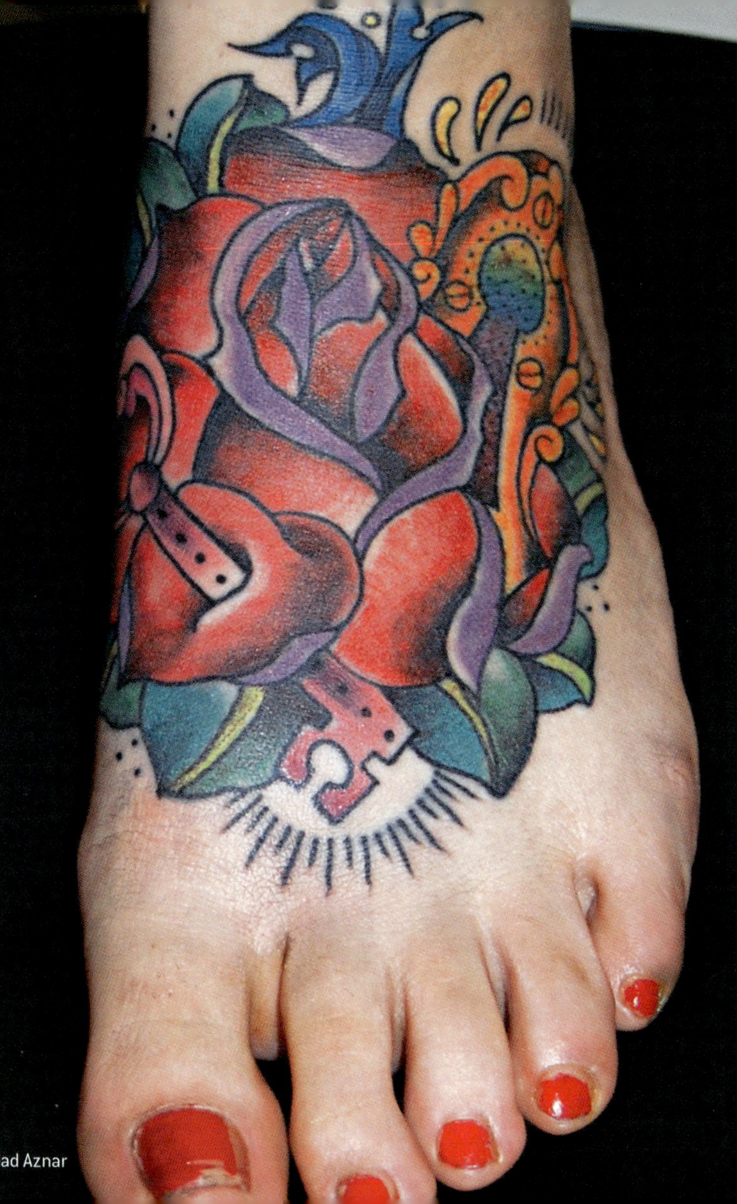

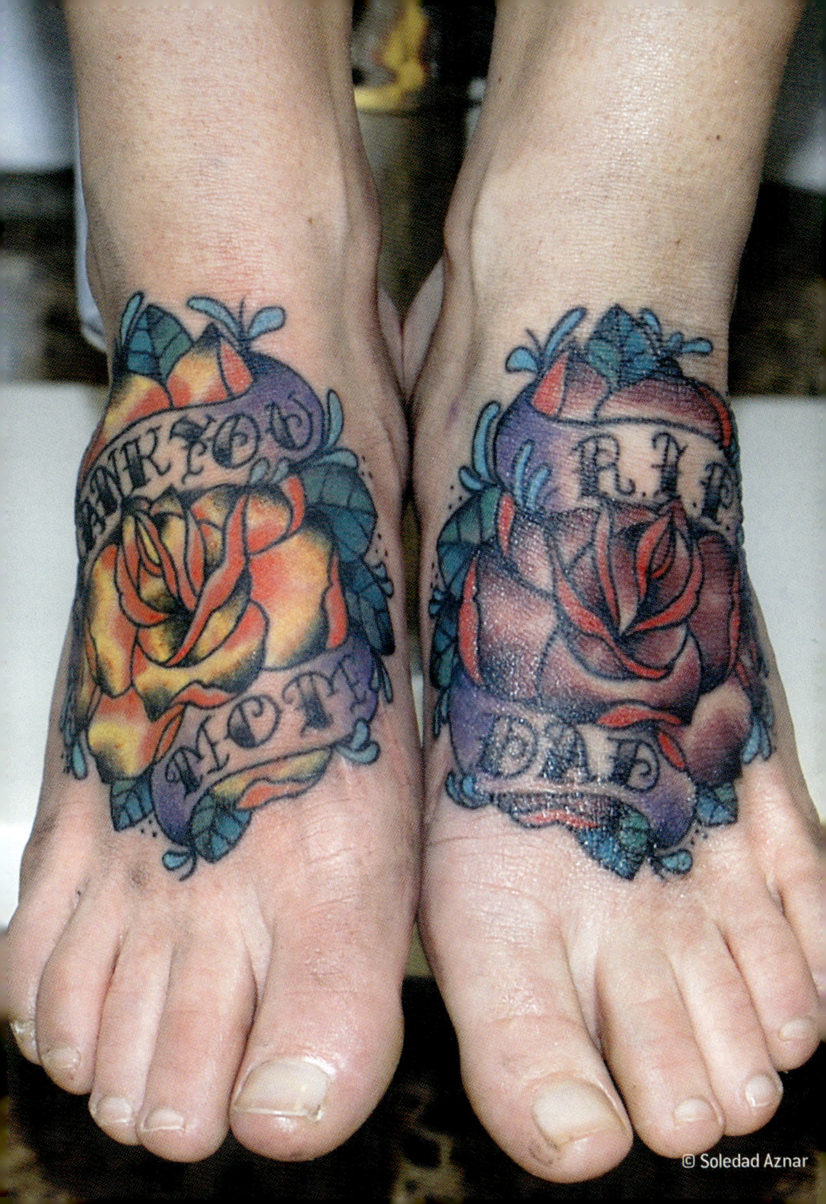

© Soledad Aznar

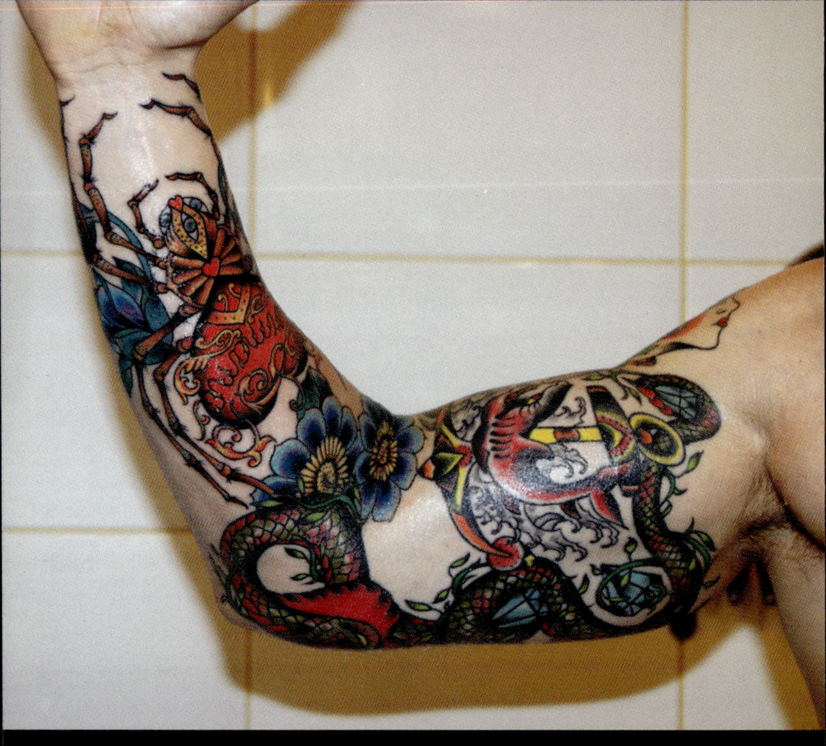

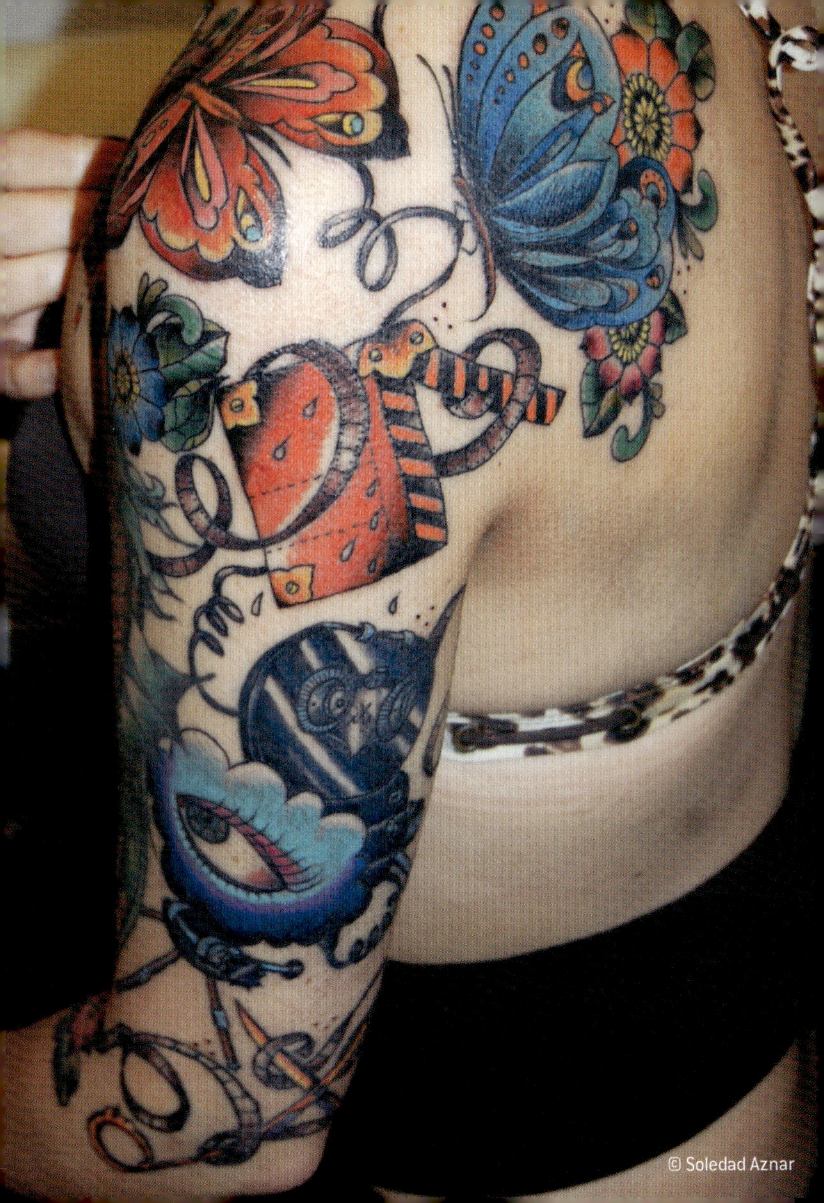
© Soledad Aznar

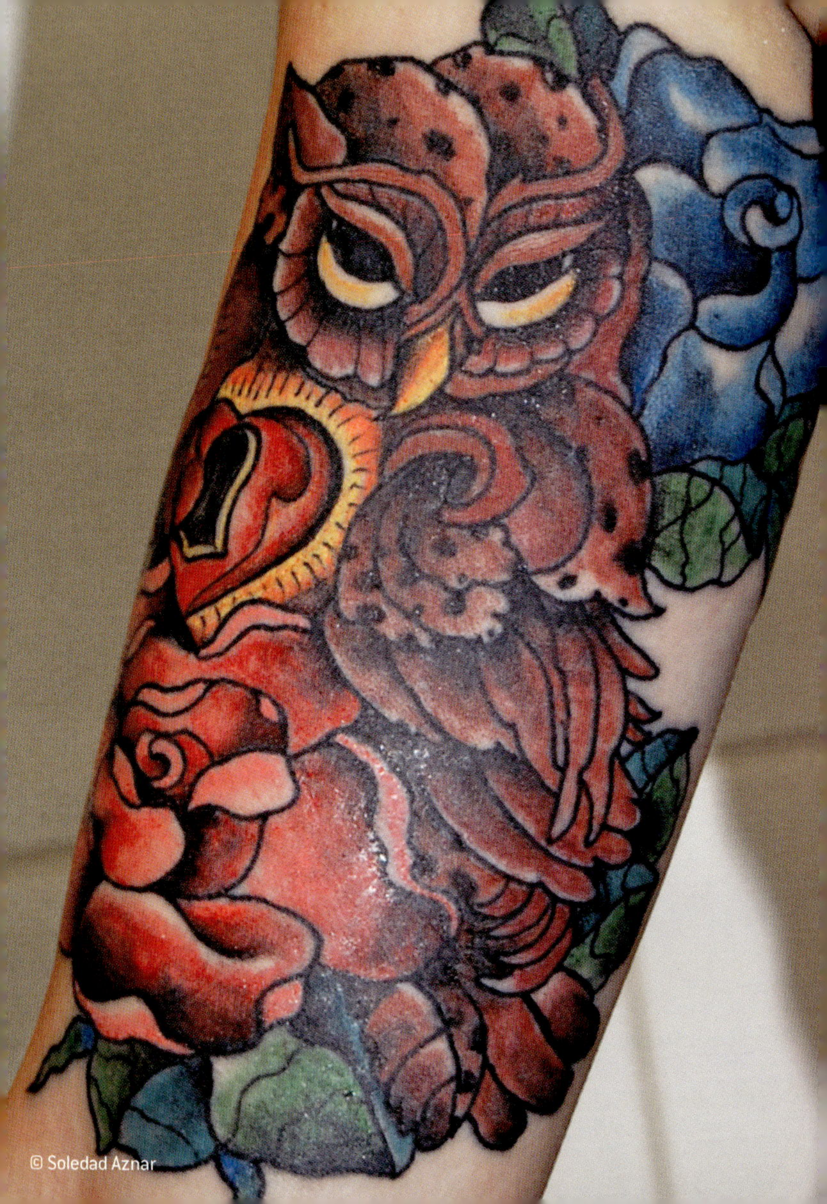

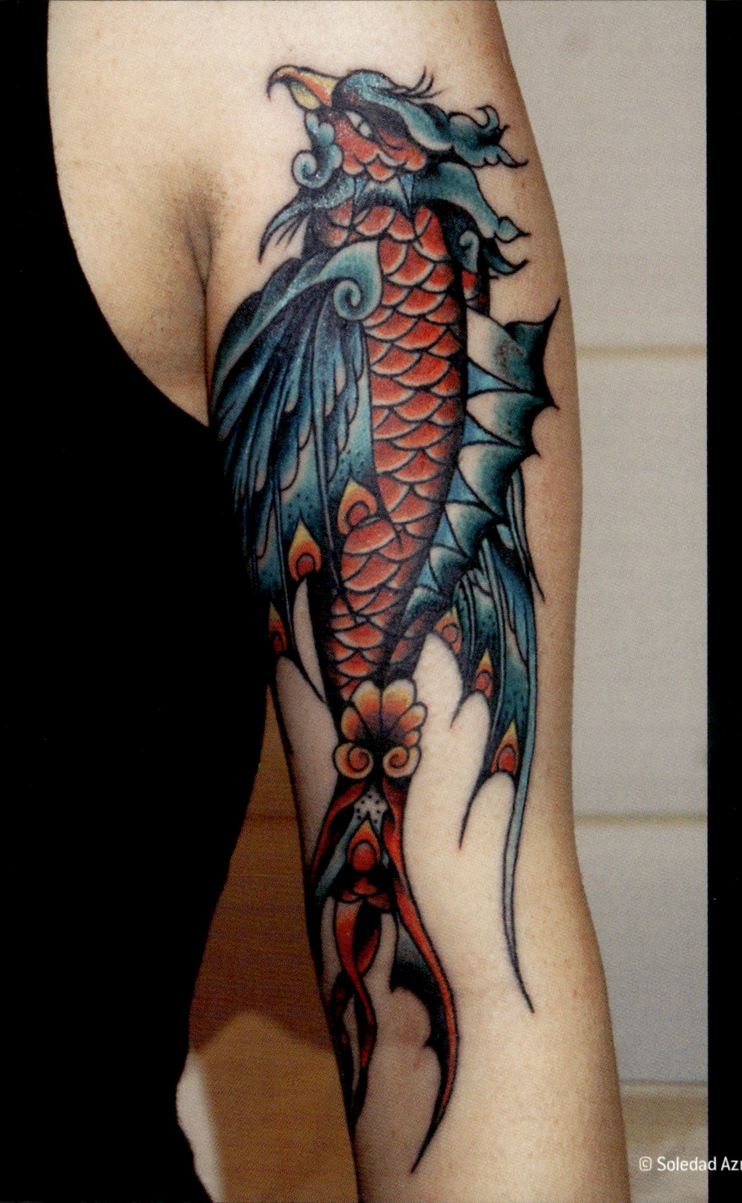
© Soledad Aznar

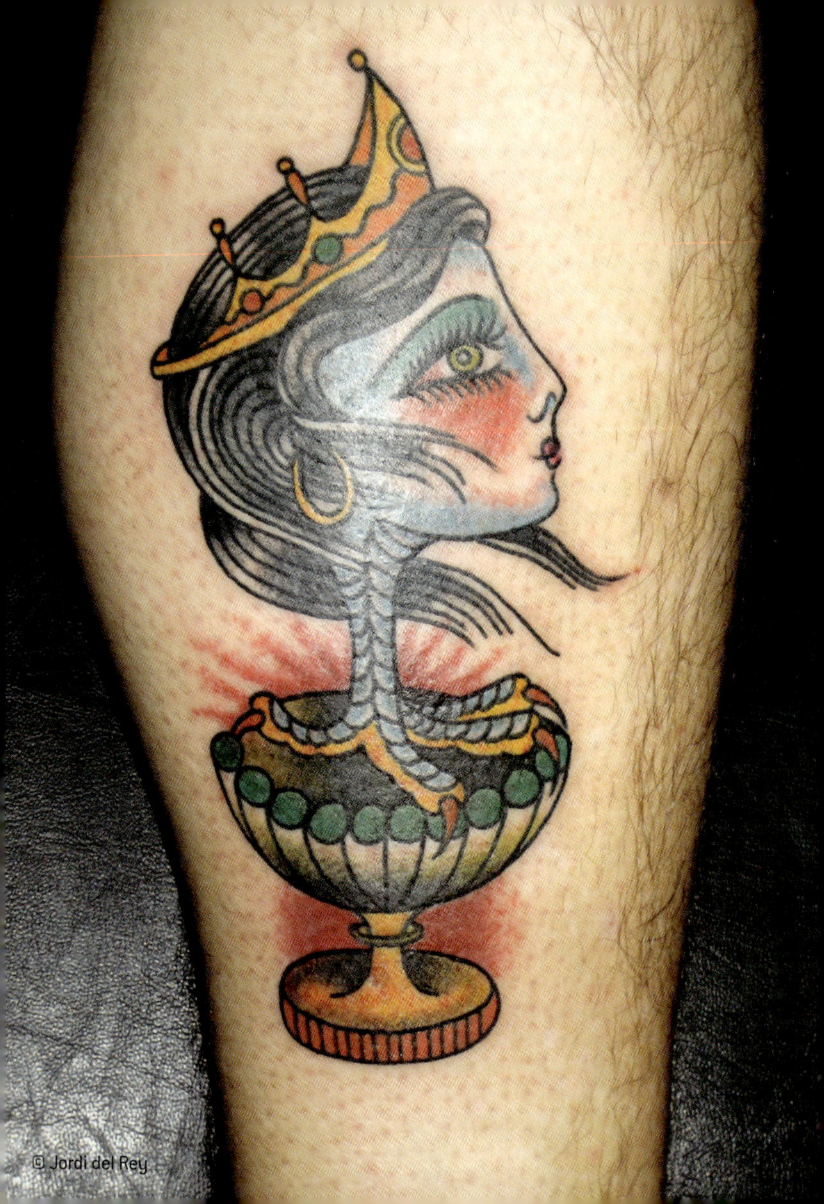

© Jordi del Rey

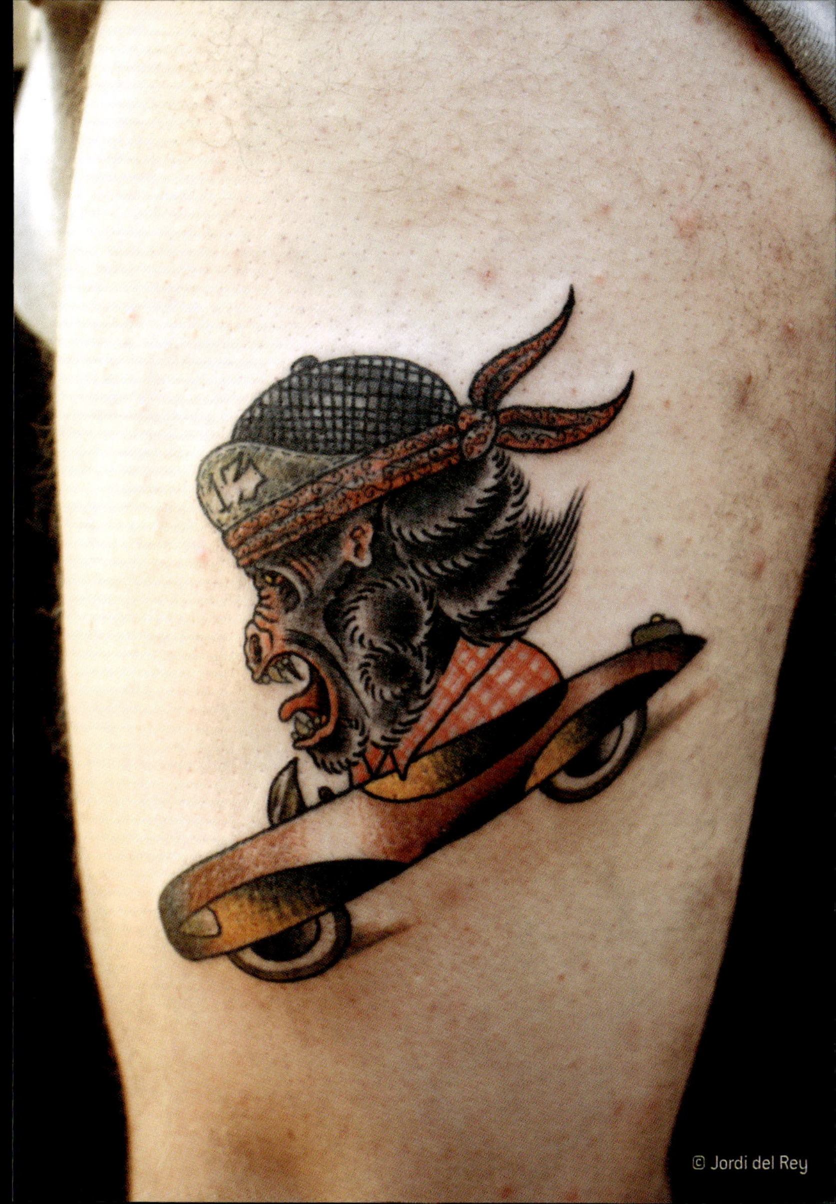

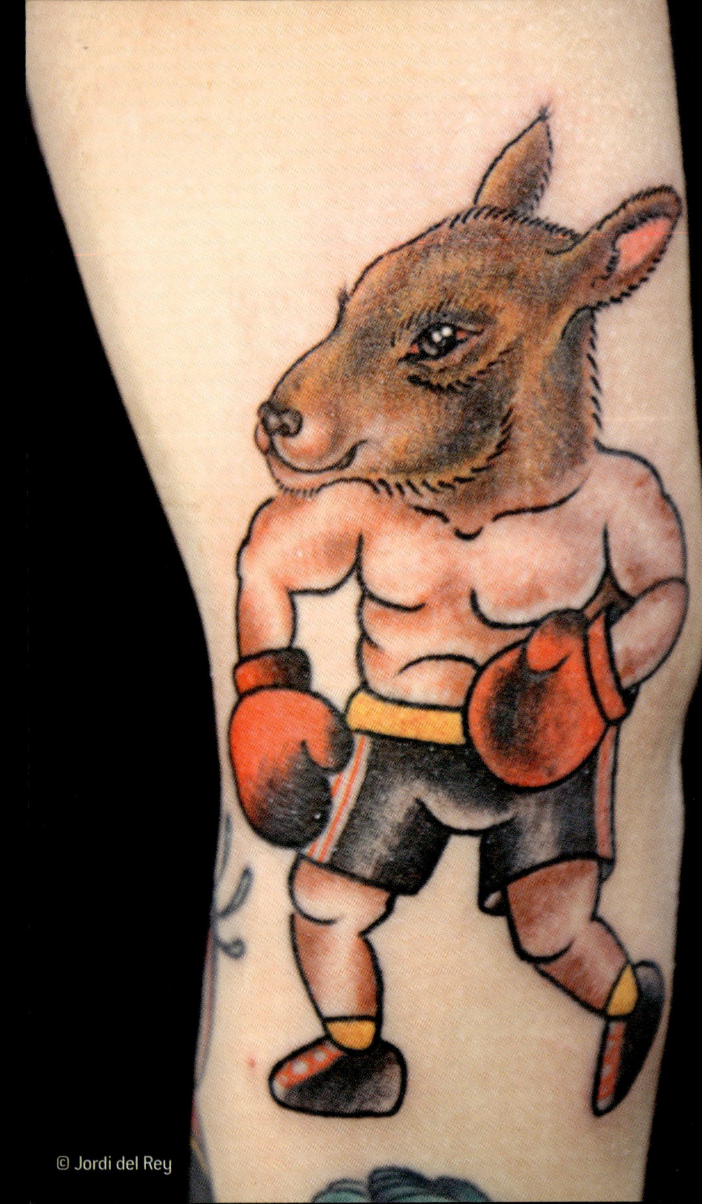

© Jordi del Rey

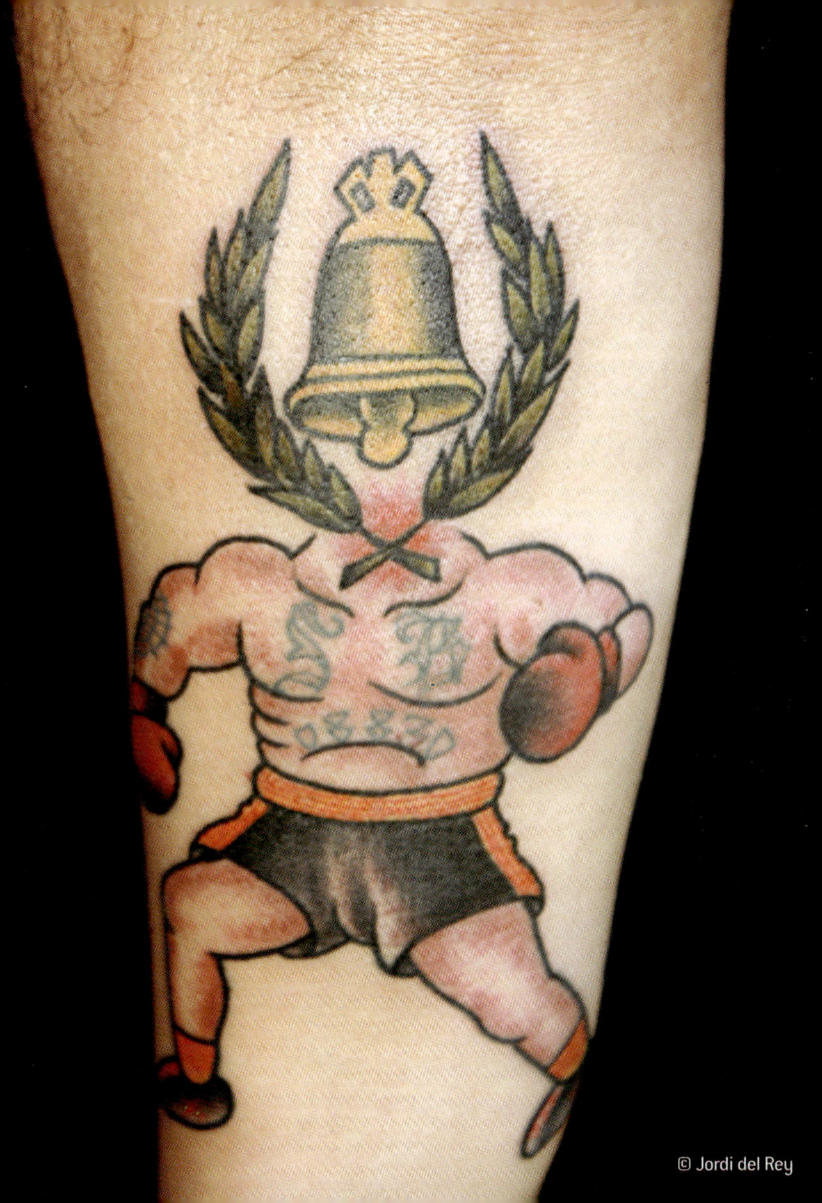

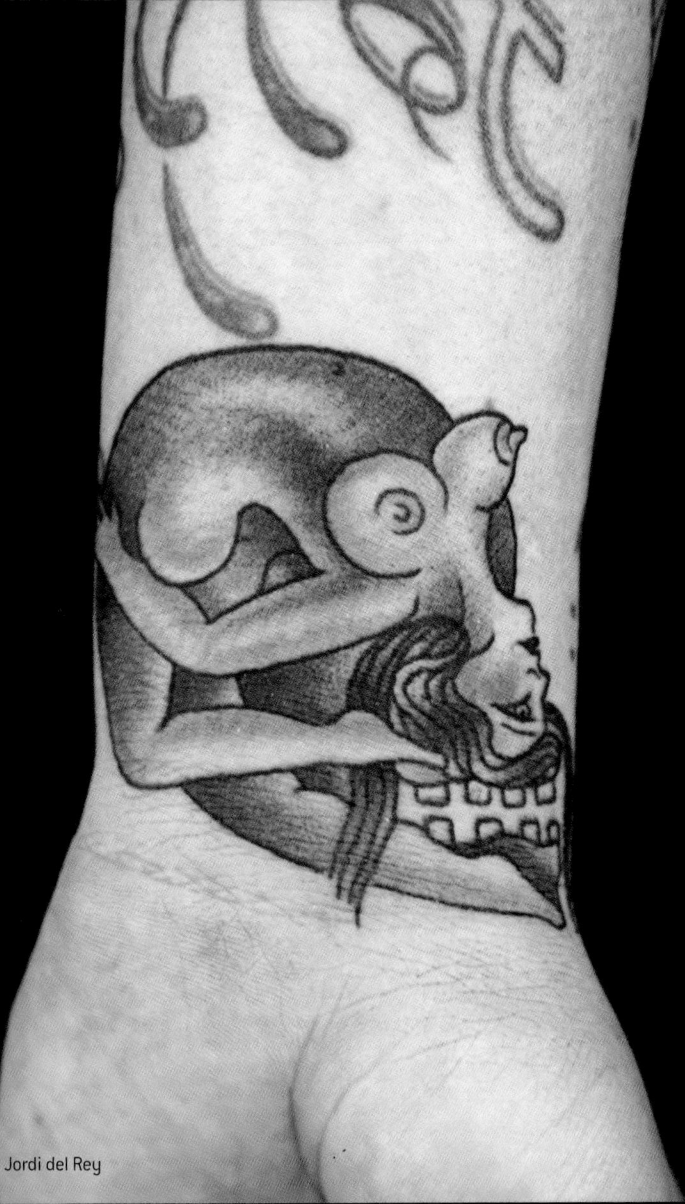

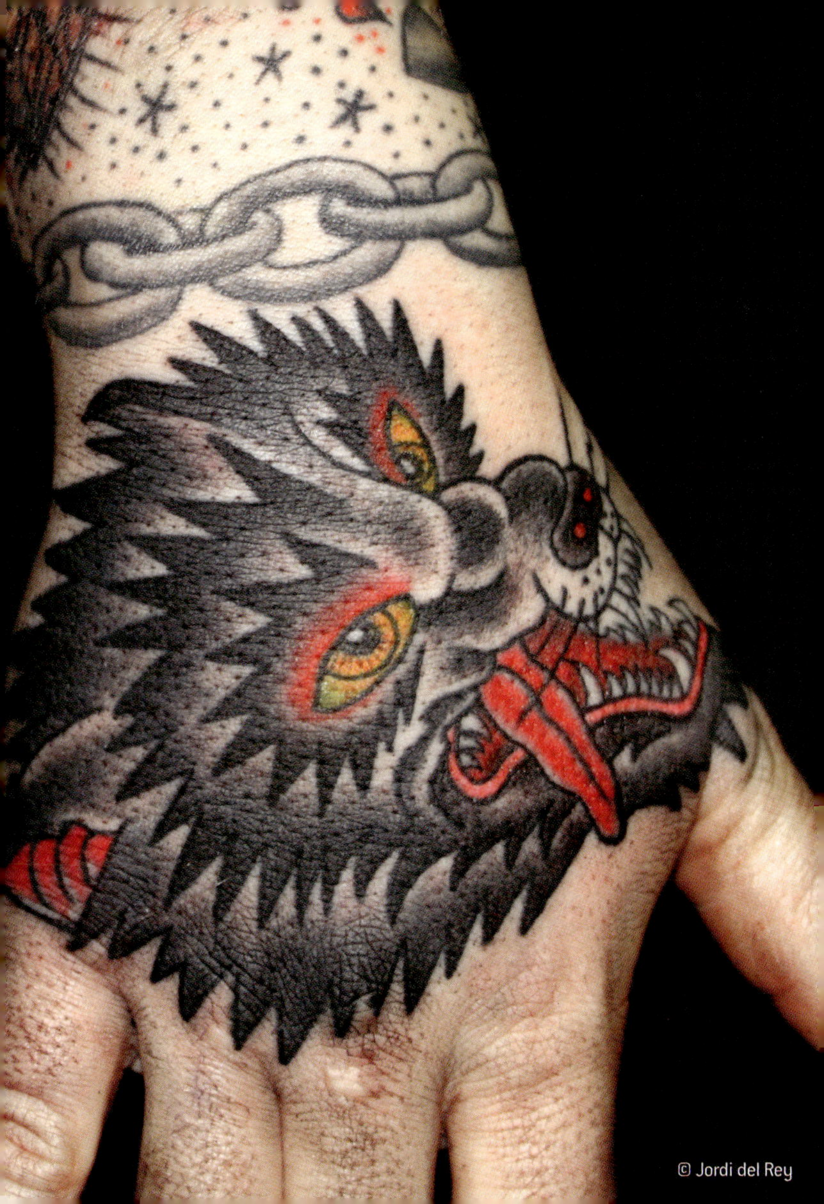

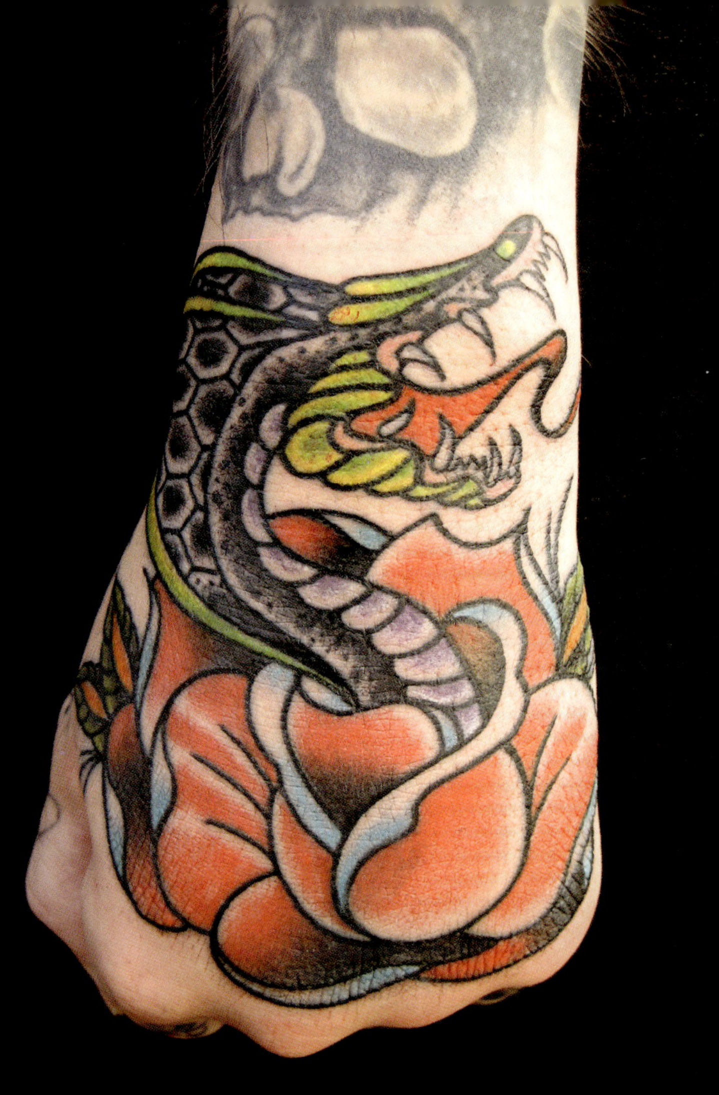

© Jordi del Rey

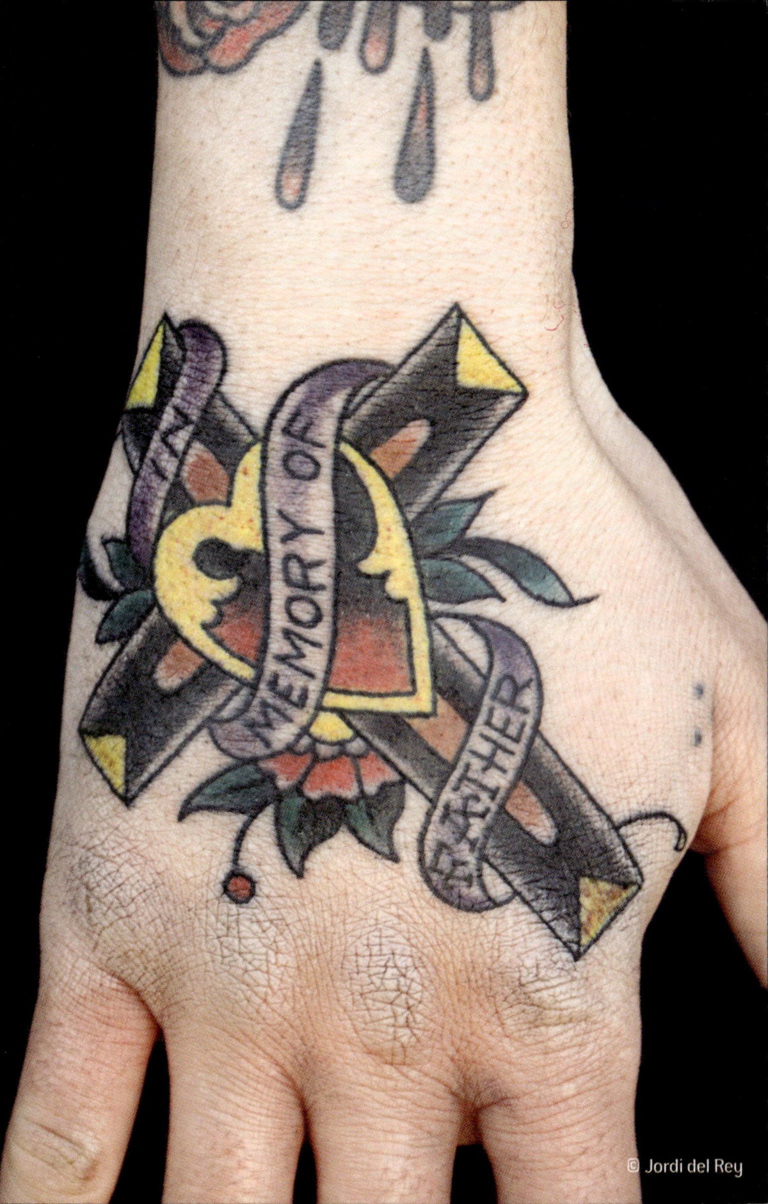

IN
MEMORY OF
FATHER

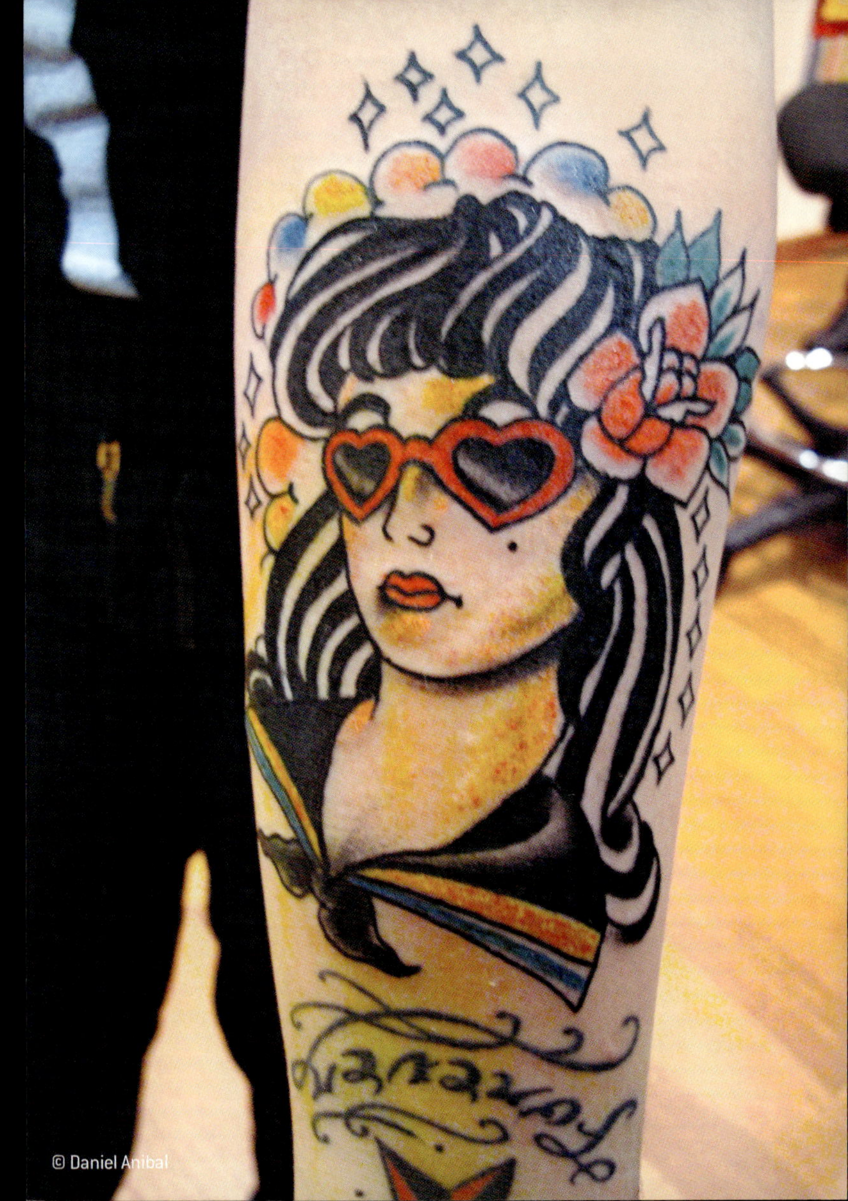

© Daniel Anibal

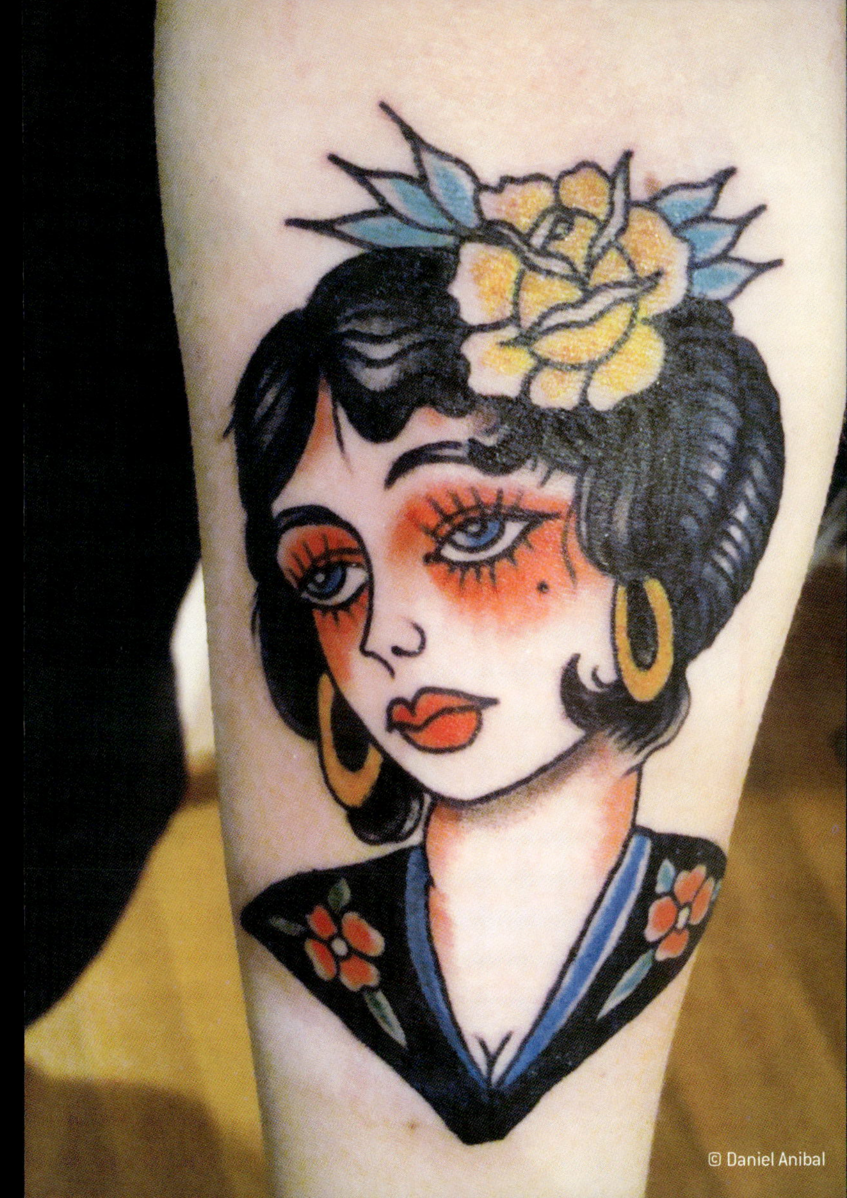

© Daniel Anibal

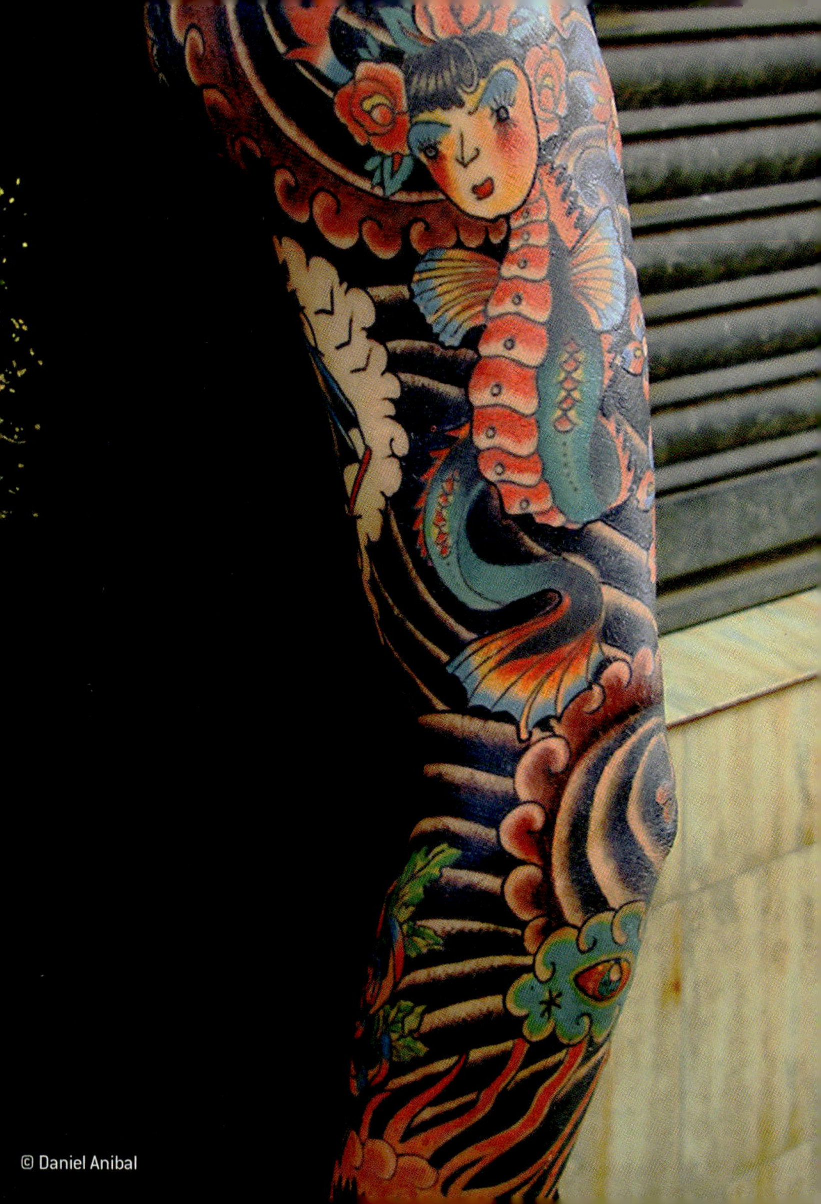

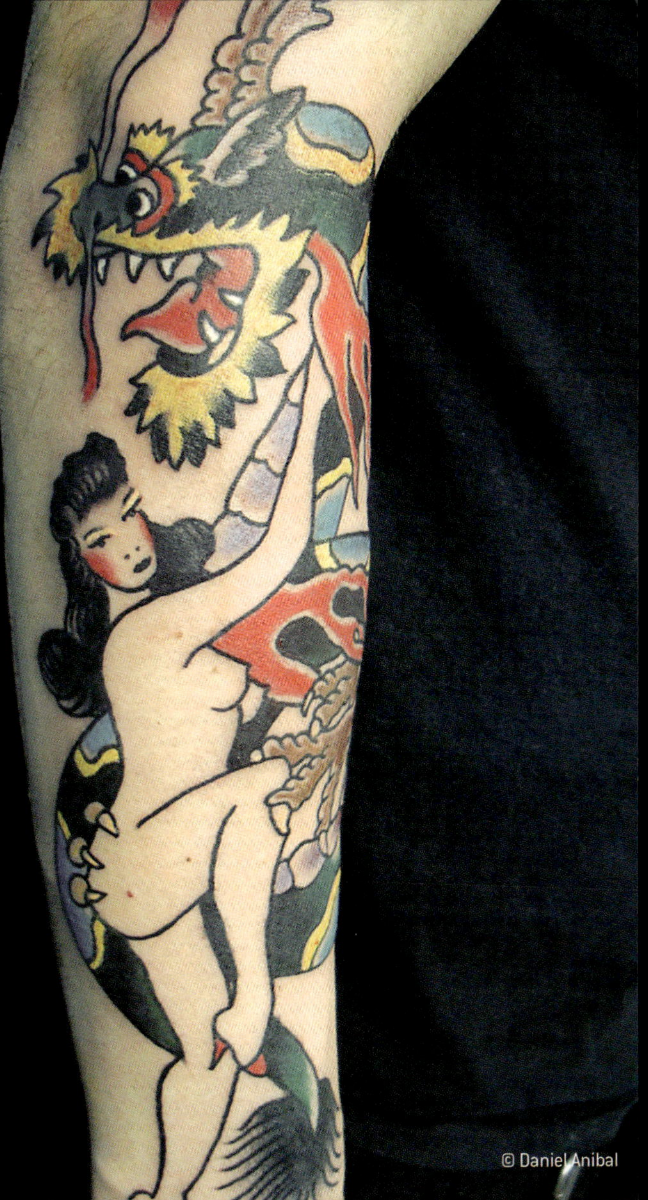
© Daniel Anibal

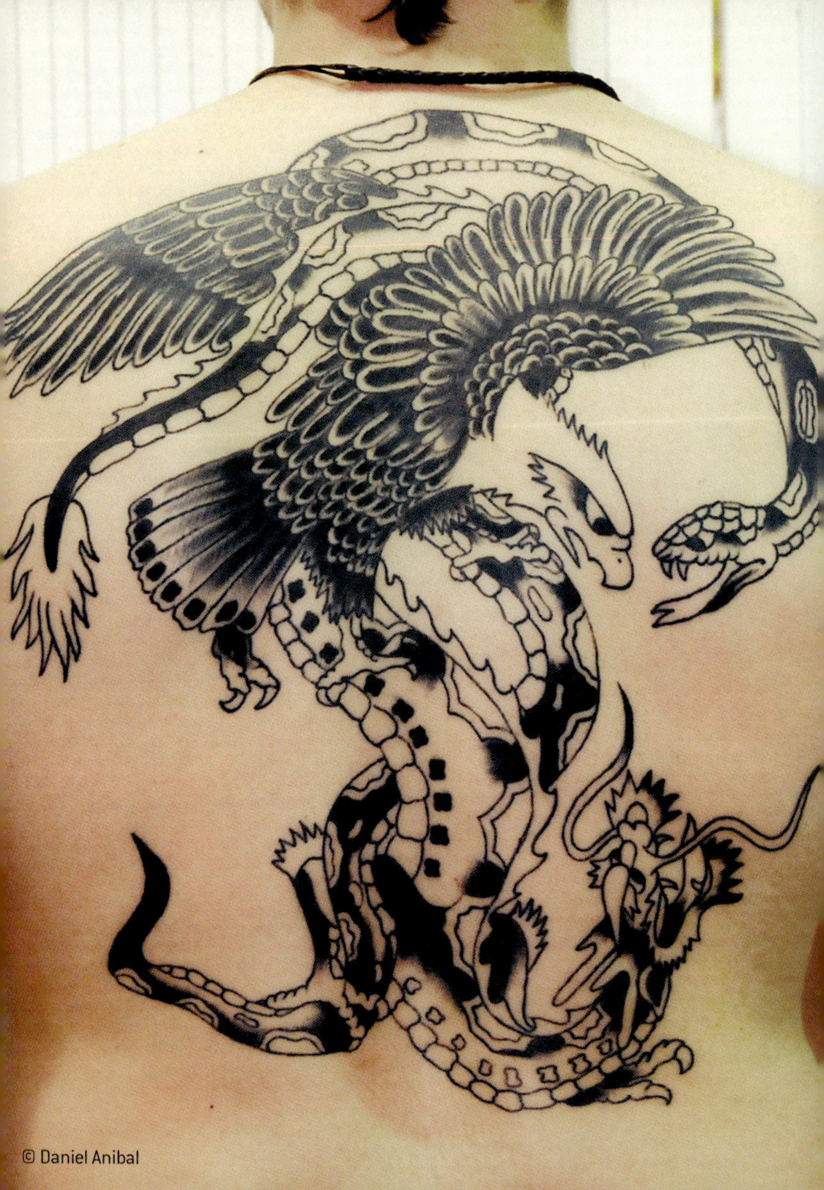

© Daniel Anibal

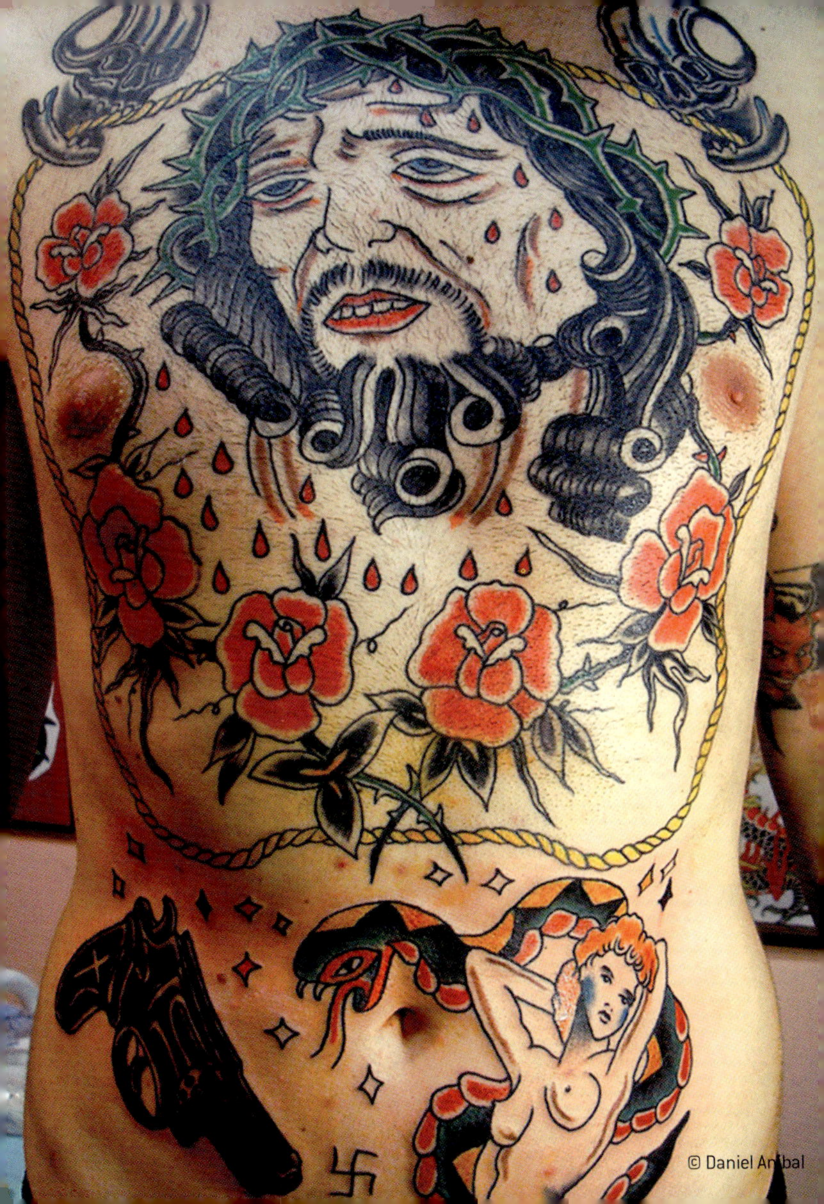
© Daniel Aníbal

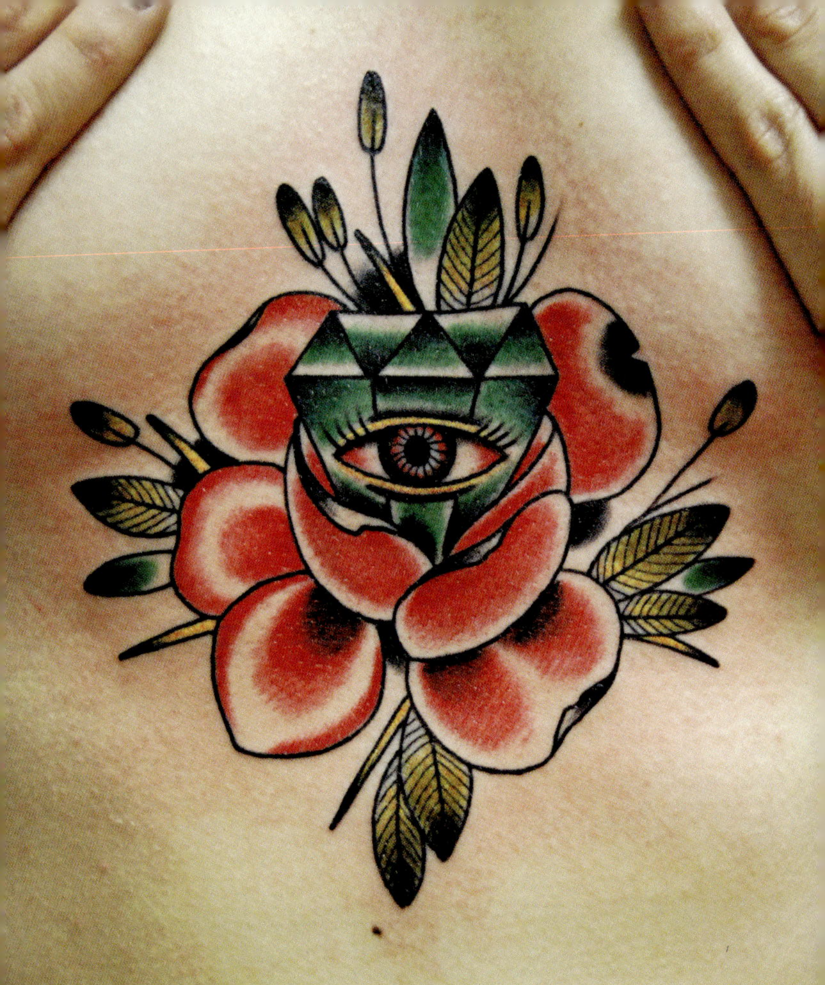

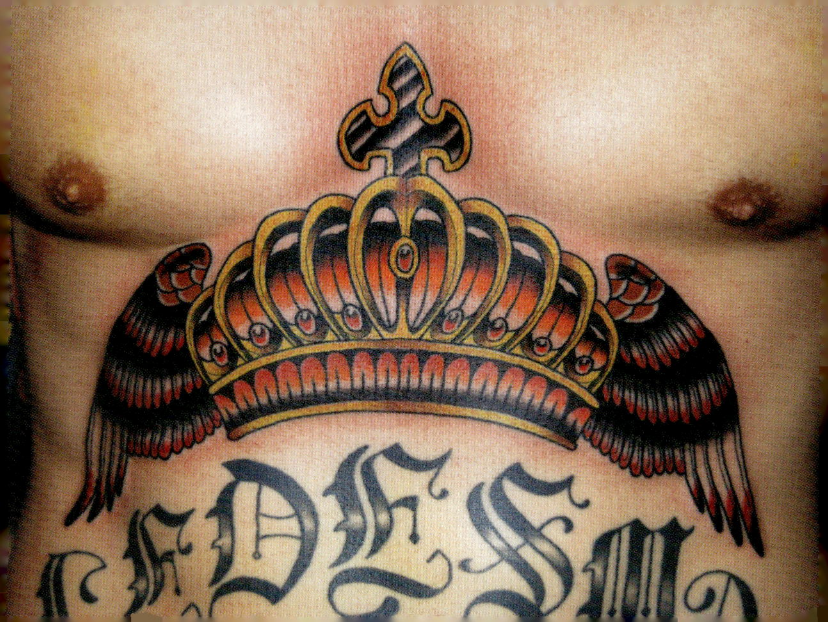
DESM

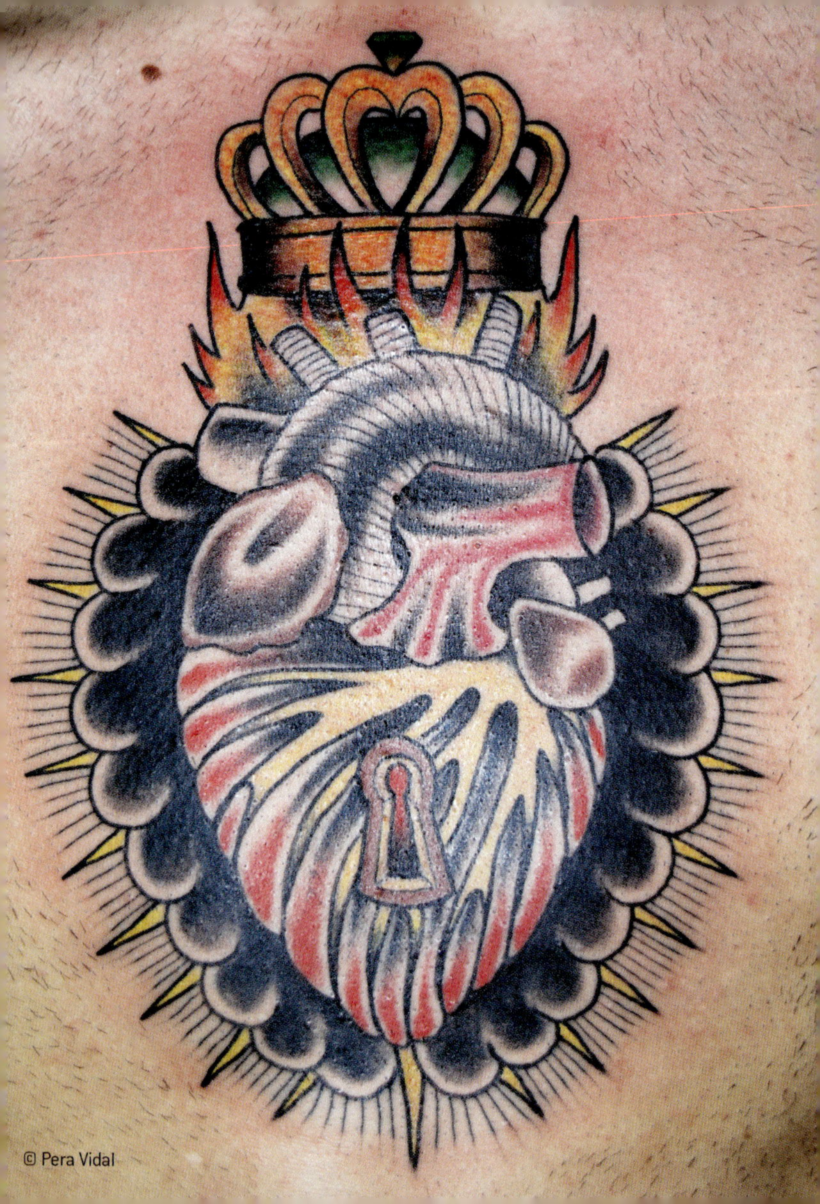
© Pera Vidal

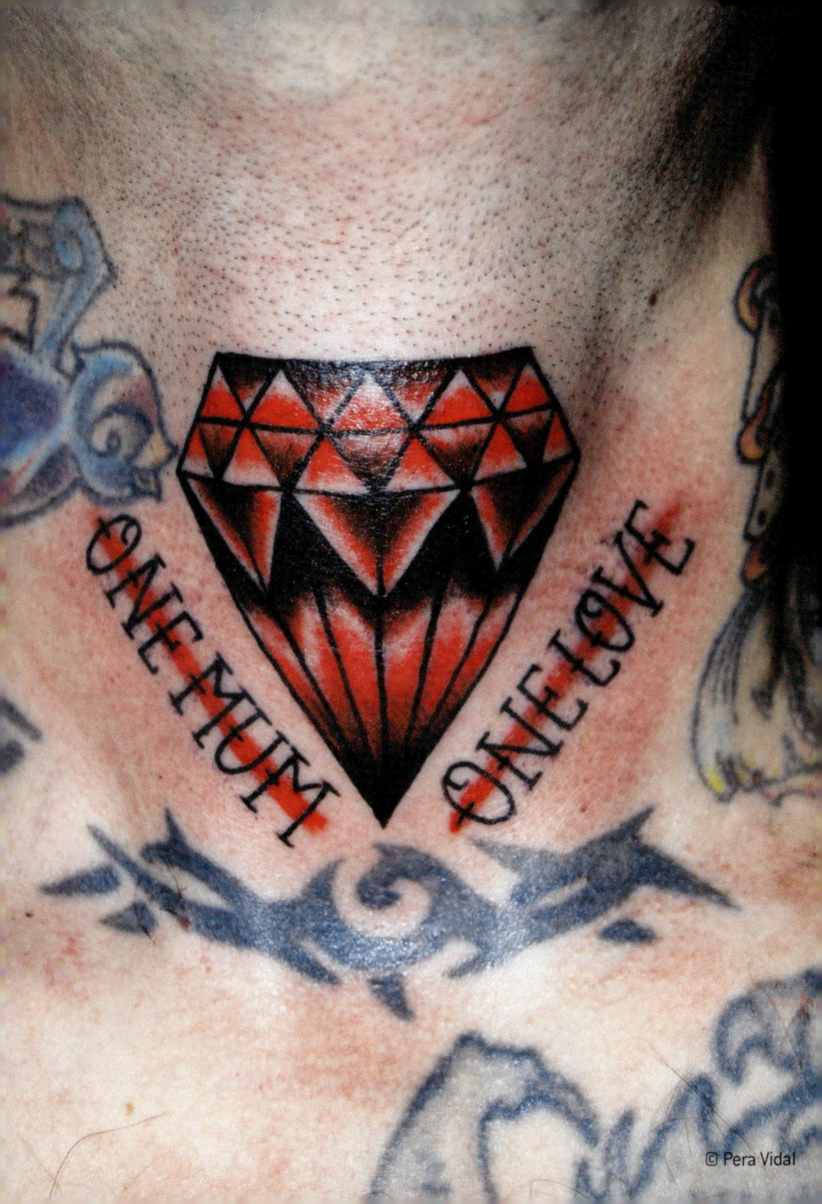

ONE MUM
ONE LOVE

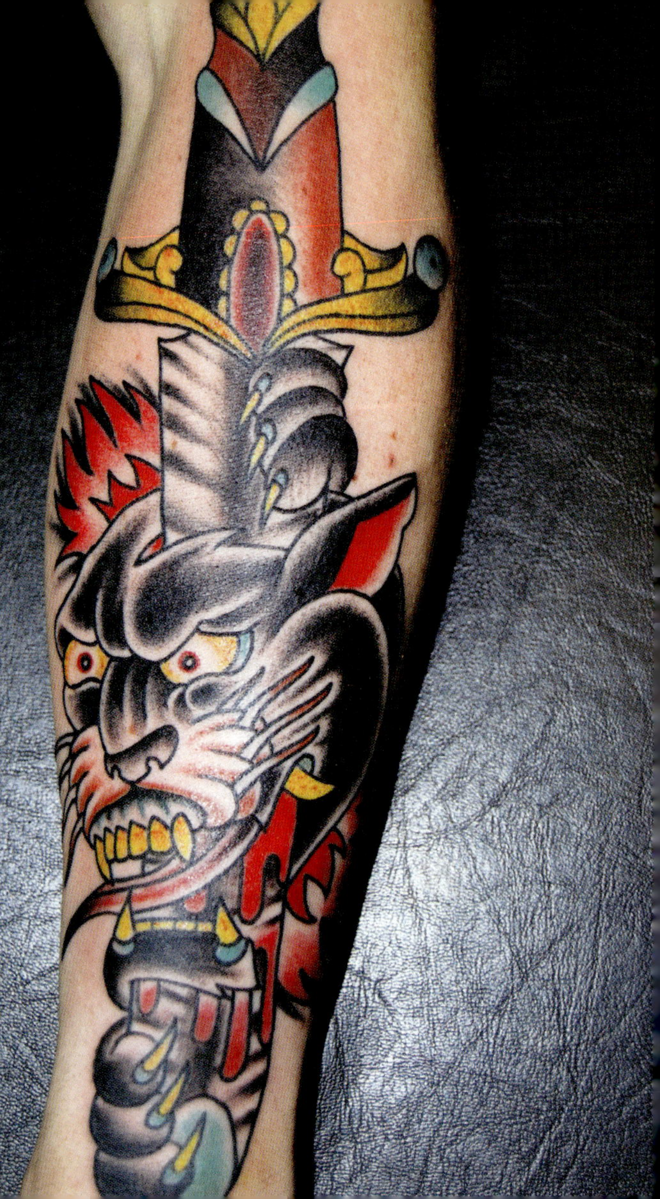

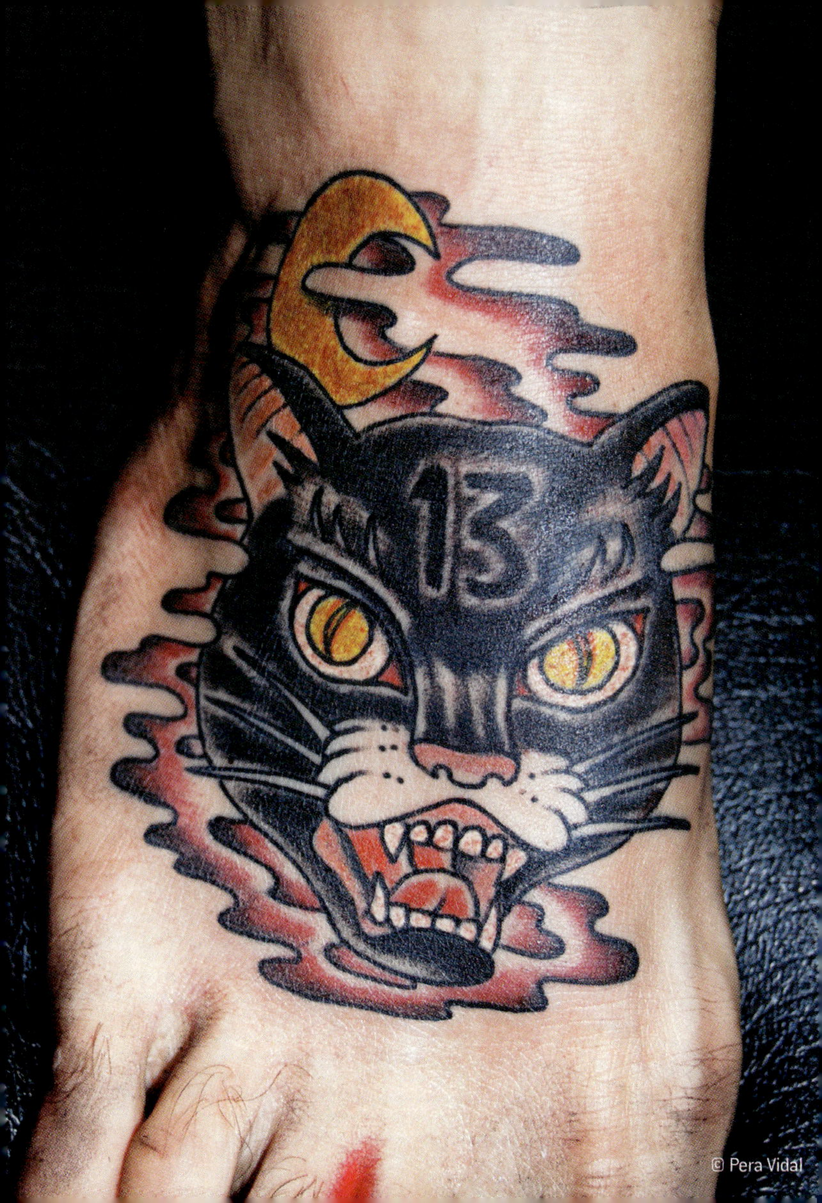
13

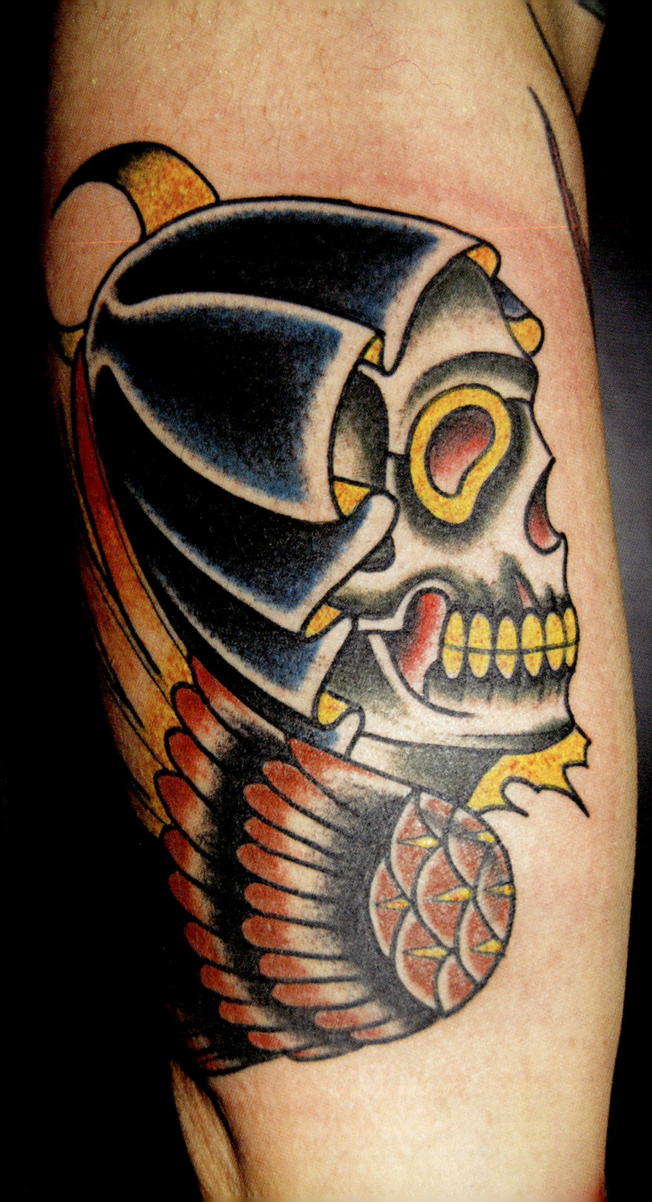

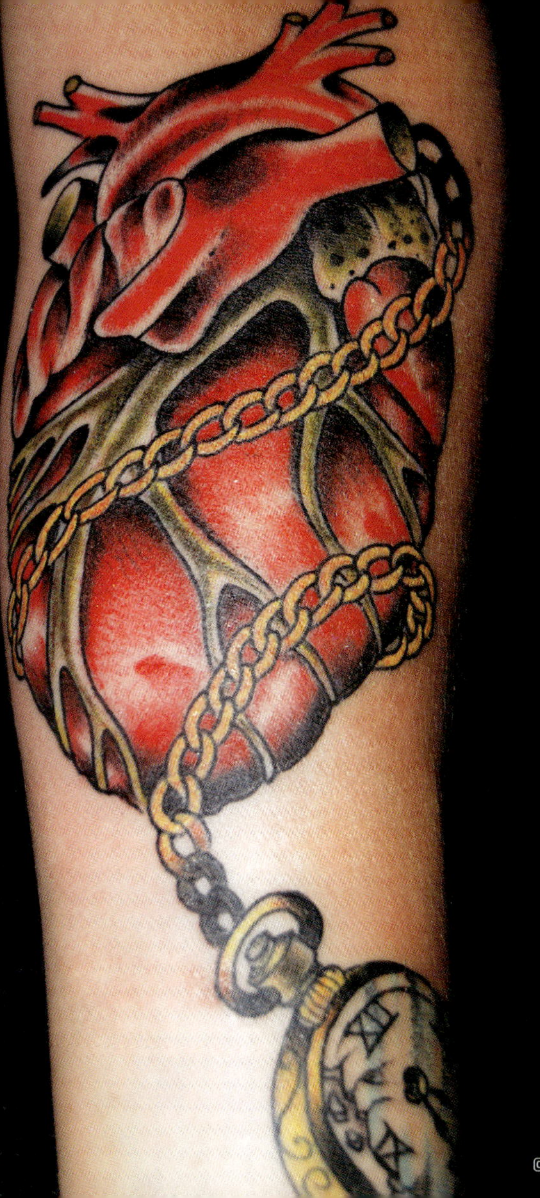

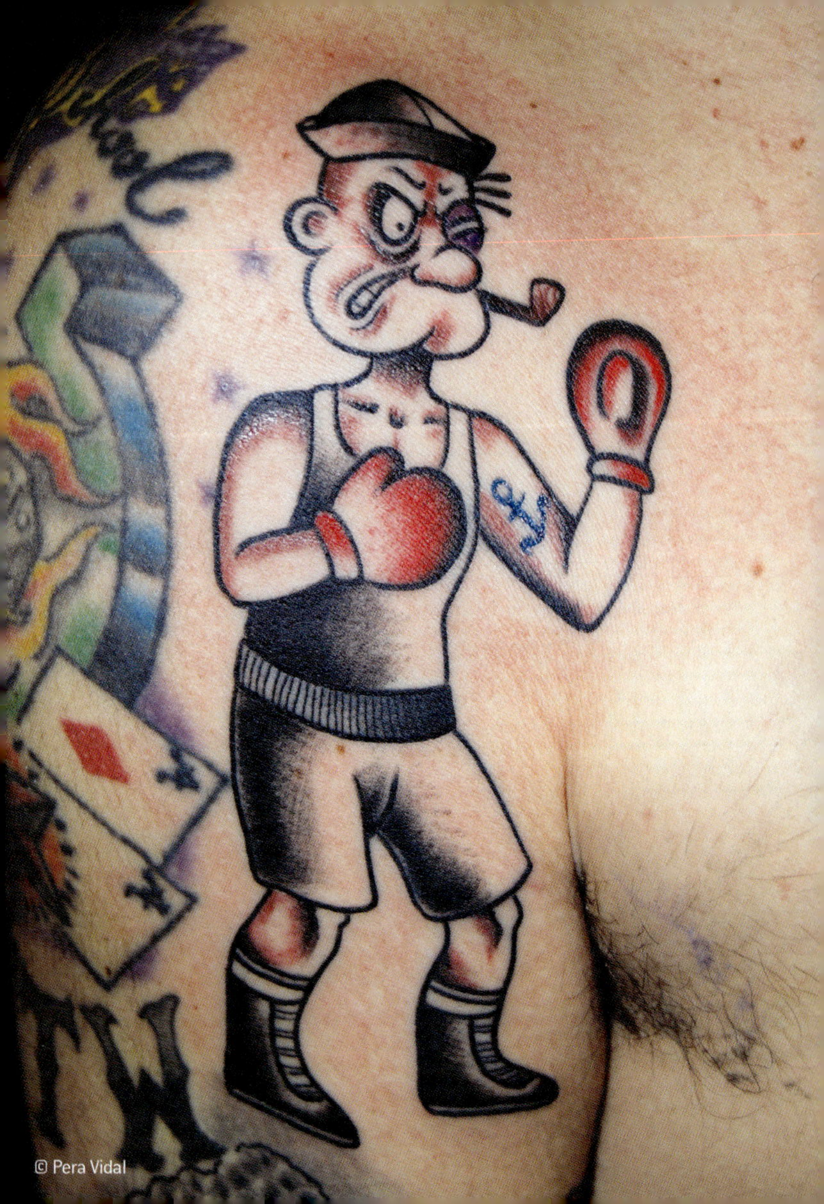

© Pera Vidal

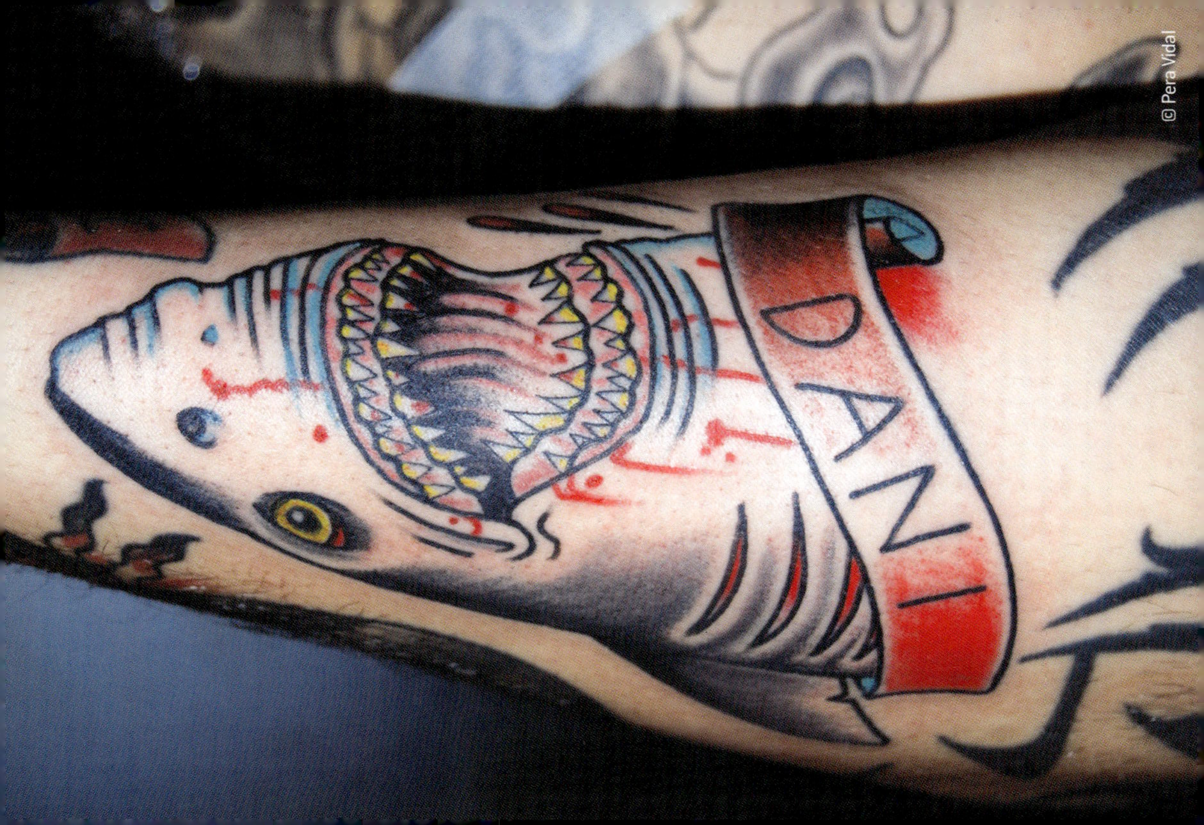
DANI

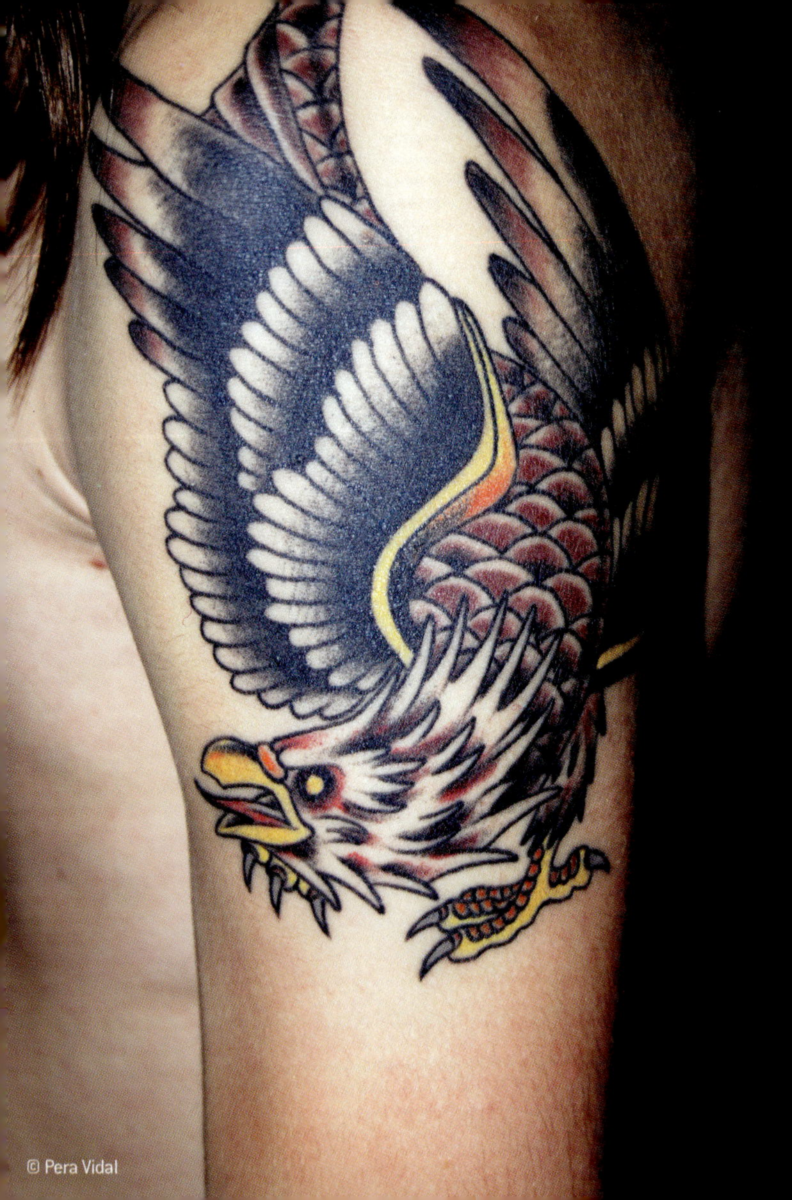

© Pera Vidal

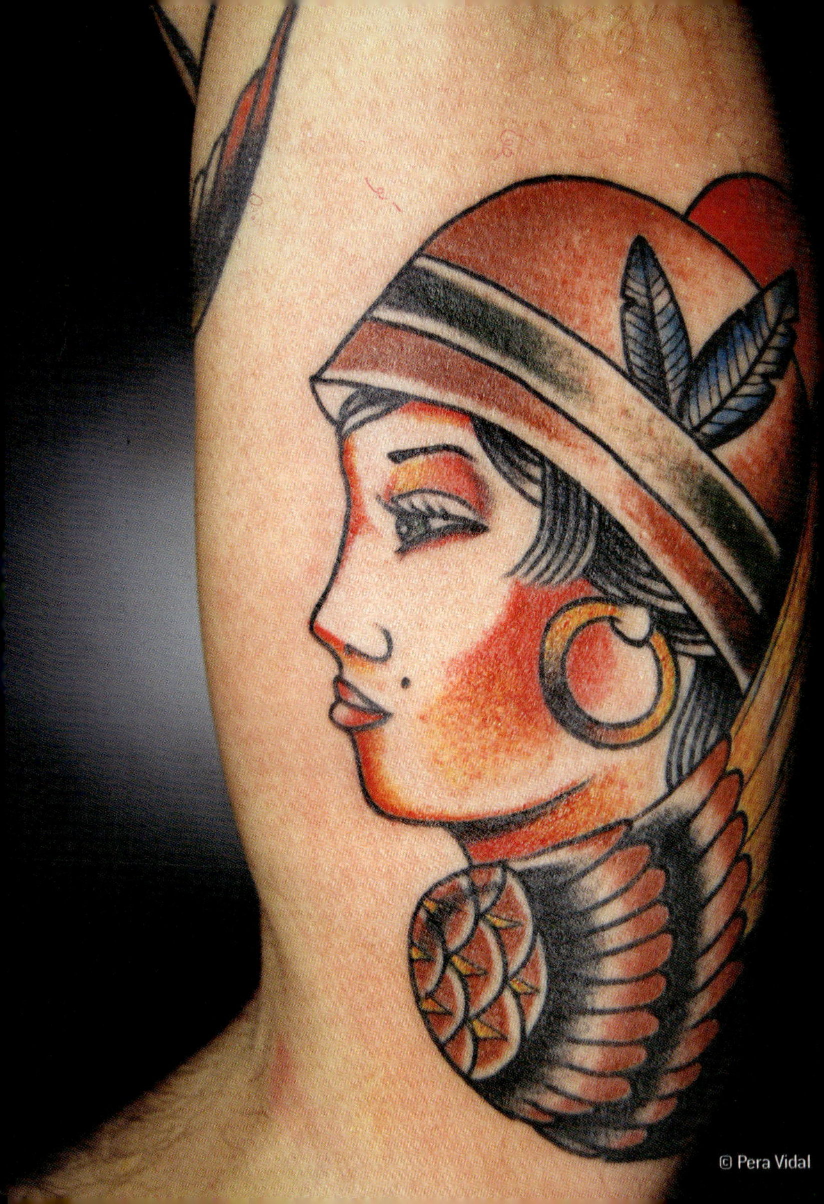

© Pera Vidal

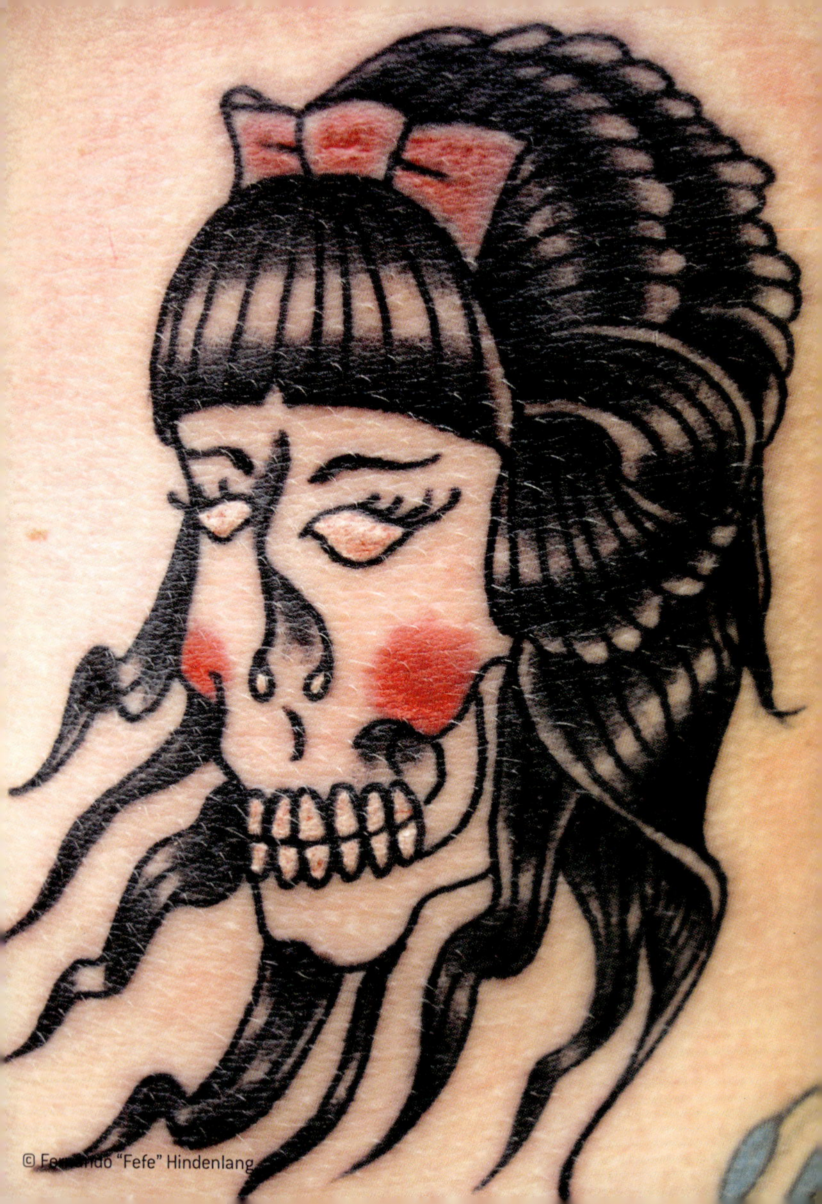

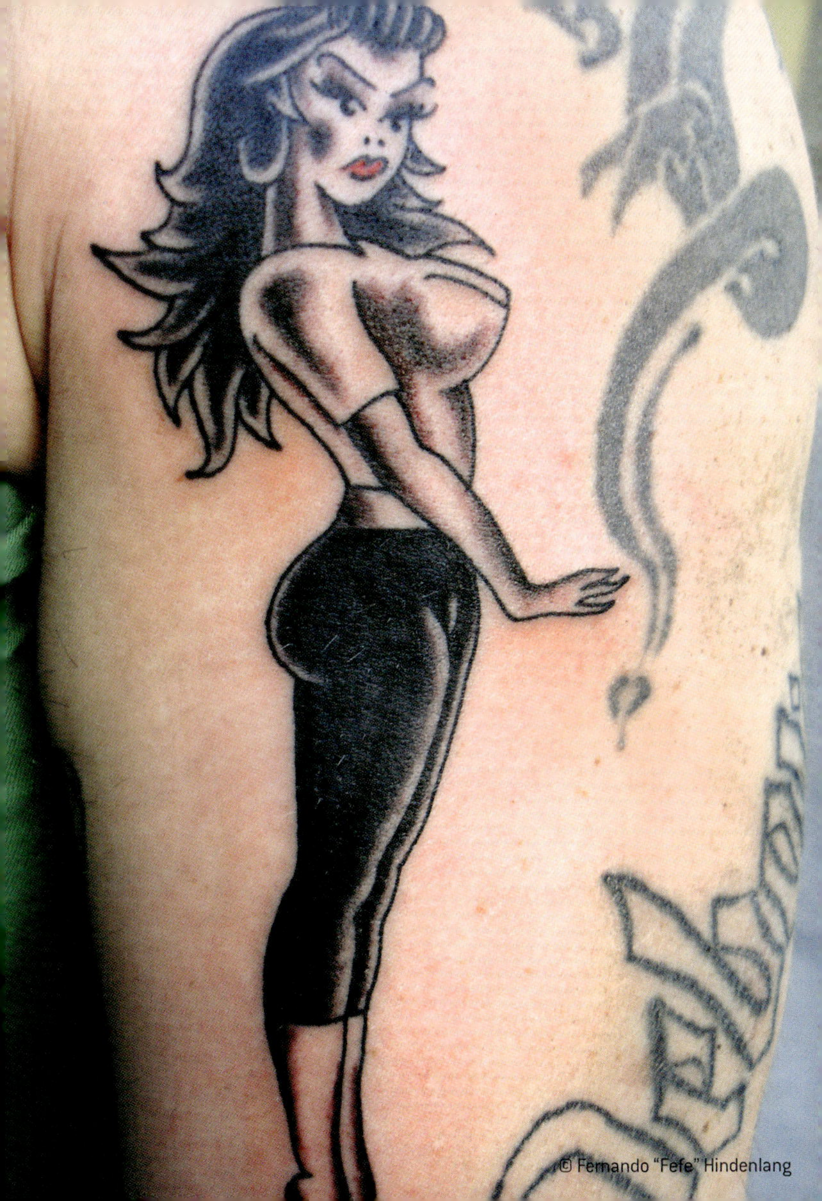
© Fernando "Fefe" Hindenlang

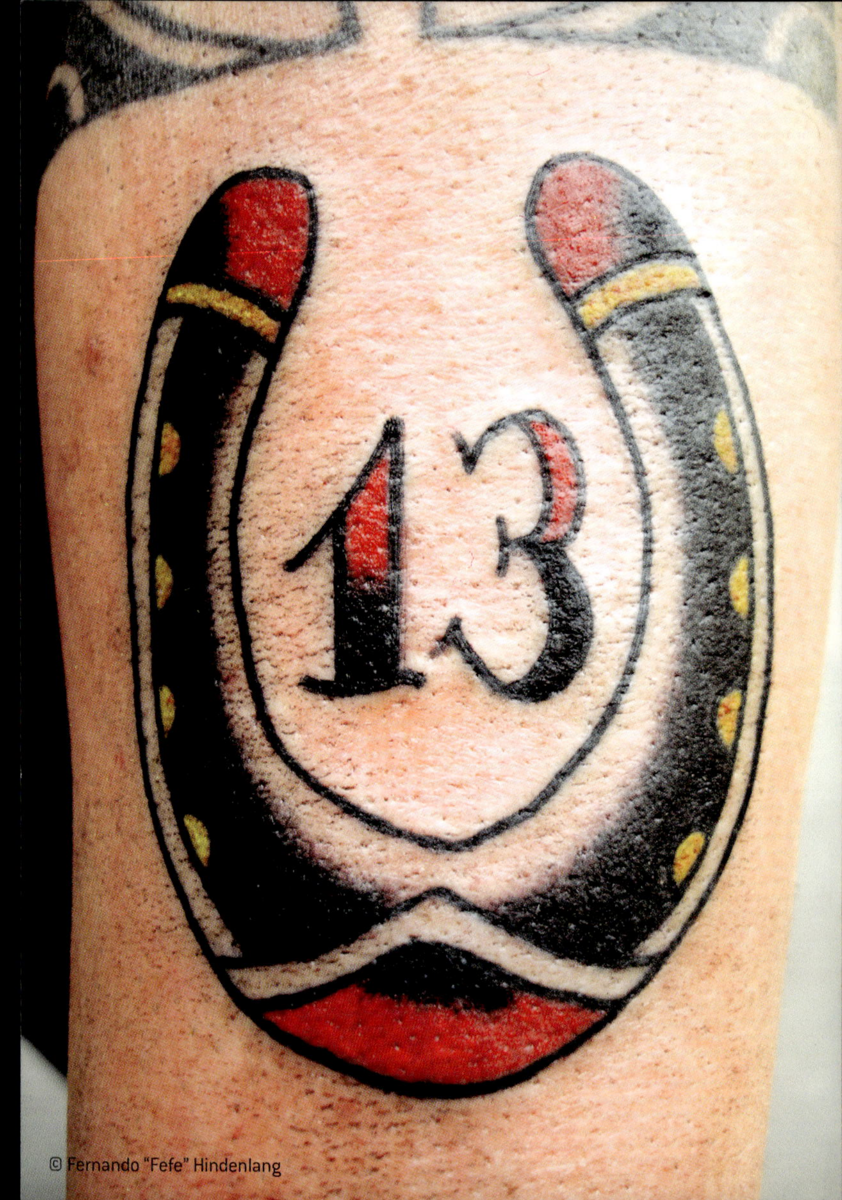

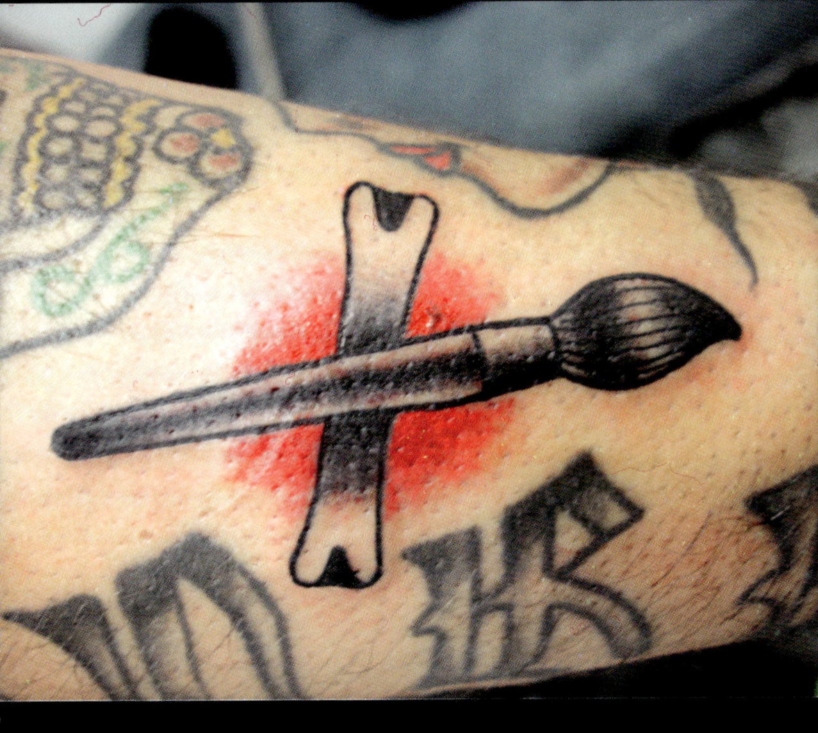

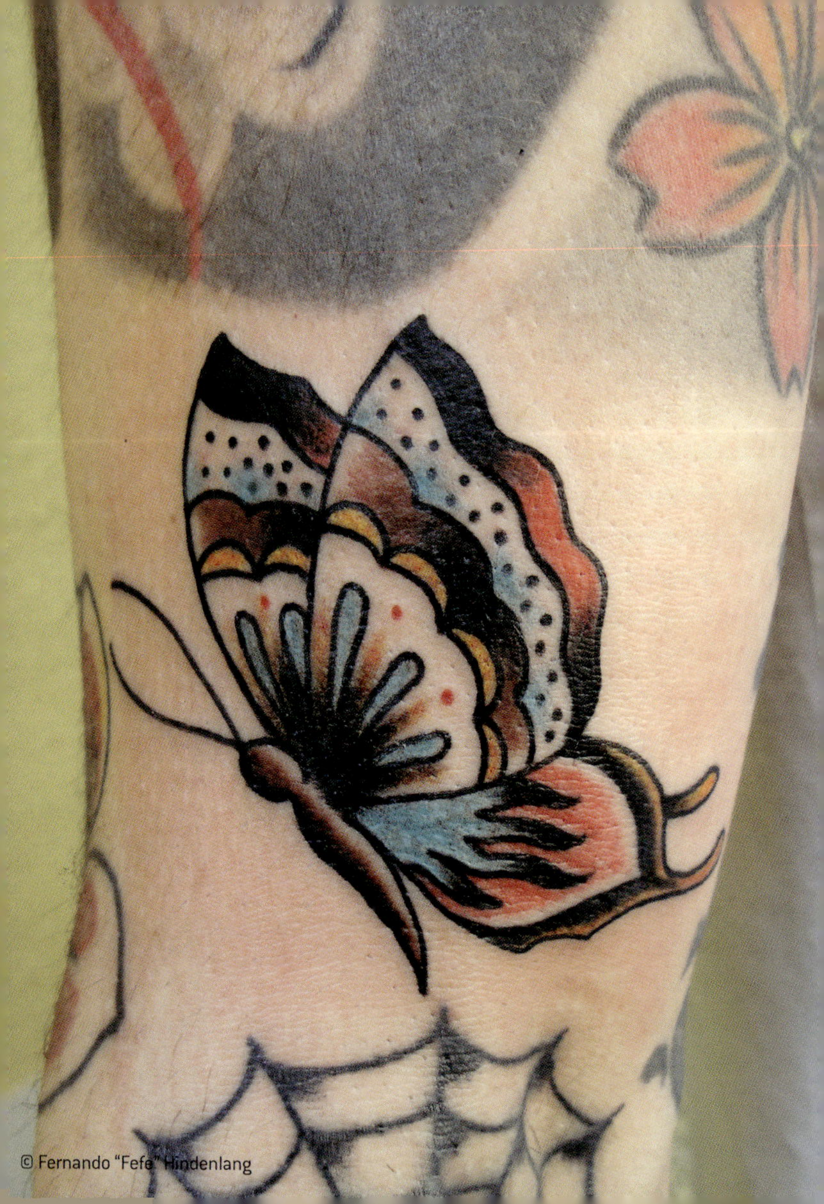

© Fernando "Fefe" Hindenlang

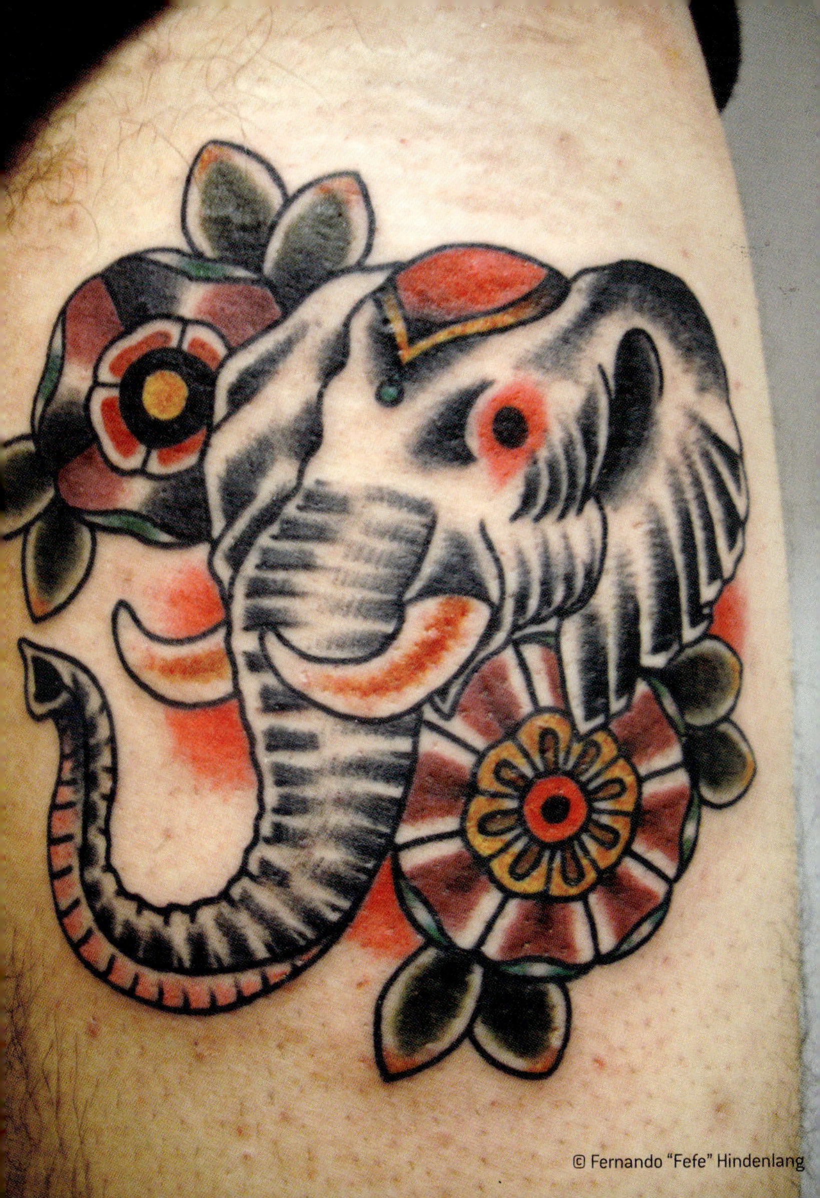

© Fernando "Fefe" Hindenlang

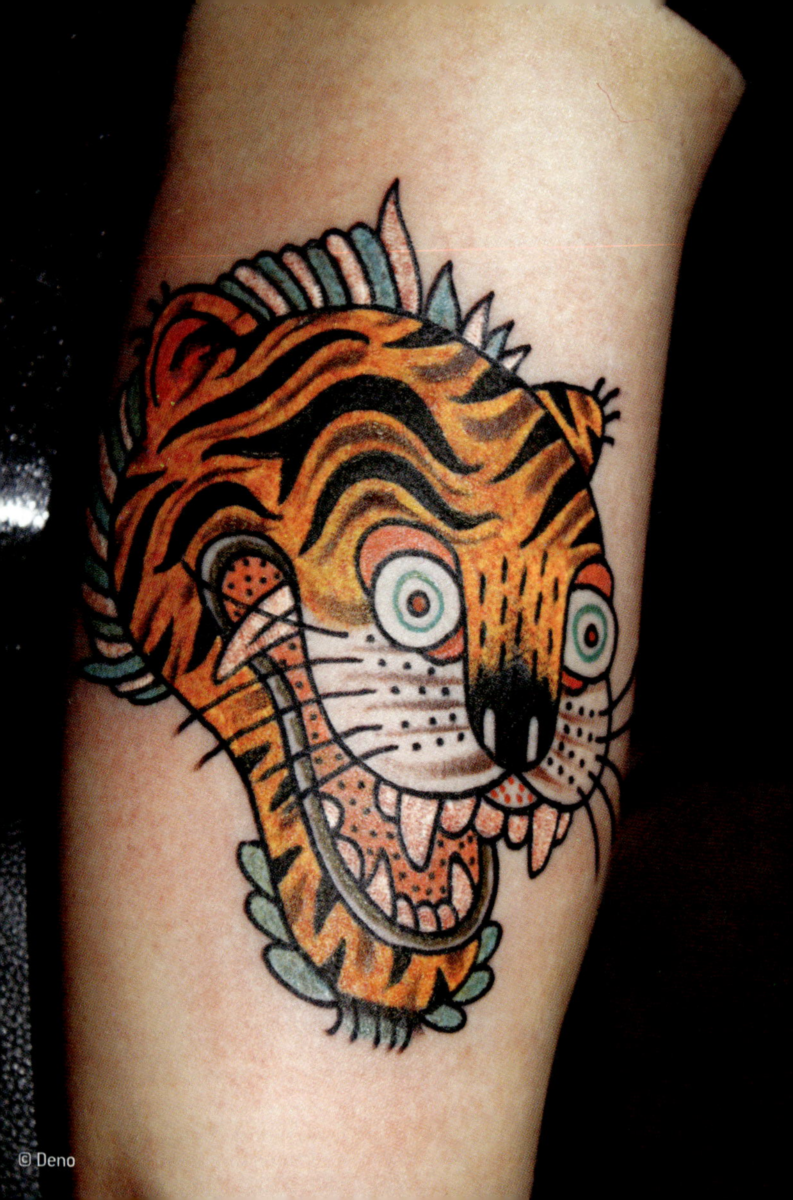
© Deno

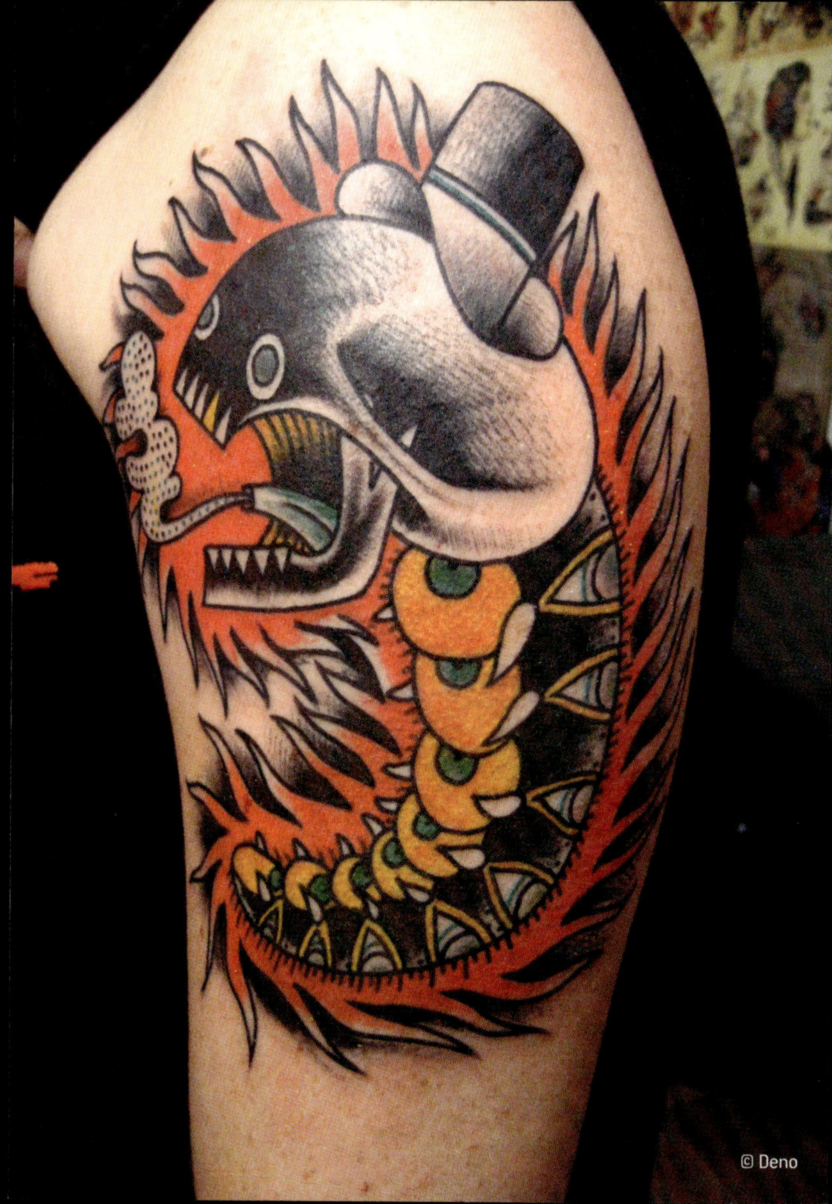
© Deno

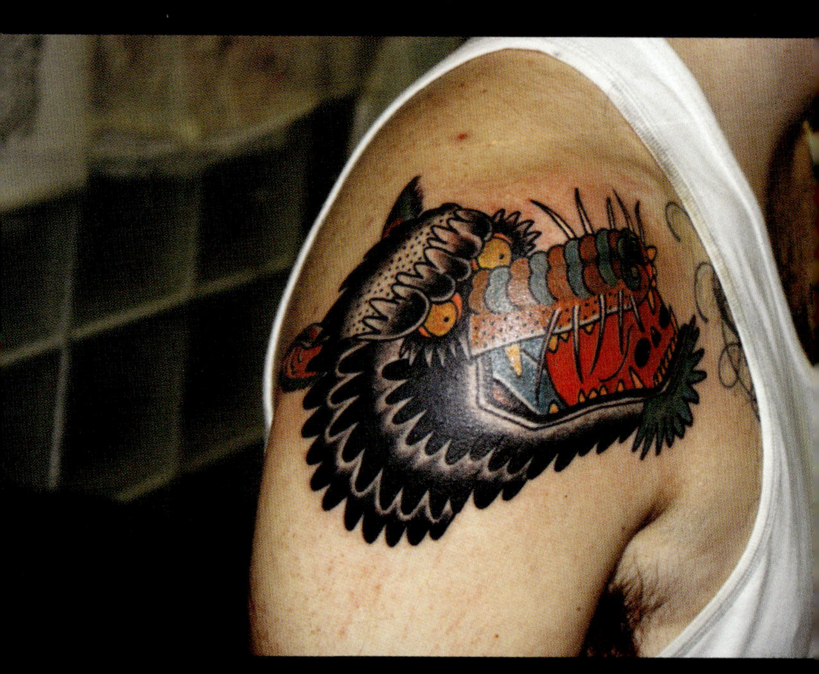

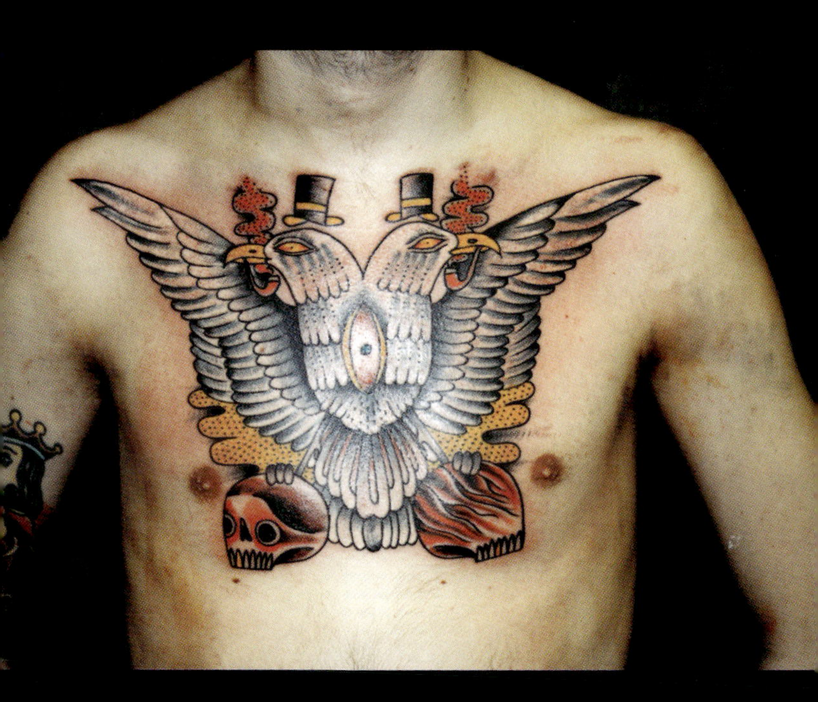

© Deno

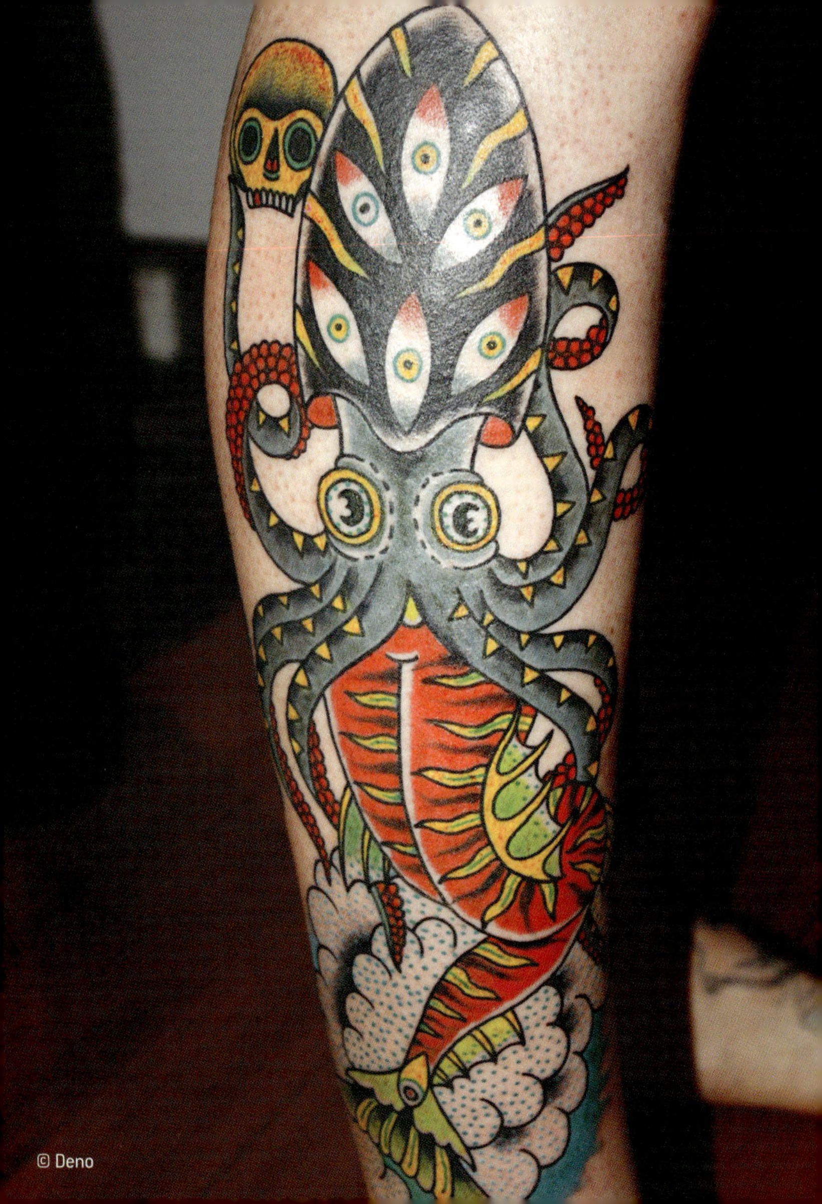
© Deno

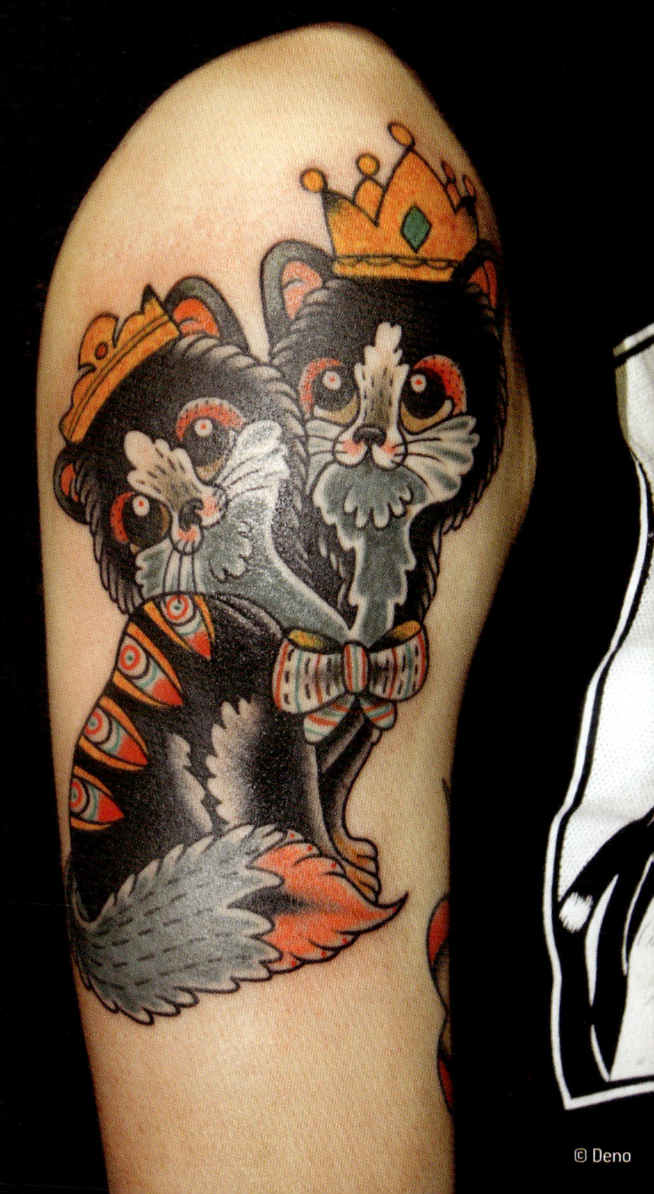

© Deno

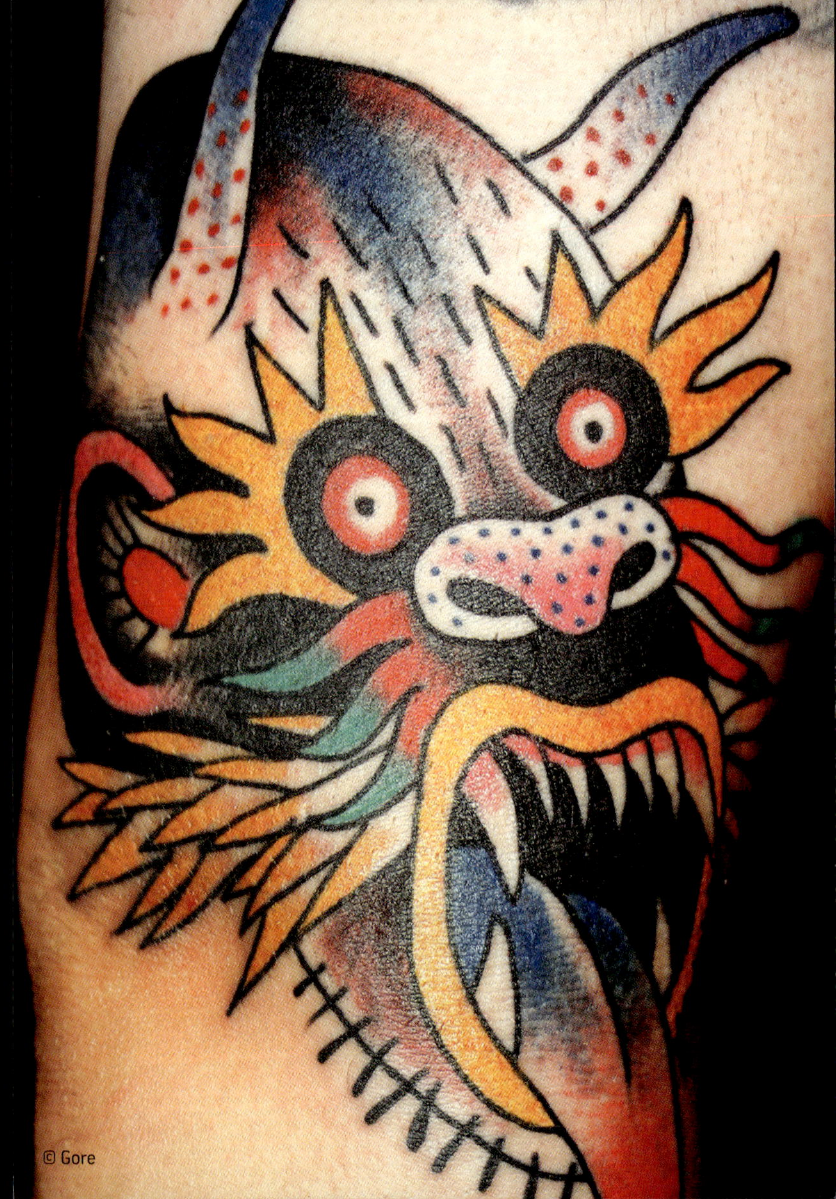
© Gore

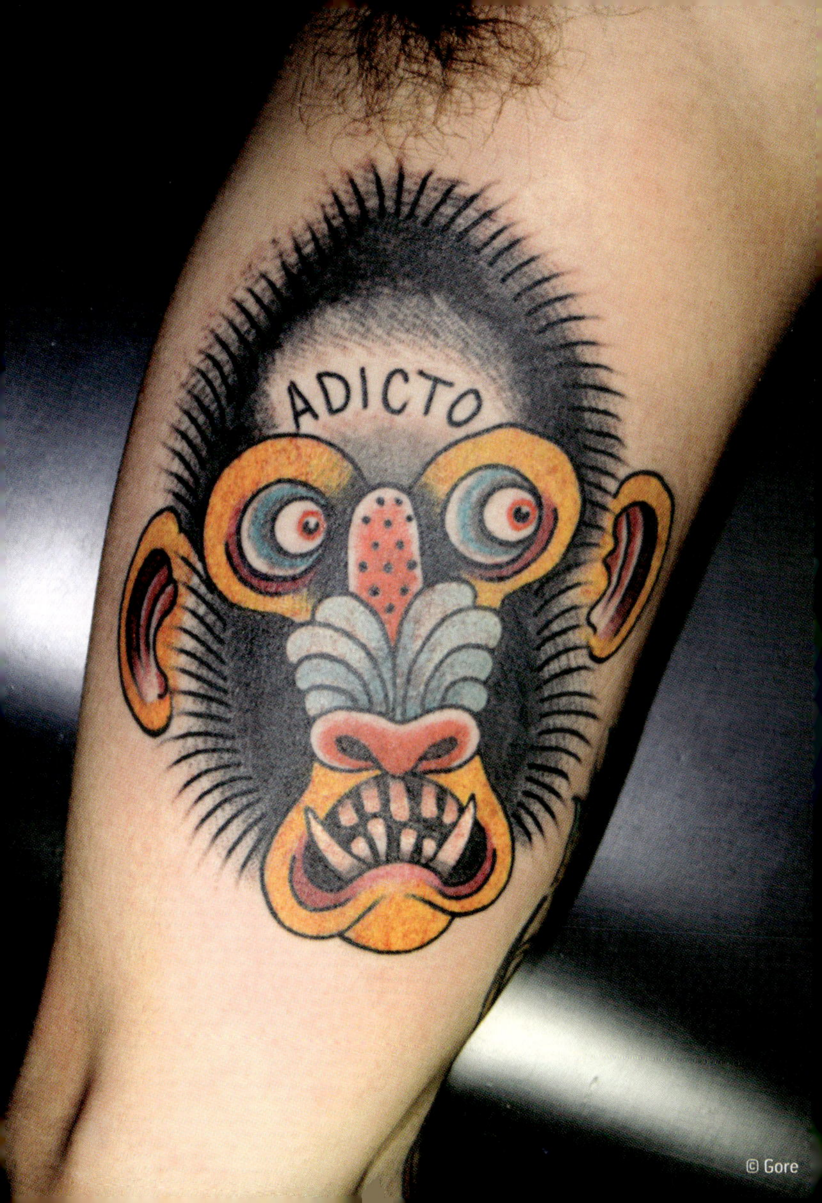
ADICTO

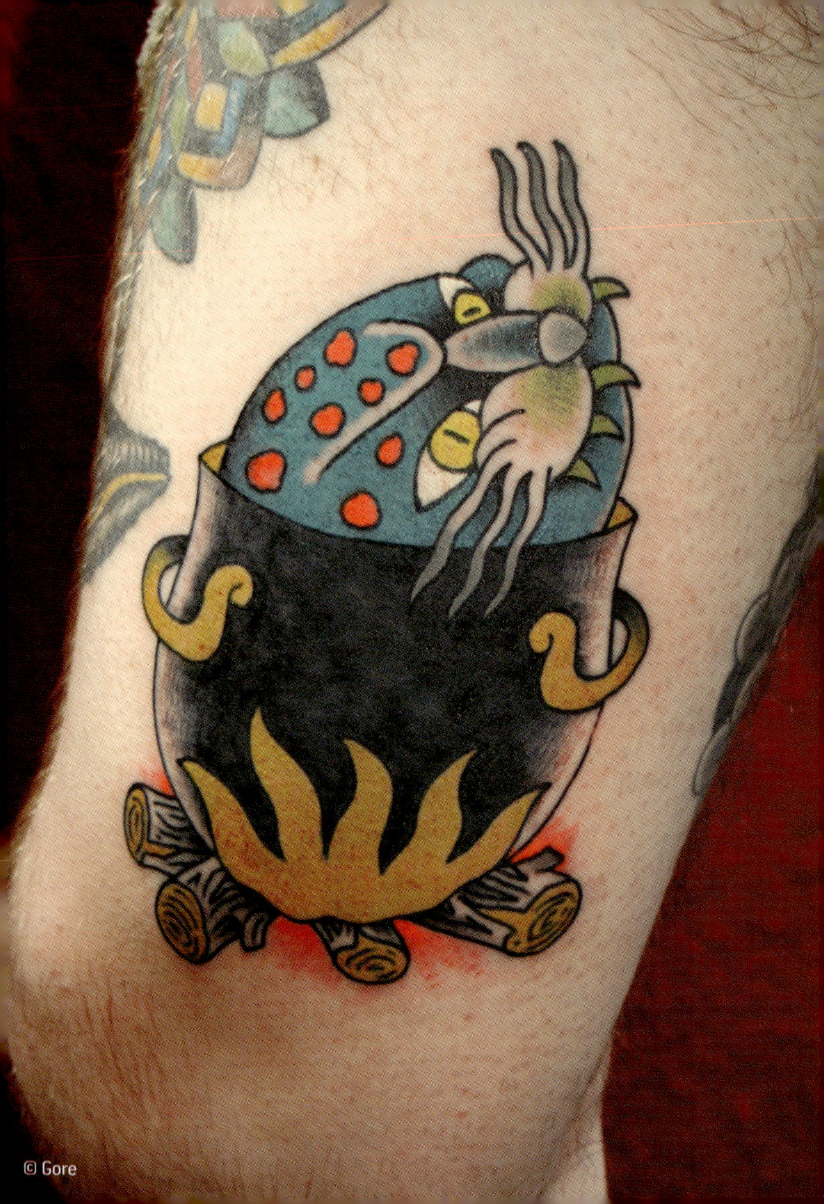
© Gore

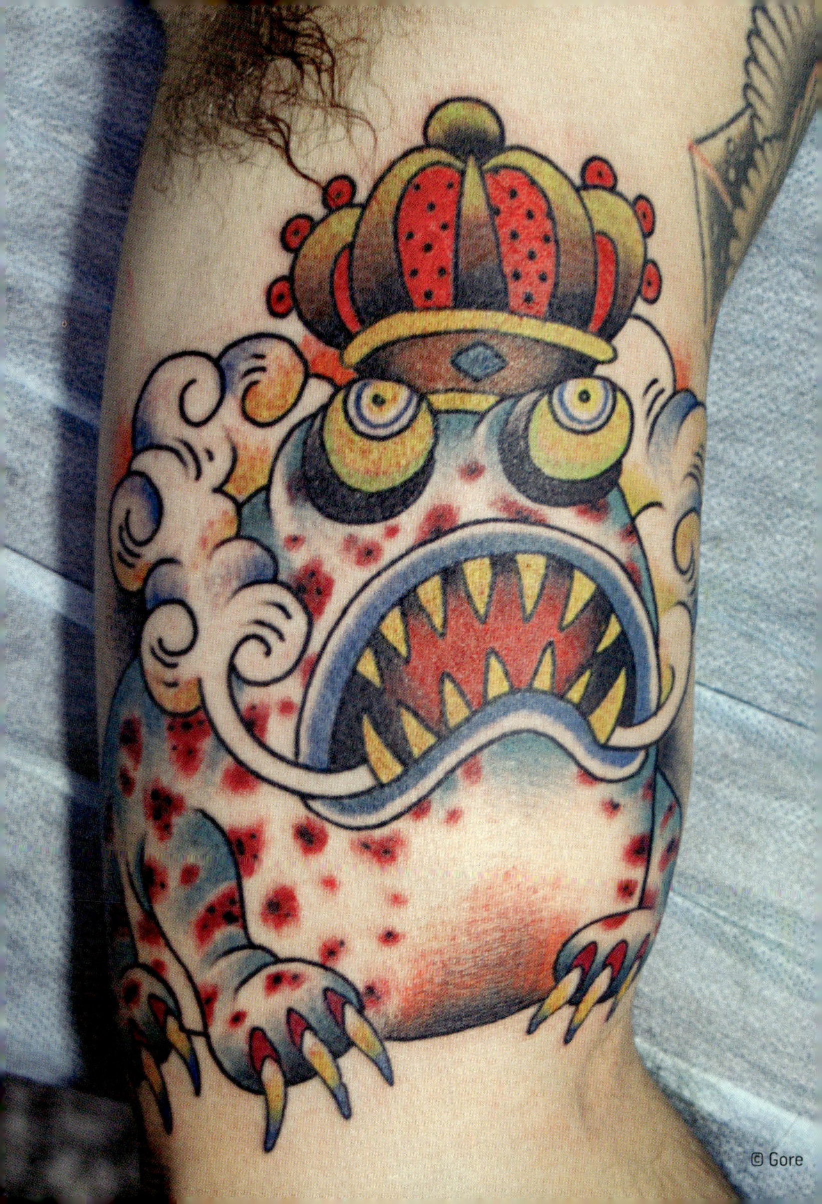

© Gore

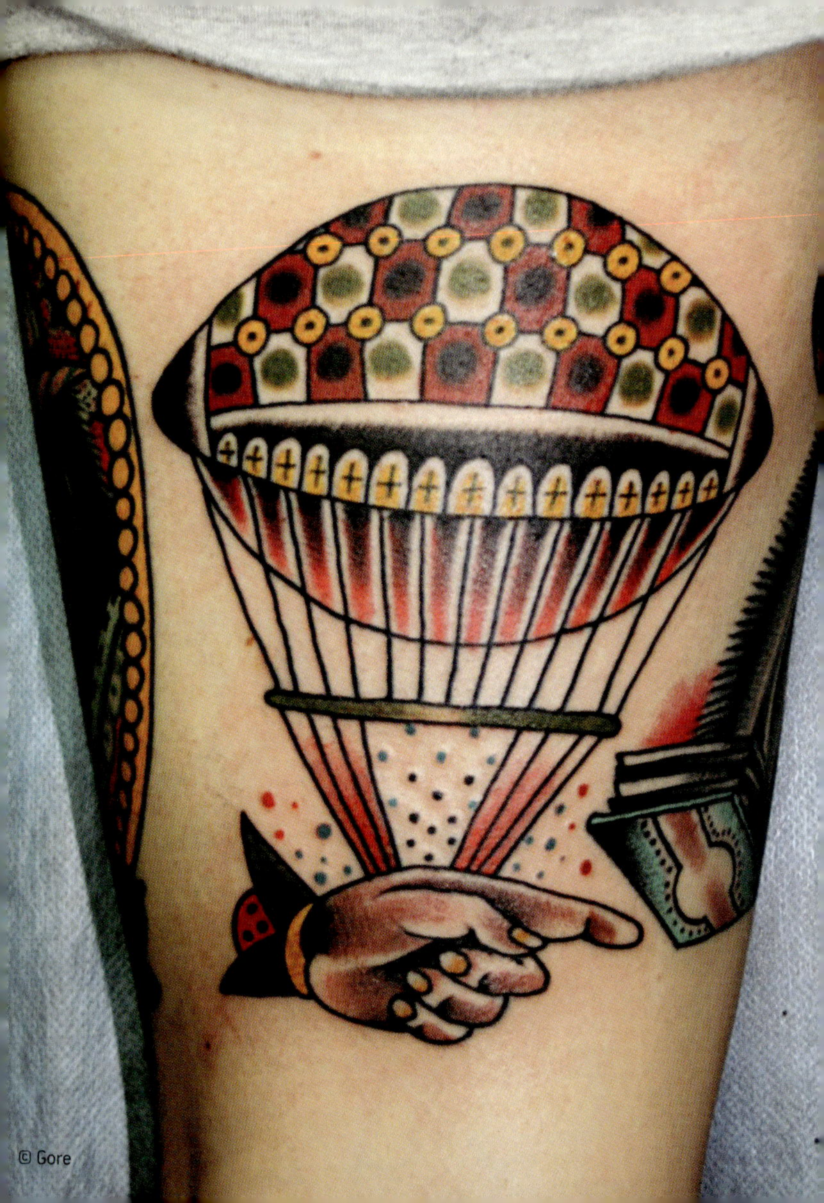

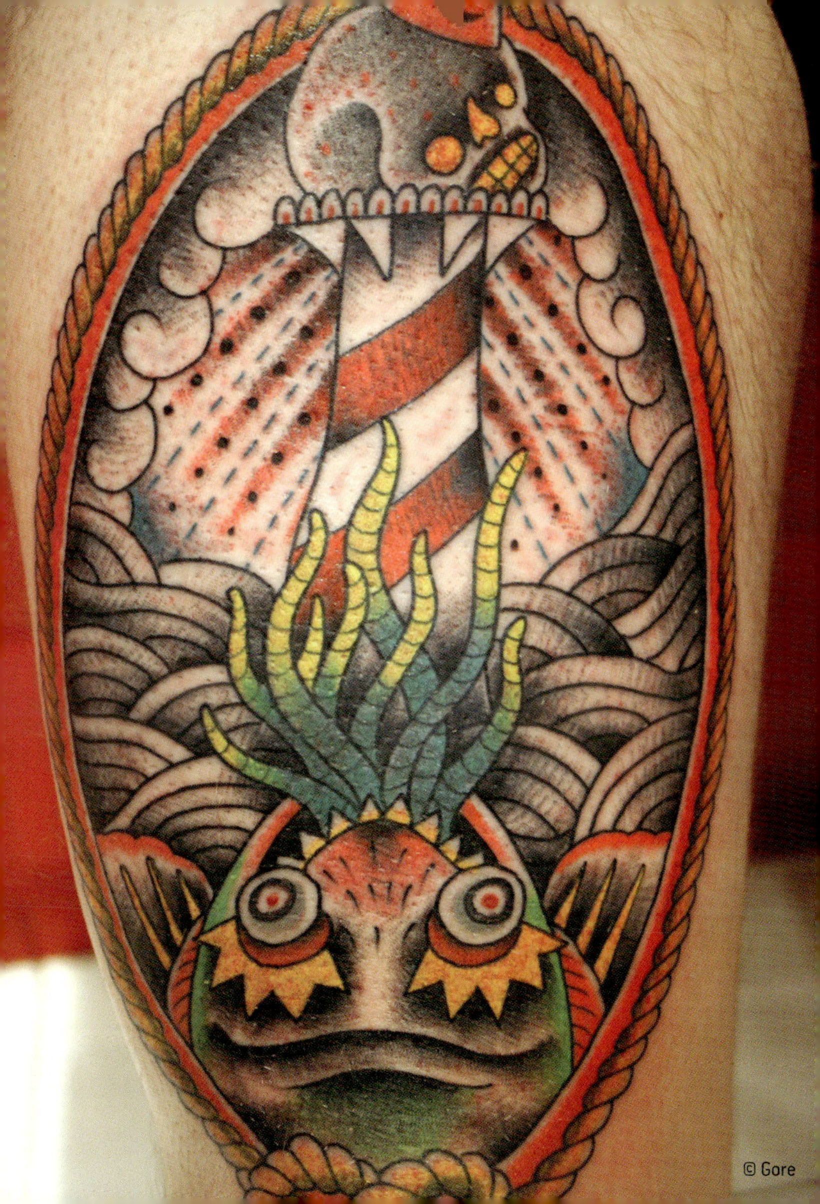
© Gore

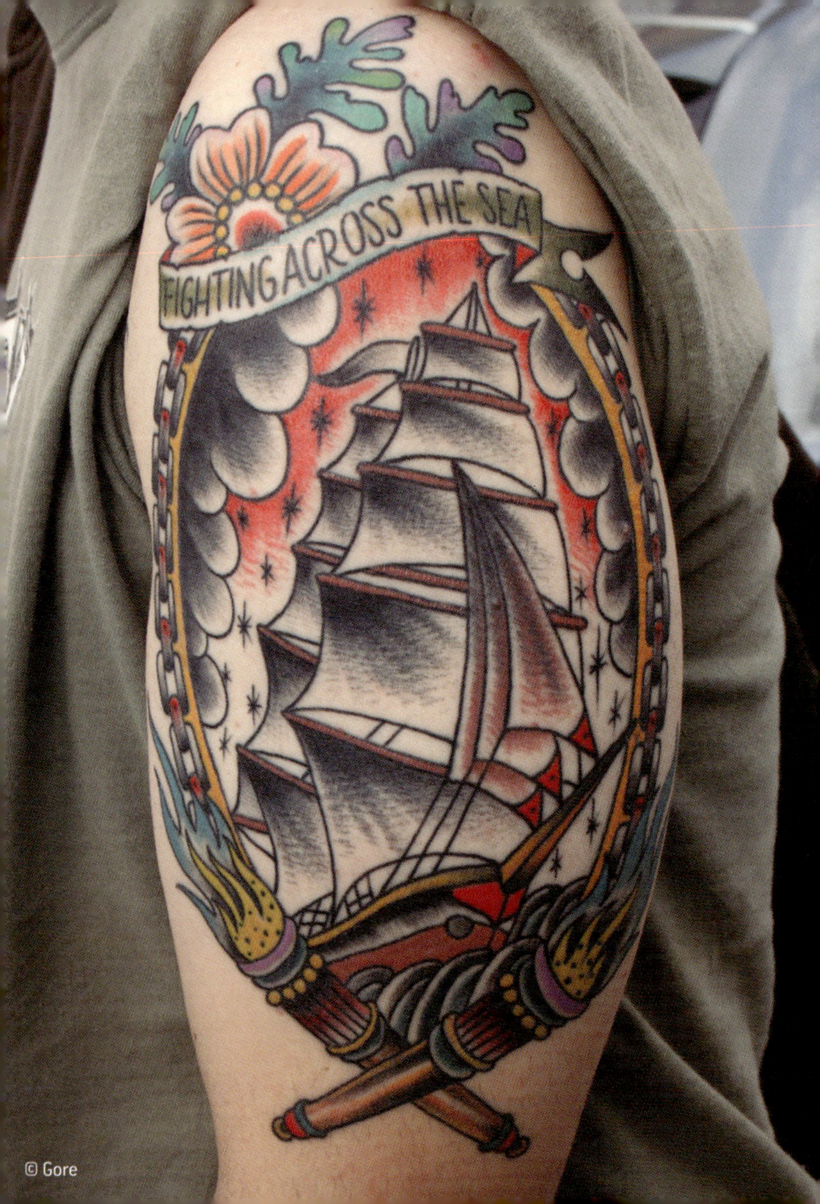

FIGHTING ACROSS THE SEA
© Gore

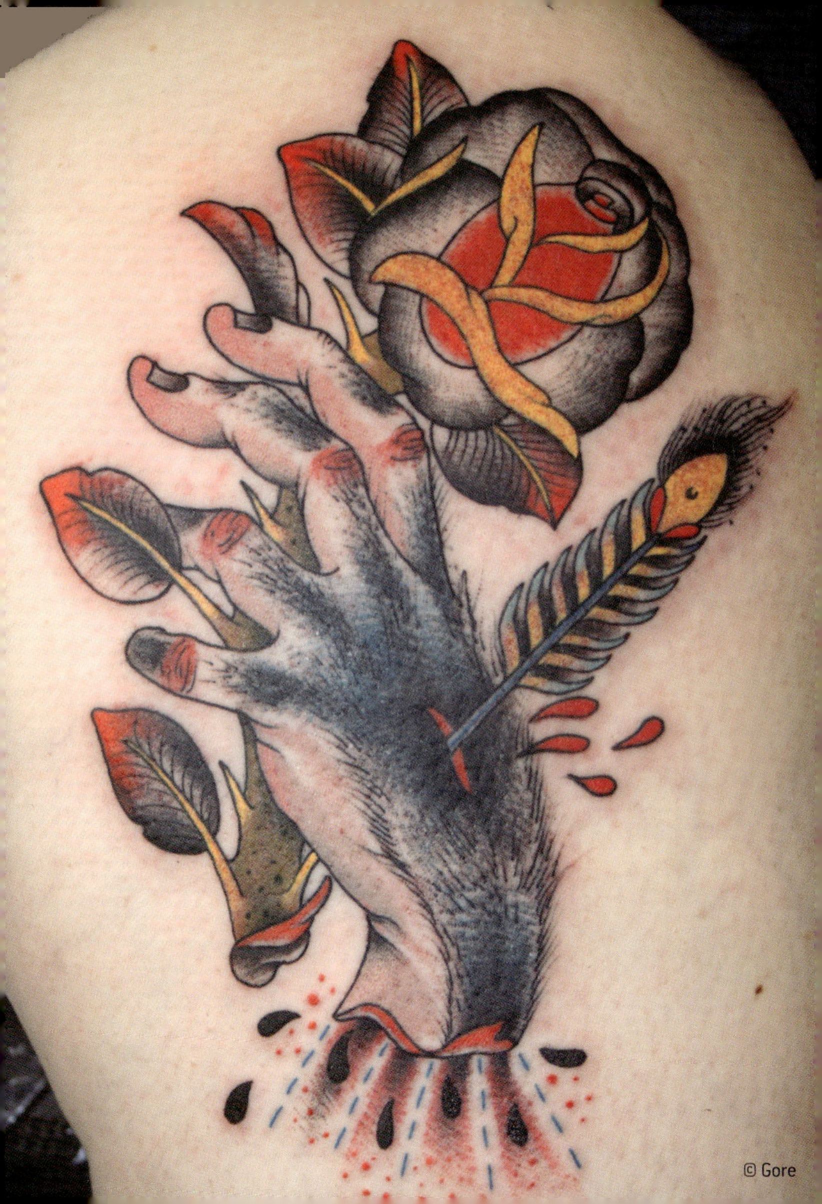
© Gore

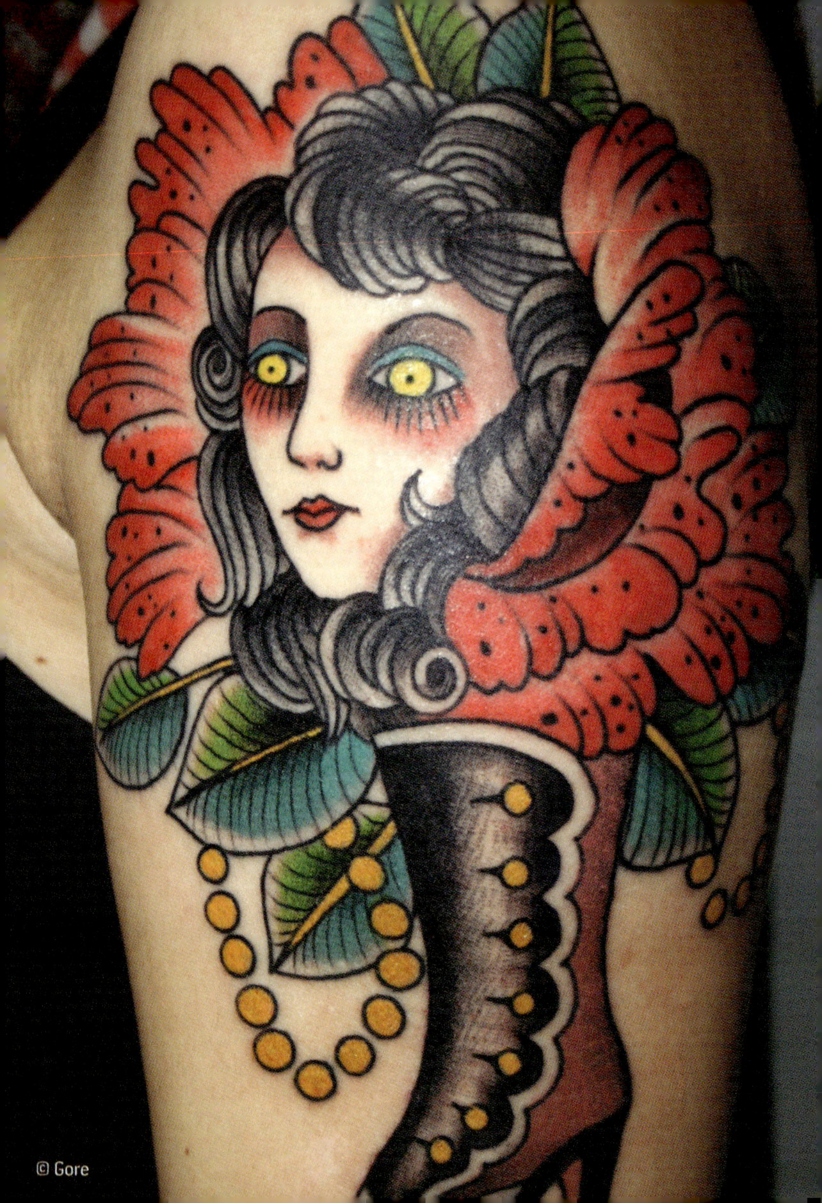
© Gore

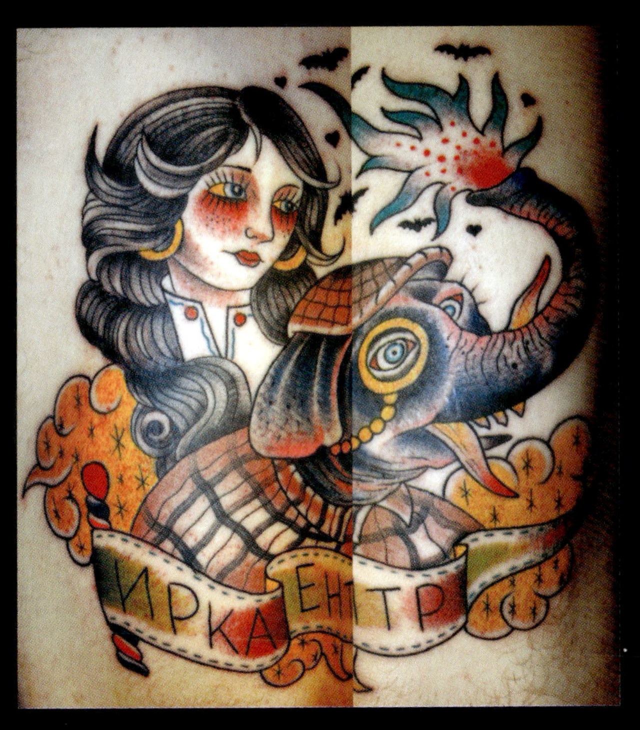

© Gore

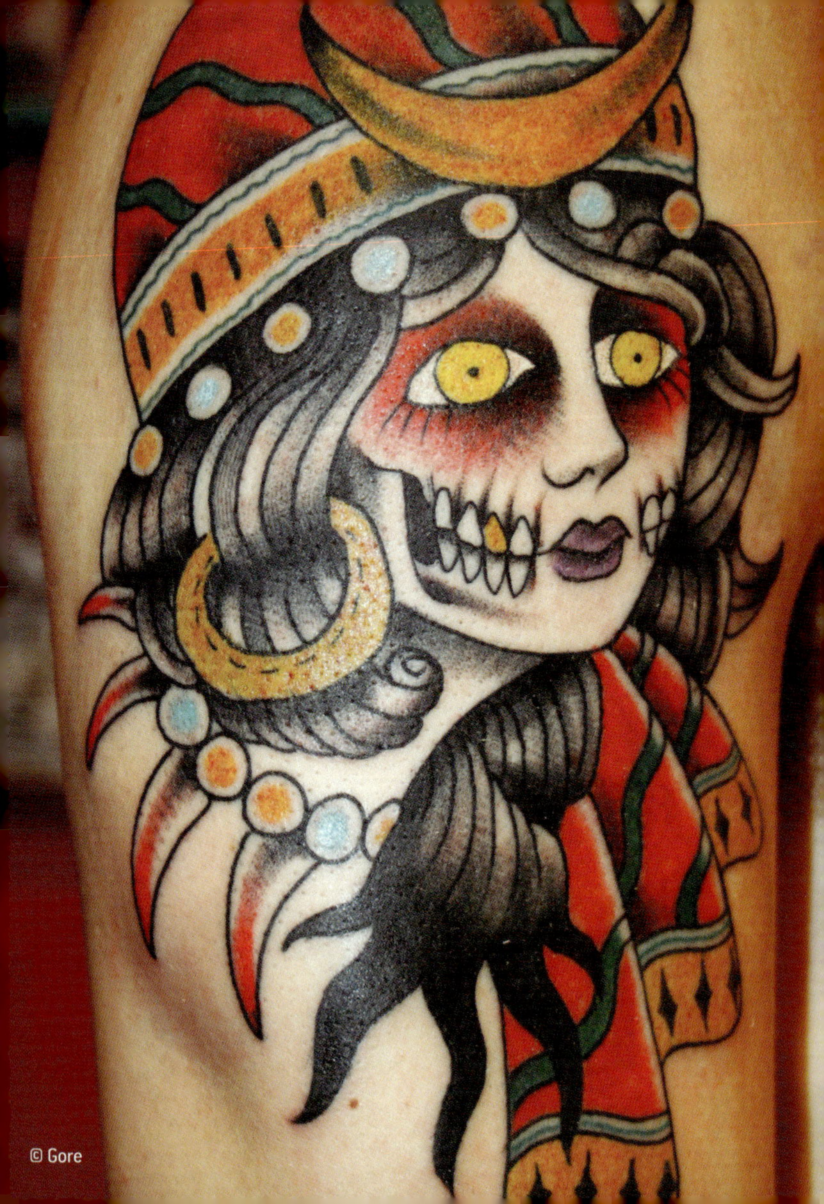

© Gore

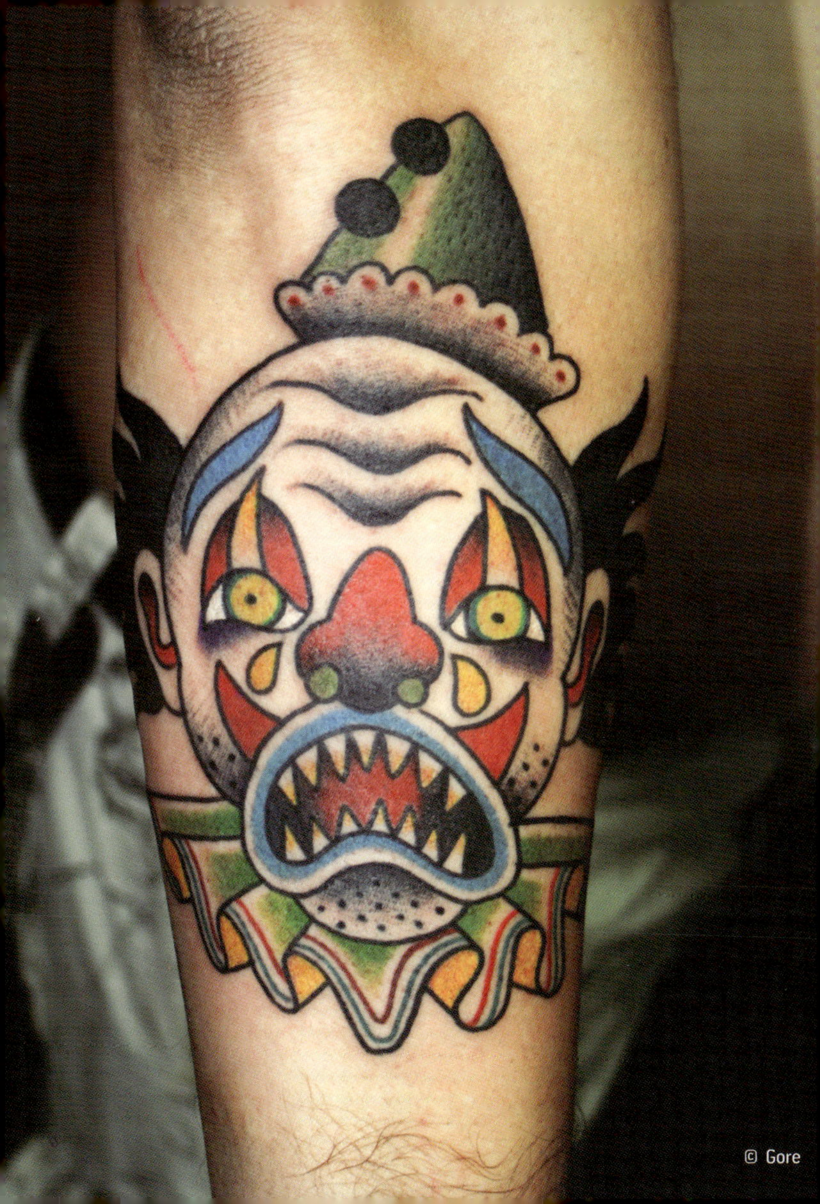

© Gore

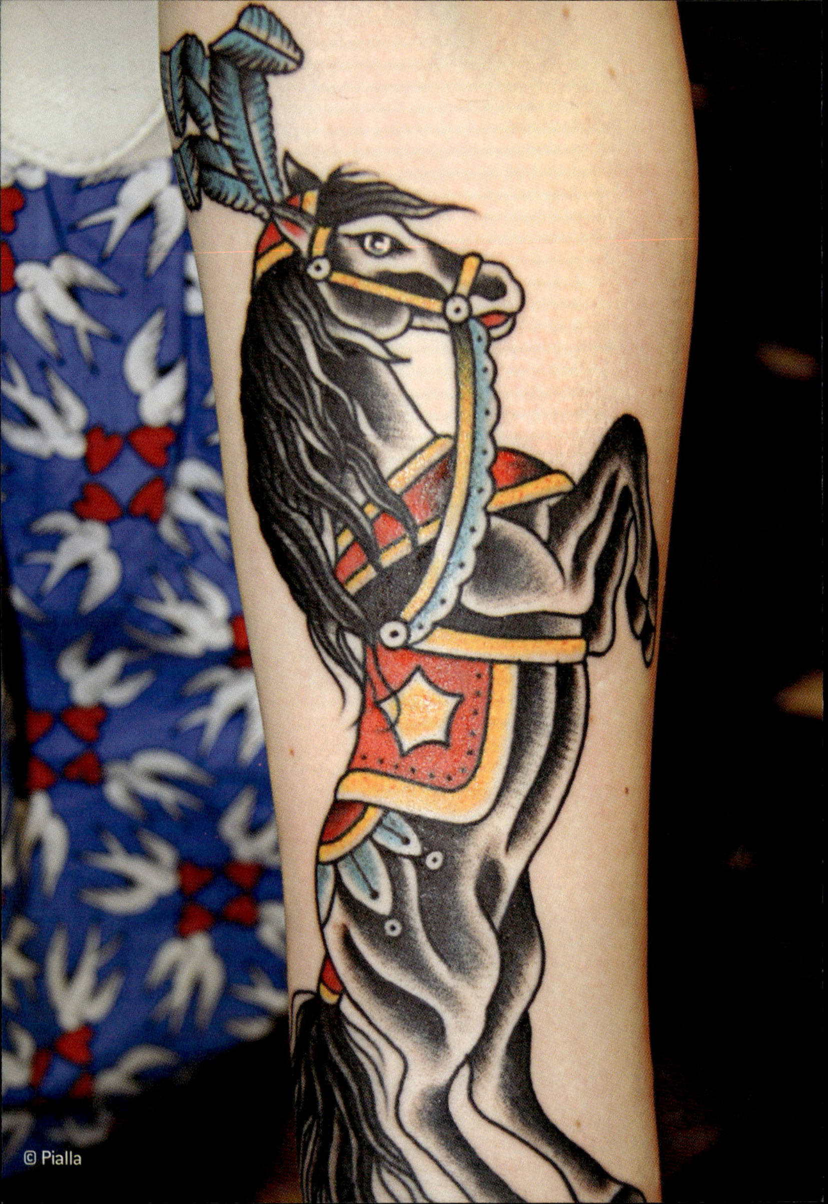

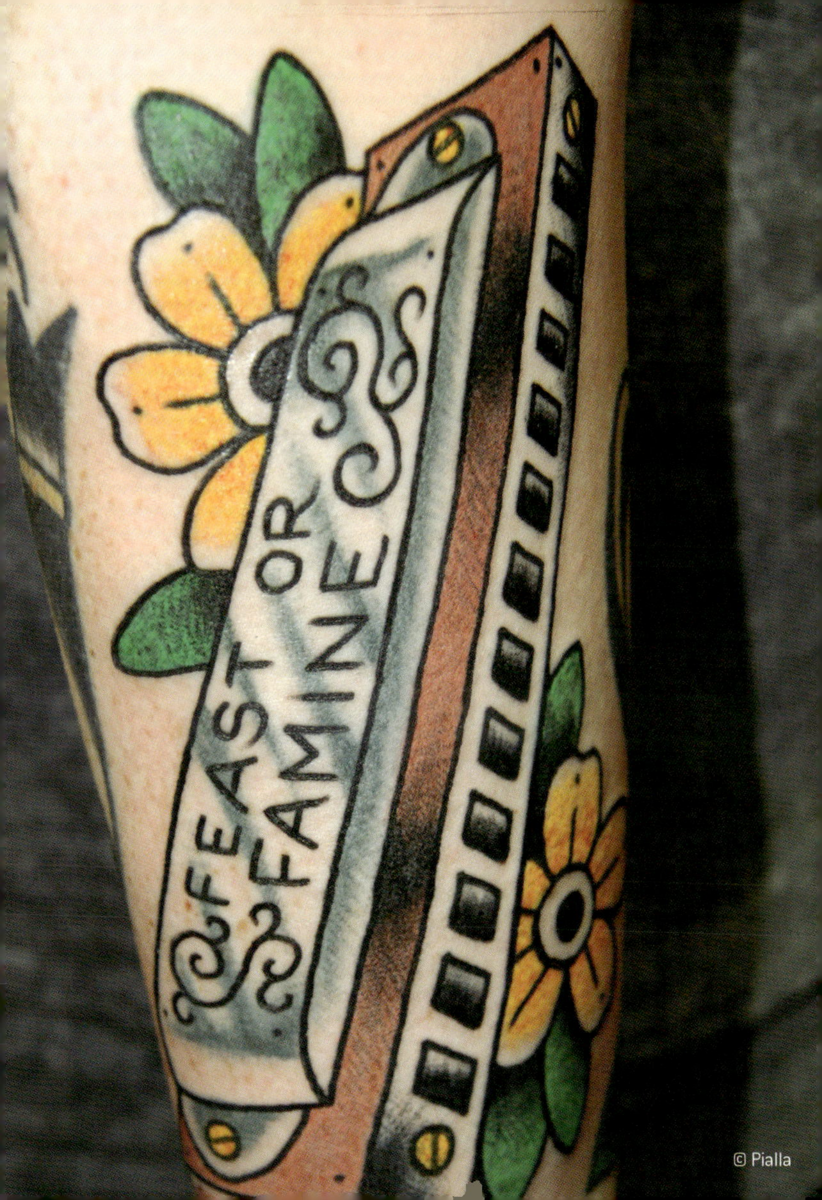
FEAST OR FAMINE

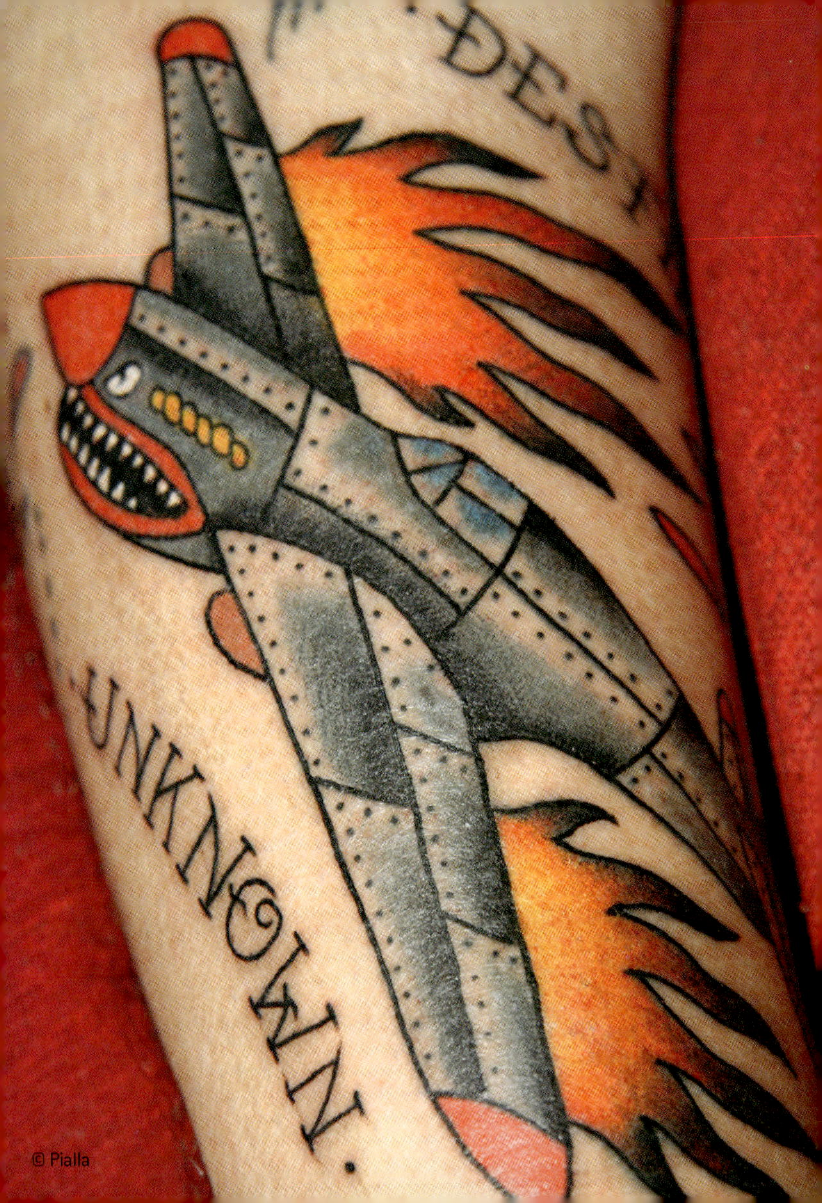

DESI
UNKNOWN.
© Pialla

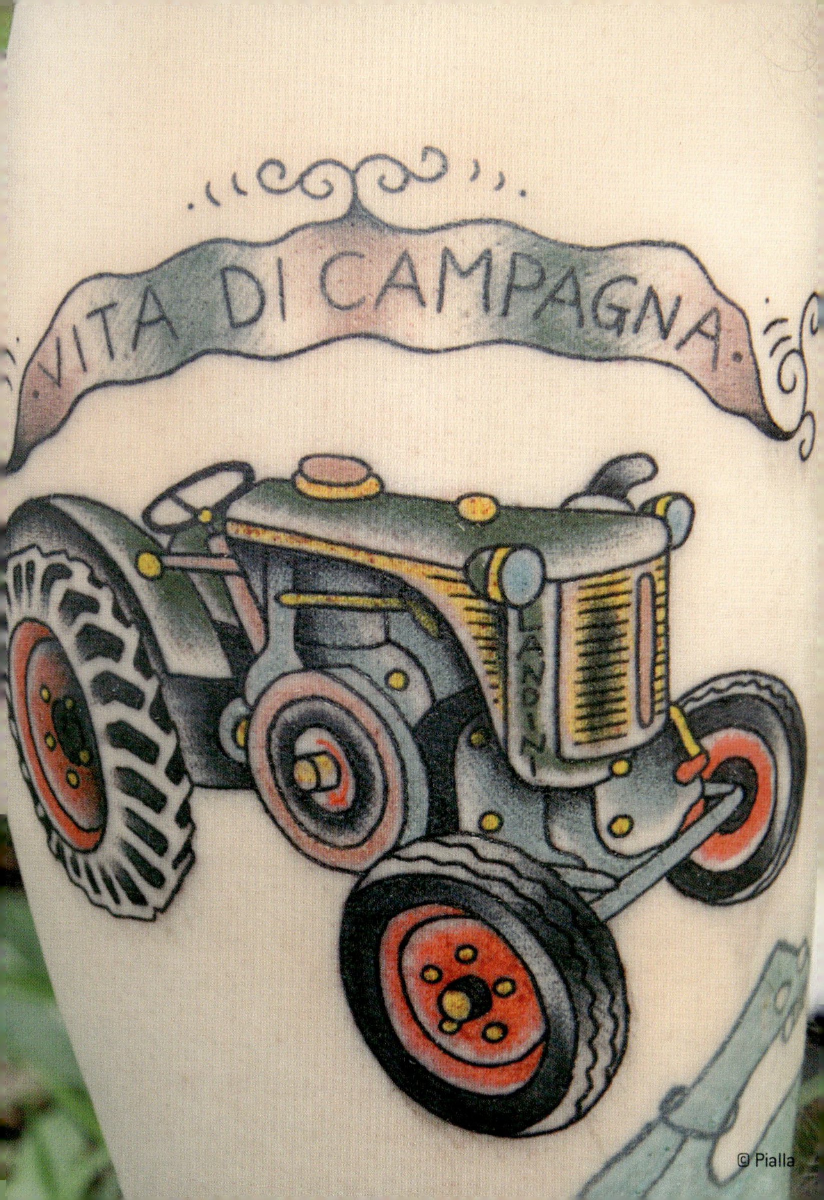
VITA DI CAMPAGNA.
LANDINI
© Pialla

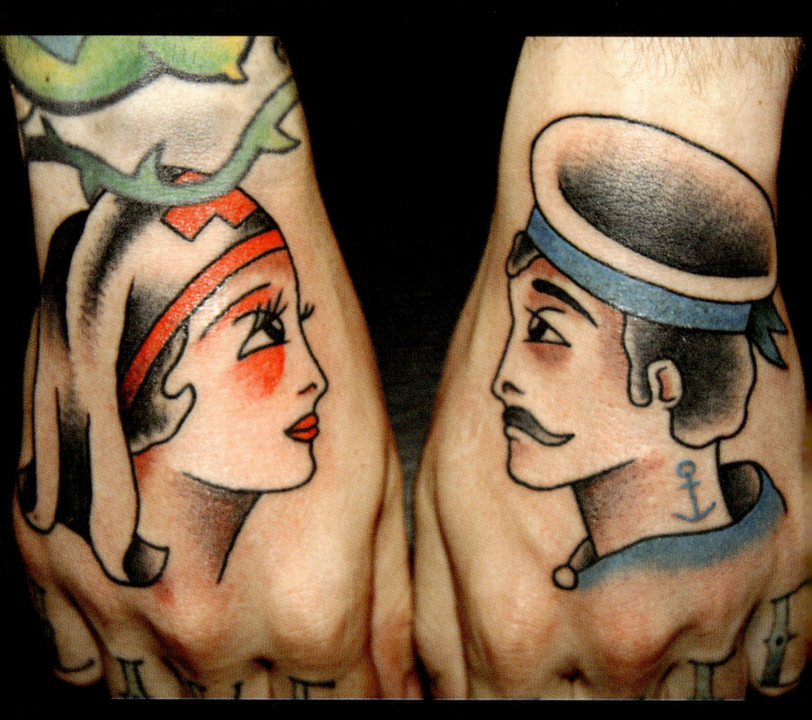

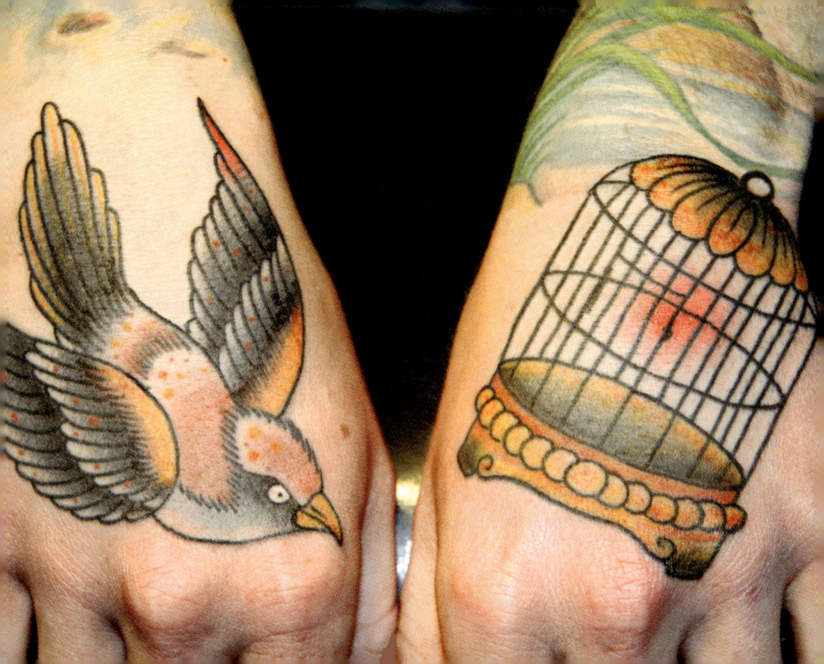

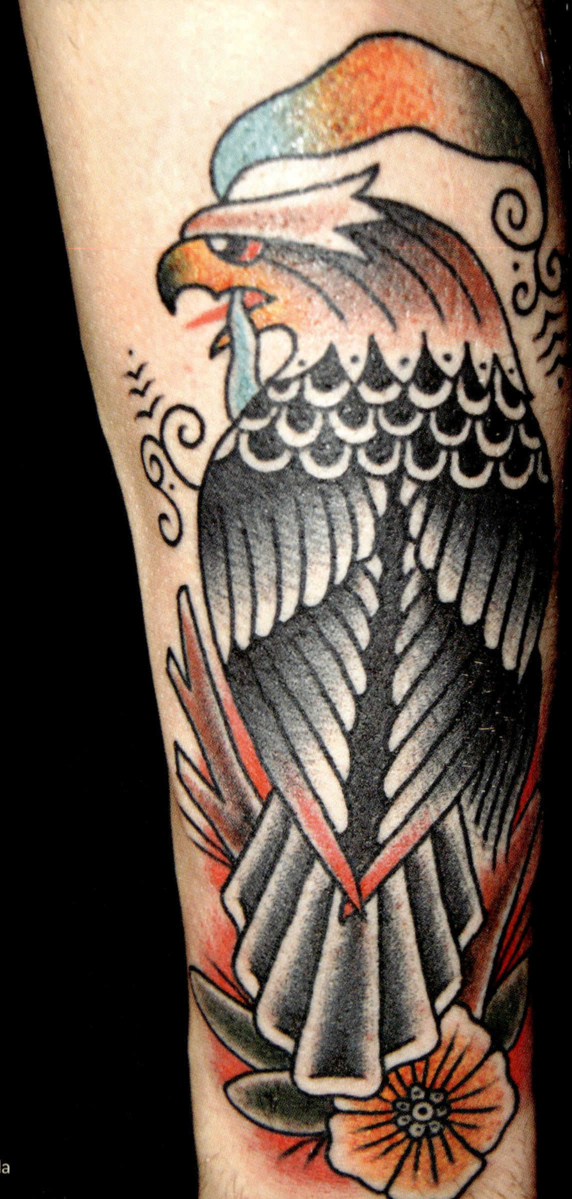
© Pialla

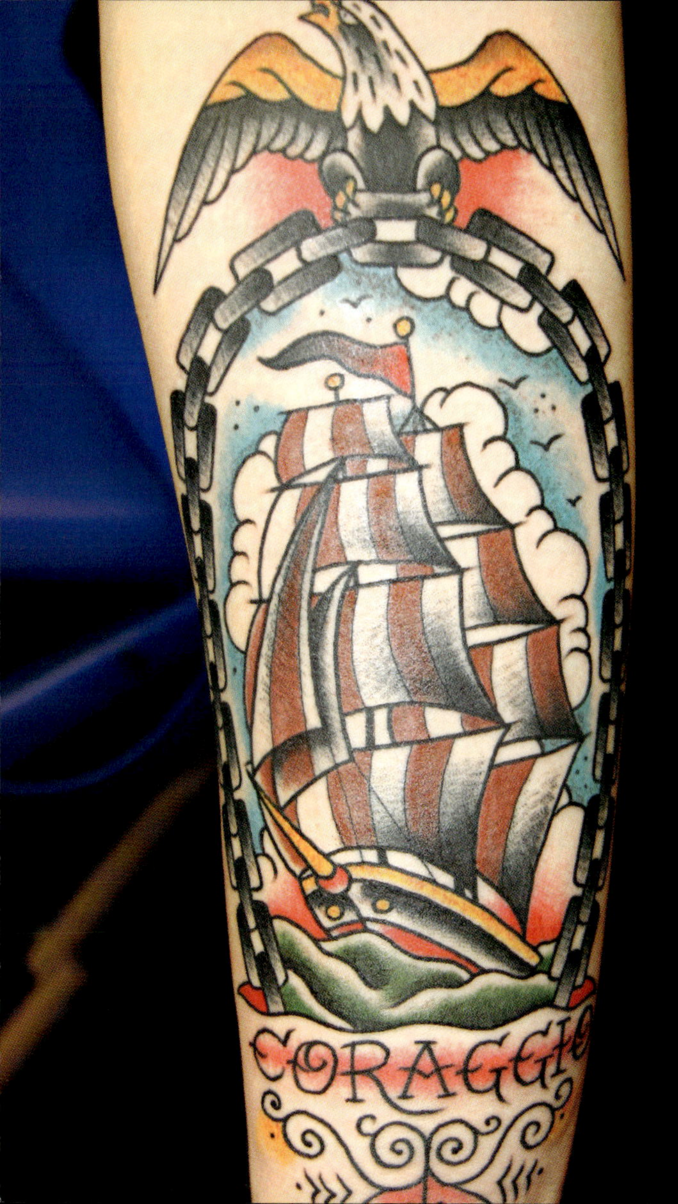
CORAGGIO

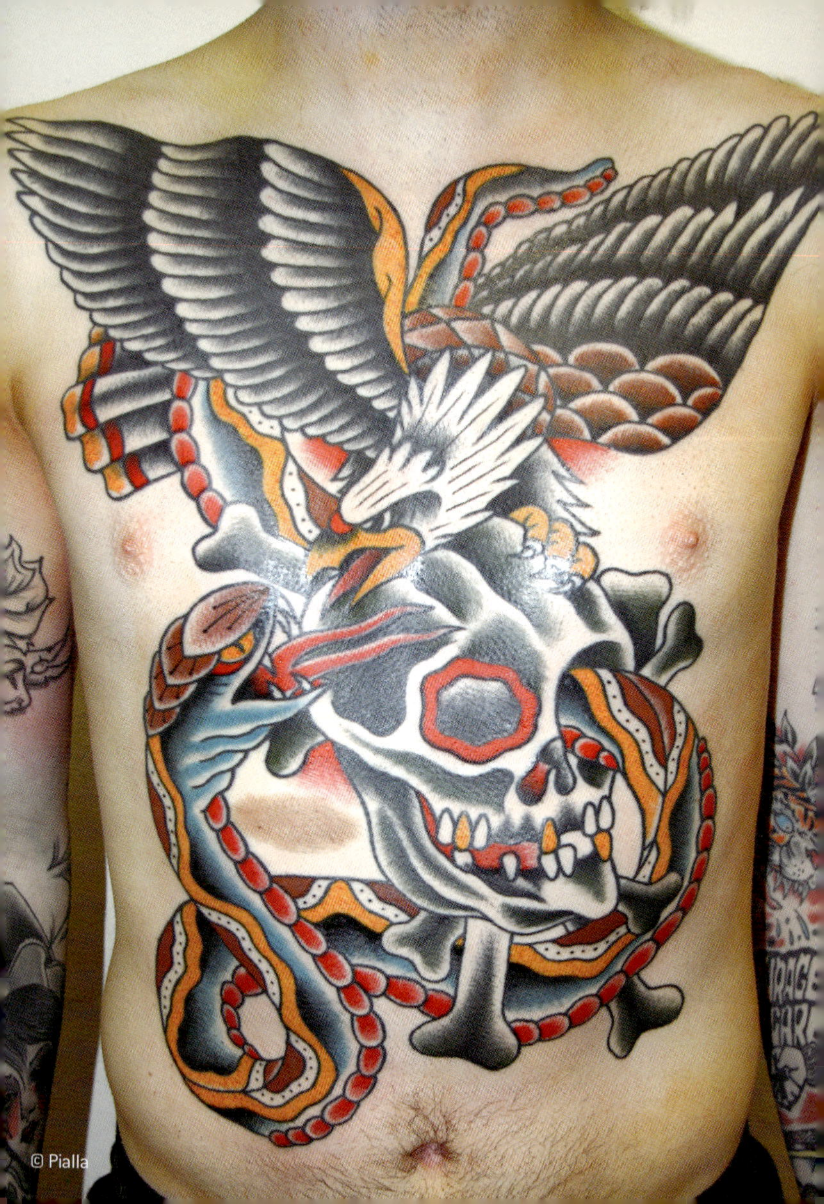
© Pialla

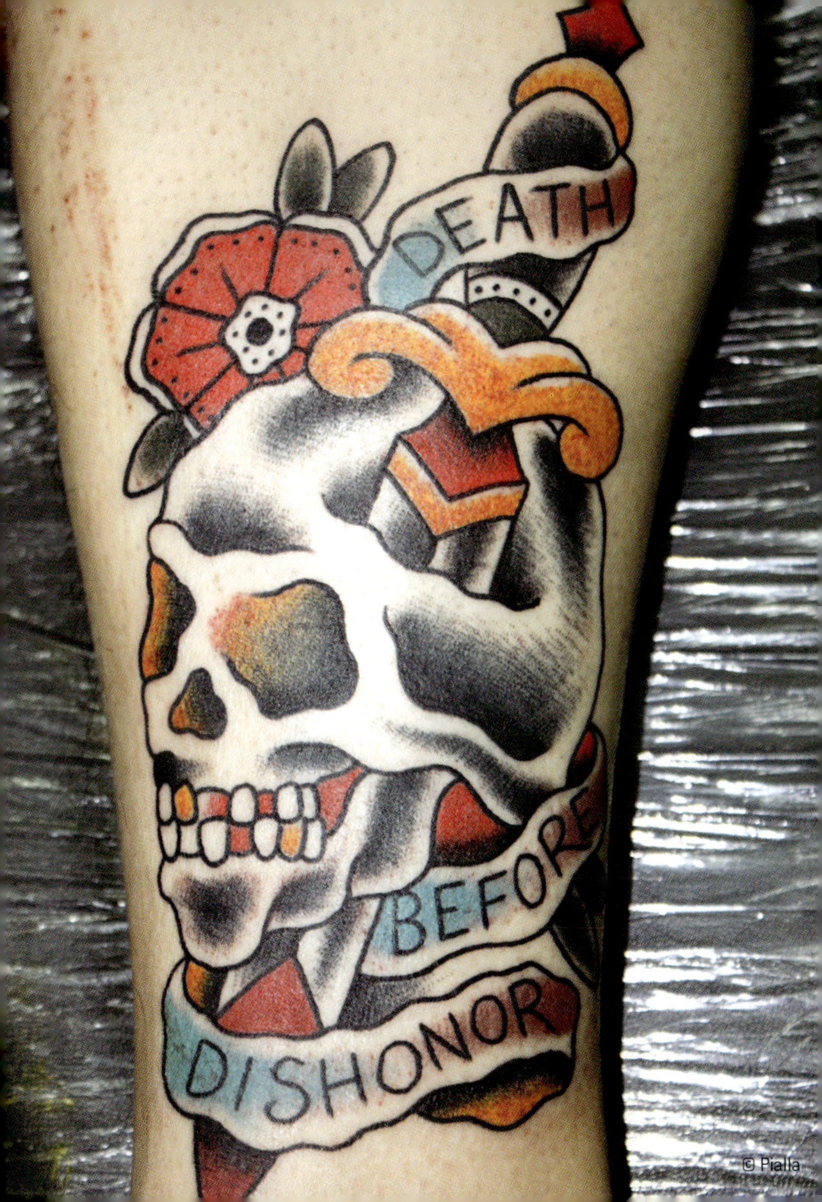
DEATH
BEFORE
DISHONOR

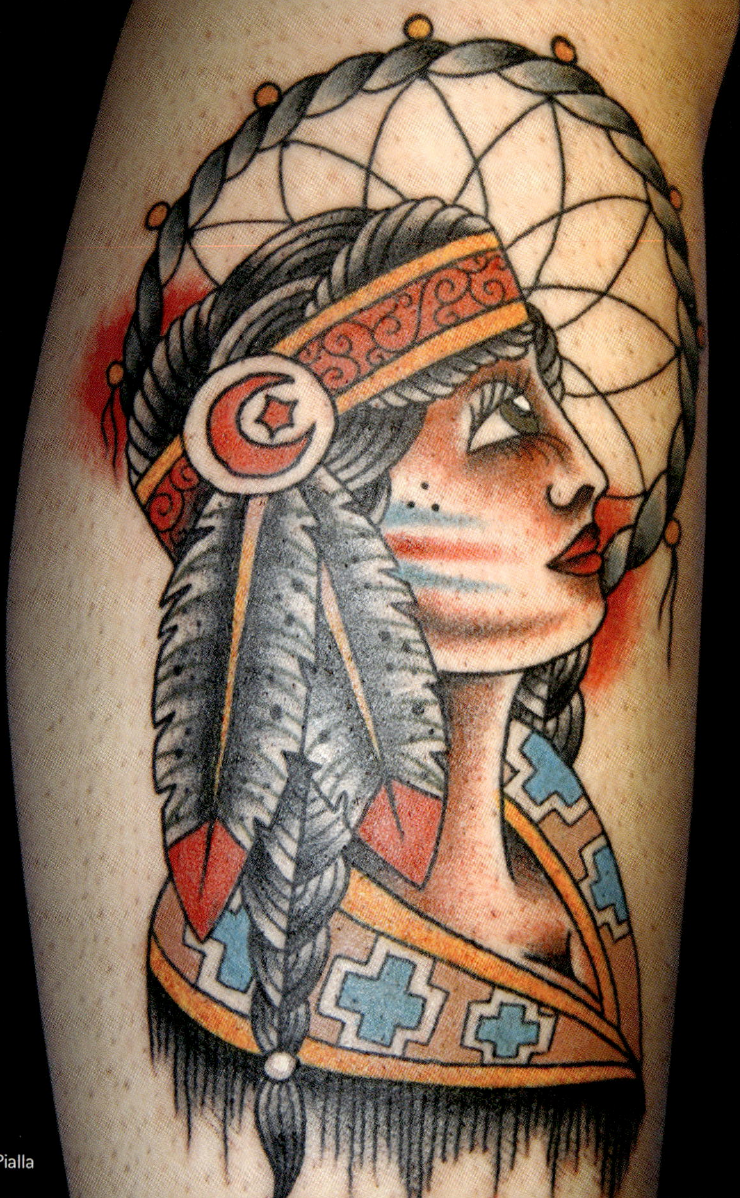
© Pialla

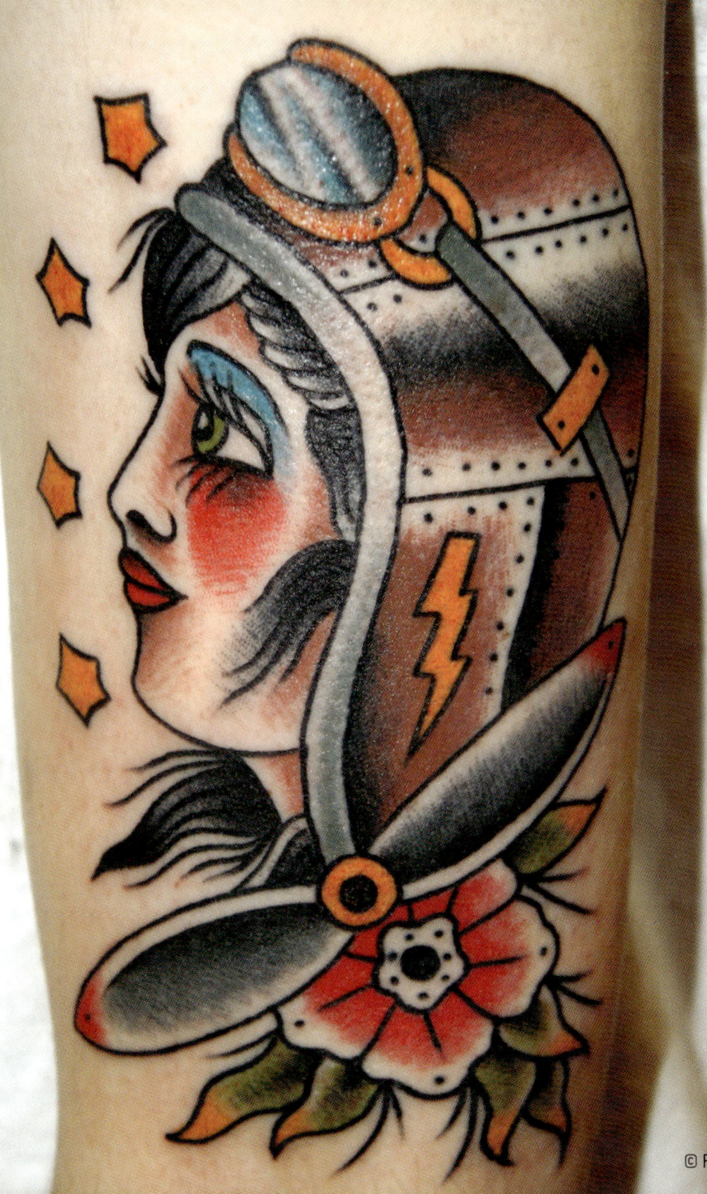

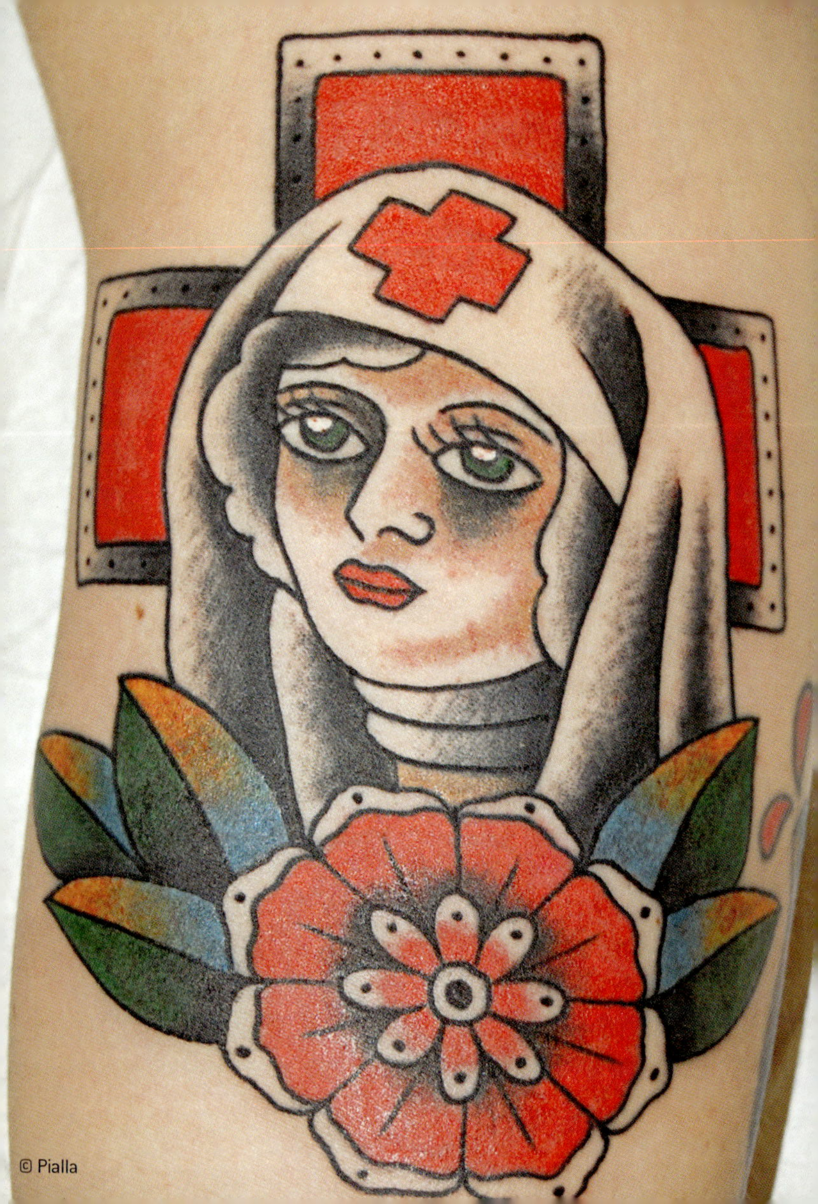
© Pialla

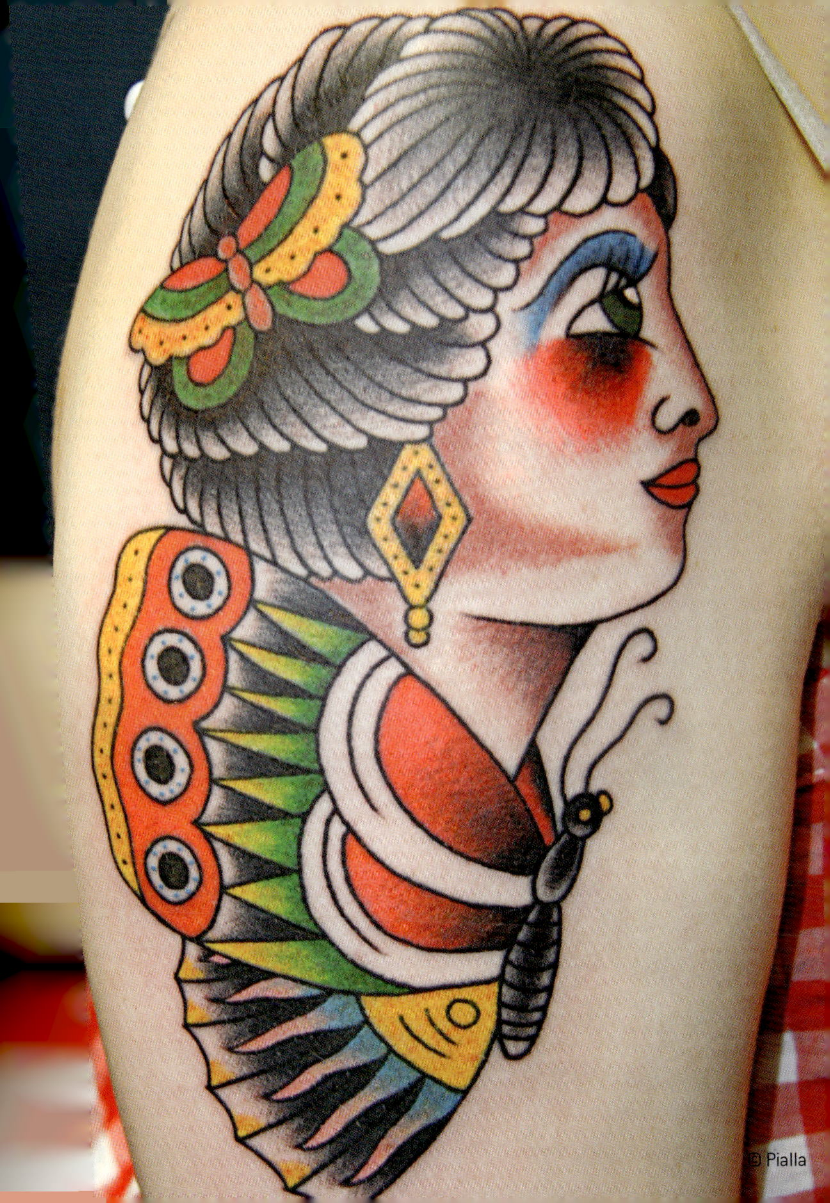
© Pialla

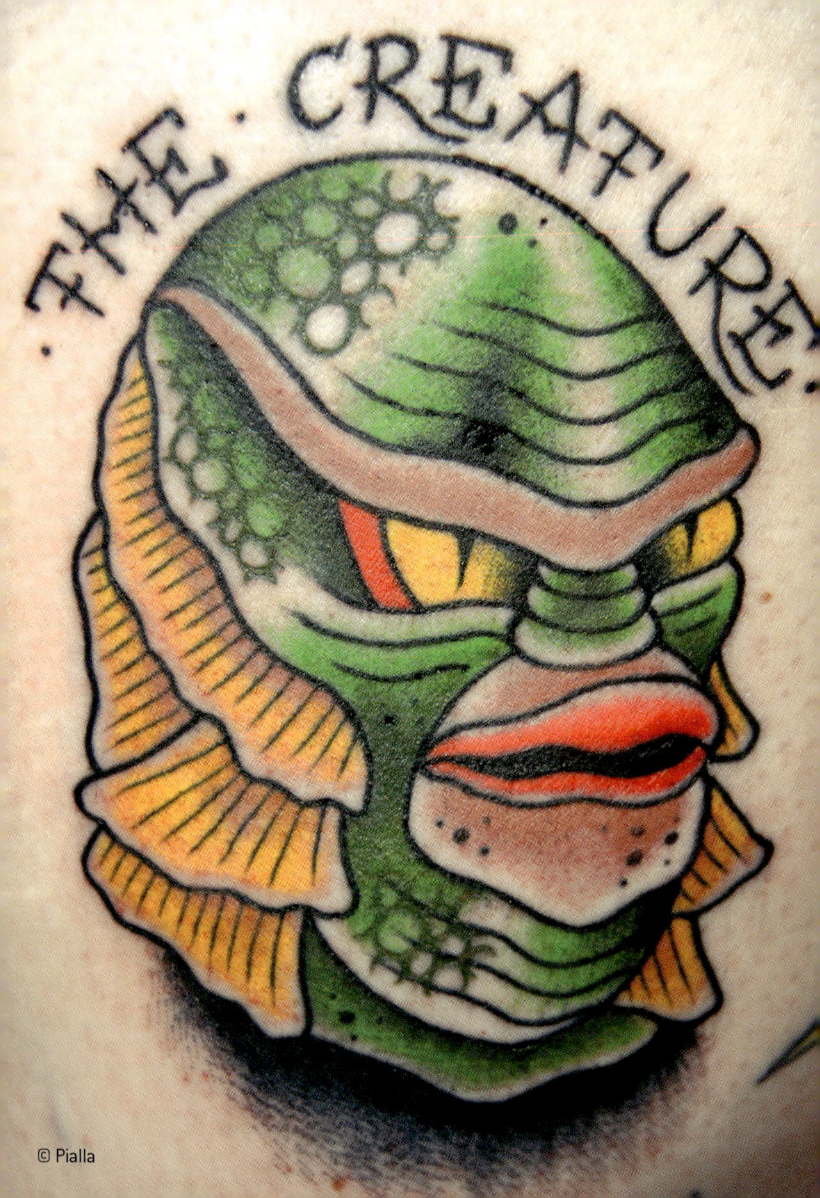
·THE · CREATURE·
© Pialla

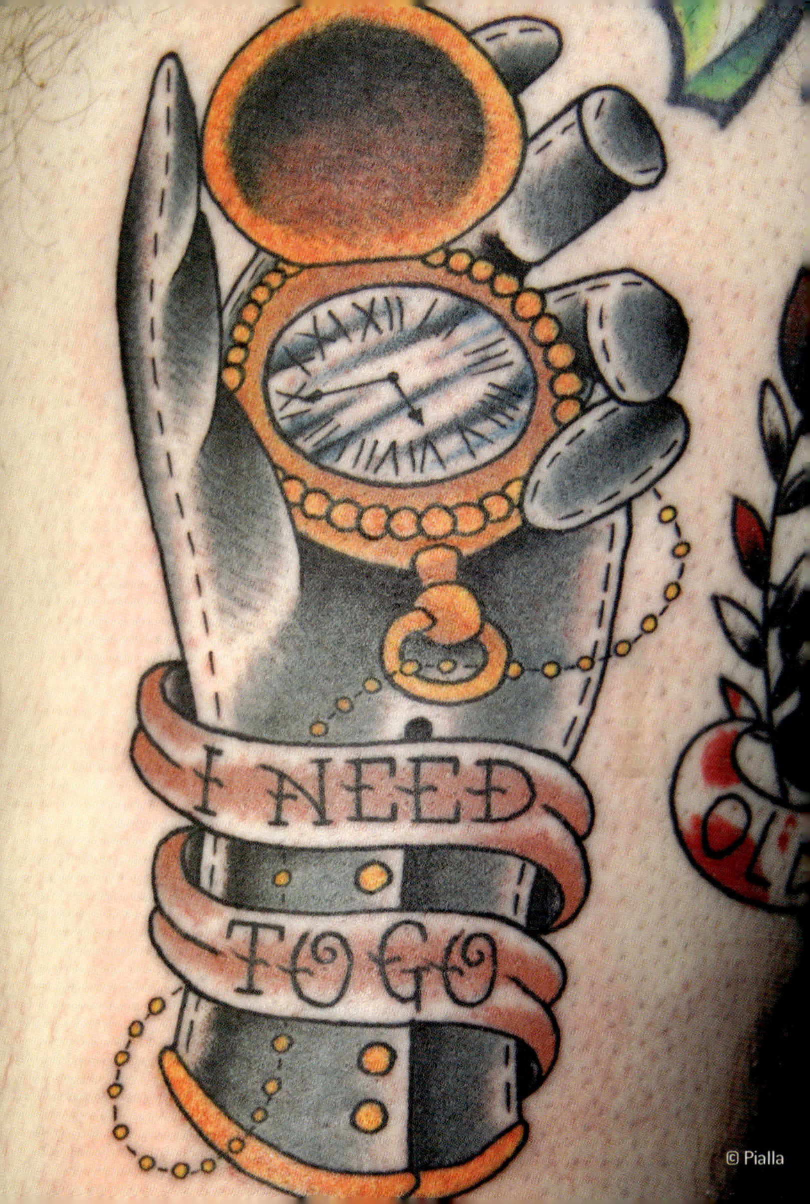

I NEED
TO GO

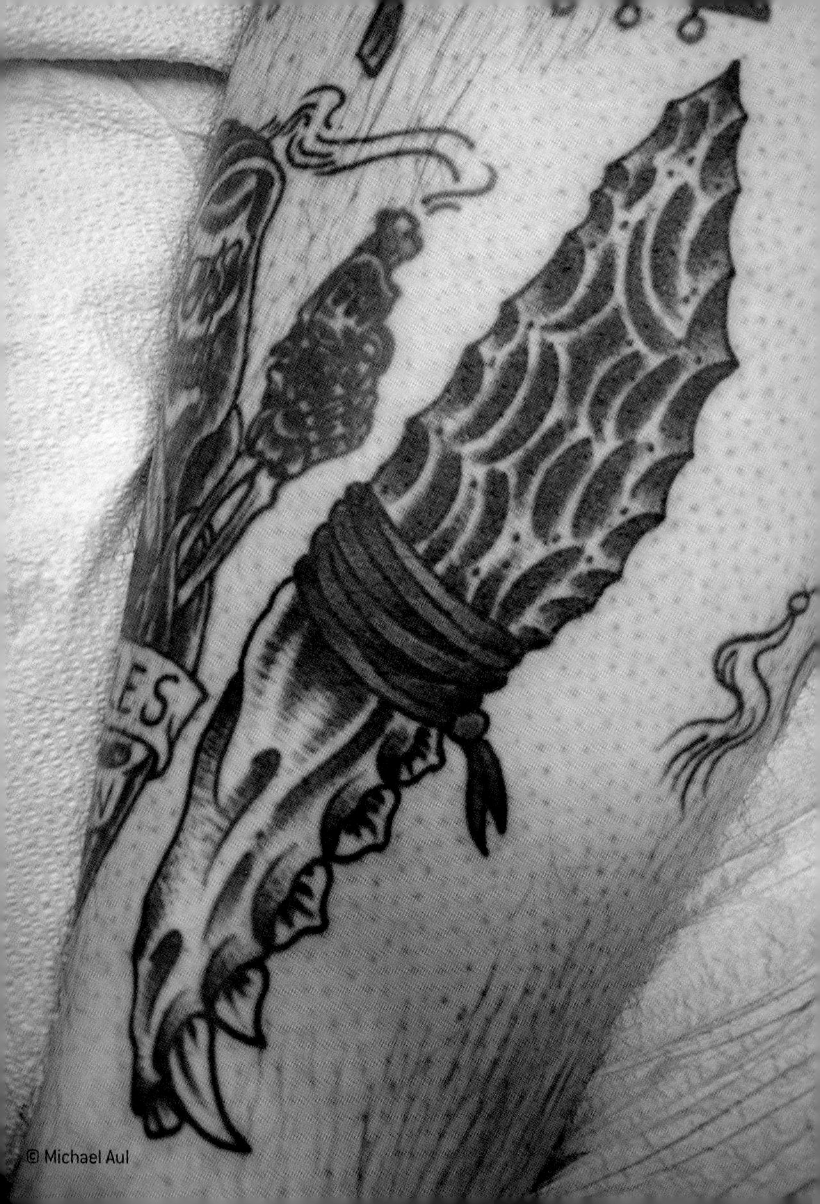

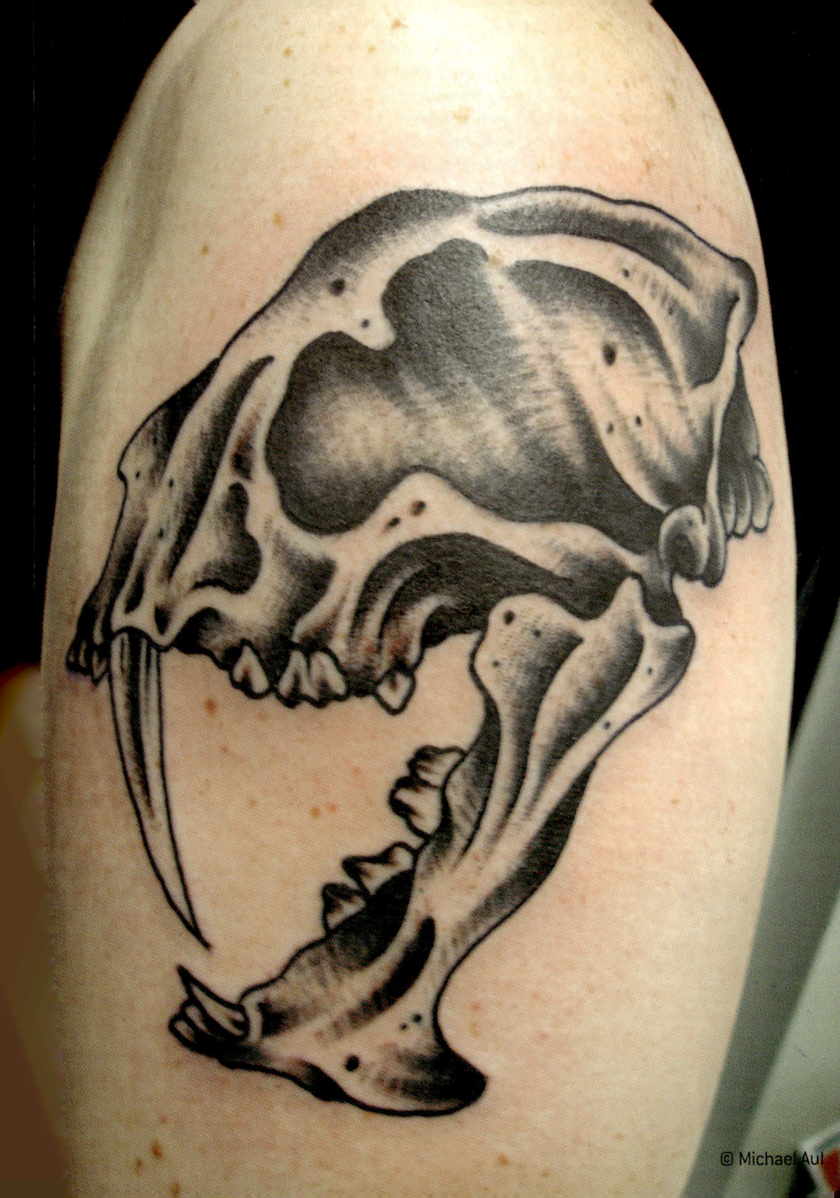

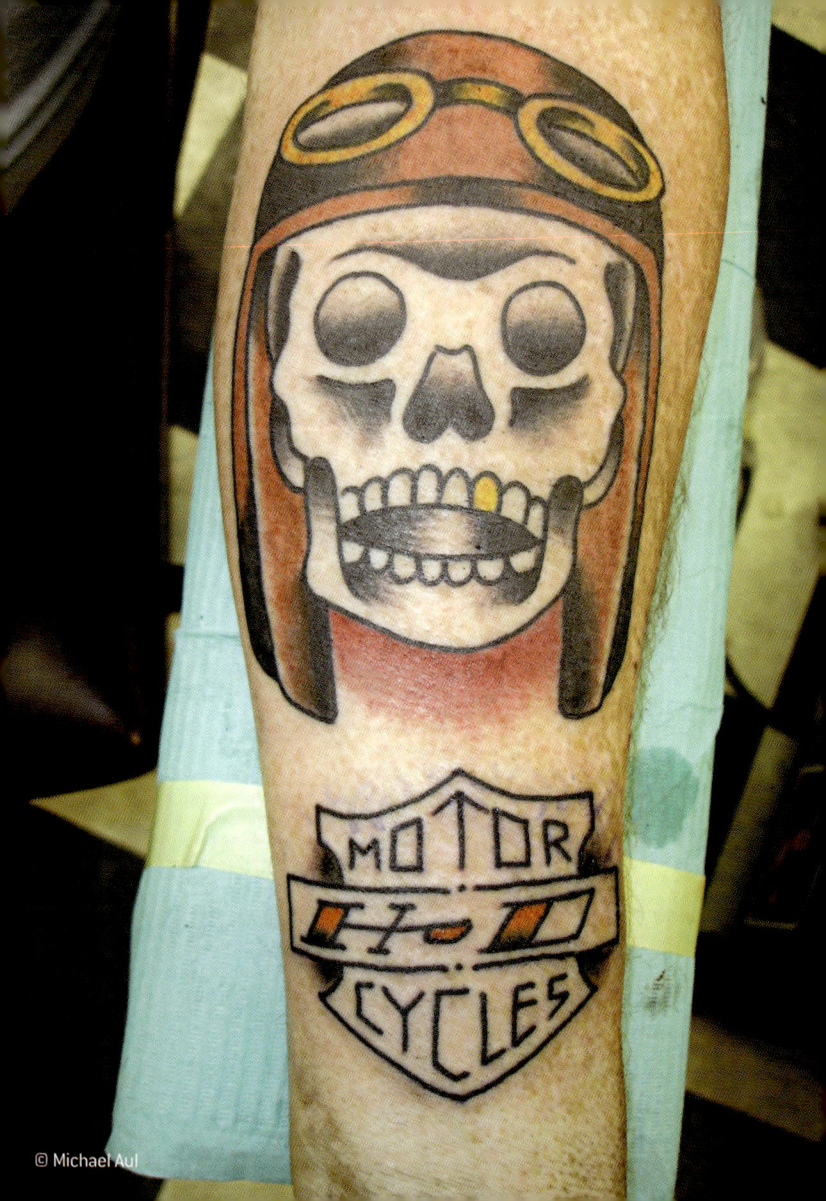

MOTOR
CYCLES

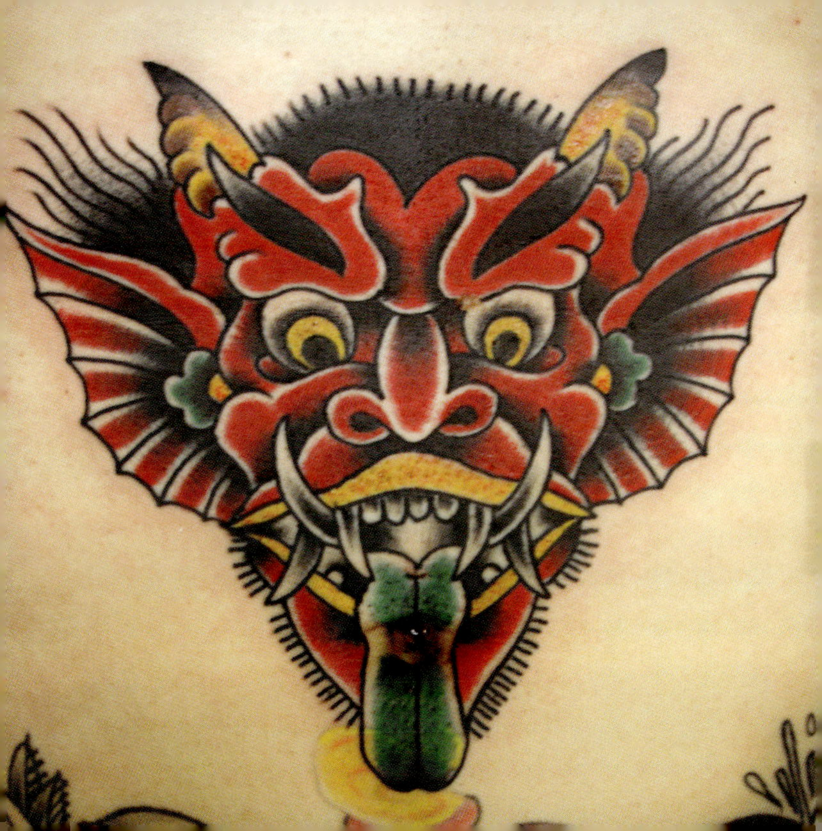

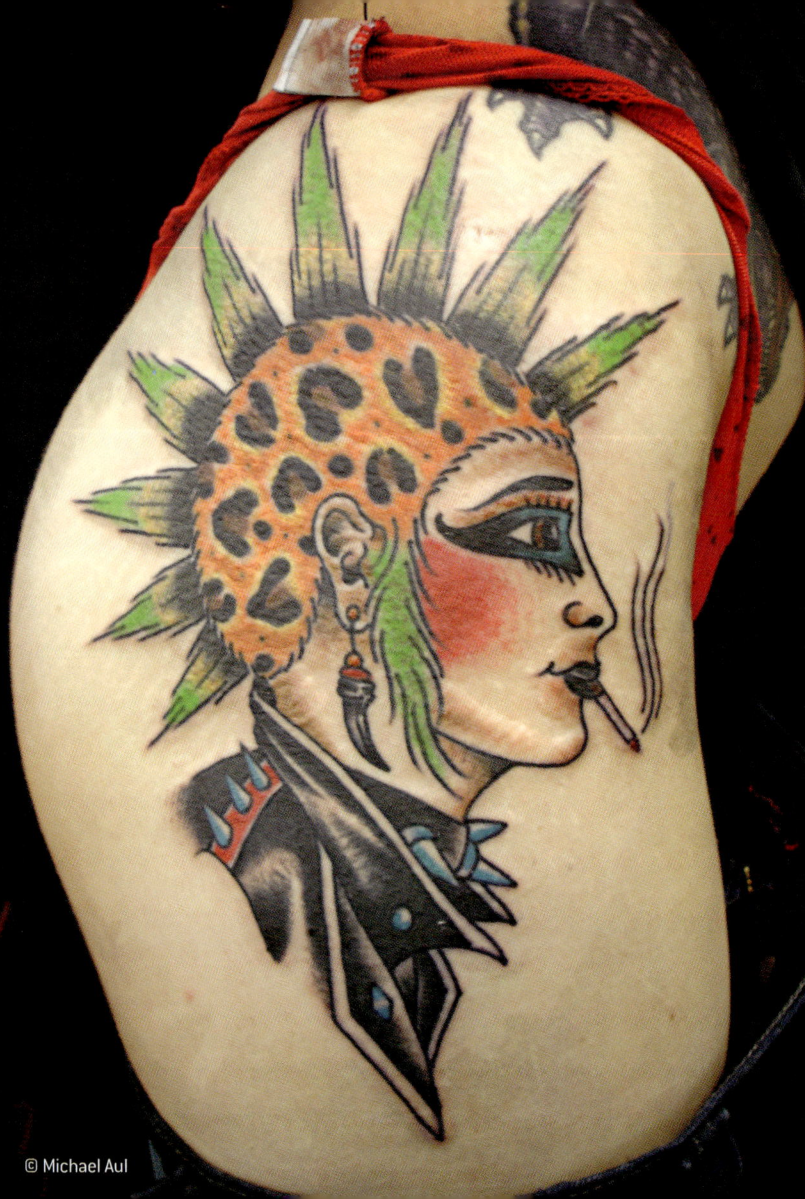
© Michael Aul

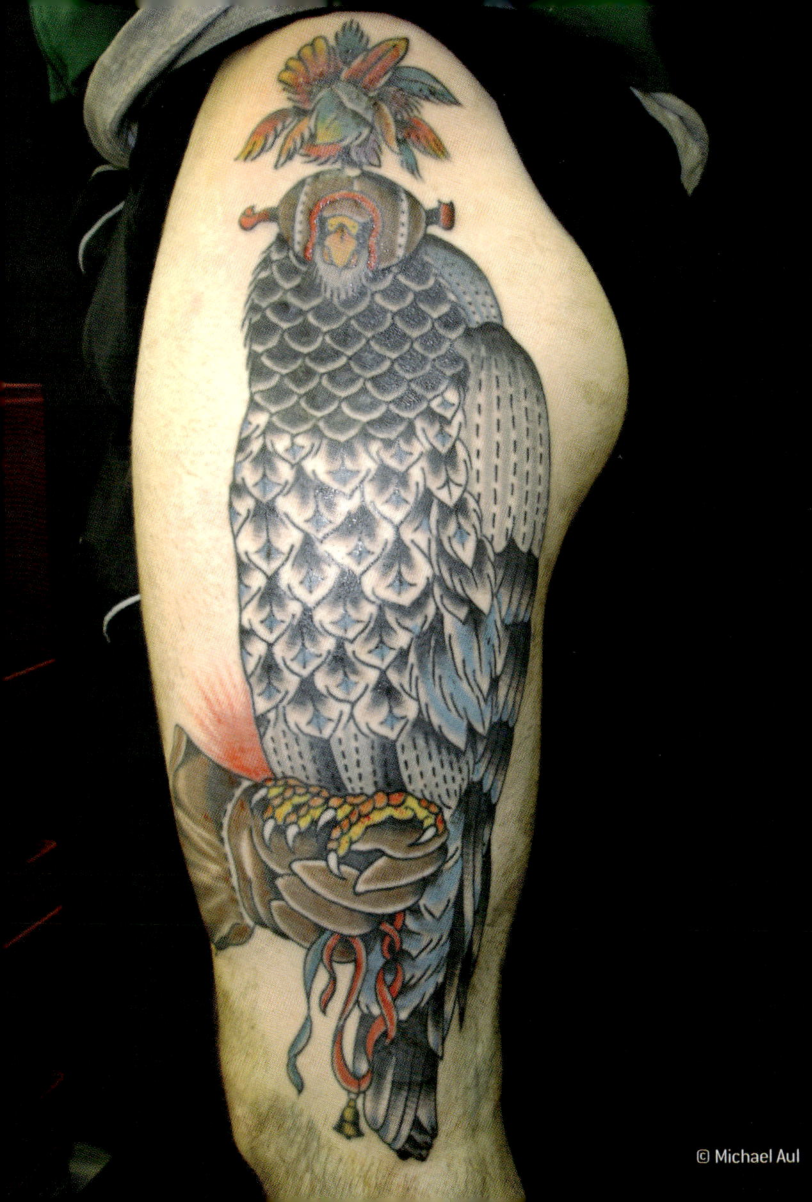
© Michael Aul

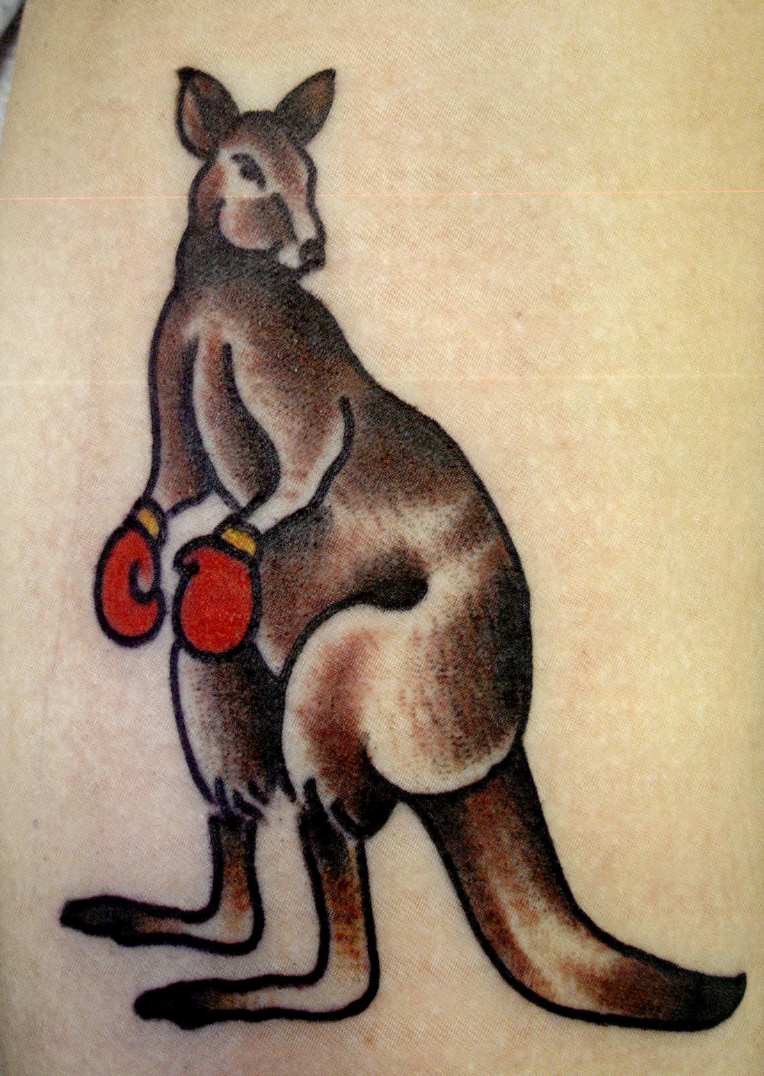

© Michael Aul

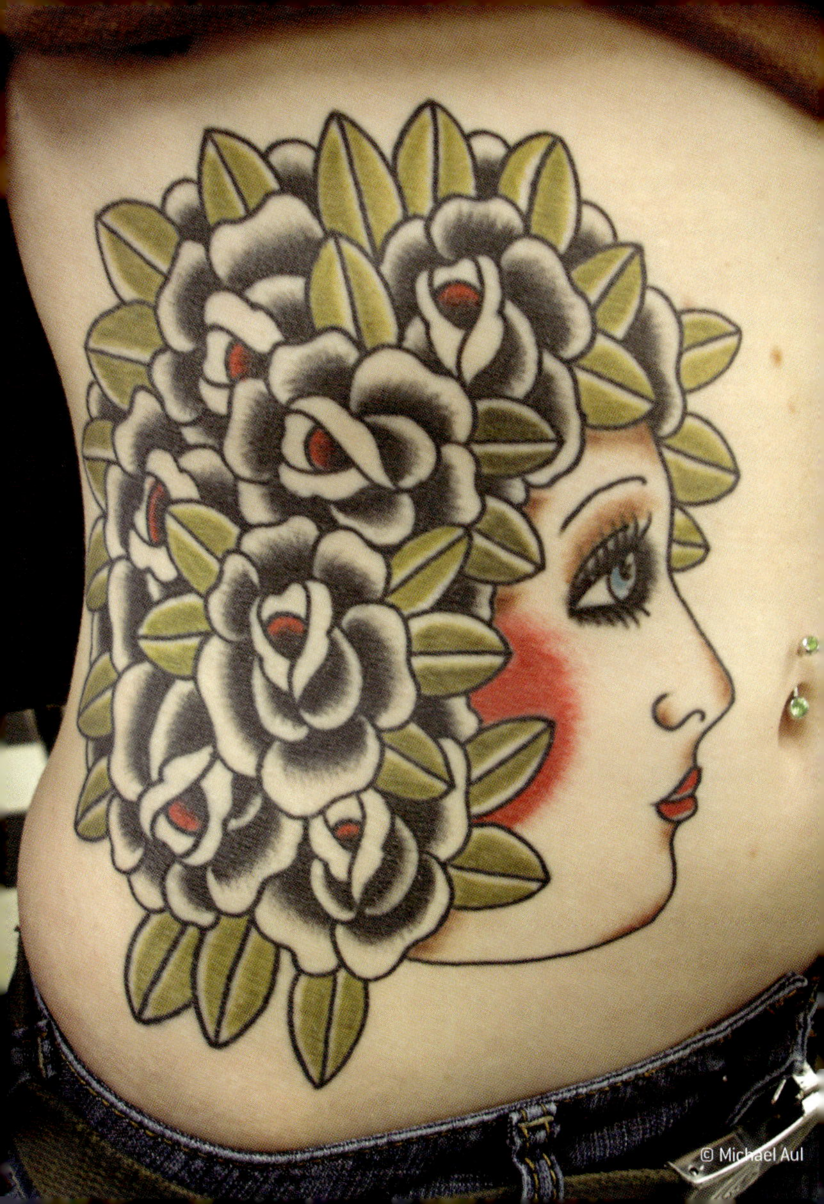
© Michael Aul

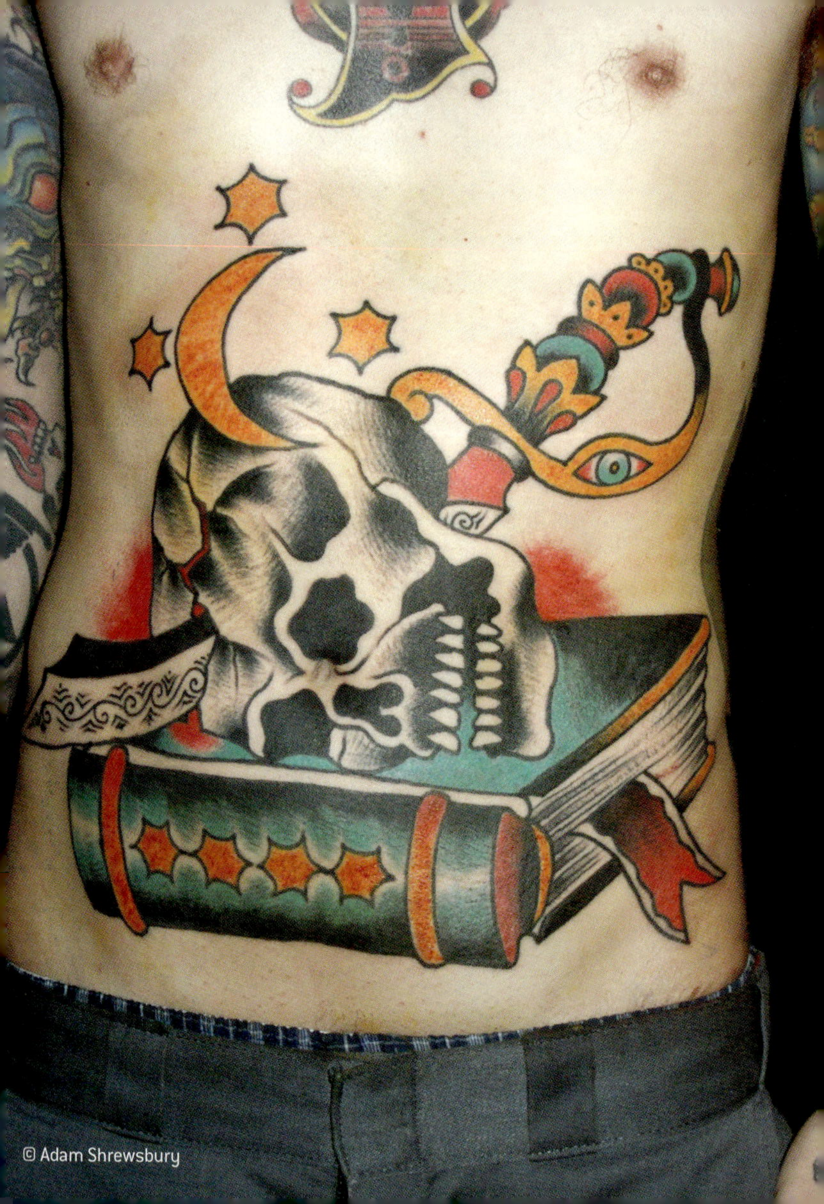

© Adam Shrewsbury

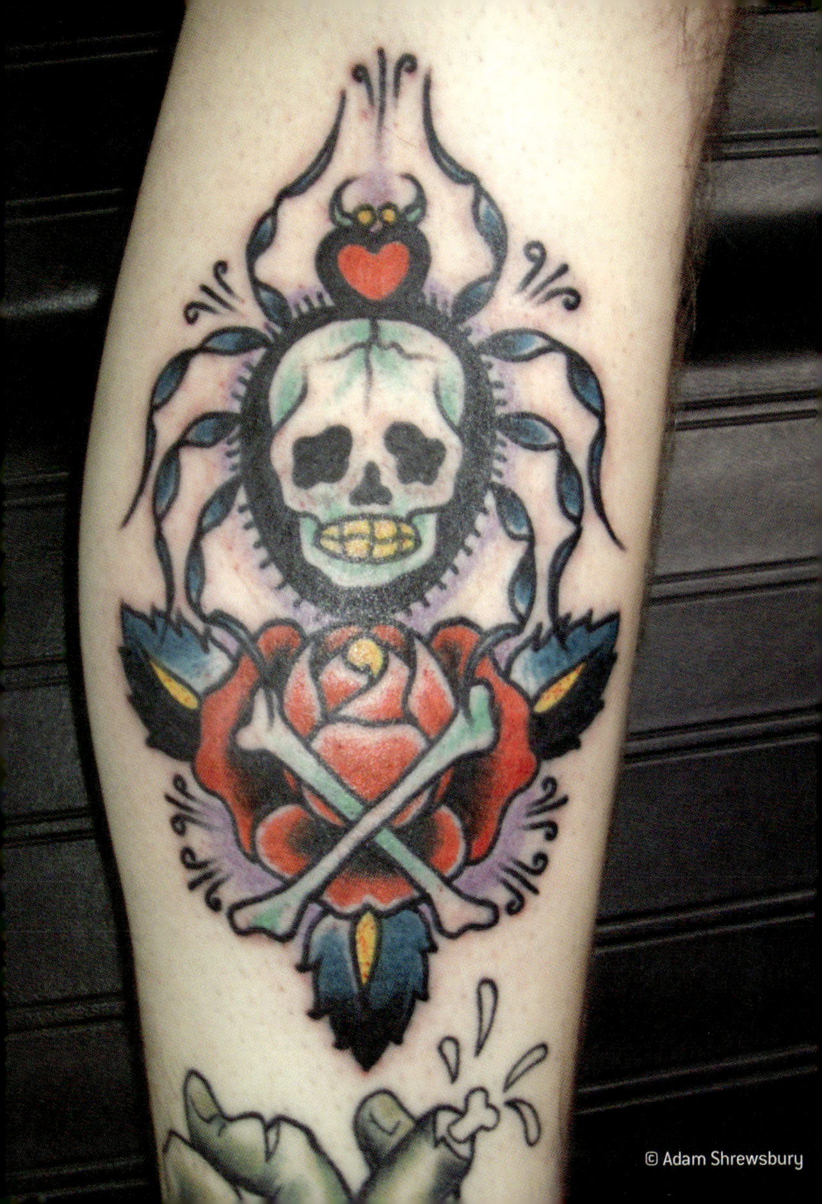
© Adam Shrewsbury

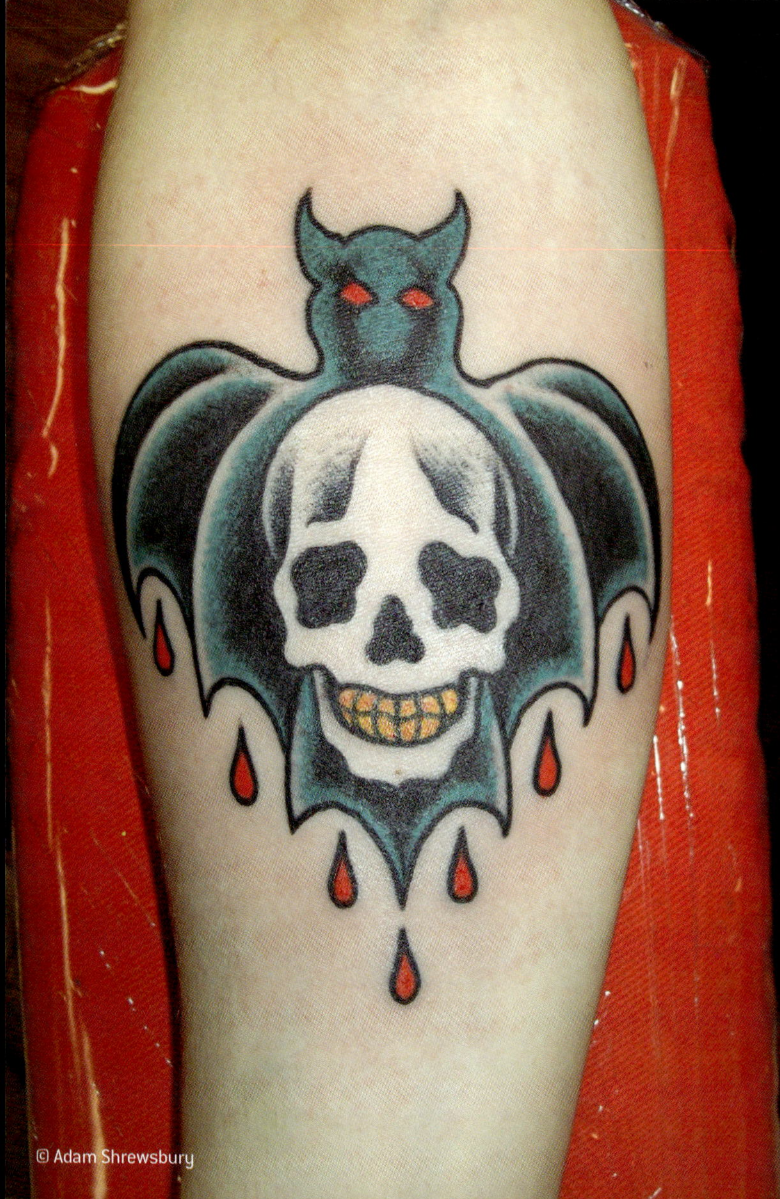

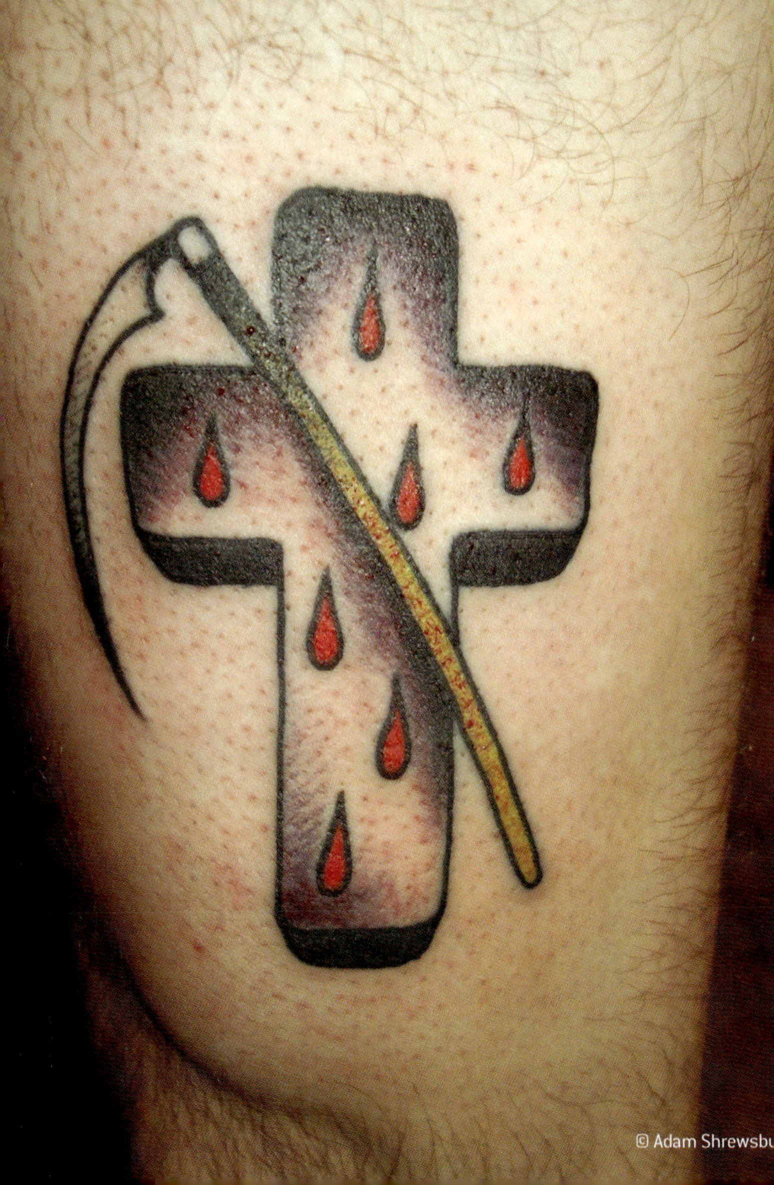
© Adam Shrewsbury

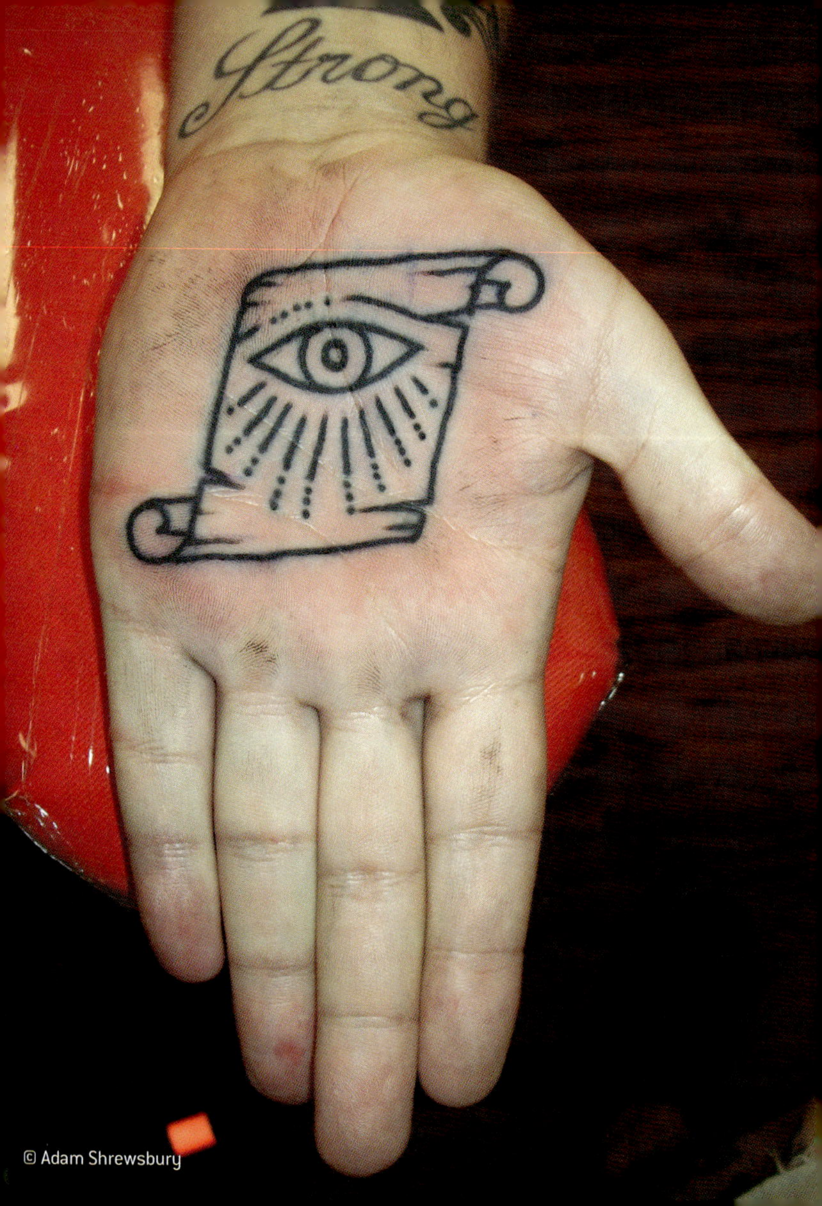

© Adam Shrewsbury

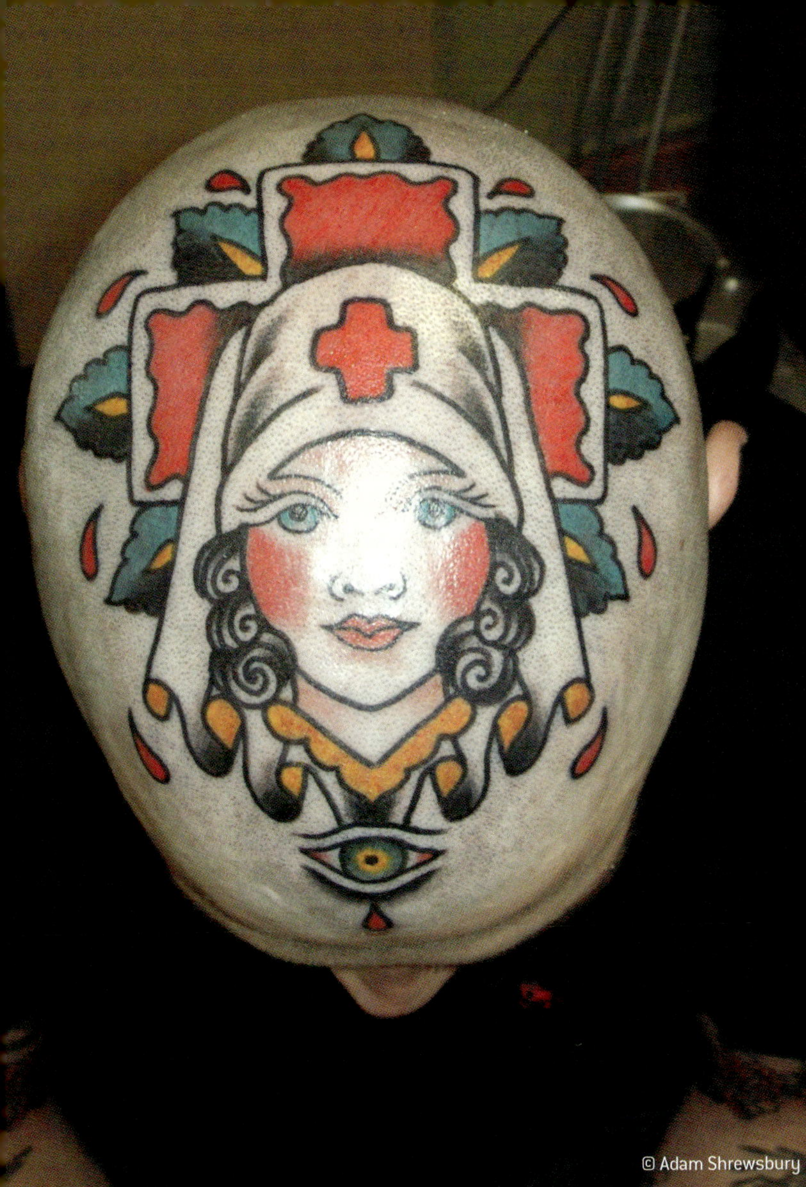
© Adam Shrewsbury

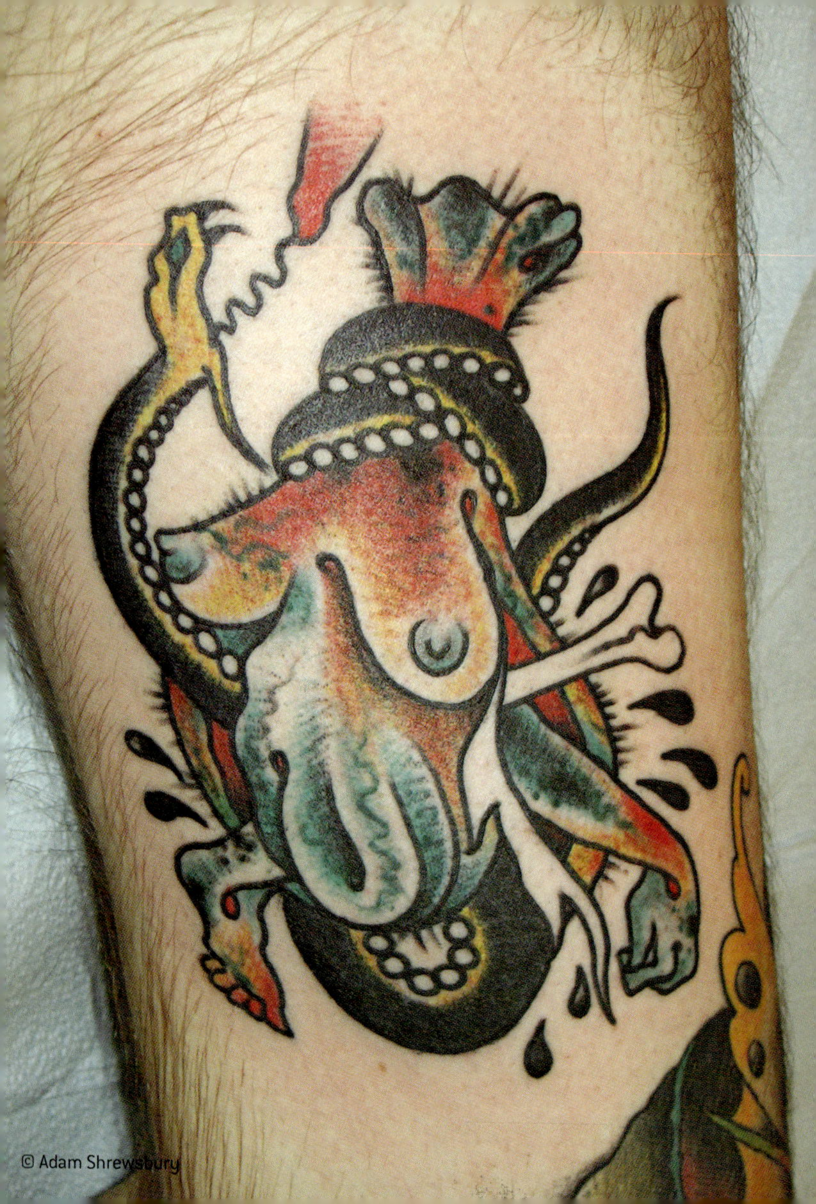
© Adam Shrewsbury

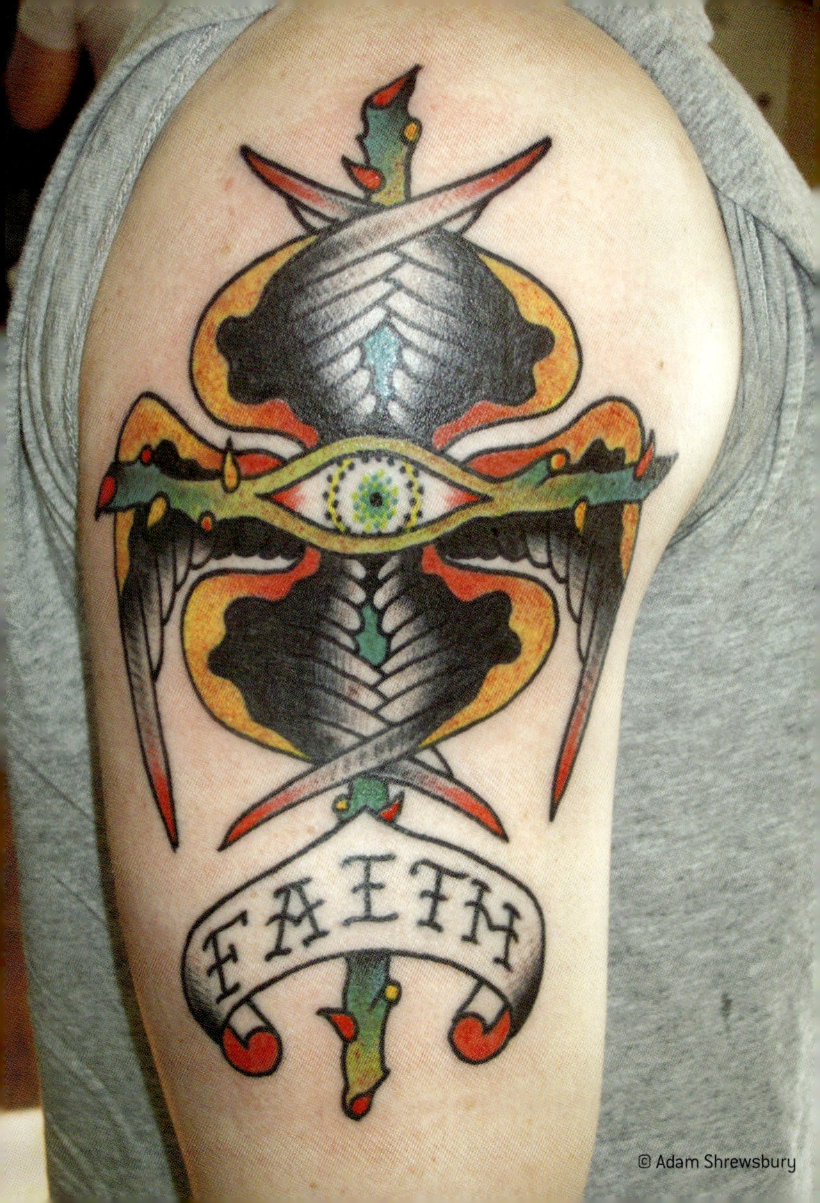

FAITH

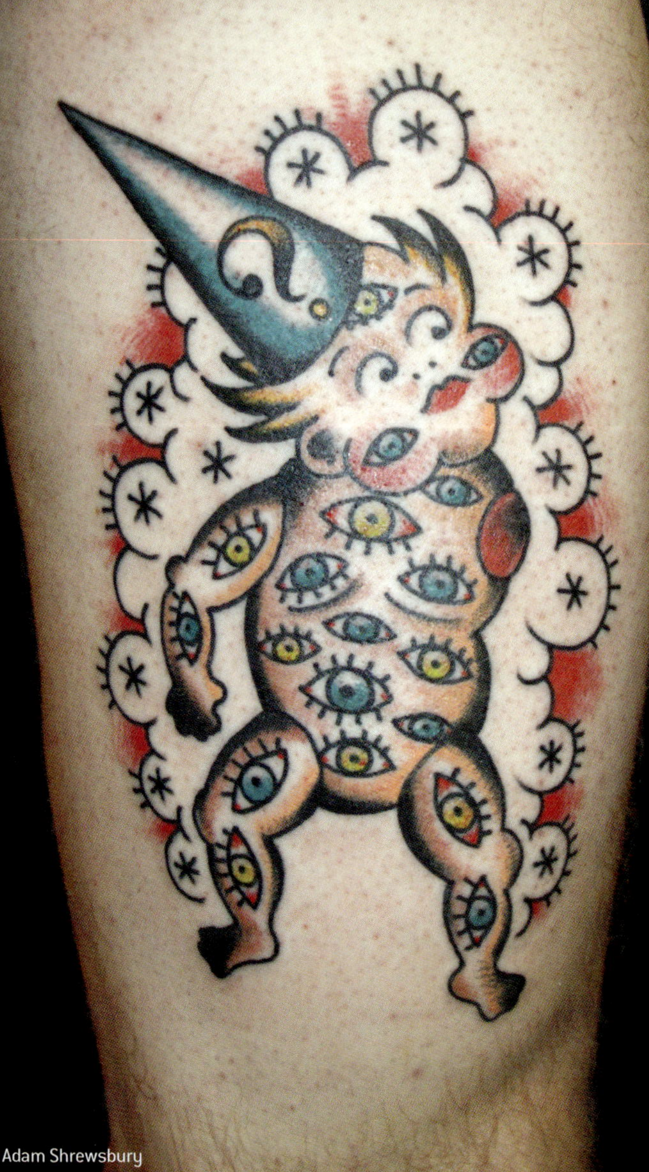

© Adam Shrewsbury

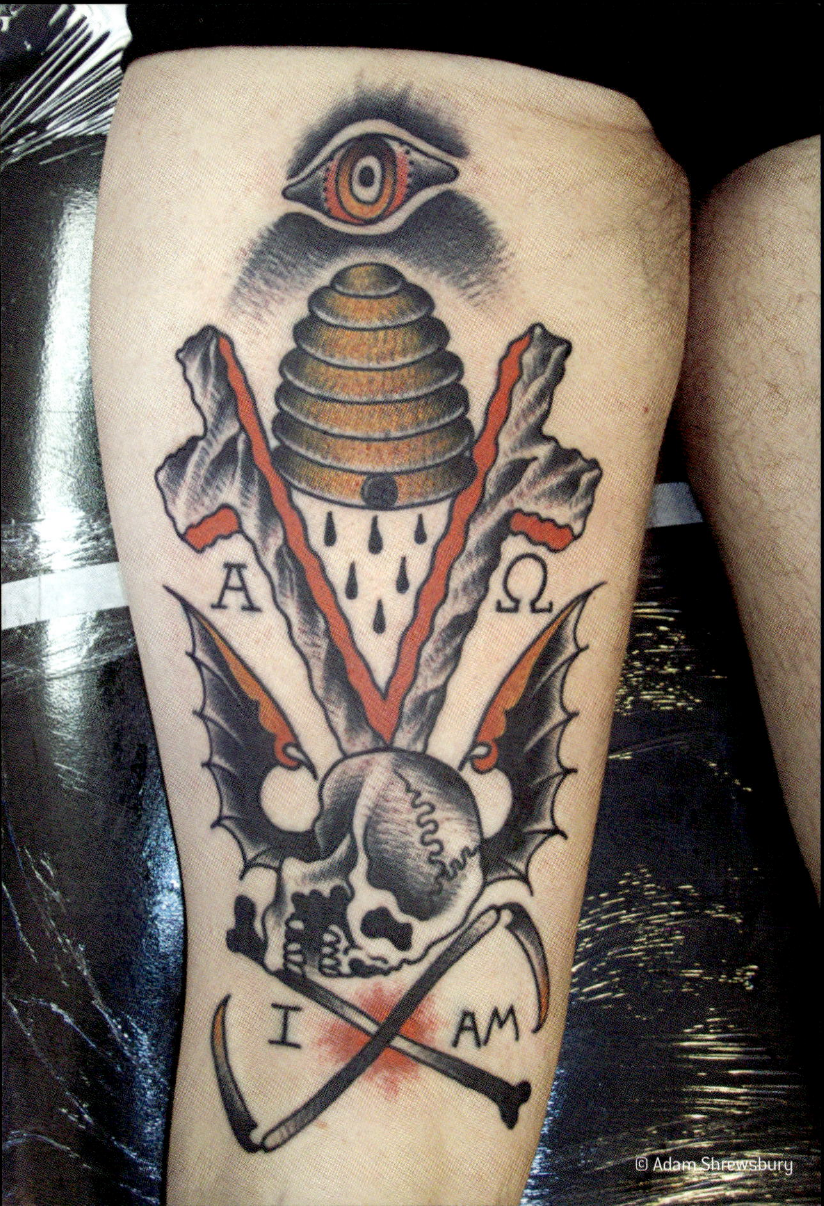

A
Ω
I
AM

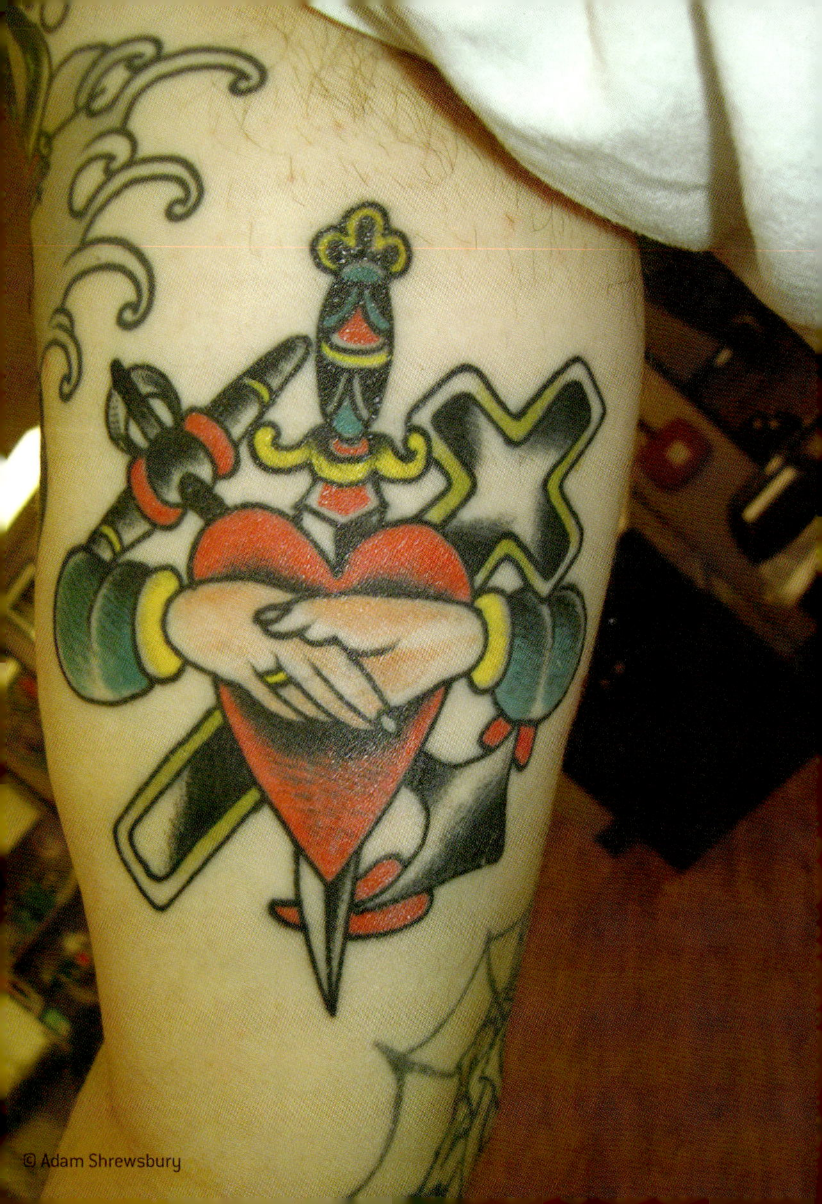
© Adam Shrewsbury

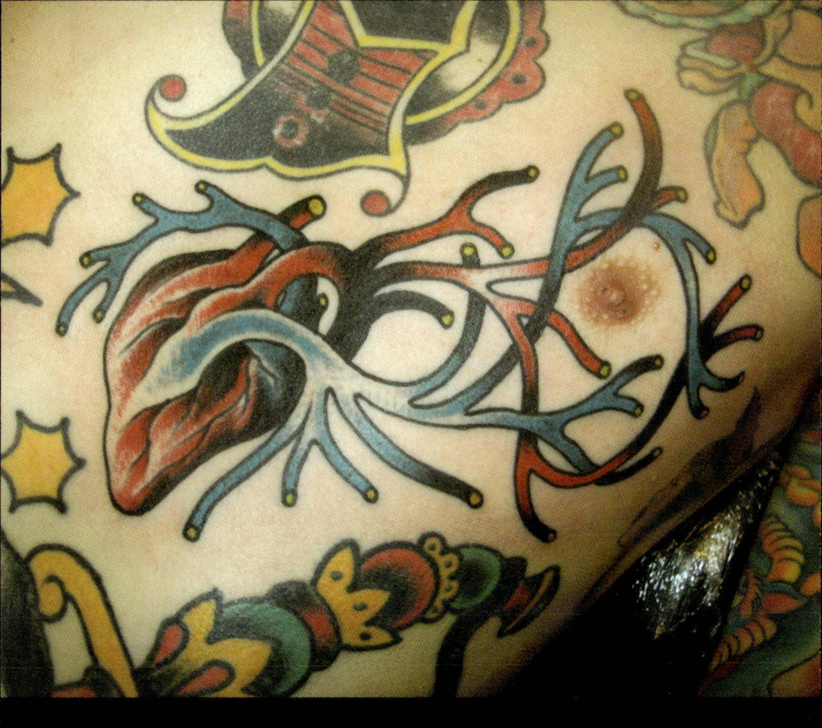

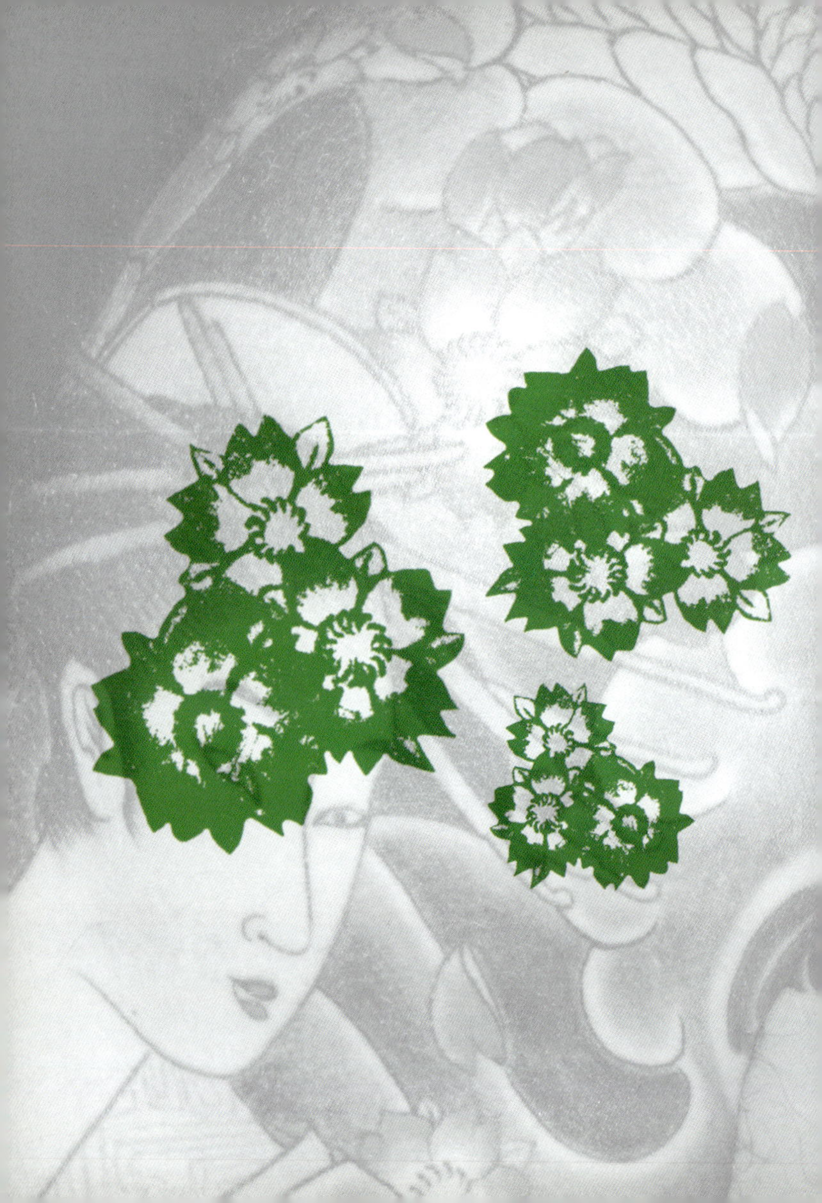

Japanese tattoos

Tatouages japonais

Japanische Tätowierungen

Japanse tatoeages

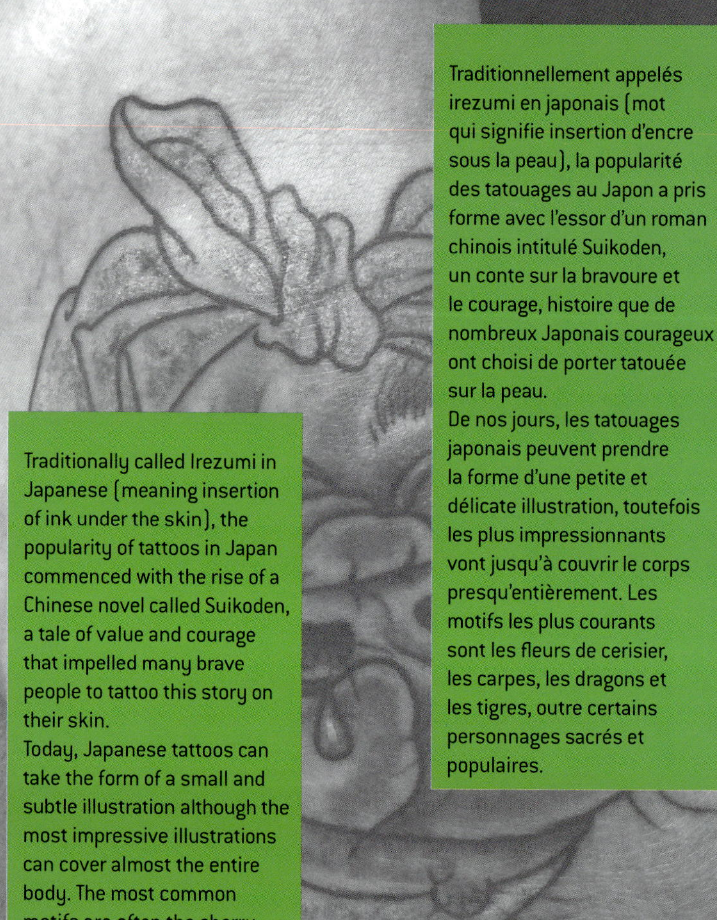

Traditionally called Irezumi in Japanese (meaning insertion of ink under the skin), the popularity of tattoos in Japan commenced with the rise of a Chinese novel called Suikoden, a tale of value and courage that impelled many brave people to tattoo this story on their skin.
Today, Japanese tattoos can take the form of a small and subtle illustration although the most impressive illustrations can cover almost the entire body. The most common motifs are often the cherry blossoms, carps, dragons and tigers, as well as other sacred and popular characters.

Traditionnellement appelés irezumi en japonais (mot qui signifie insertion d'encre sous la peau), la popularité des tatouages au Japon a pris forme avec l'essor d'un roman chinois intitulé Suikoden, un conte sur la bravoure et le courage, histoire que de nombreux Japonais courageux ont choisi de porter tatouée sur la peau.
De nos jours, les tatouages japonais peuvent prendre la forme d'une petite et délicate illustration, toutefois les plus impressionnants vont jusqu'à couvrir le corps presqu'entièrement. Les motifs les plus courants sont les fleurs de cerisier, les carpes, les dragons et les tigres, outre certains personnages sacrés et populaires.

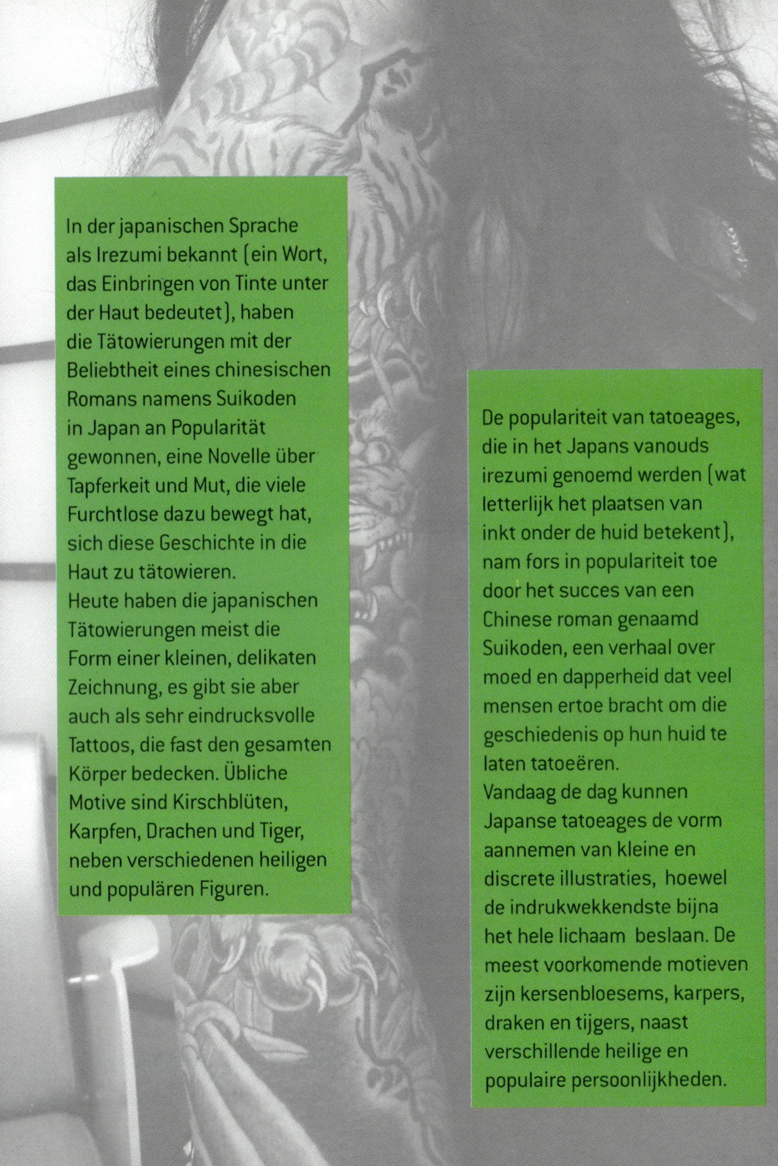

In der japanischen Sprache
als Irezumi bekannt (ein Wort,
das Einbringen von Tinte unter
der Haut bedeutet), haben
die Tätowierungen mit der
Beliebtheit eines chinesischen
Romans namens Suikoden
in Japan an Popularität
gewonnen, eine Novelle über
Tapferkeit und Mut, die viele
Furchtlose dazu bewegt hat,
sich diese Geschichte in die
Haut zu tätowieren.
Heute haben die japanischen
Tätowierungen meist die
Form einer kleinen, delikaten
Zeichnung, es gibt sie aber
auch als sehr eindrucksvolle
Tattoos, die fast den gesamten
Körper bedecken. Übliche
Motive sind Kirschblüten,
Karpfen, Drachen und Tiger,
neben verschiedenen heiligen
und populären Figuren.

De populariteit van tatoeages,
die in het Japans vanouds
irezumi genoemd werden (wat
letterlijk het plaatsen van
inkt onder de huid betekent),
nam fors in populariteit toe
door het succes van een
Chinese roman genaamd
Suikoden, een verhaal over
moed en dapperheid dat veel
mensen ertoe bracht om die
geschiedenis op hun huid te
laten tatoeëren.
Vandaag de dag kunnen
Japanse tatoeages de vorm
aannemen van kleine en
discrete illustraties, hoewel
de indrukwekkendste bijna
het hele lichaam beslaan. De
meest voorkomende motieven
zijn kersenbloesems, karpers,
draken en tijgers, naast
verschillende heilige en
populaire persoonlijkheden.

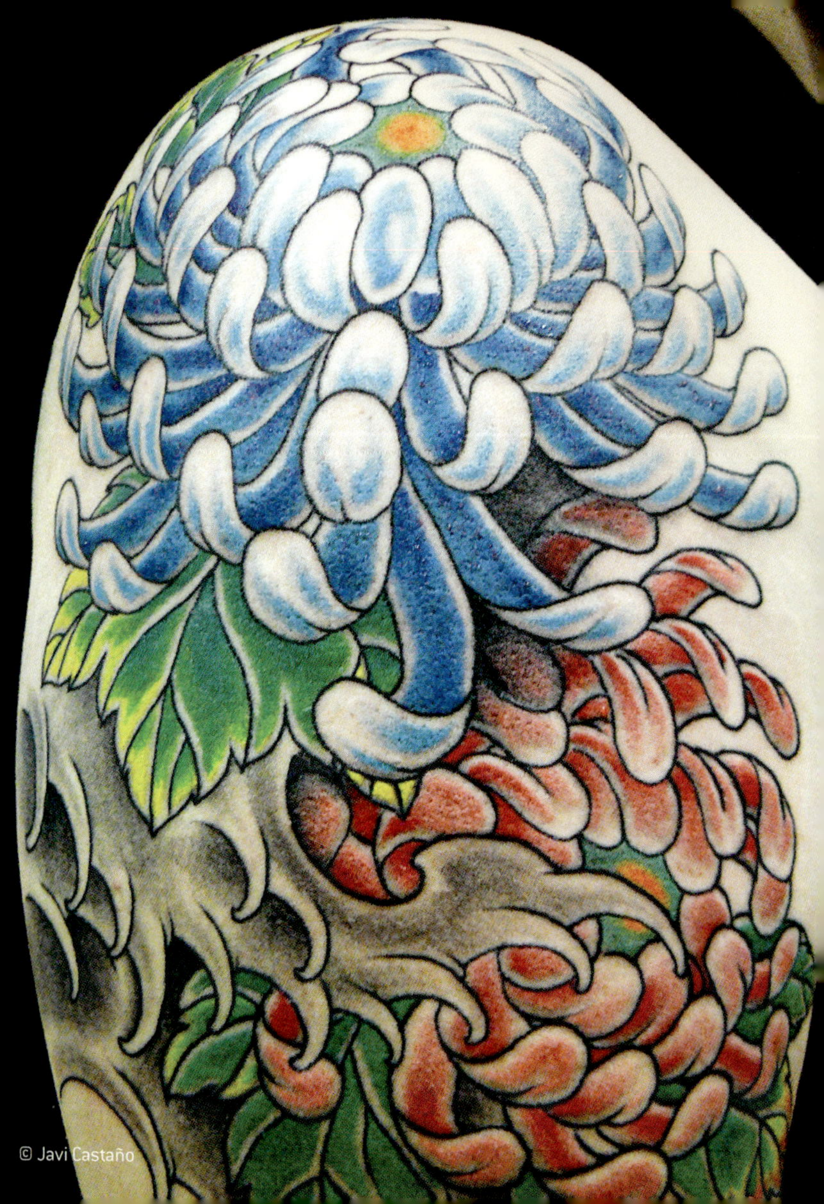
© Javi Castaño

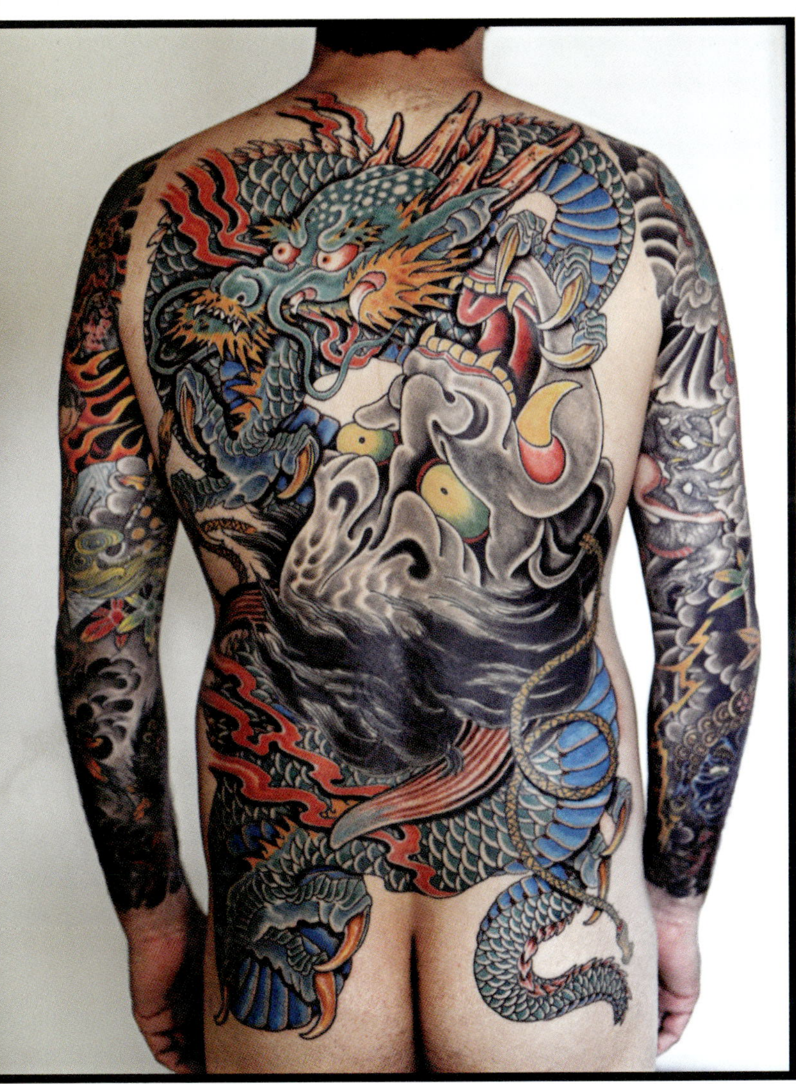

© Javi Castaño

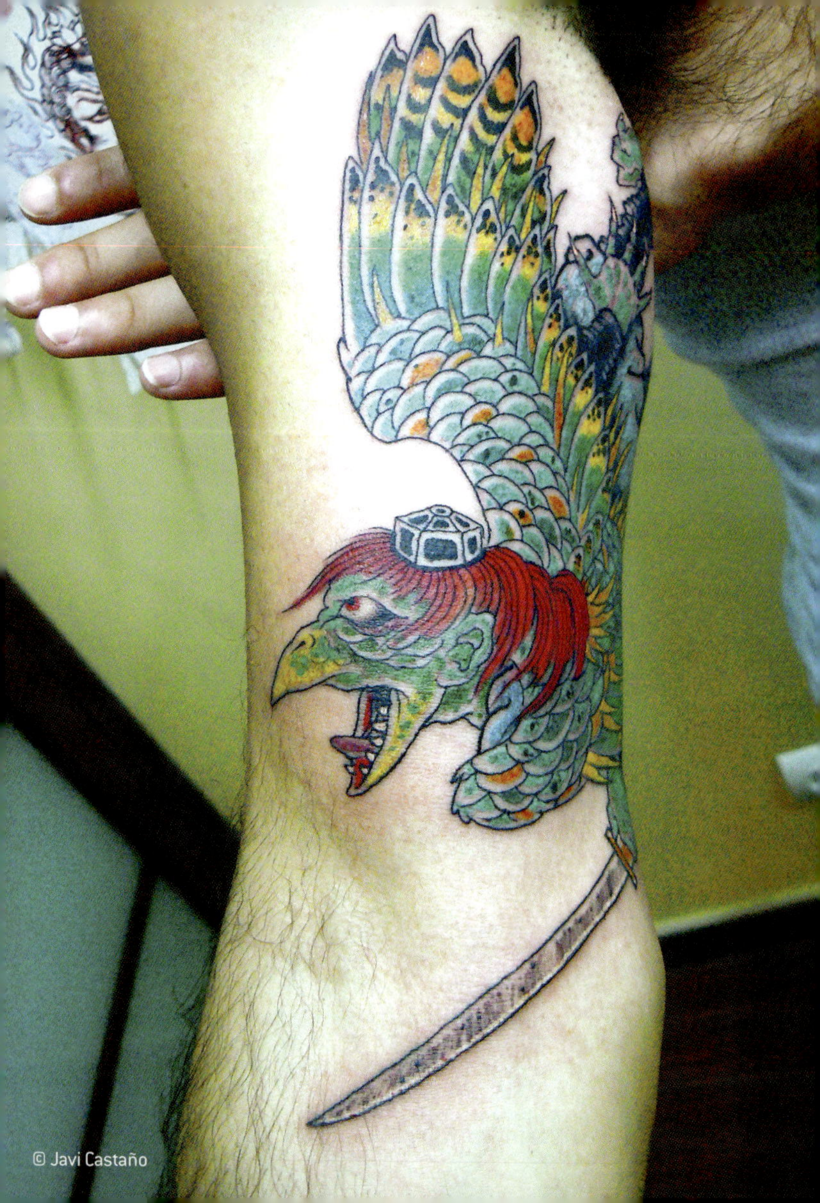

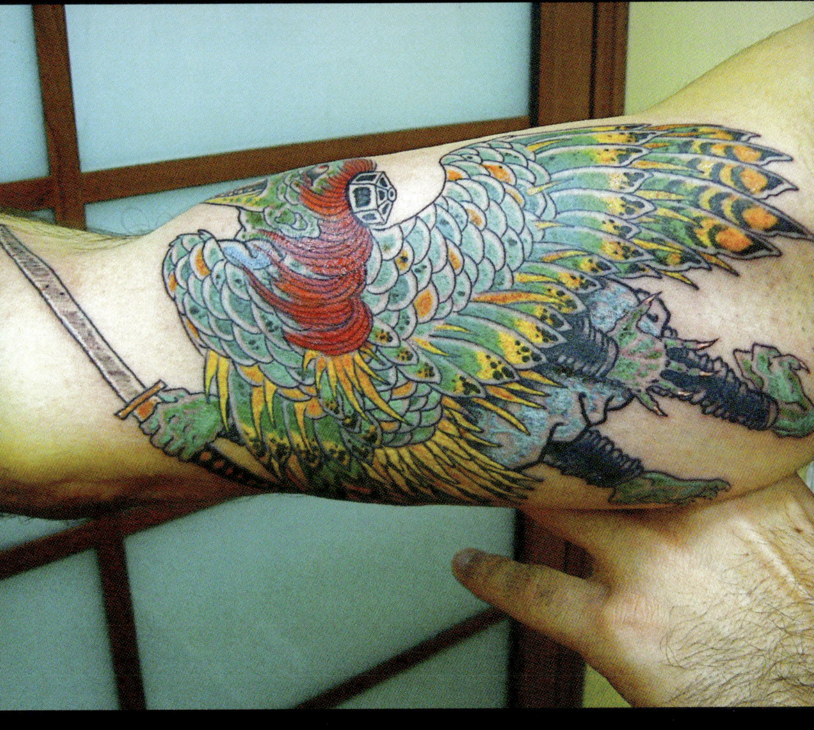

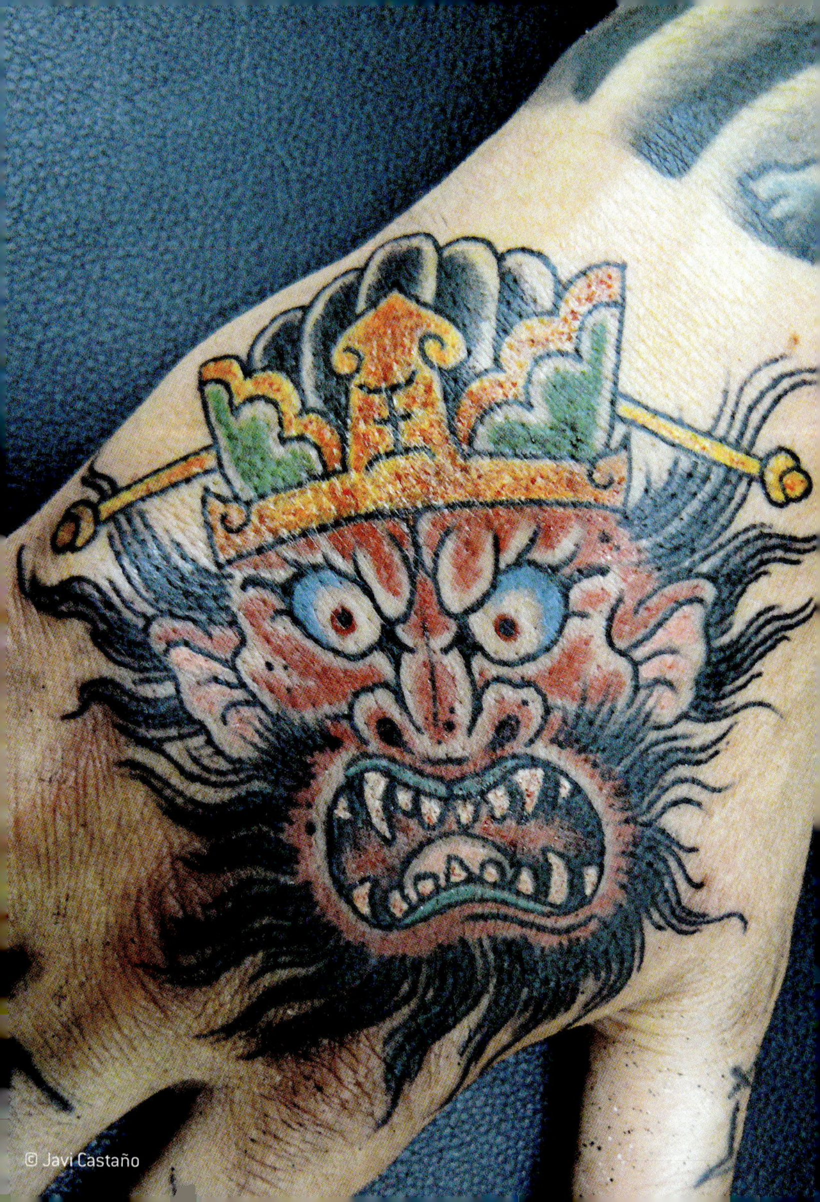

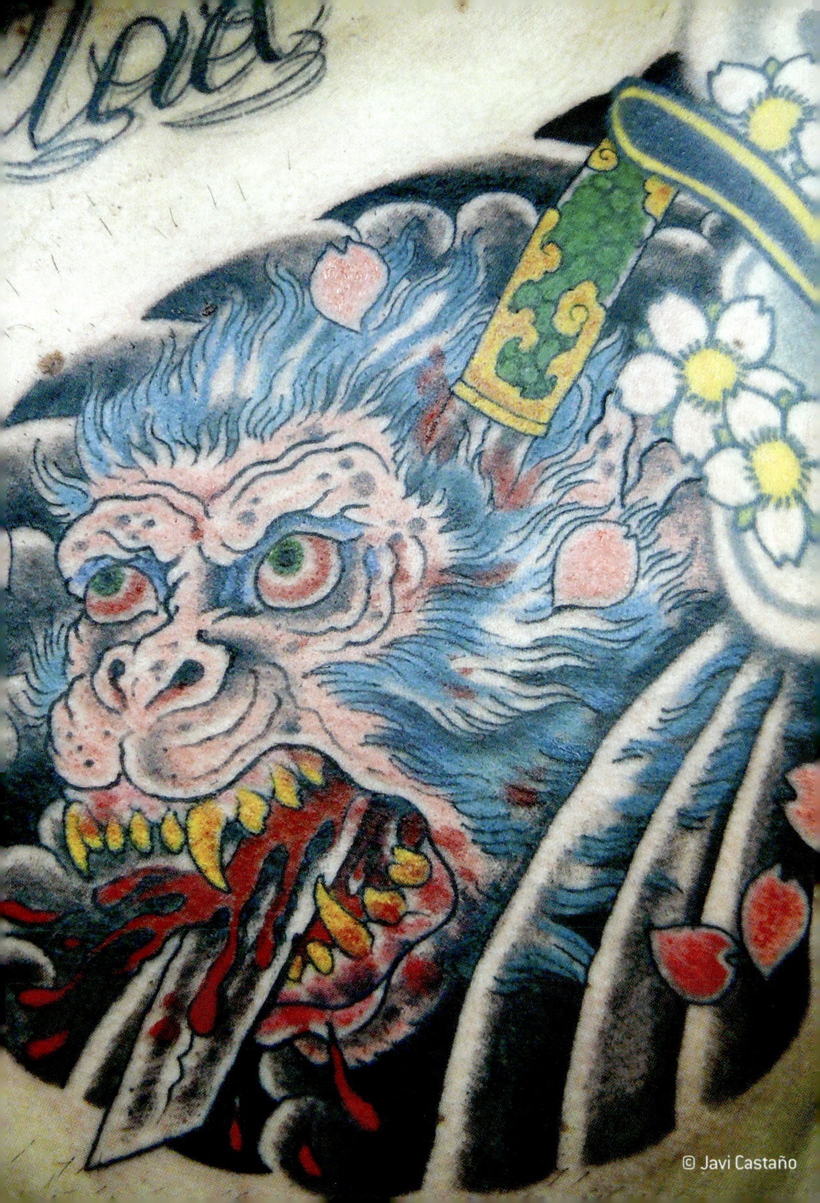
© Javi Castaño

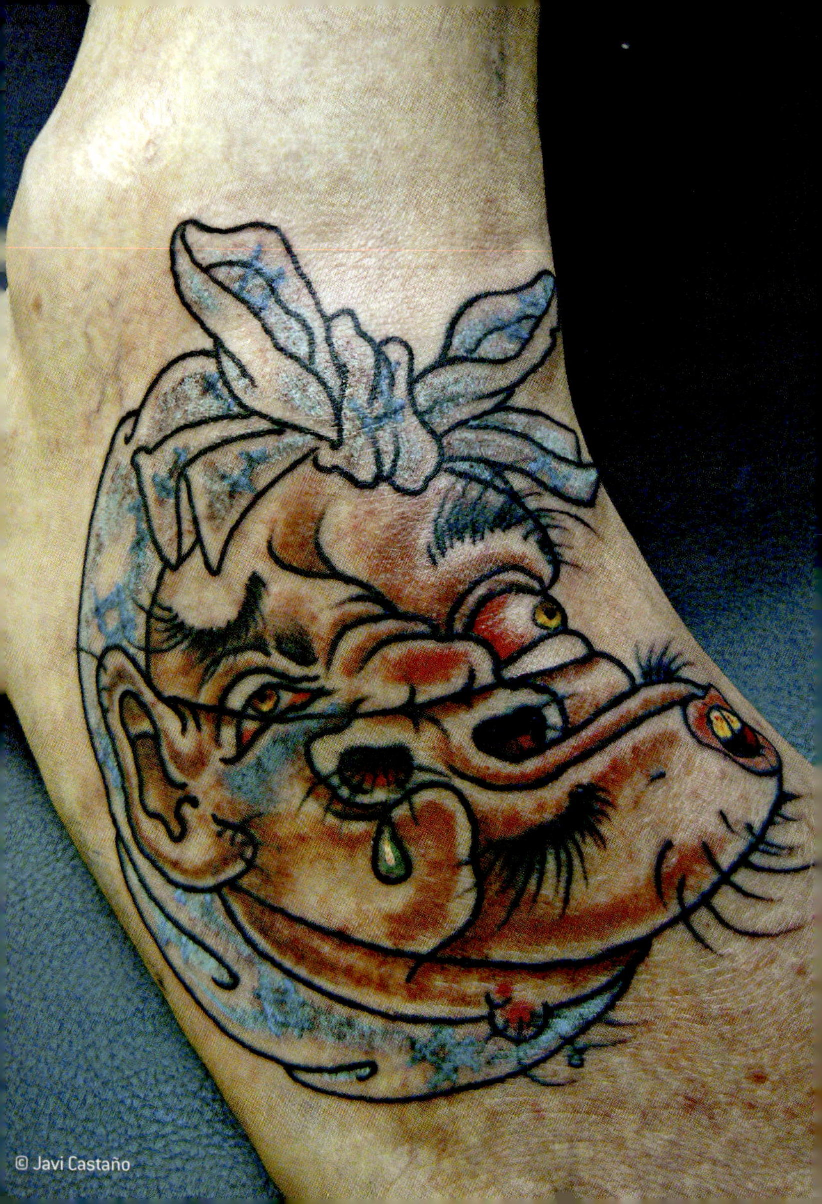

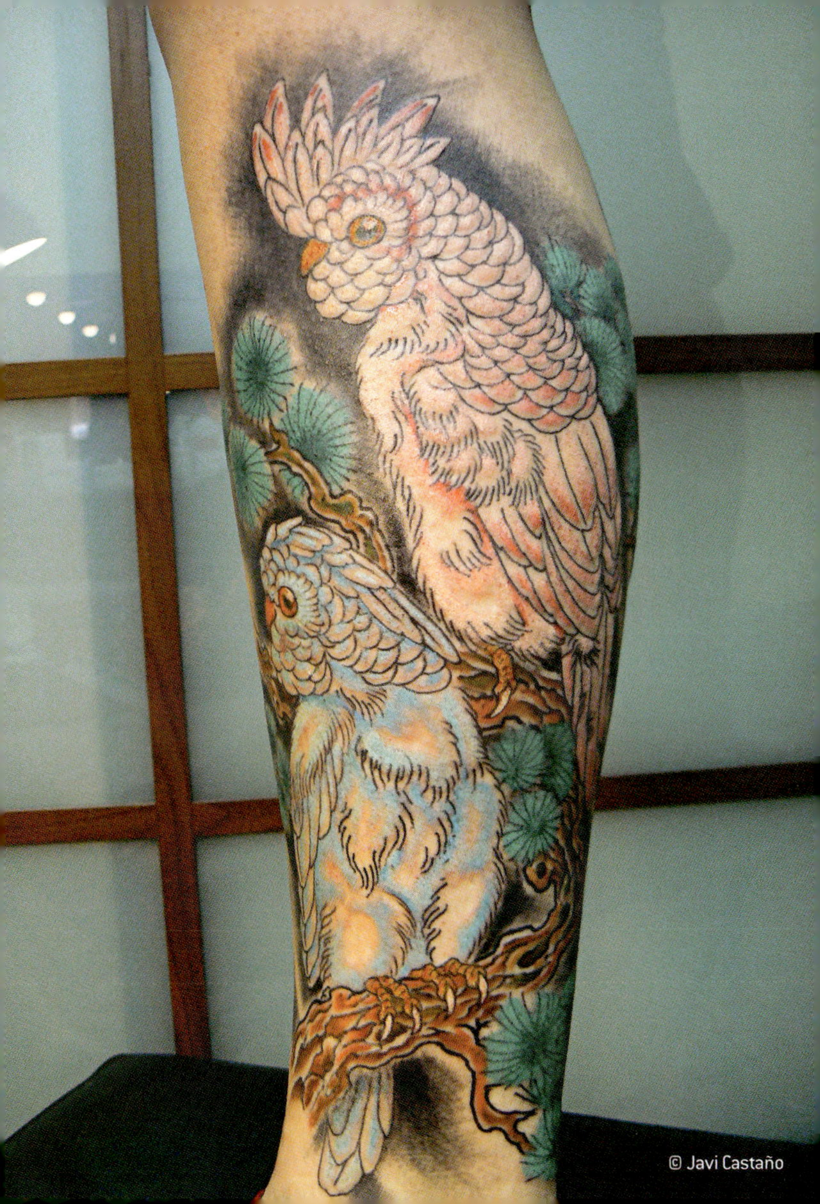
© Javi Castaño

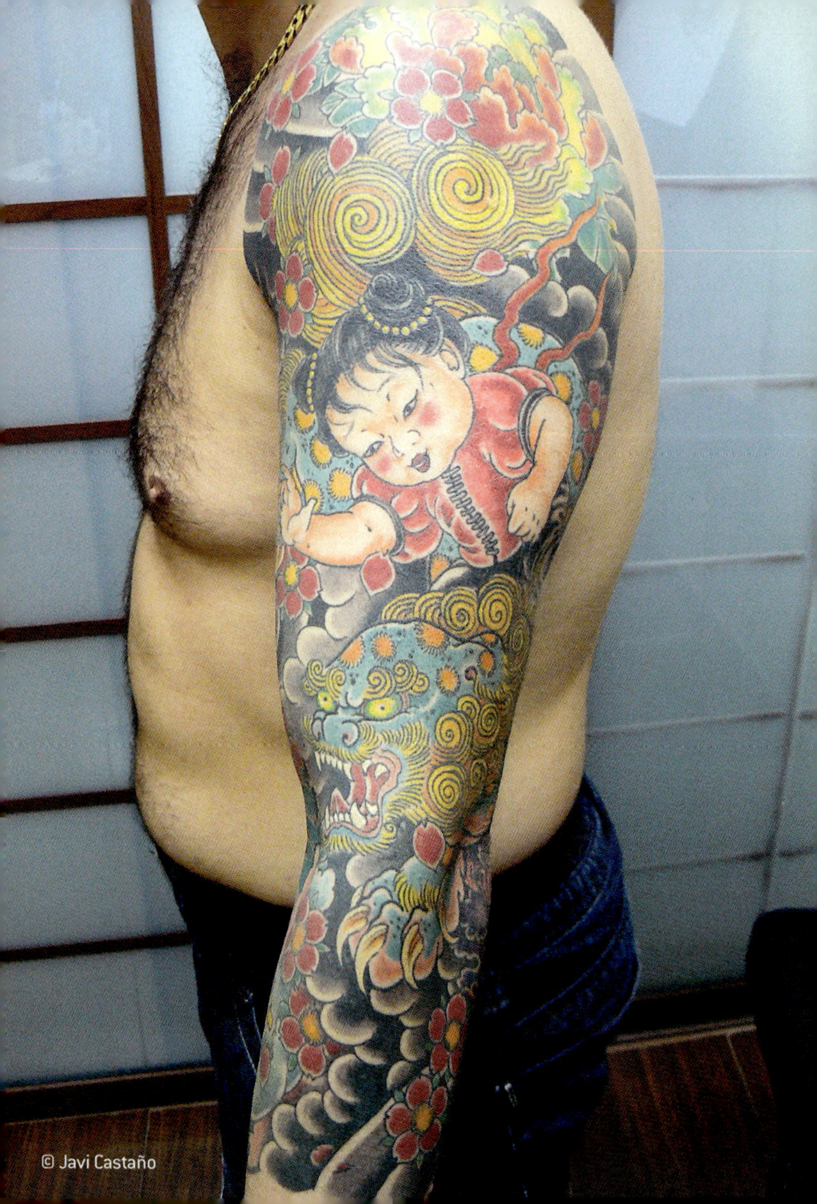

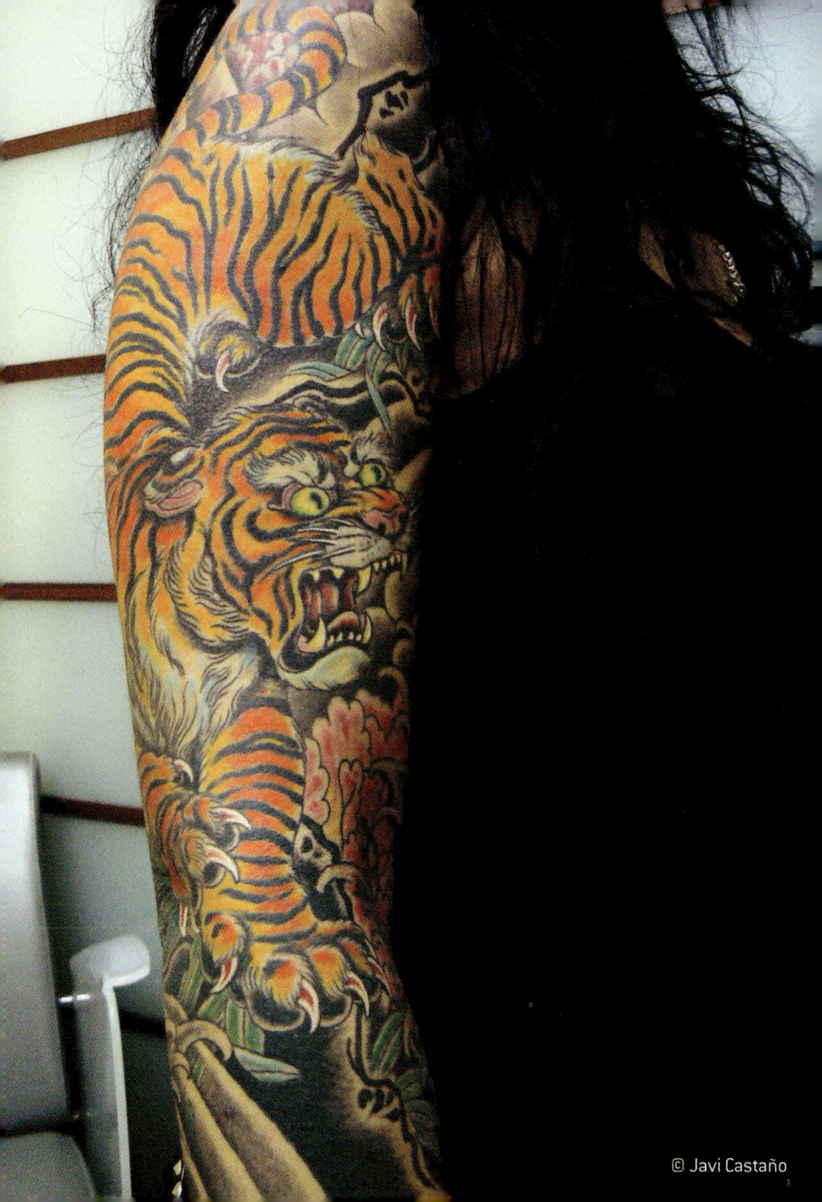
© Javi Castaño

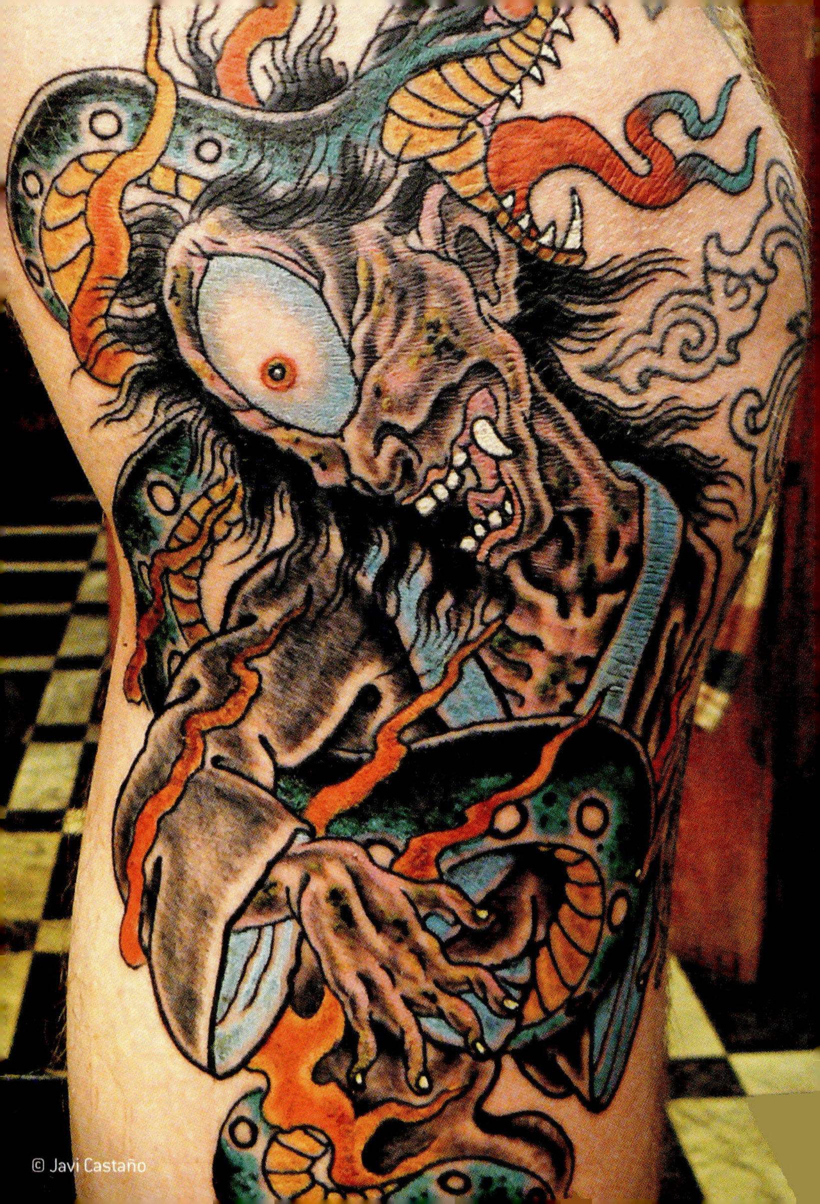
© Javi Castaño

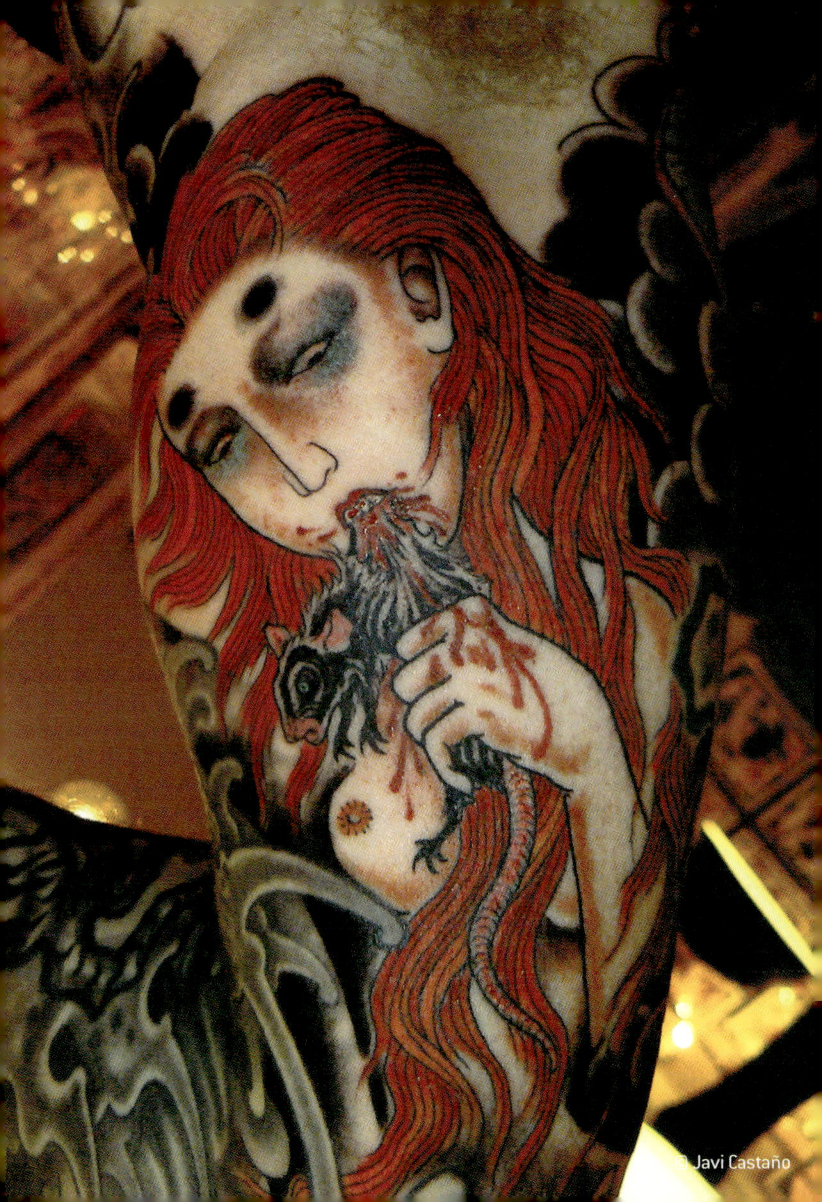

© Javi Castaño

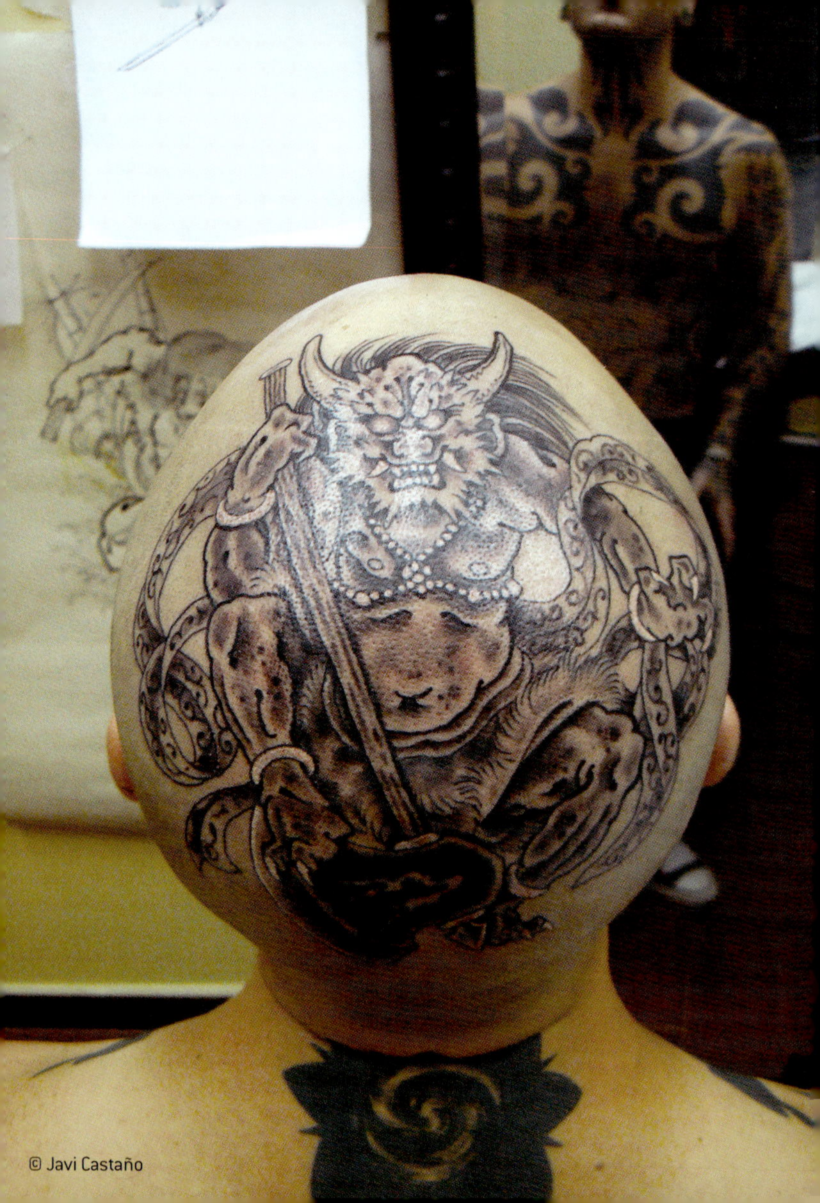

© Javi Castaño

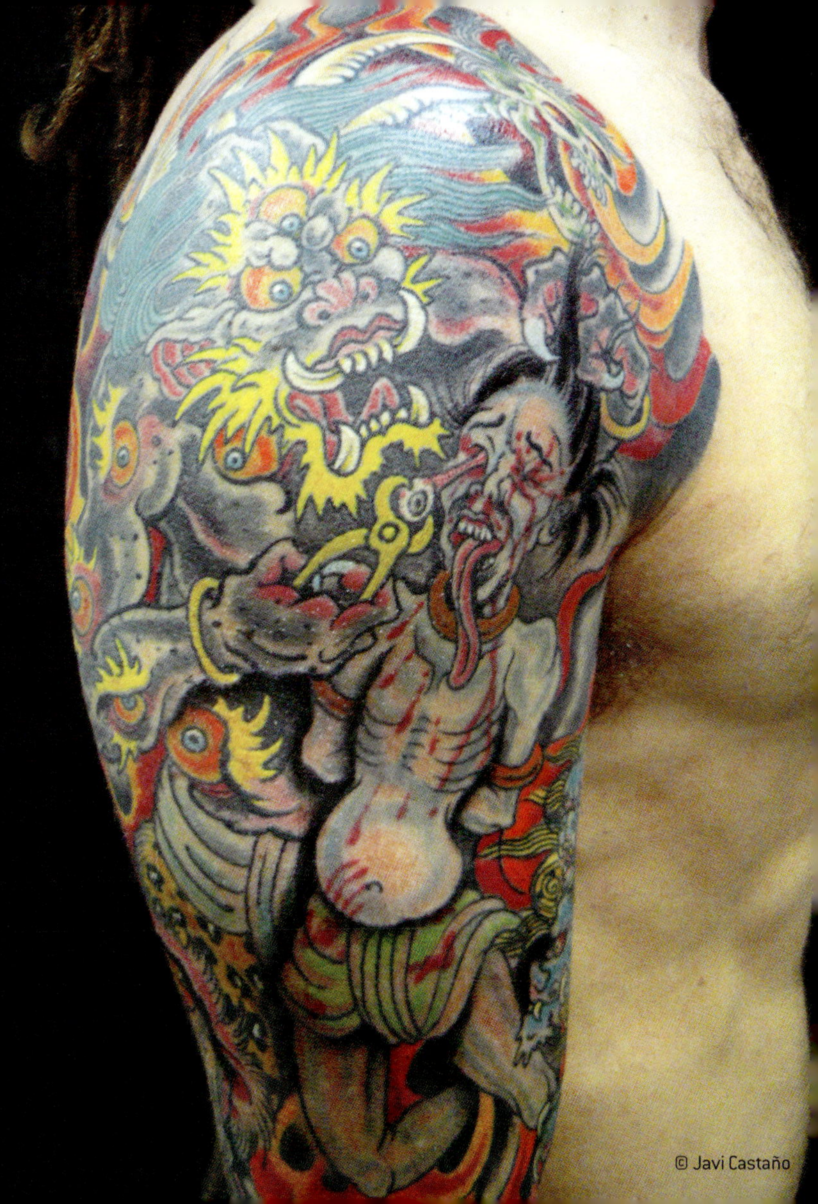

© Javi Castaño

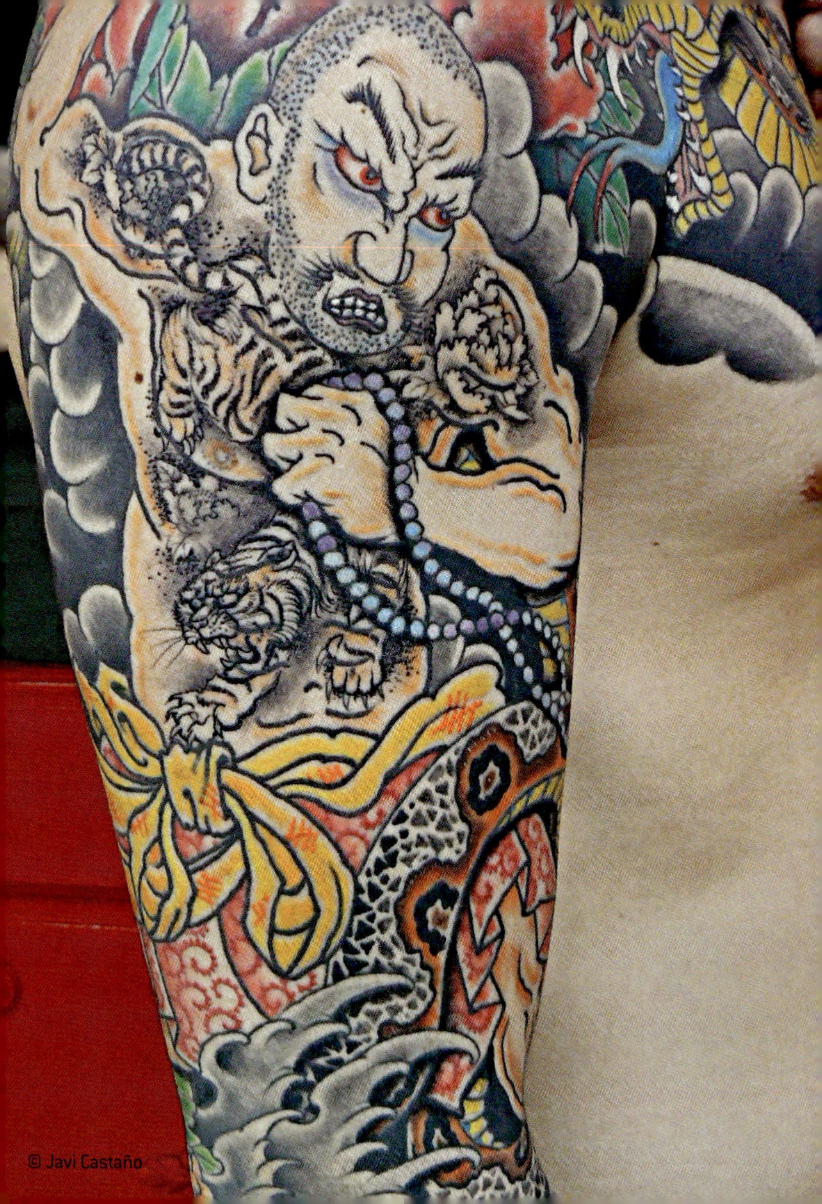
© Javi Castaño

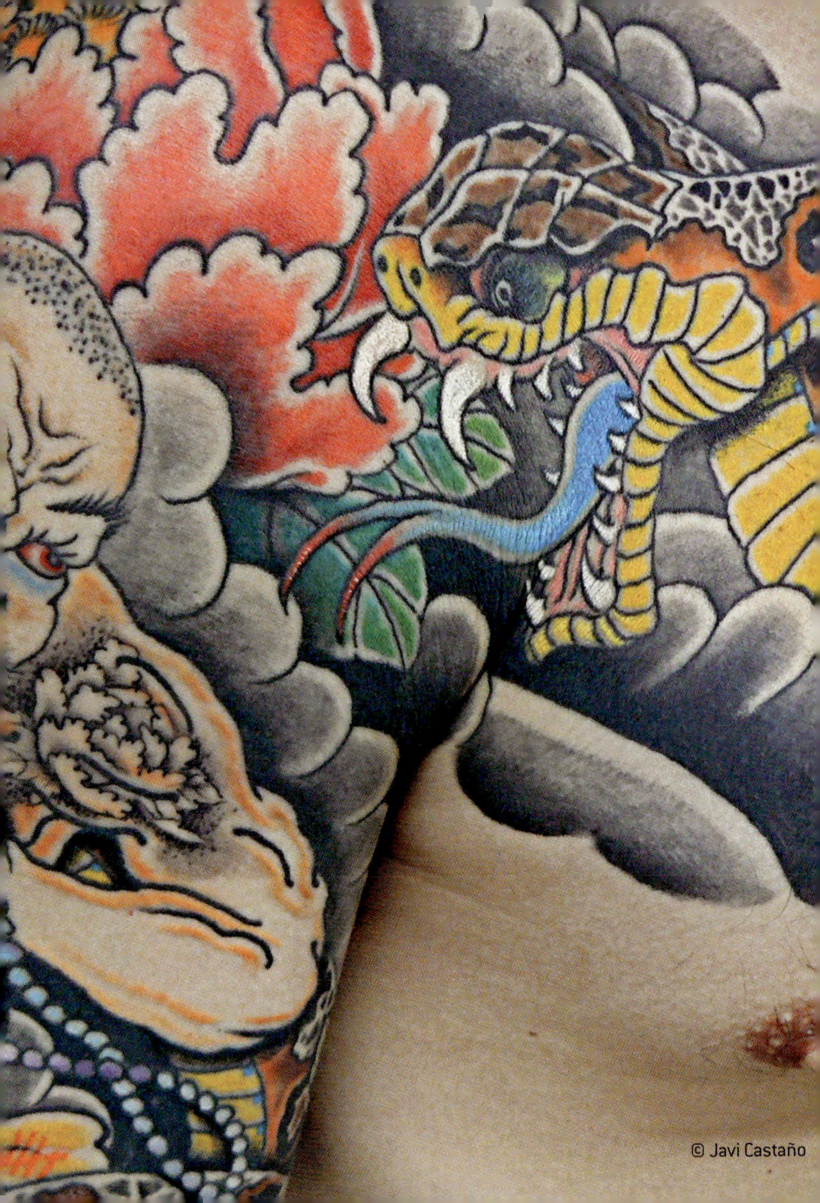

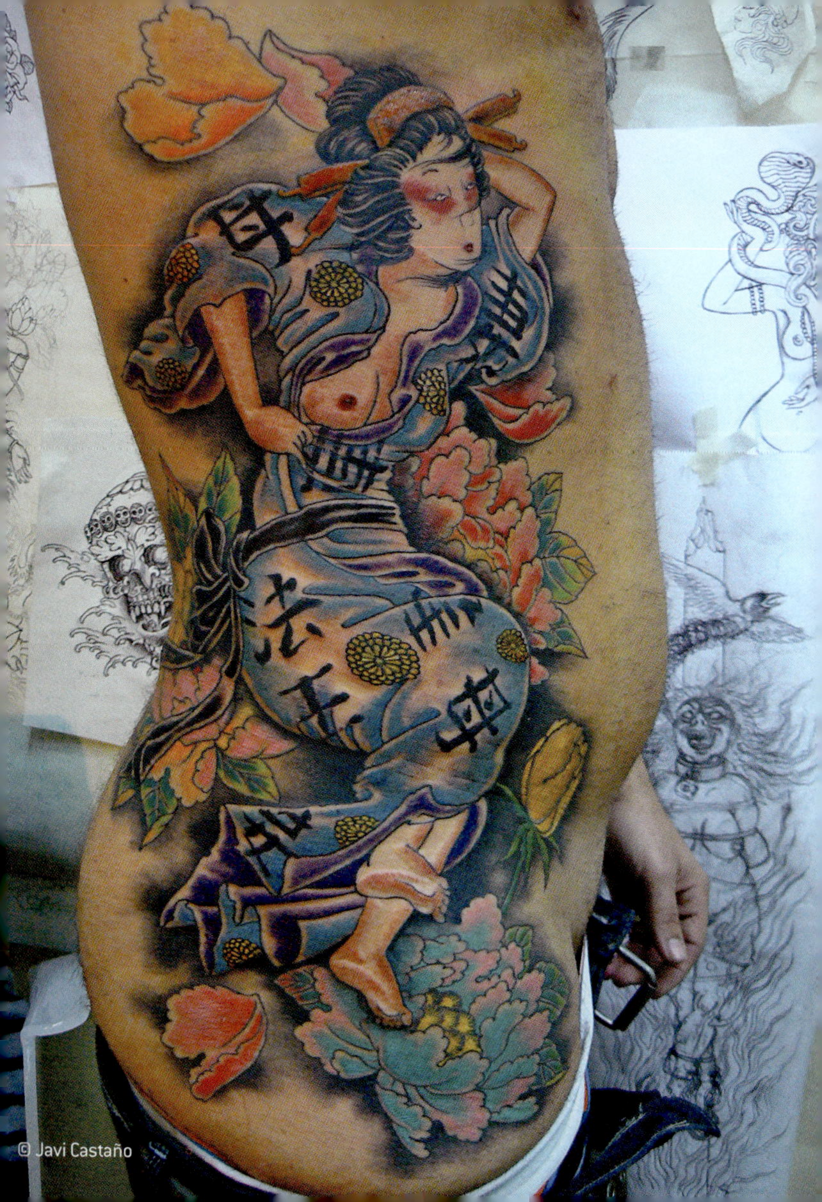
© Javi Castaño

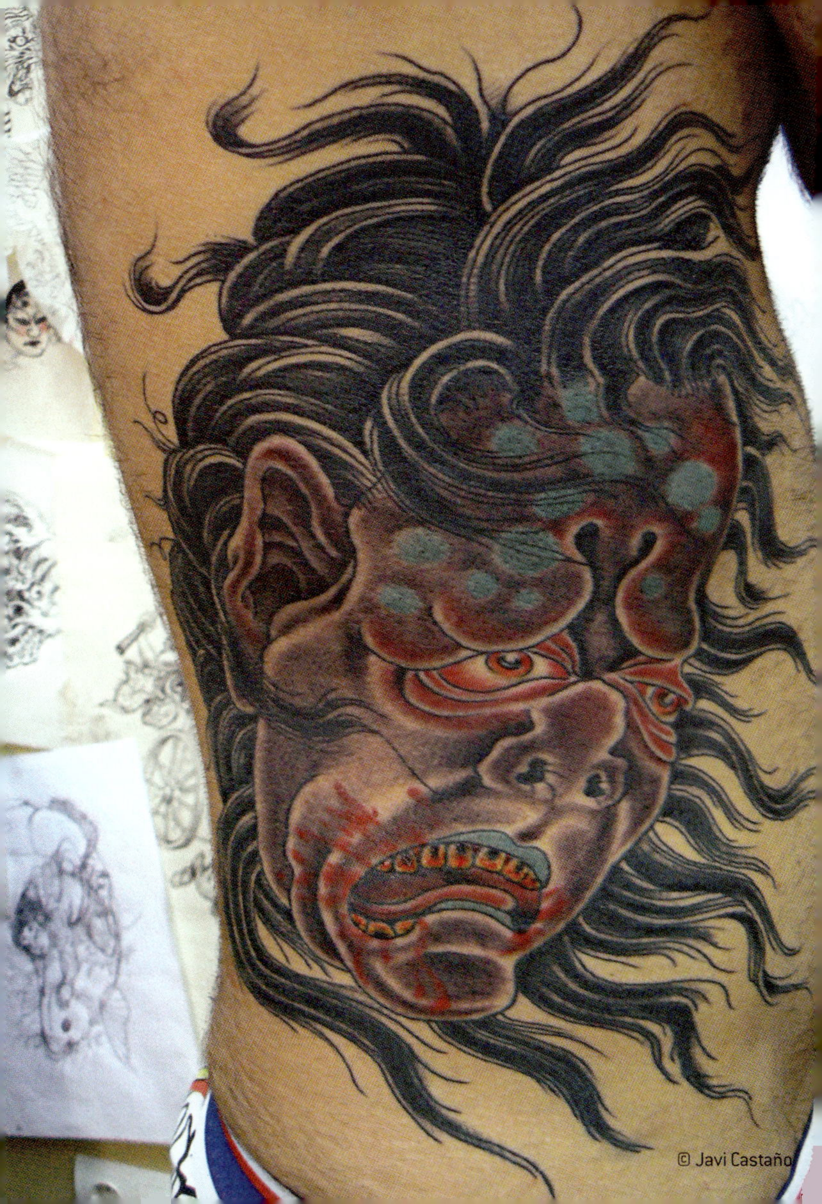

© Javi Castaño

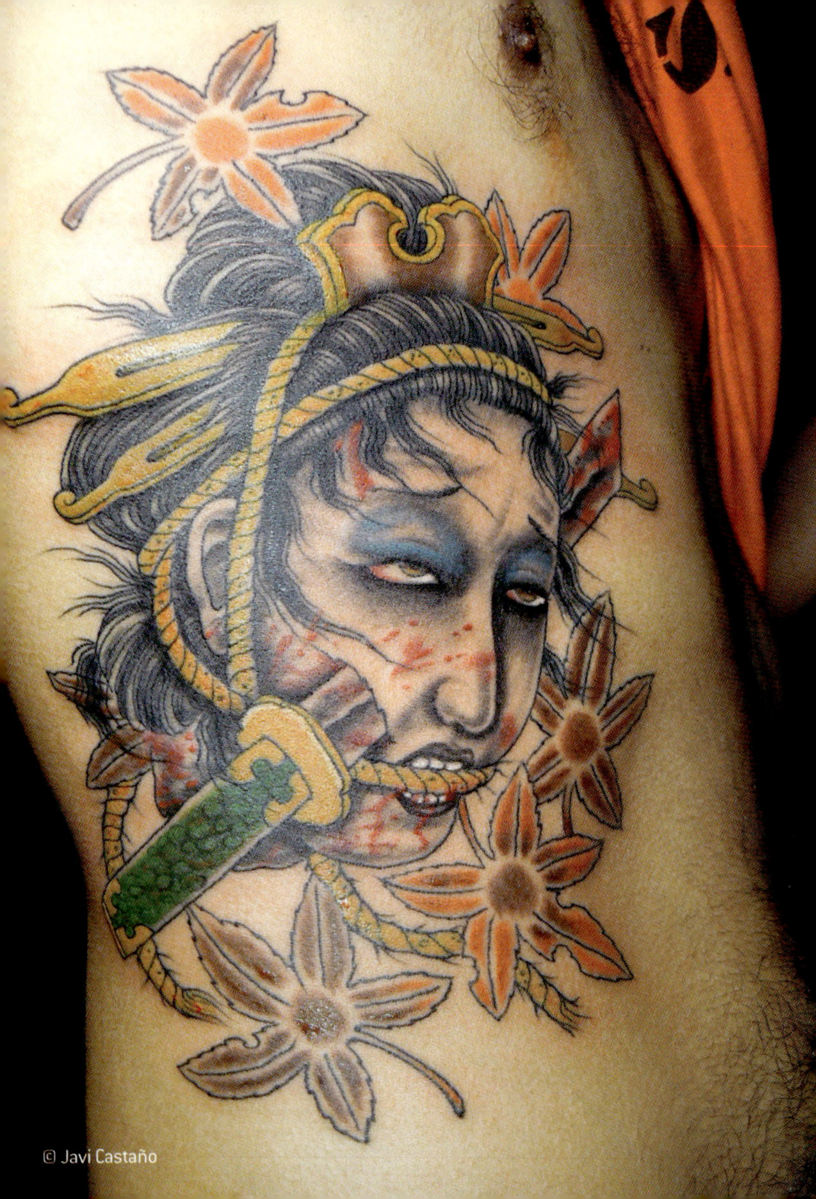

© Javi Castaño

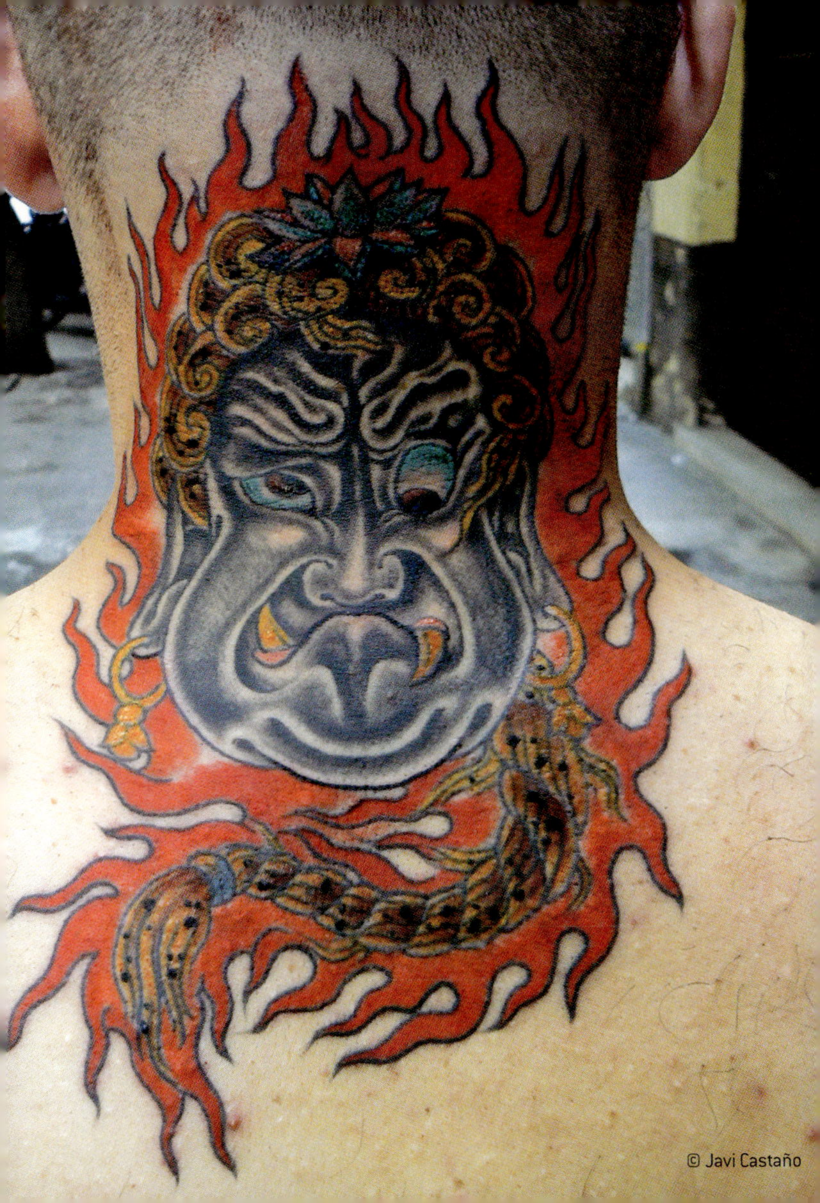

© Javi Castaño

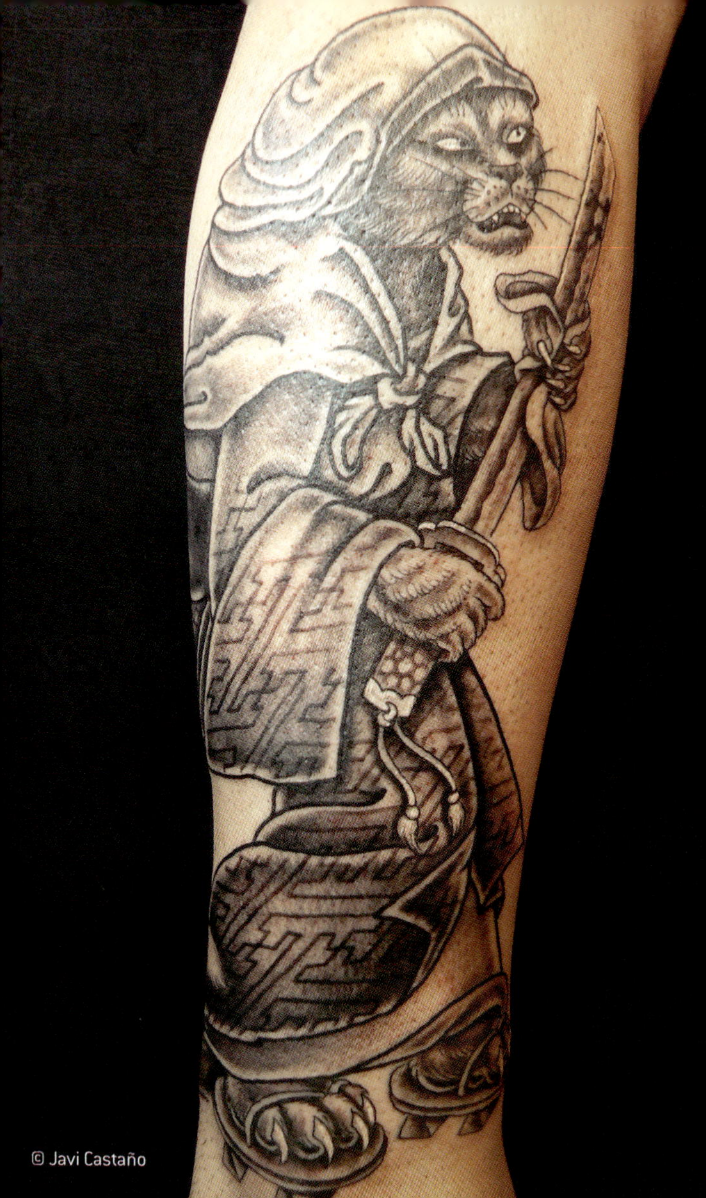

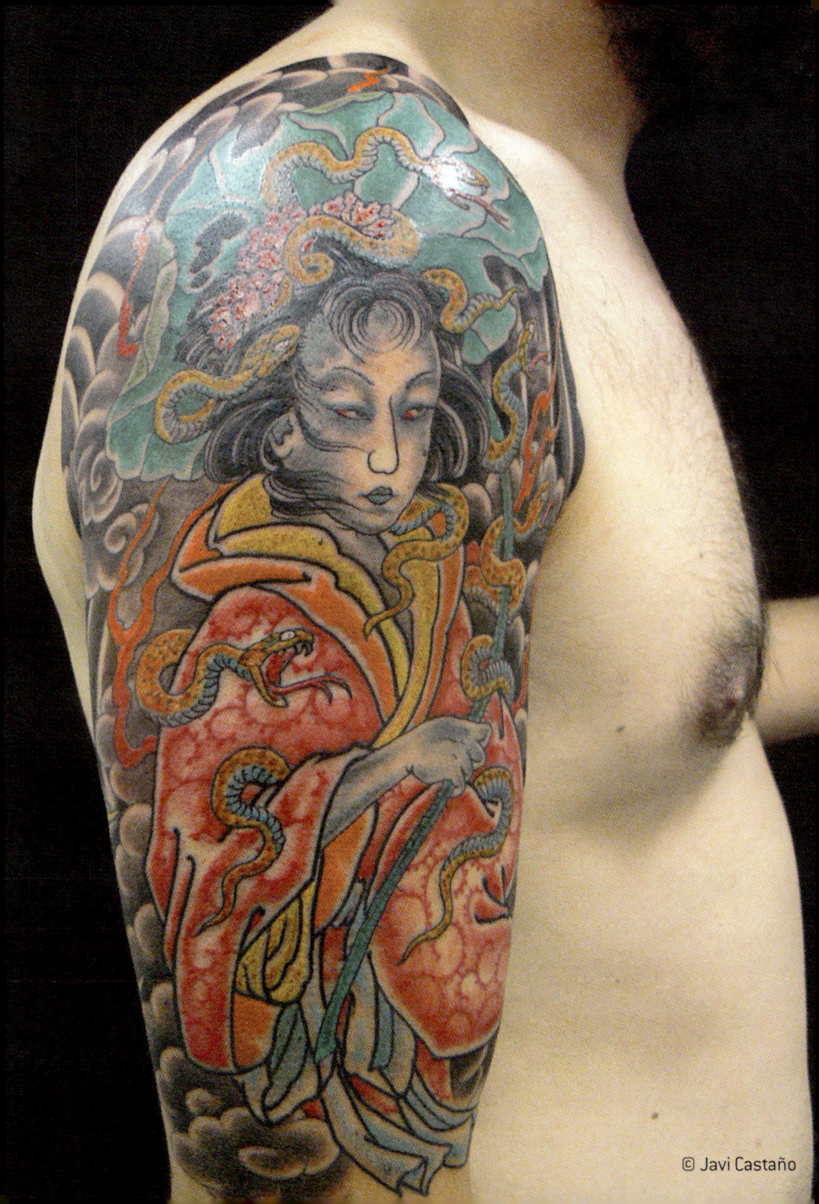

© Javi Castaño

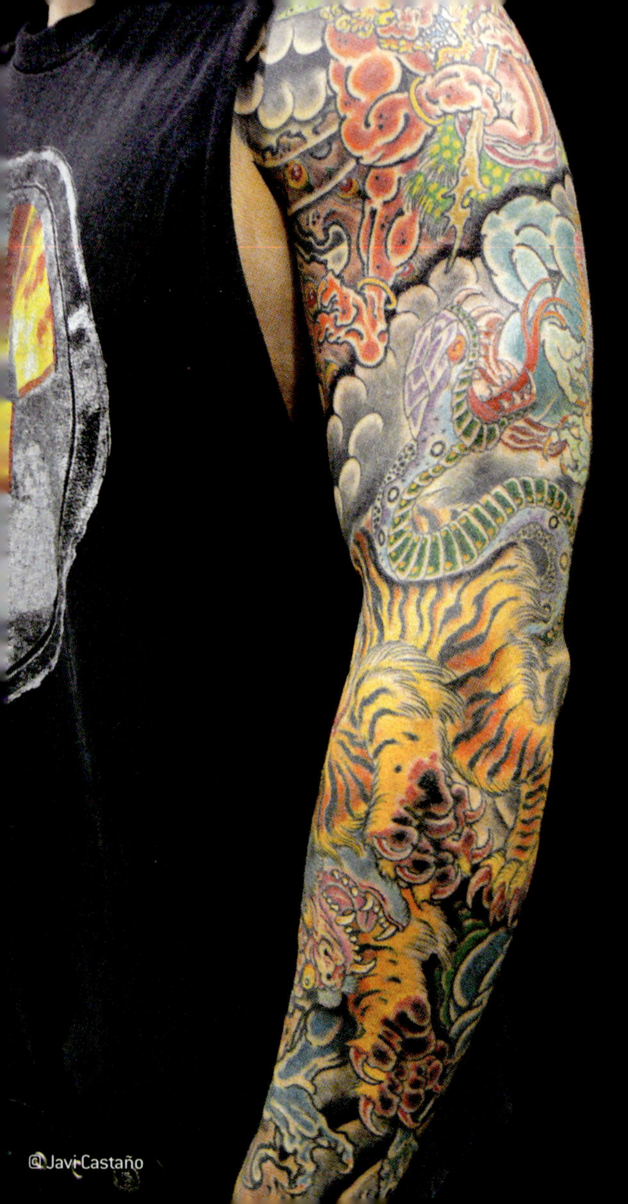
@JaviCastaño

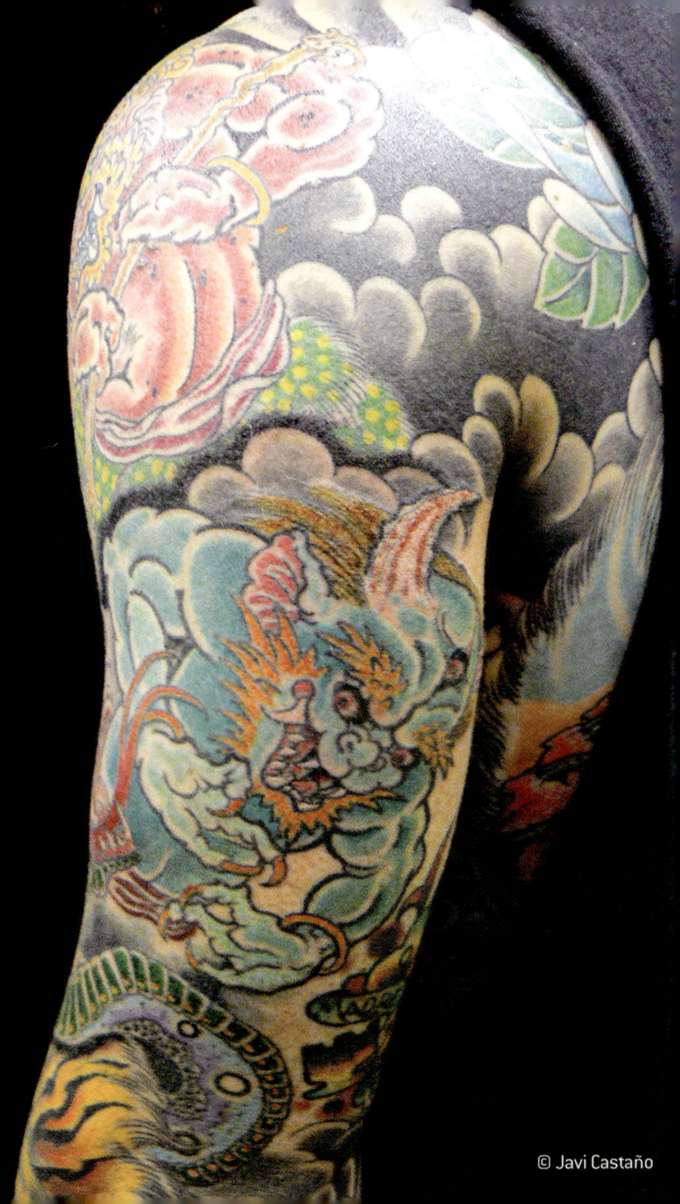

© Javi Castaño

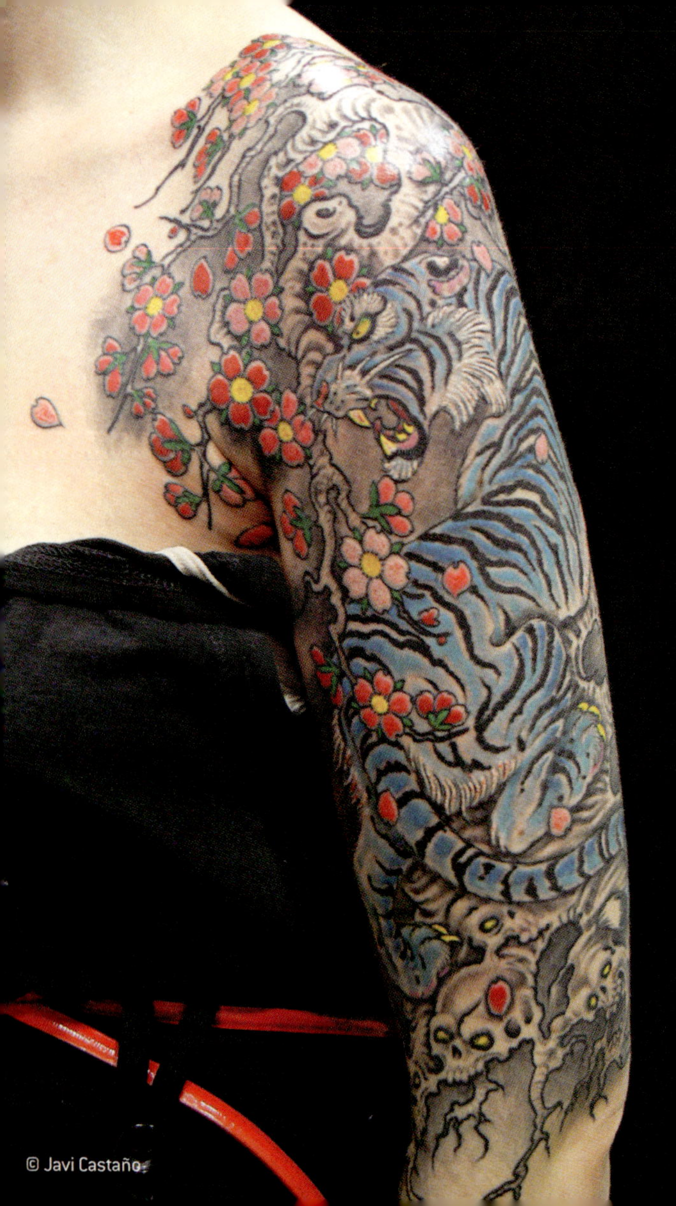

© Javi Castaño

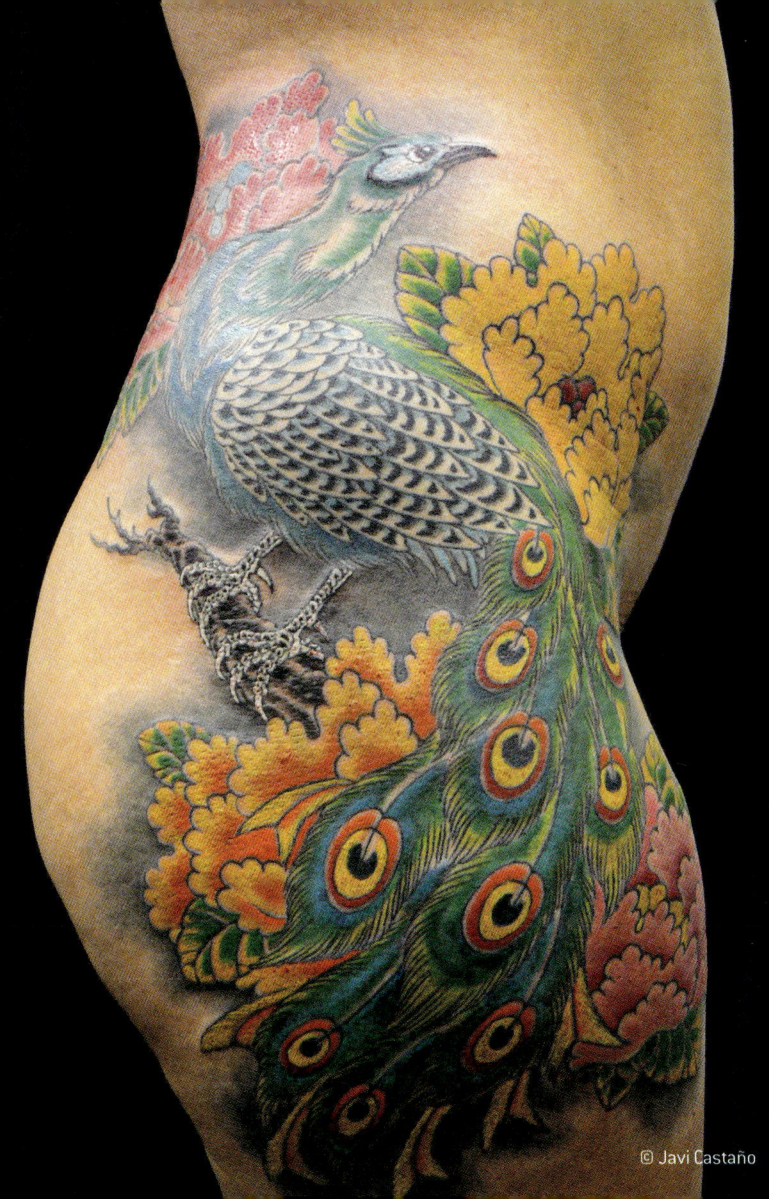
© Javi Castaño

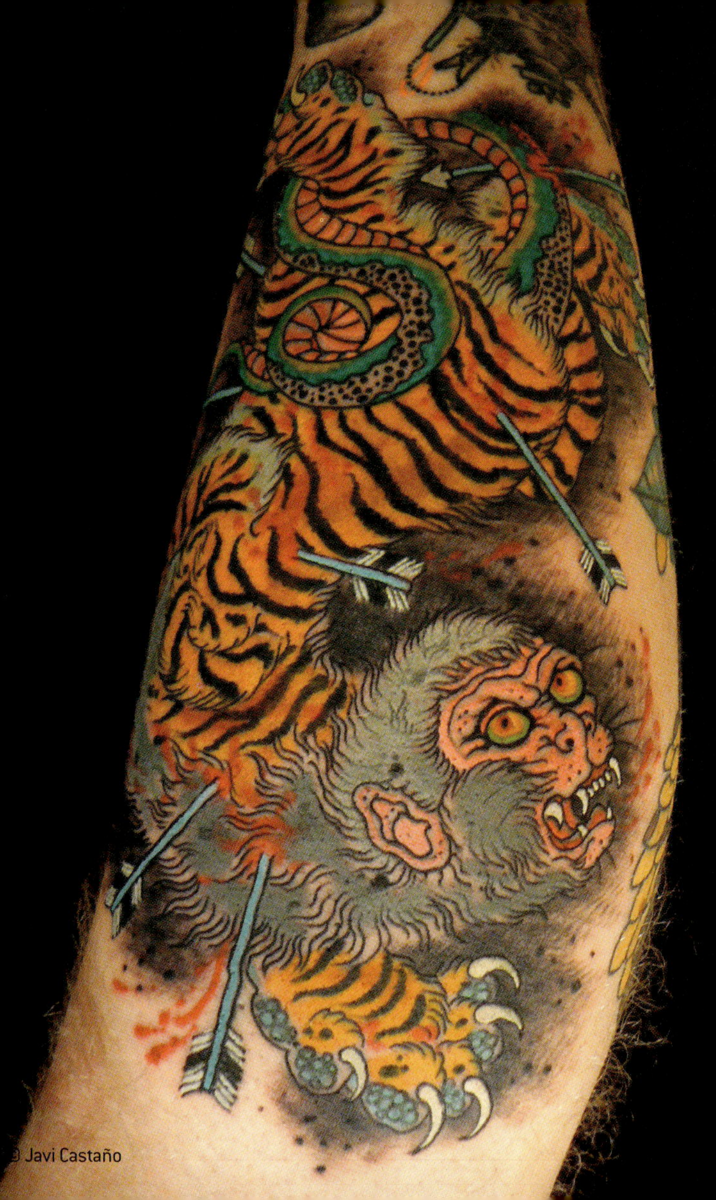

© Javi Castaño

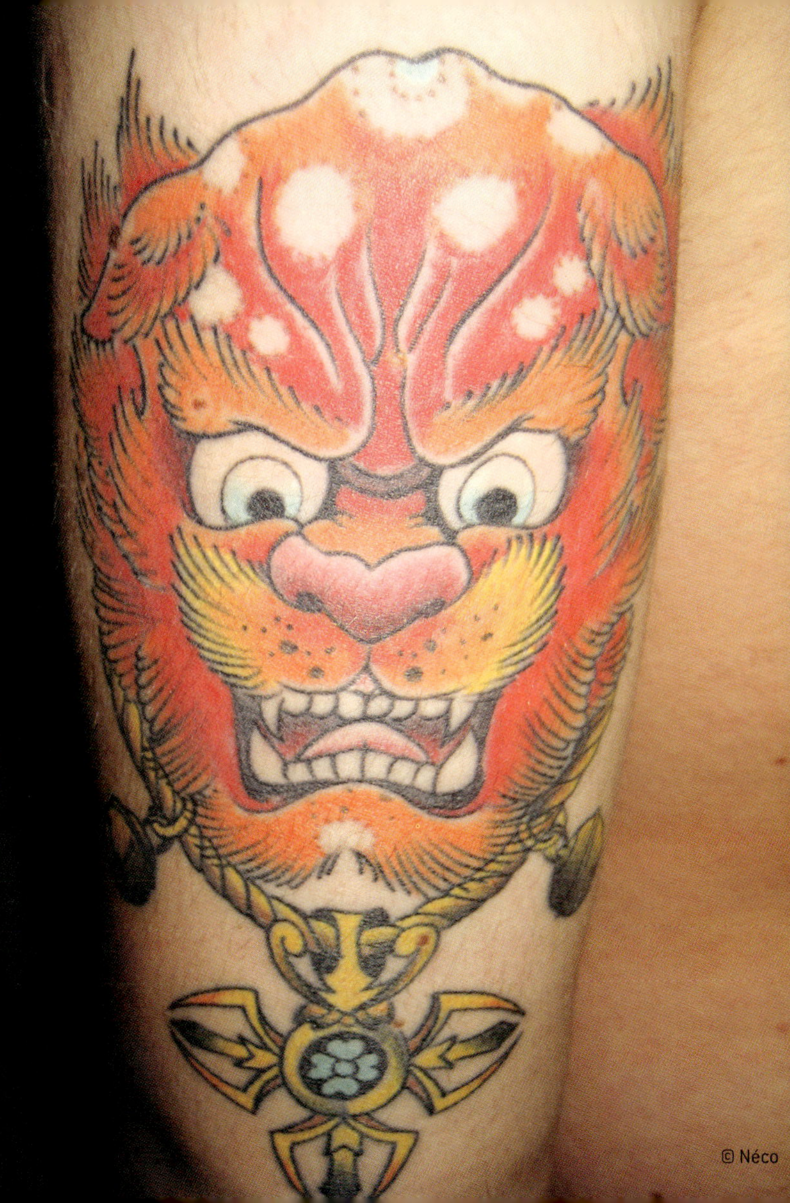
© Néco

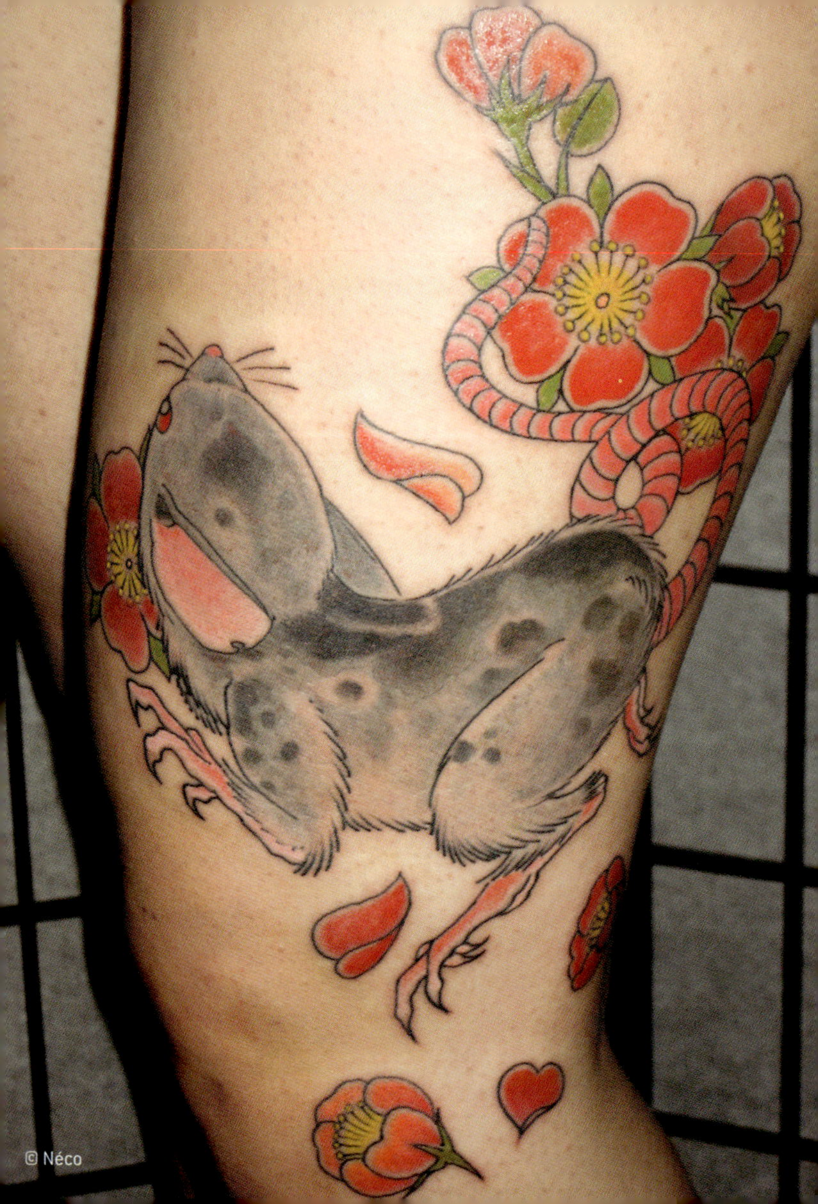
© Néco

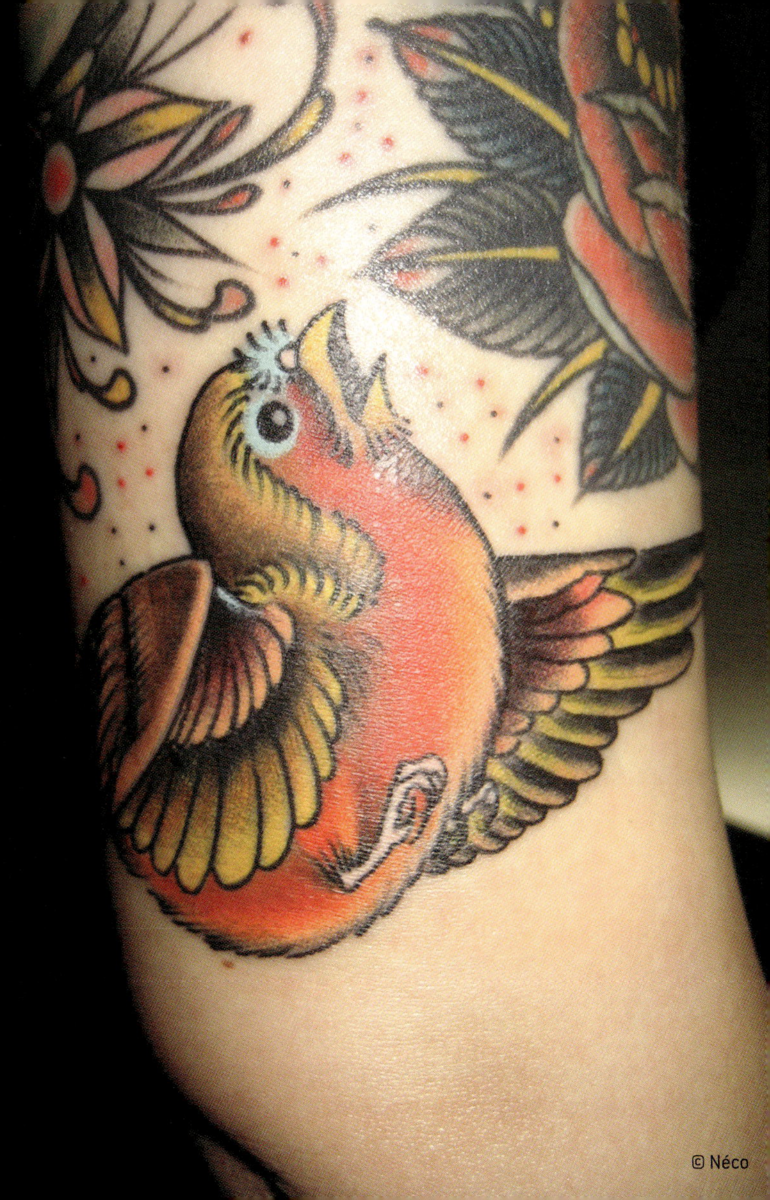

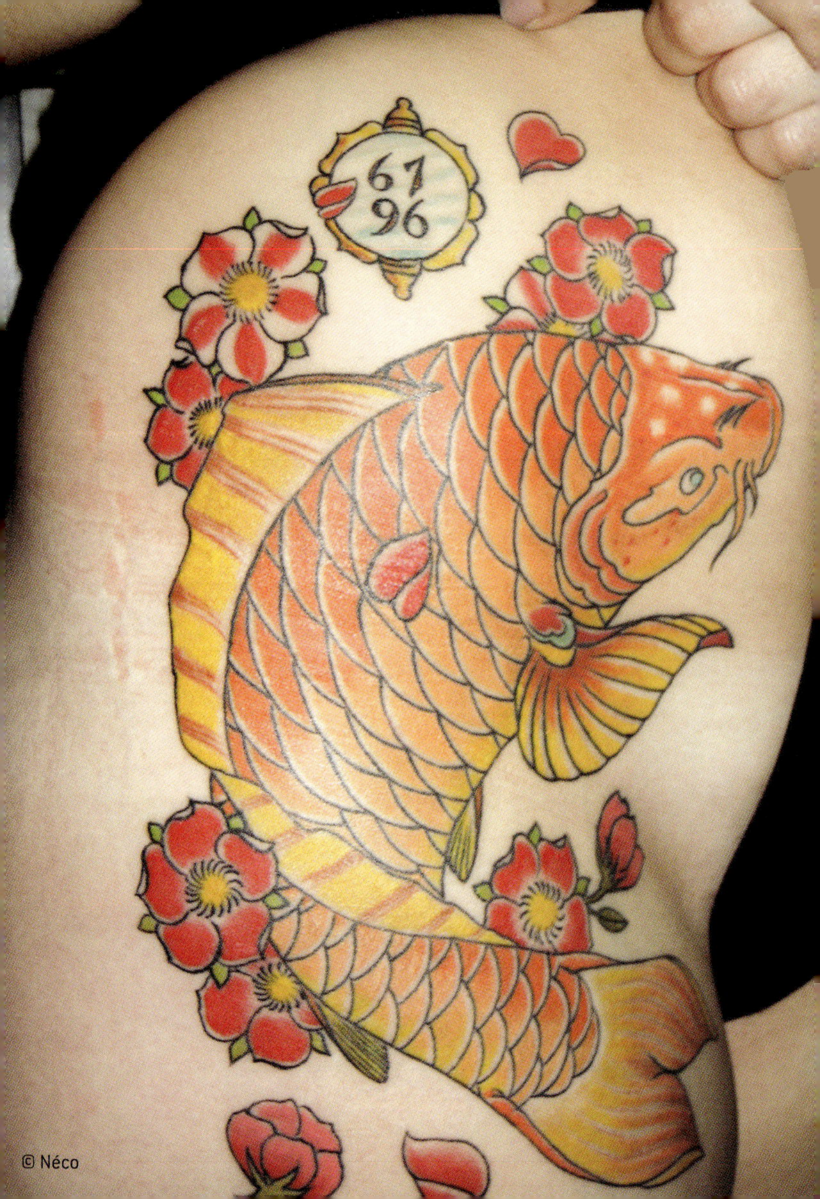
67
96

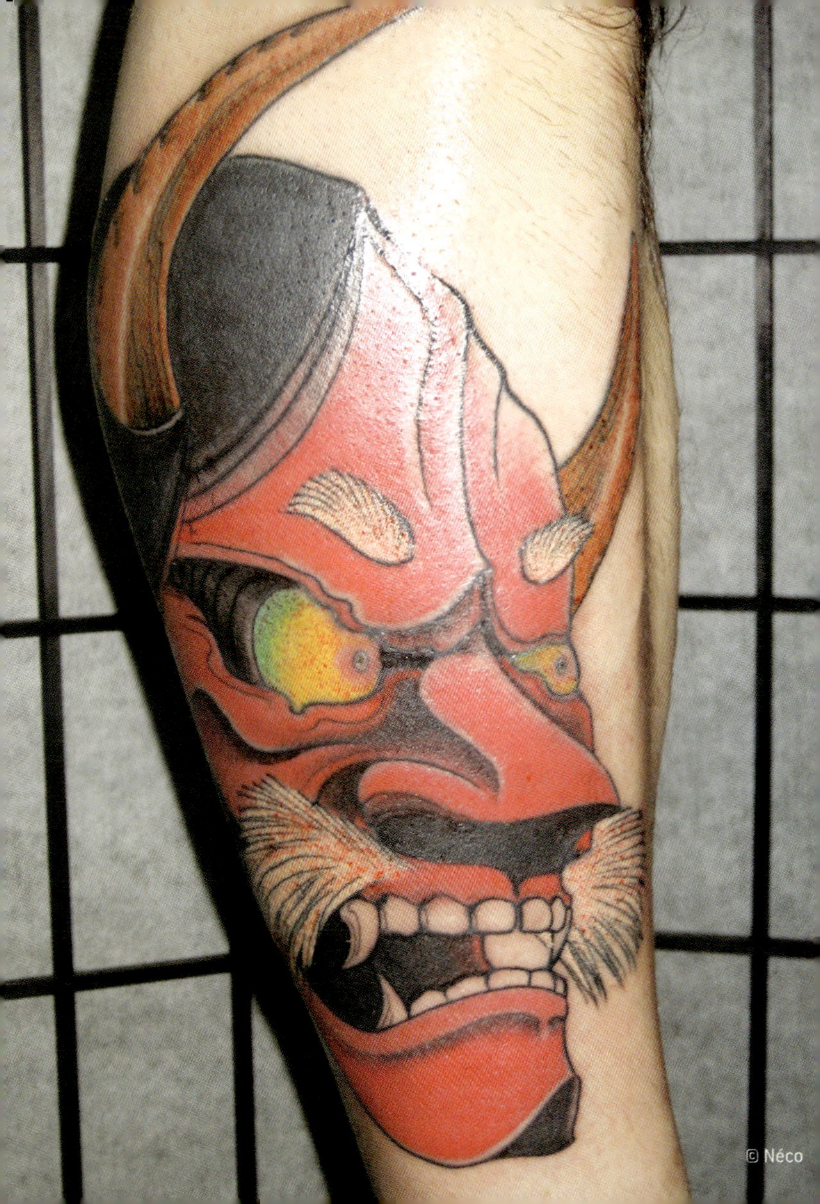
© Néco

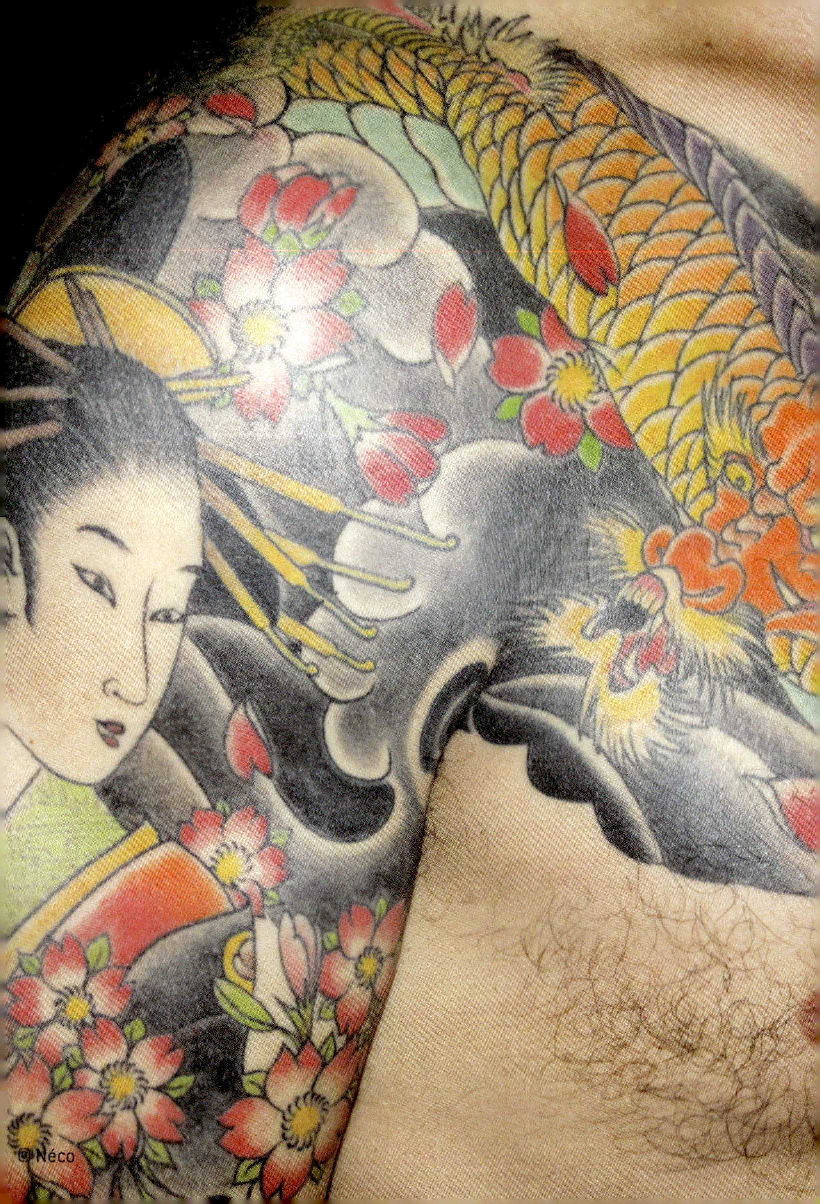

©Néco

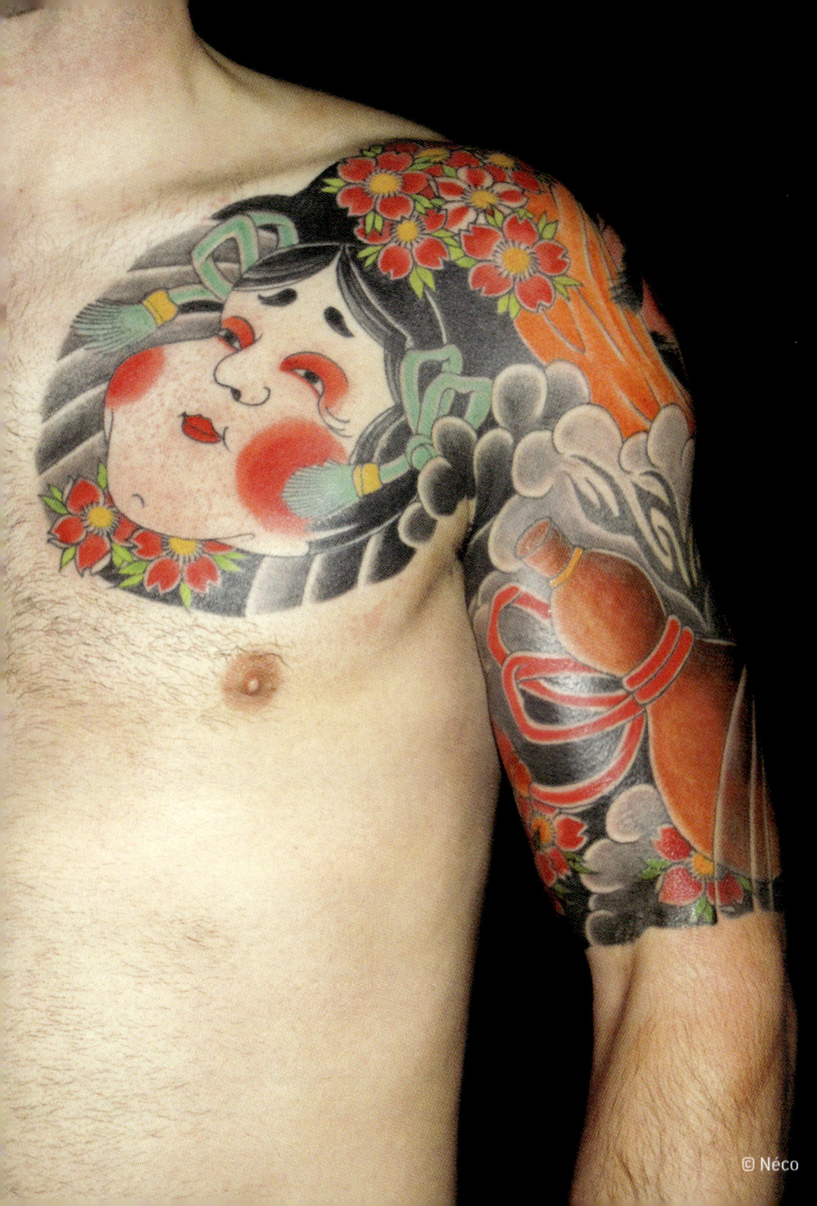
© Néco

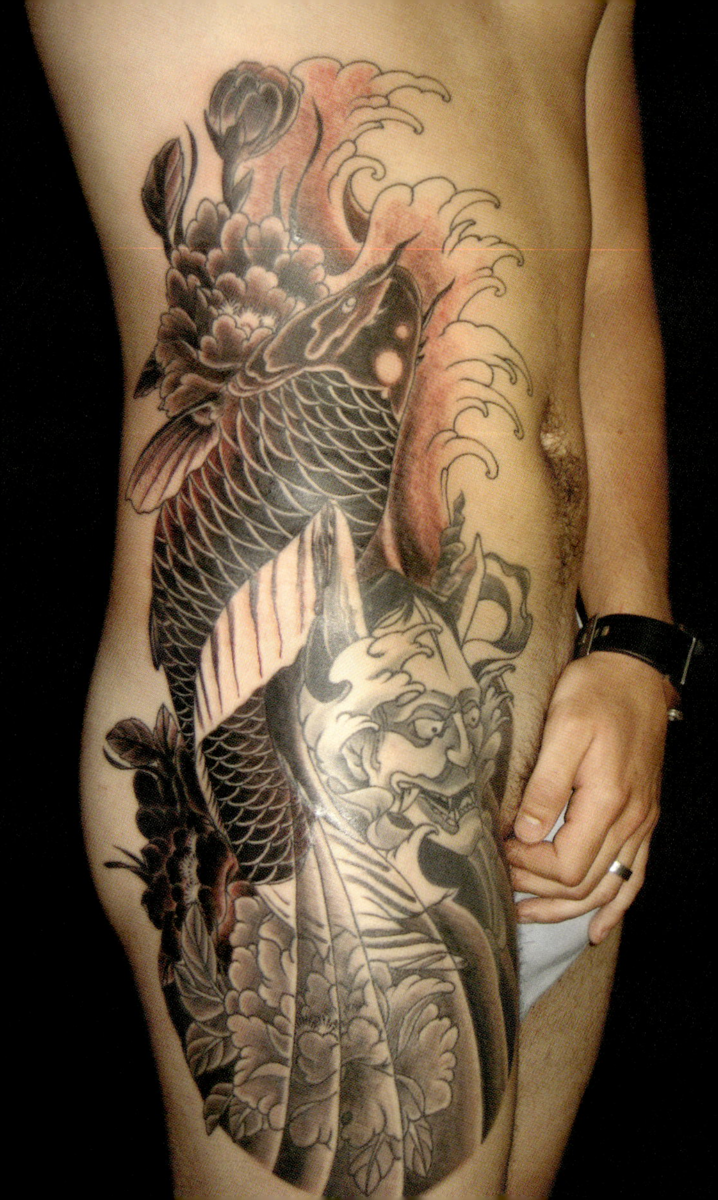

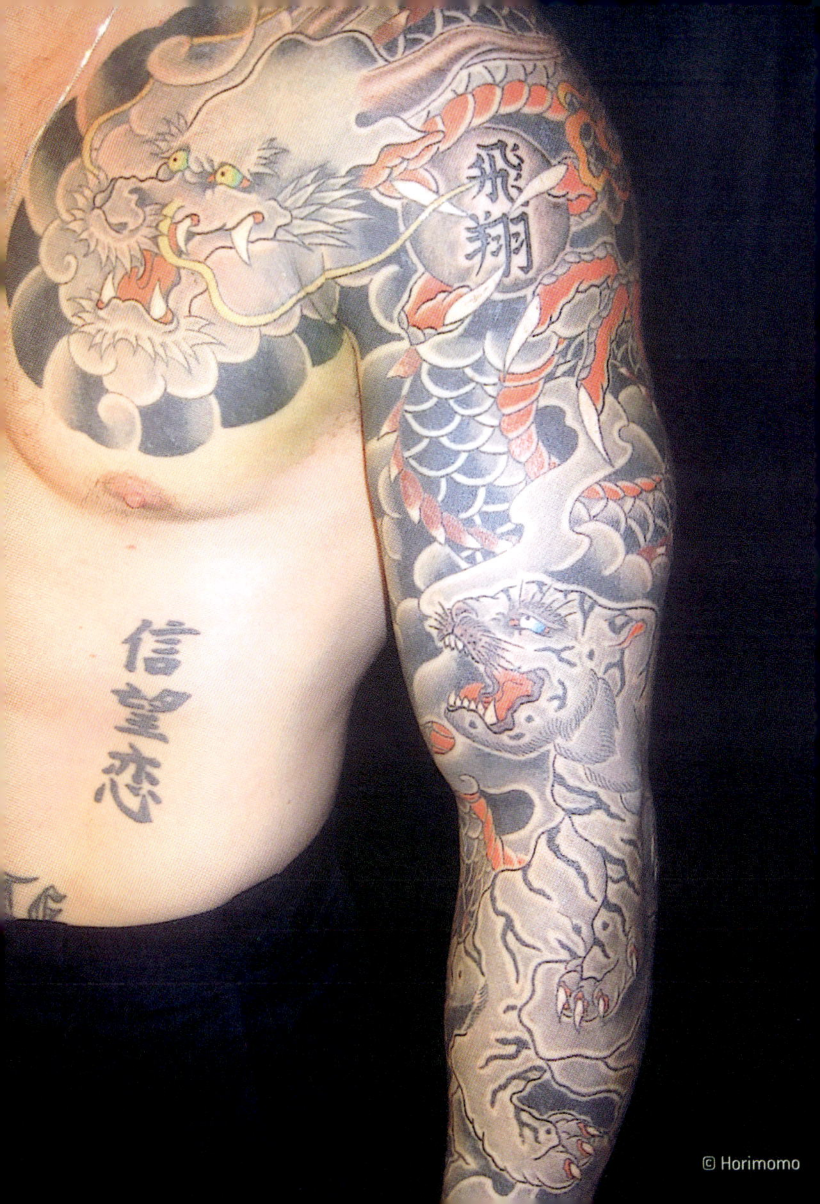
飛翔
信望恋

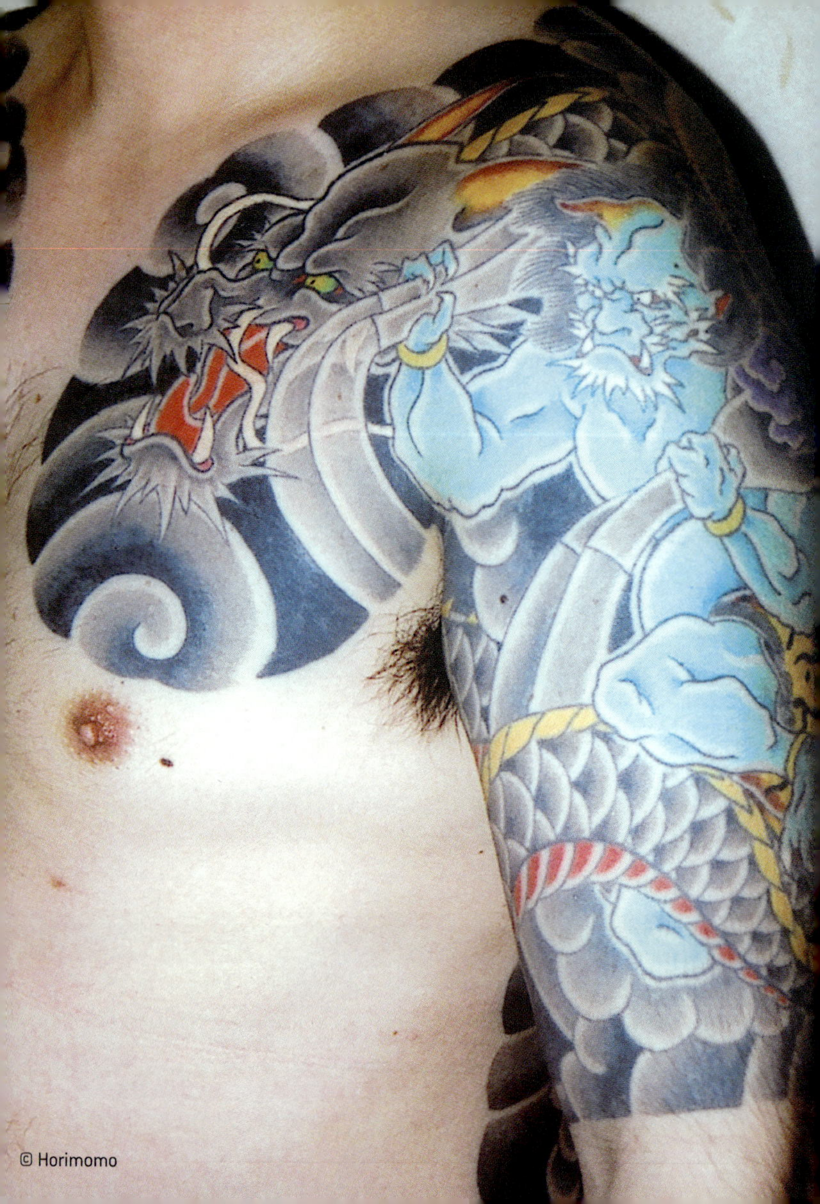

© Horimomo

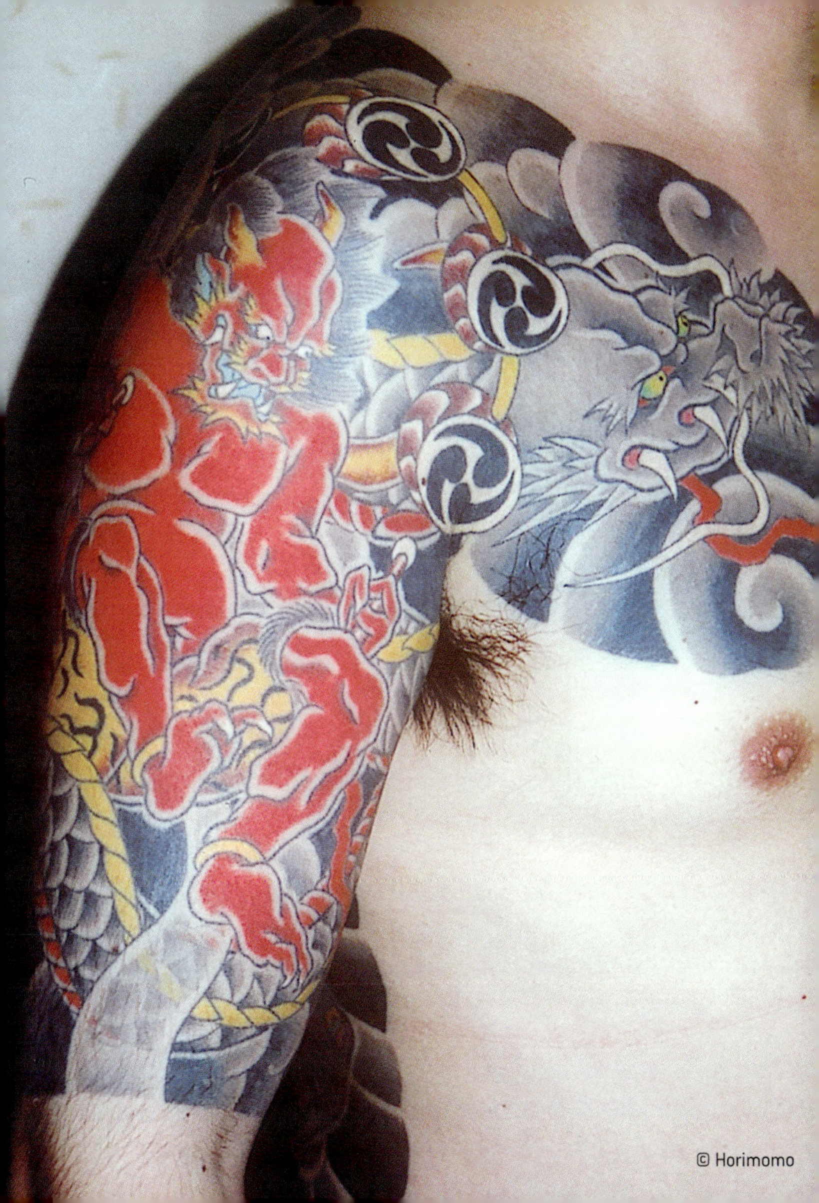

© Horimomo

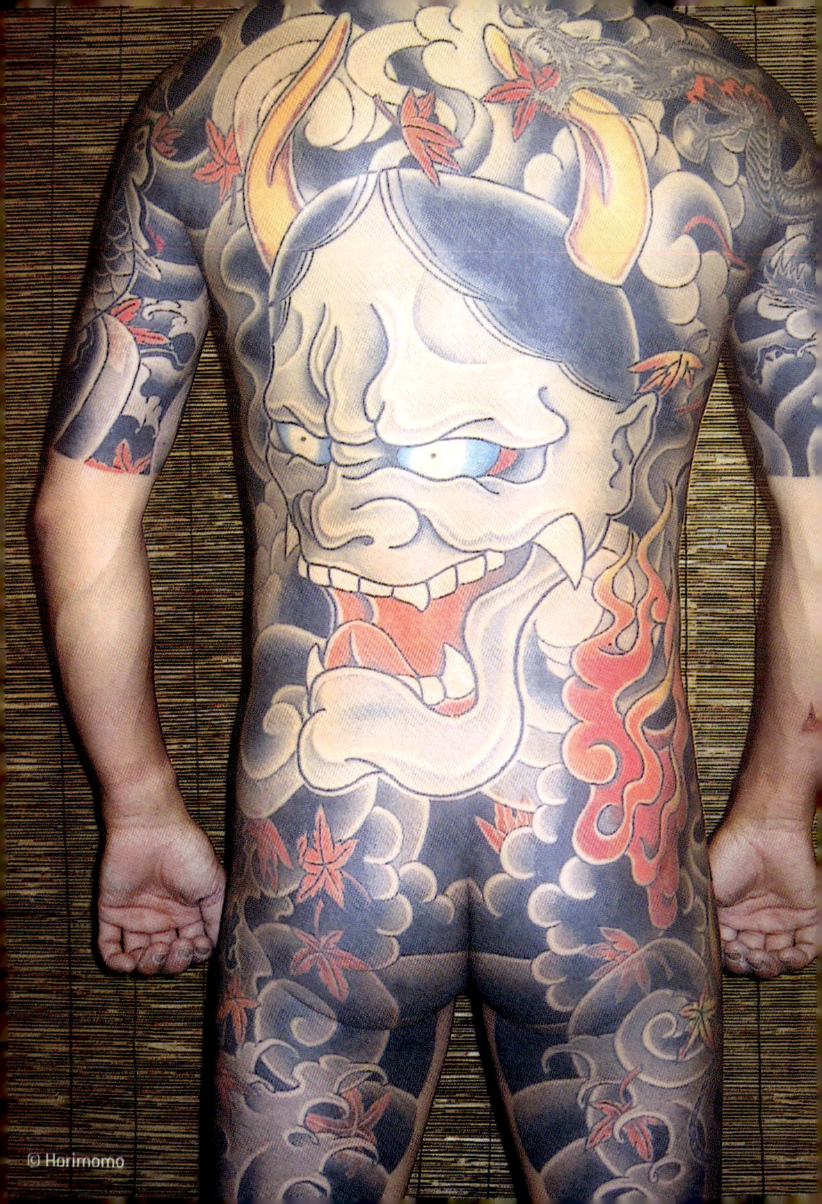
© Horimomo

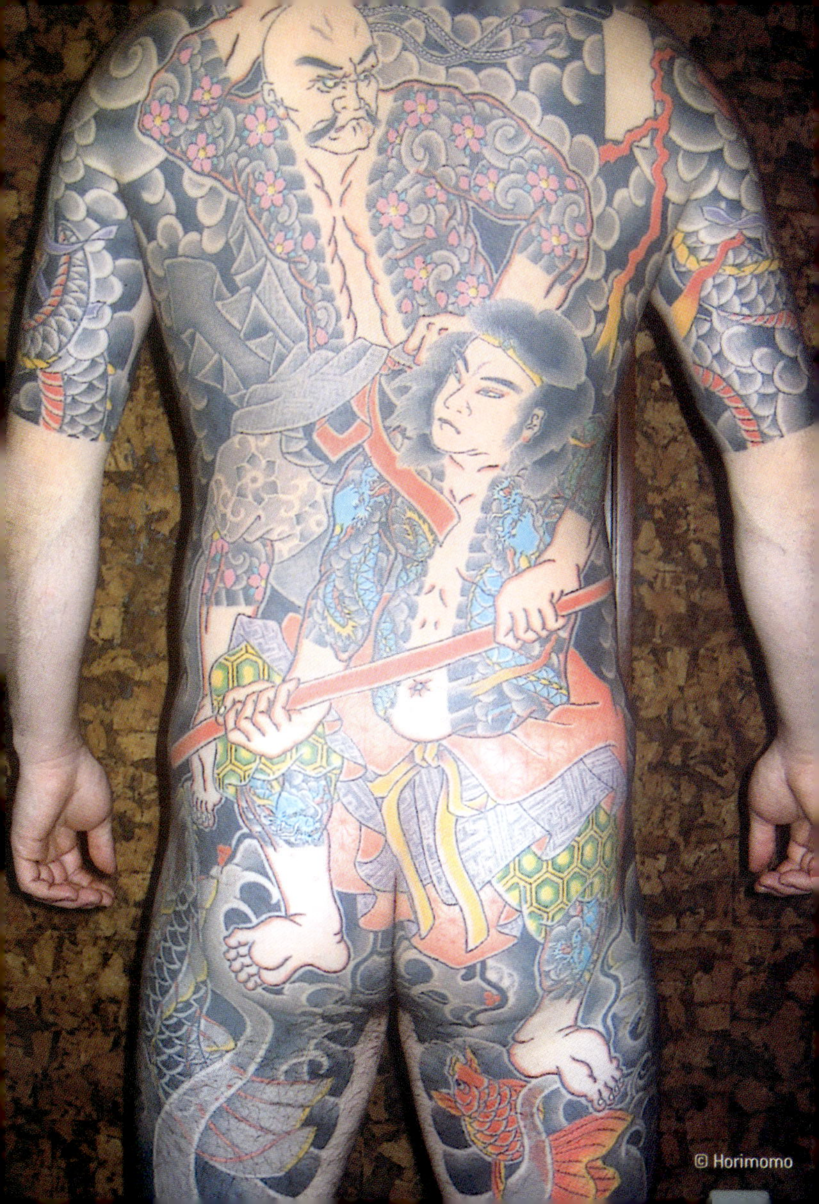
© Horimomo

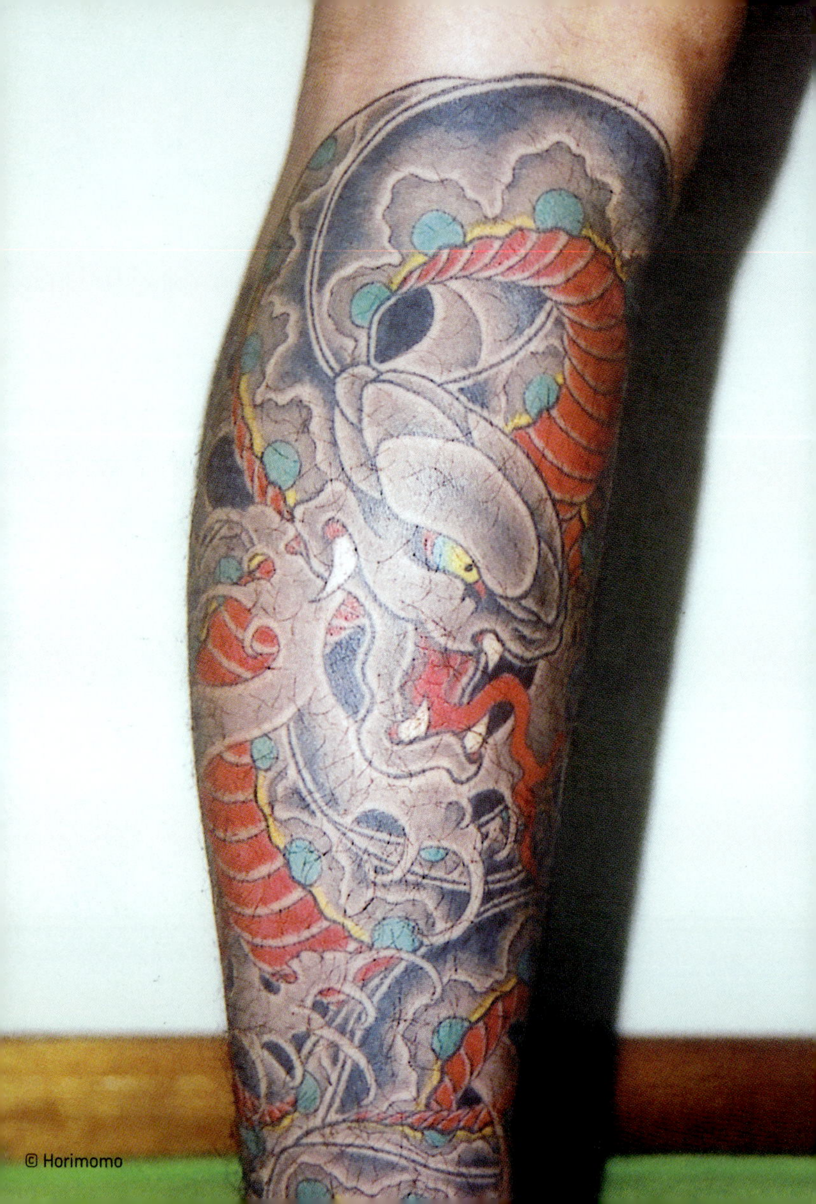

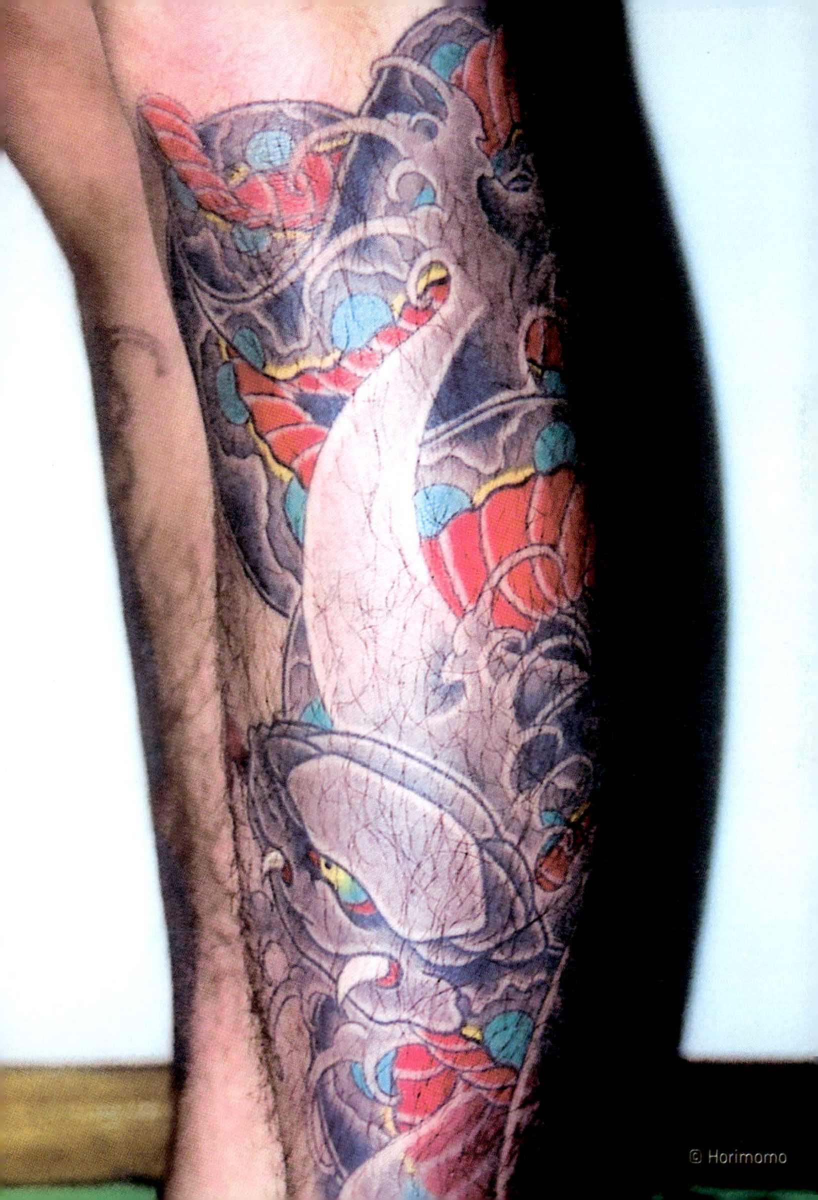
© Horimomo

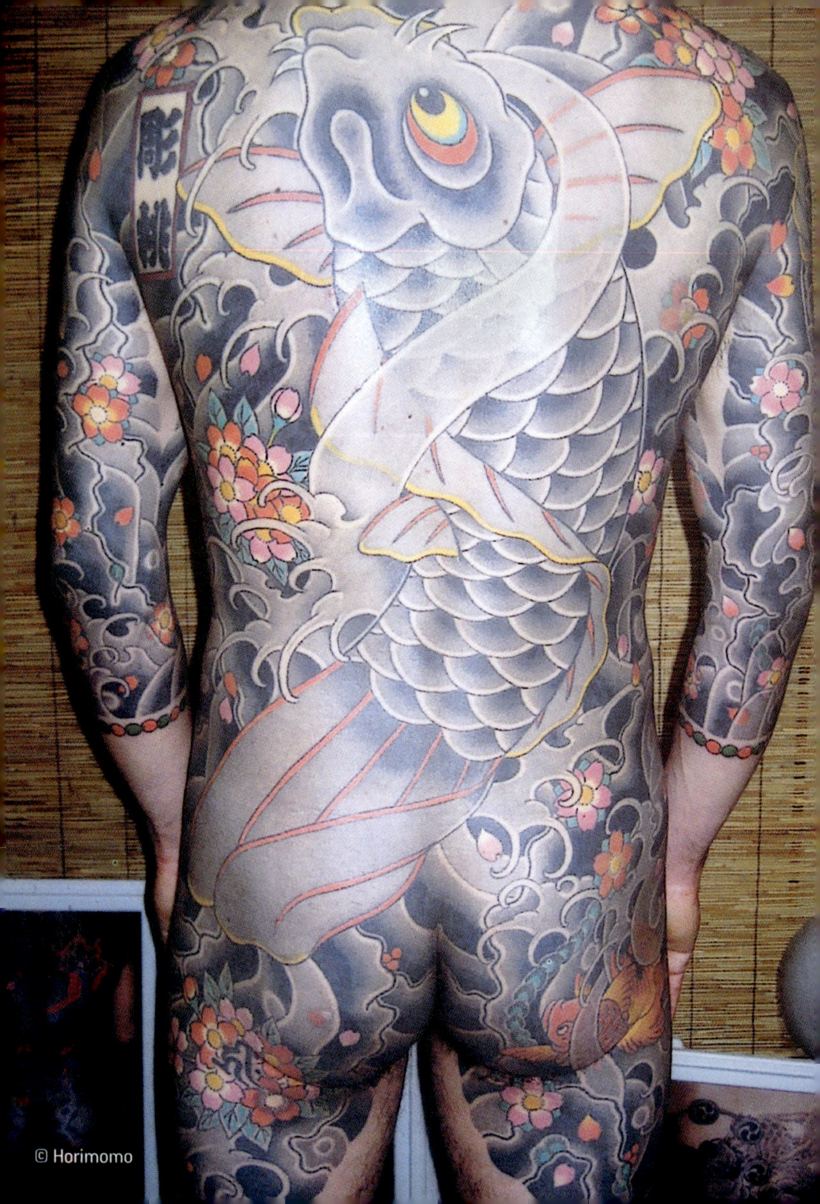
© Horimomo

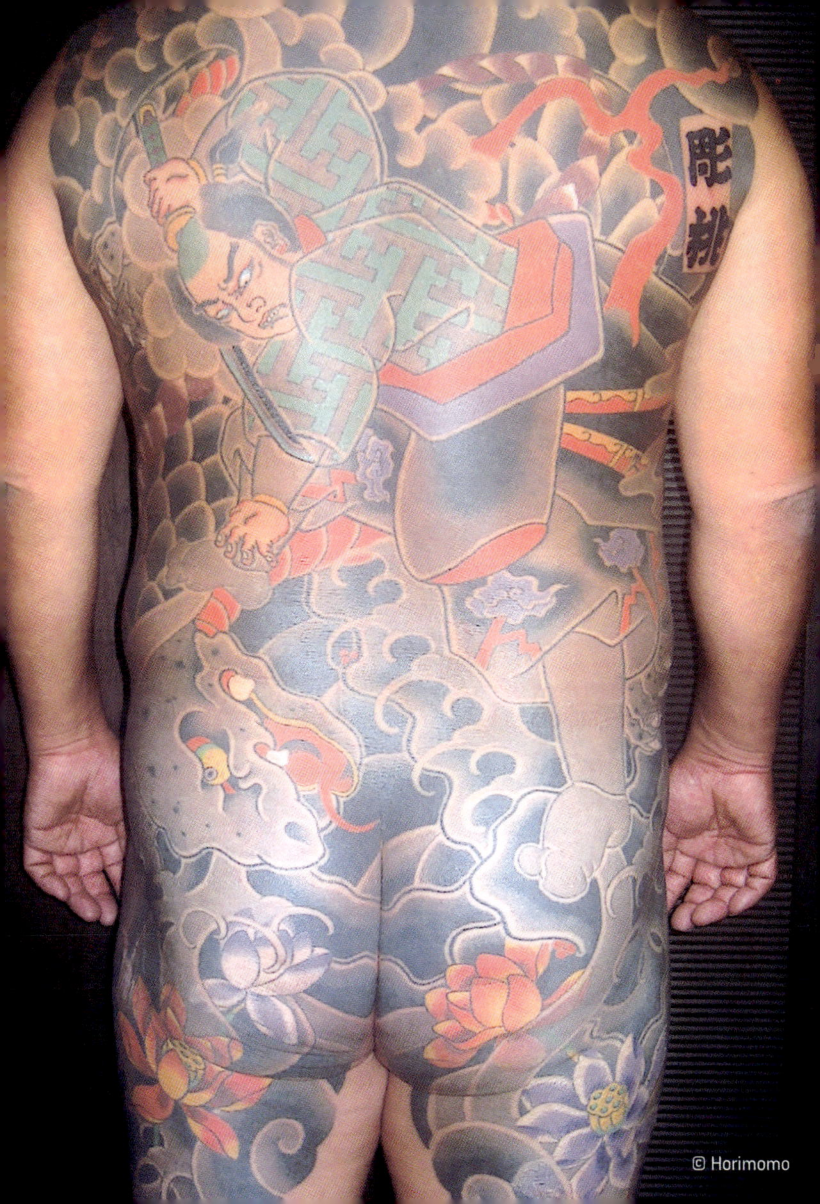
彫桃

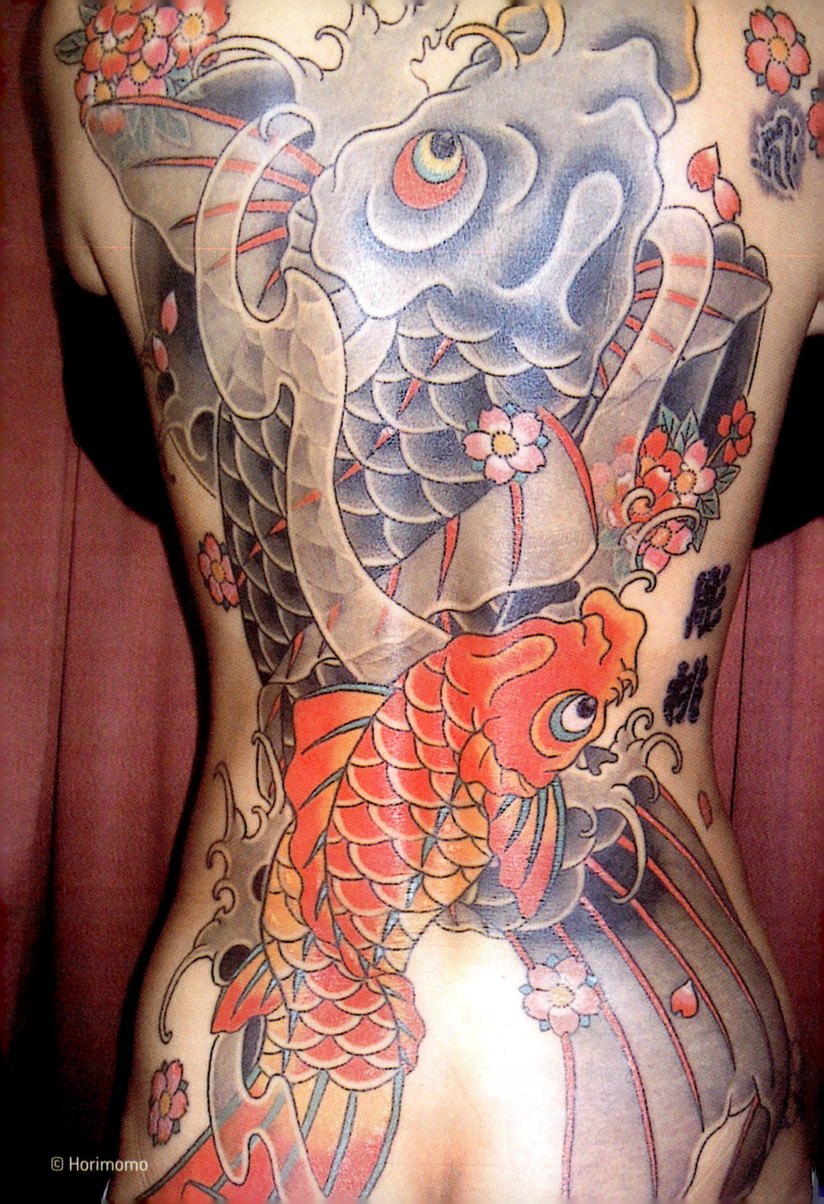
© Horimomo

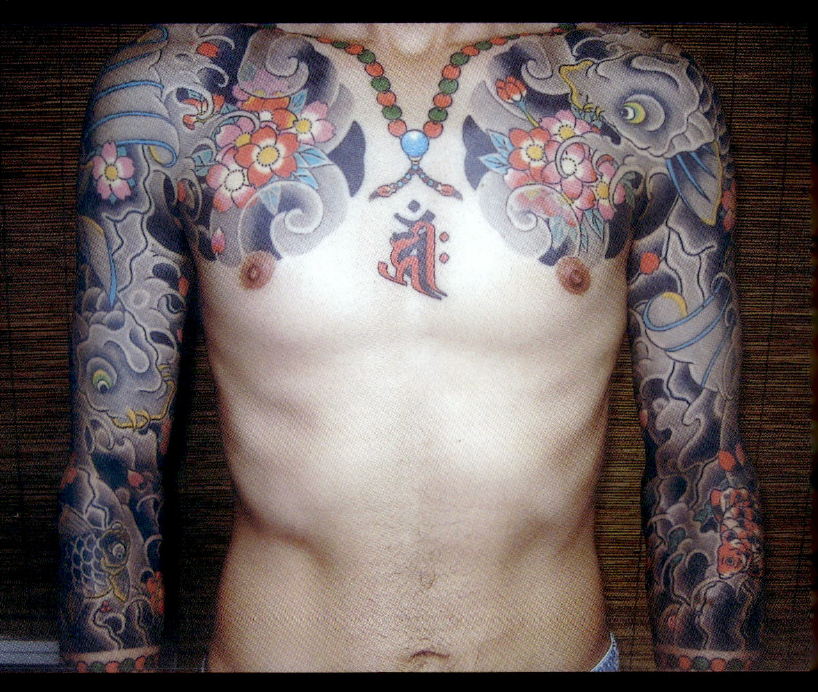

© Horimomo

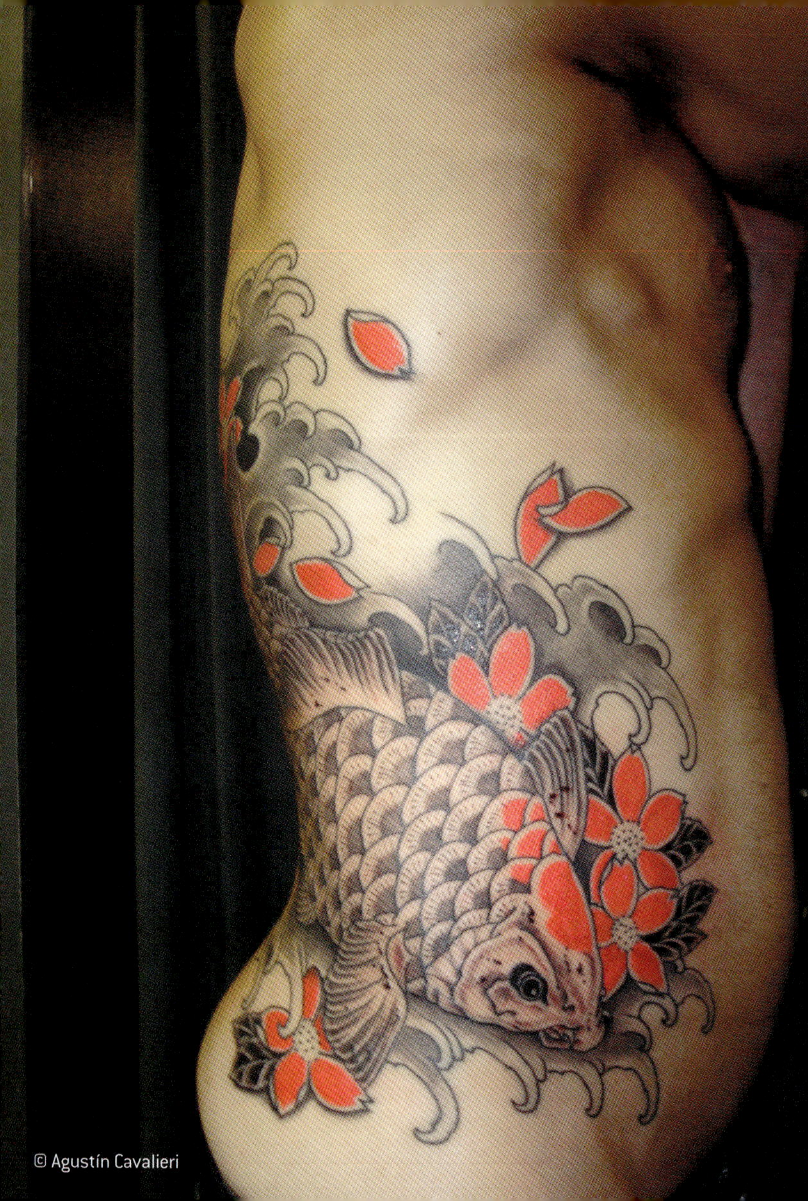
© Agustín Cavalieri

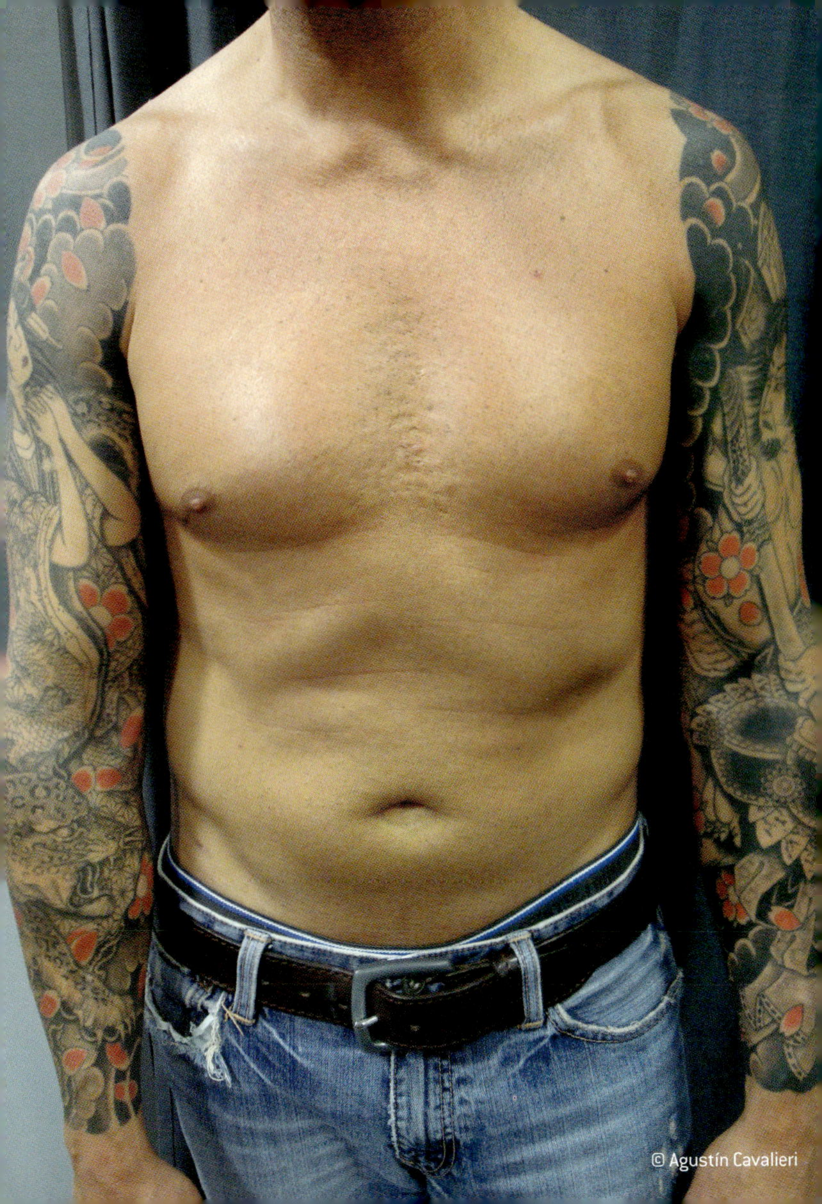
© Agustín Cavalieri

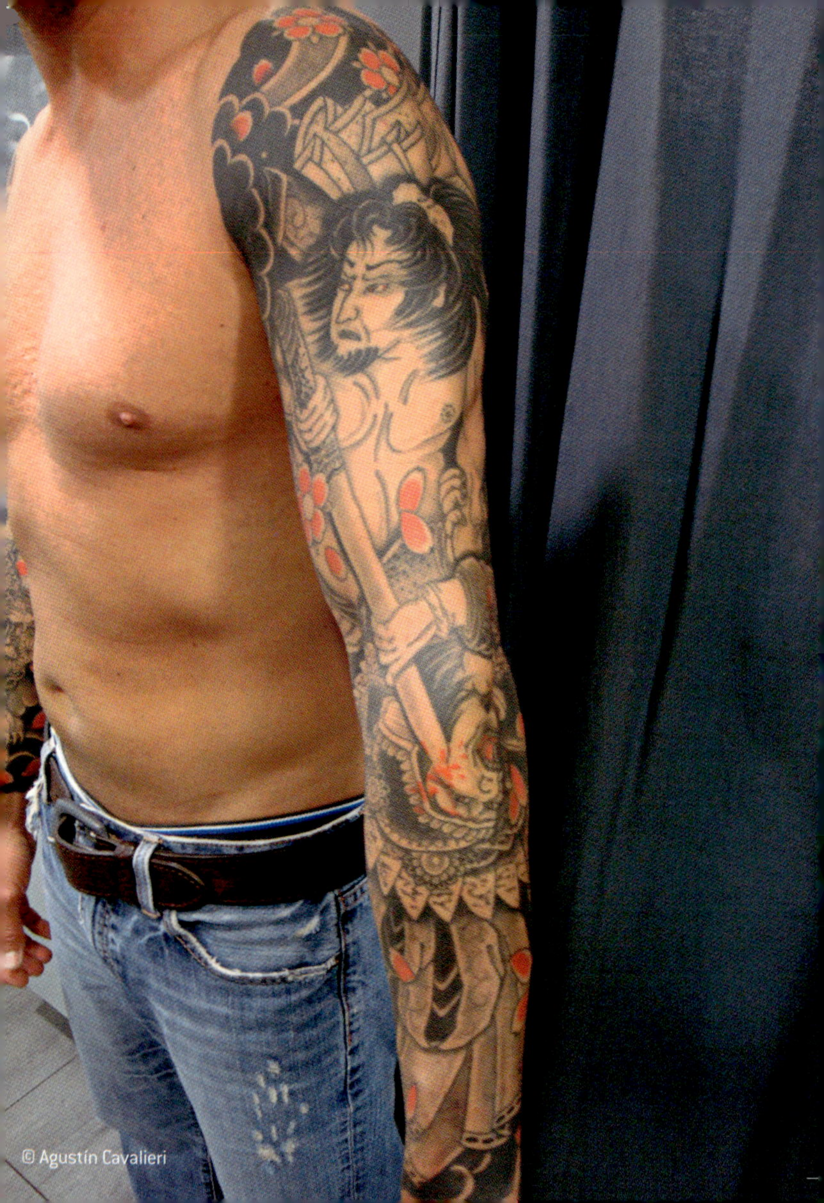
© Agustín Cavalieri

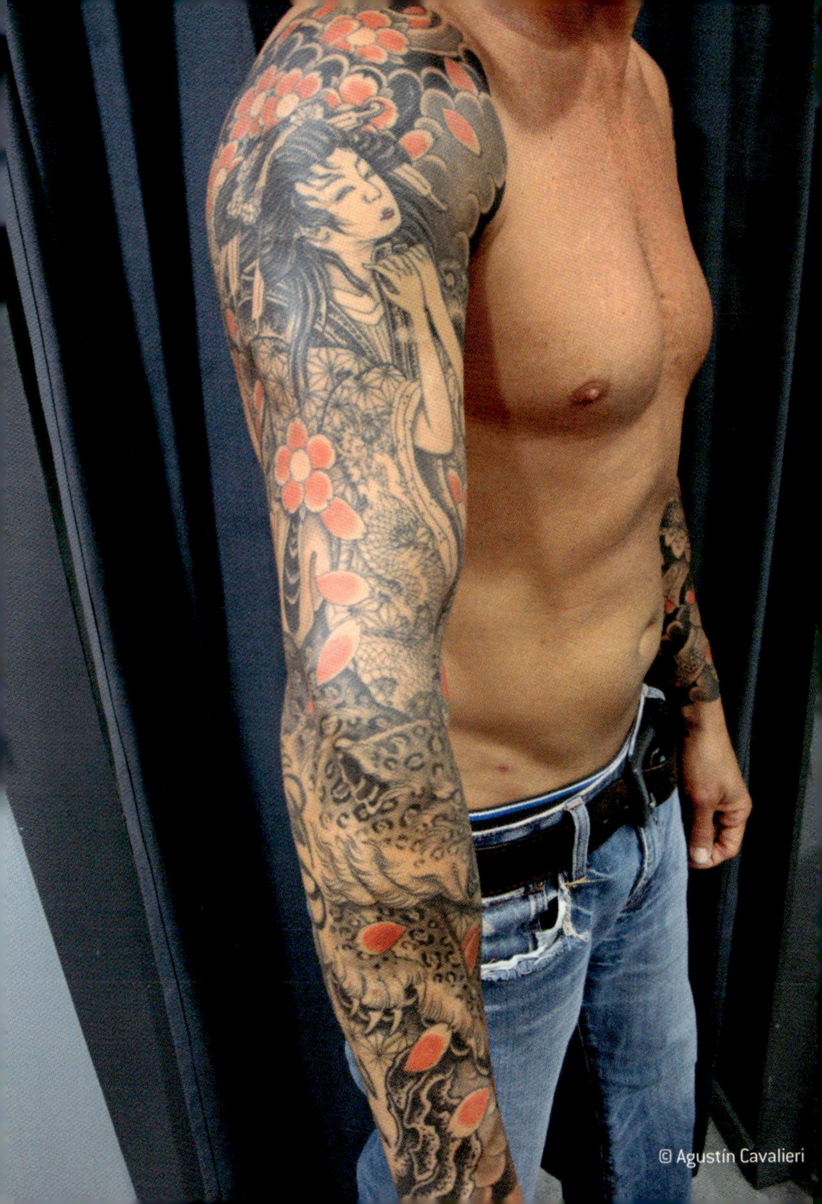
© Agustín Cavalieri

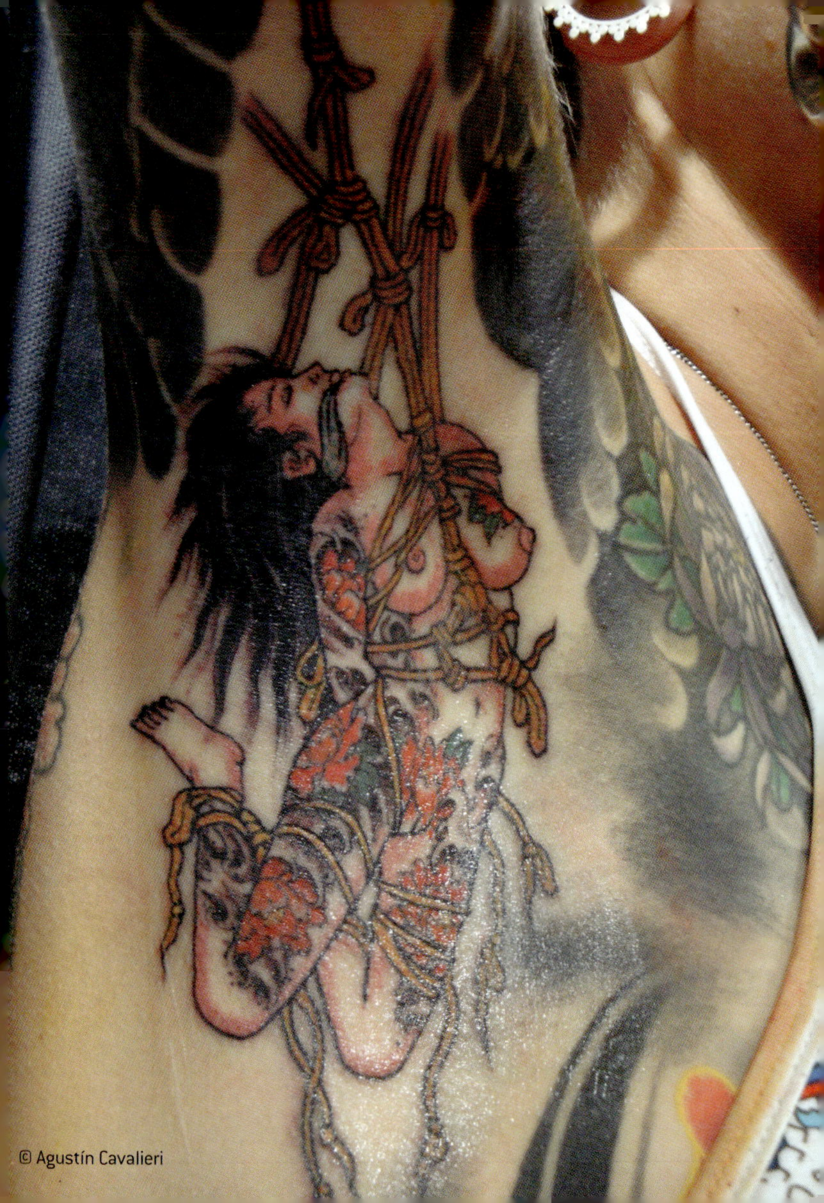

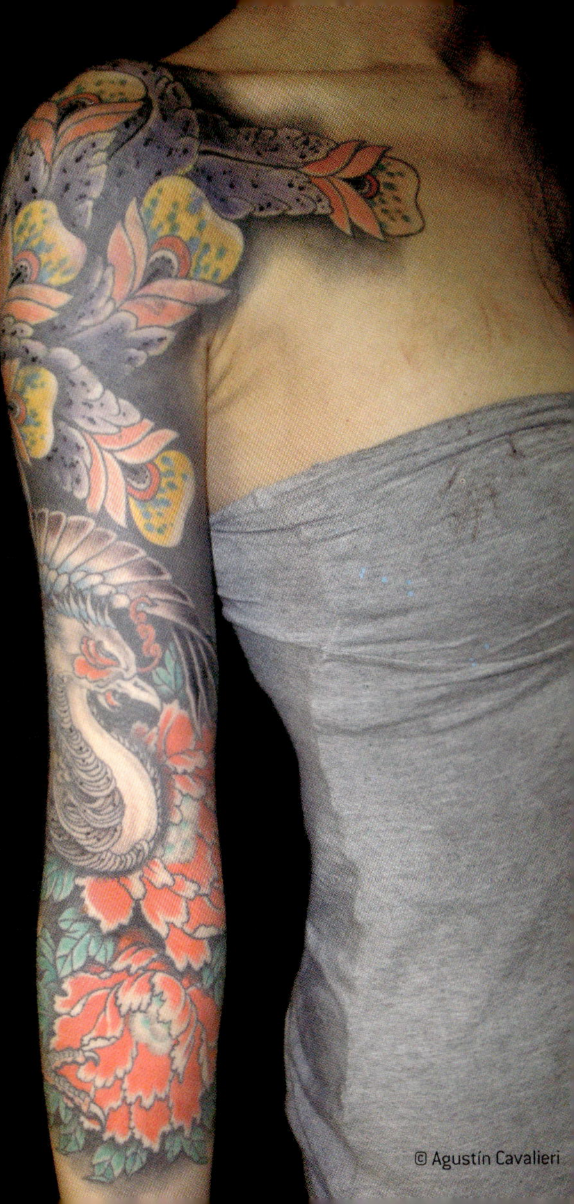

© Agustín Cavalieri

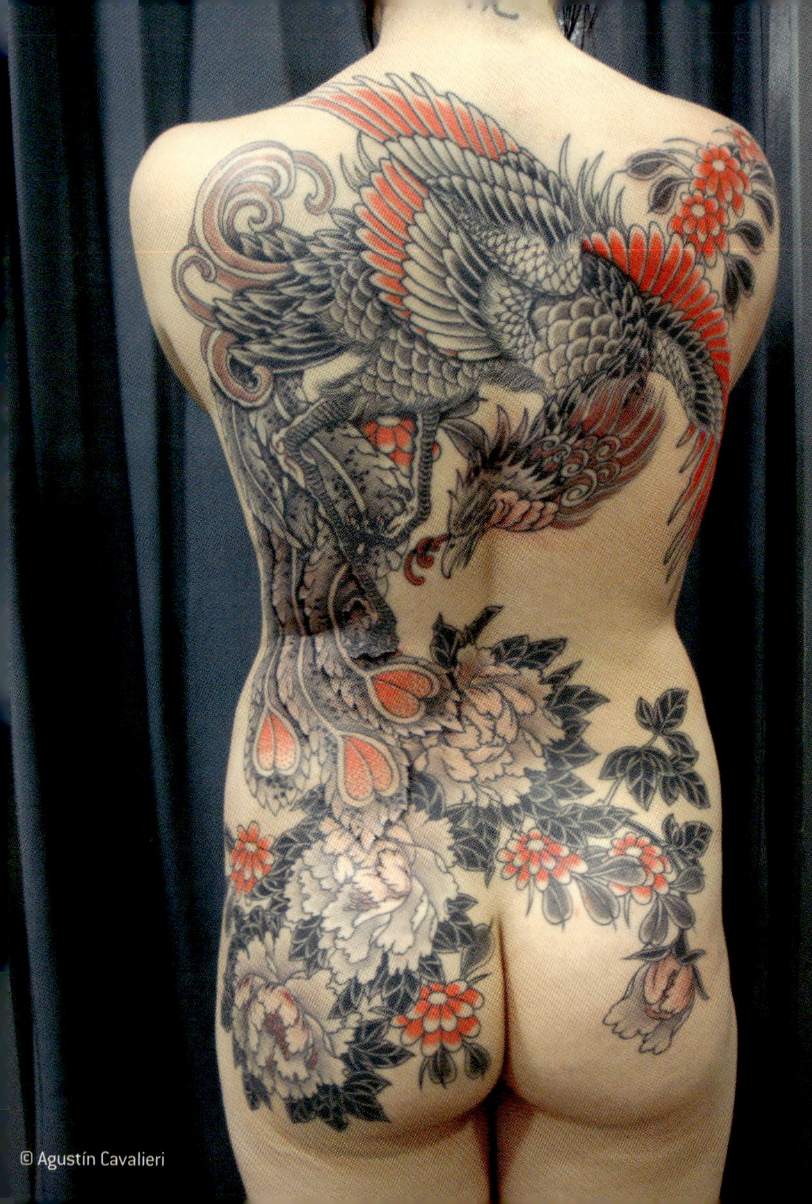

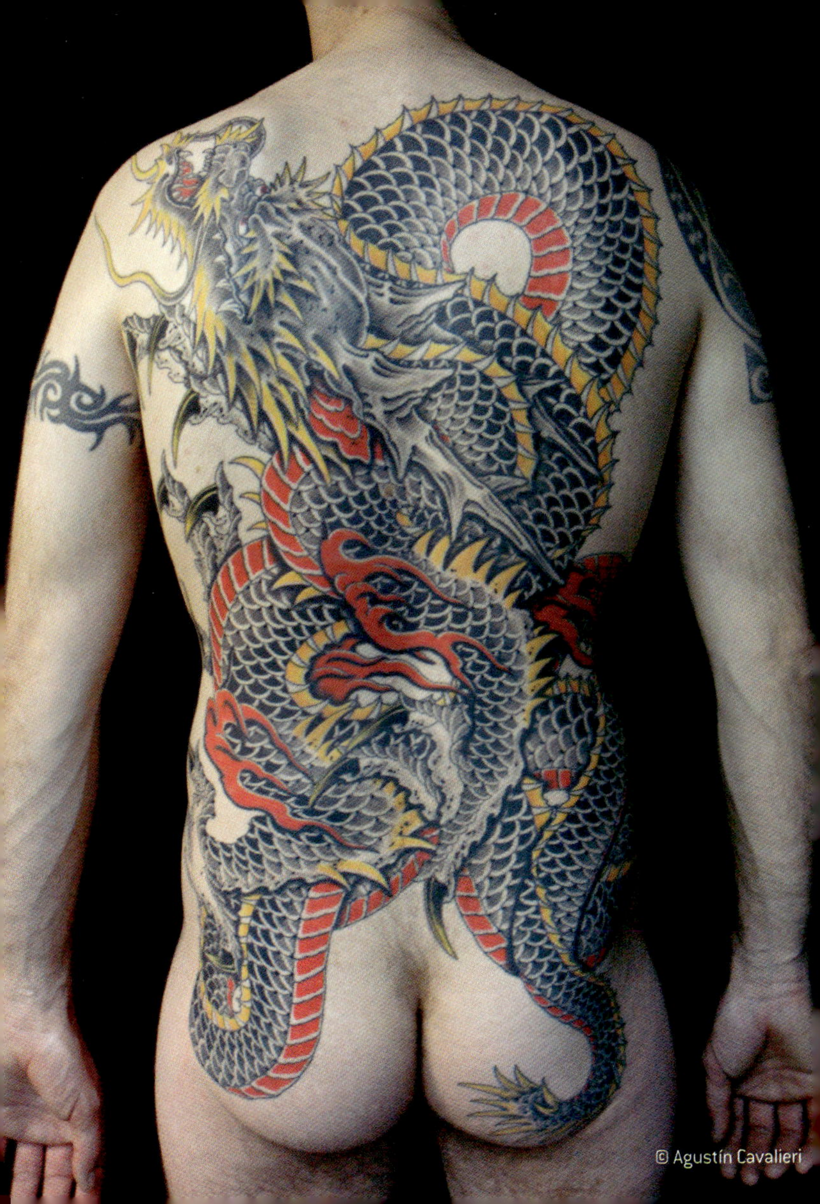
© Agustín Cavalieri

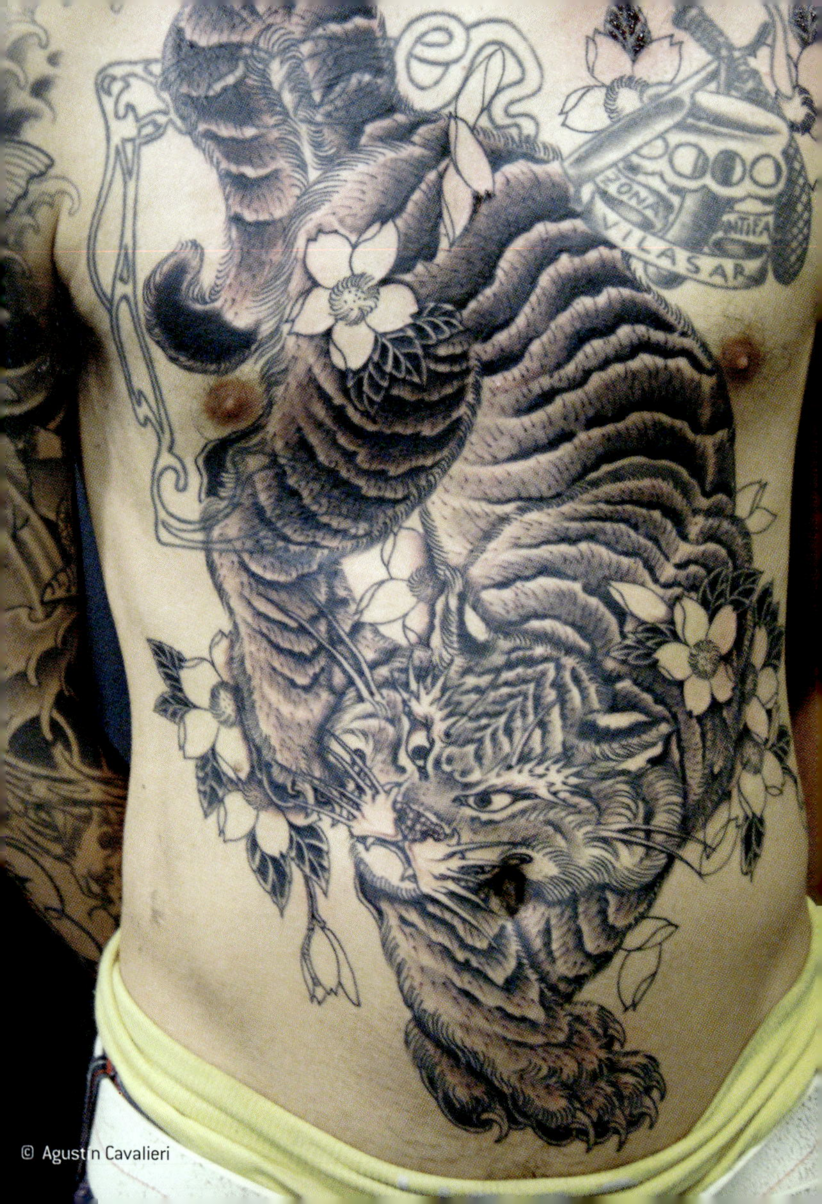

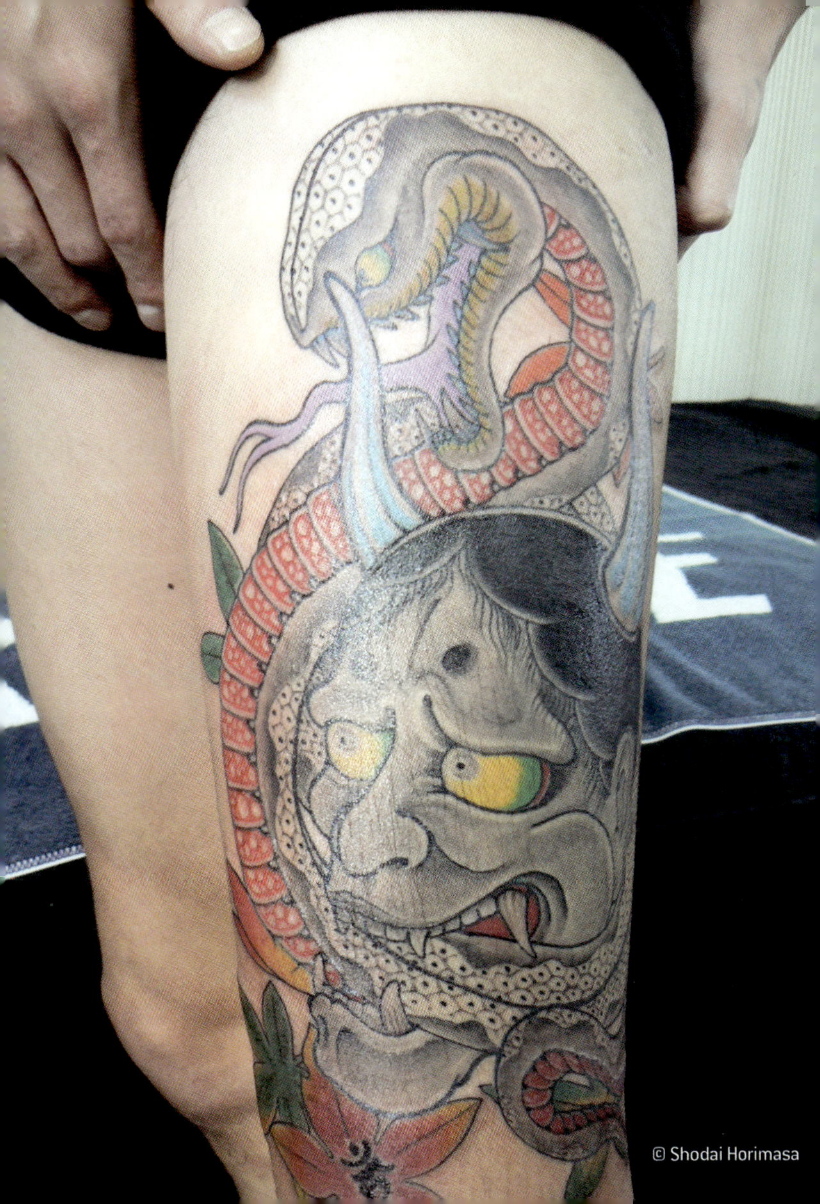

© Shodai Horimasa

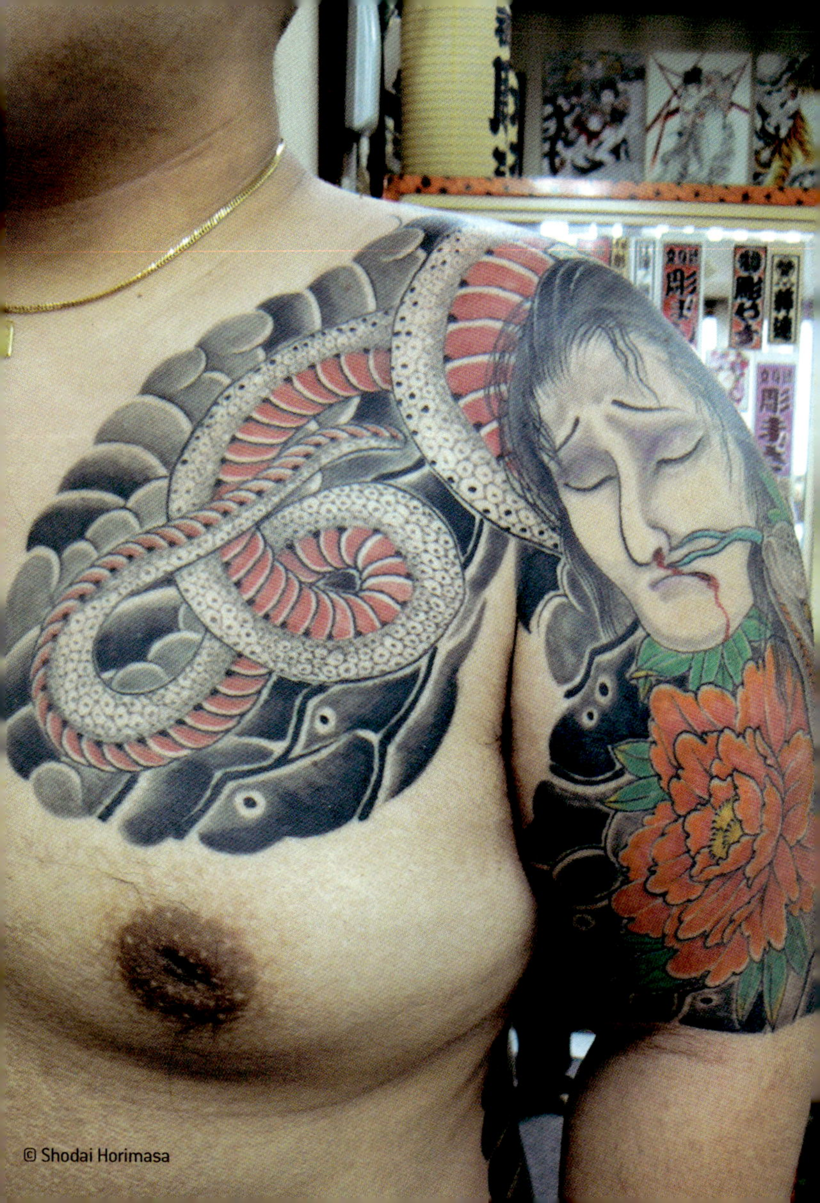
© Shodai Horimasa

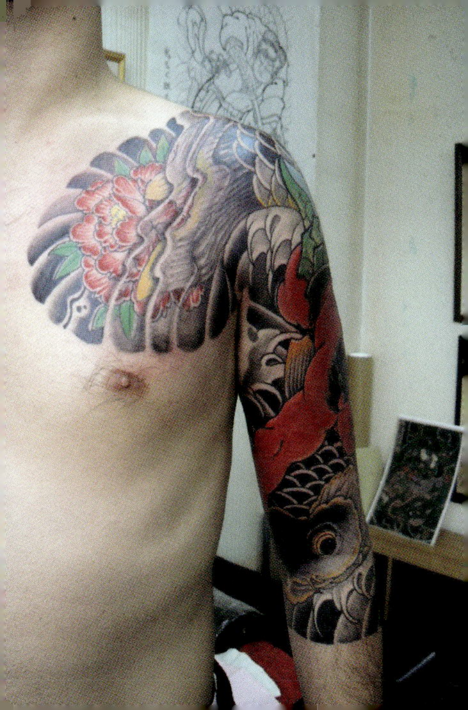

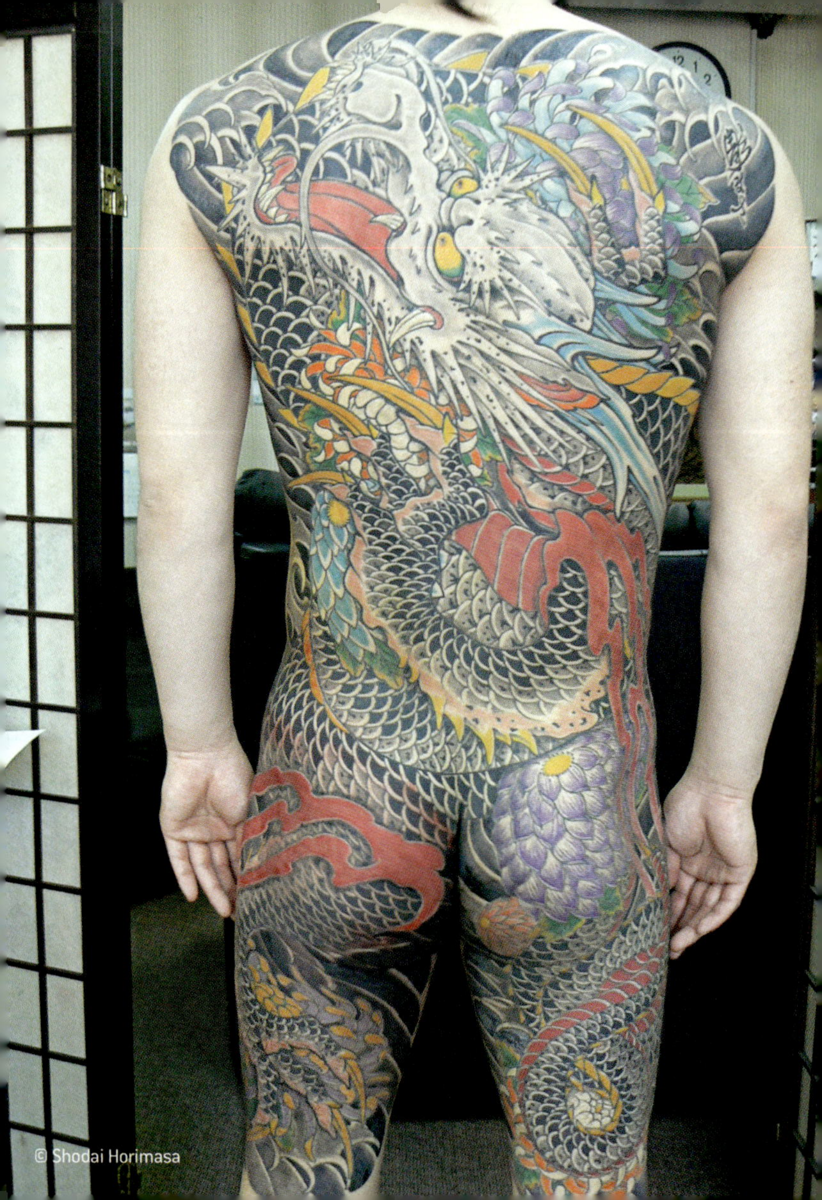
© Shodai Horimasa

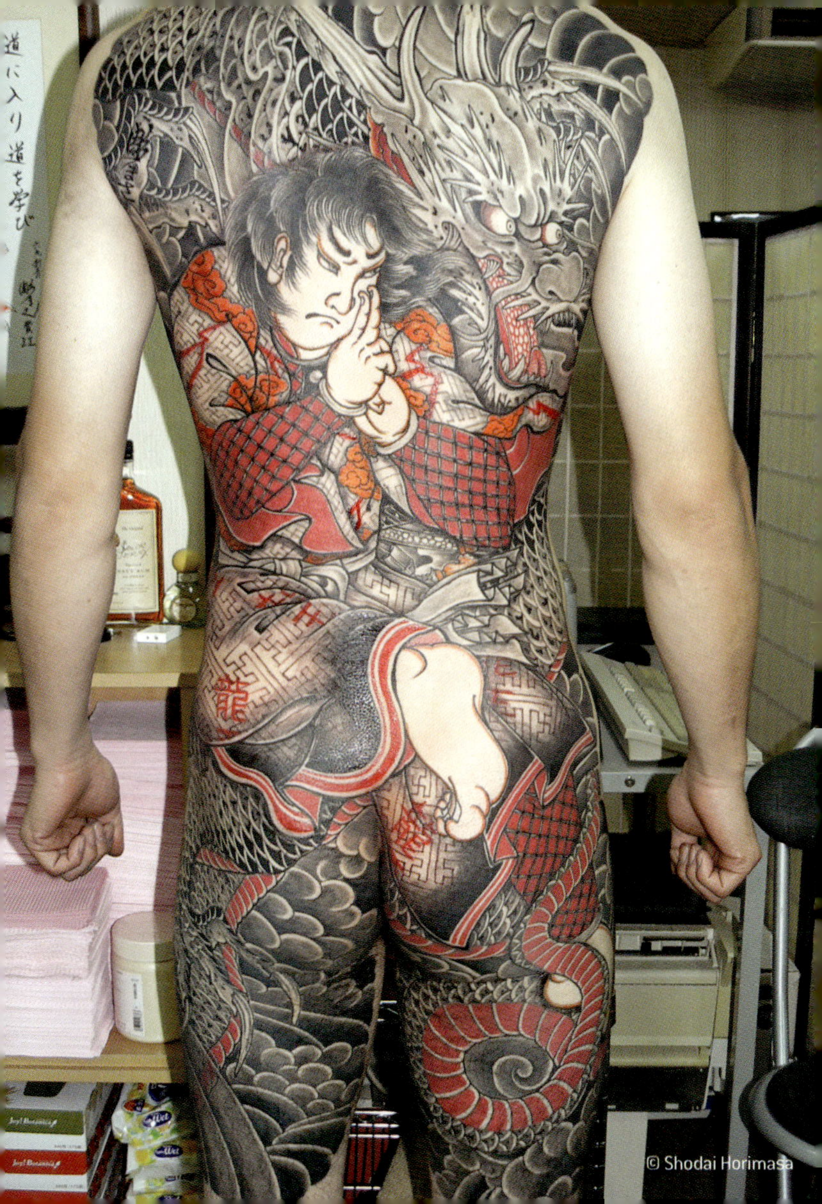
道に入り道を学び

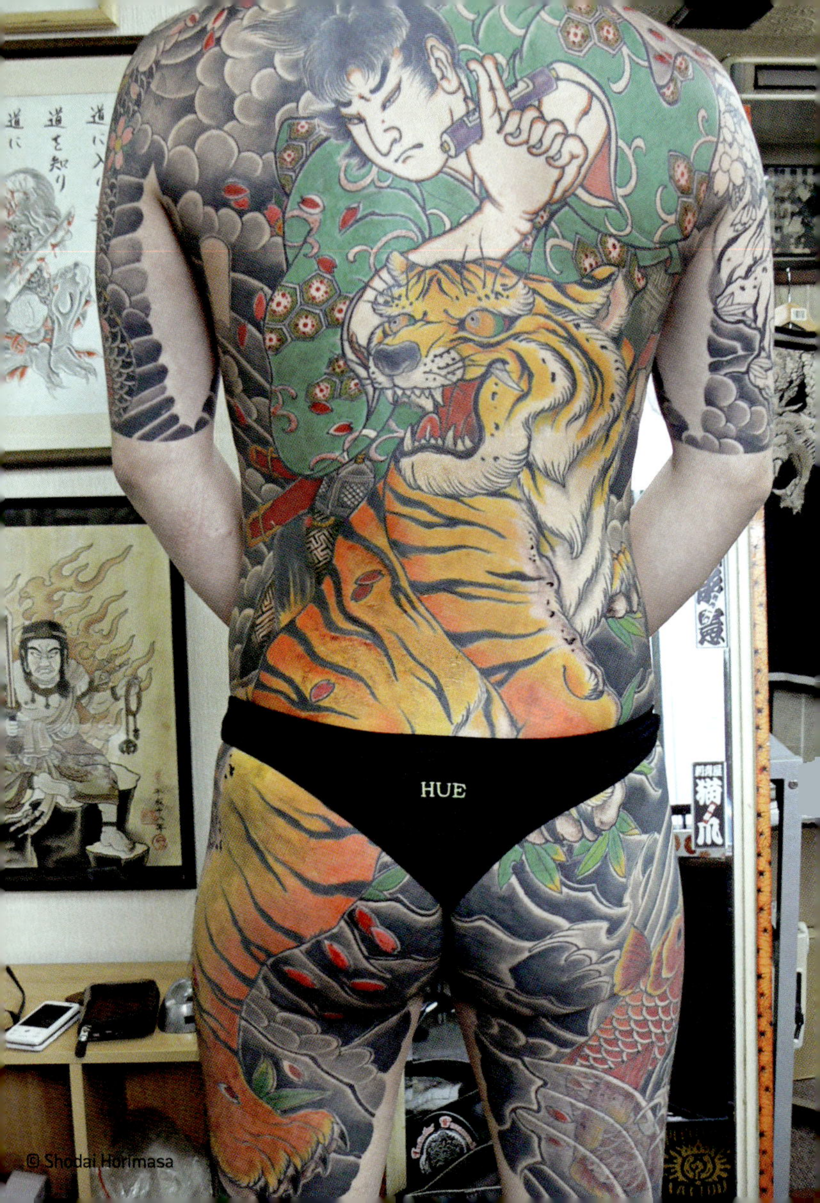
HUE

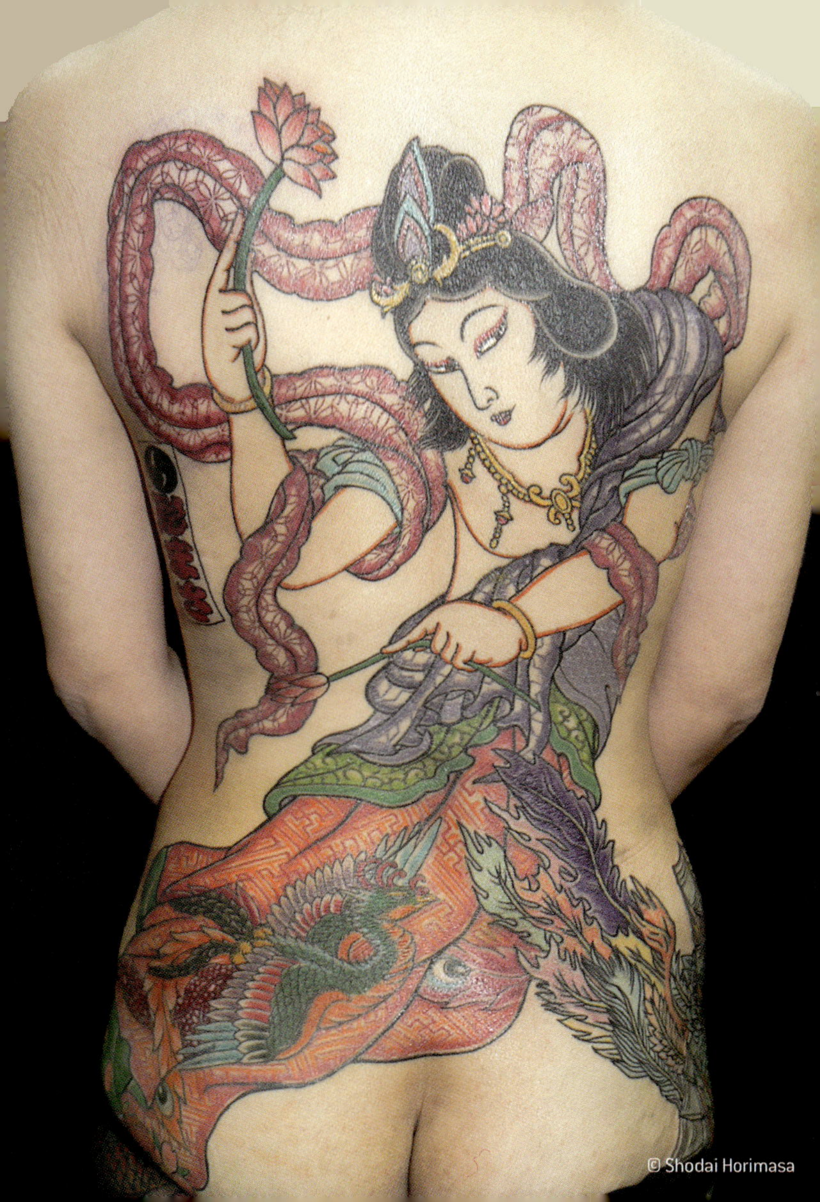

© Shodai Horimasa

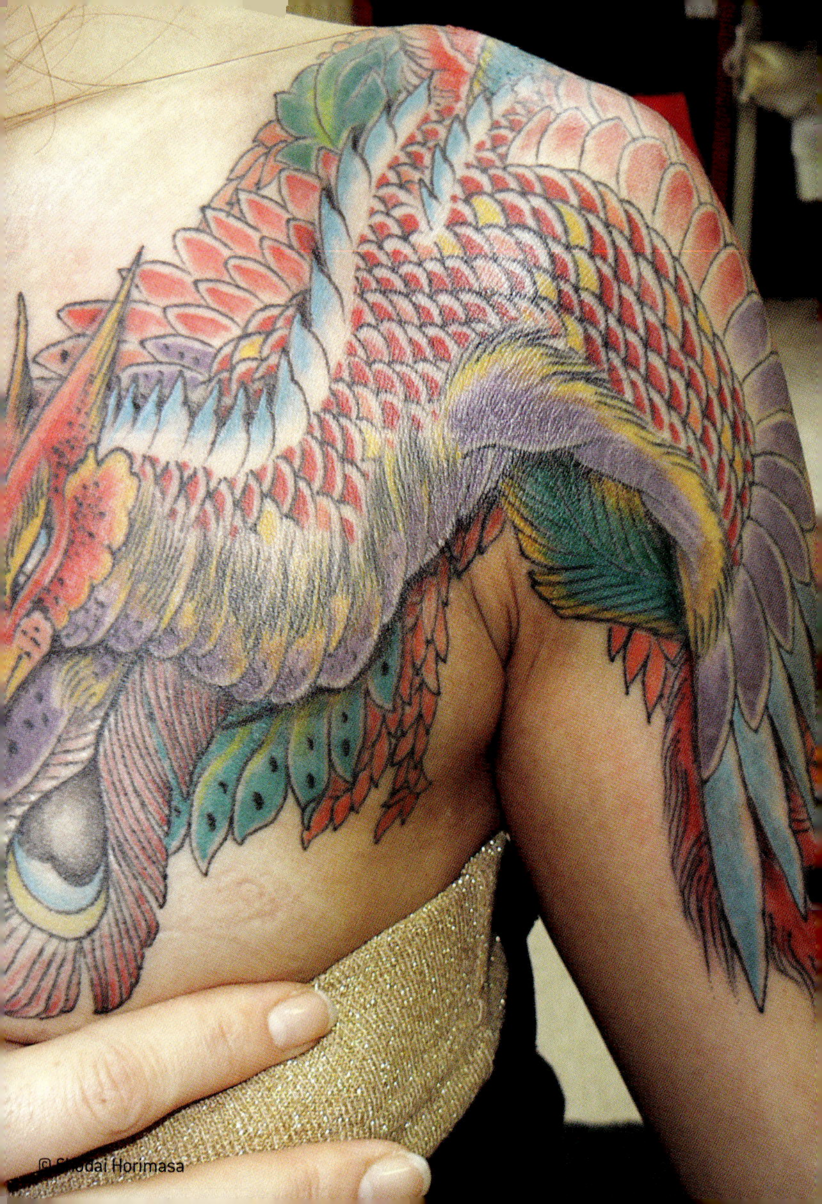
© Shodai Horimasa

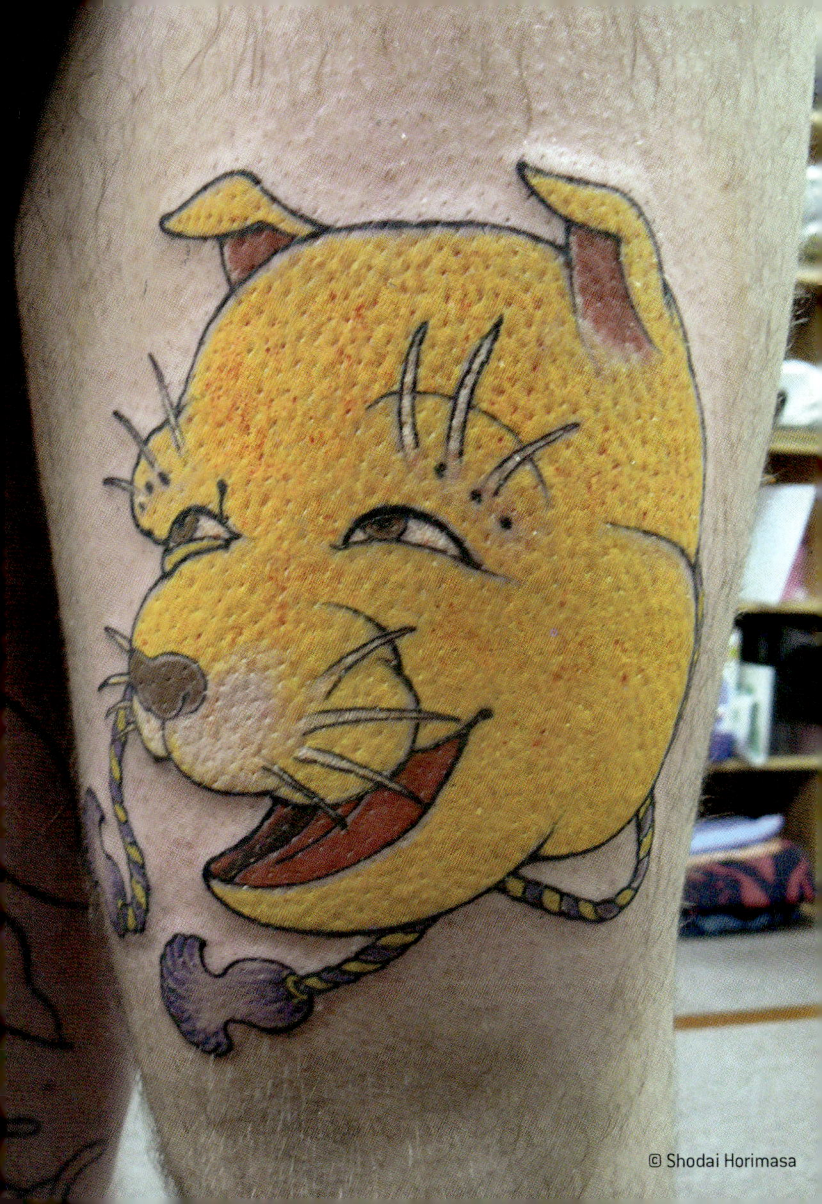

© Shodai Horimasa

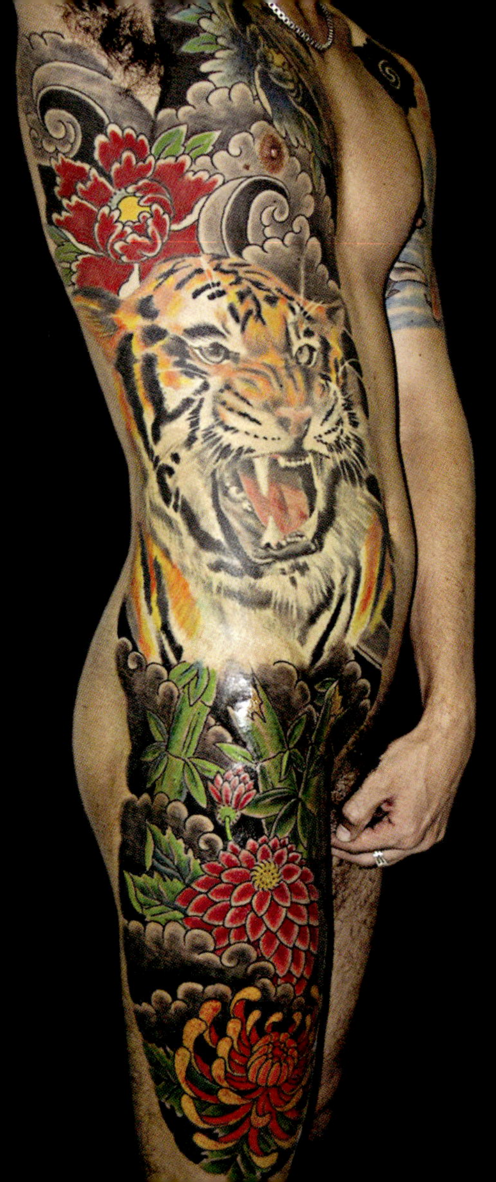

© Chío

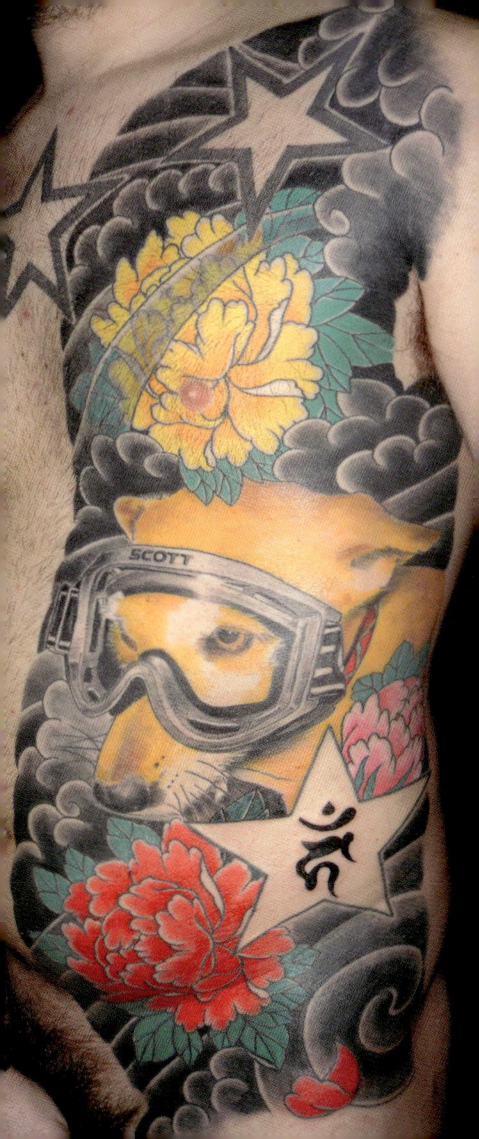
SCOTT

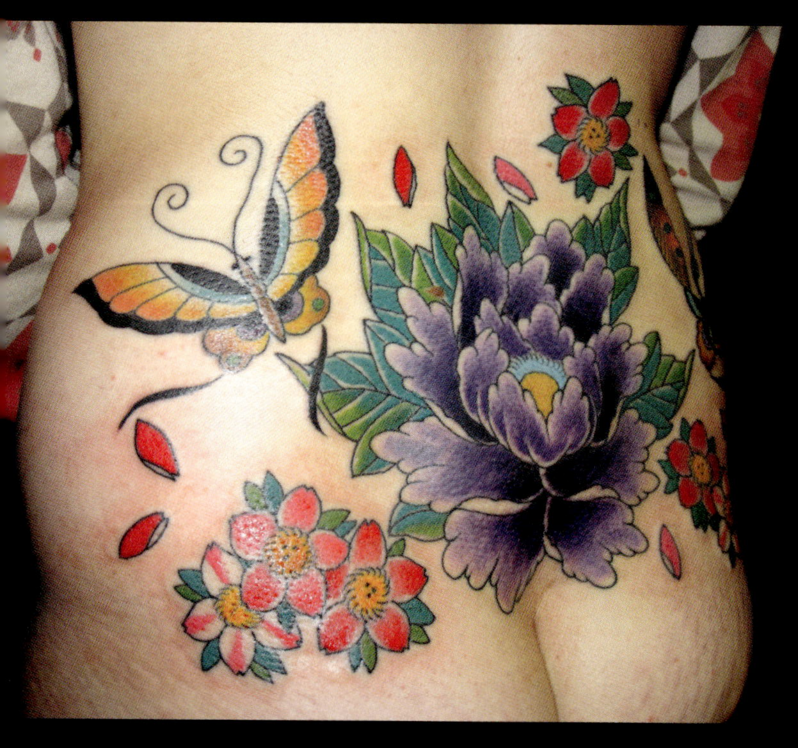

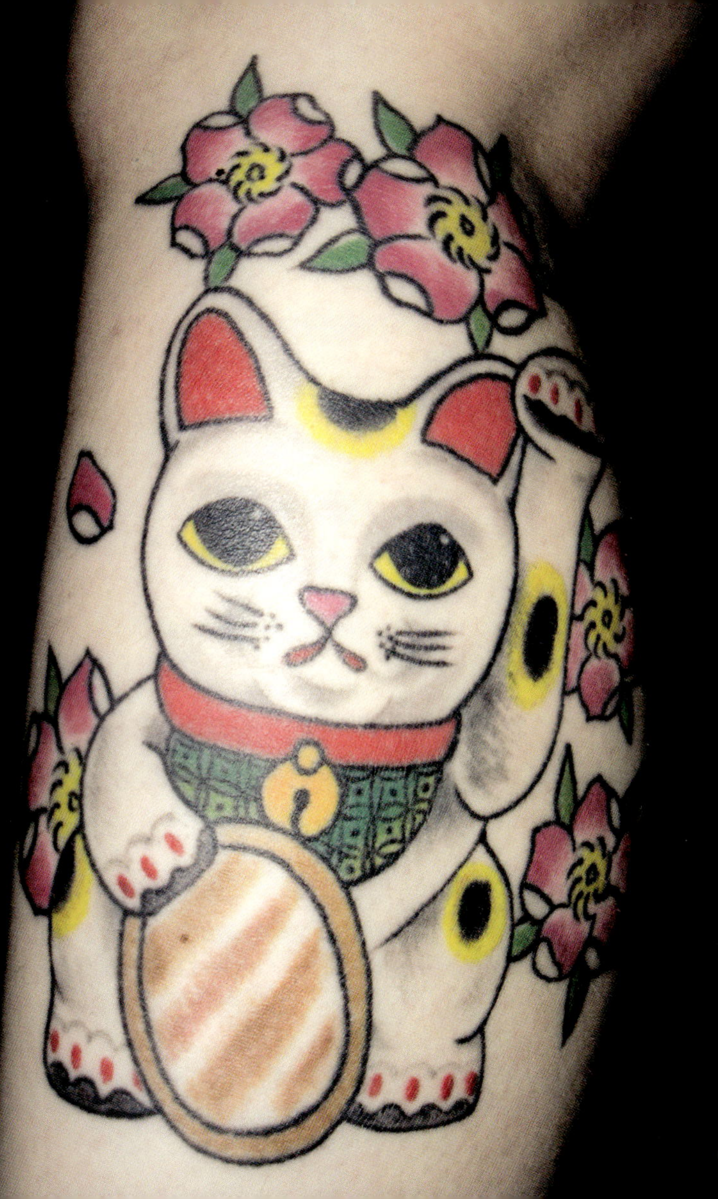
© Chío

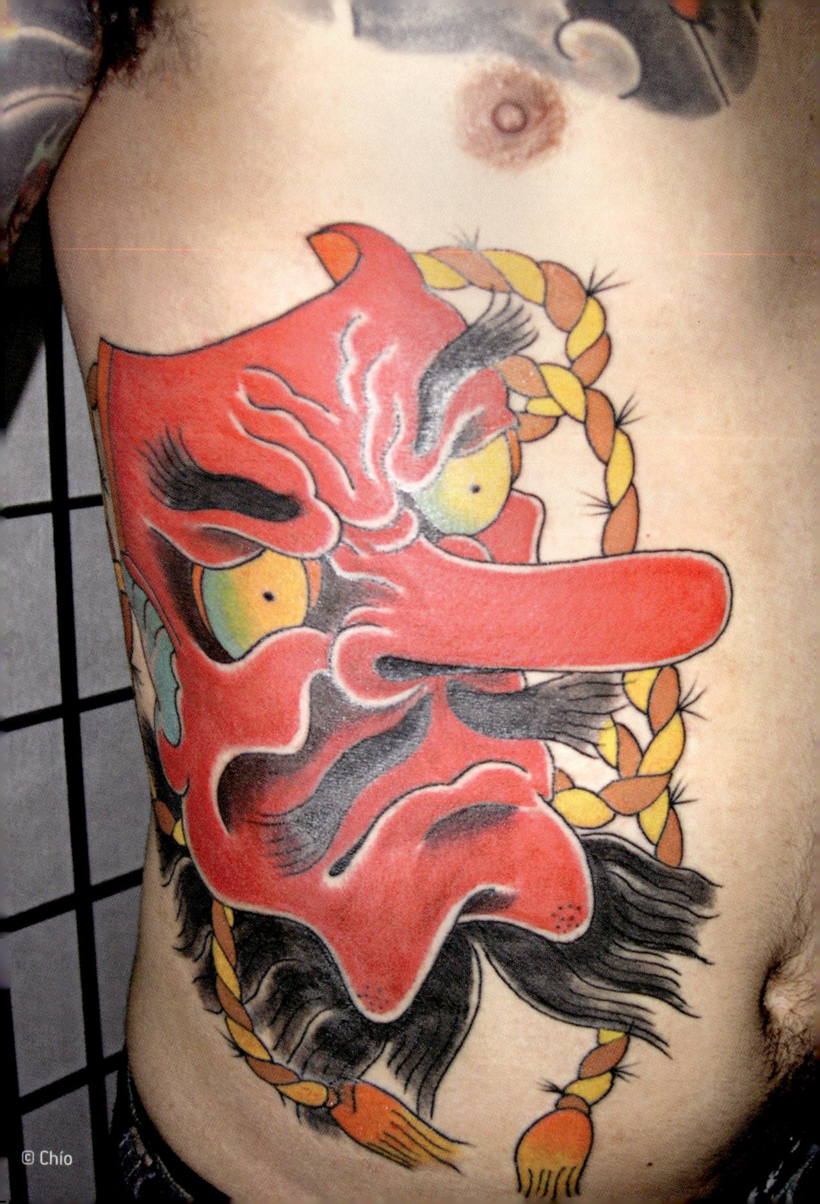
© Chío

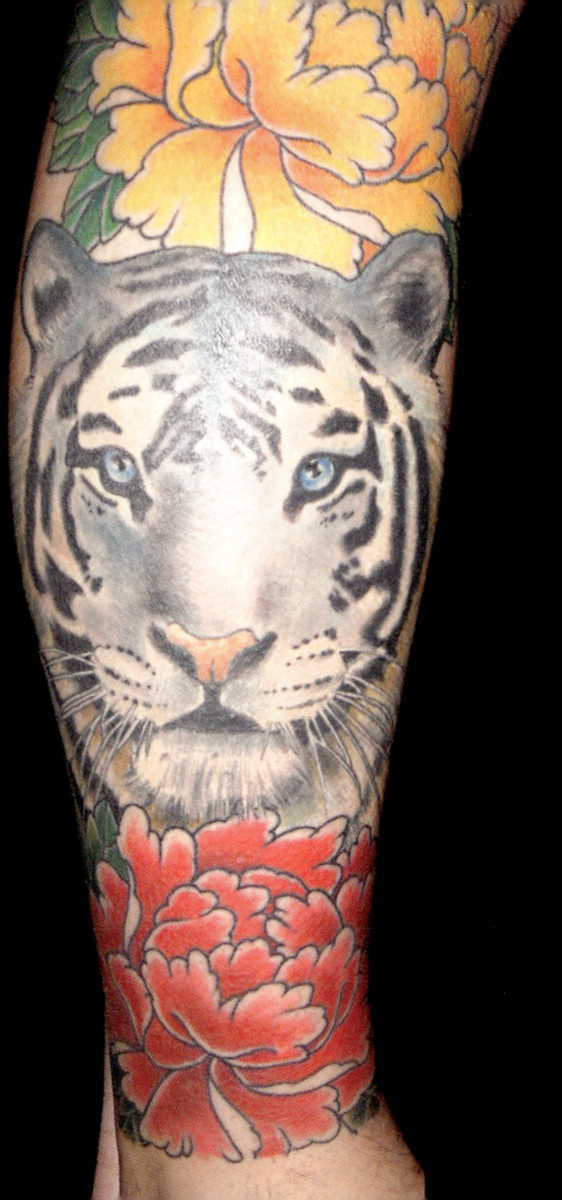

© Chío

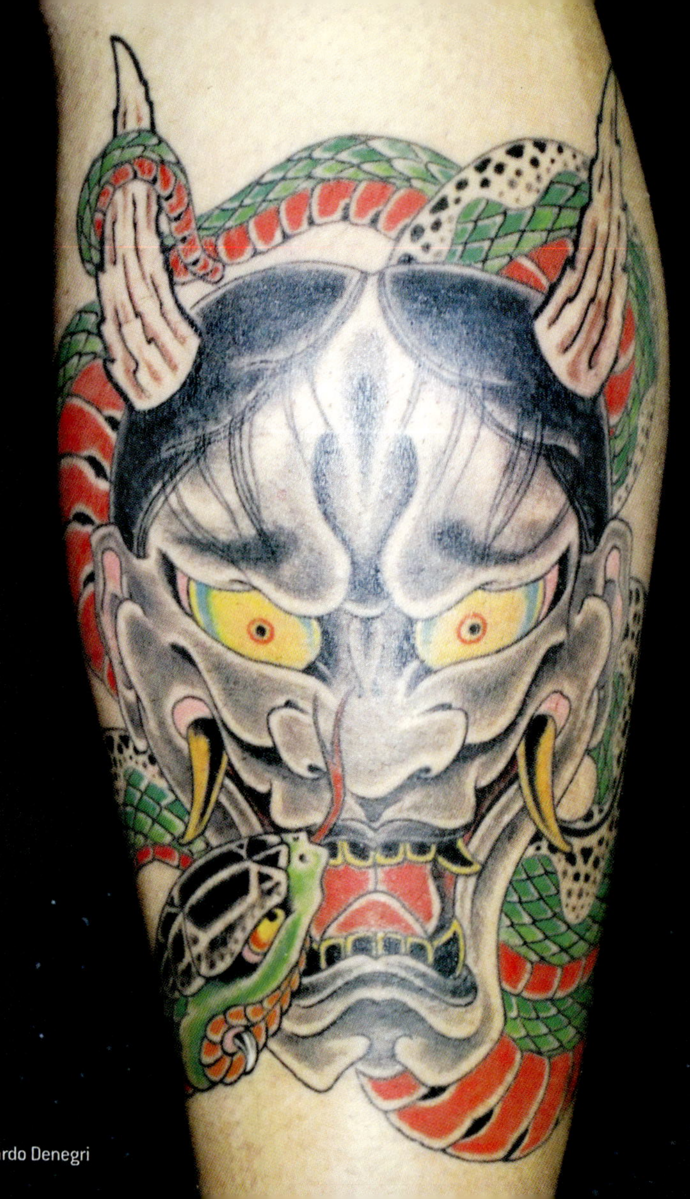

© Leonardo Denegri

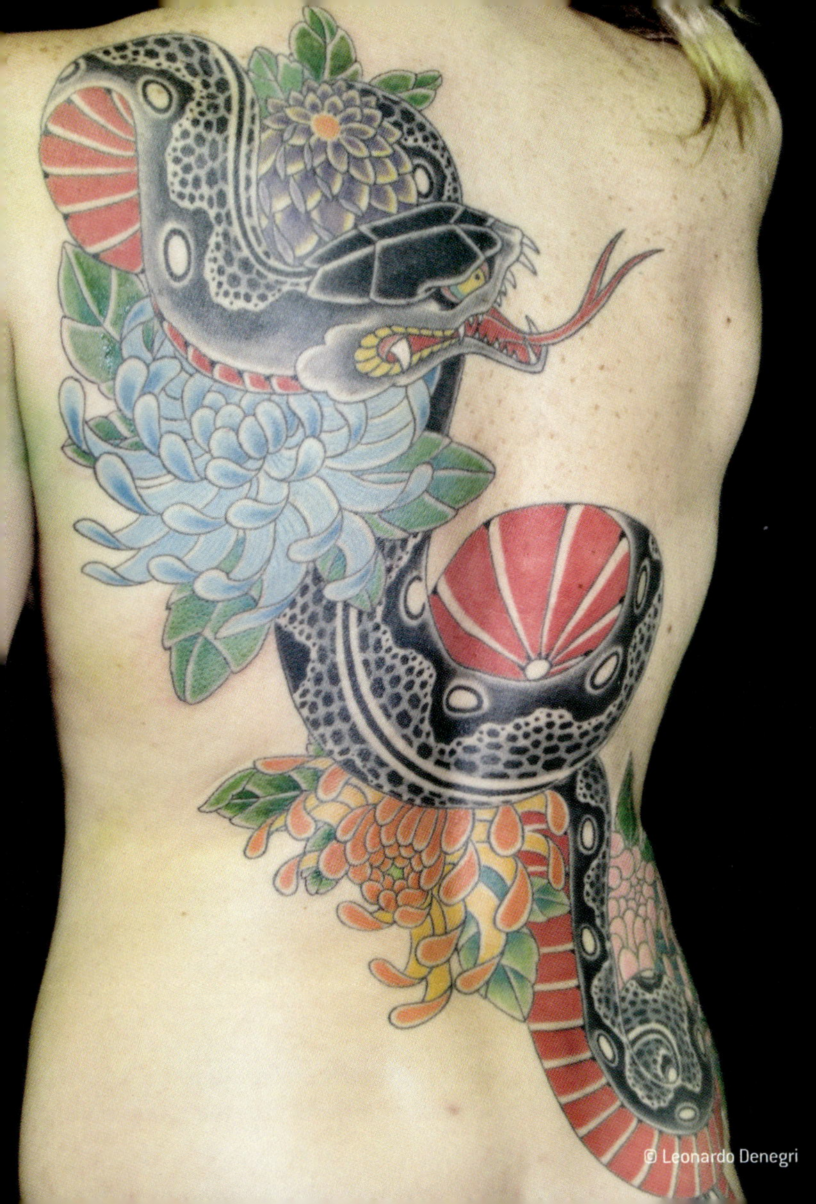
© Leonardo Denegri

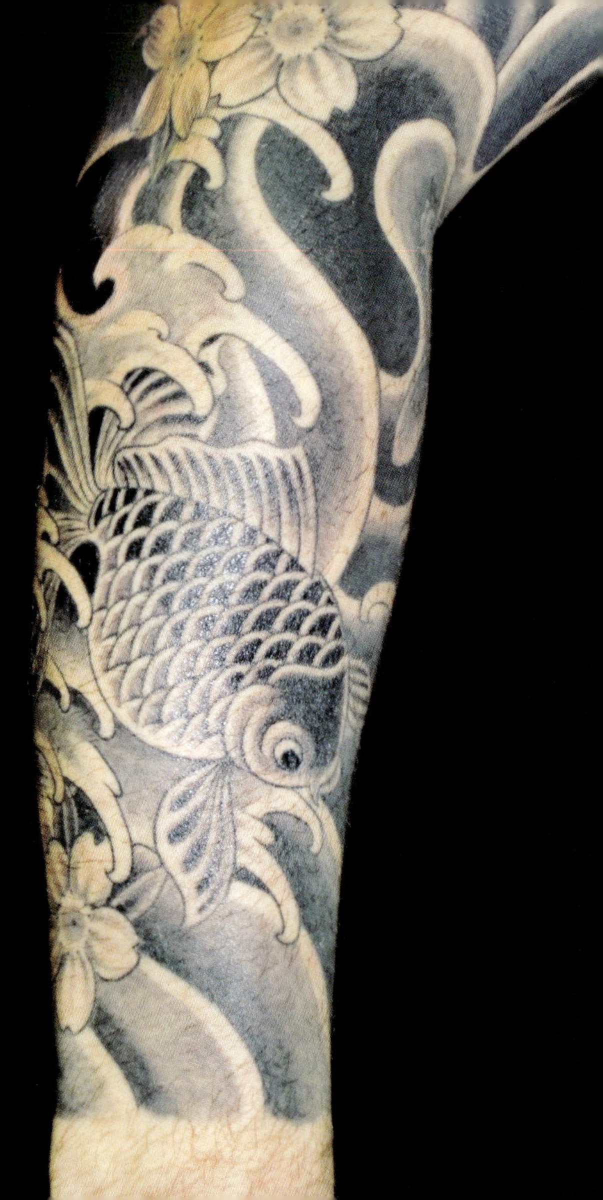

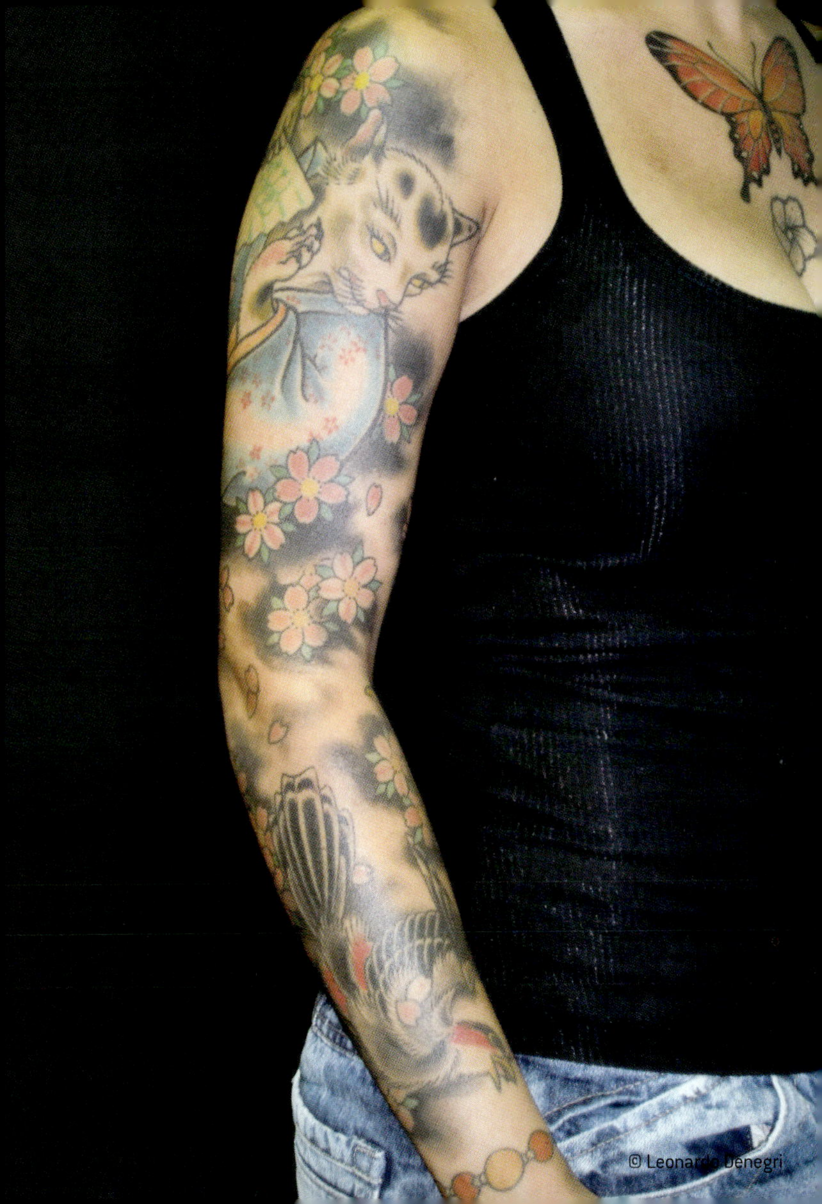
© Leonardo Denegri

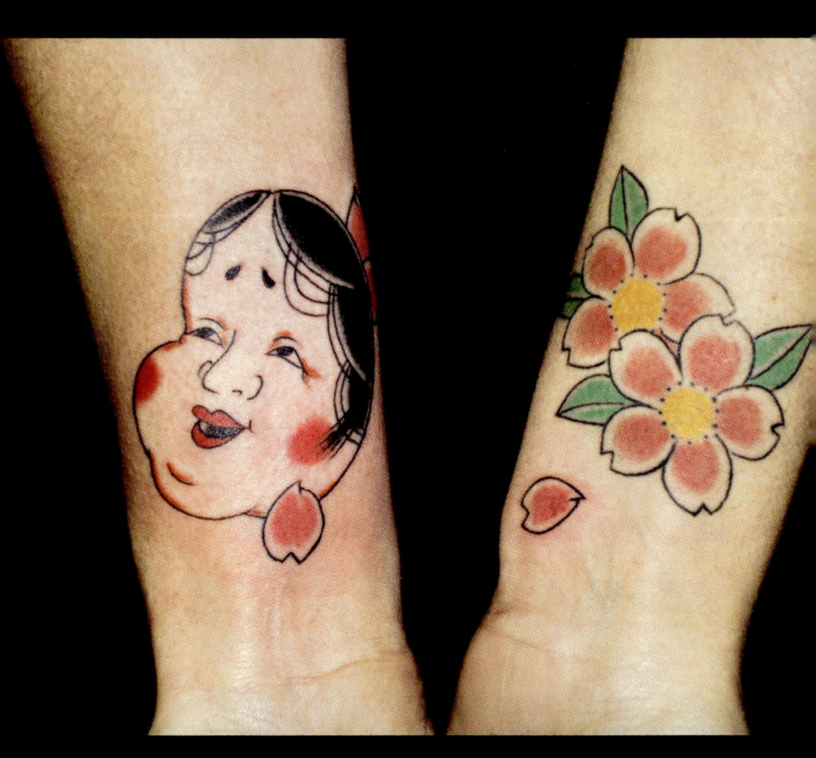

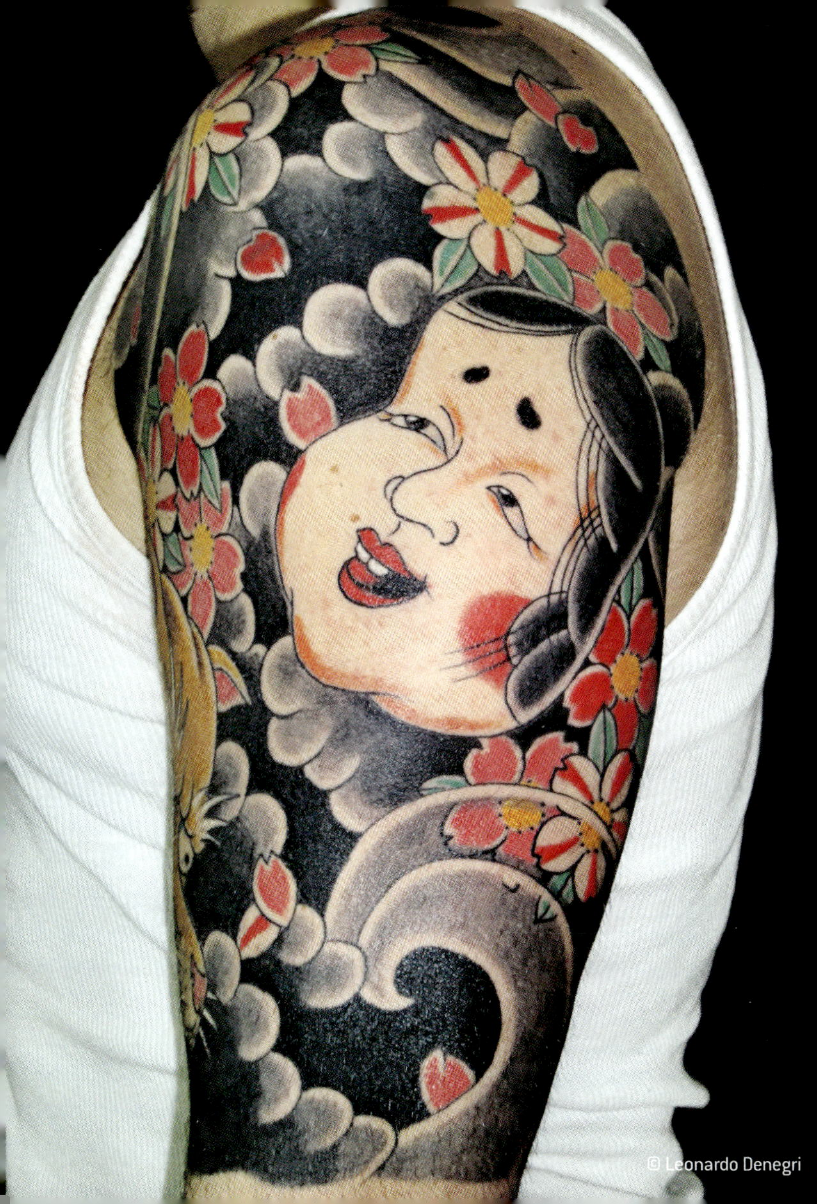
© Leonardo Denegri

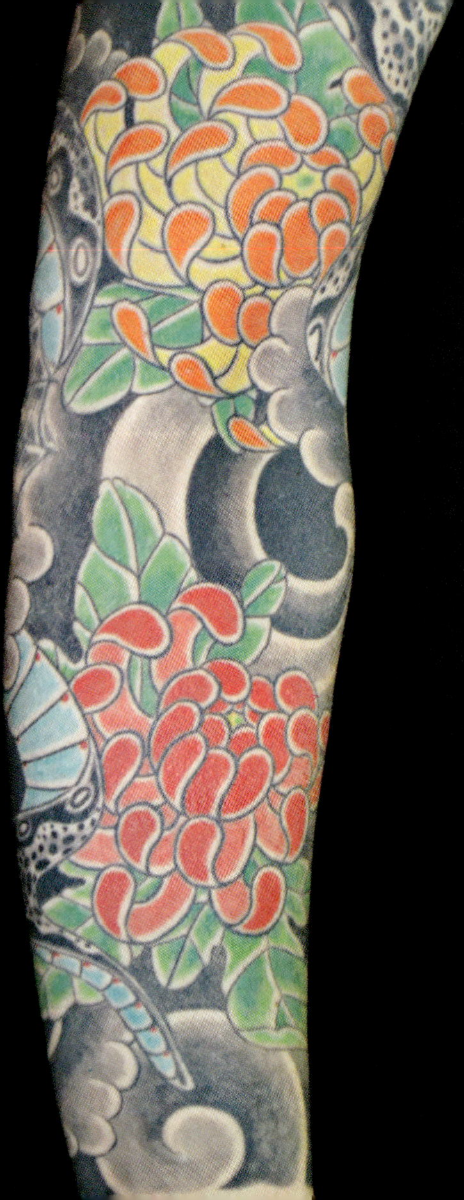

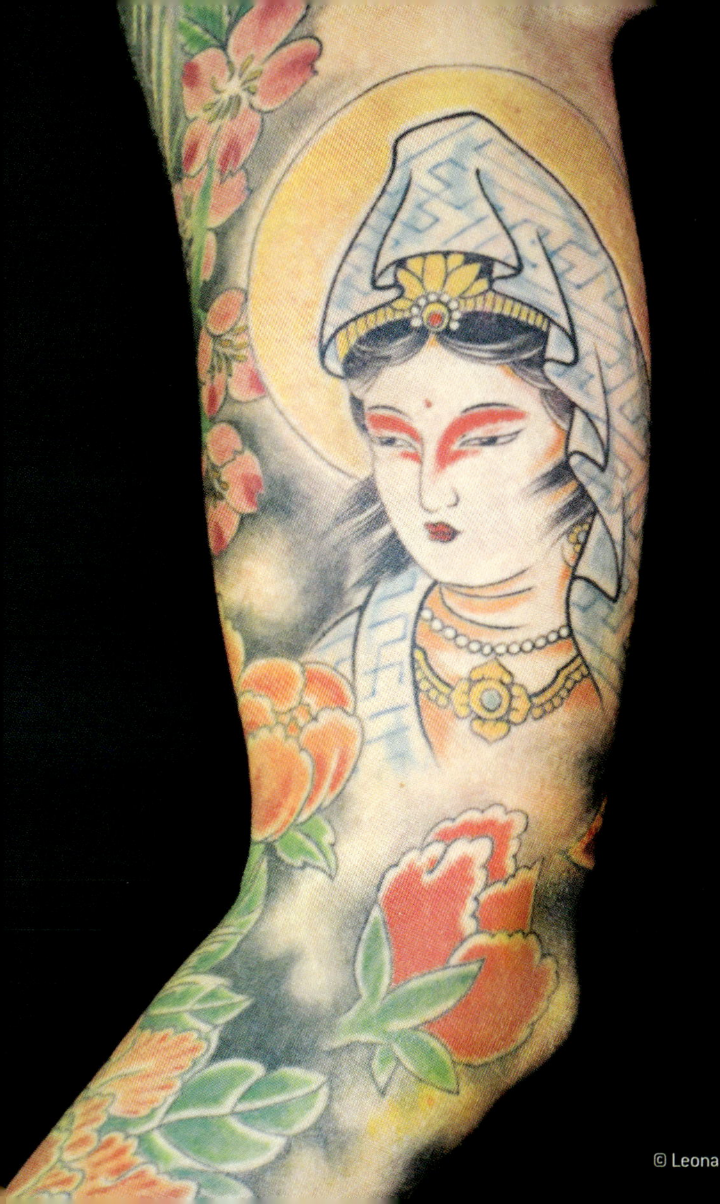

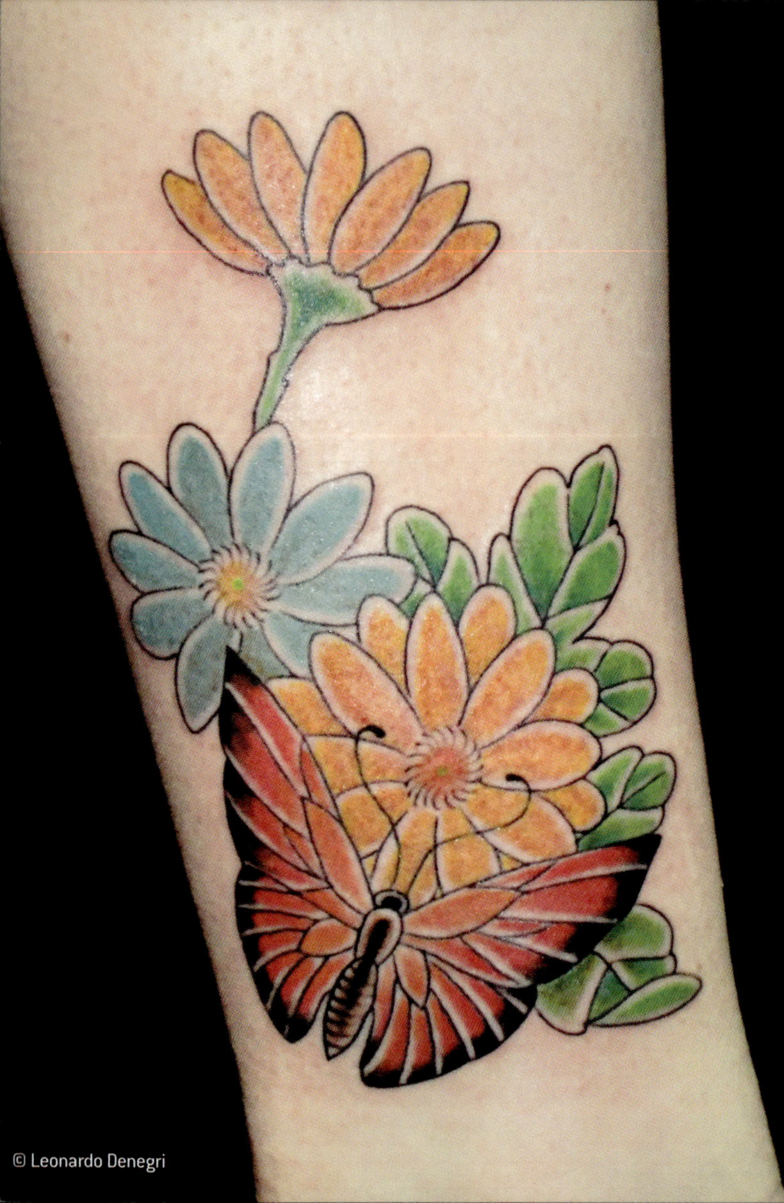

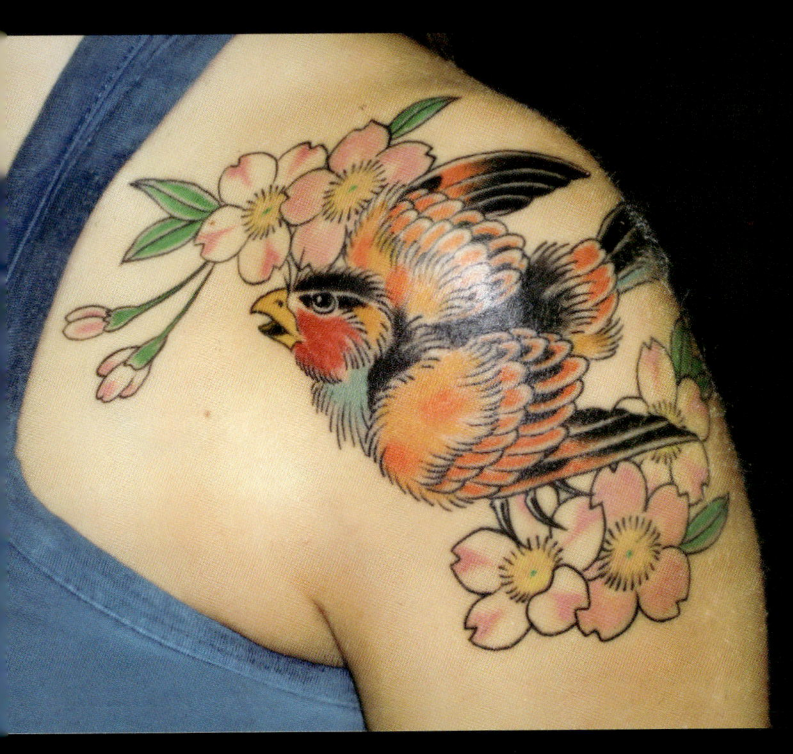

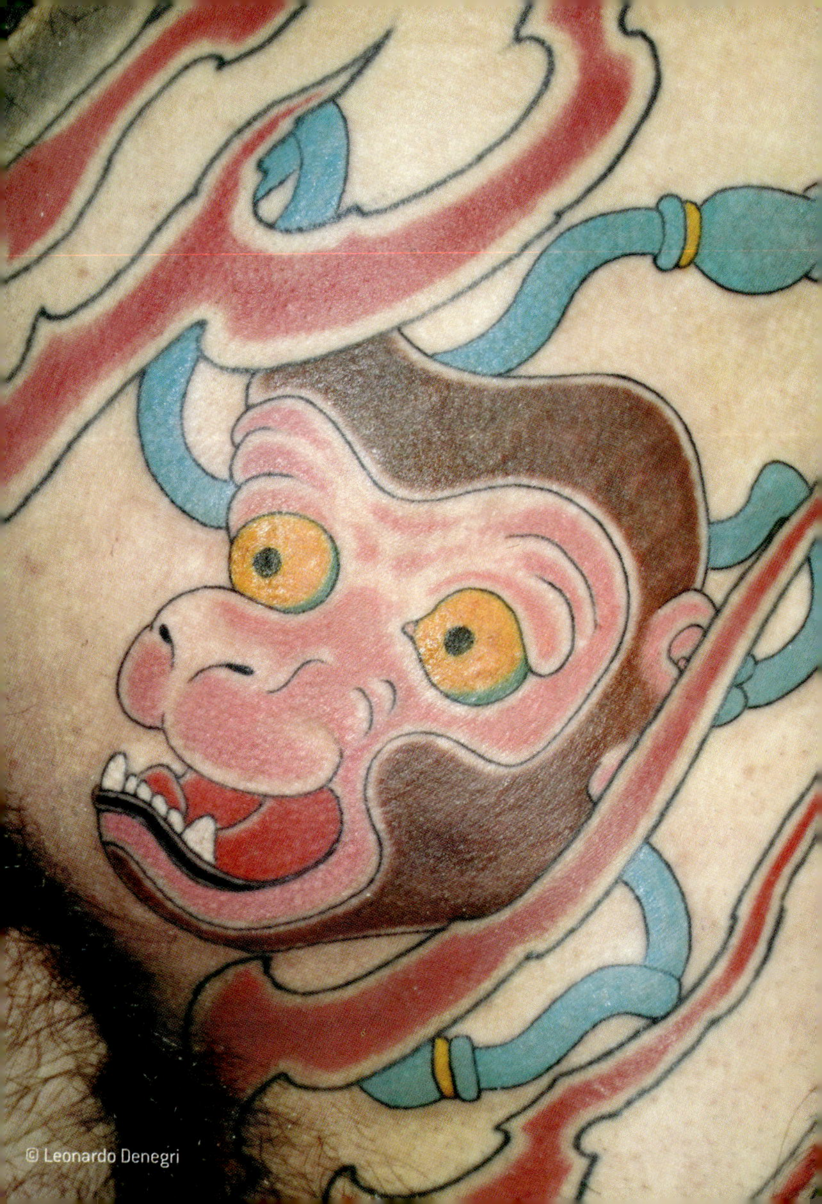
© Leonardo Denegri

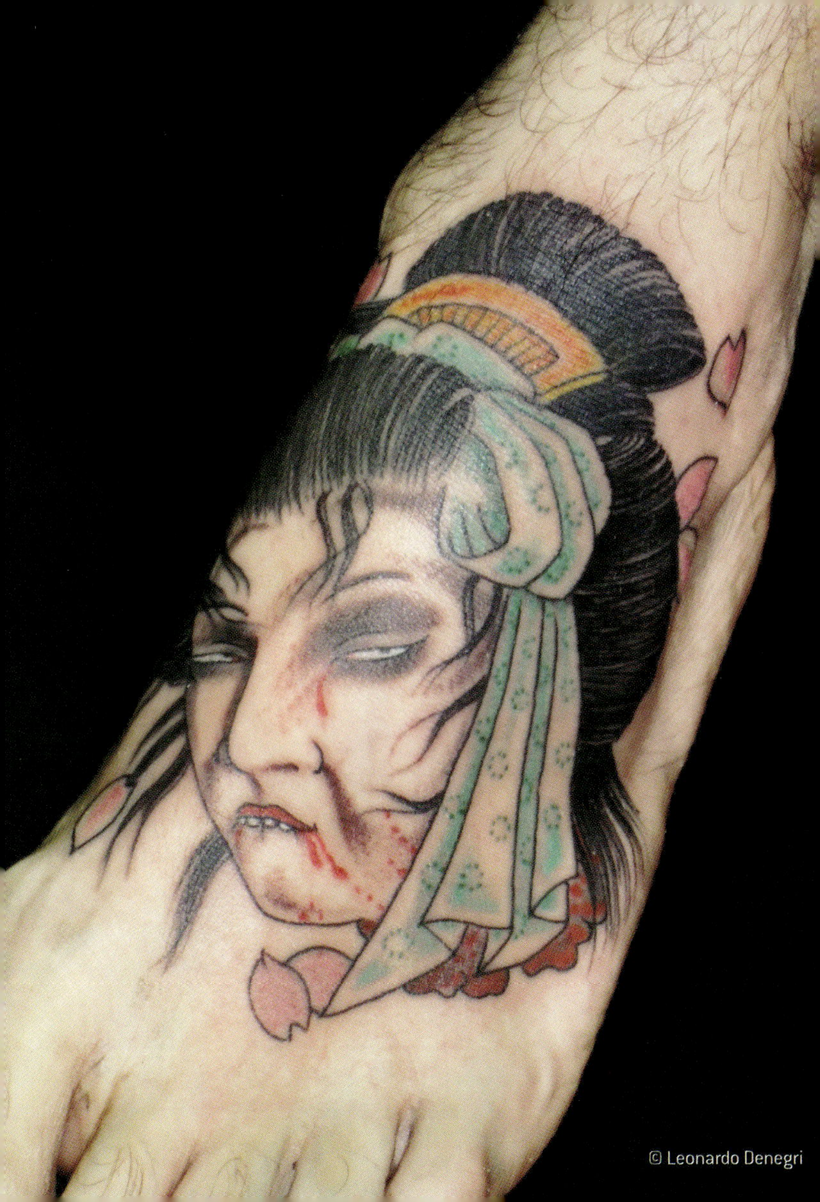

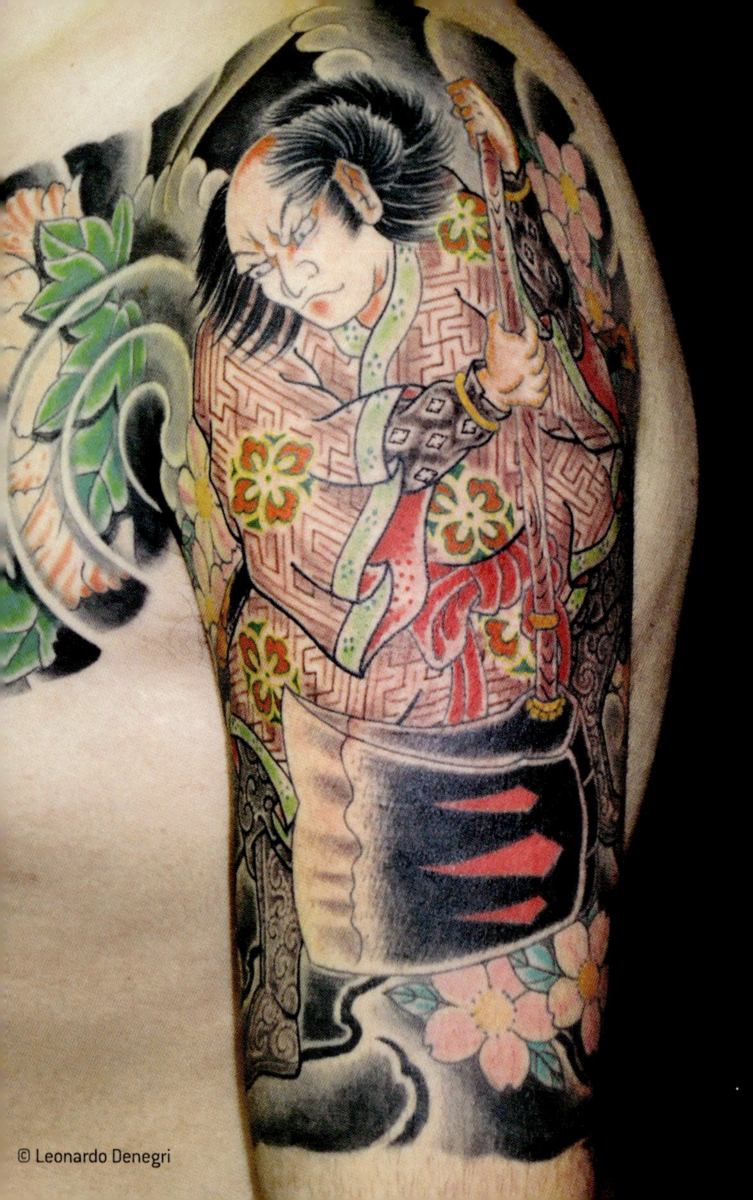

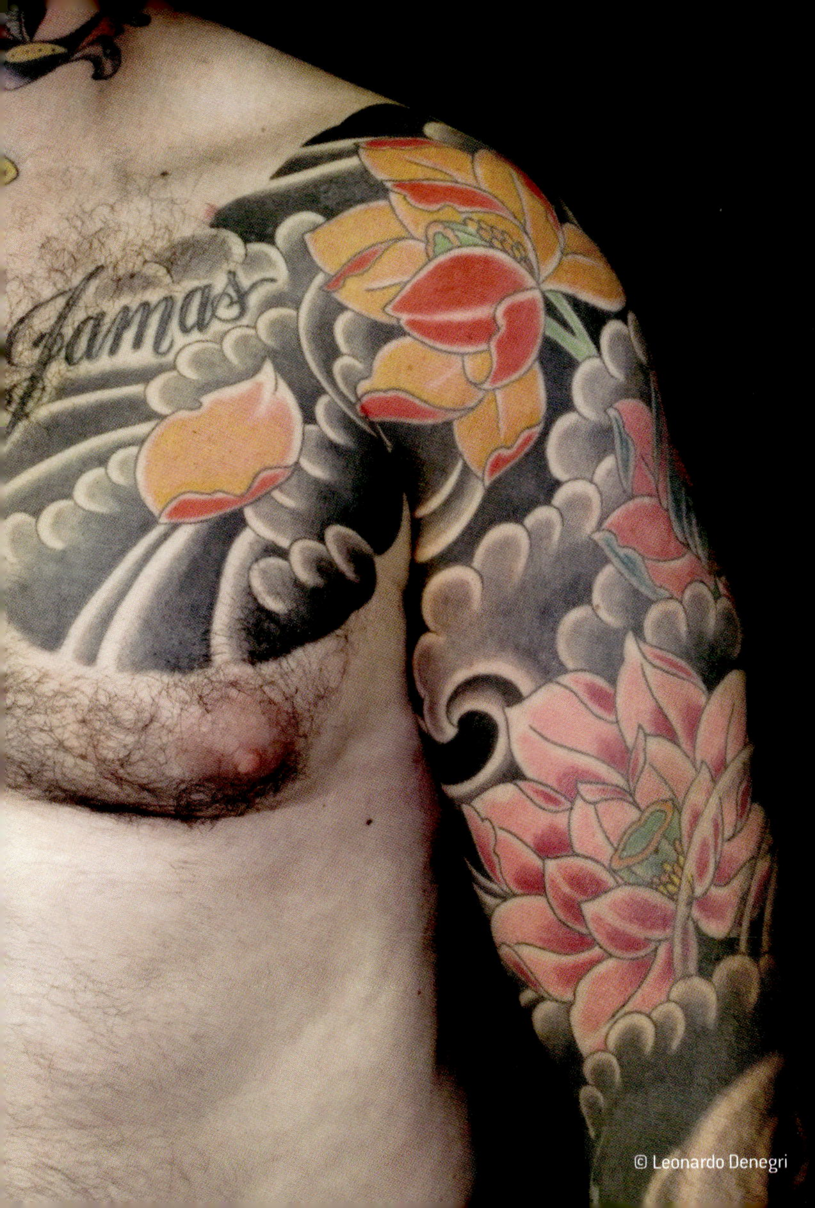
Jamas

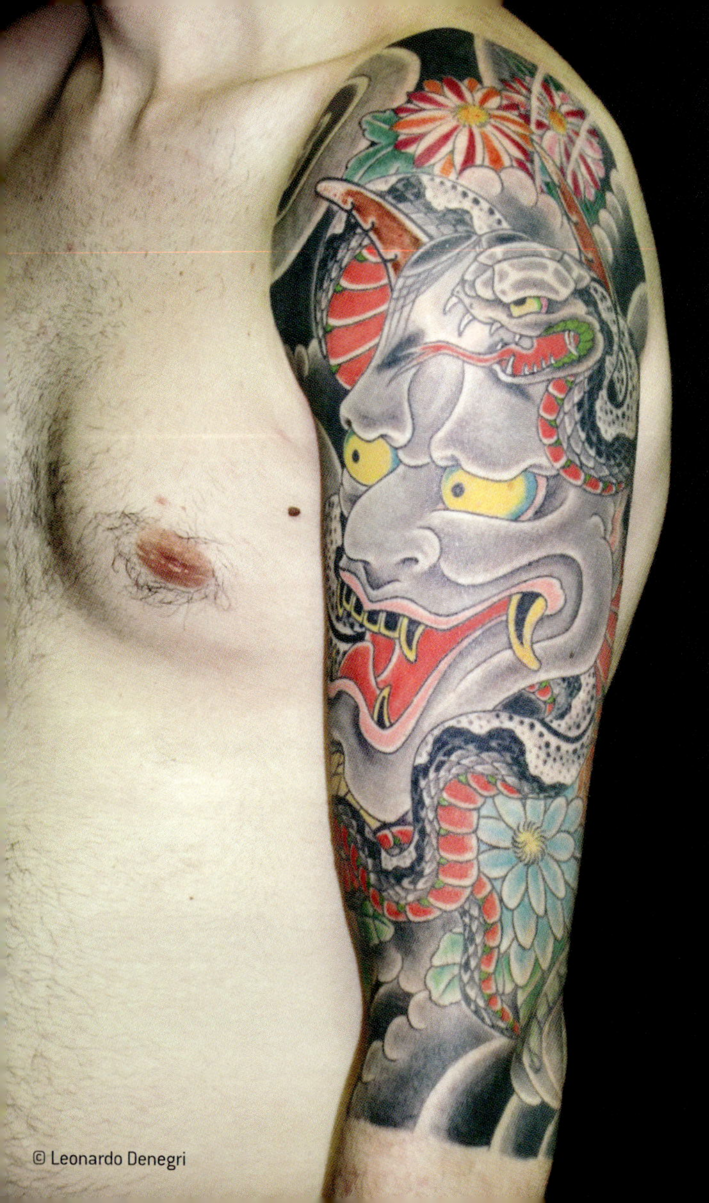
© Leonardo Denegri

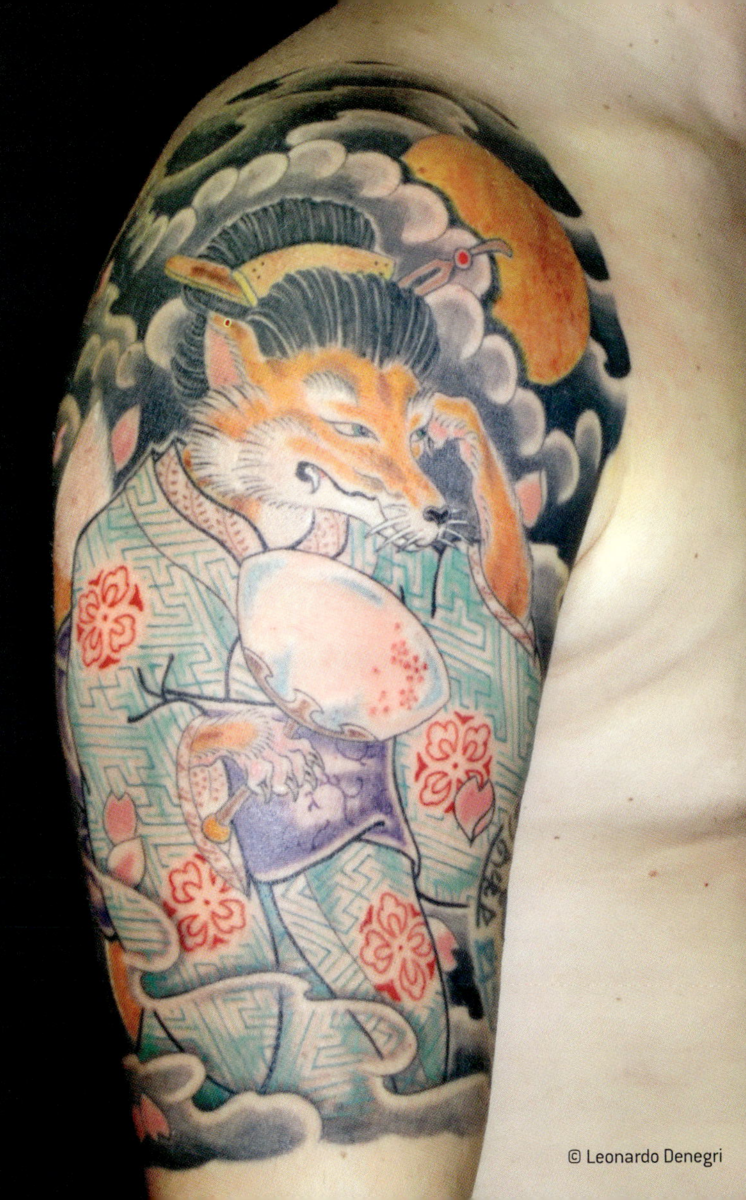

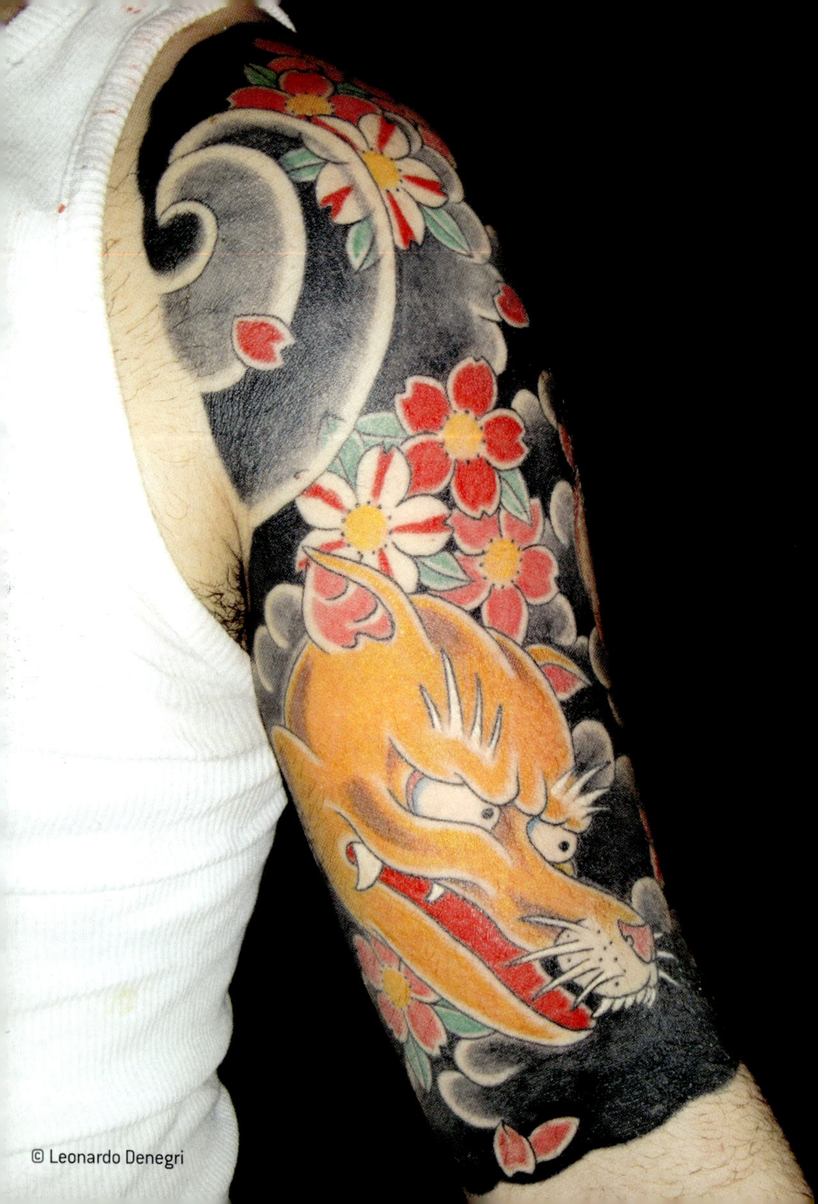

© Leonardo Denegri

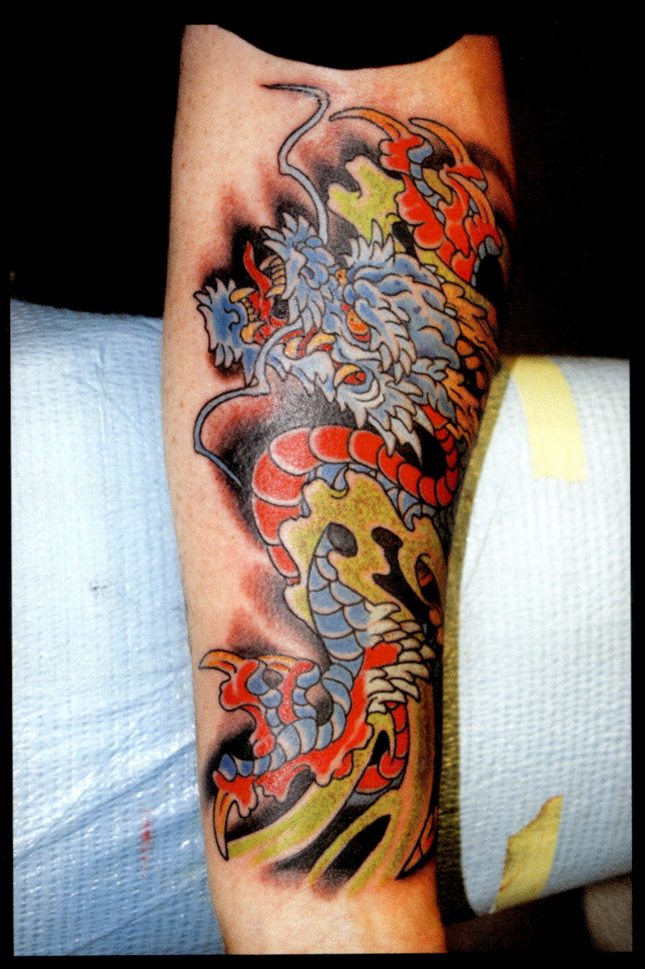

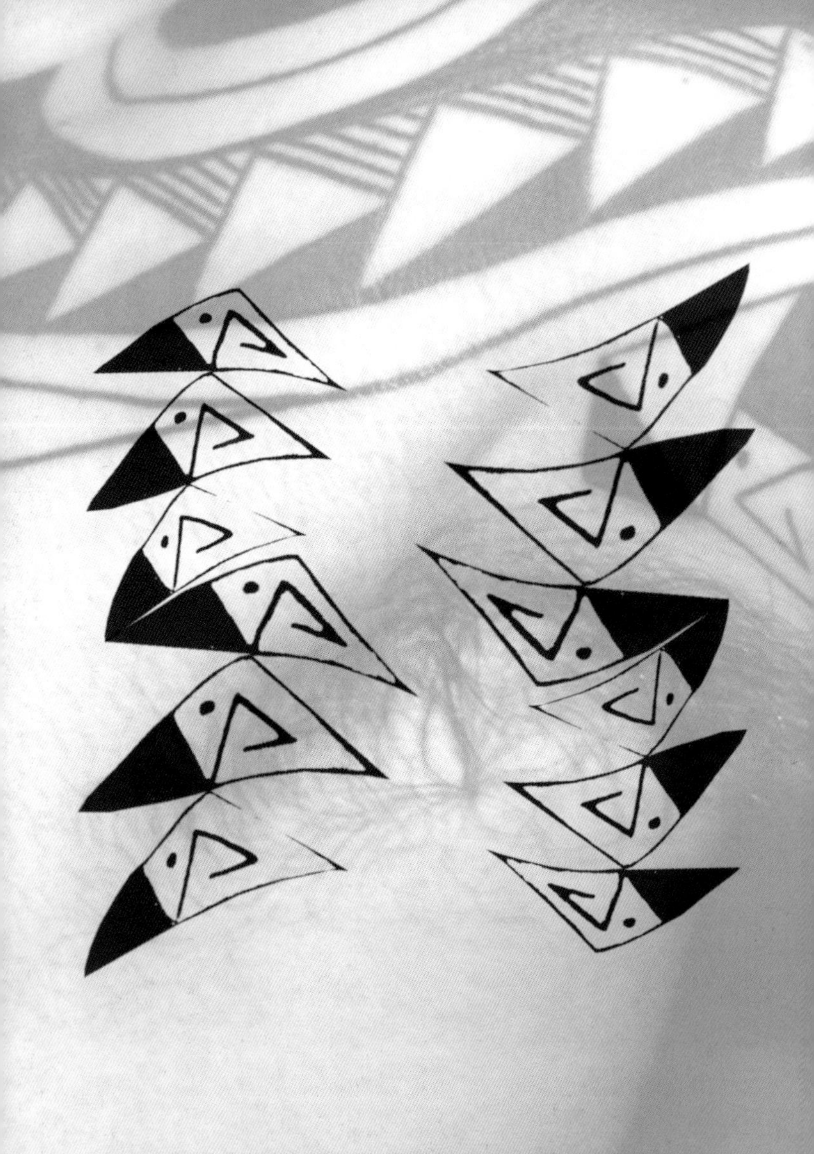

Black Ink

Black Ink

Black Ink

Black Ink

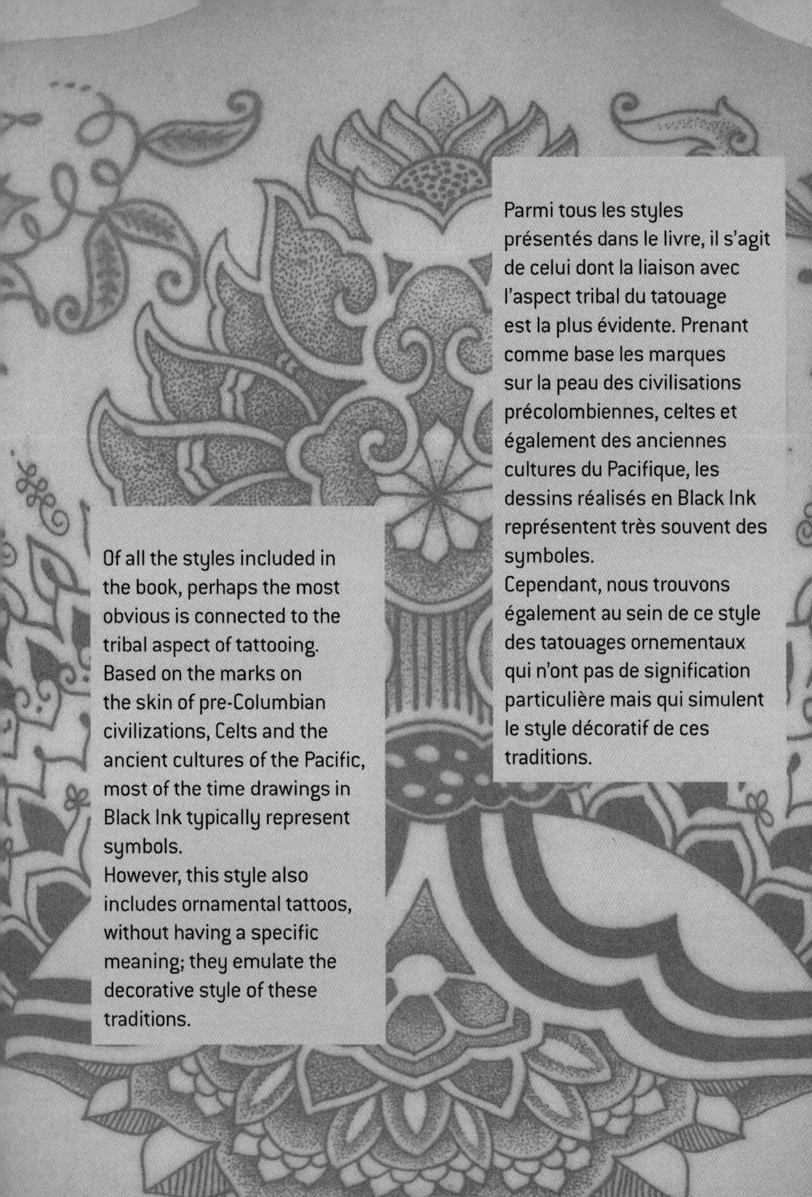

Of all the styles included in the book, perhaps the most obvious is connected to the tribal aspect of tattooing. Based on the marks on the skin of pre-Columbian civilizations, Celts and the ancient cultures of the Pacific, most of the time drawings in Black Ink typically represent symbols.
However, this style also includes ornamental tattoos, without having a specific meaning; they emulate the decorative style of these traditions.

Parmi tous les styles présentés dans le livre, il s'agit de celui dont la liaison avec l'aspect tribal du tatouage est la plus évidente. Prenant comme base les marques sur la peau des civilisations précolombiennes, celtes et également des anciennes cultures du Pacifique, les dessins réalisés en Black Ink représentent très souvent des symboles.
Cependant, nous trouvons également au sein de ce style des tatouages ornementaux qui n'ont pas de signification particulière mais qui simulent le style décoratif de ces traditions.

Van alle stijlen die in dit boek zijn opgenomen, wordt deze wellicht het duidelijkst in verband gebracht met het tribale aspect van de tatoeage. Door als uitgangspunt de tekens op de huid bij precolumbiaanse of Keltische beschavingen en ook bij de oude culturen van de Stille Oceaan te nemen, beelden de tekeningen in Black Ink vaak symbolen uit.
Binnen deze stijl kunnen we echter ook decoratieve tatoeages vinden die, zonder dat ze een concrete betekenis hebben, de decoratieve stijl van deze tradities proberen te evenaren.

Von allen in diesem Buch enthaltenen Stilen ist dieser vielleicht derjenige, der die engste Verbindung zum Stammesaspekt von Tätowierungen bewahrt. Die in Black Ink gezeichneten Tattoos zeigen häufig Symbole, indem sie als Grundlage die Hautmarkierungen der amerikanischen, keltischen Urvölker und auch der alten Stämme des Pazifiks nehmen. In diesem Stil finden wir aber auch ornamentale Tätowierungen ohne eine konkrete Bedeutung, die einfach nur den dekorativen Stil dieser Traditionen nachempfinden.

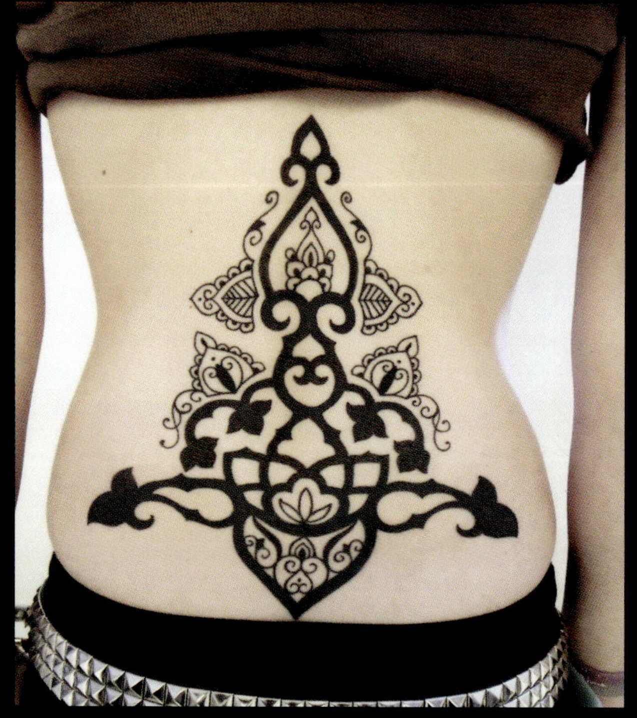

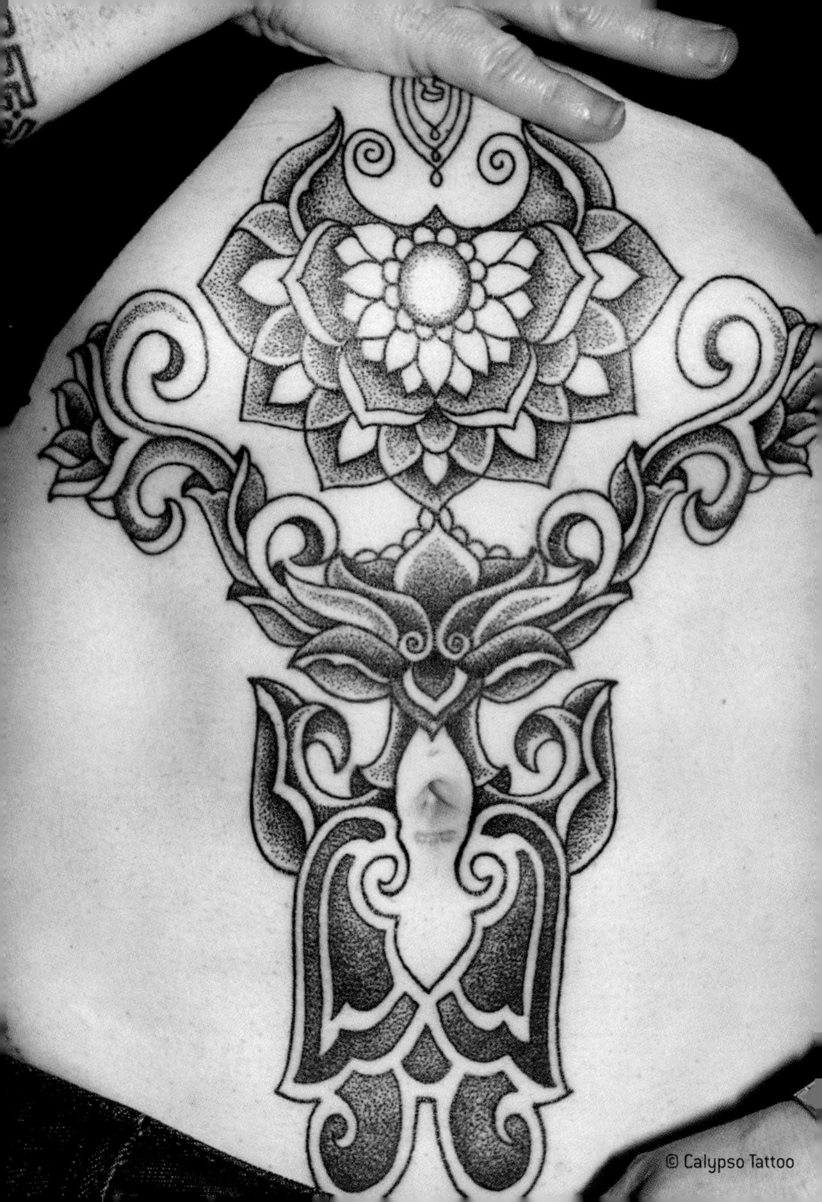
© Calypso Tattoo

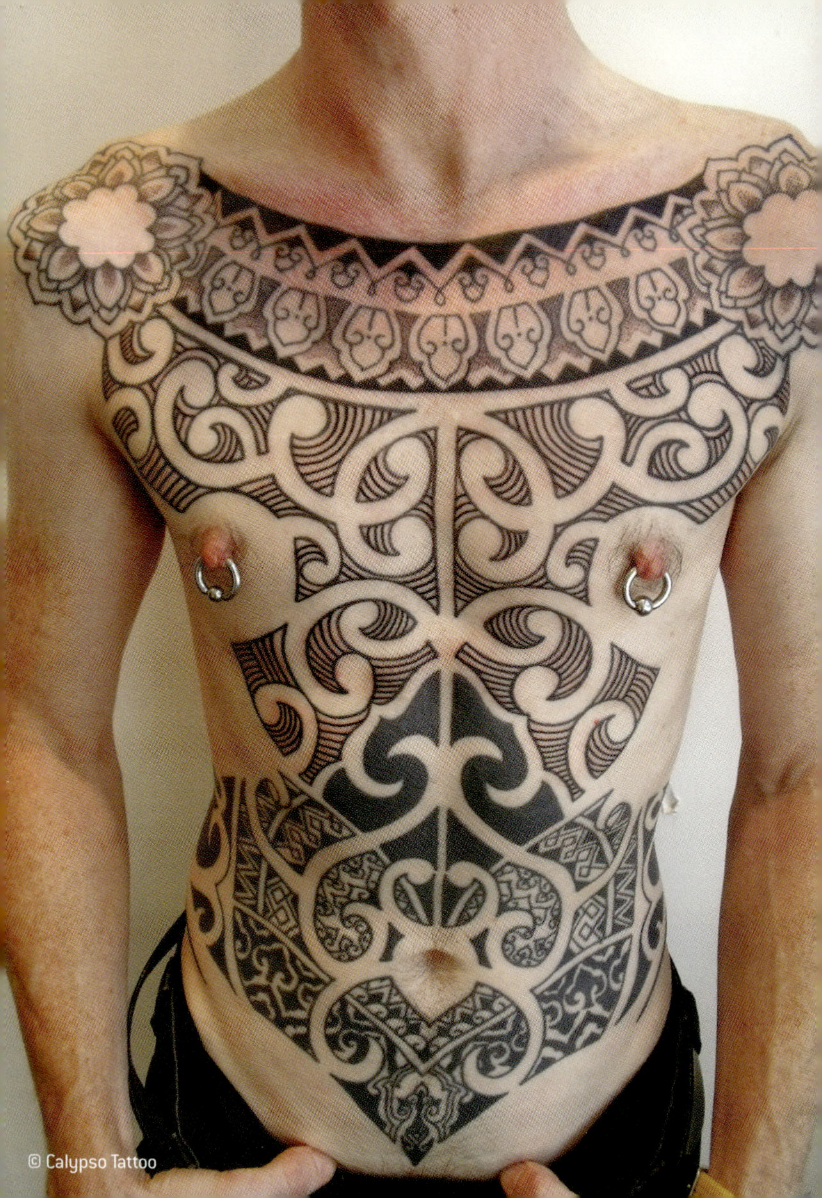
© Calypso Tattoo

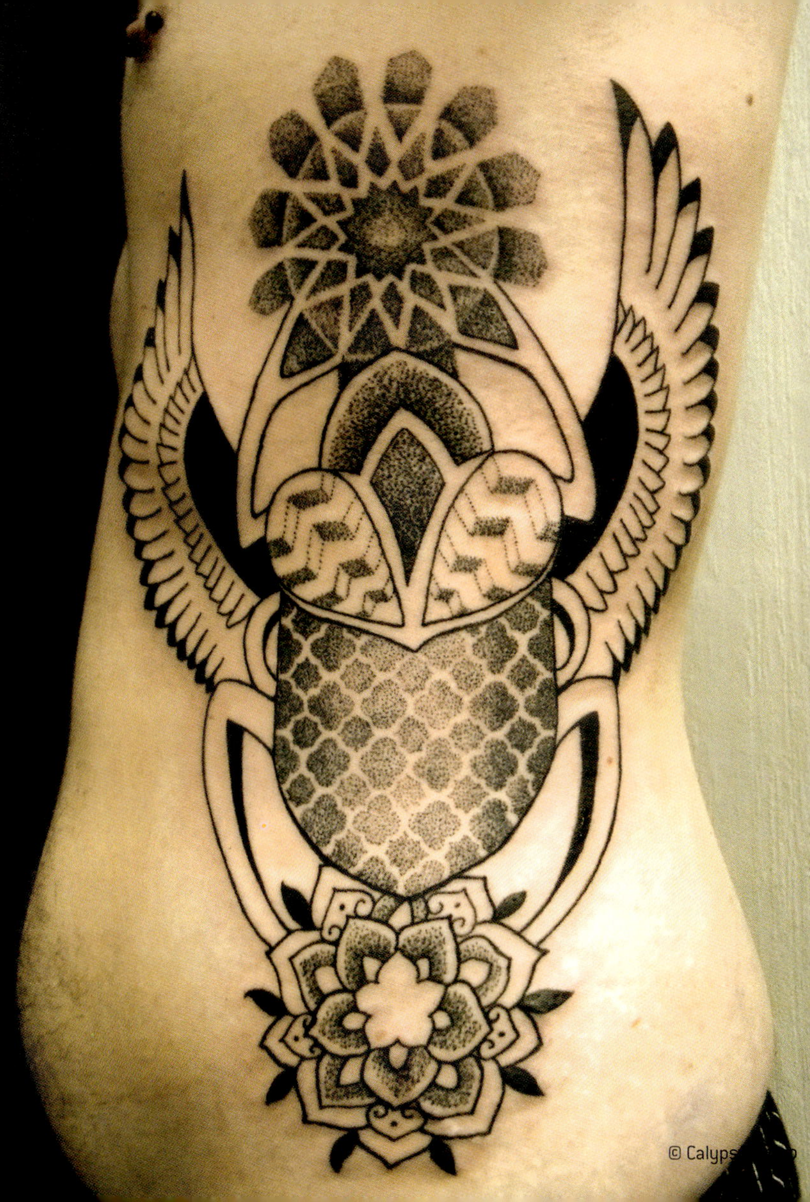
© Calypso

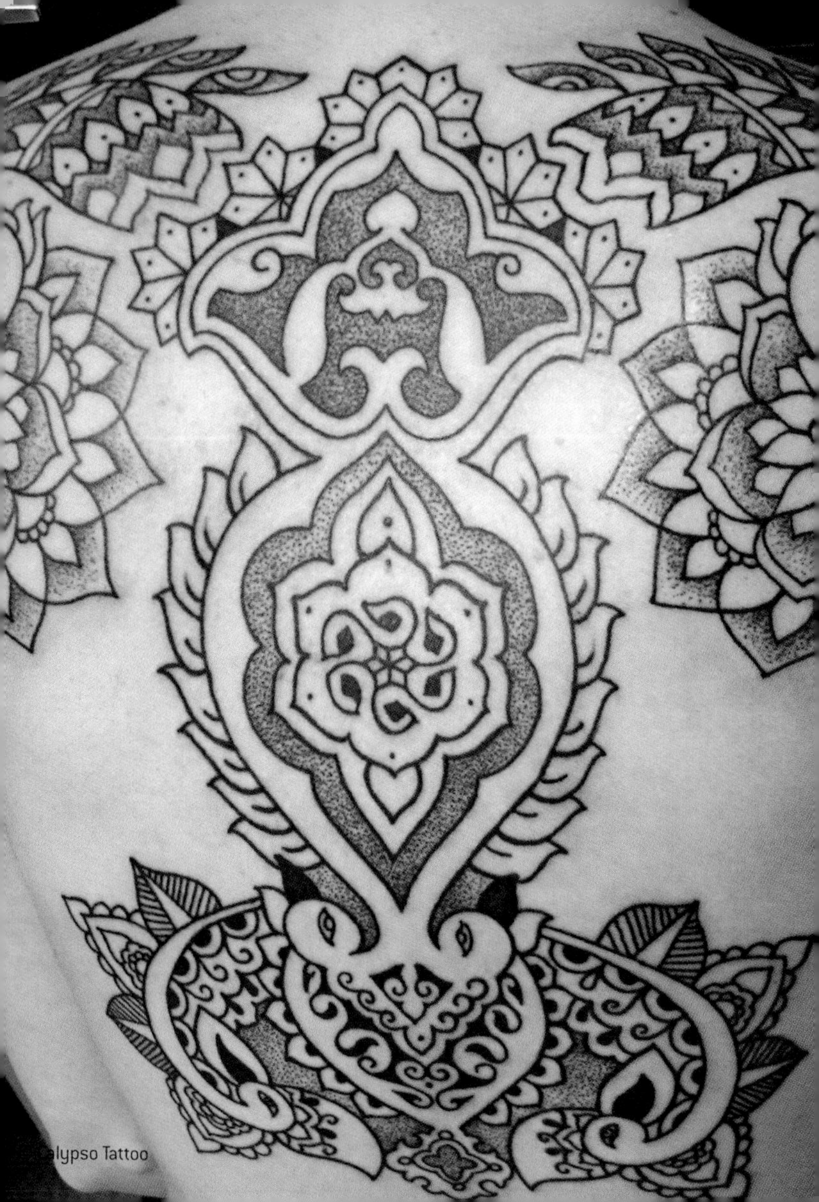

Calypso Tattoo

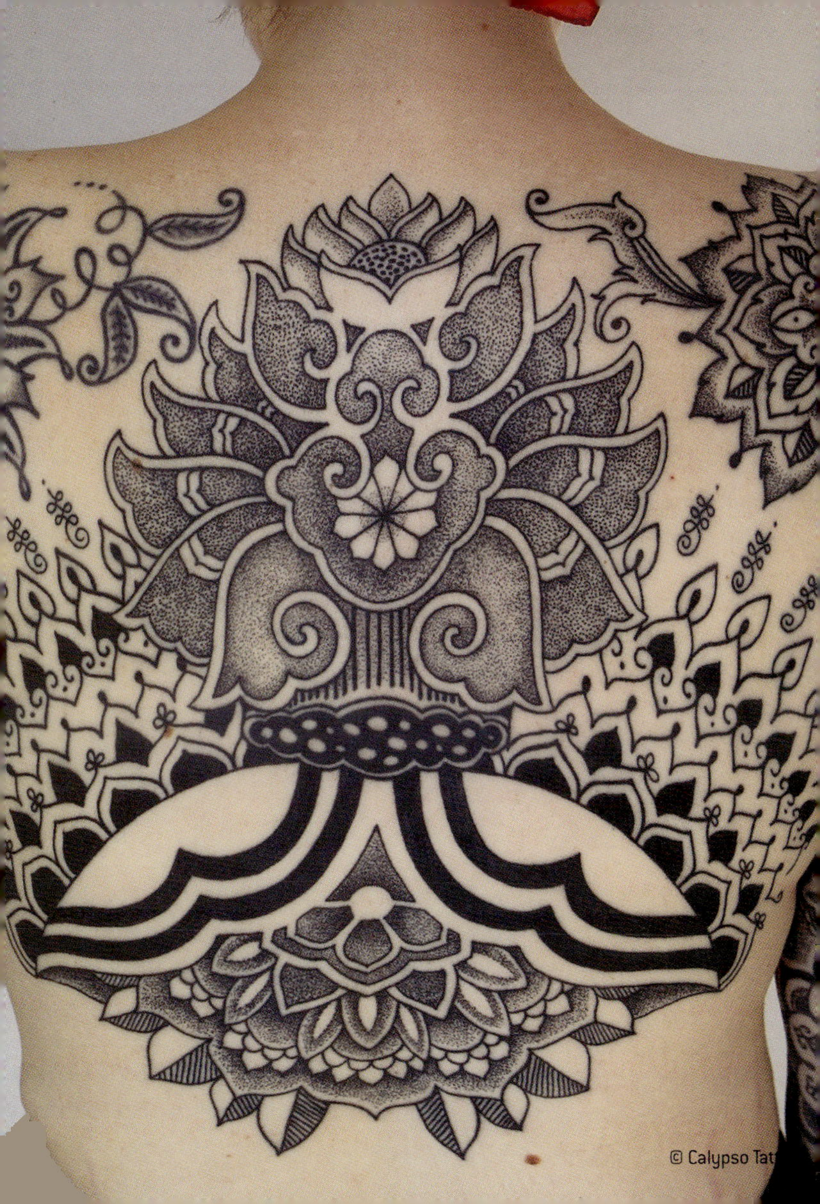
© Calypso Tat

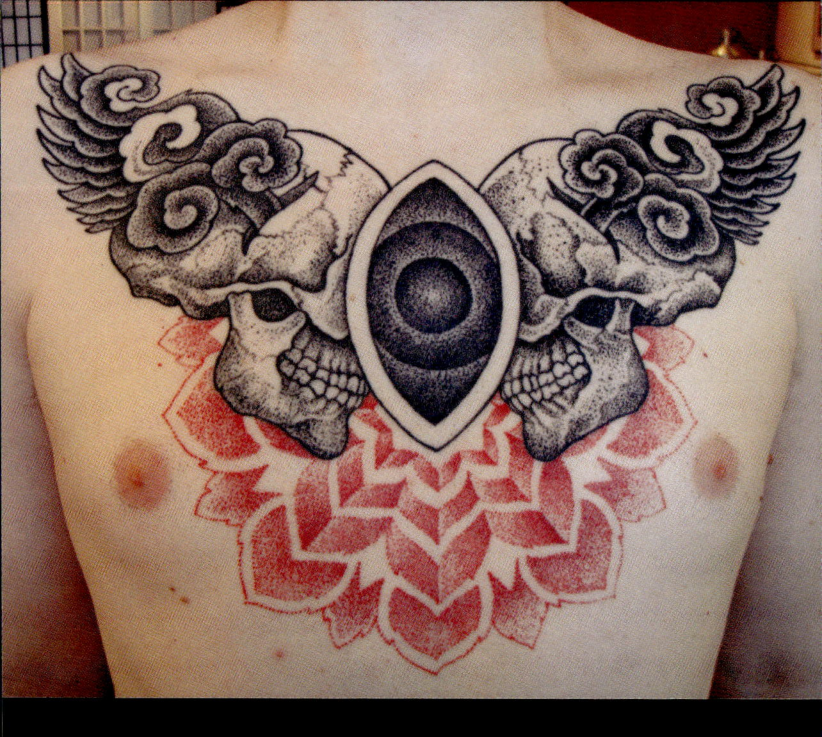

© Calypso Tattoo

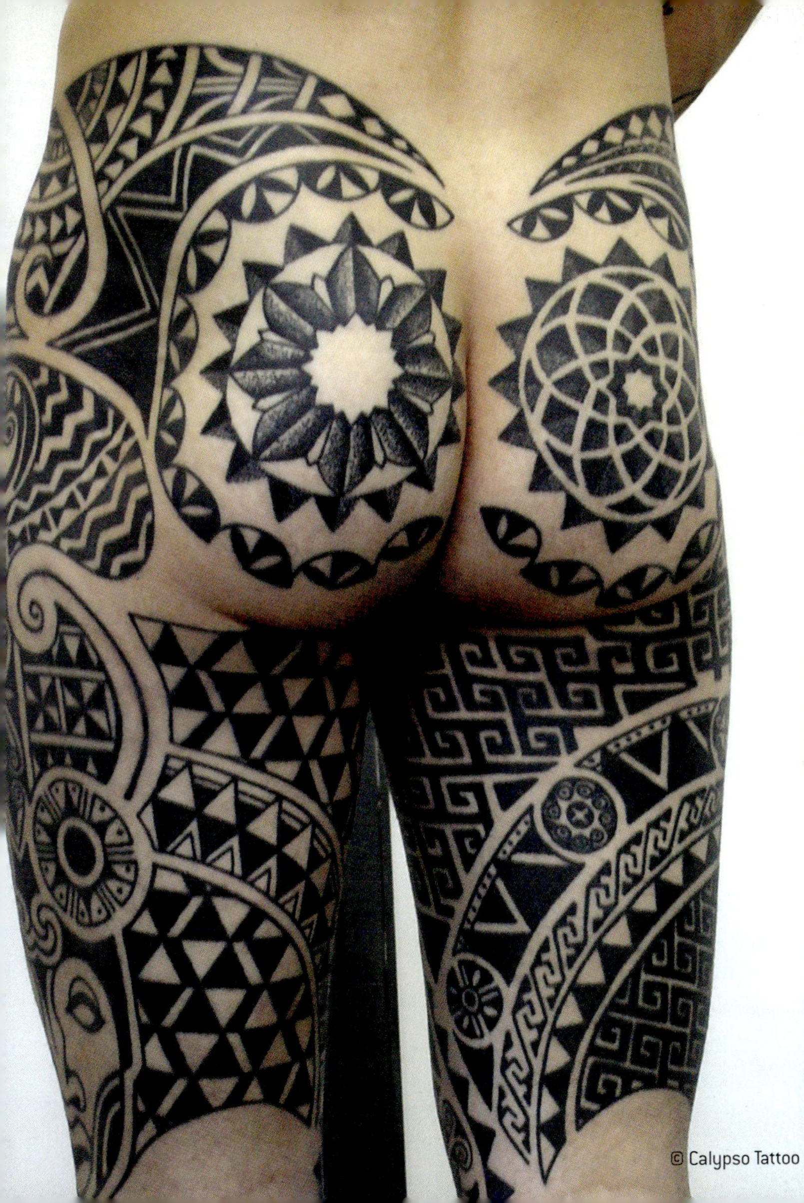
© Calypso Tattoo

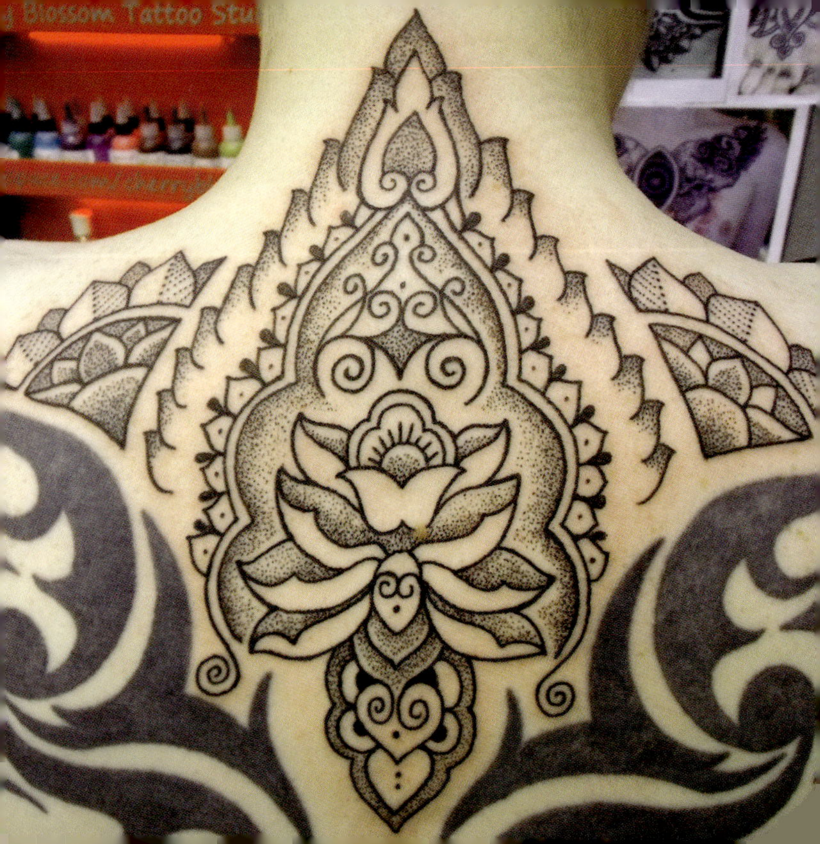
Blossom Tattoo Stu

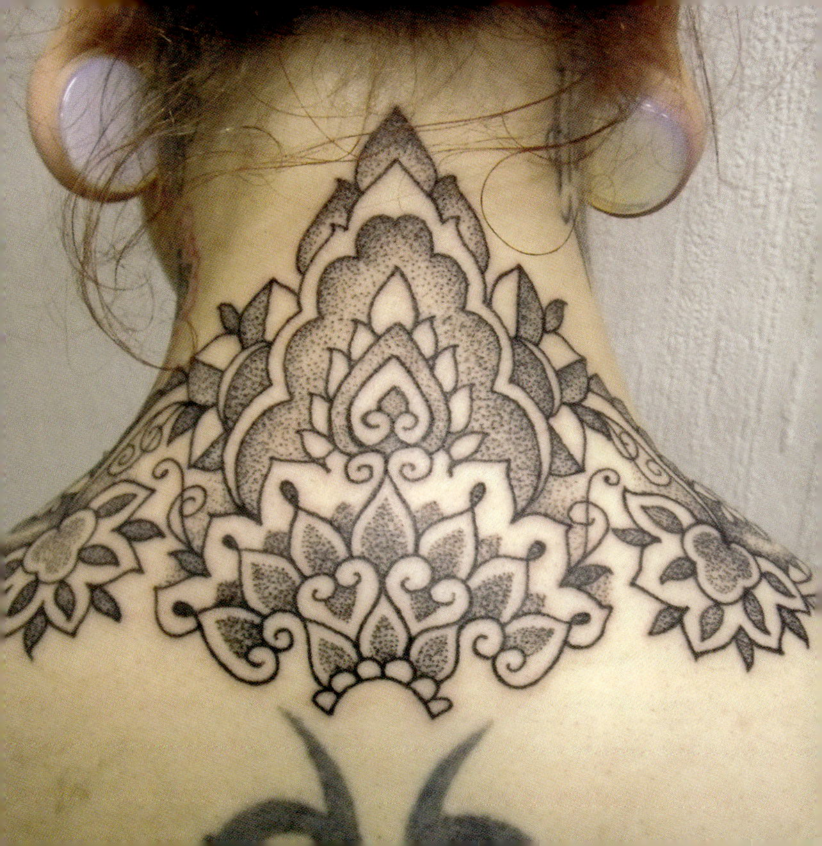

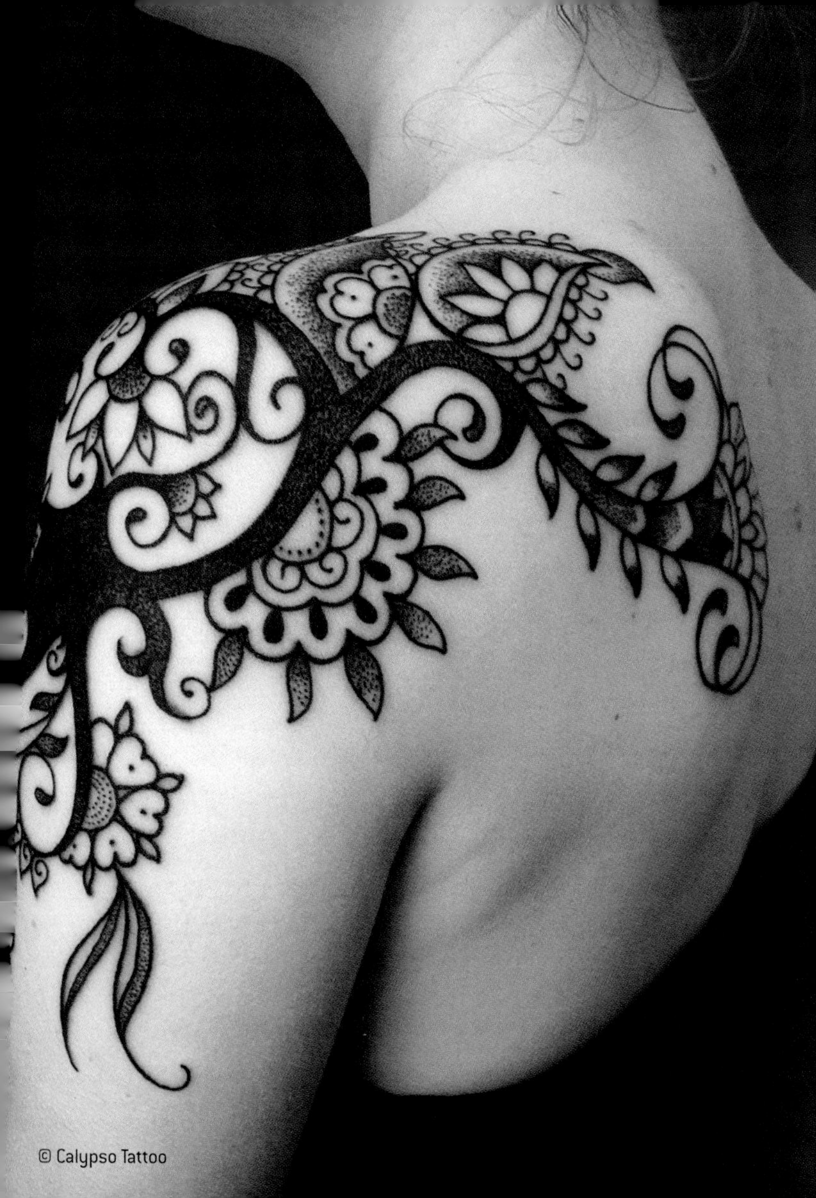

© Calypso Tattoo

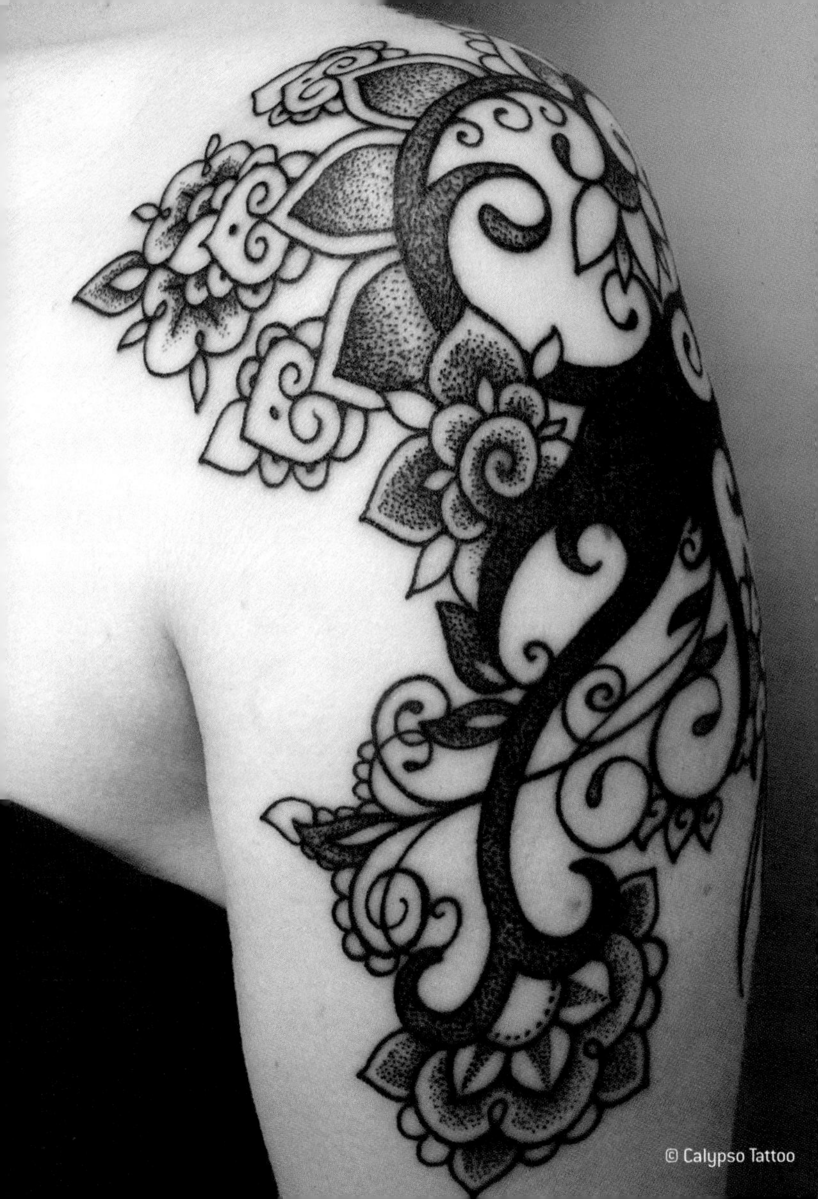
© Calypso Tattoo

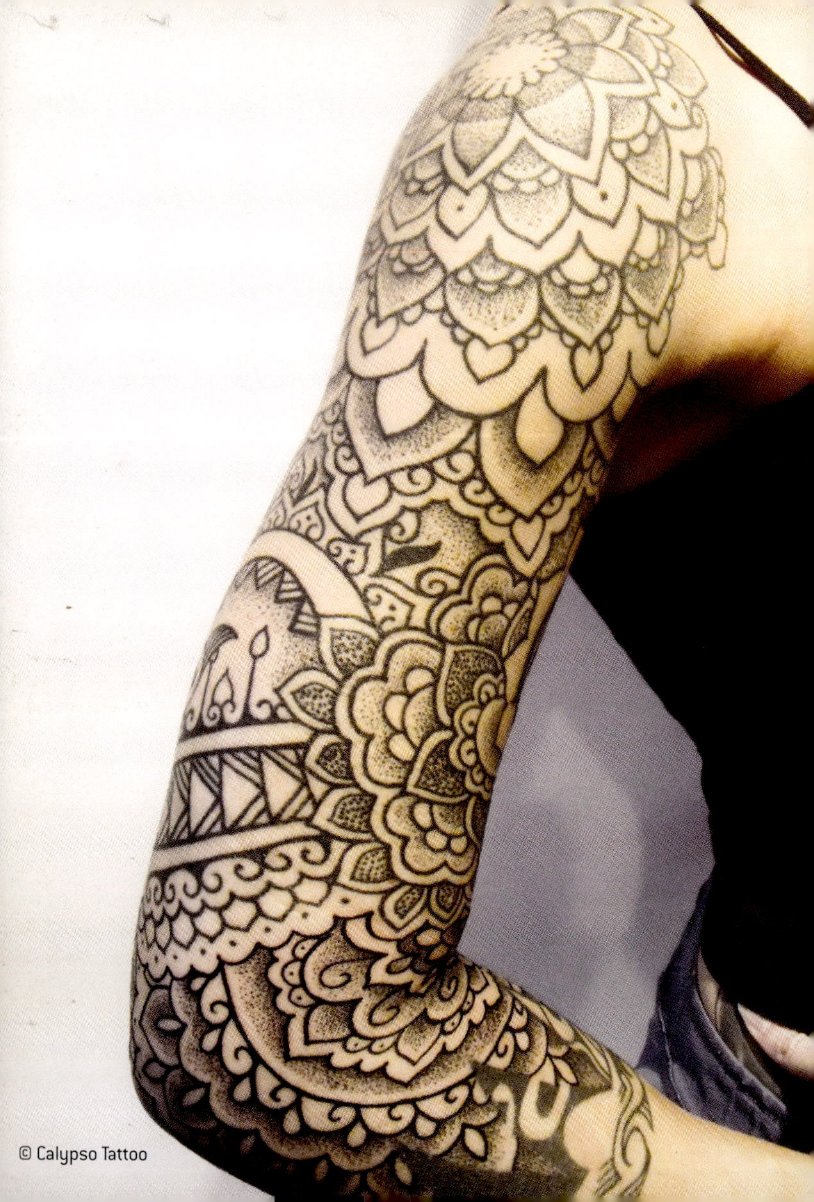

© Calypso Tattoo

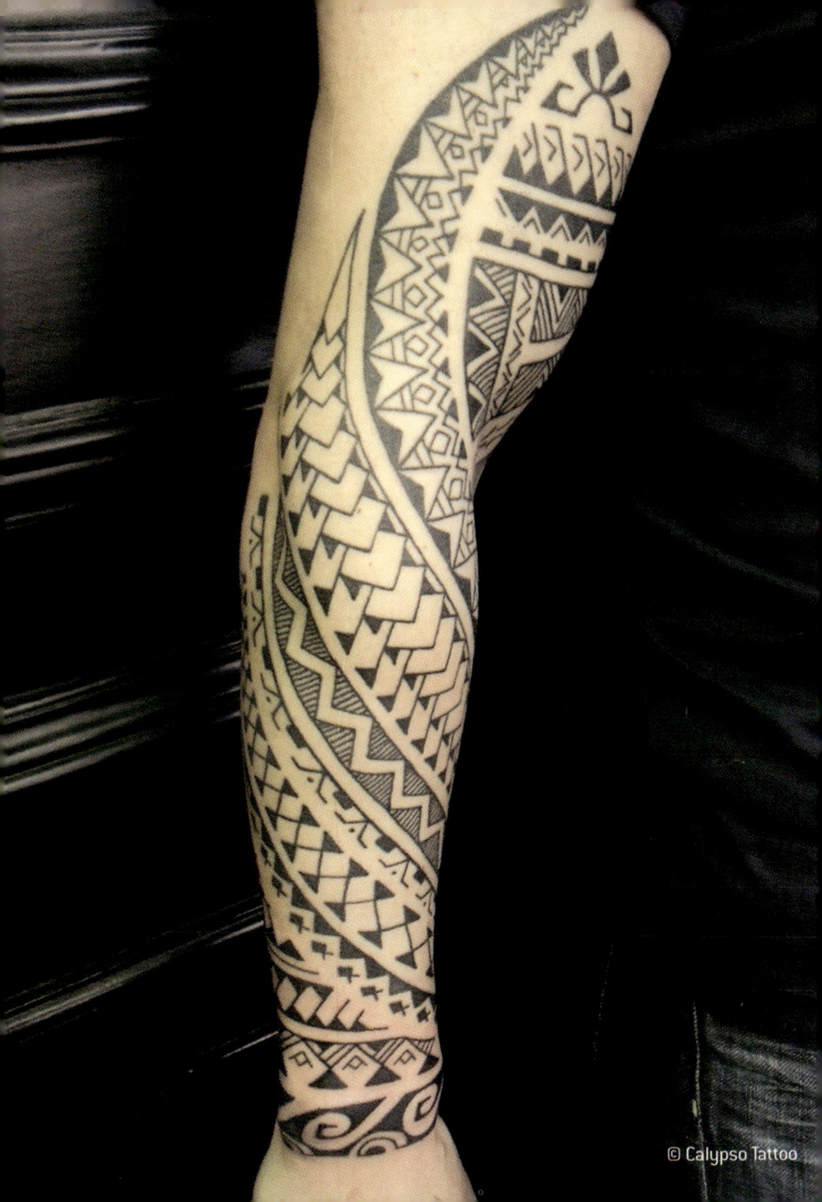
© Calypso Tattoo

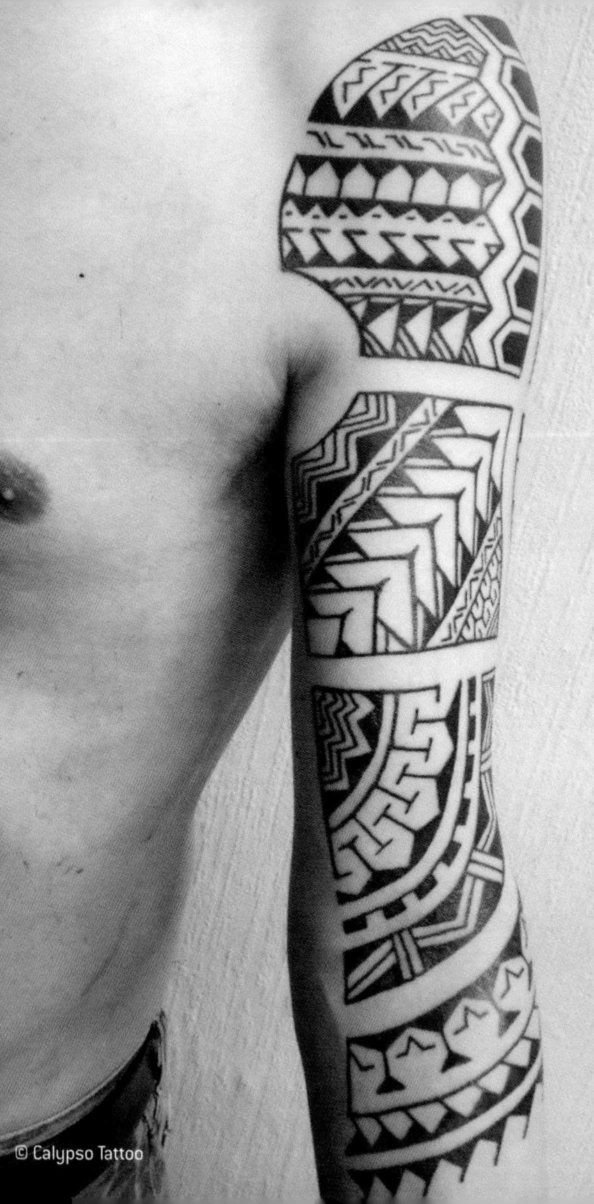

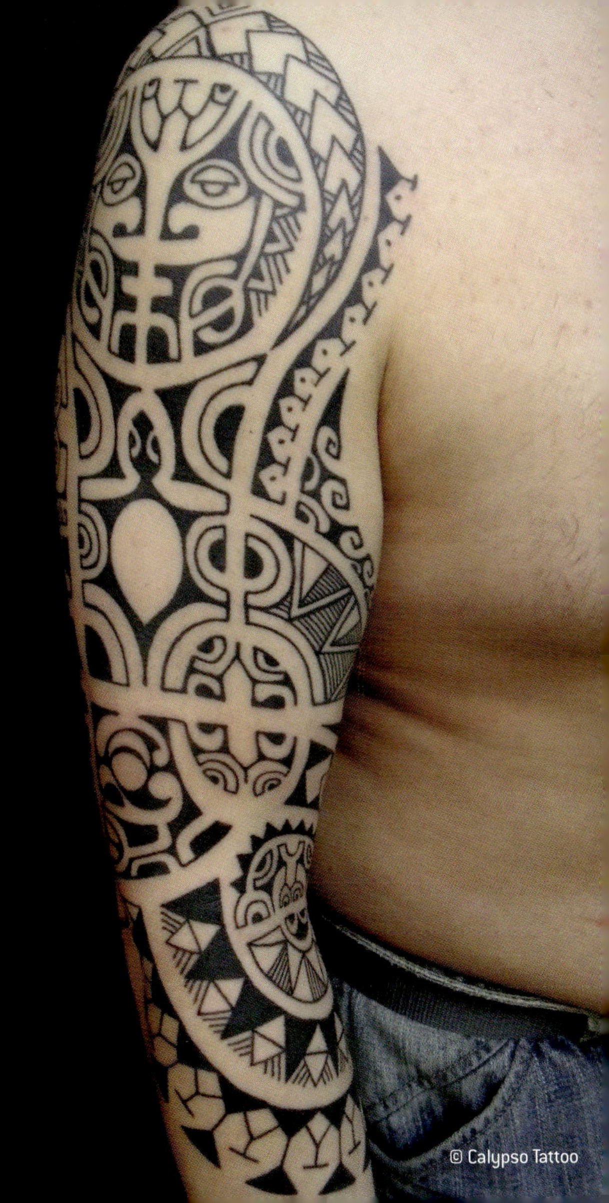
© Calypso Tattoo

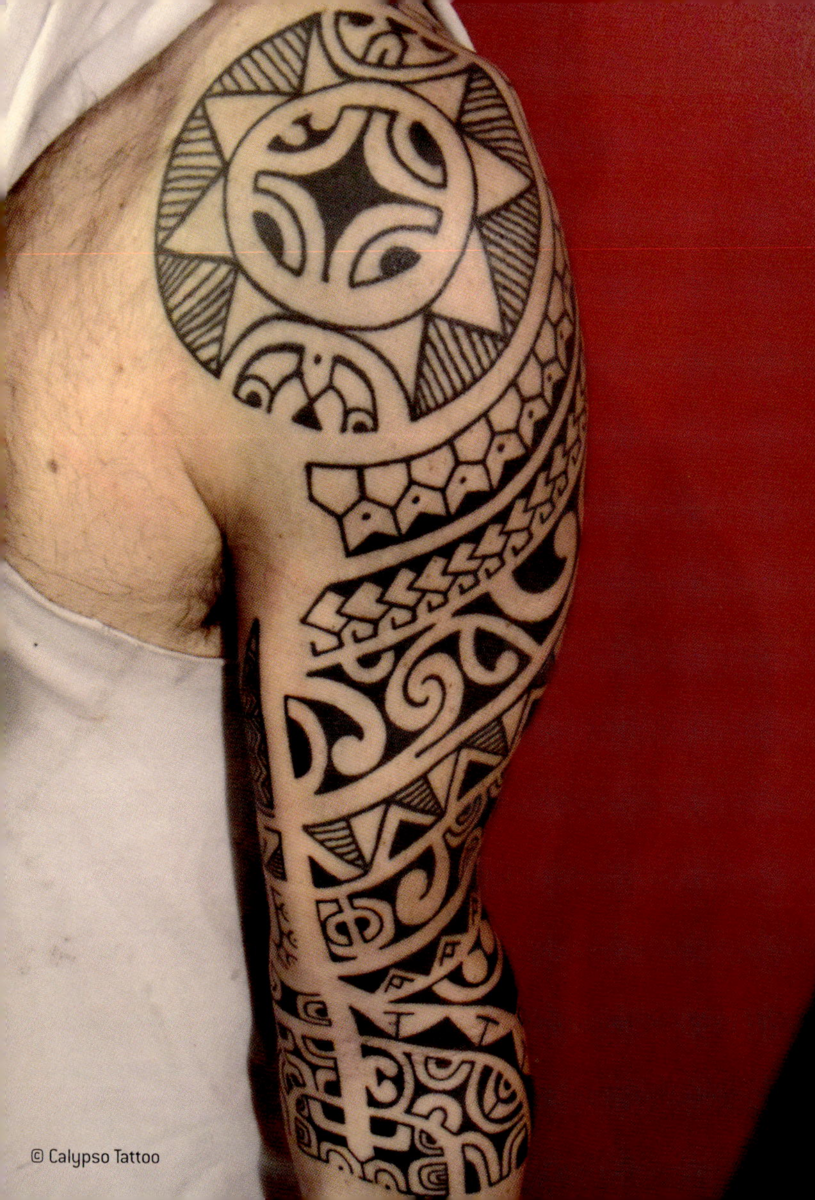

© Calypso Tattoo

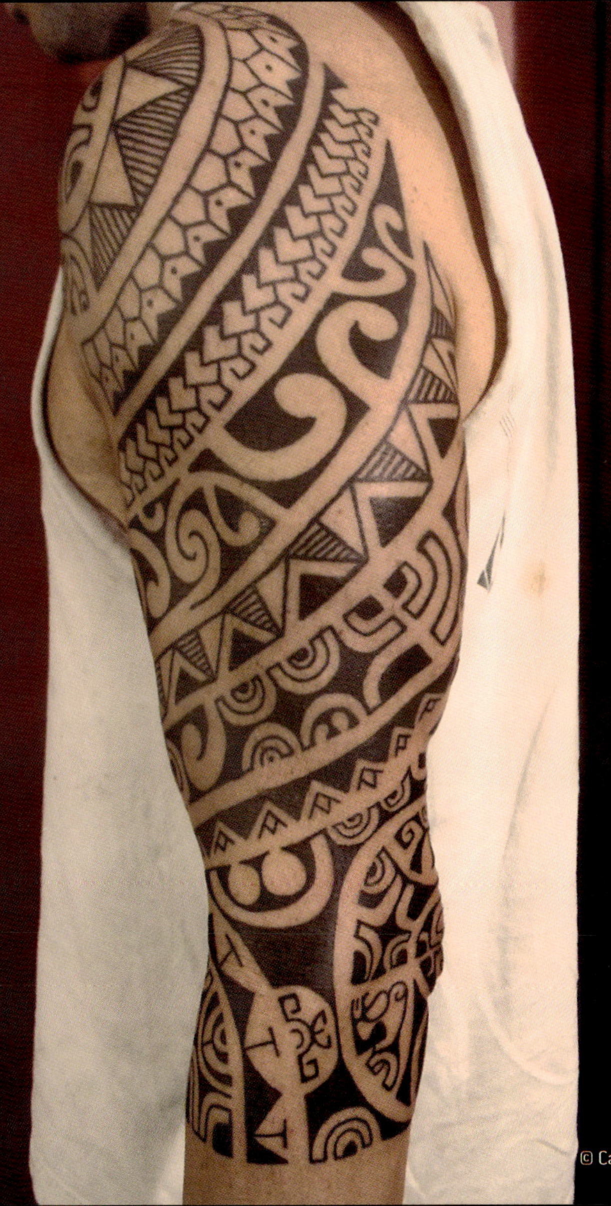

© Calypso Tattoo

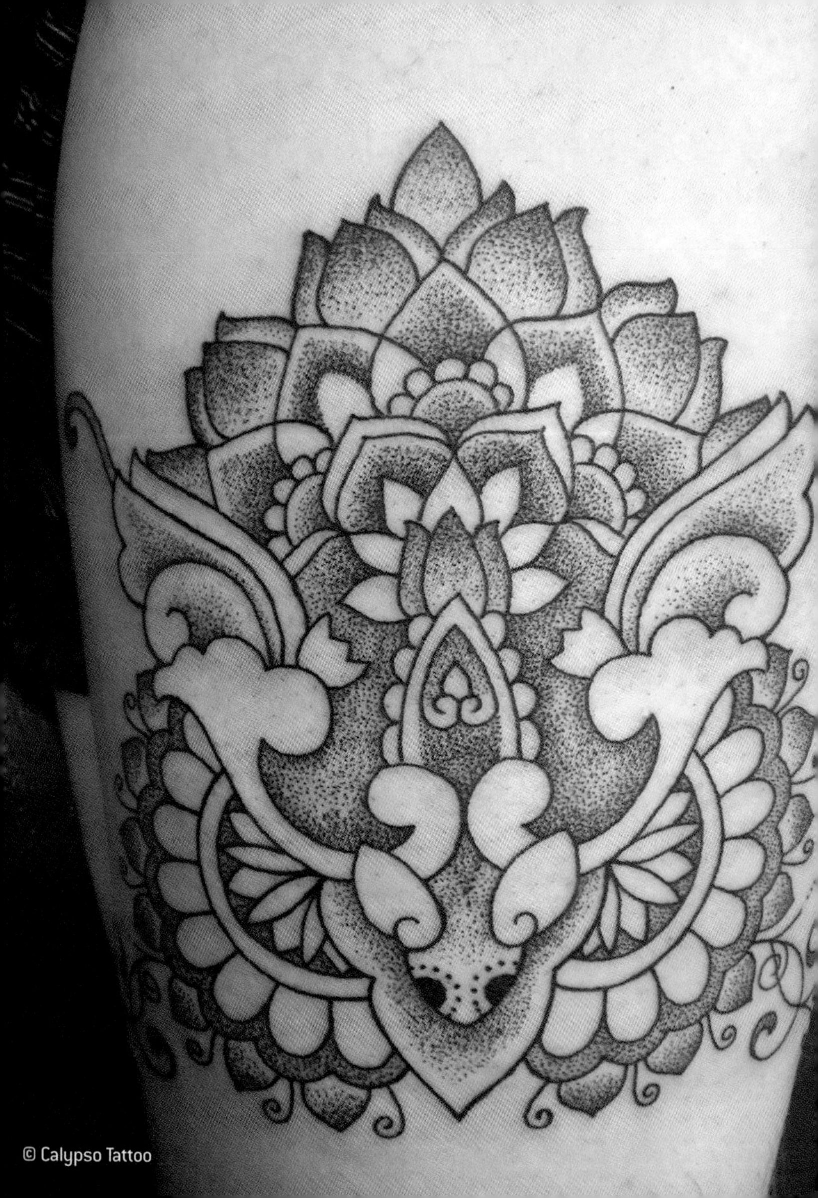
© Calypso Tattoo

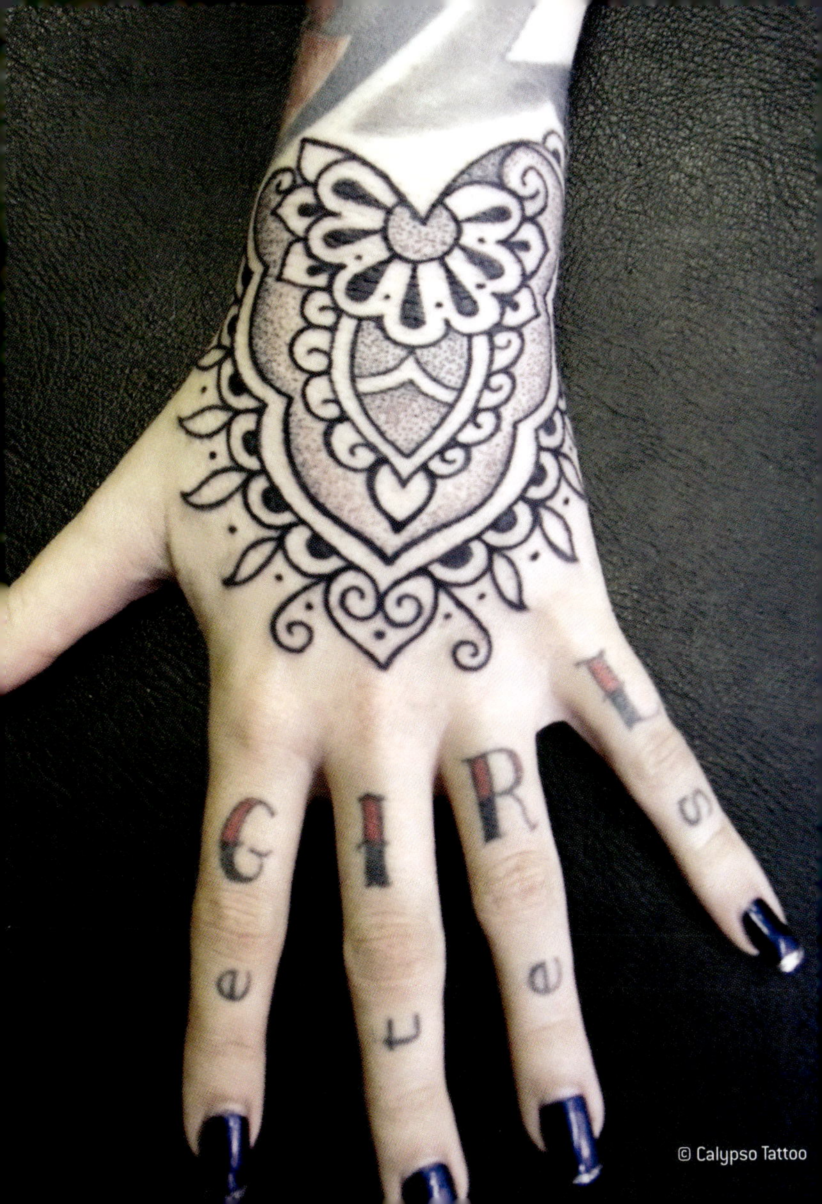

GIRL
S
G
e
t
t
e

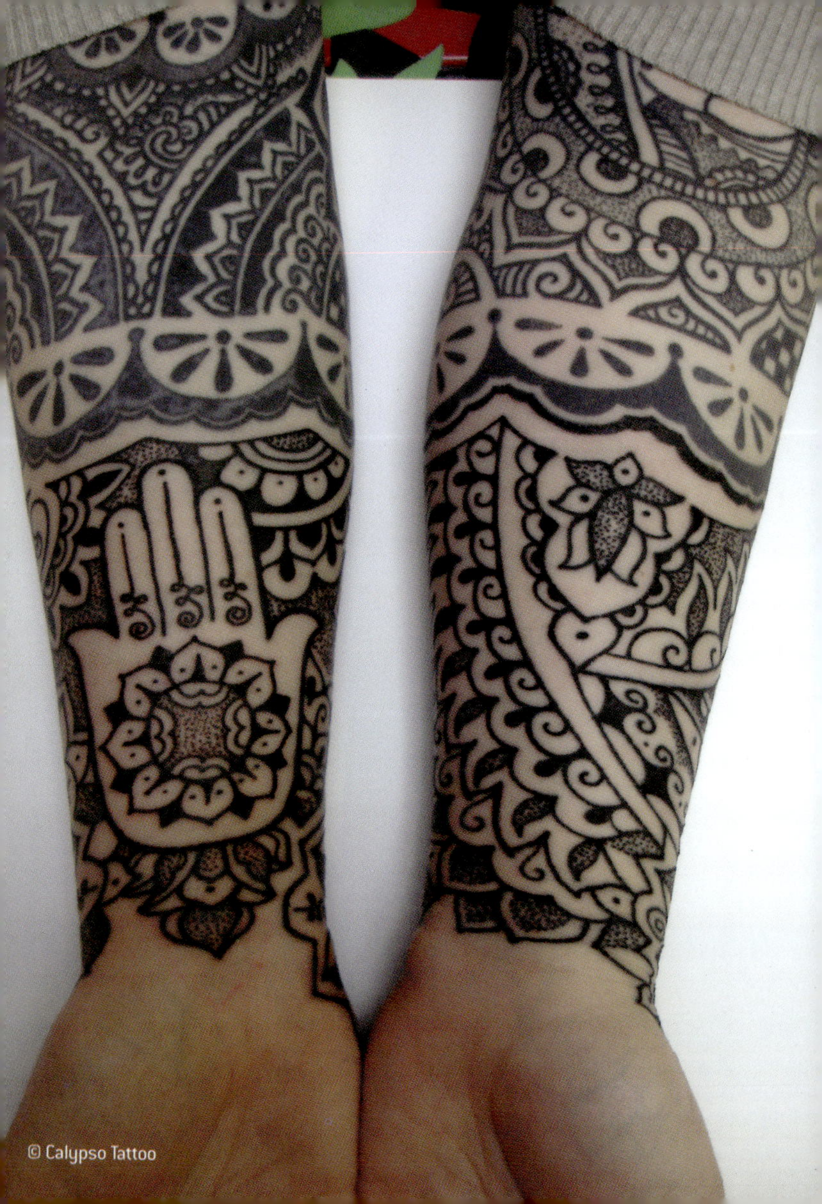
© Calypso Tattoo

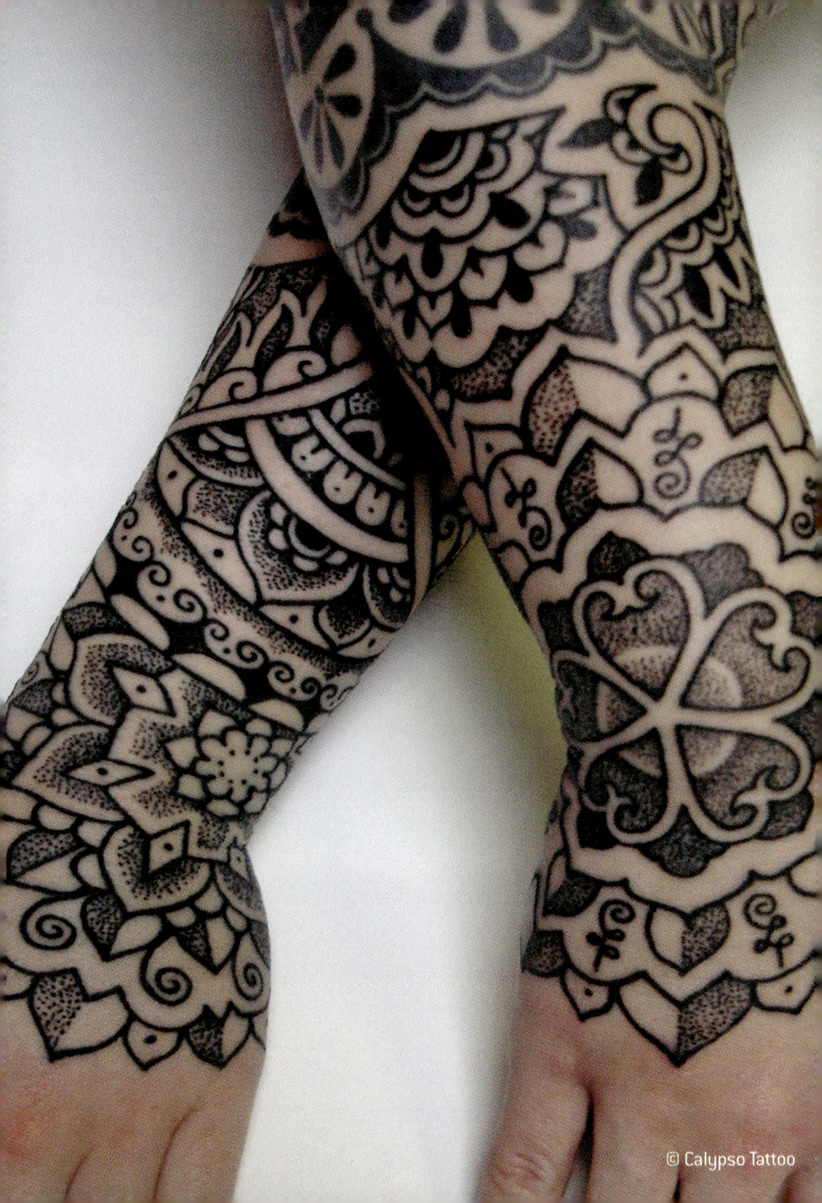
© Calypso Tattoo

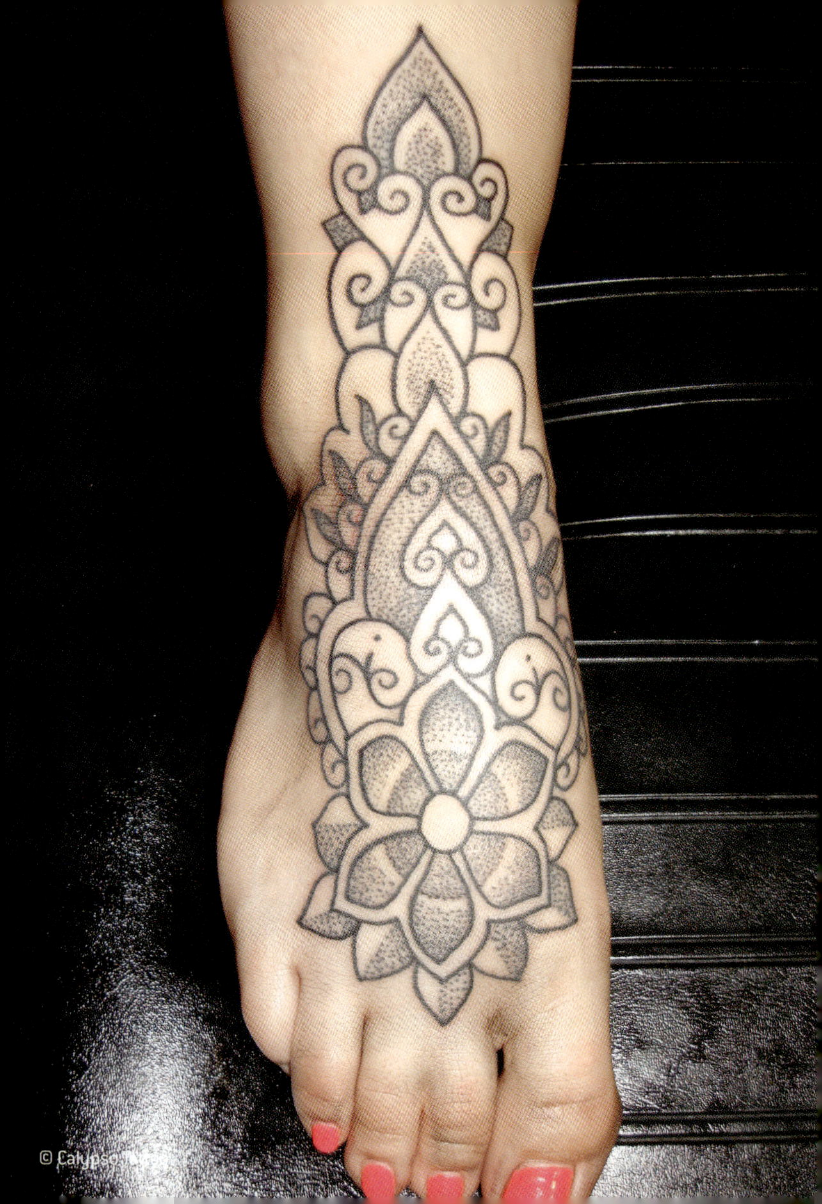
© Calypso Tattoo

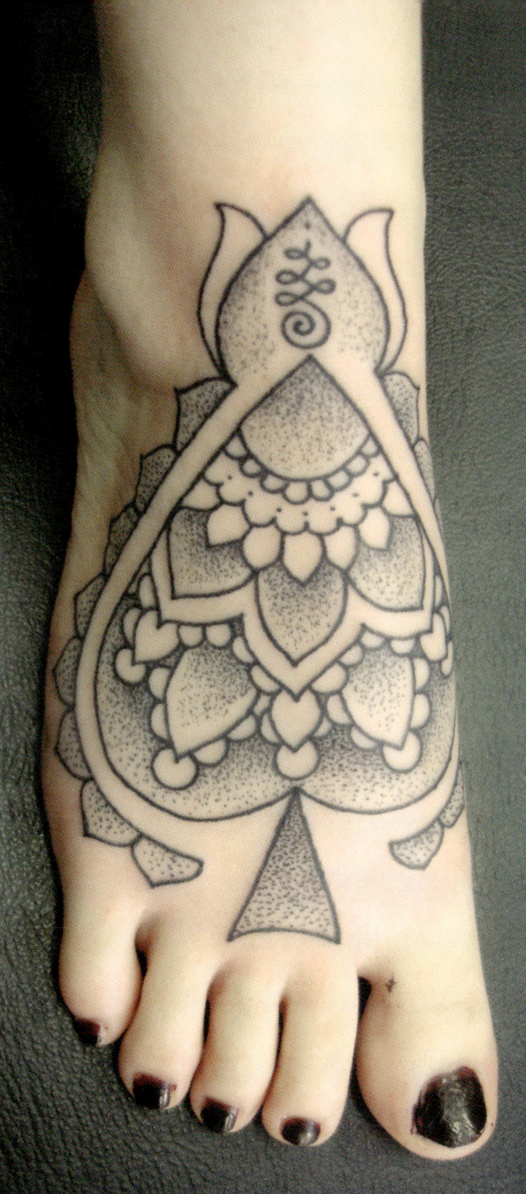
© Calypso Tattoo

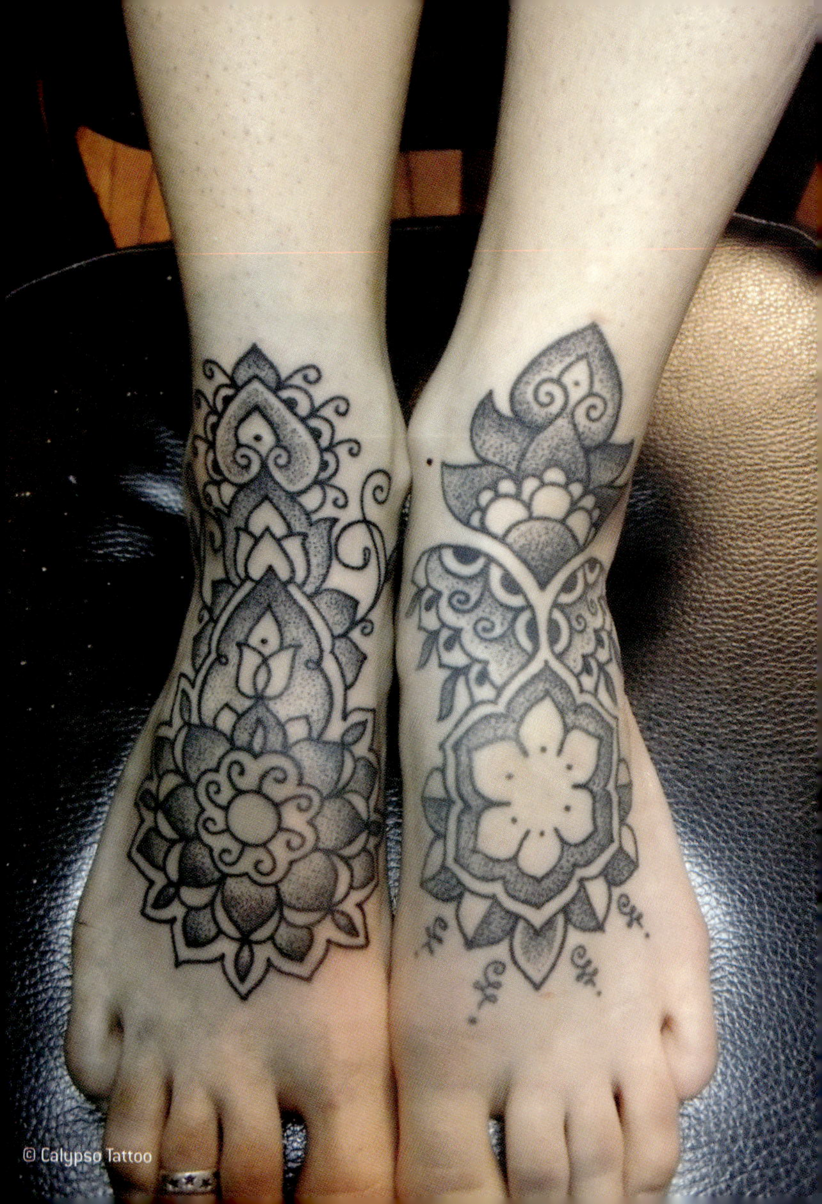
© Calypso Tattoo

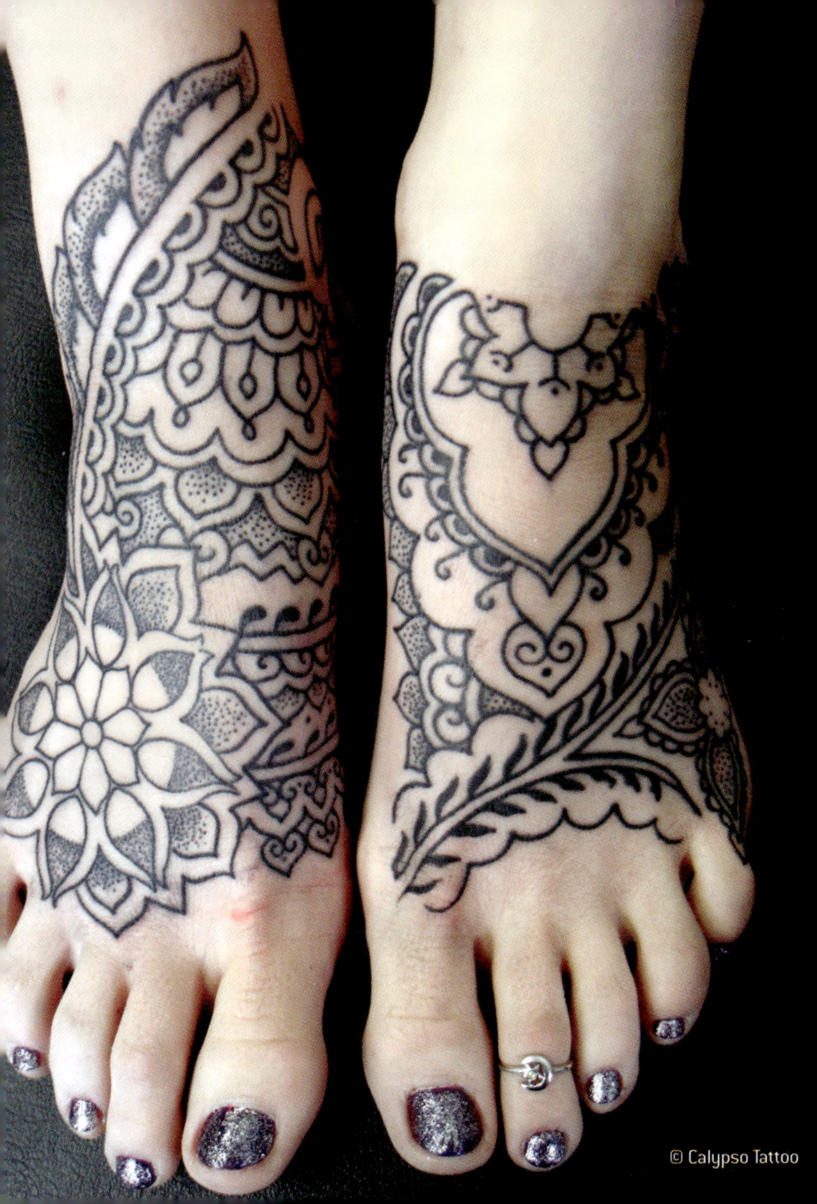
© Calypso Tattoo

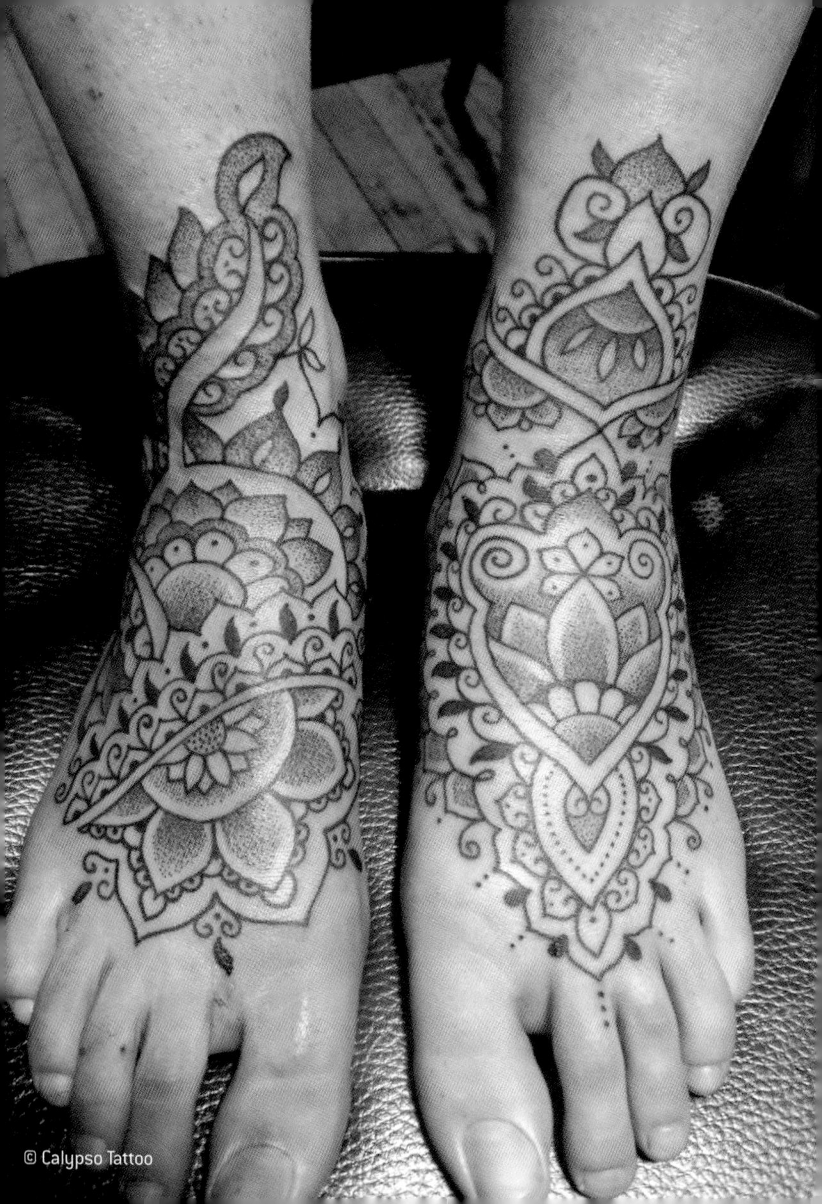
© Calypso Tattoo

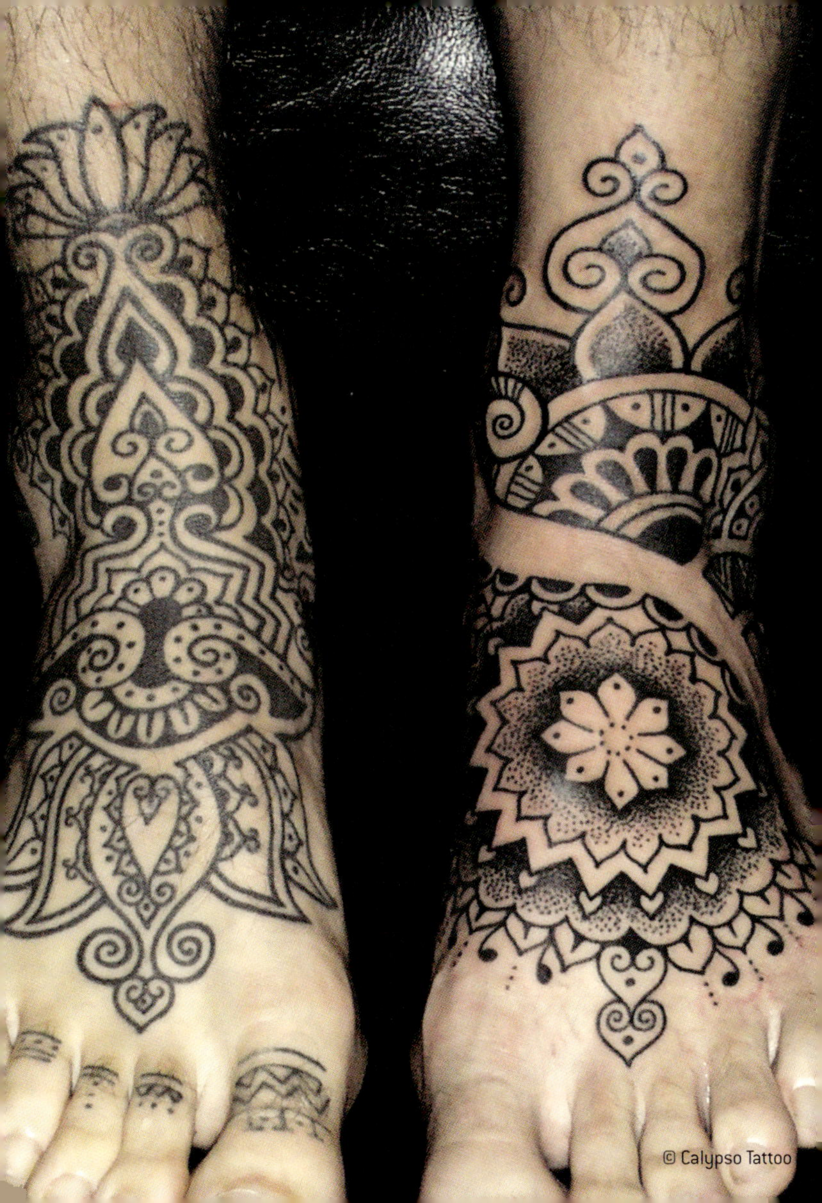
© Calypso Tattoo

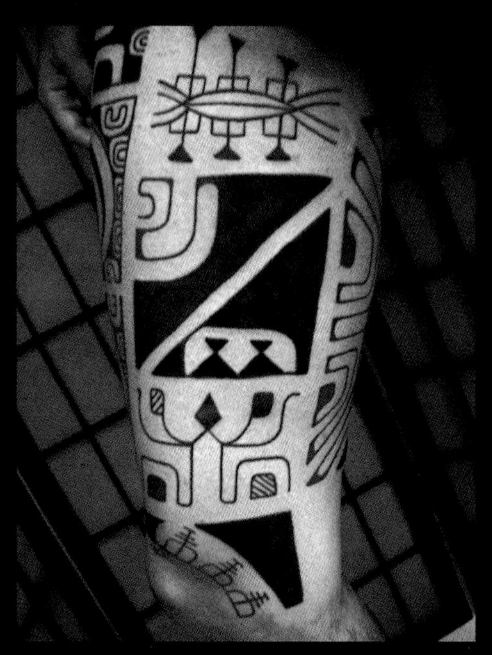

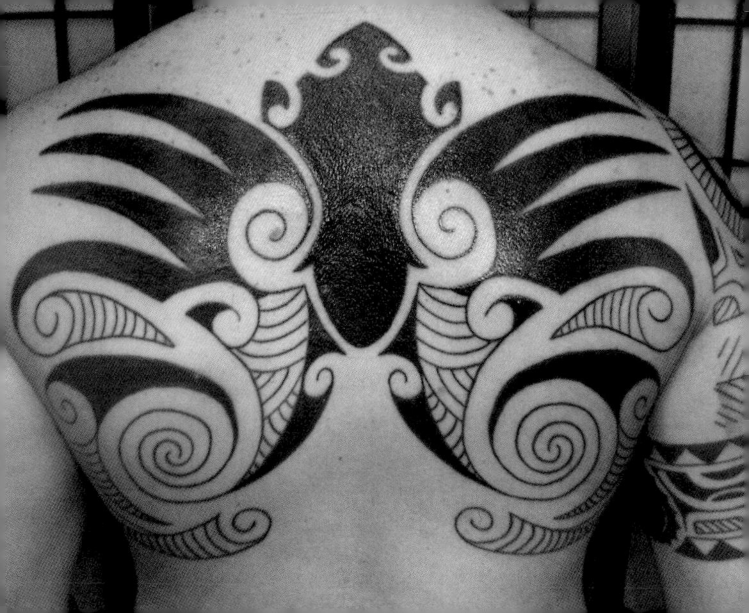

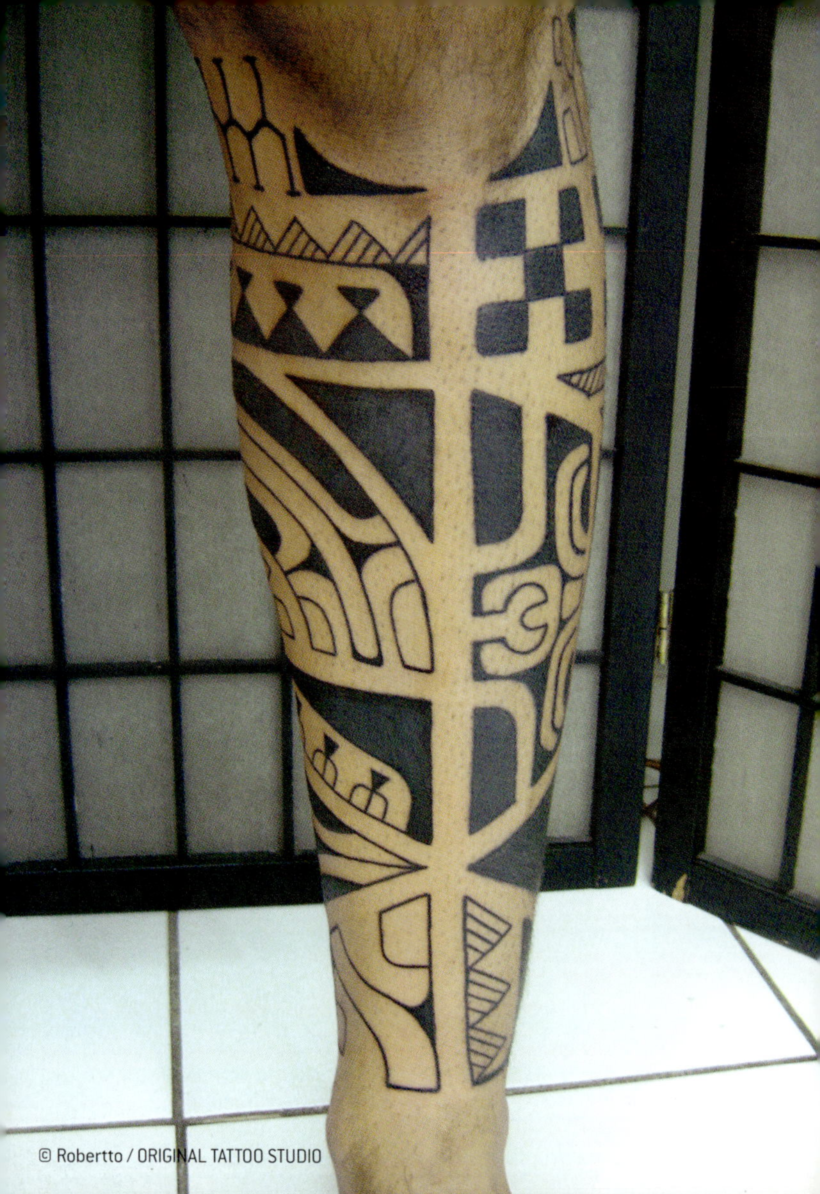

© Robertto / ORIGINAL TATTOO STUDIO

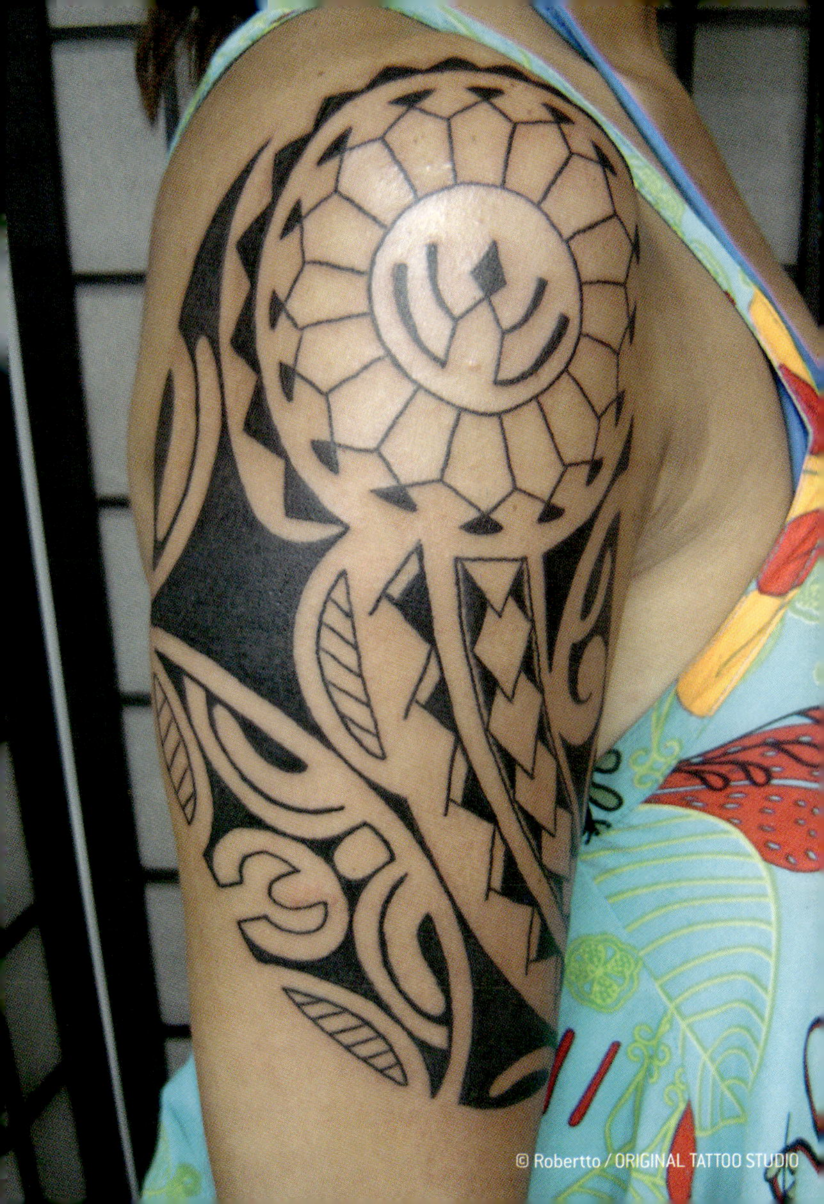
© Robertto / ORIGINAL TATTOO STUDIO

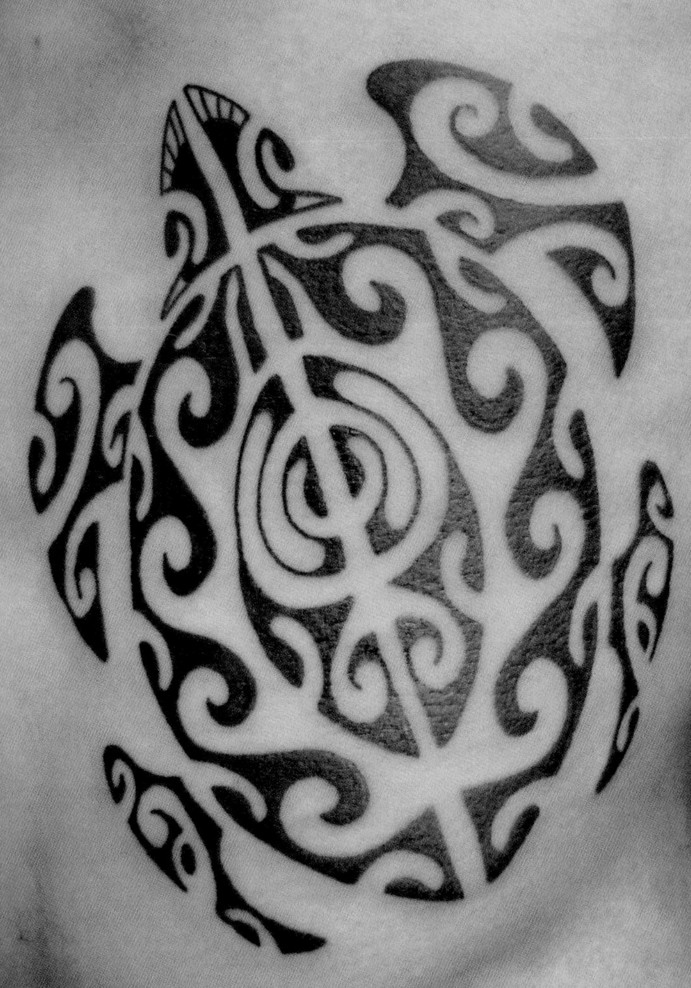

© Robertto / ORIGINAL TATTOO STUDIO

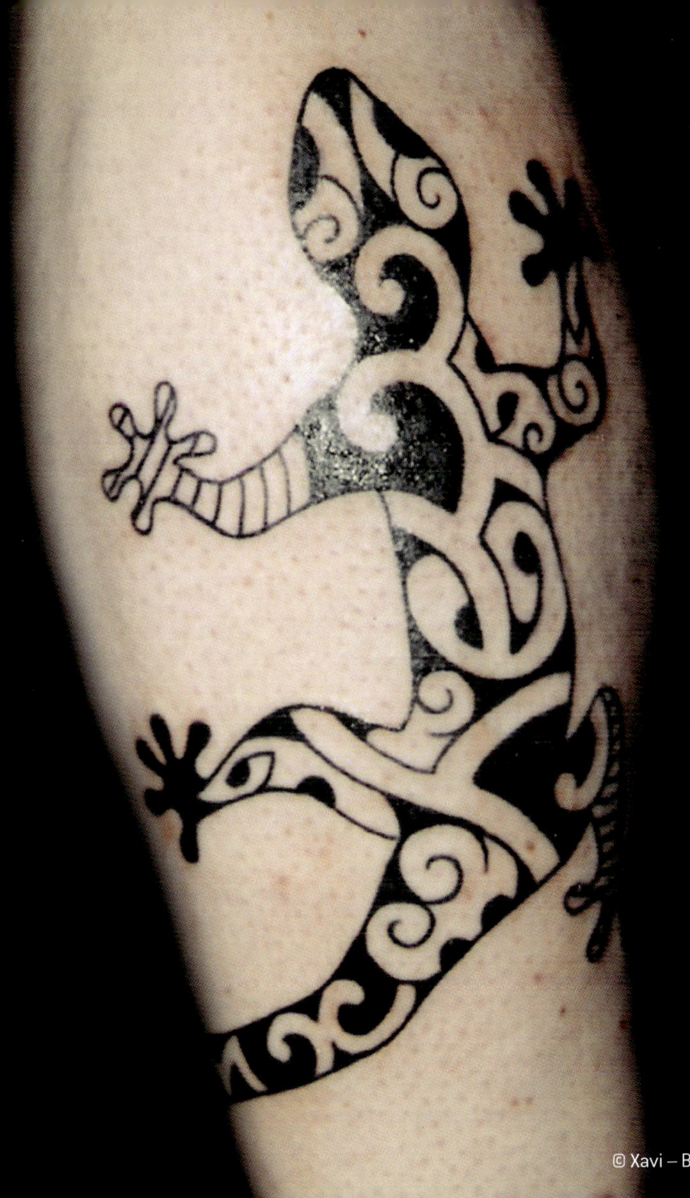

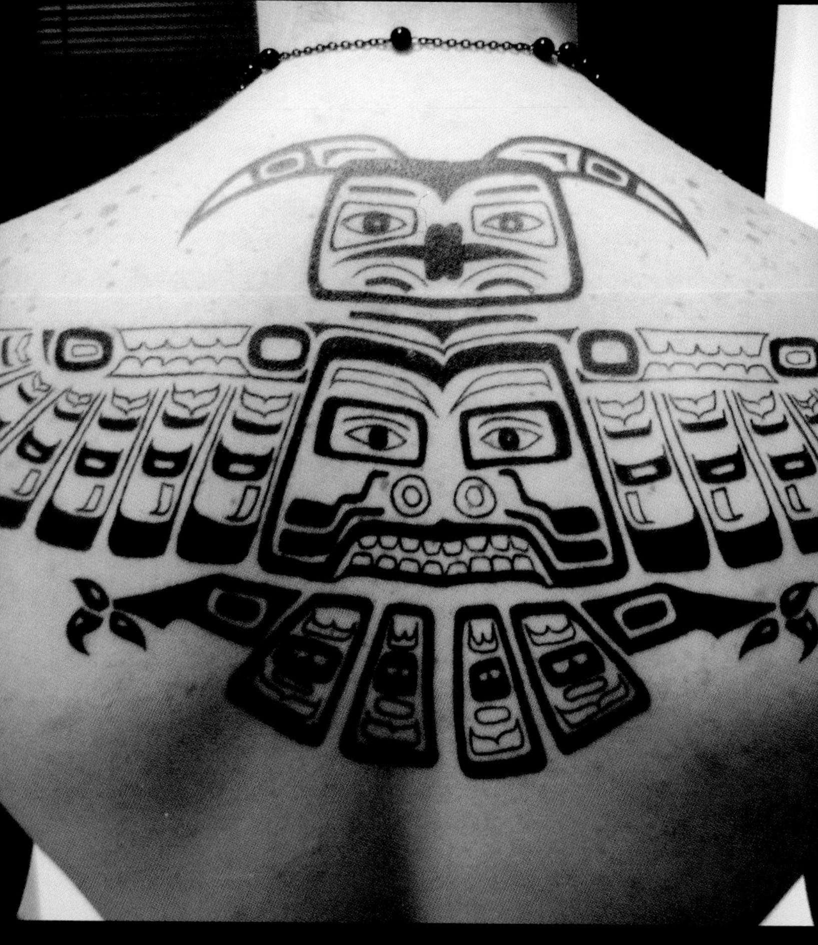

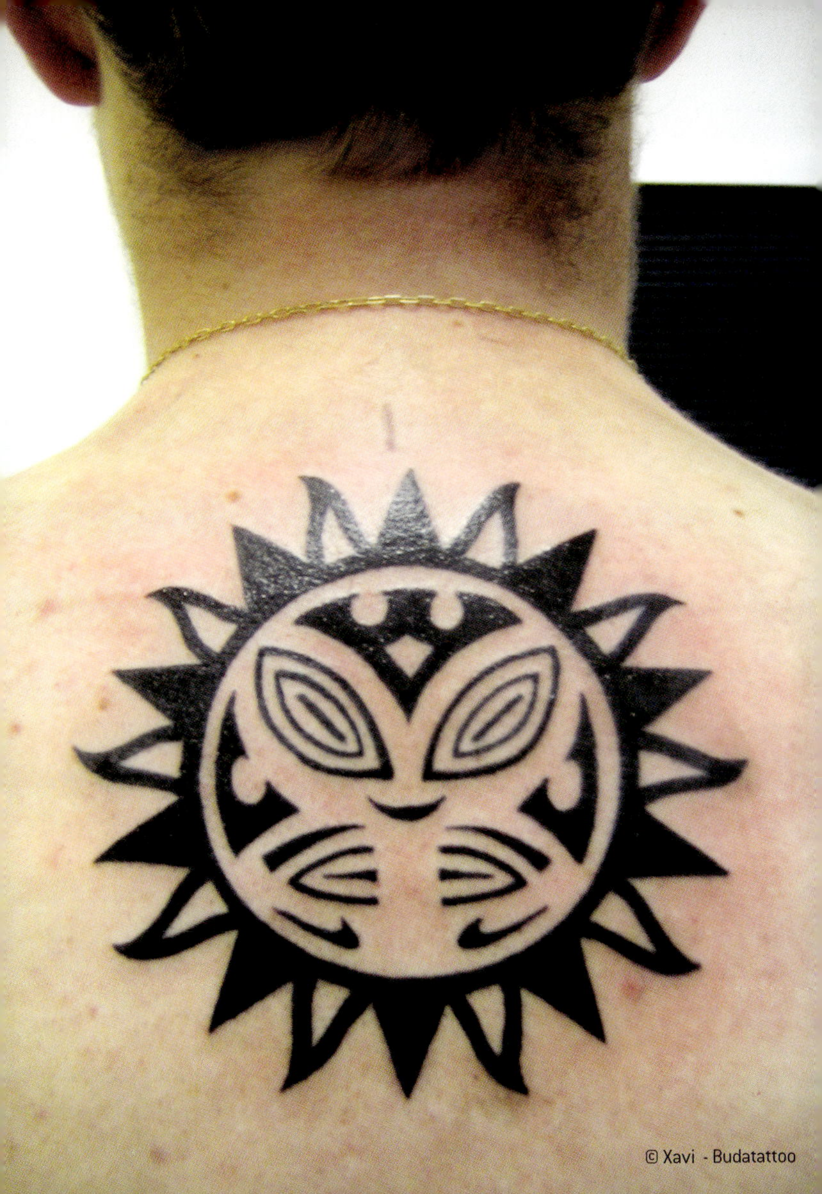
© Xavi - Budatattoo

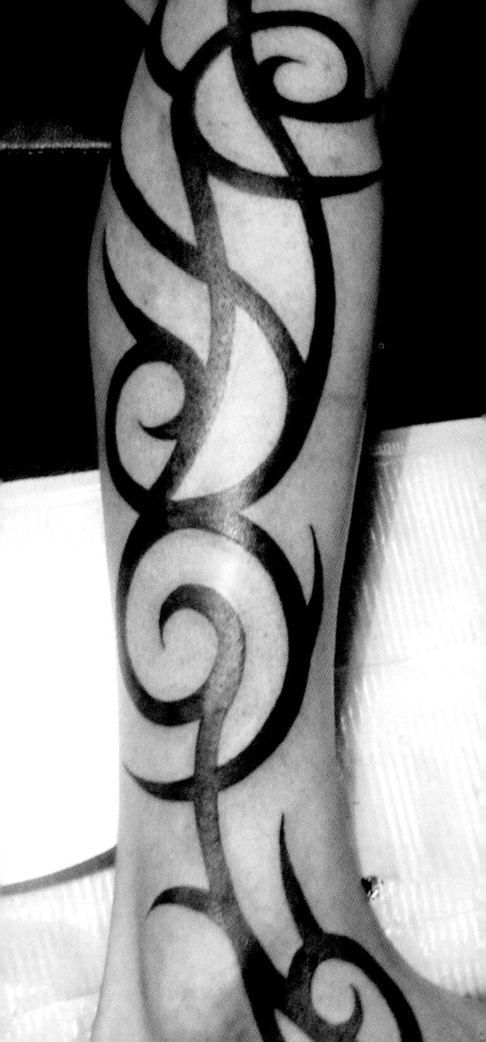

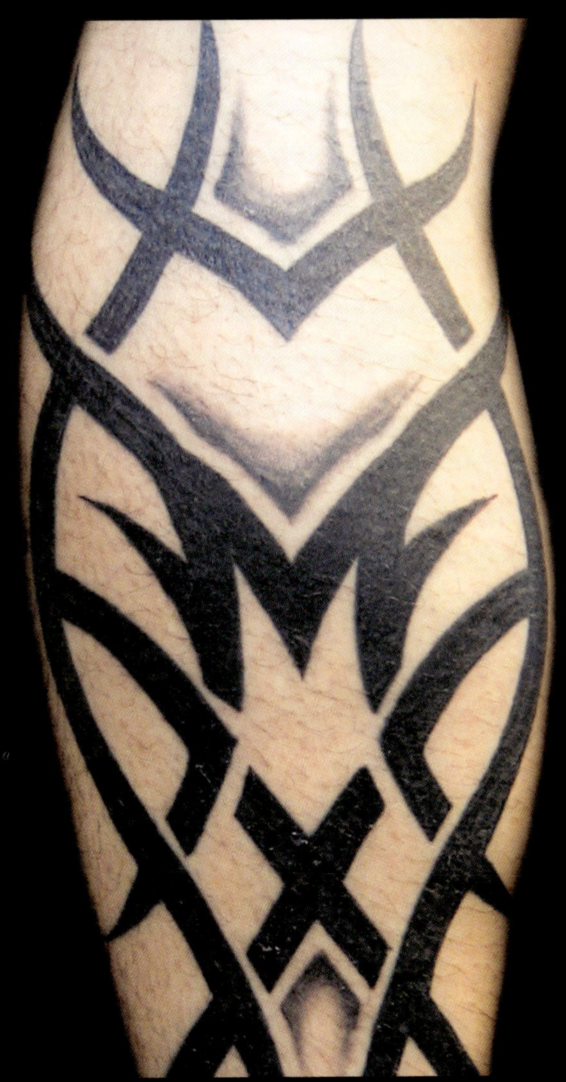

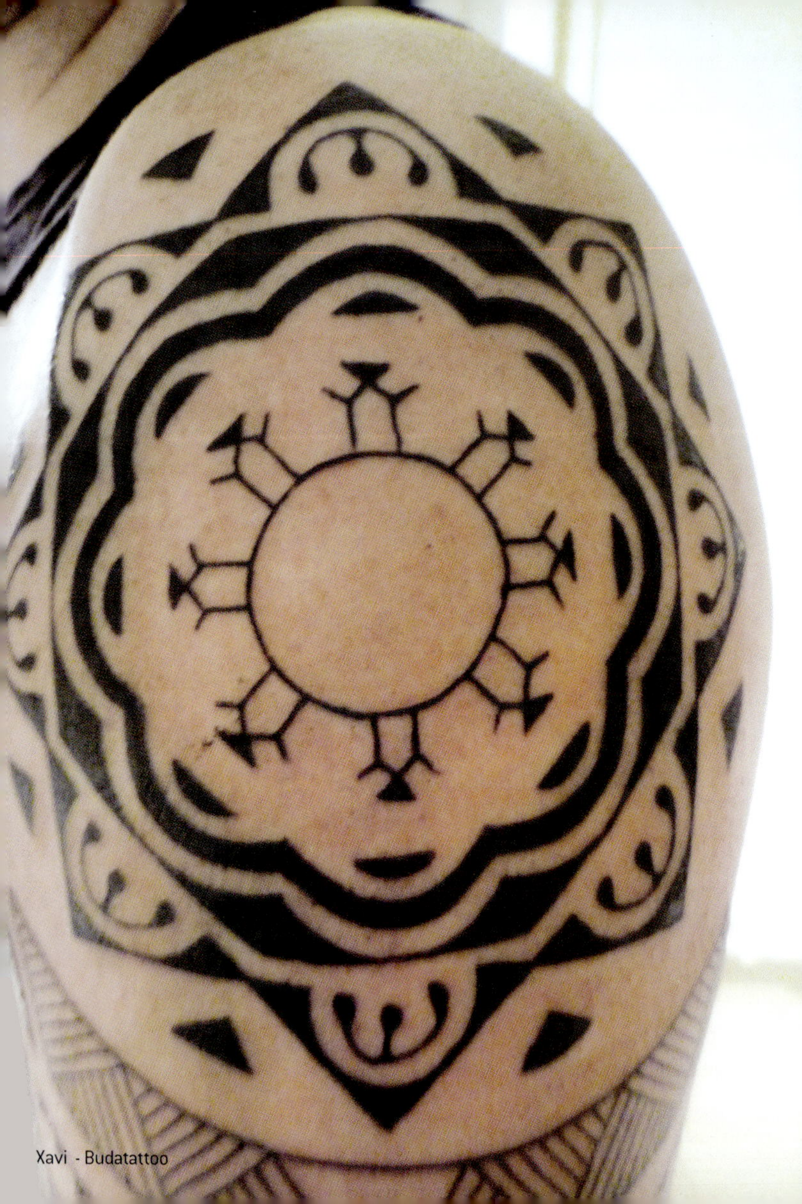

Xavi - Budatattoo

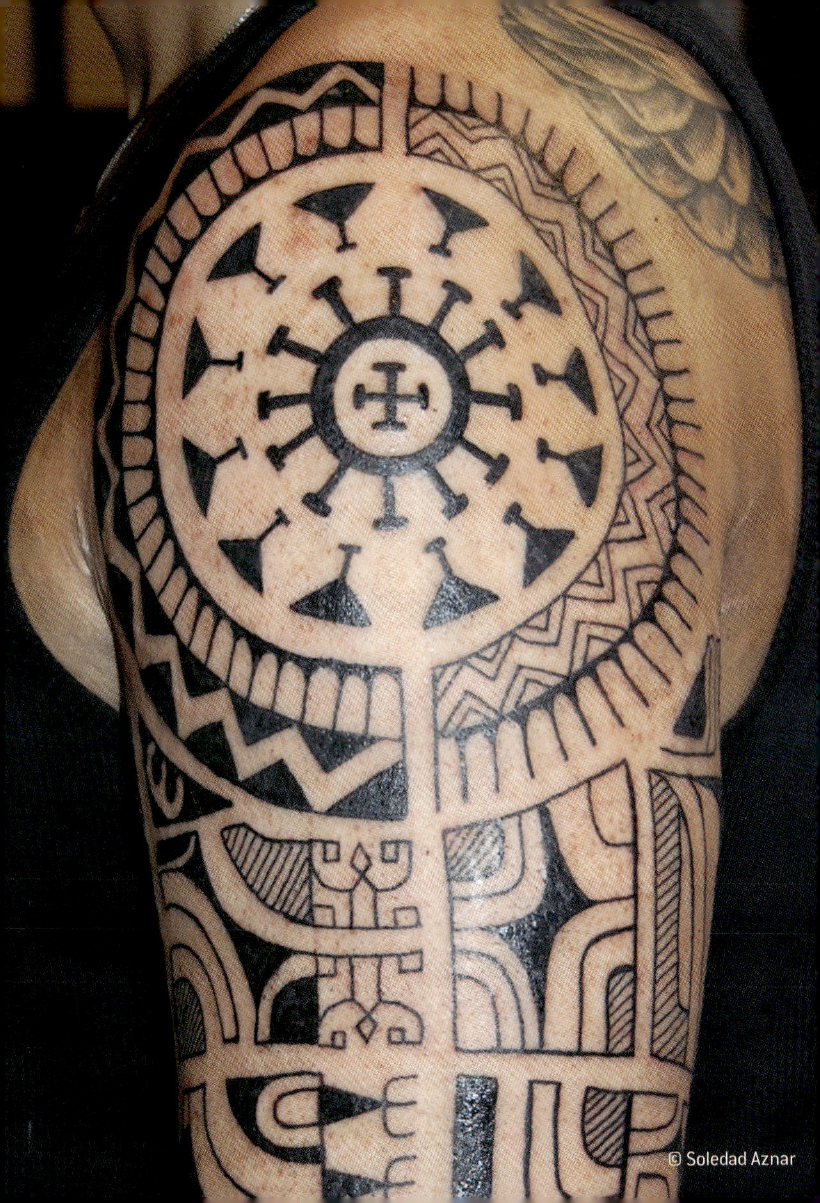

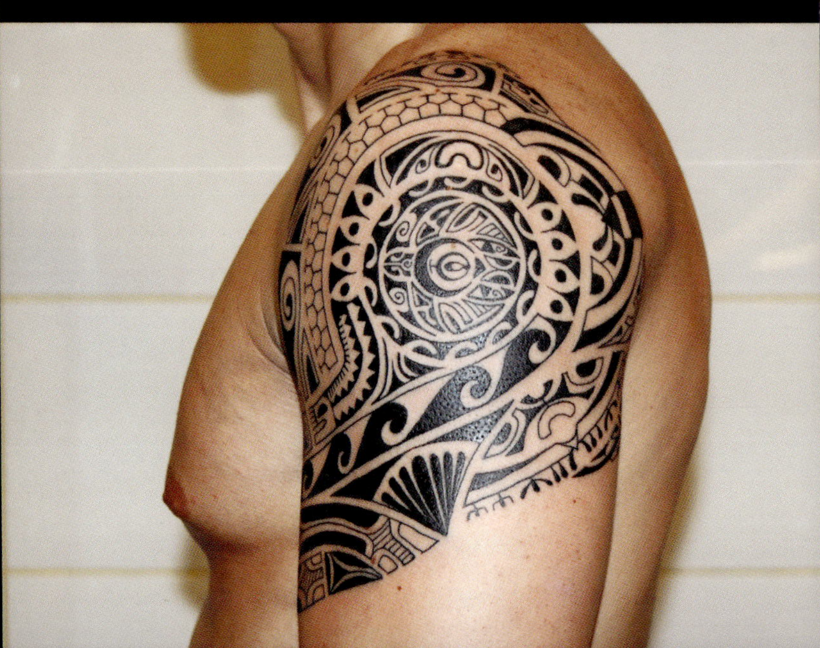

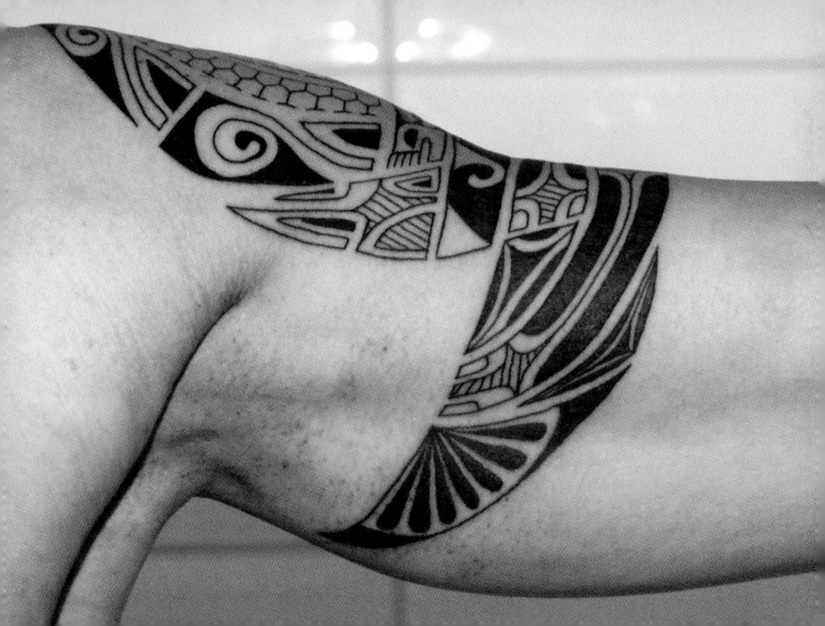

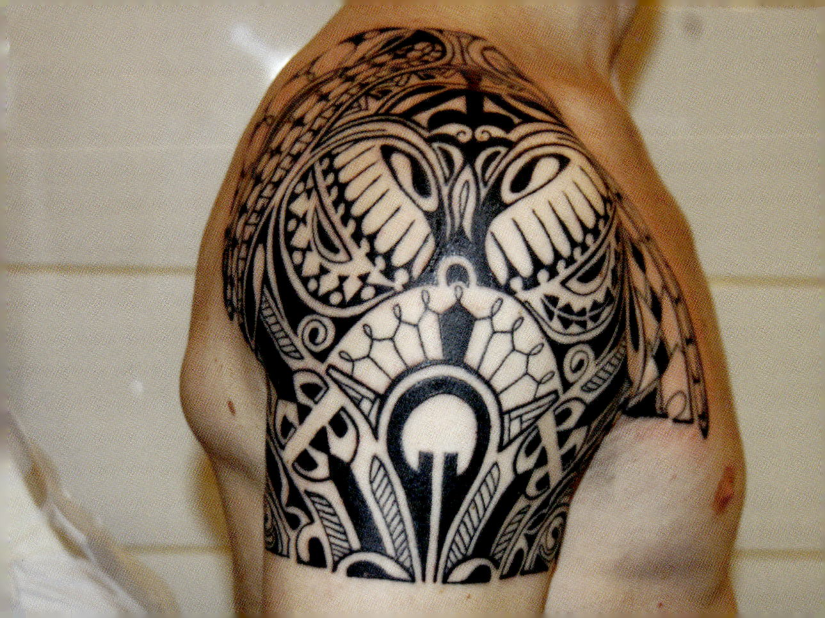

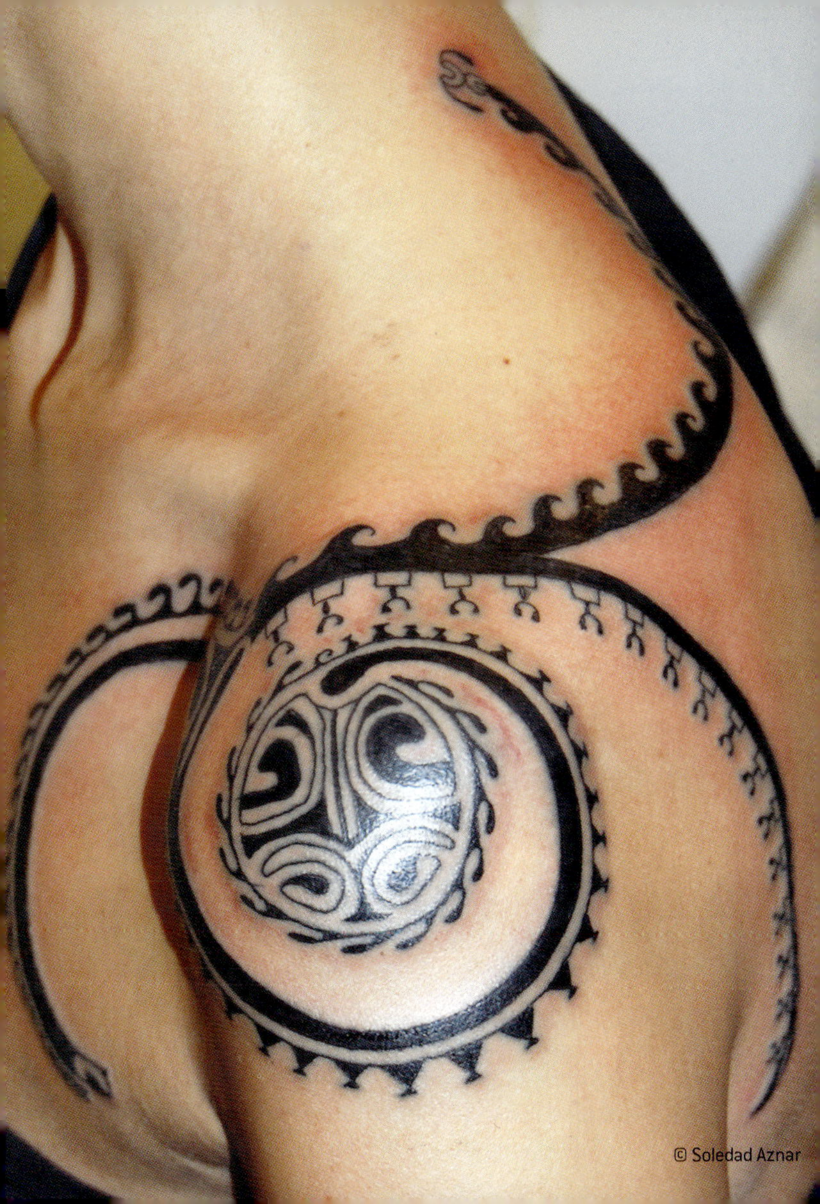

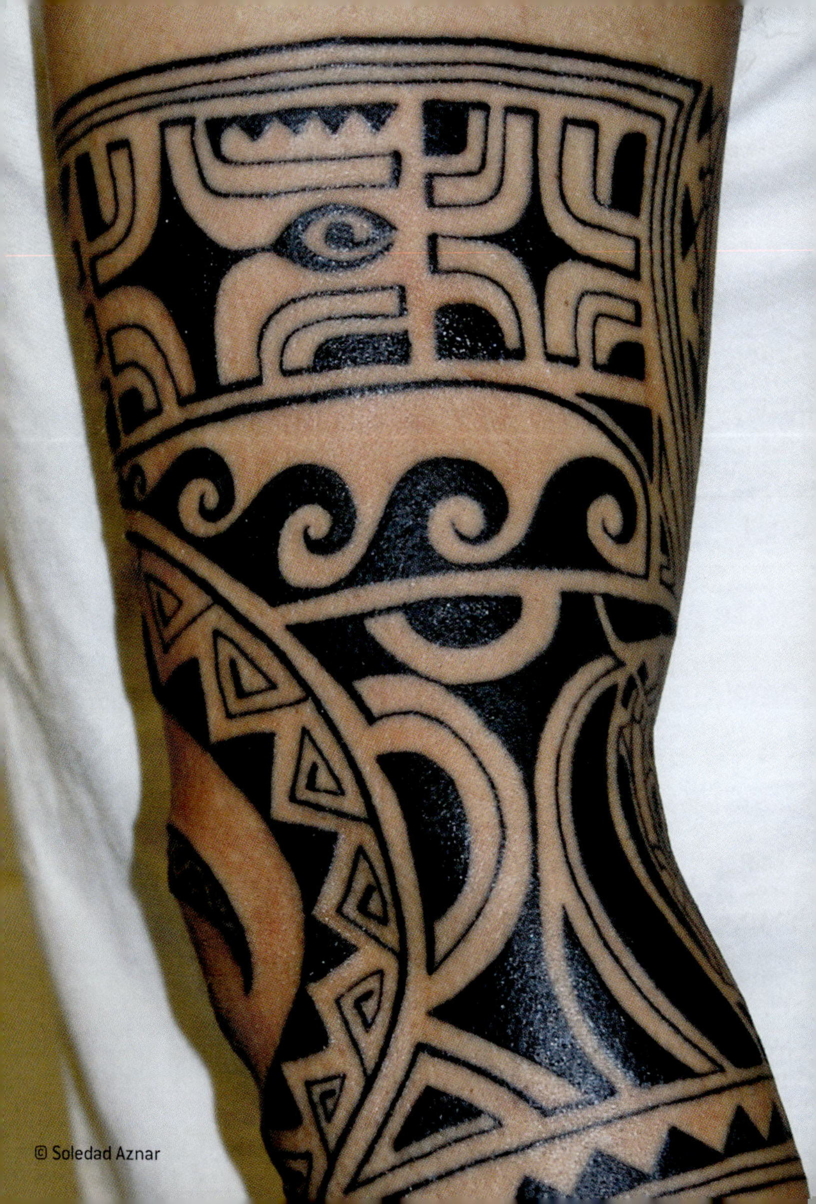

© Soledad Aznar

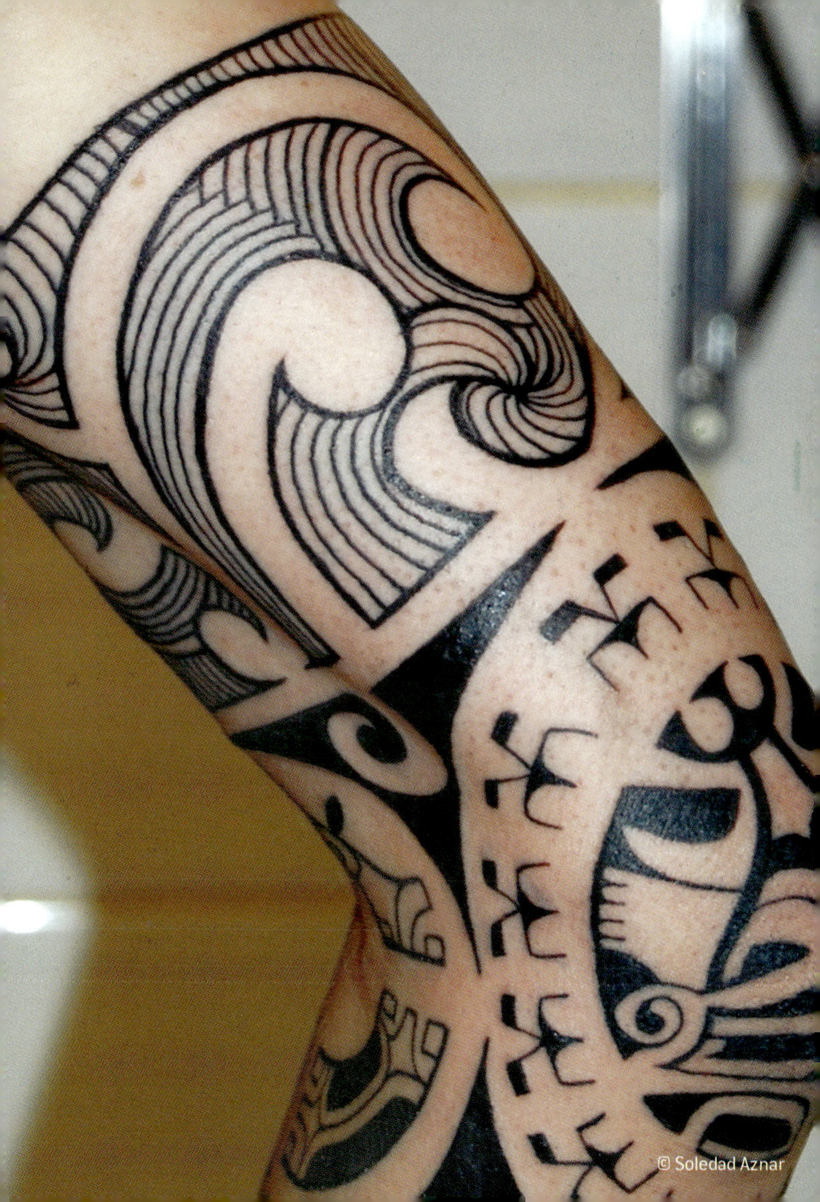

© Soledad Aznar

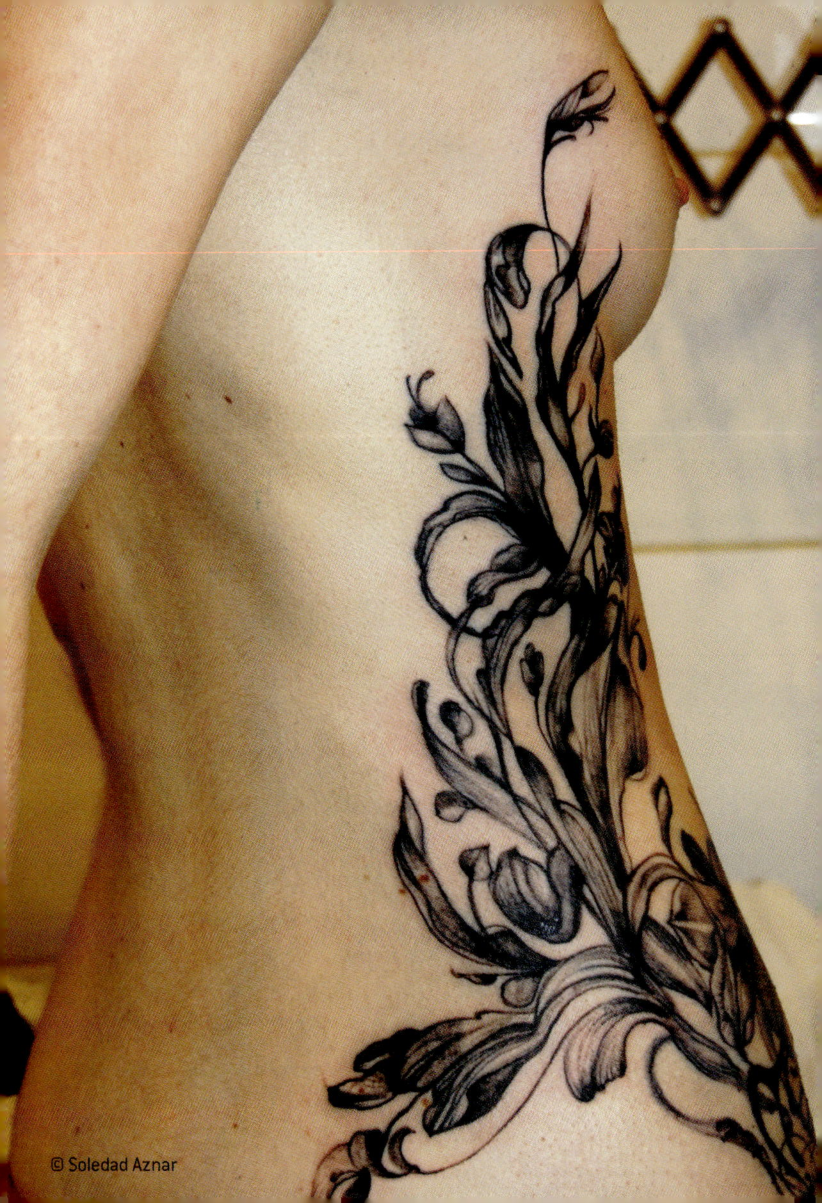

© Soledad Aznar

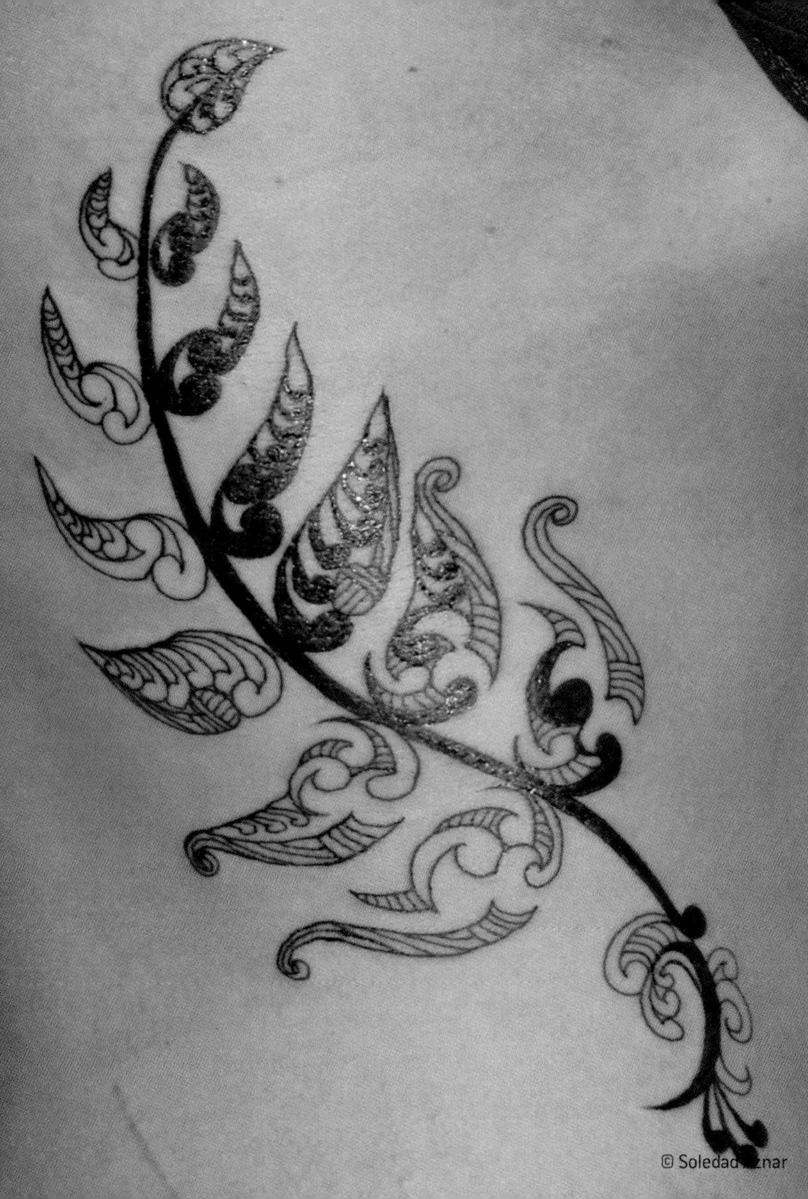
© Soledad Aznar

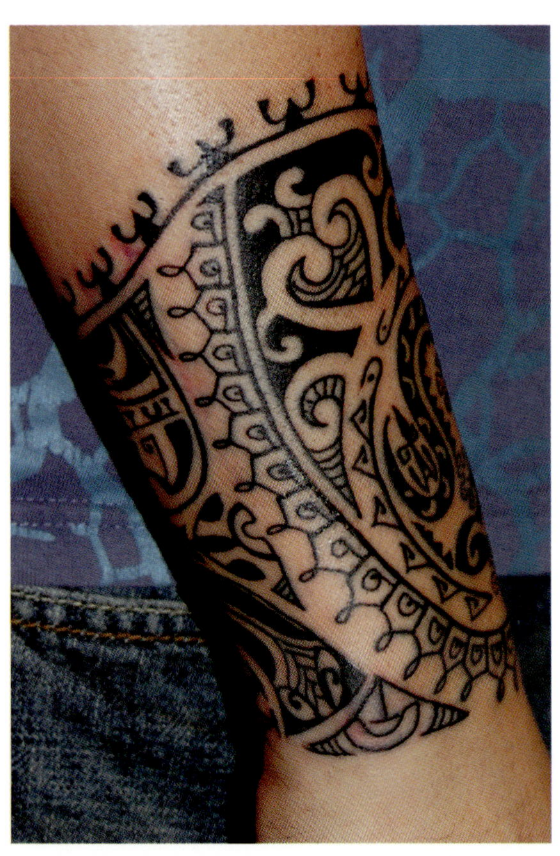

© Soledad Aznar

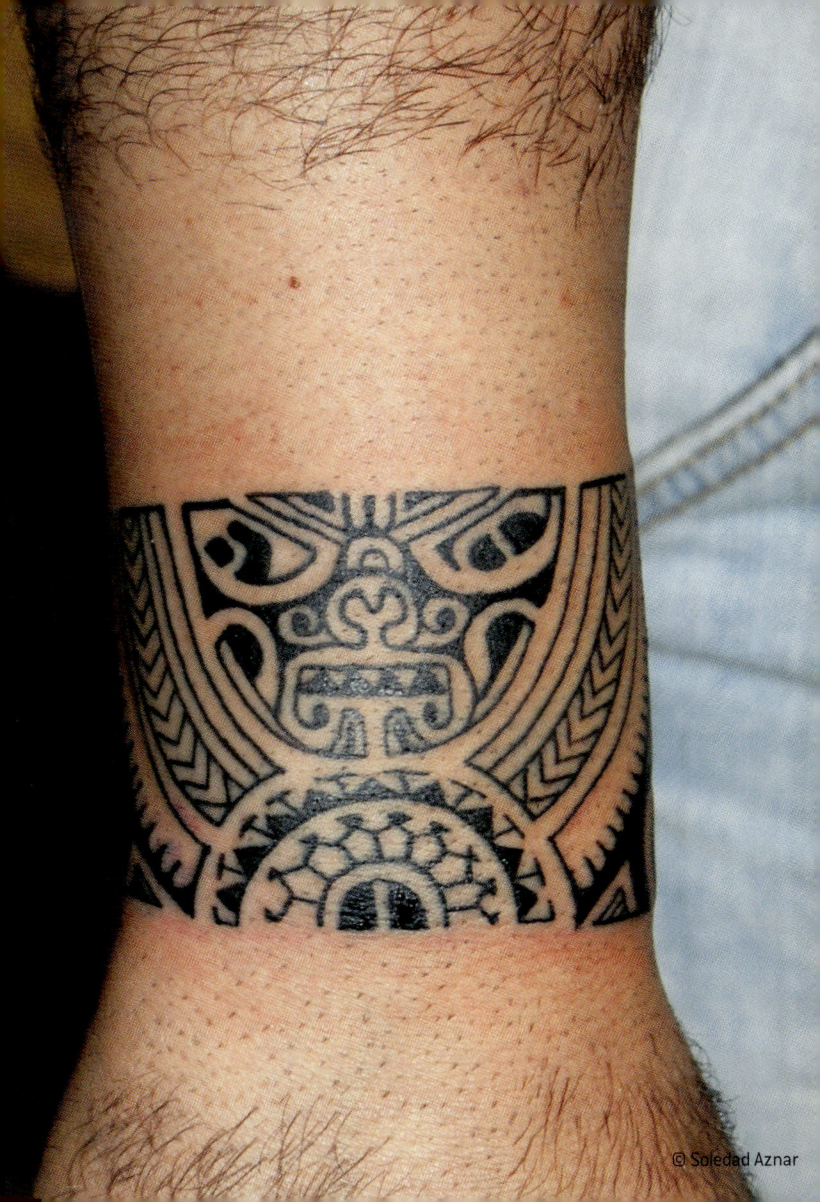

© Soledad Aznar

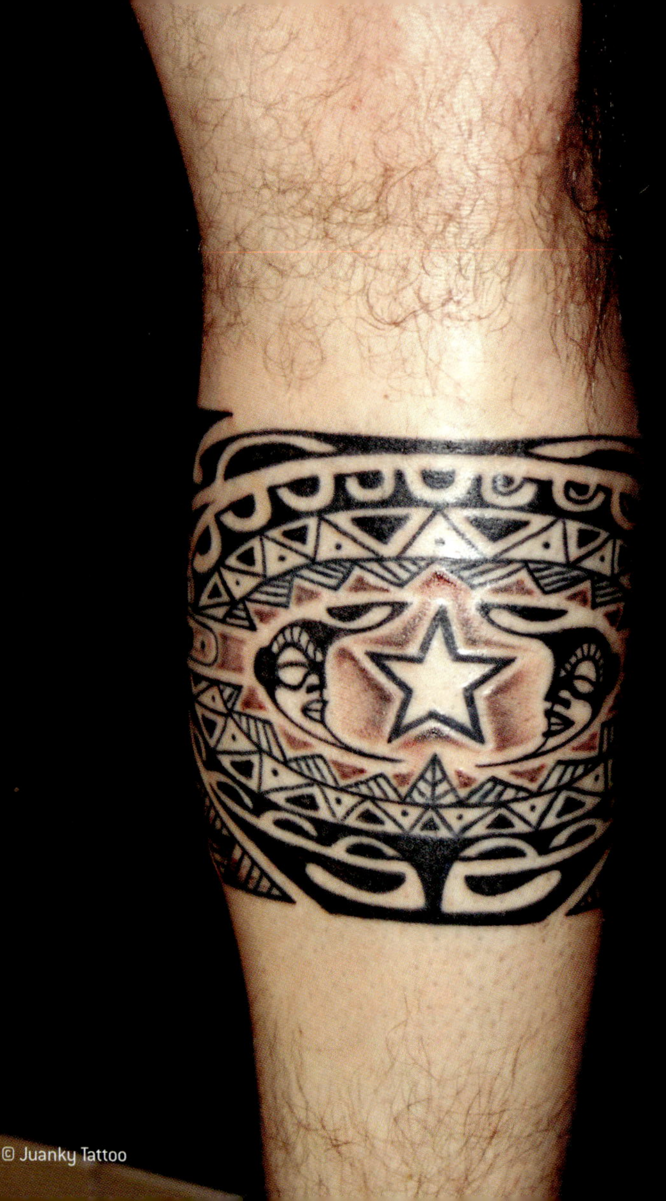
© Juanky Tattoo

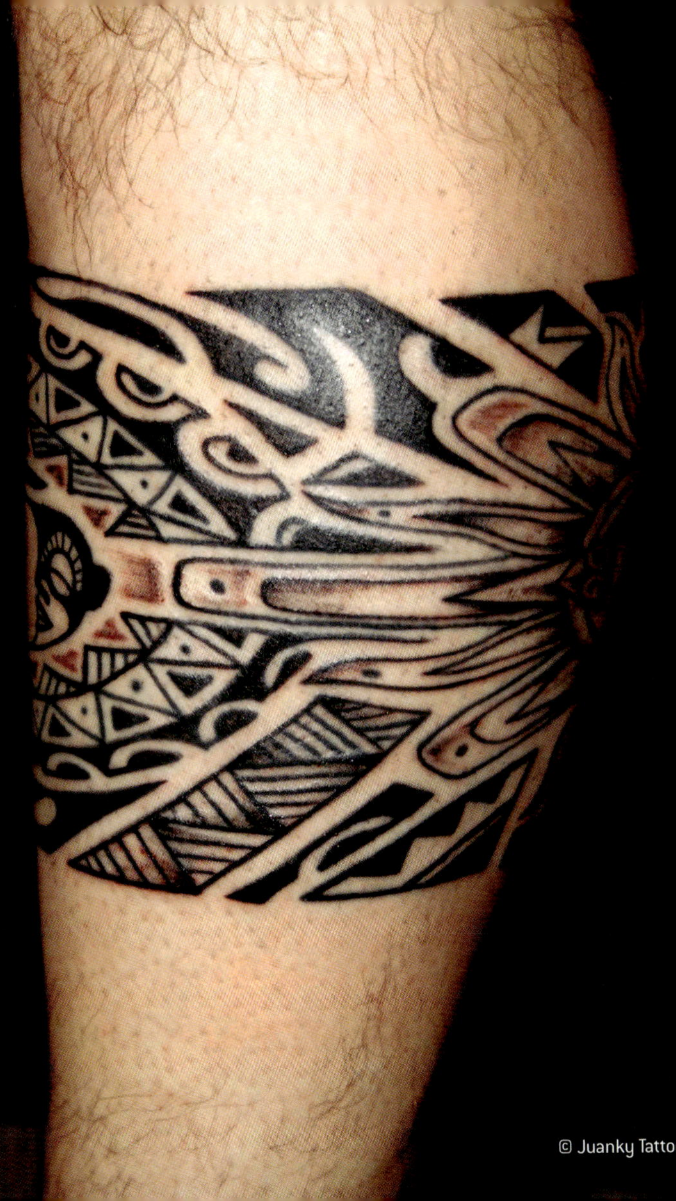
© Juanky Tattoo

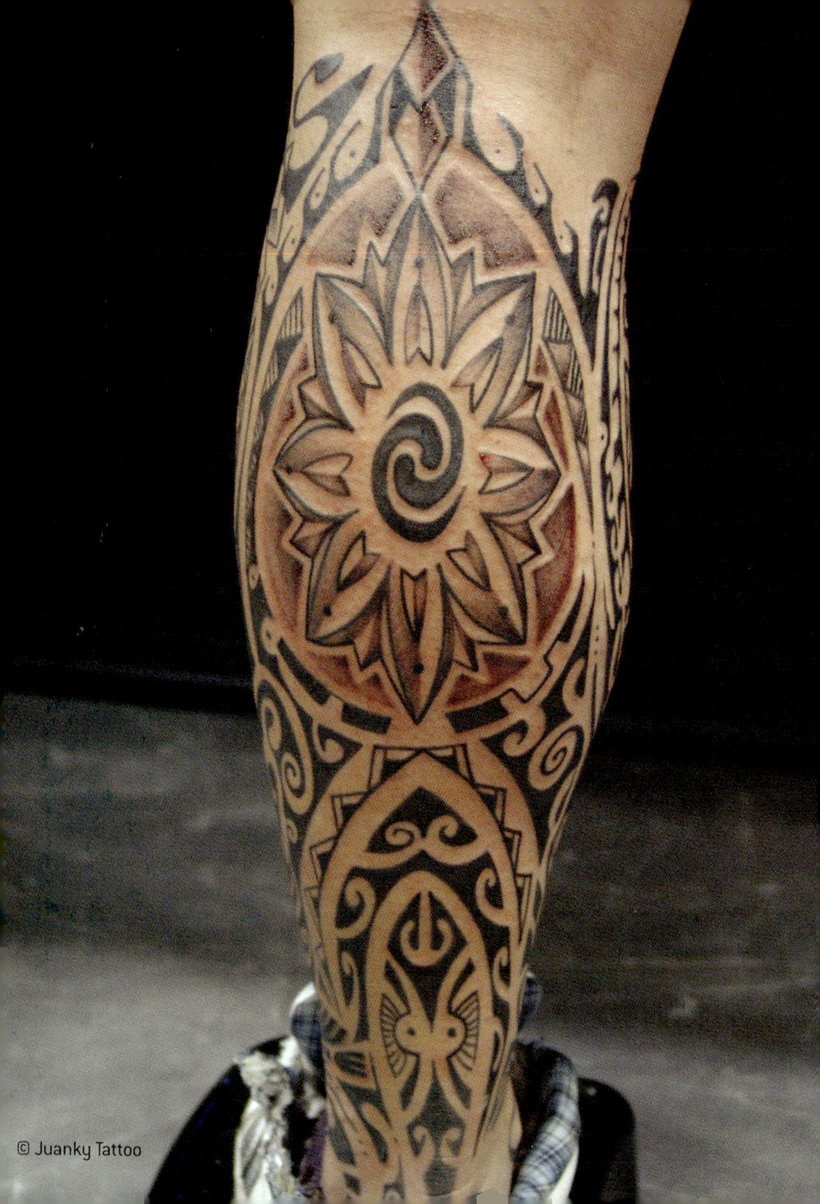

© Juanky Tattoo

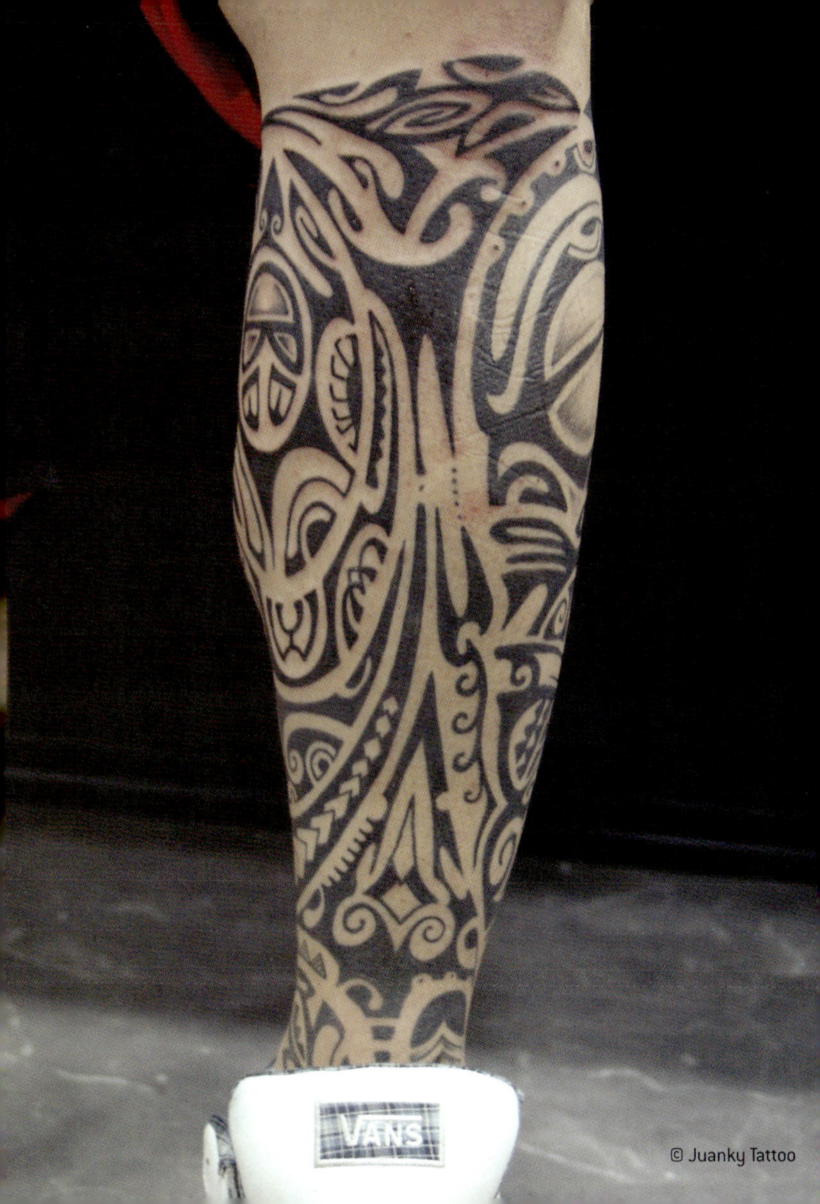

© Juanky Tattoo

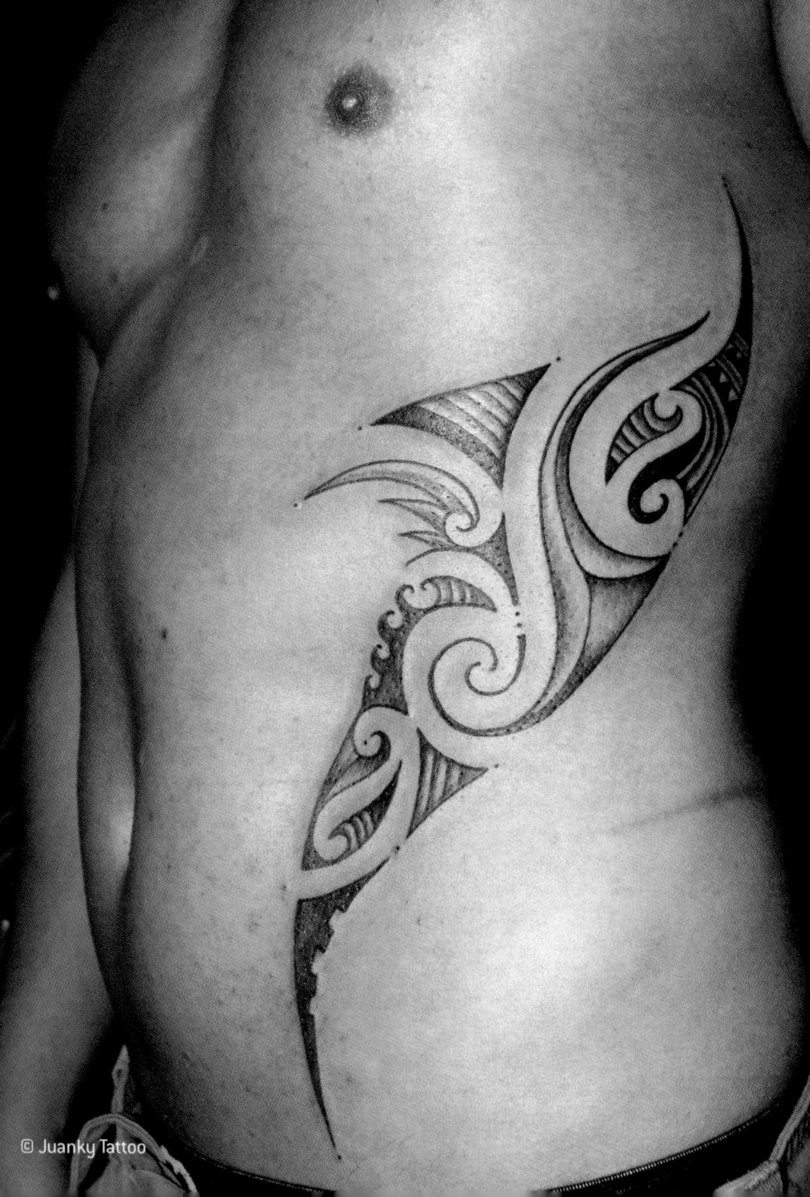
© Juanky Tattoo

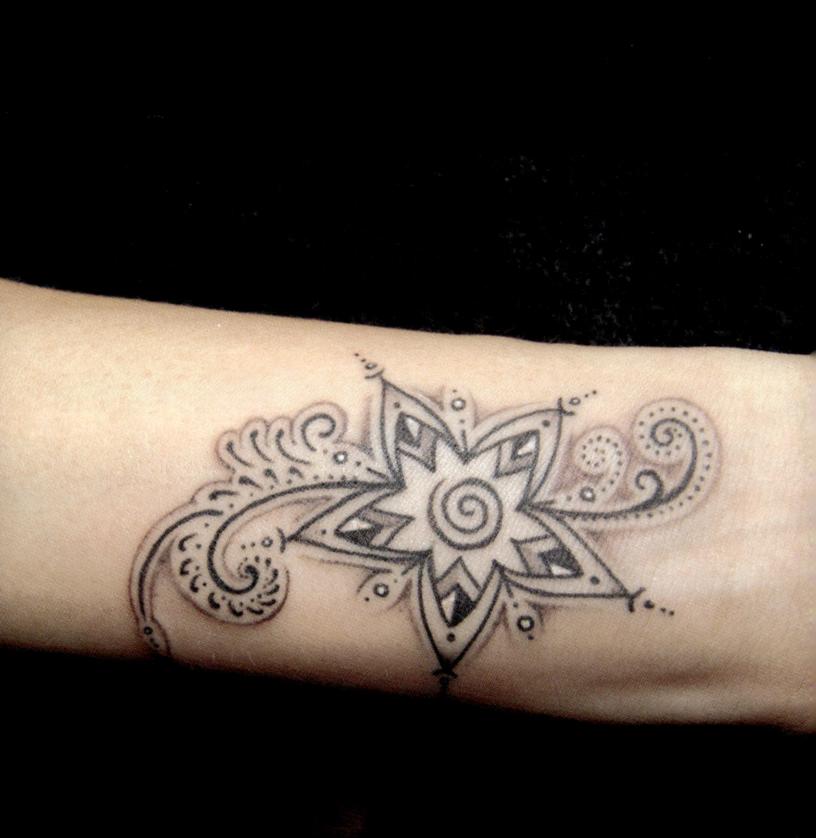

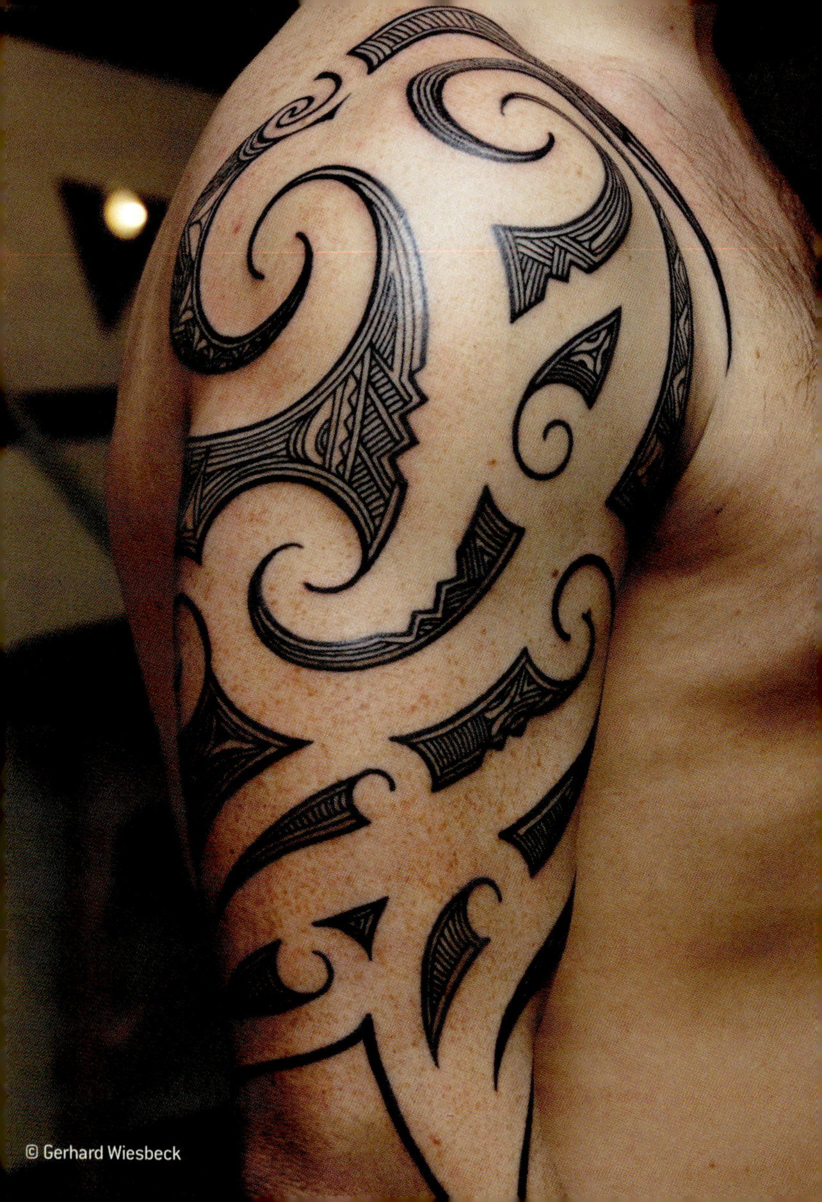
© Gerhard Wiesbeck

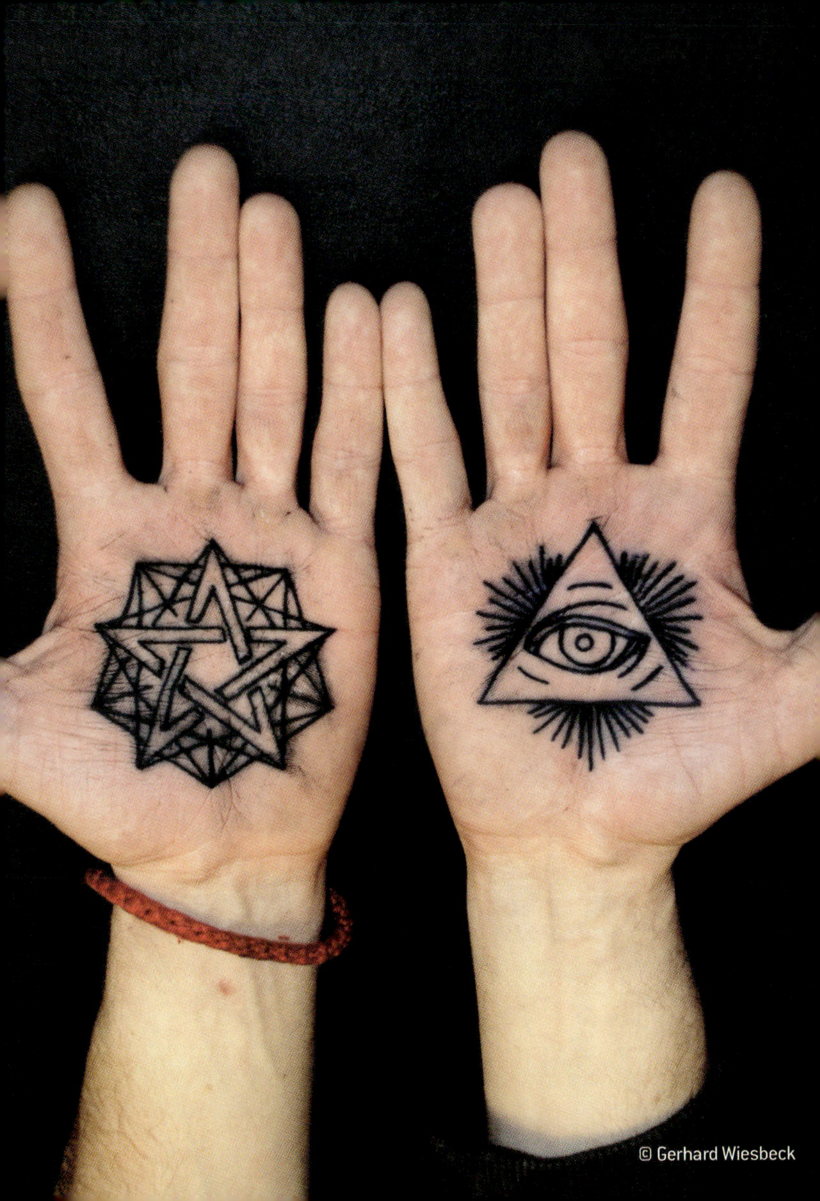
© Gerhard Wiesbeck

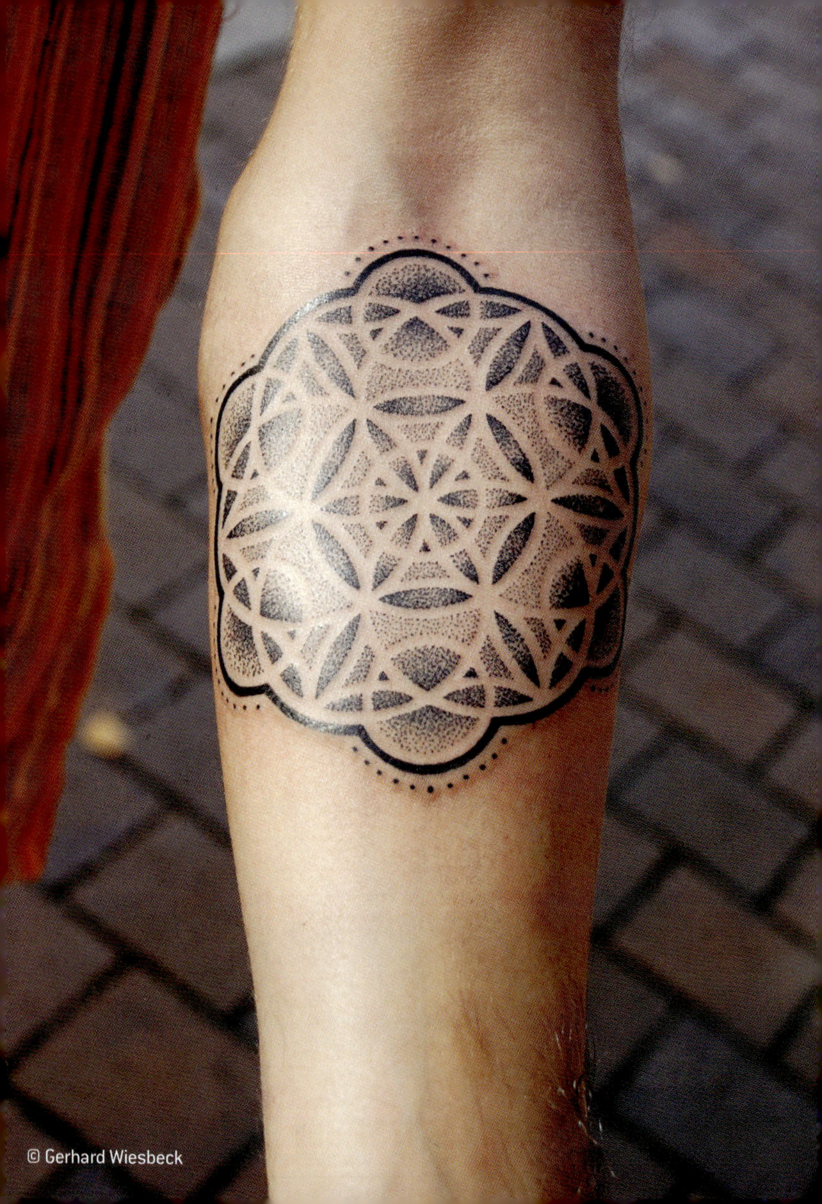

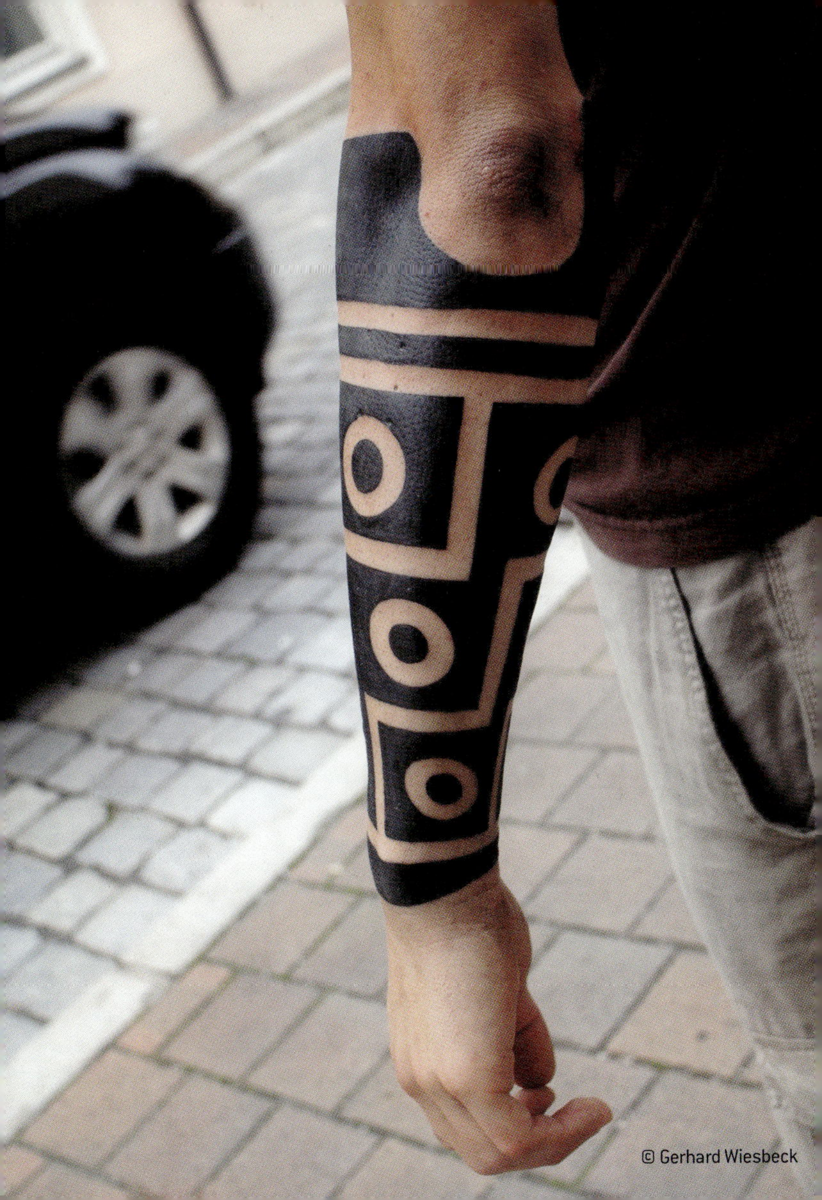
© Gerhard Wiesbeck

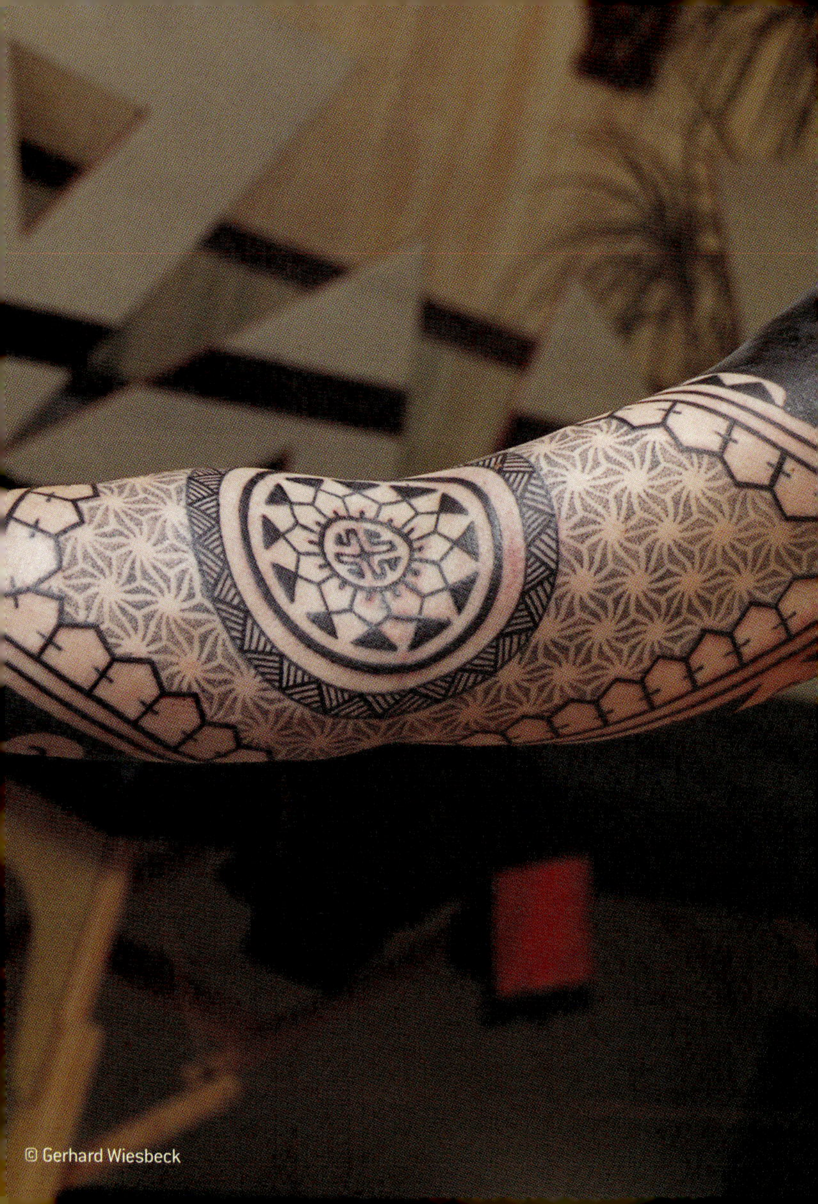

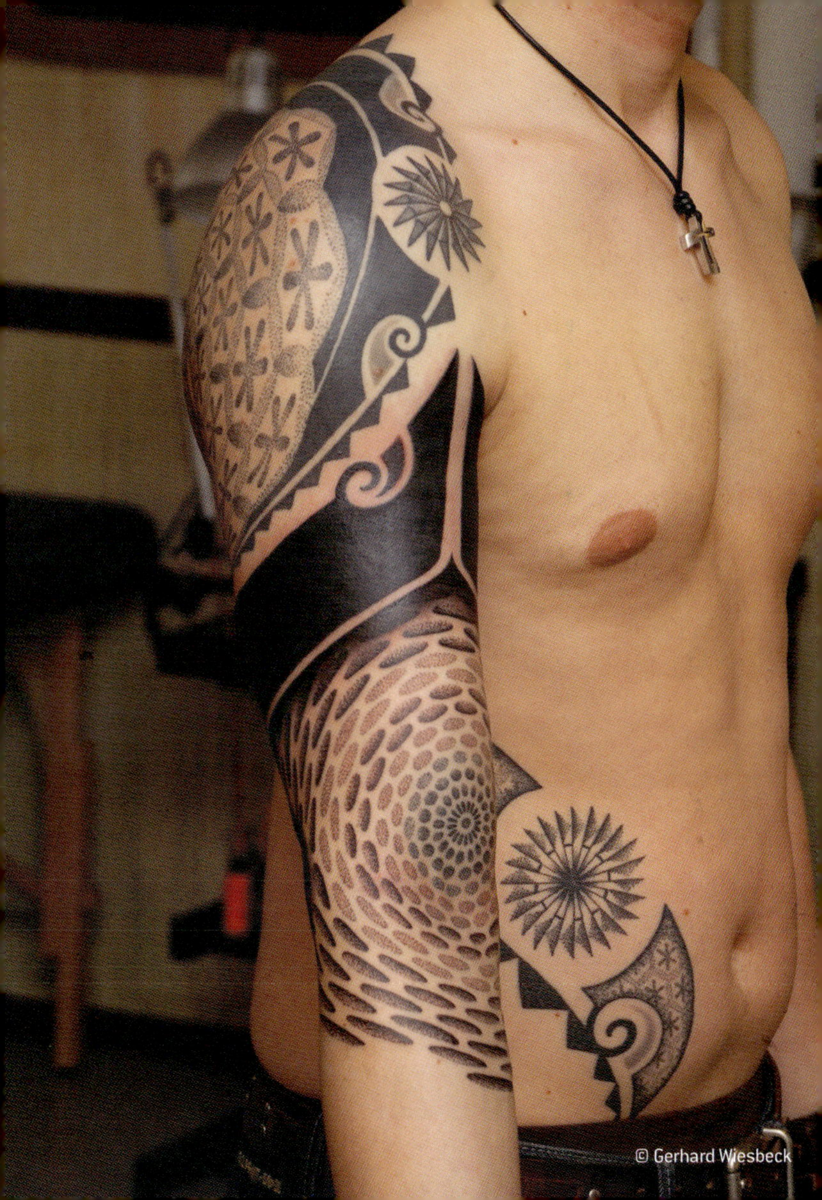

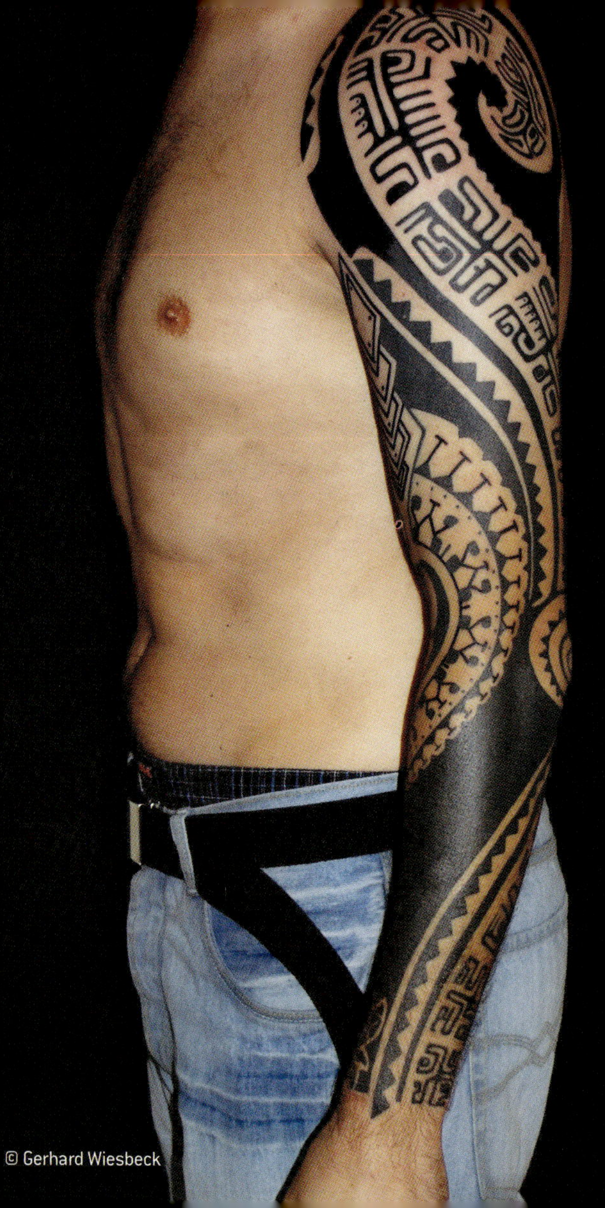

© Gerhard Wiesbeck

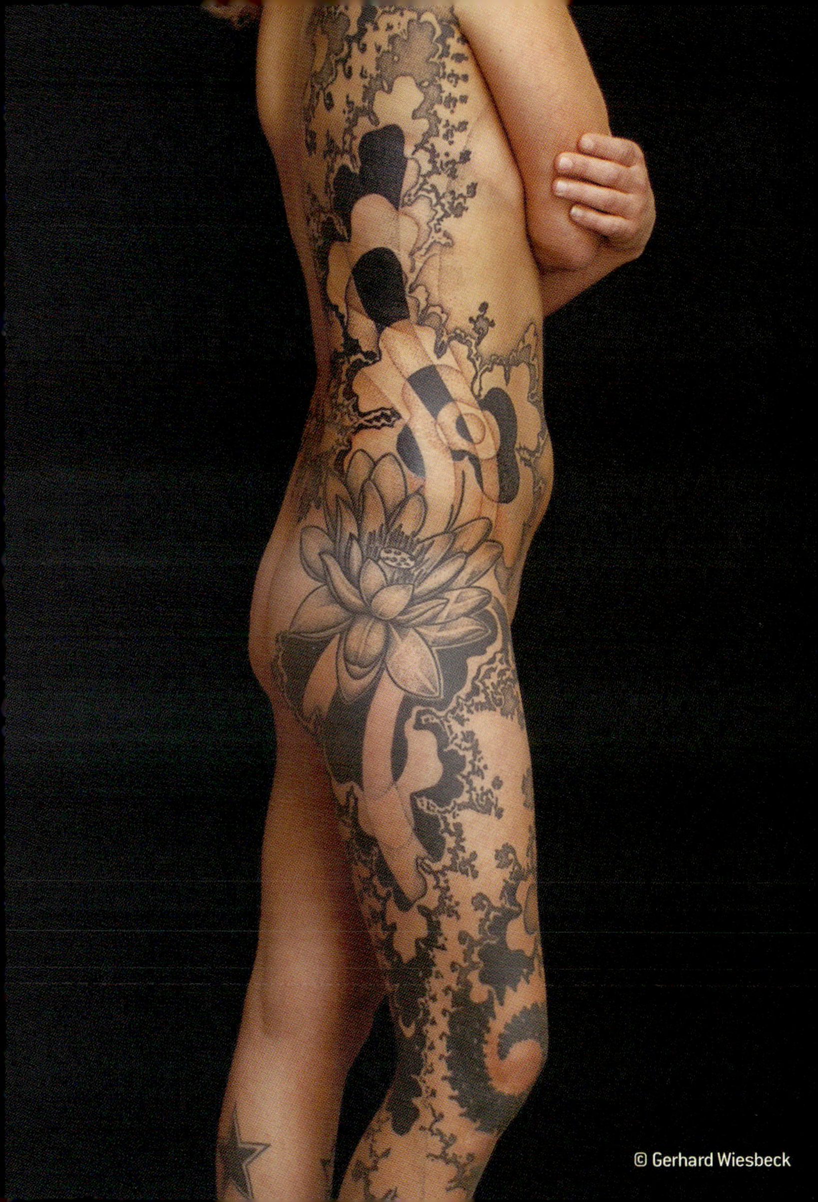
© Gerhard Wiesbeck

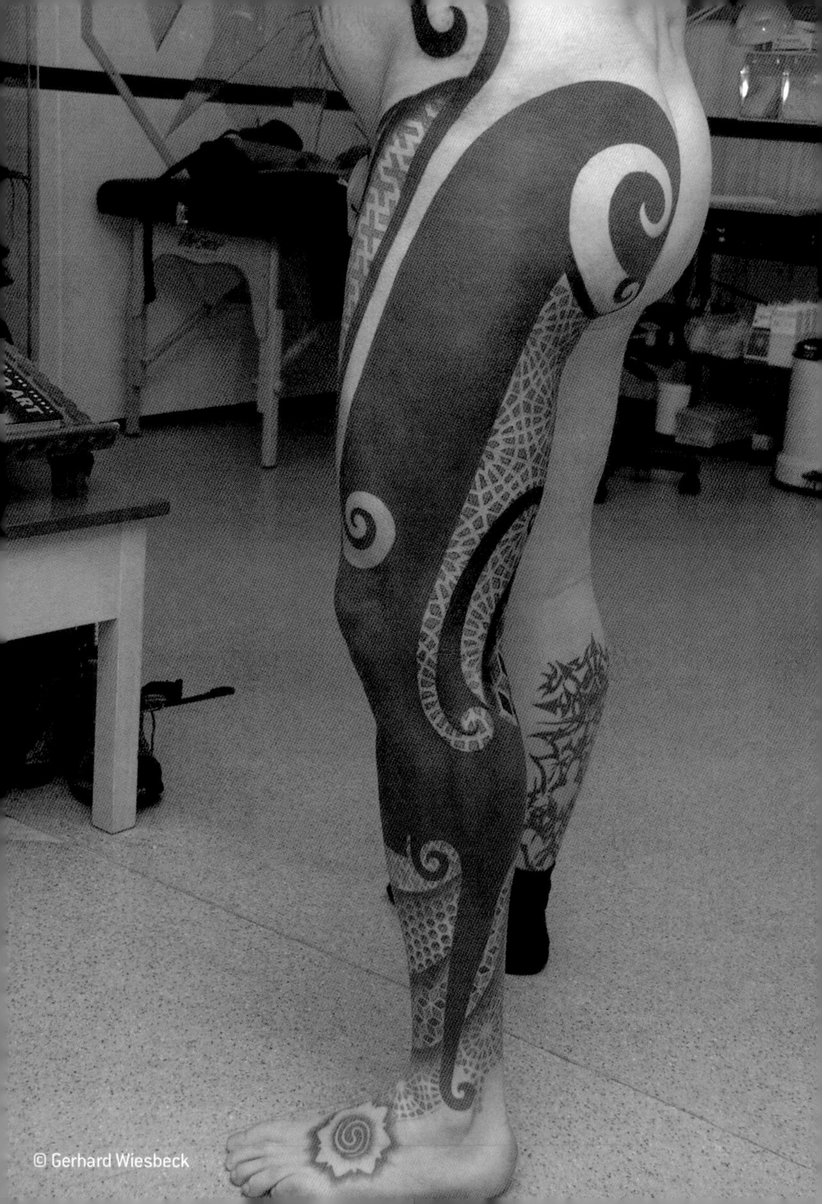

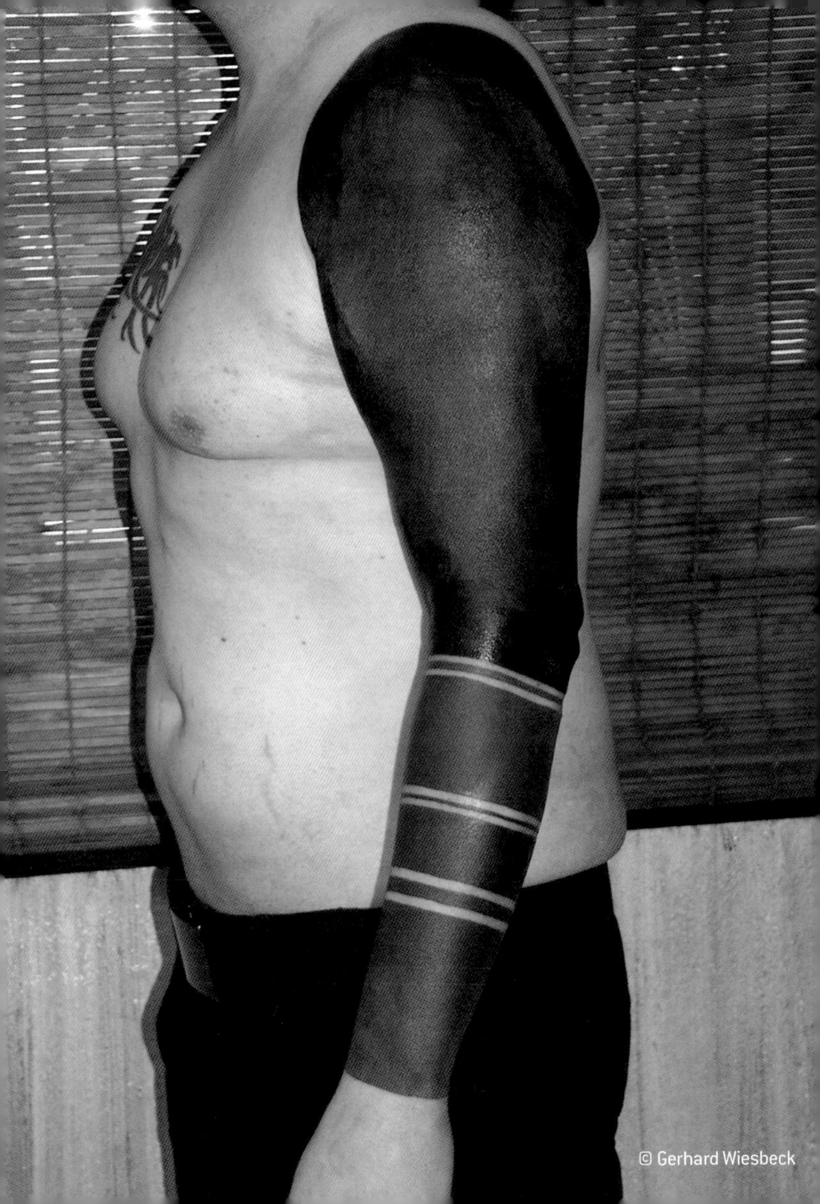

© Gerhard Wiesbeck

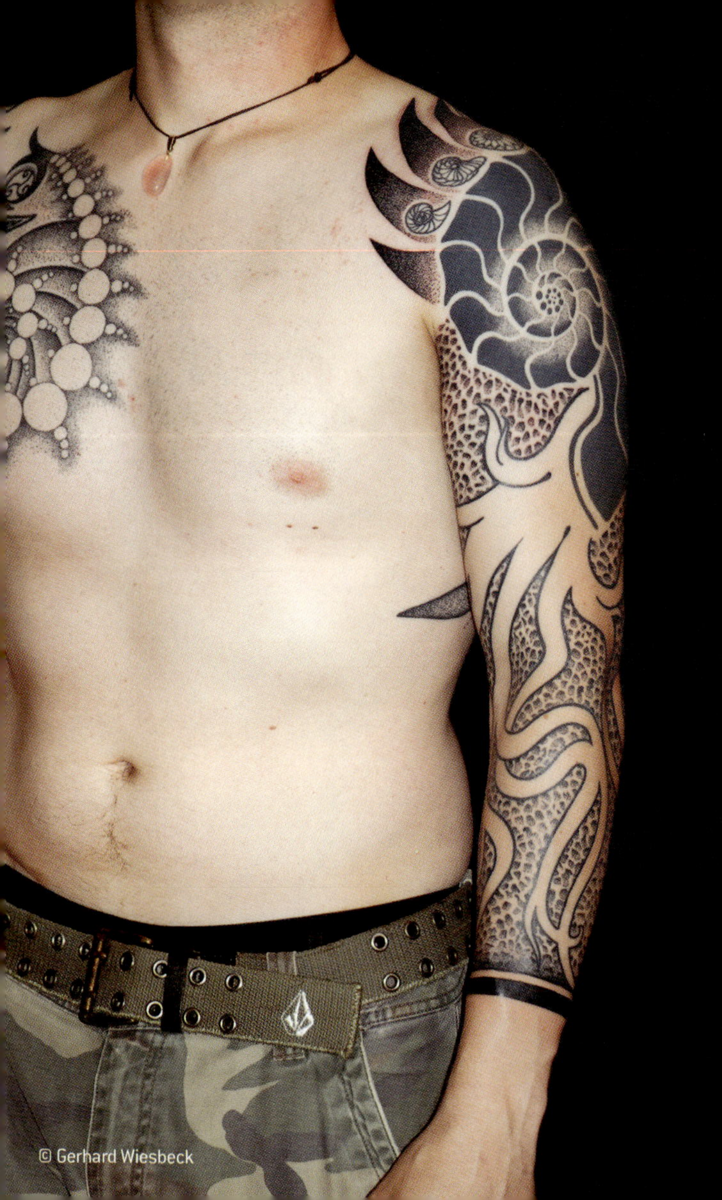

© Gerhard Wiesbeck

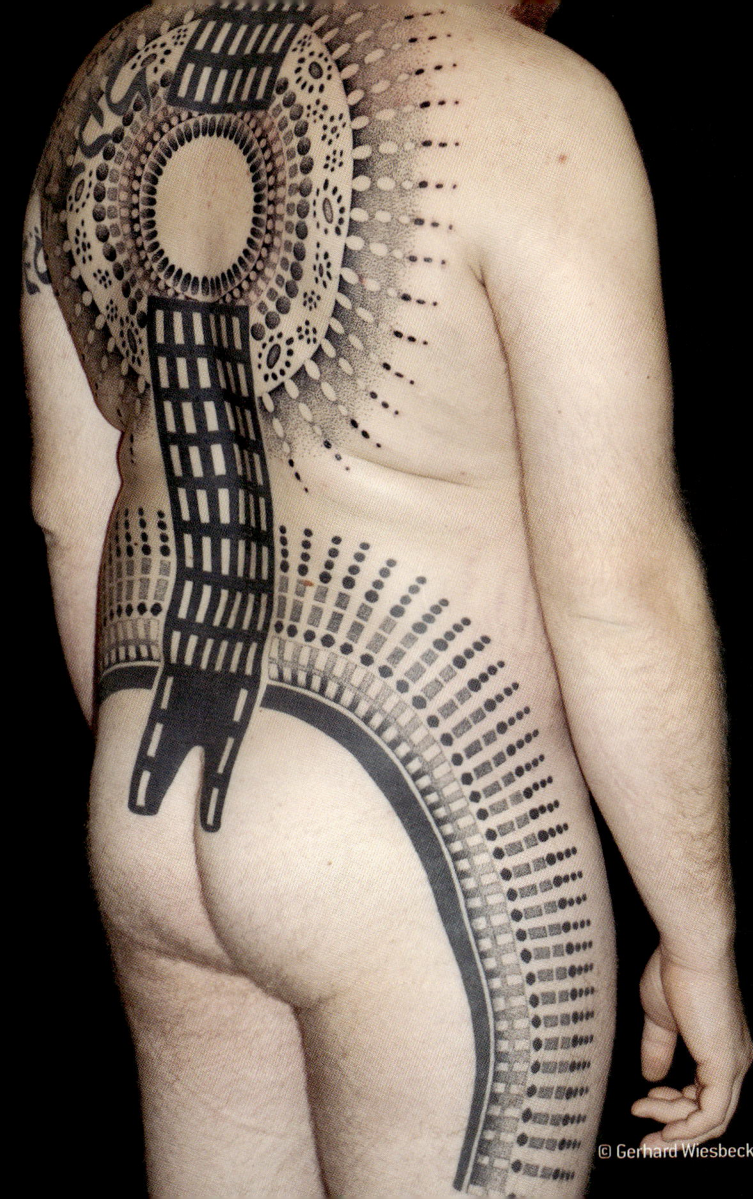
© Gerhard Wiesbeck

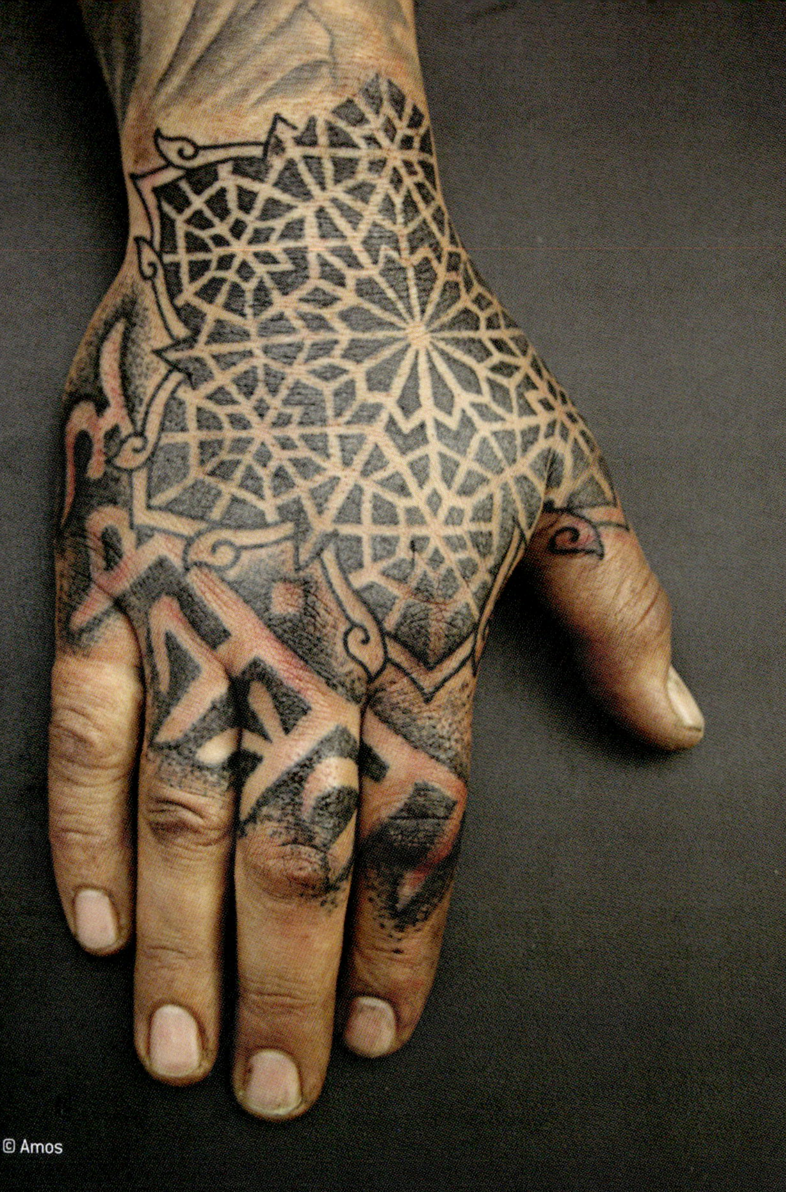
© Amos

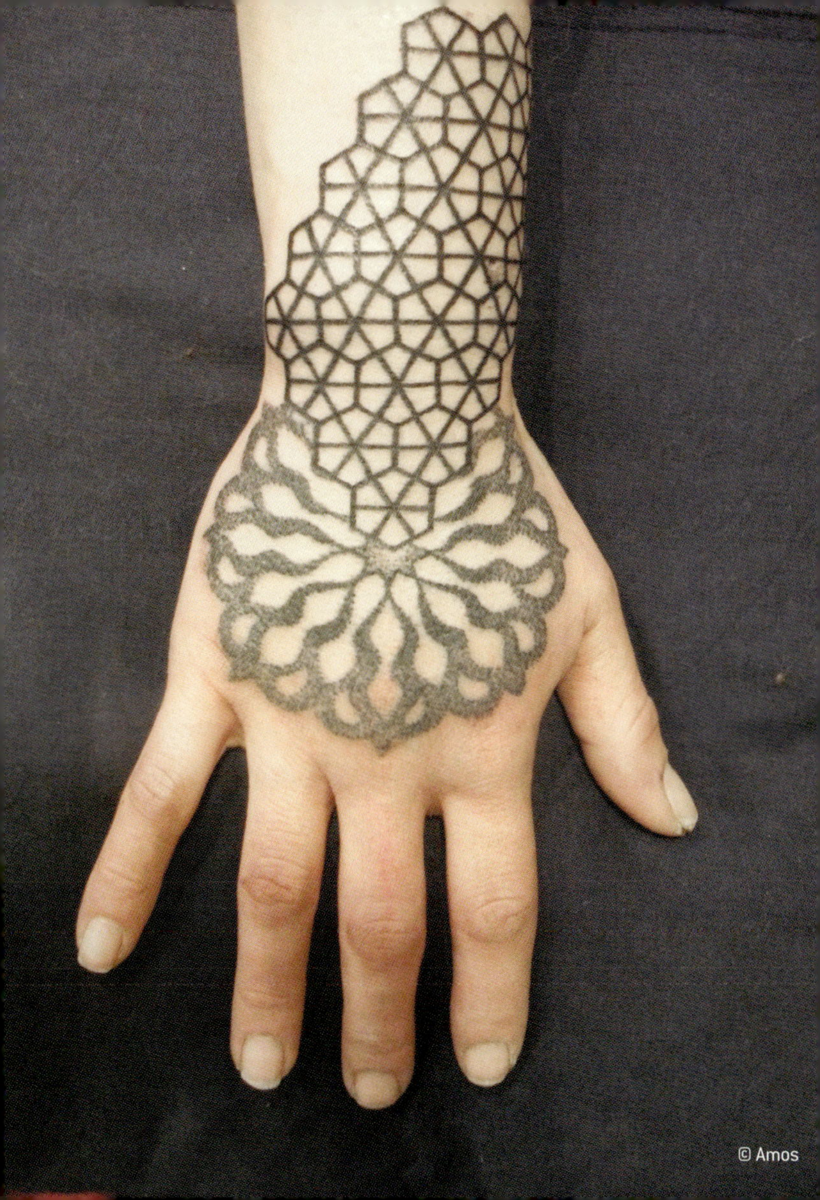
© Amos

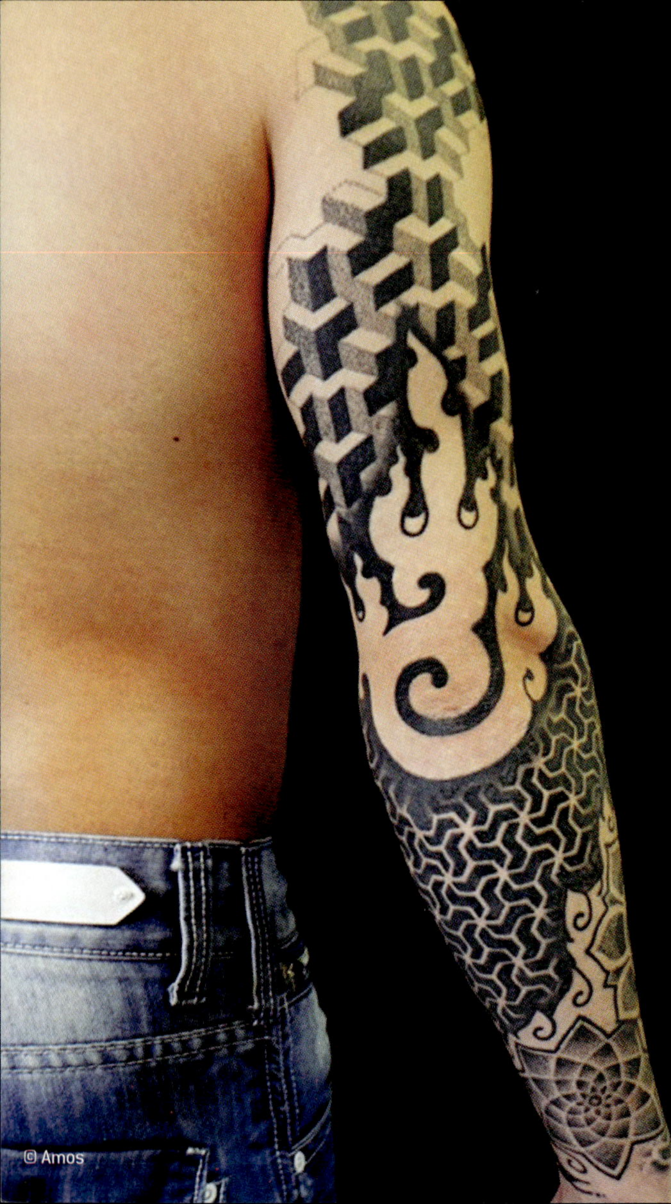
© Amos

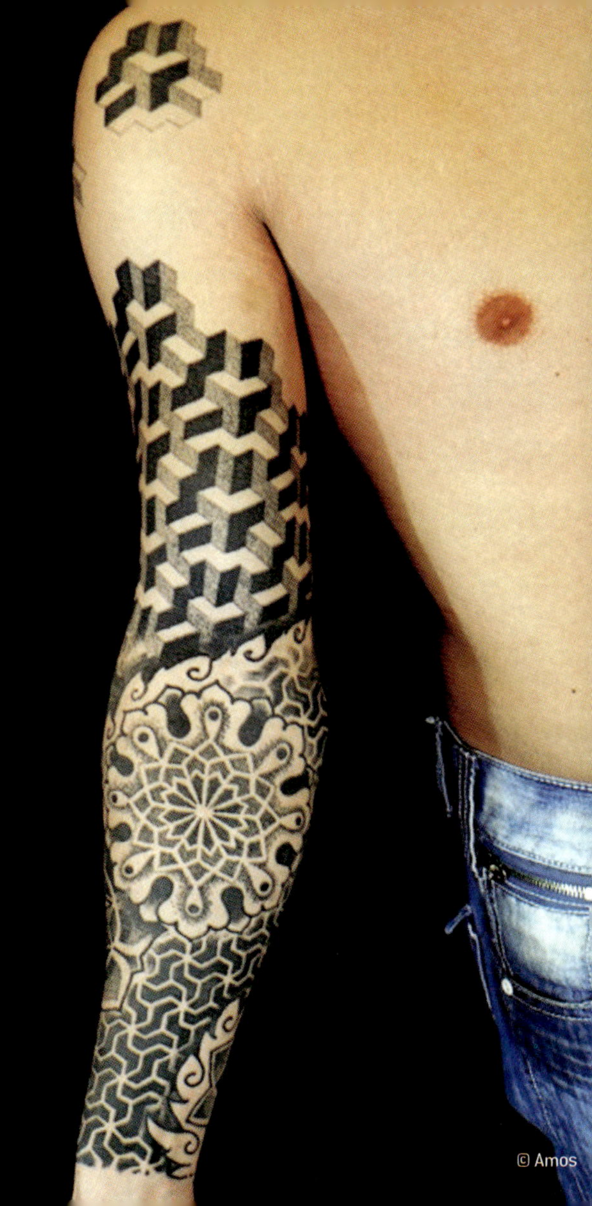
© Amos

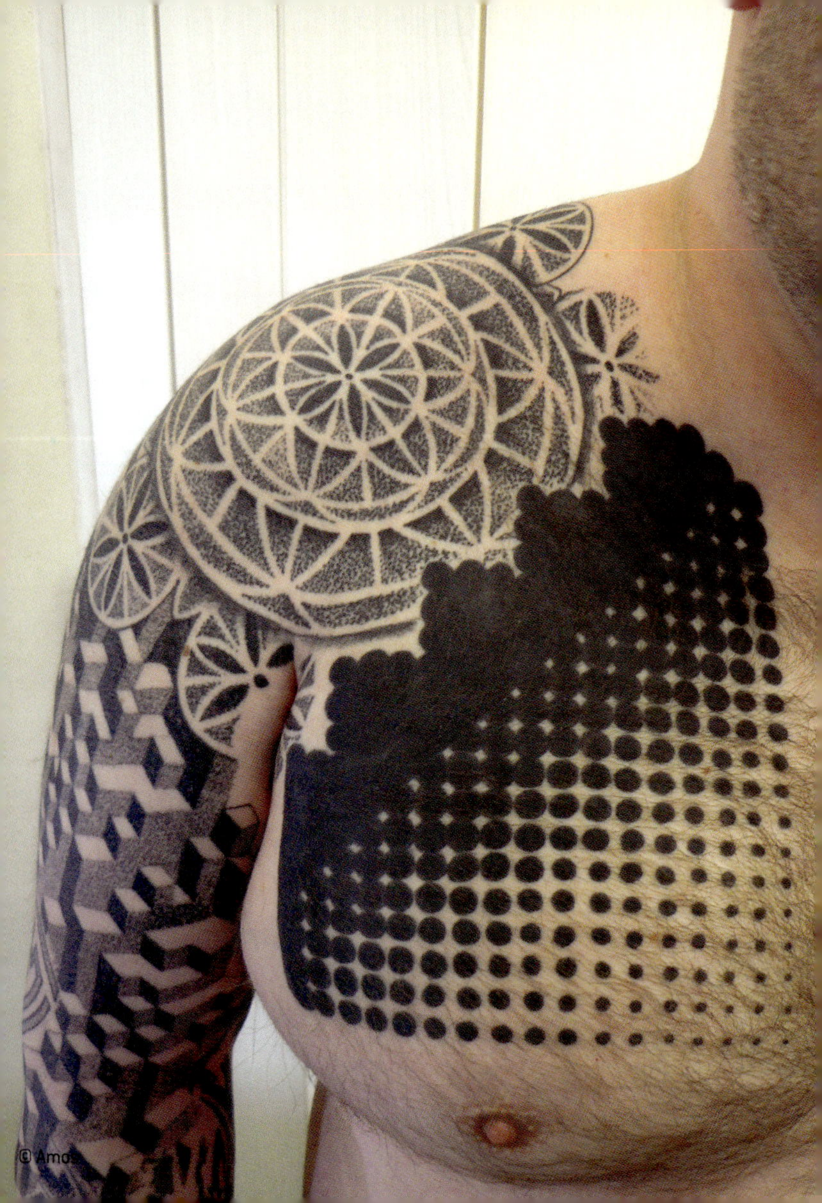

© Amos

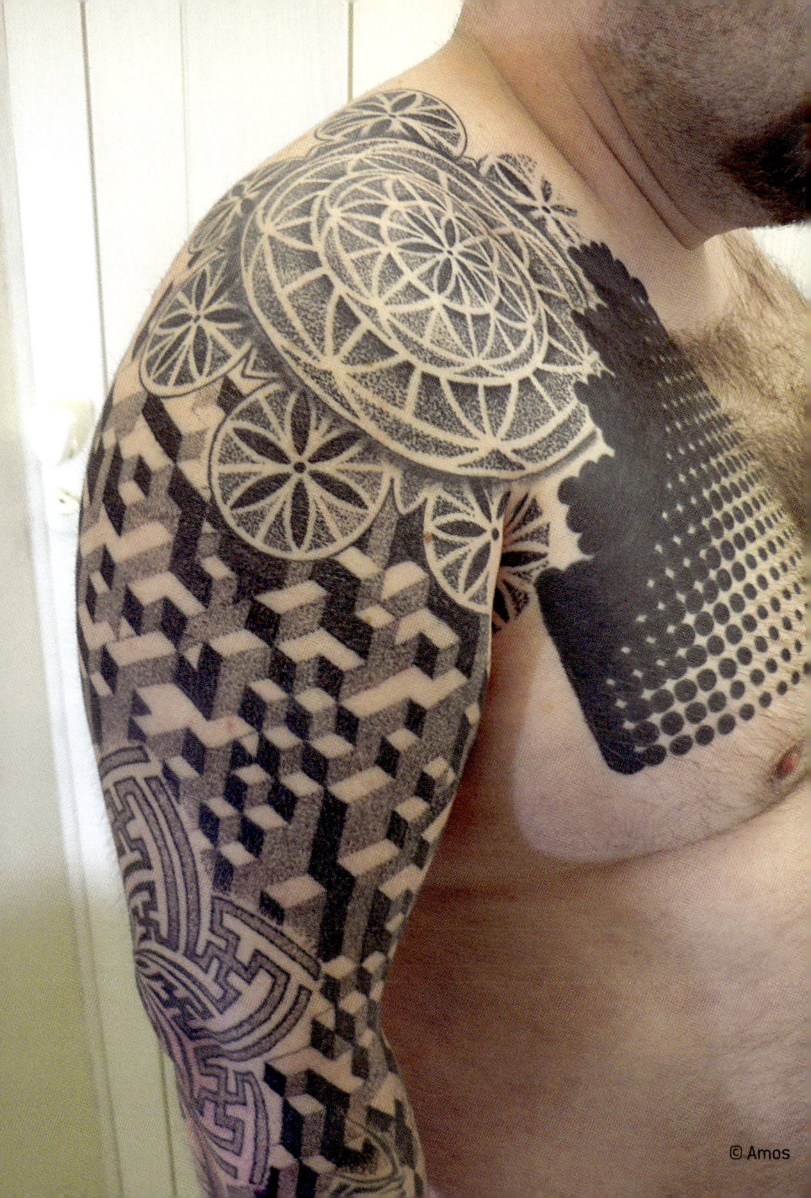
© Amos

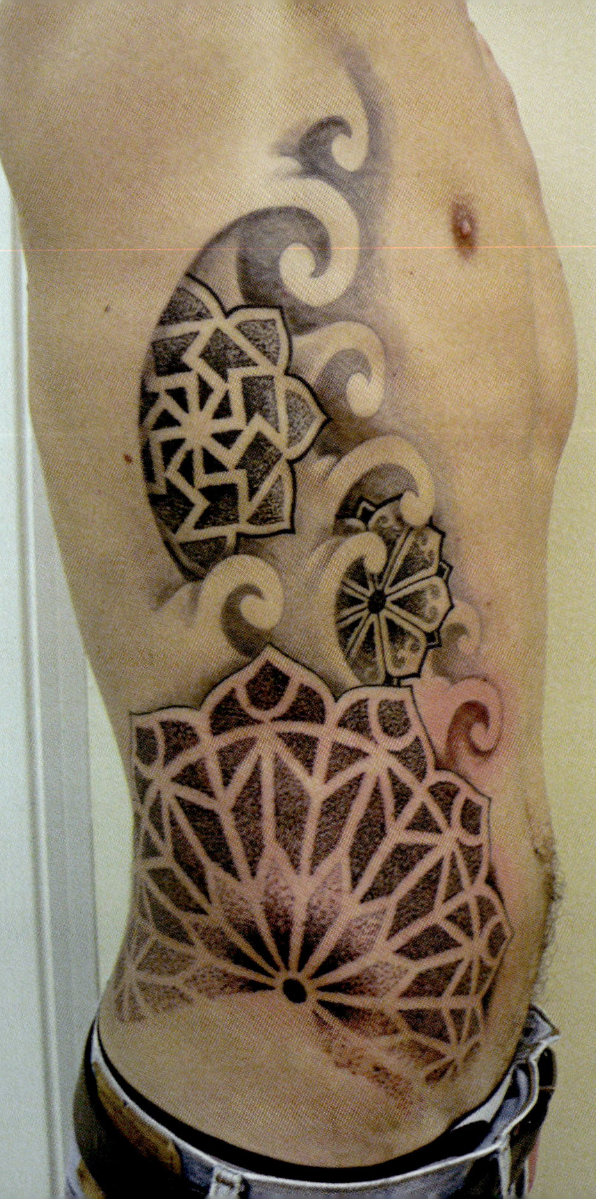

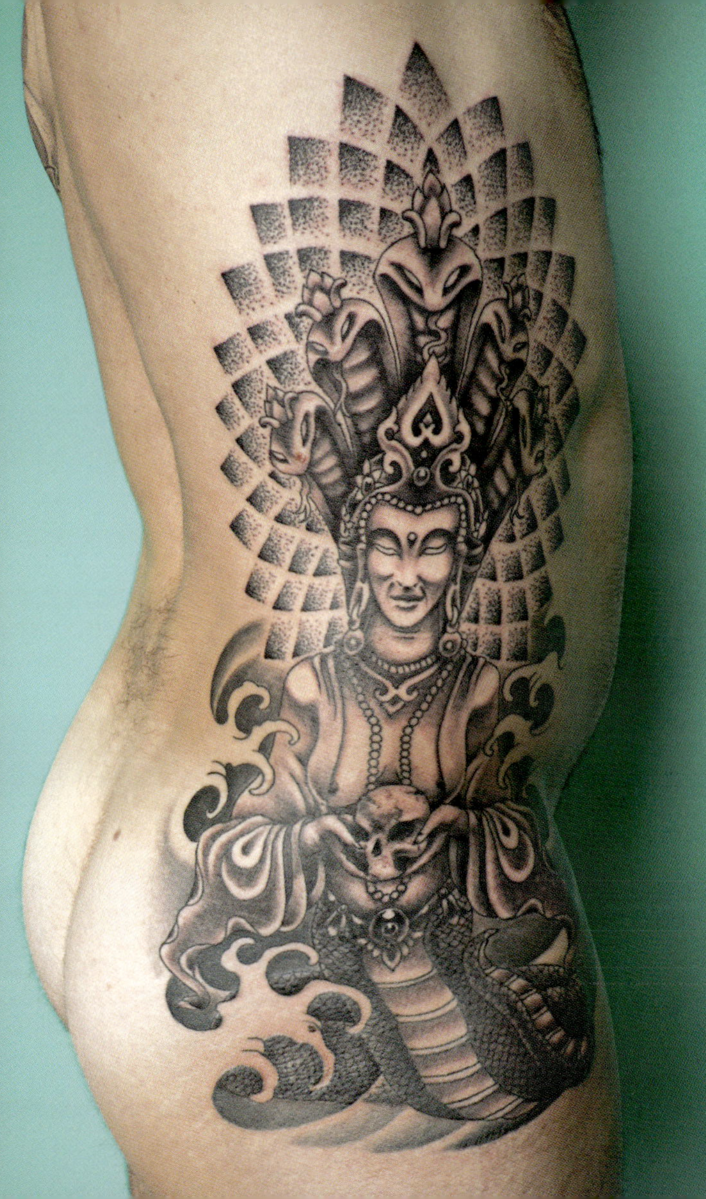
© Amos

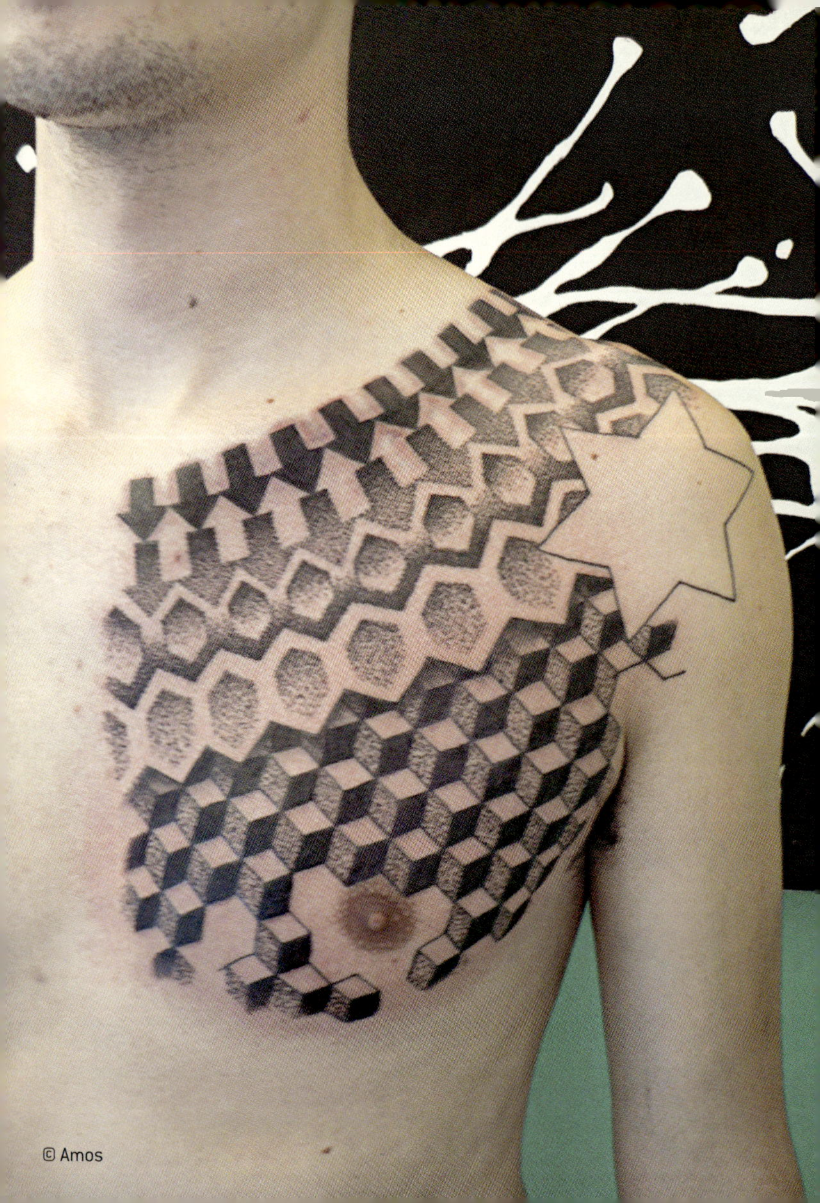
© Amos

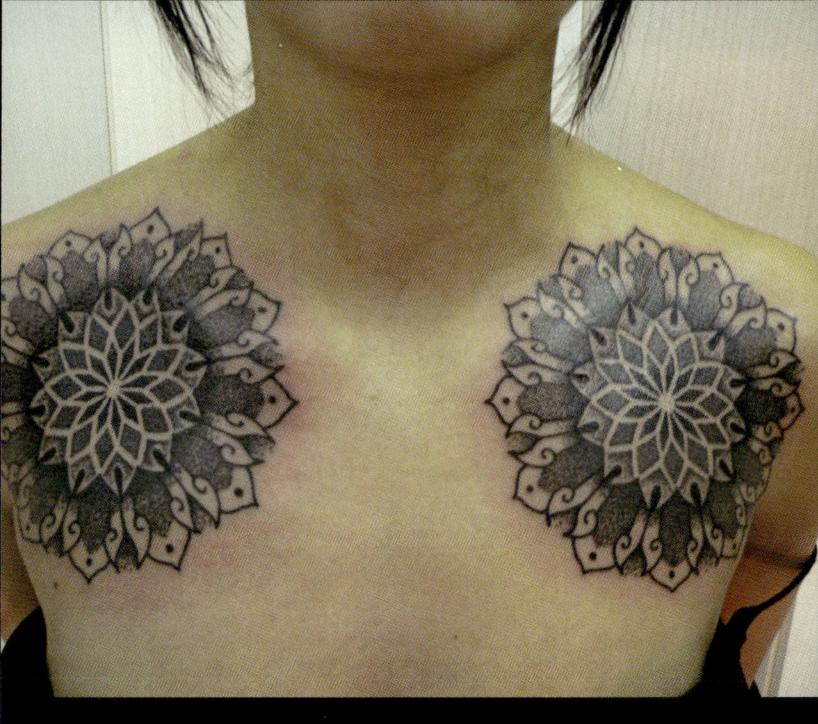

© Amos

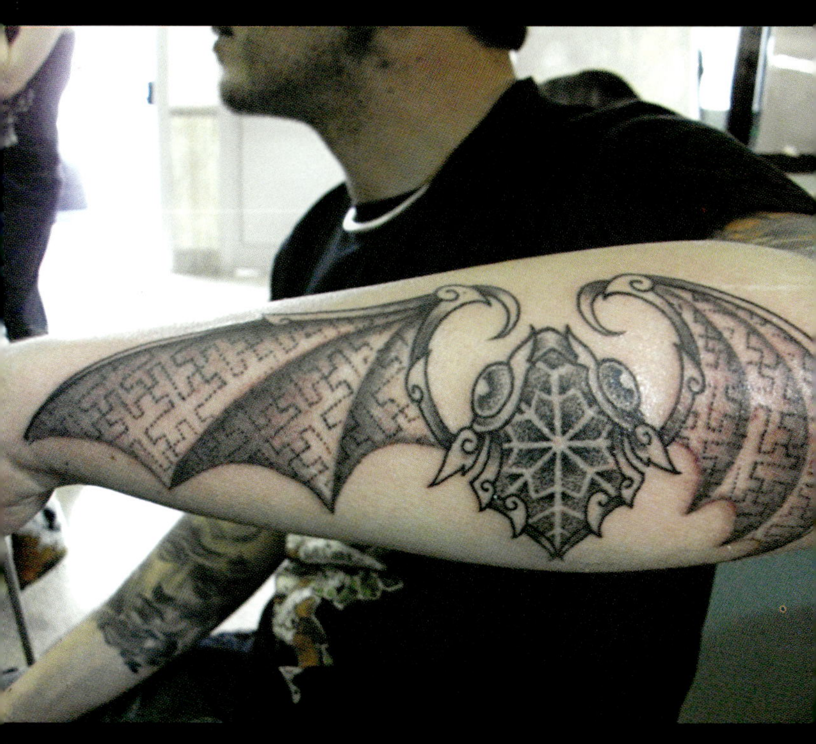

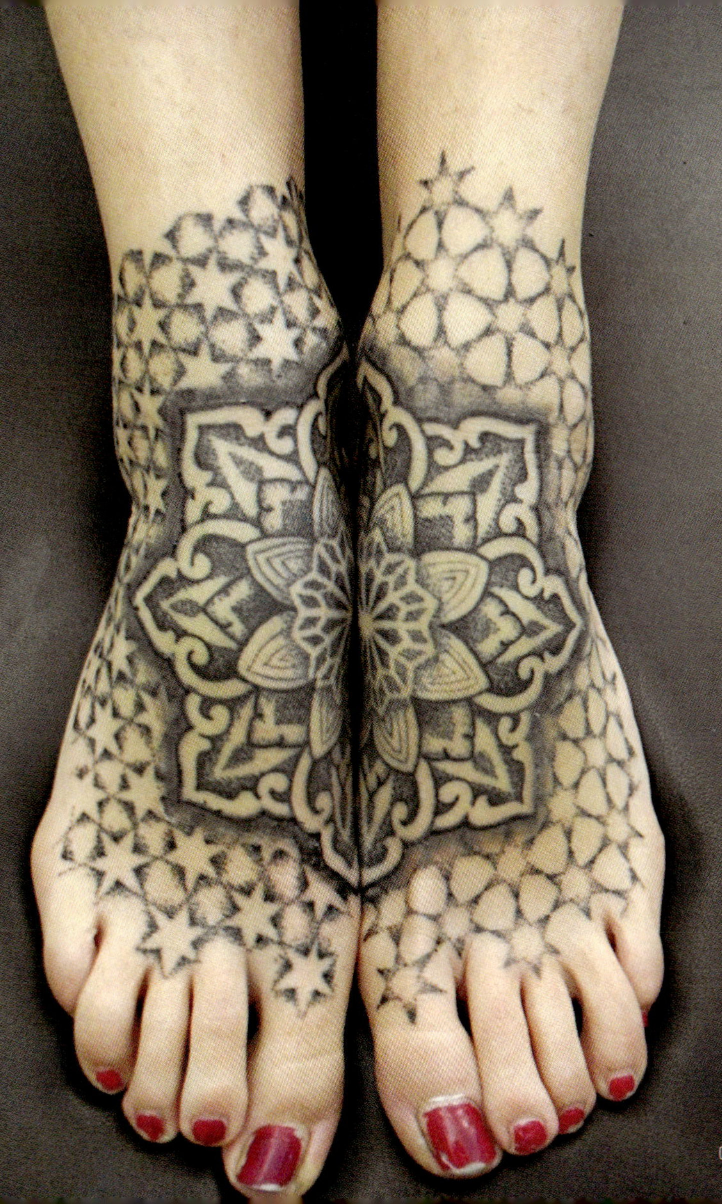
© Amos

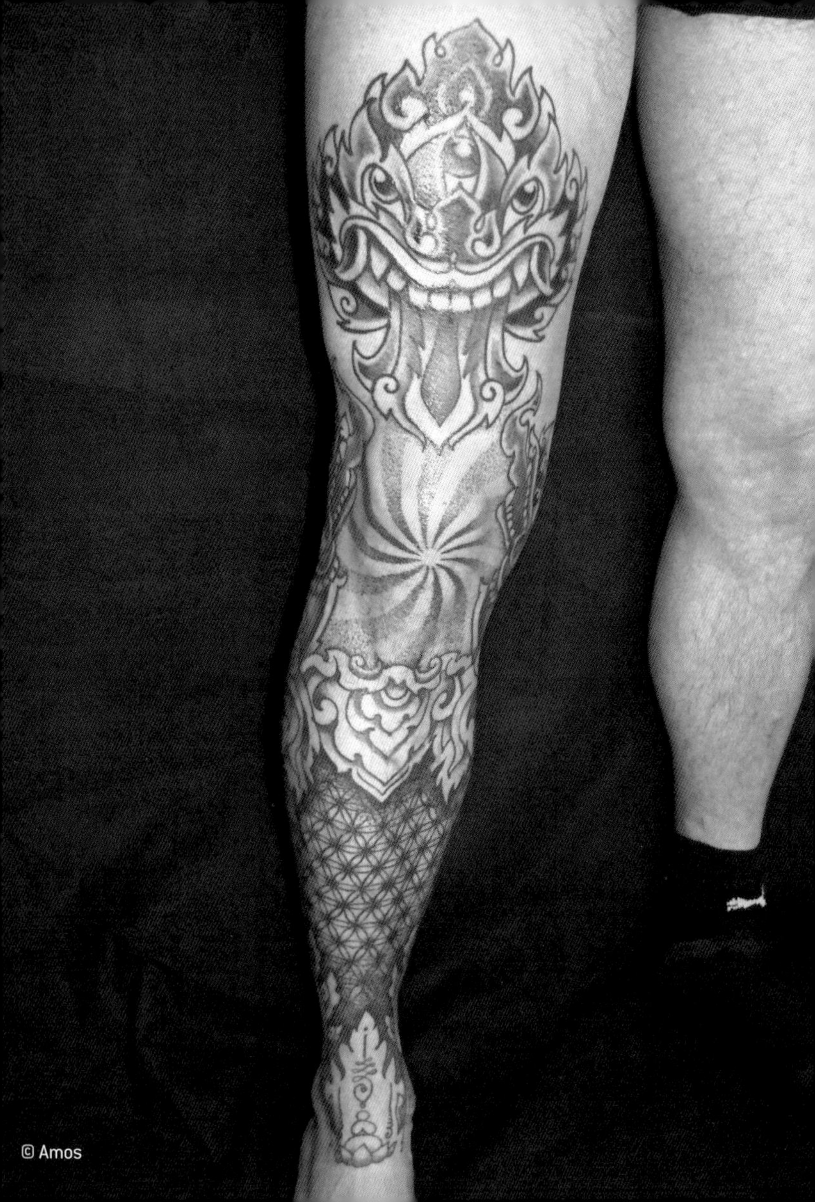
© Amos

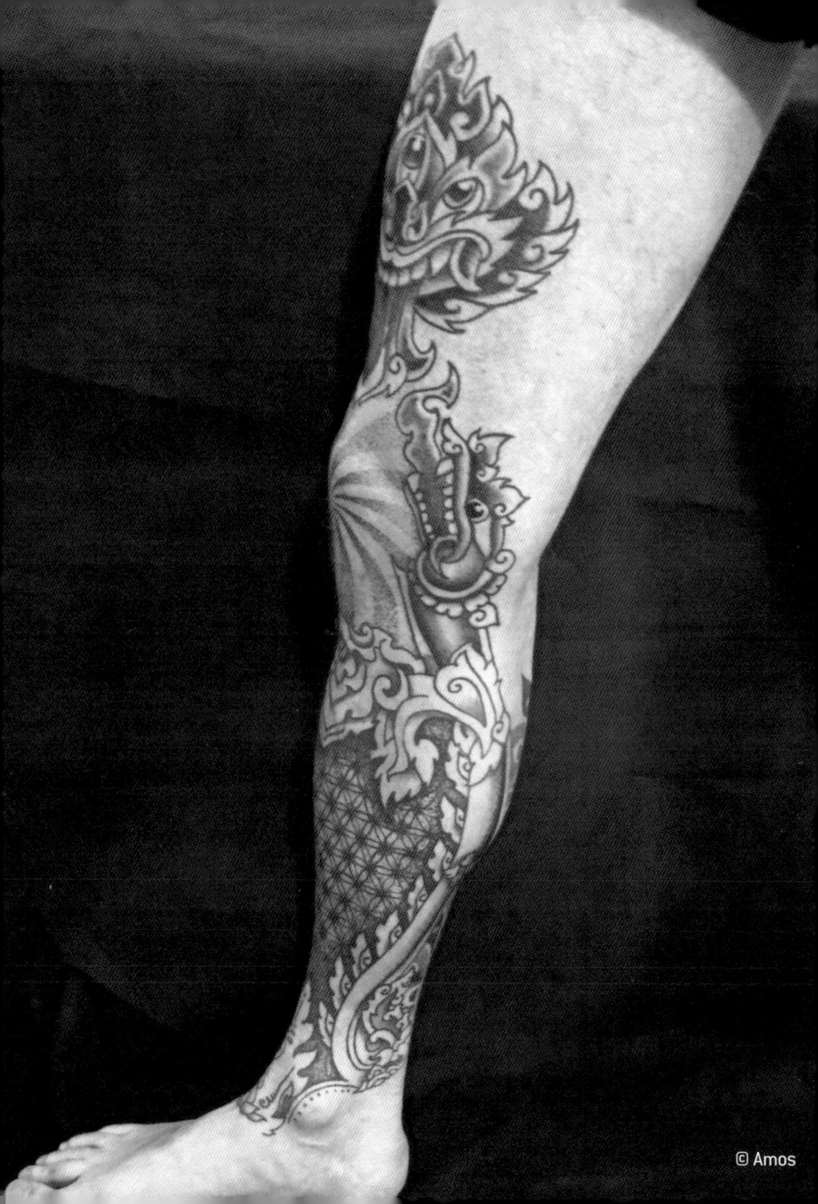
© Amos

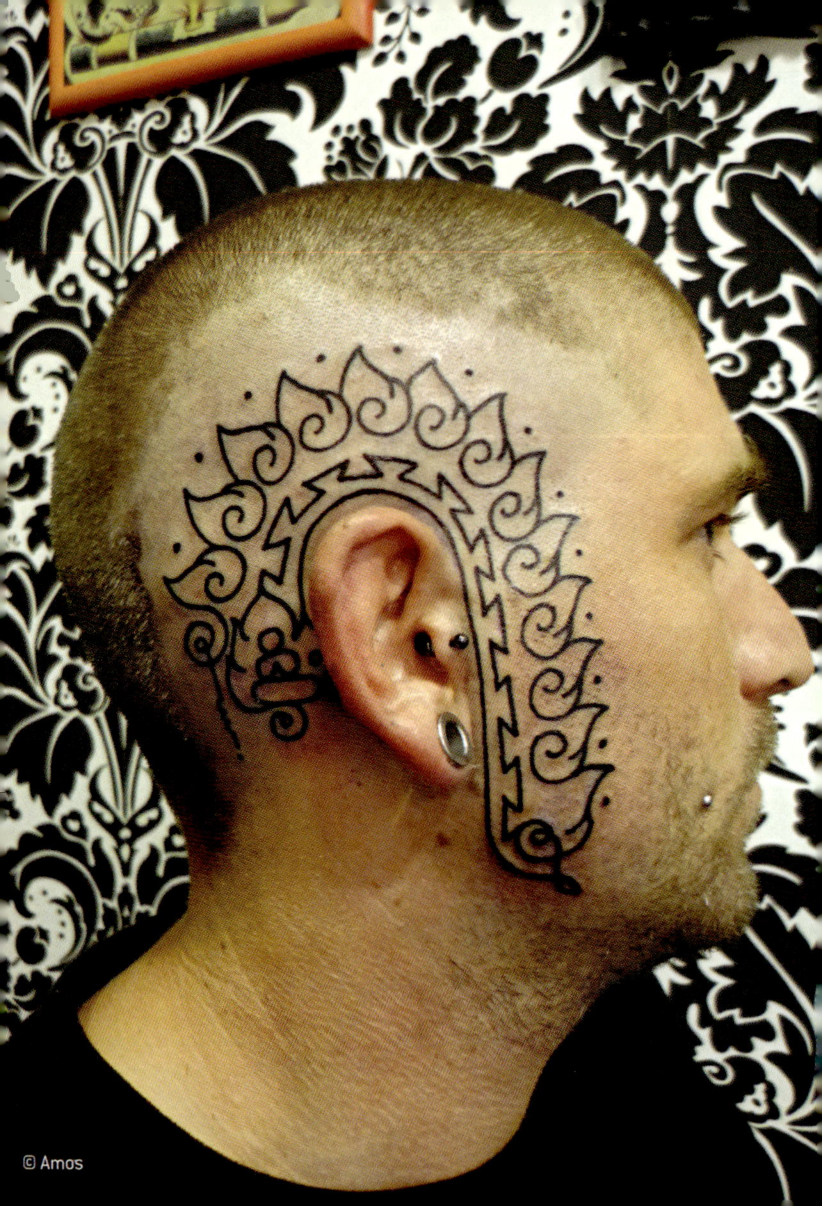
© Amos

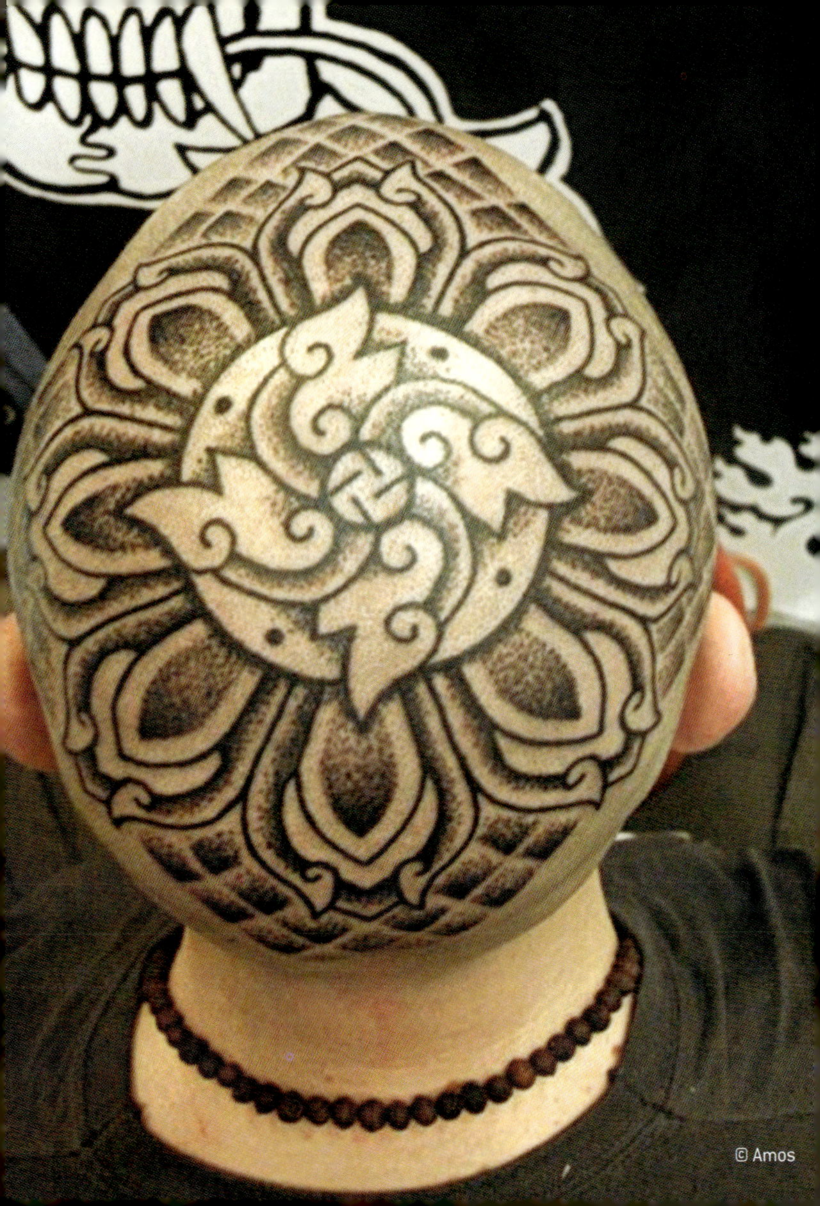
© Amos

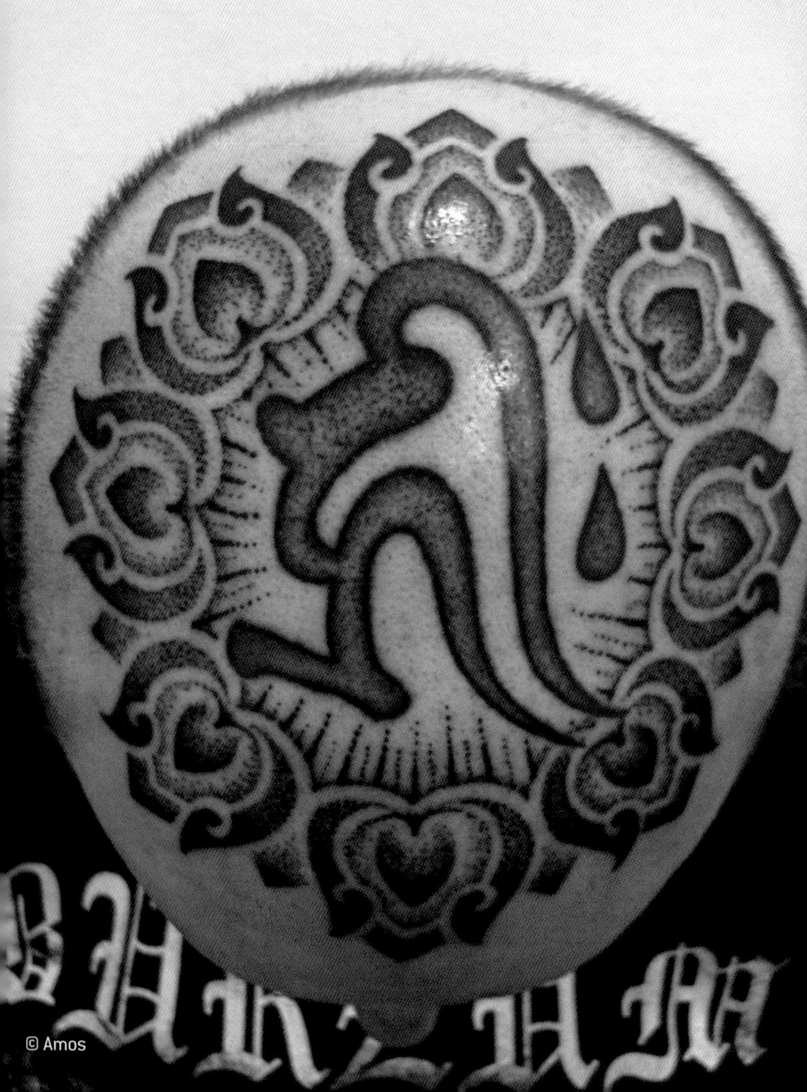

© Amos

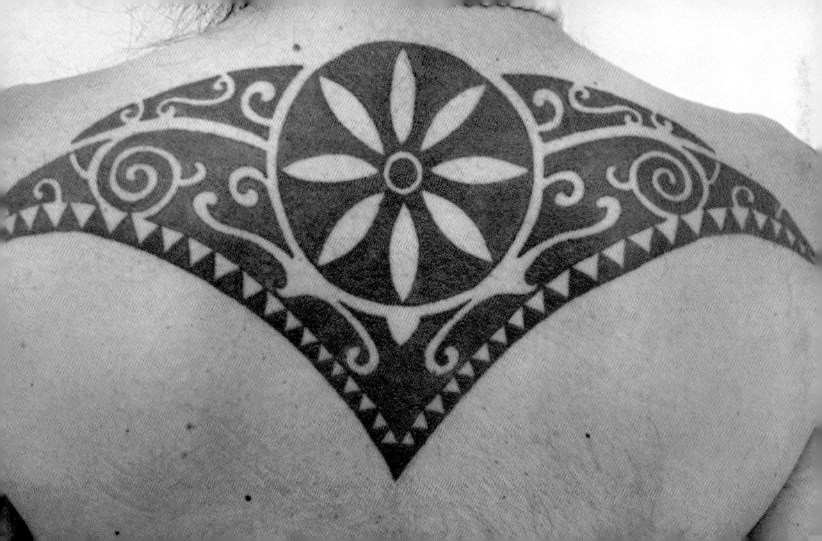

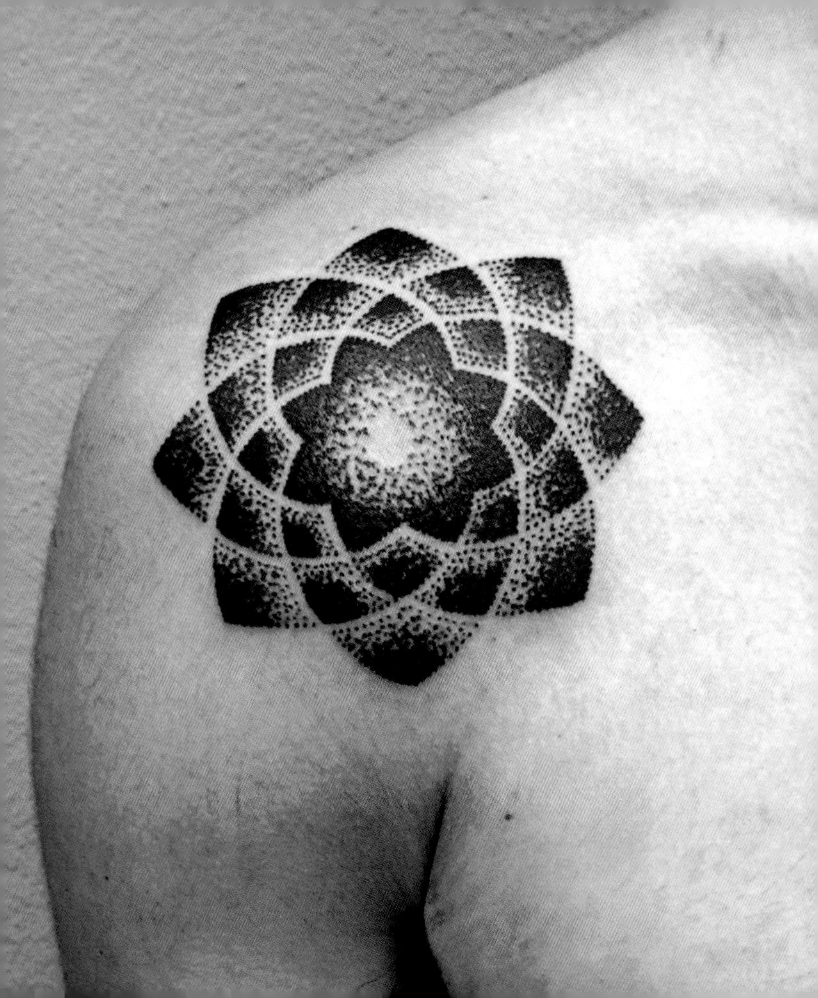

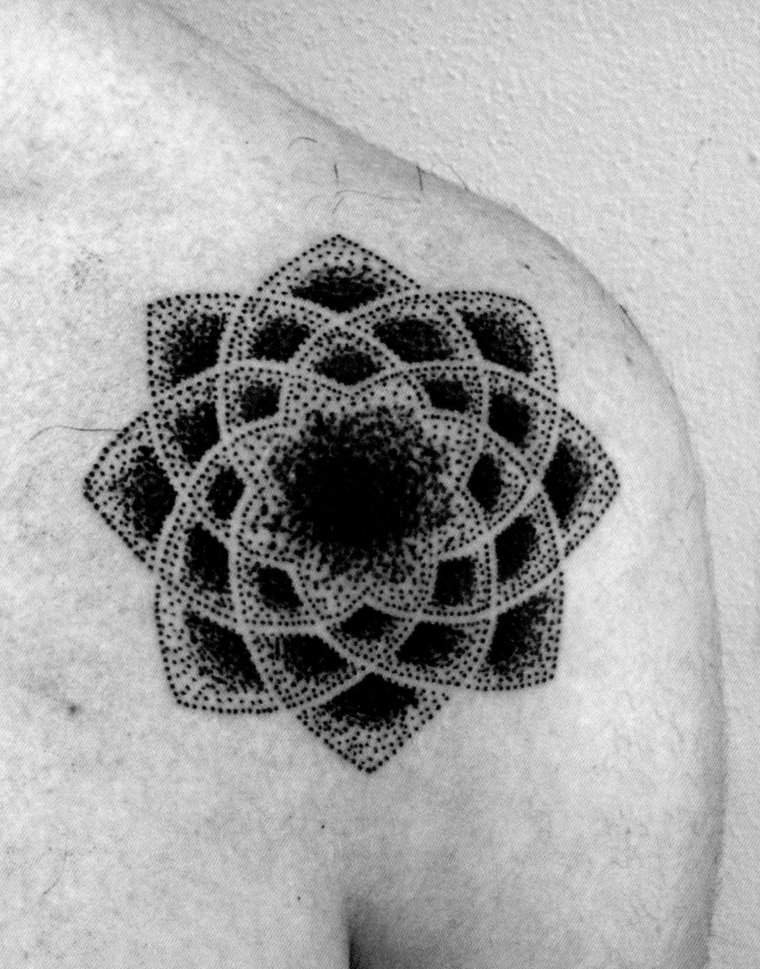

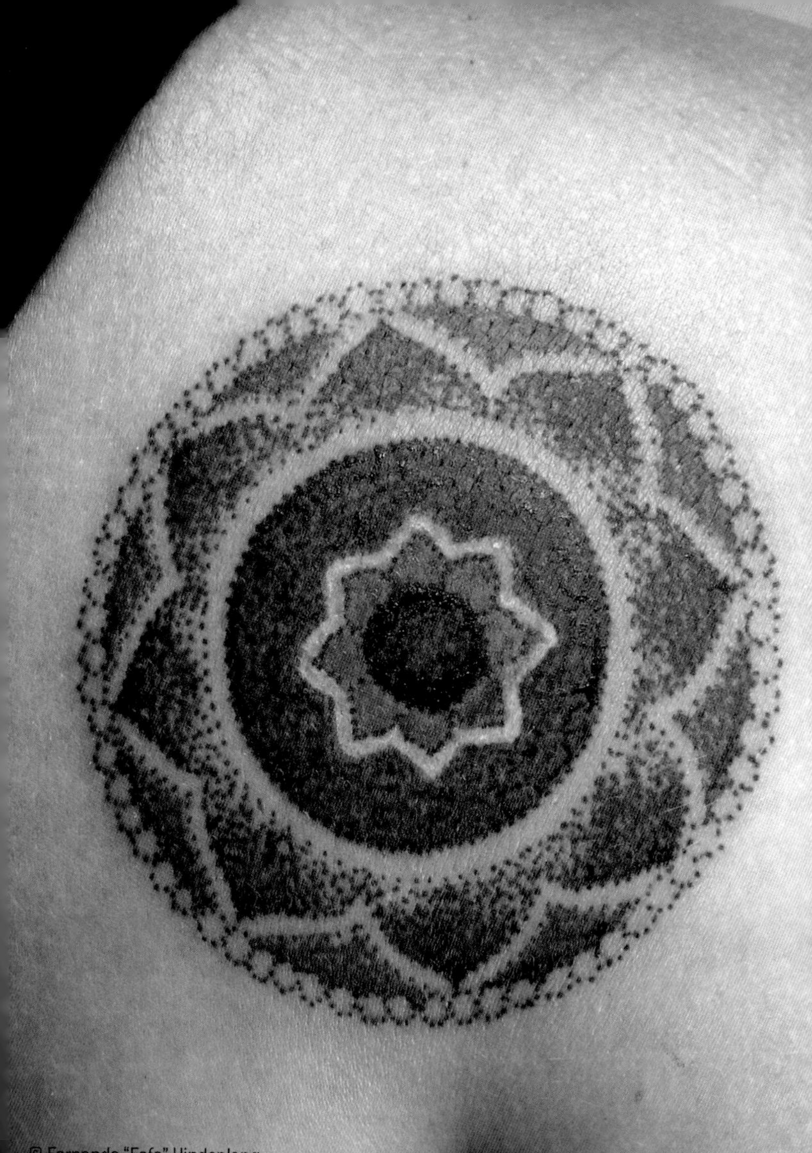

© Fernando "Fefe" Hindenlang

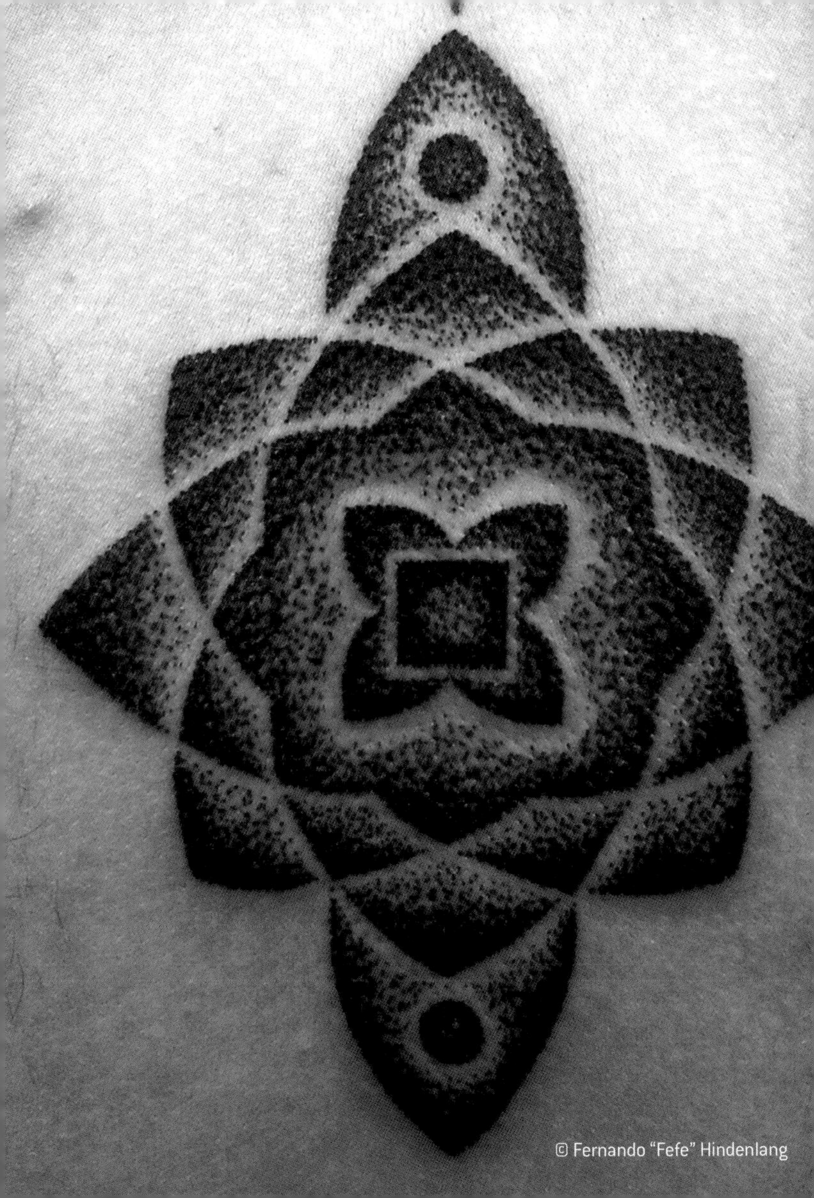
© Fernando "Fefe" Hindenlang

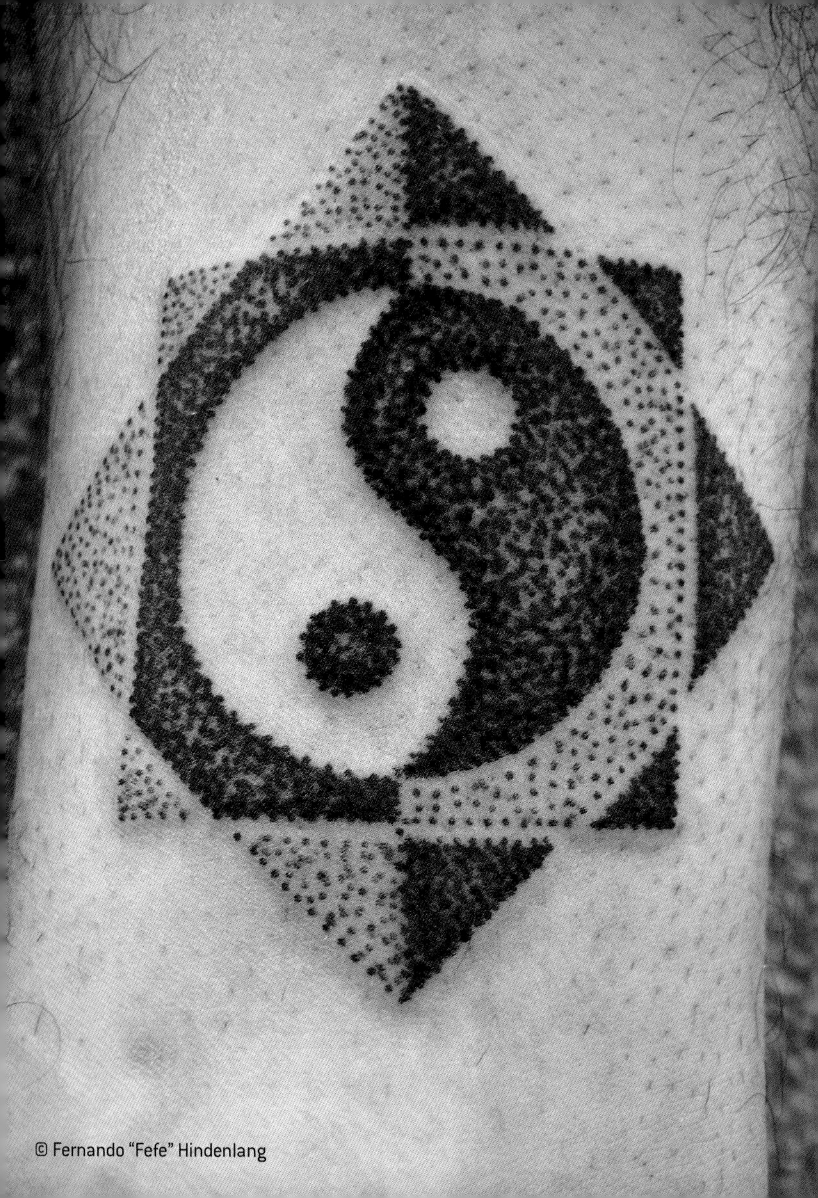

© Fernando "Fefe" Hindenlang

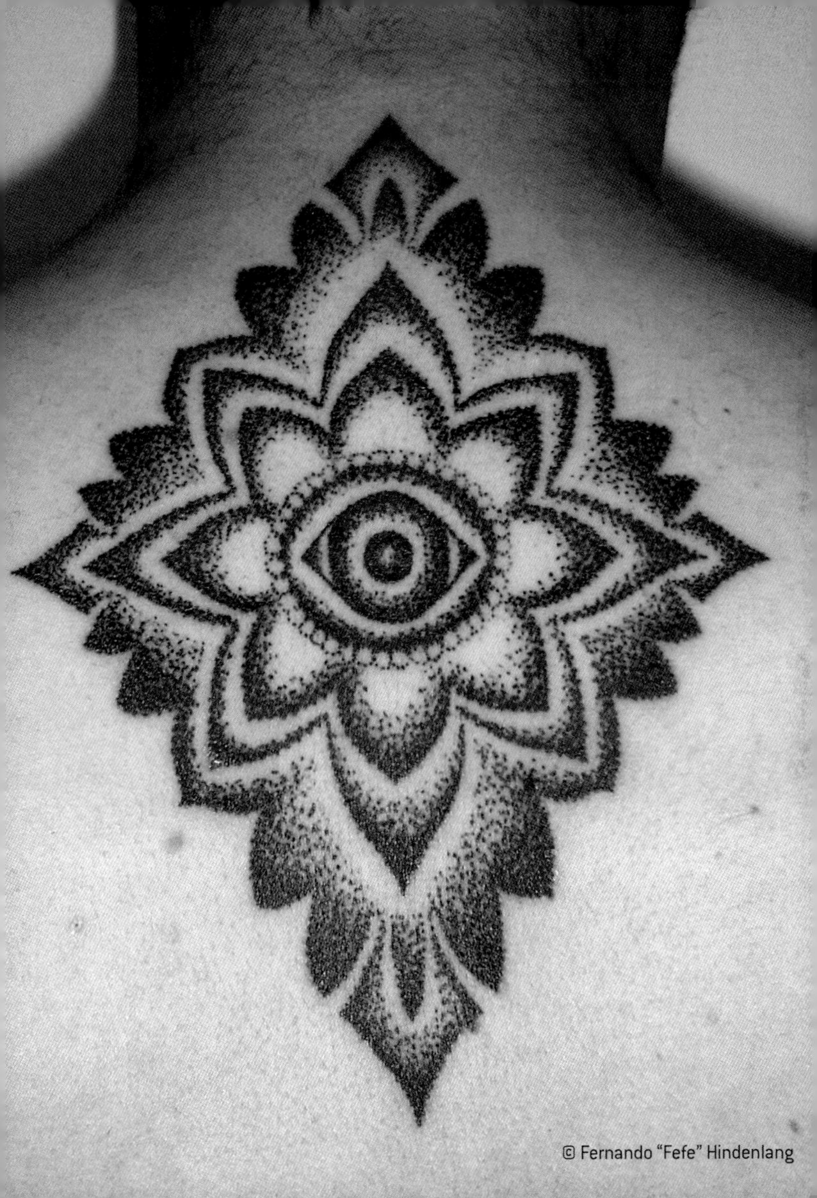

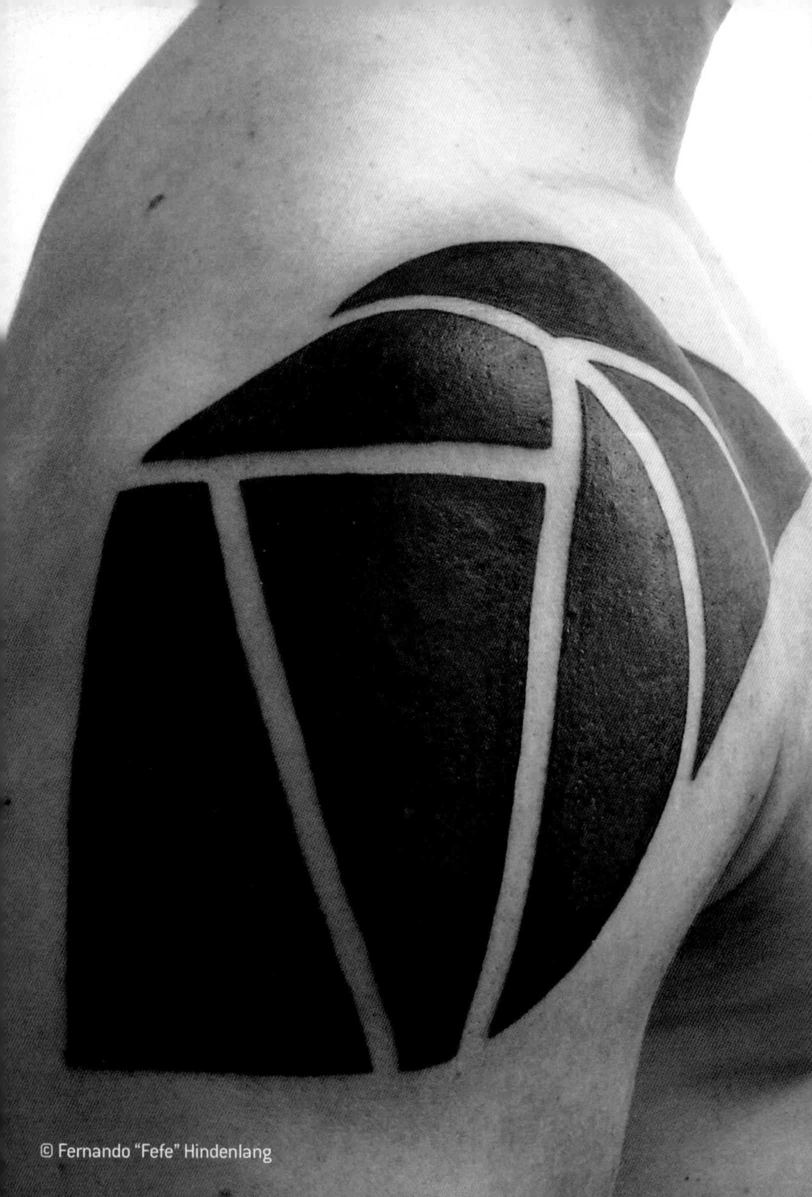
© Fernando "Fefe" Hindenlang

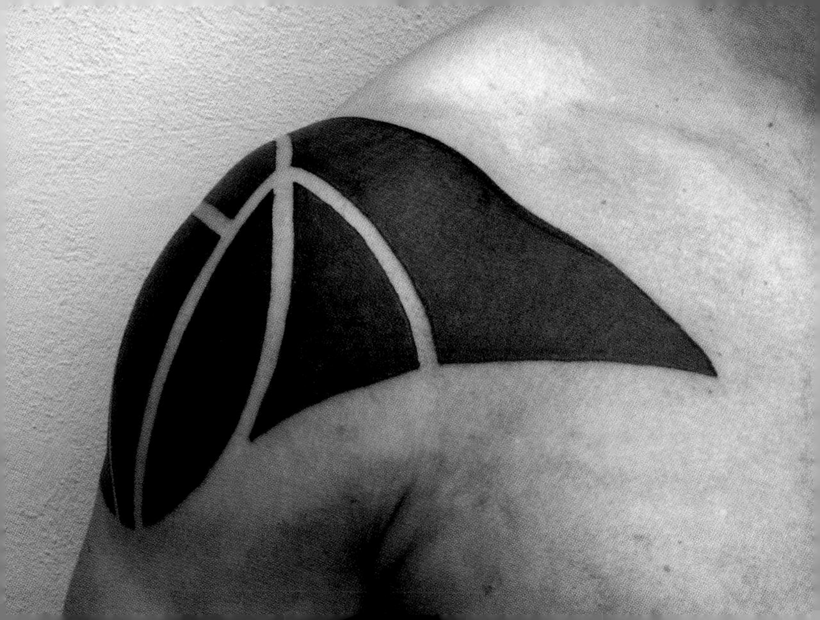

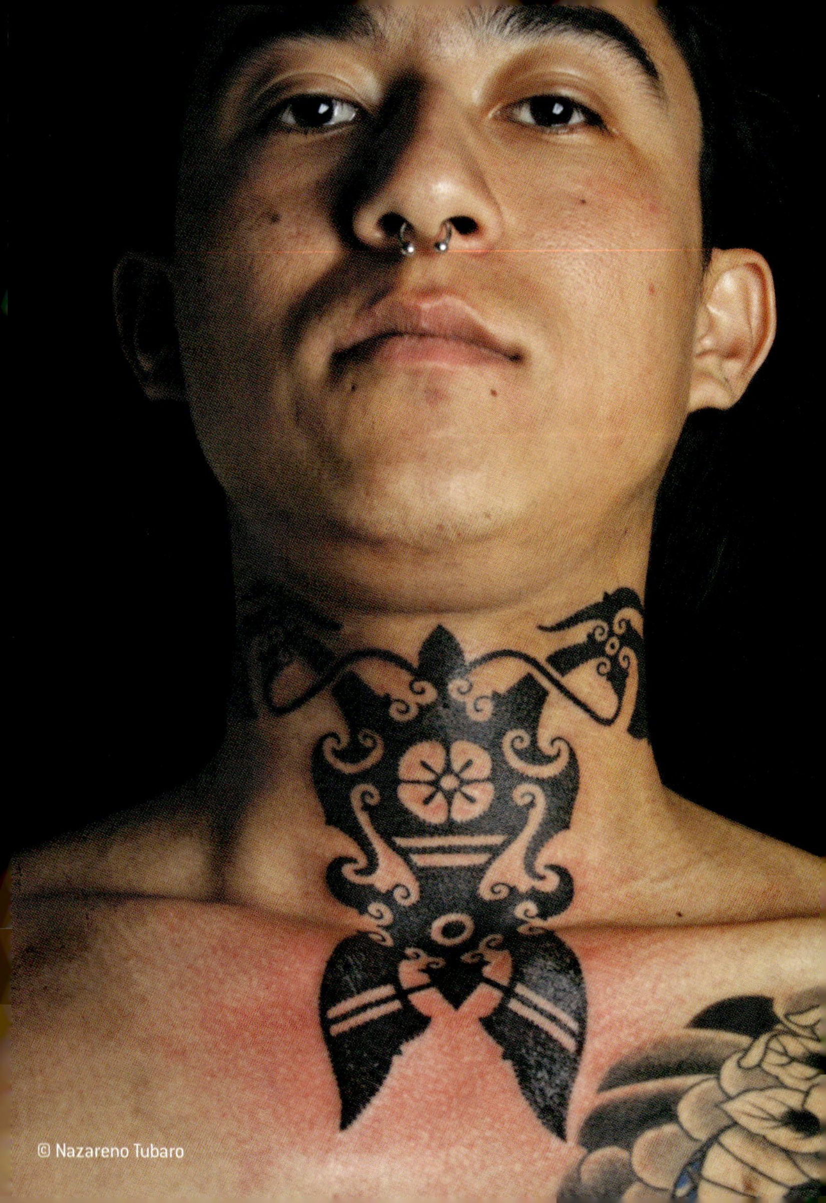
© Nazareno Tubaro

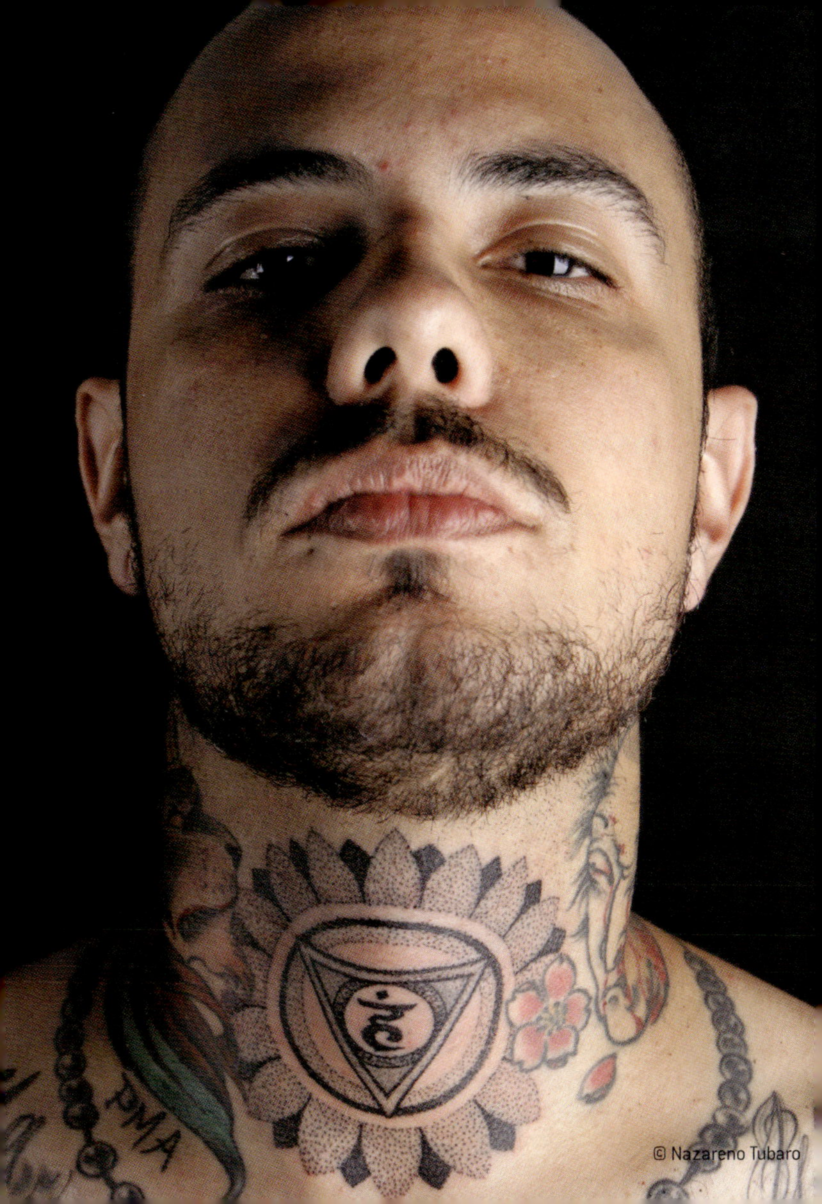
© Nazareno Tubaro

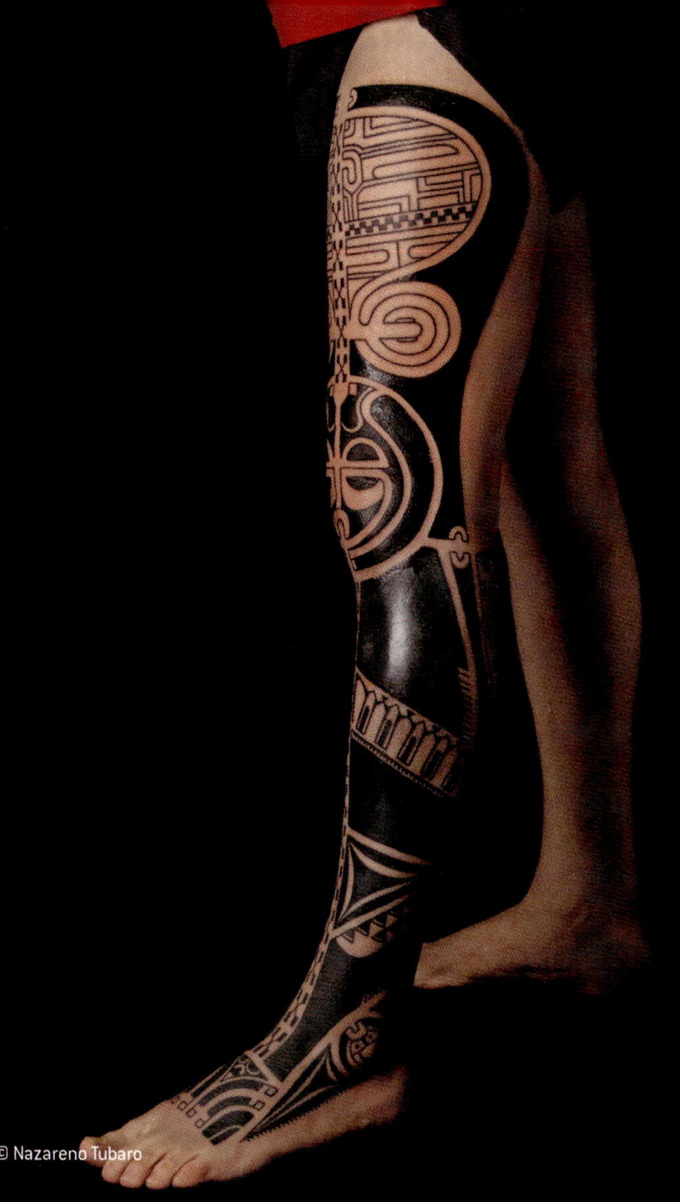

© Nazareno Tubaro

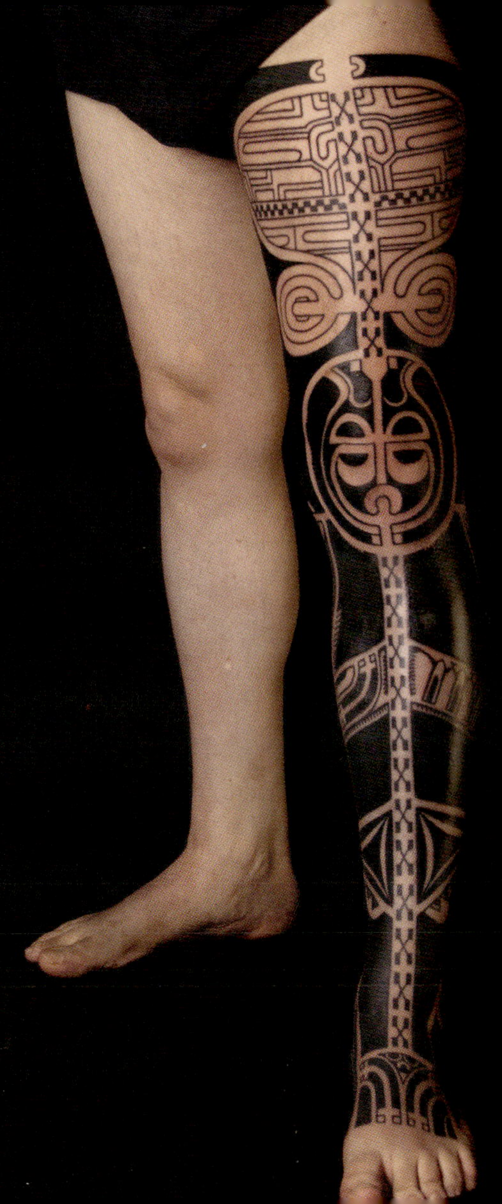

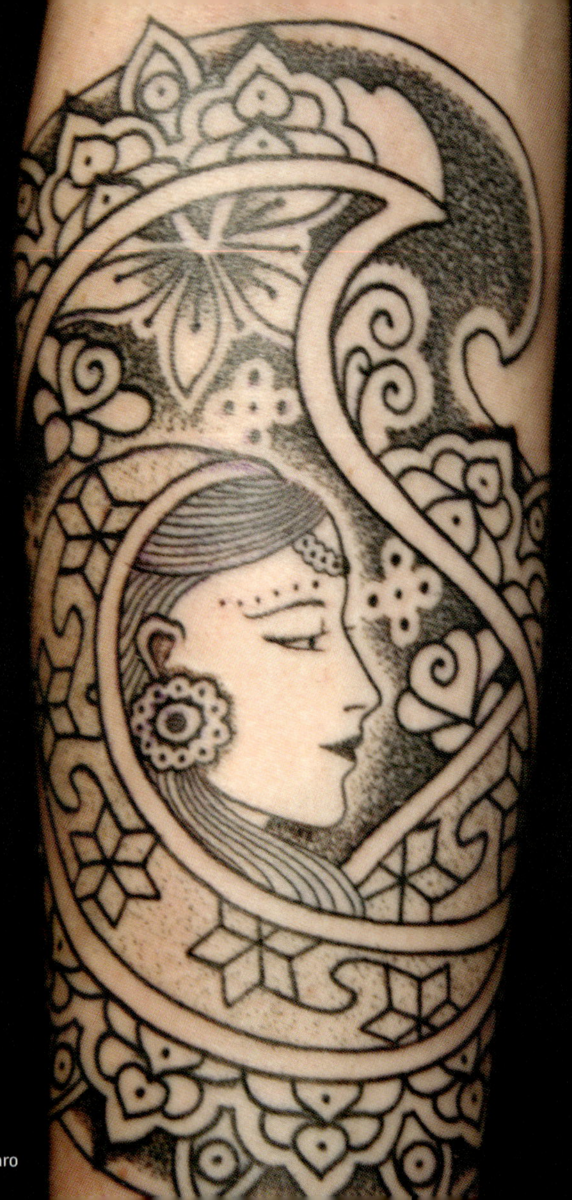

© Nazareno Tubaro

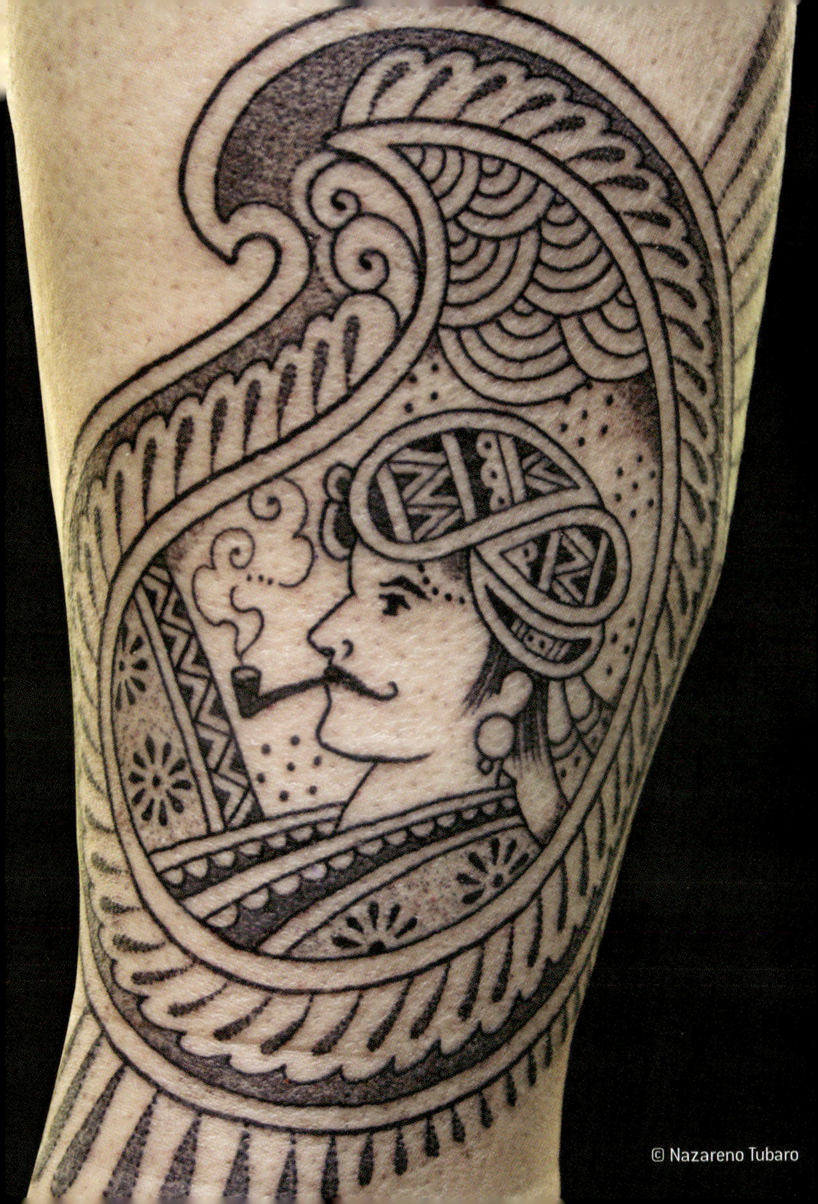
© Nazareno Tubaro

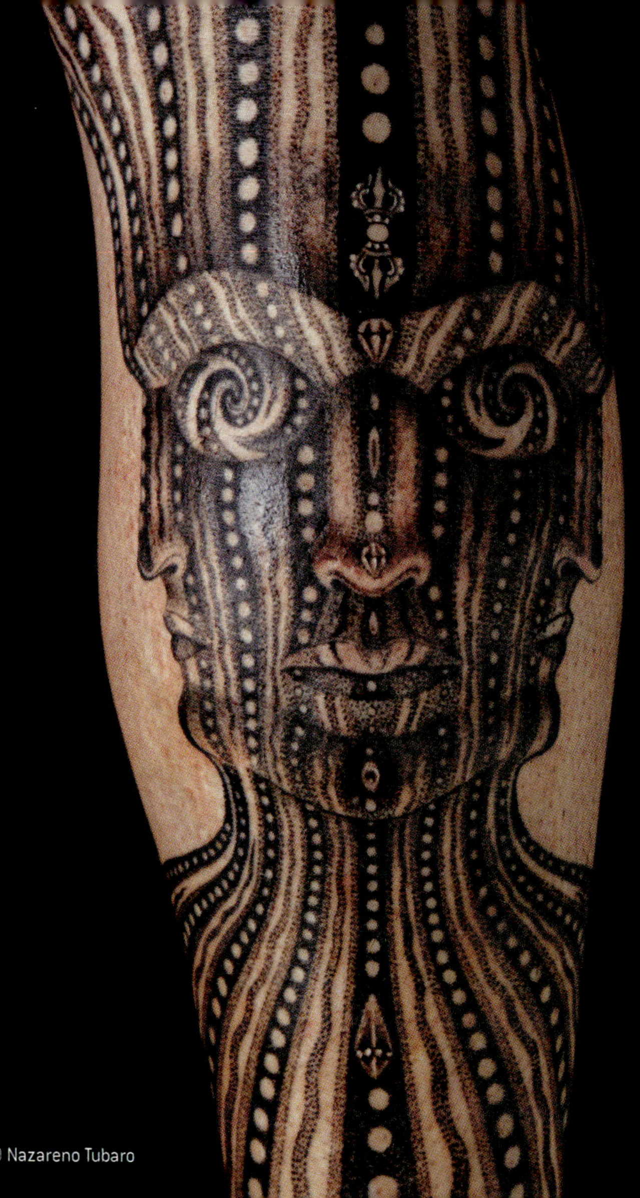

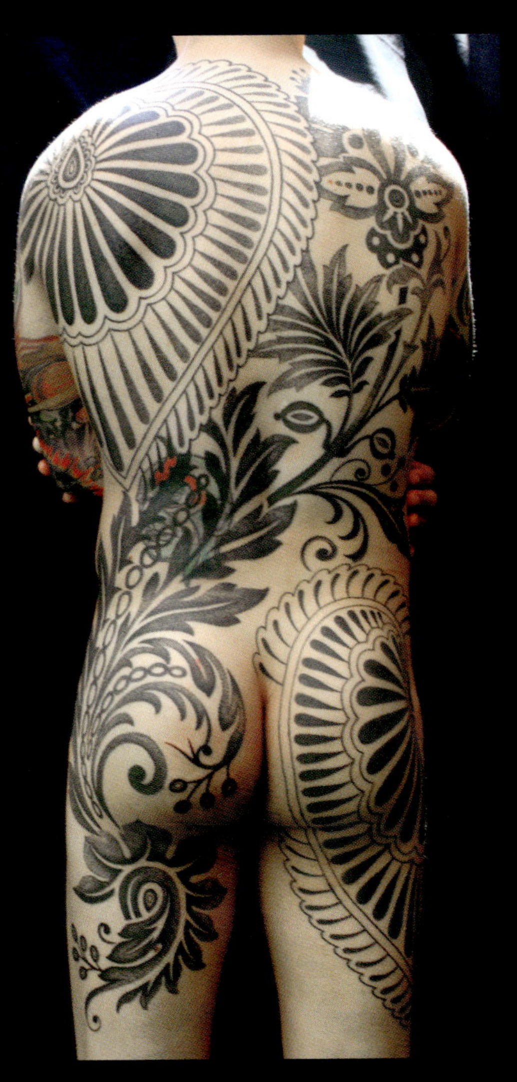

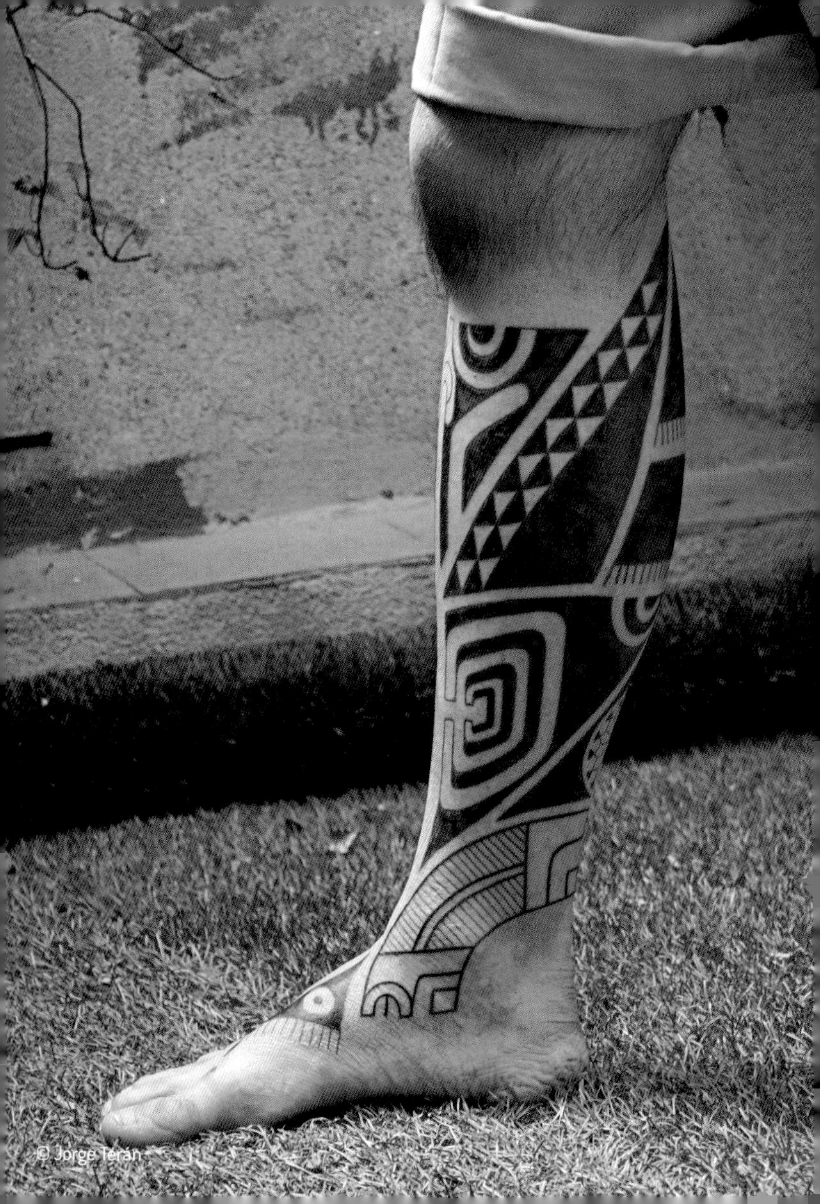
© Jorge Terán

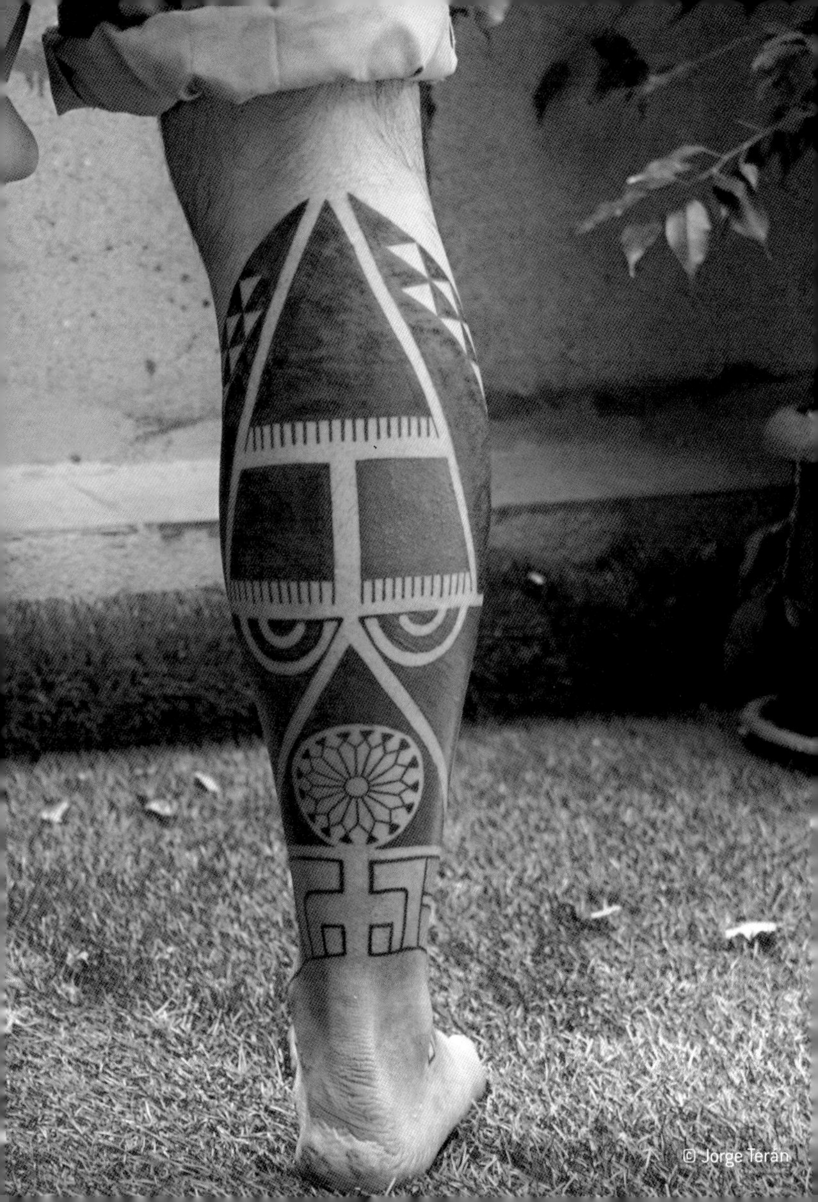

© Jorge Terán

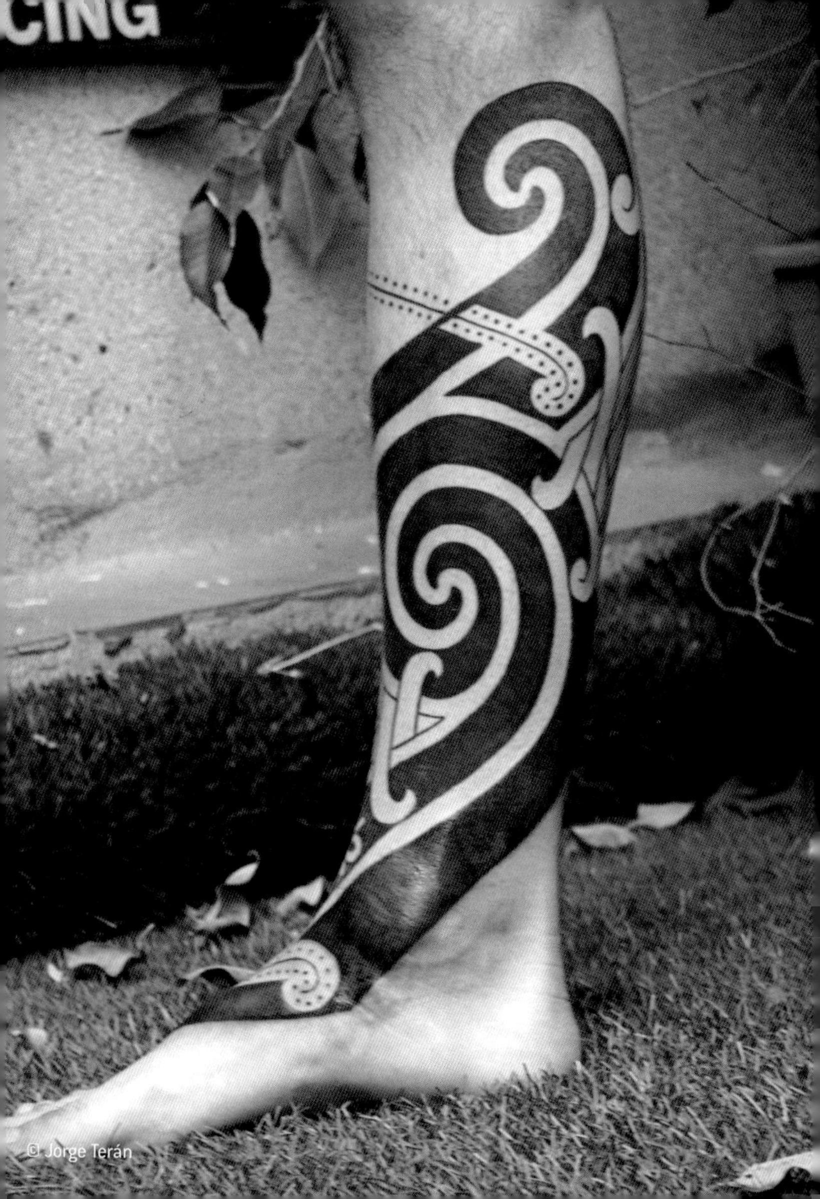
CING

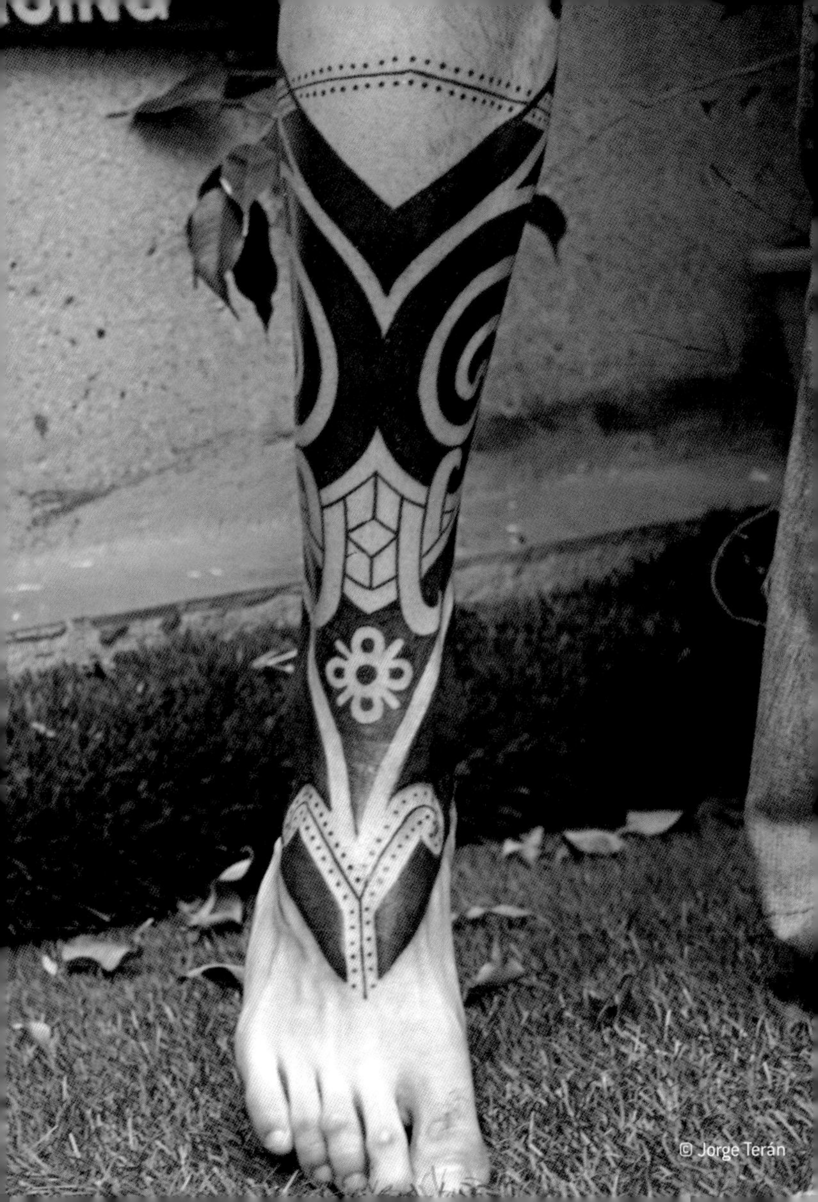

© Jorge Terán

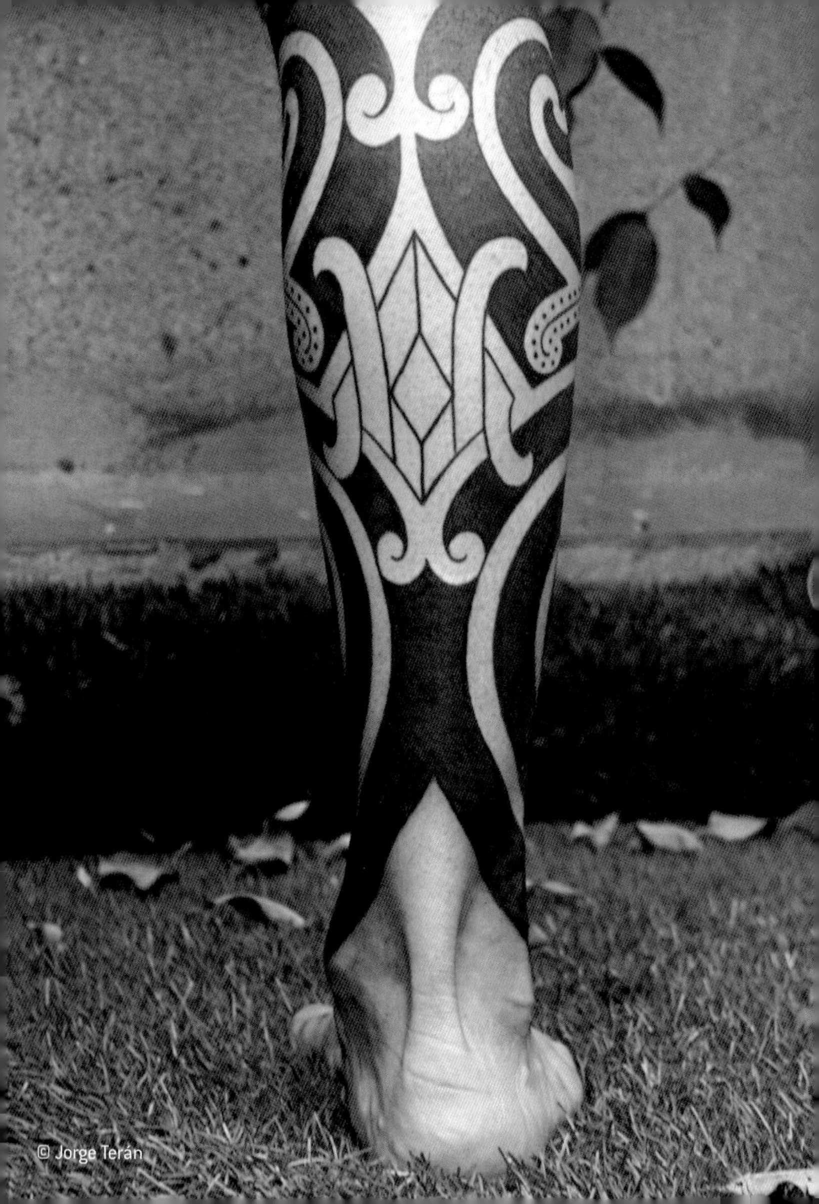

© Jorge Terán

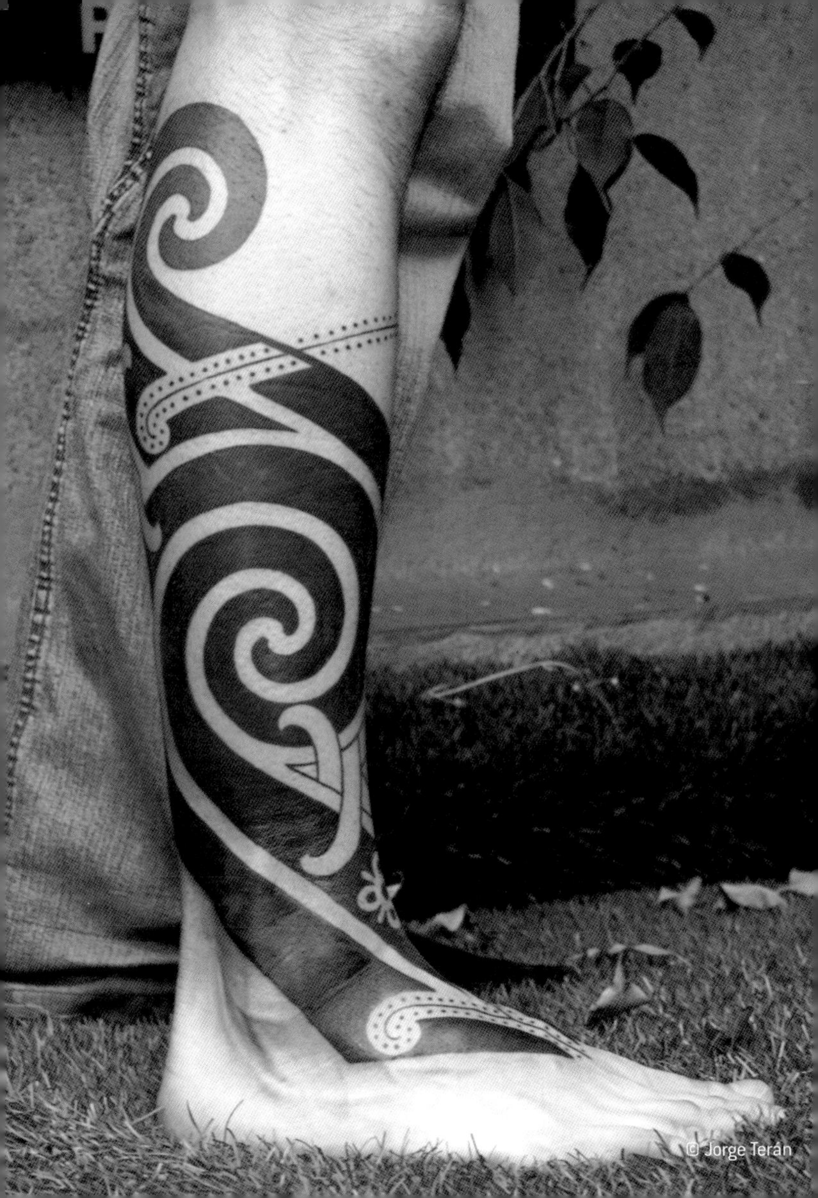
© Jorge Terán

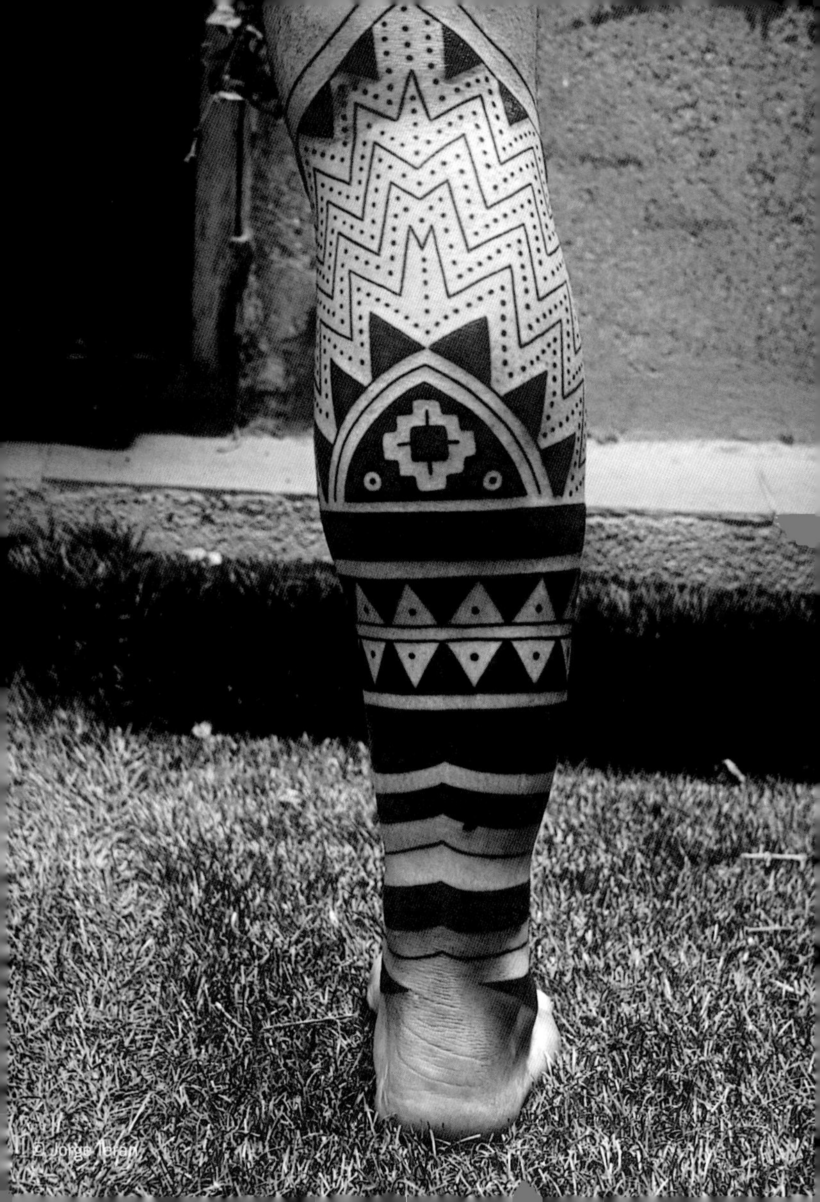
© Jorge Terán

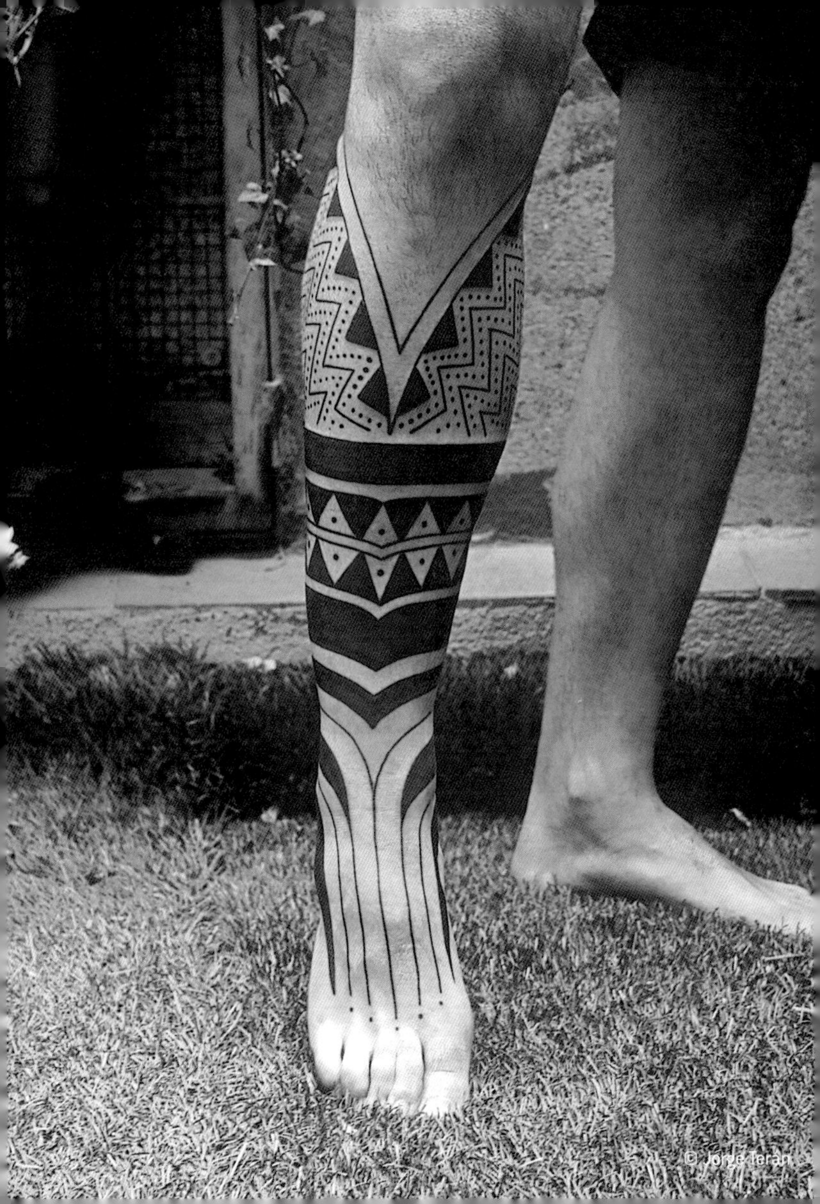© Jorge Terán

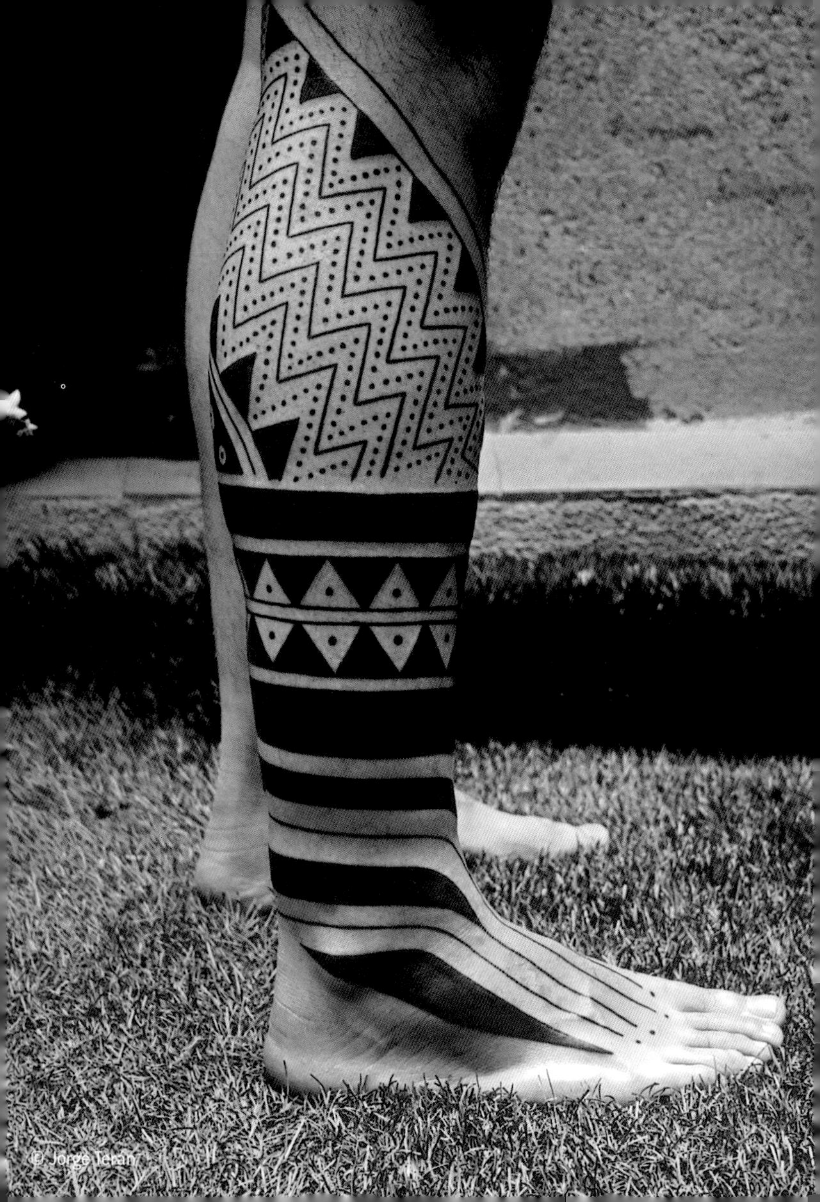
© Jorge Teran

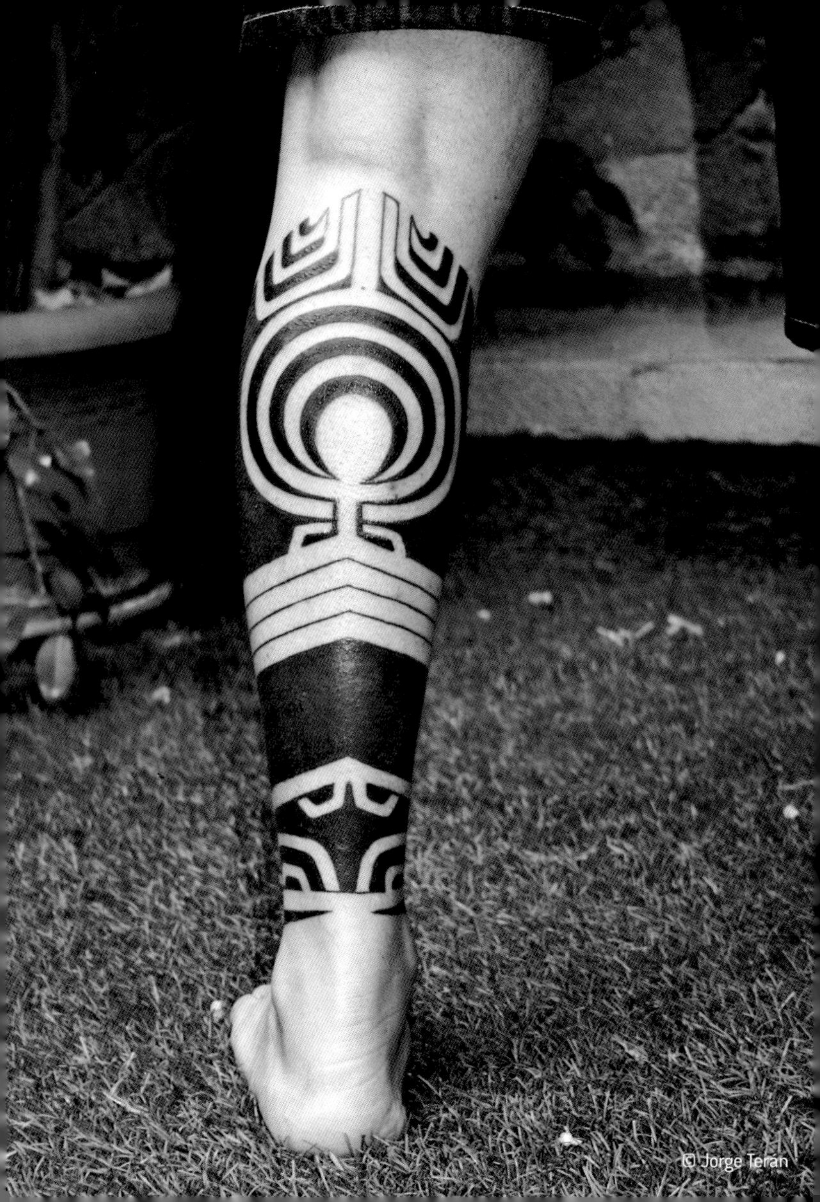
© Jorge Teran

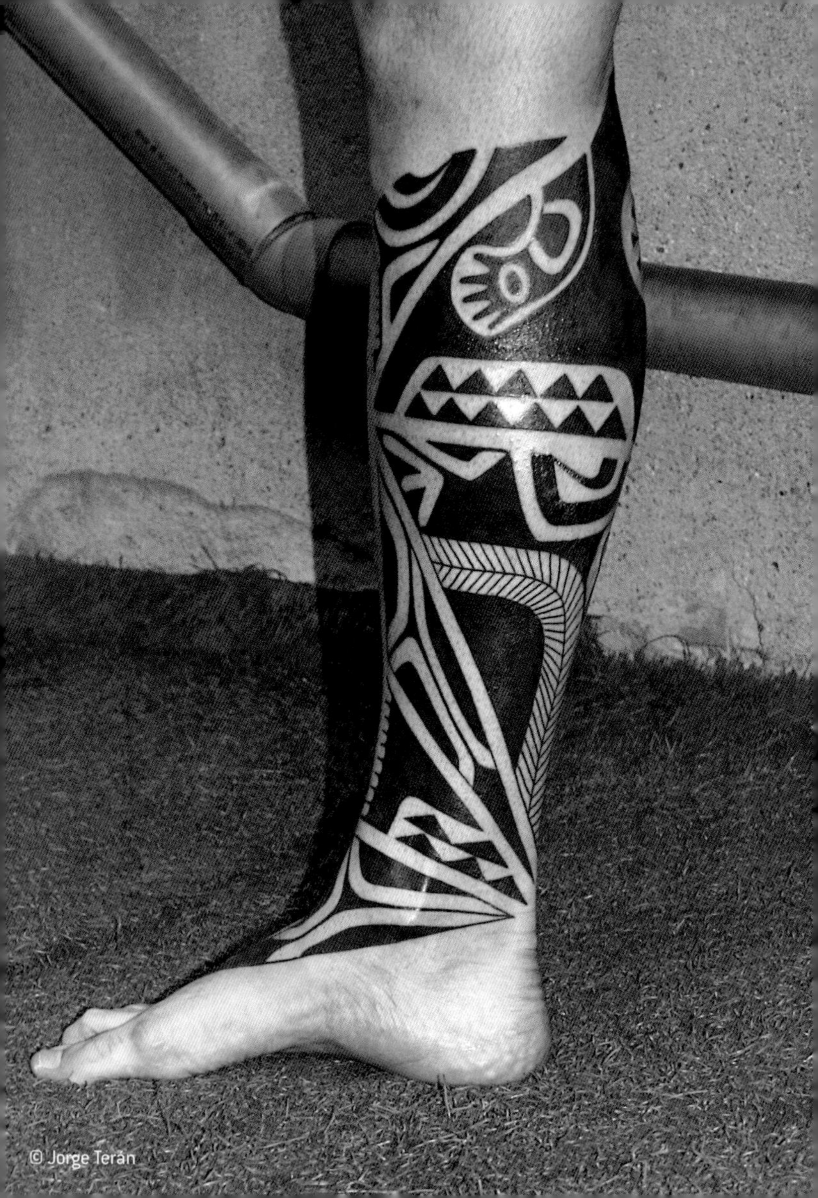

© Jorge Terán

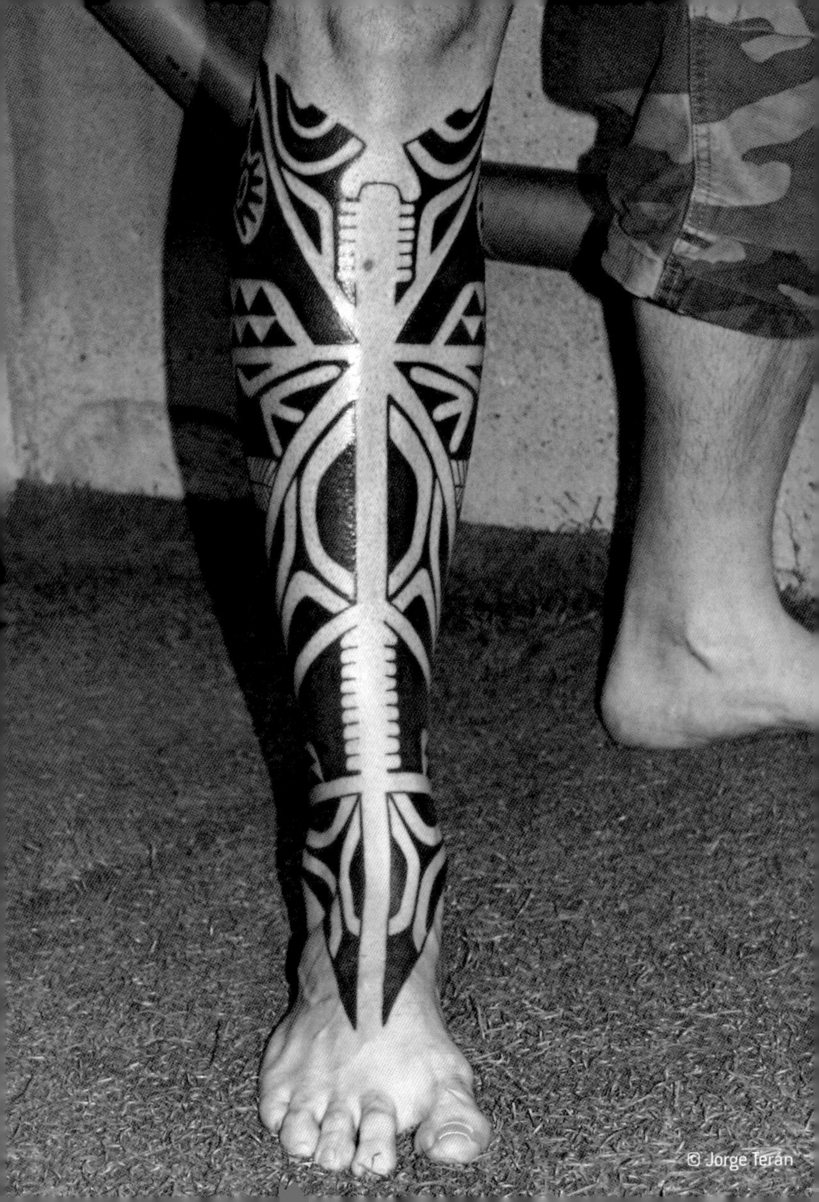
© Jorge Terán

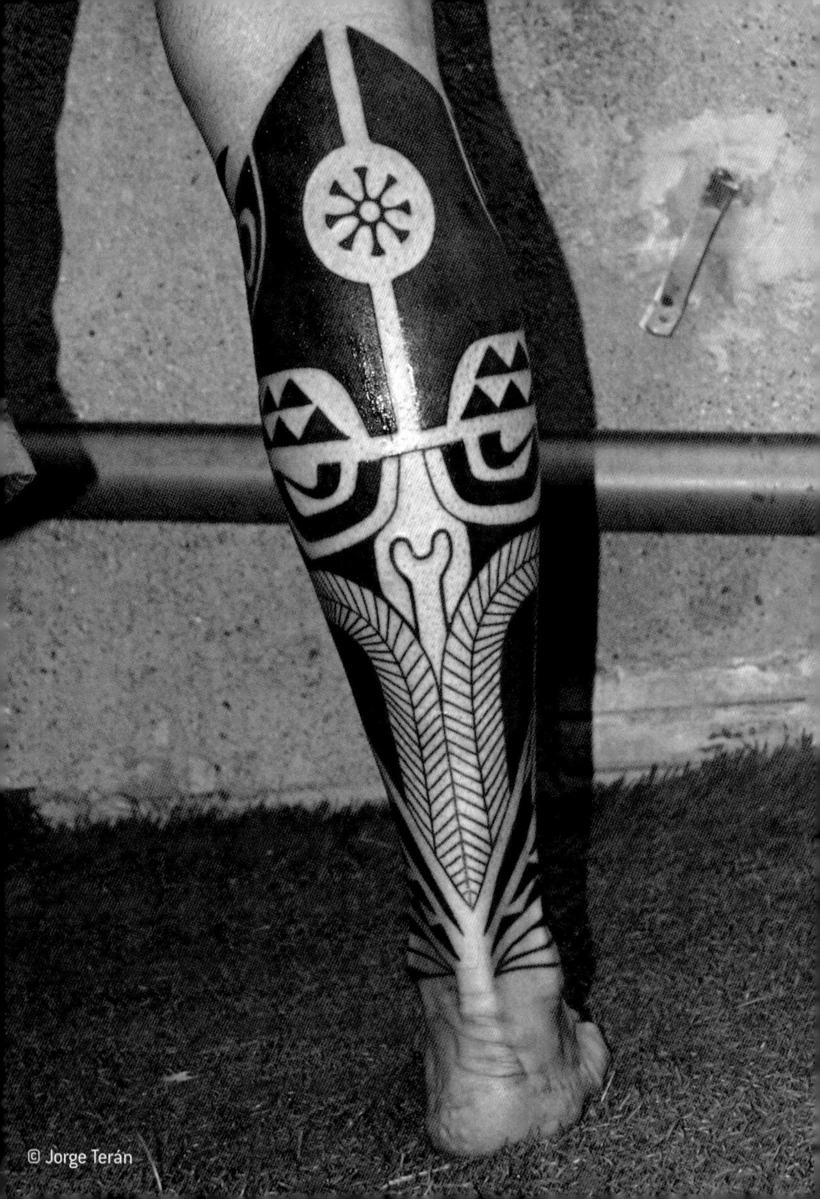

© Jorge Terán

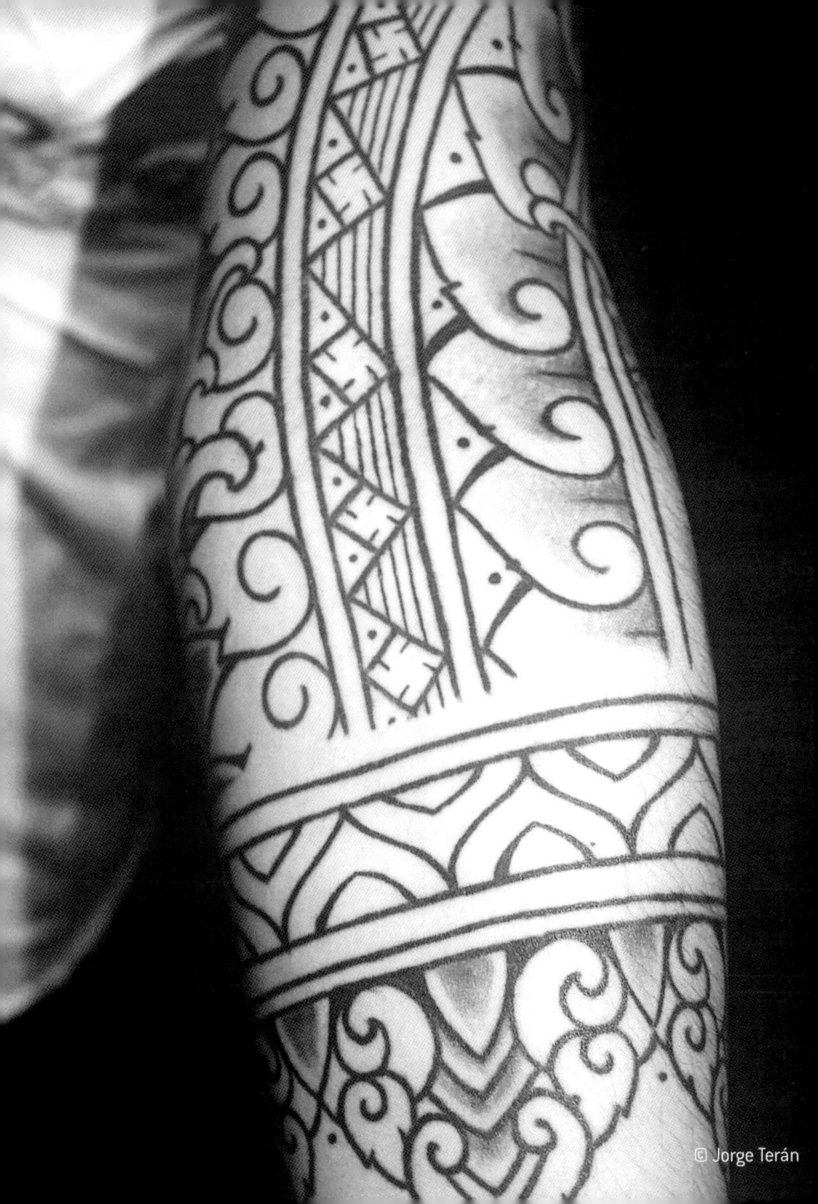
© Jorge Terán

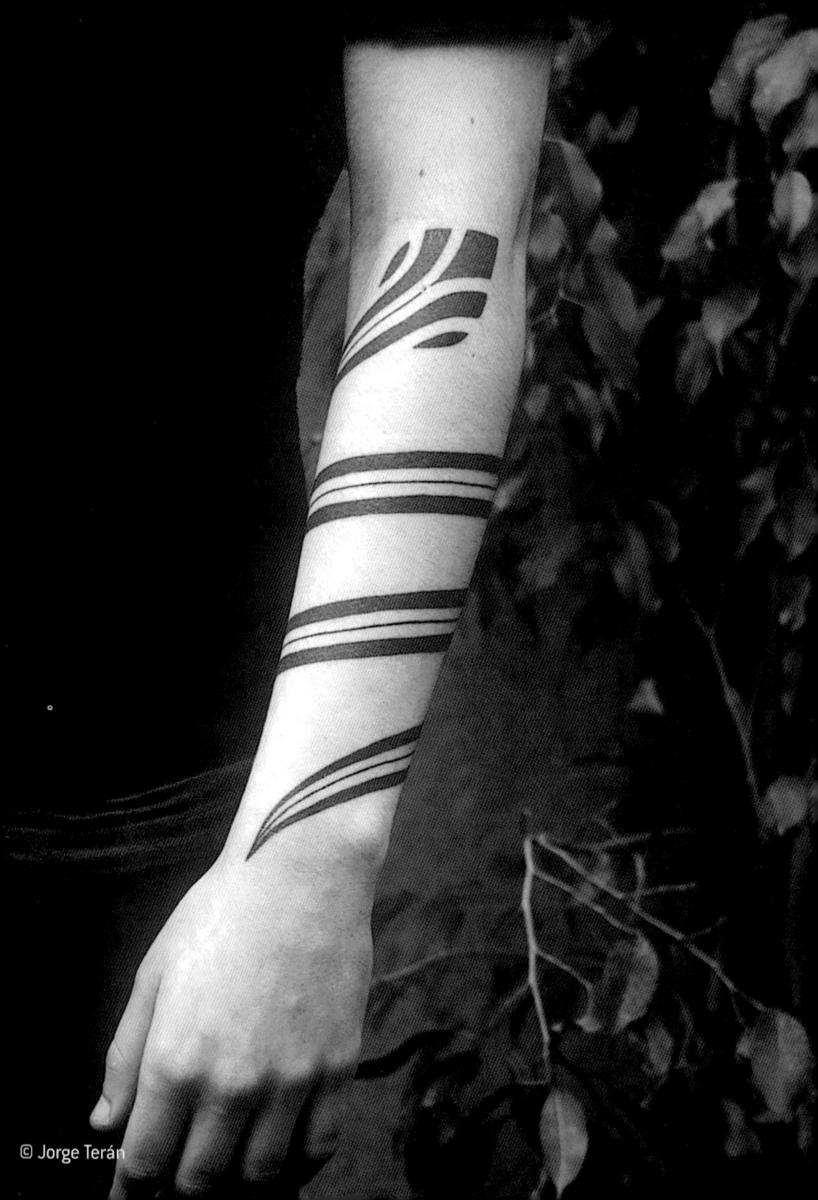
© Jorge Terán

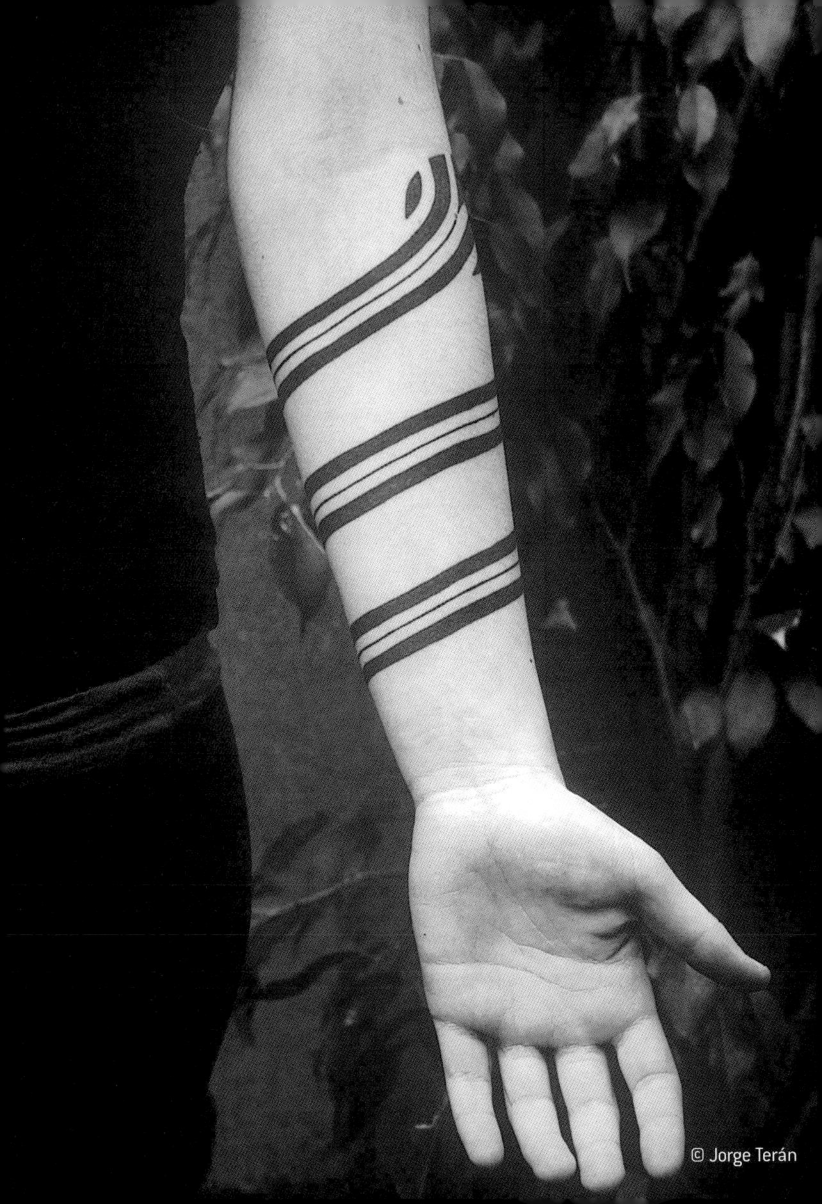
© Jorge Terán

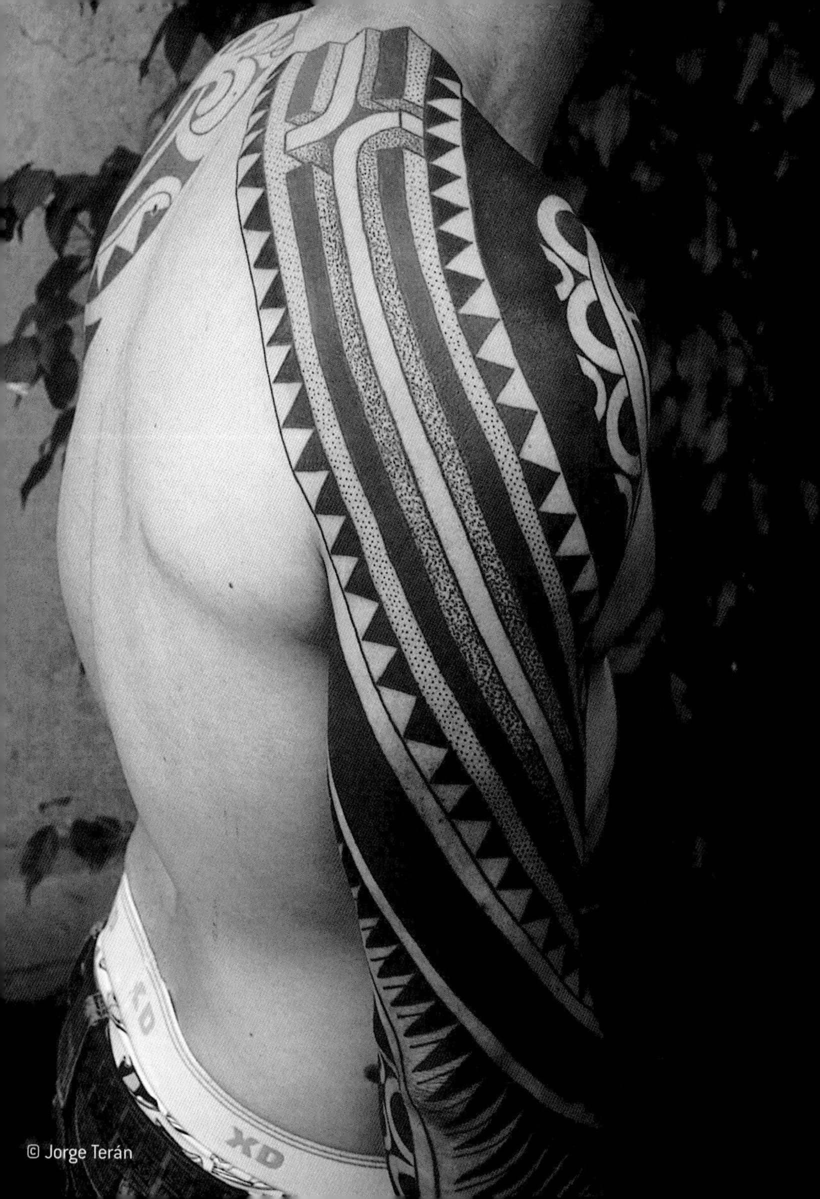
© Jorge Terán

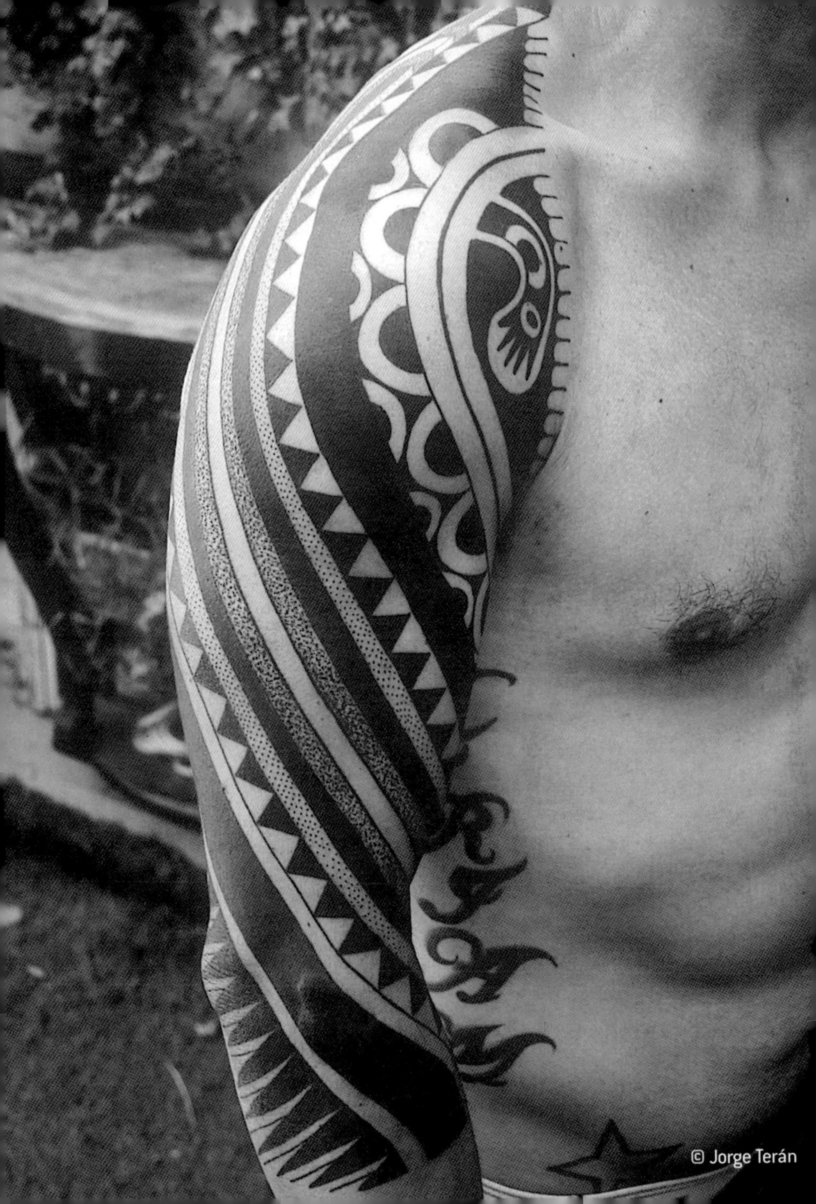
© Jorge Terán

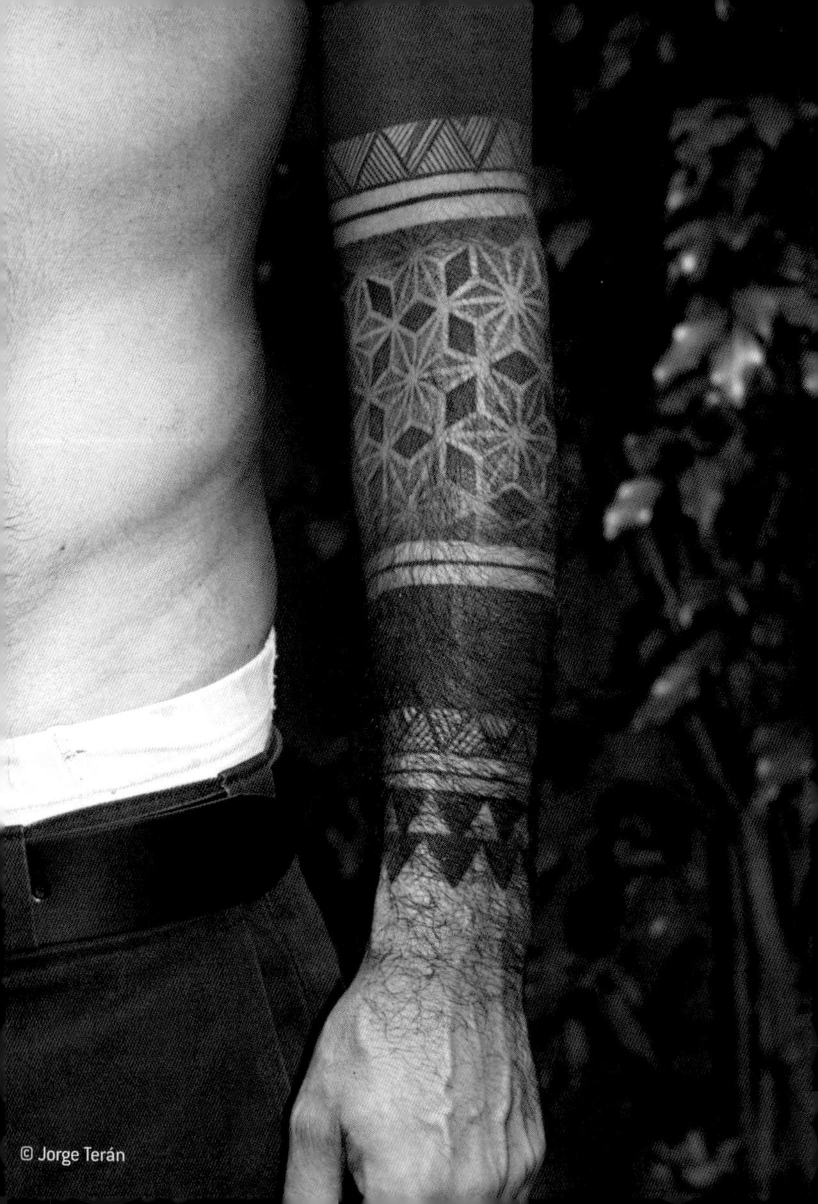
© Jorge Terán

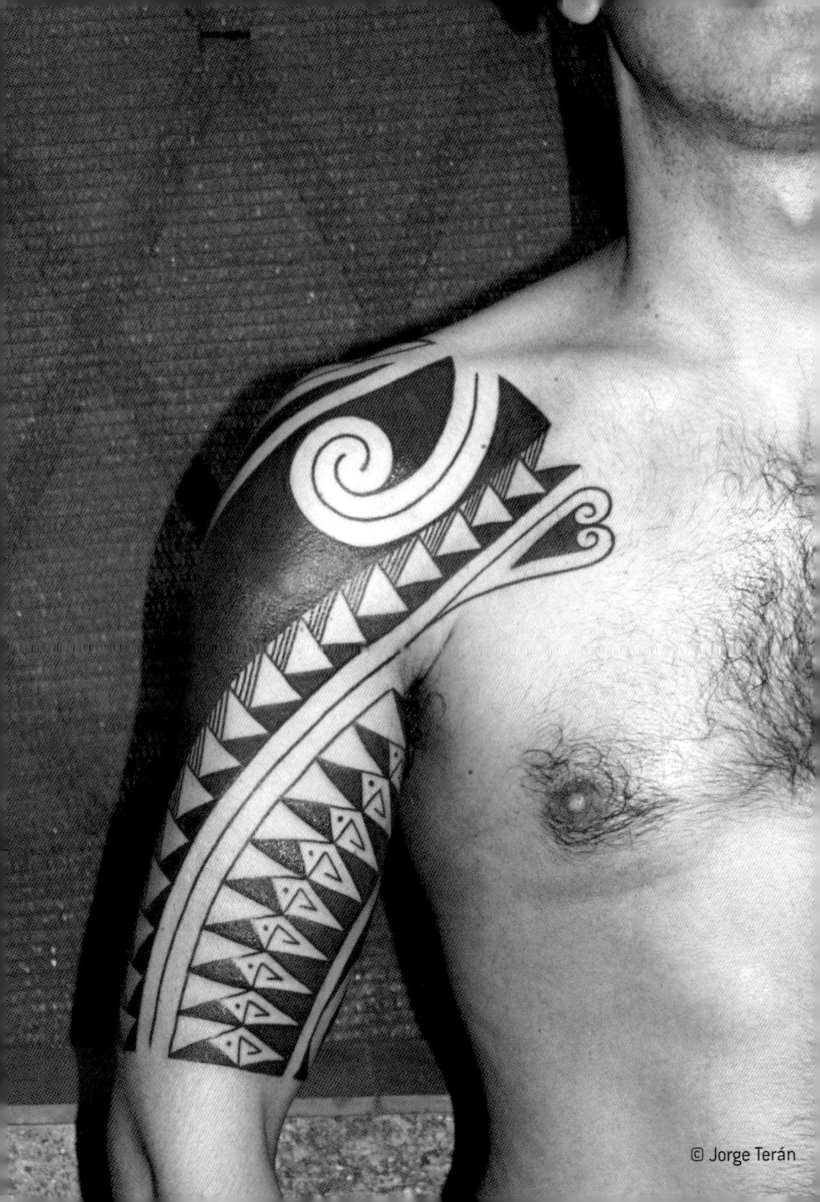

© Jorge Terán

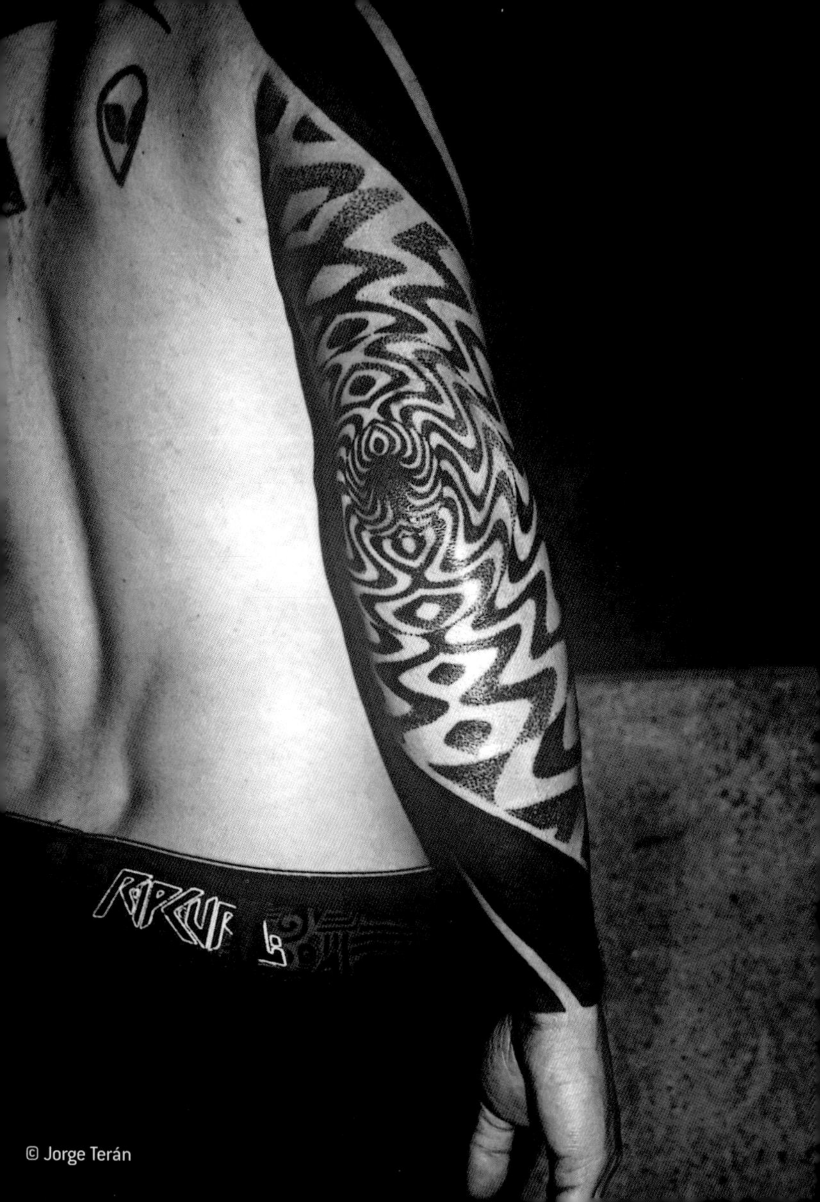
© Jorge Terán

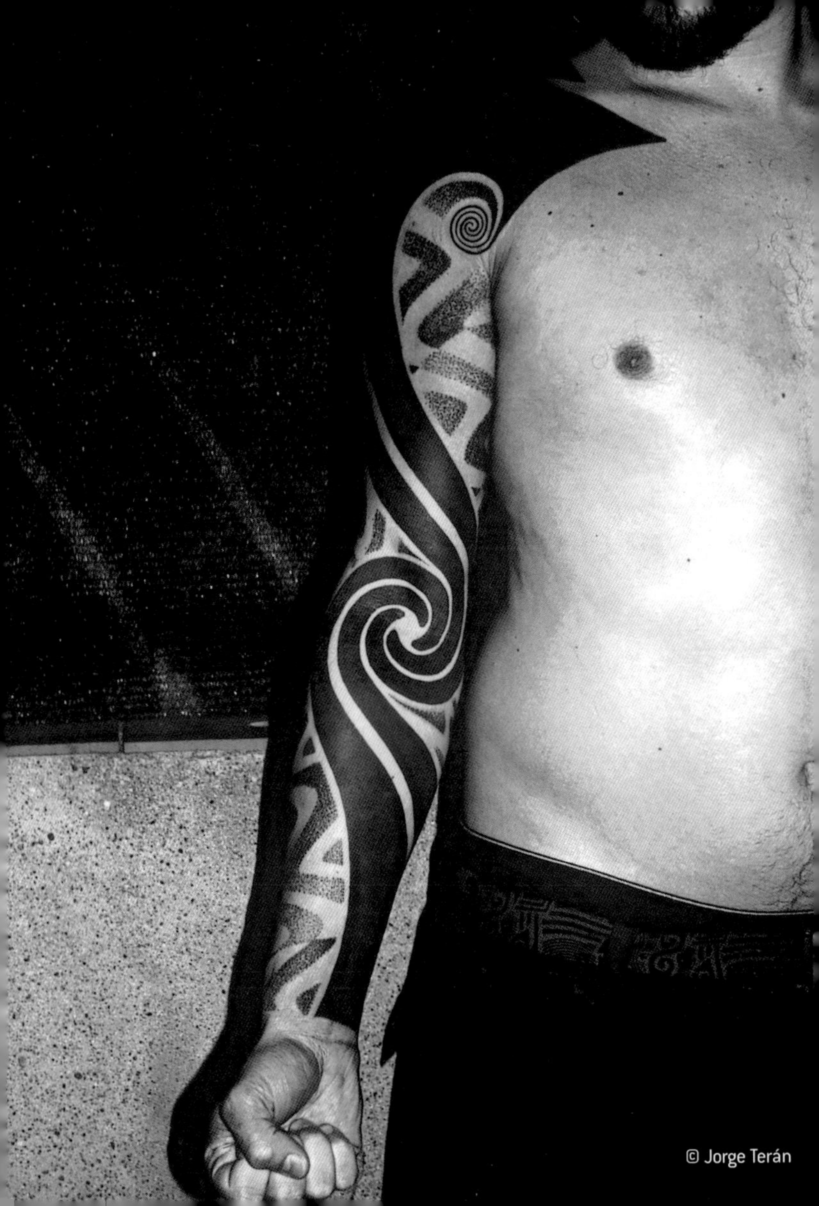

© Jorge Terán

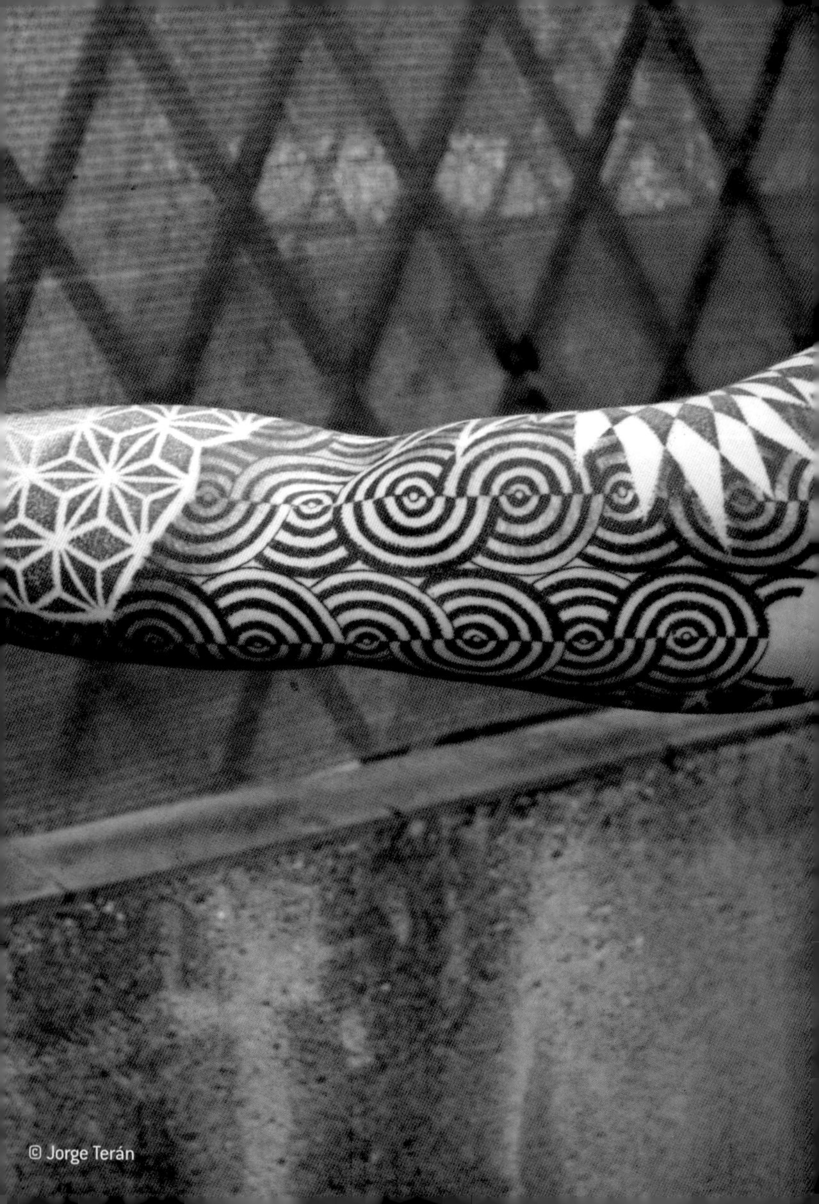

© Jorge Terán

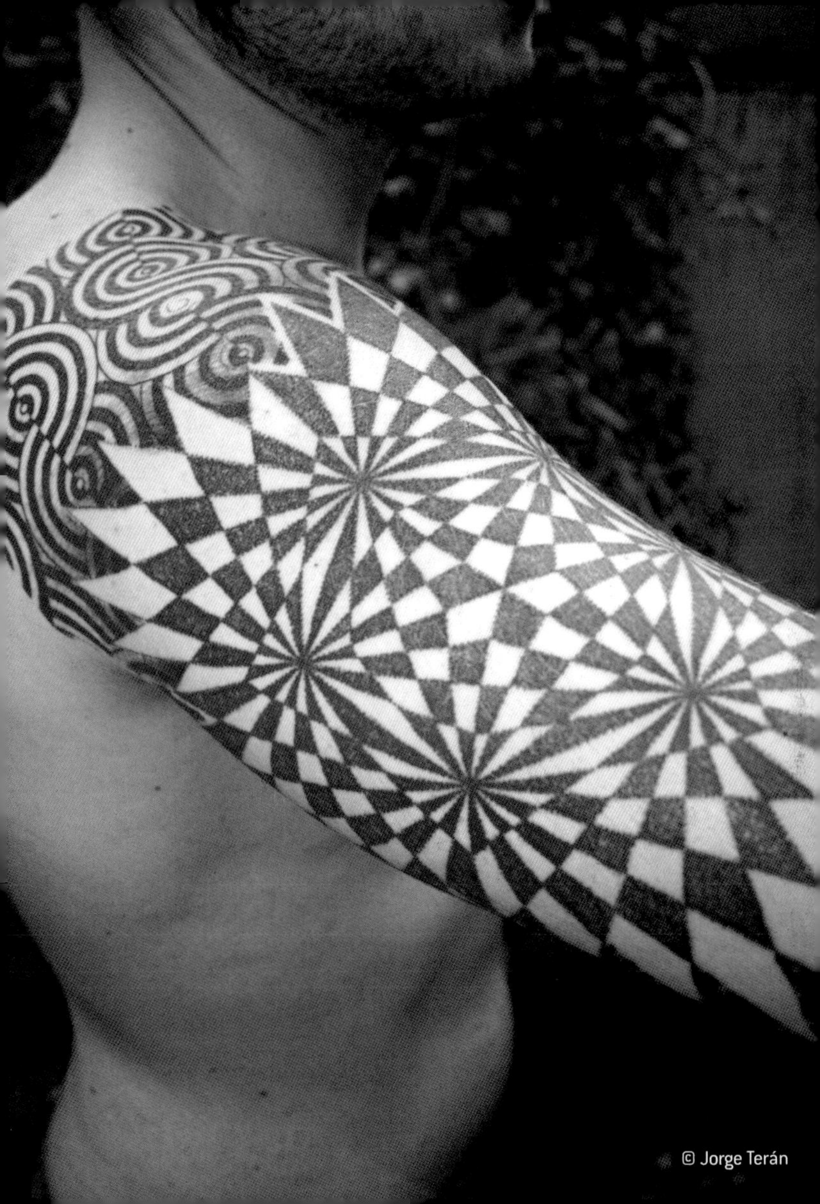

© Jorge Terán

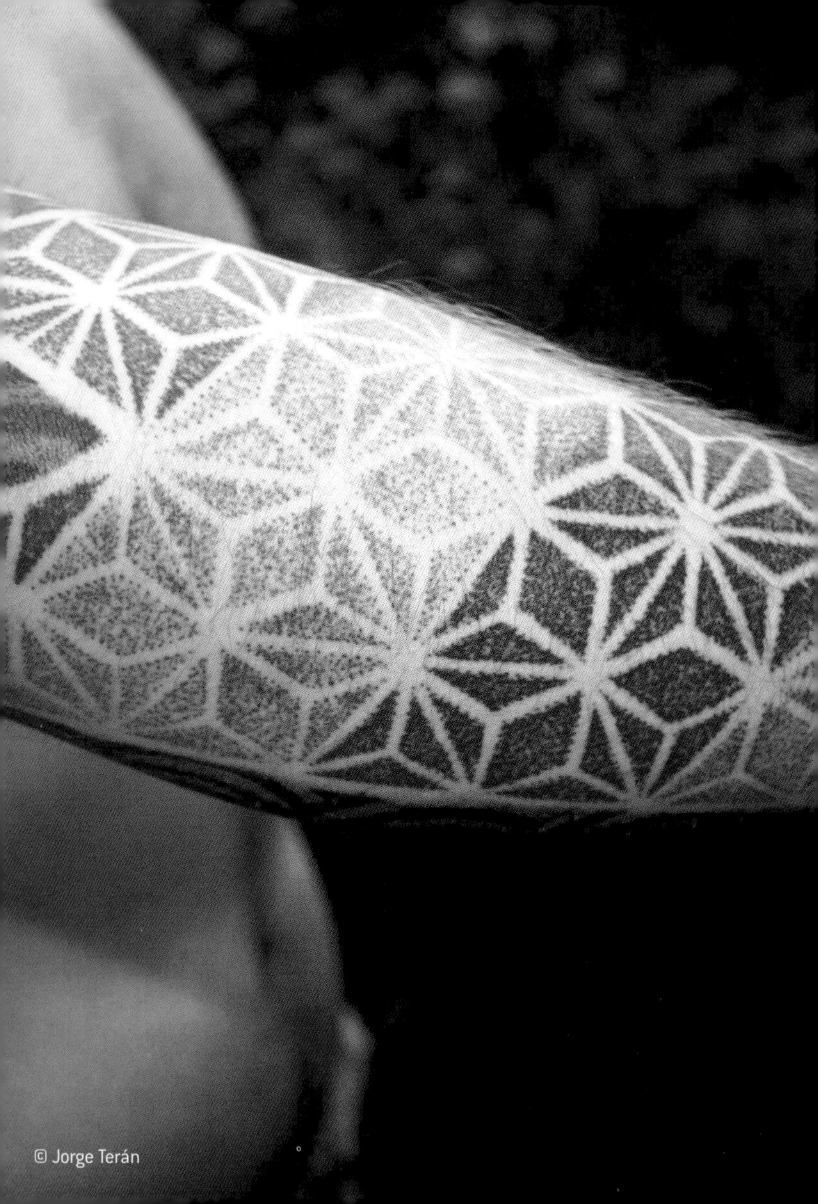

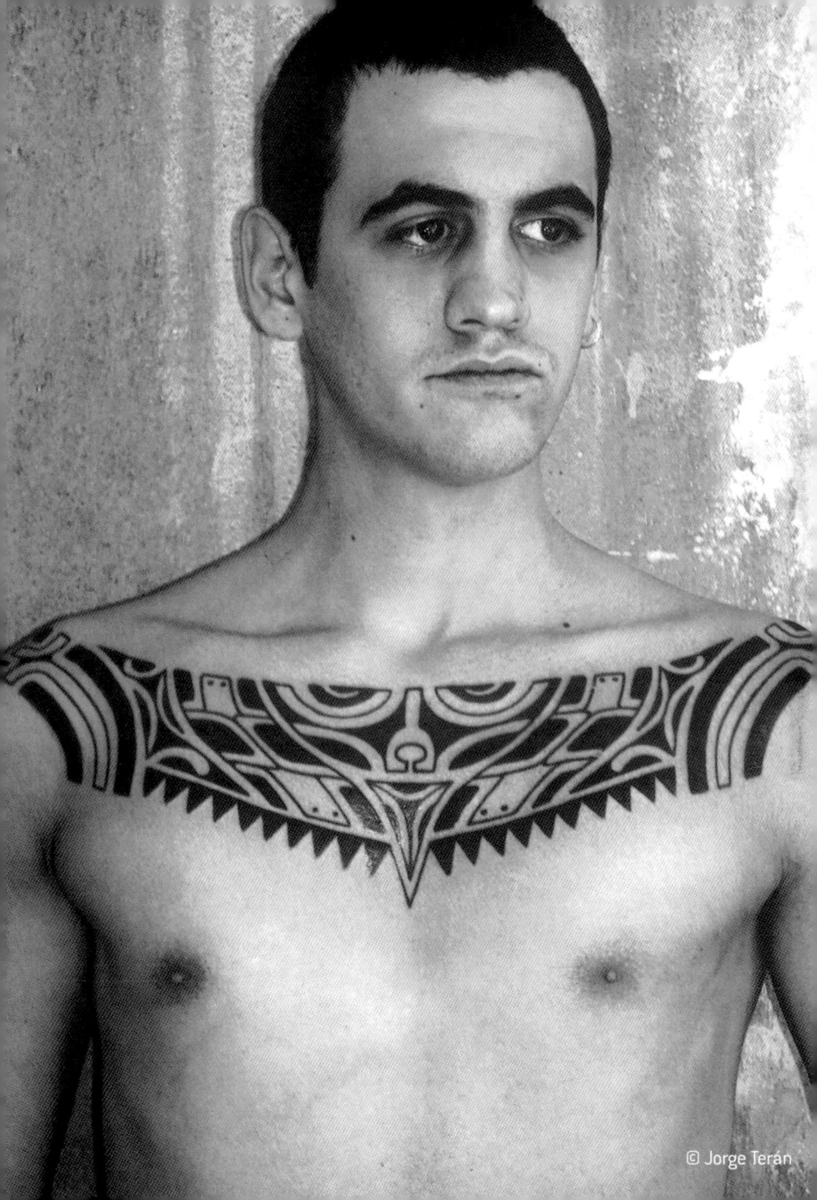
© Jorge Terán

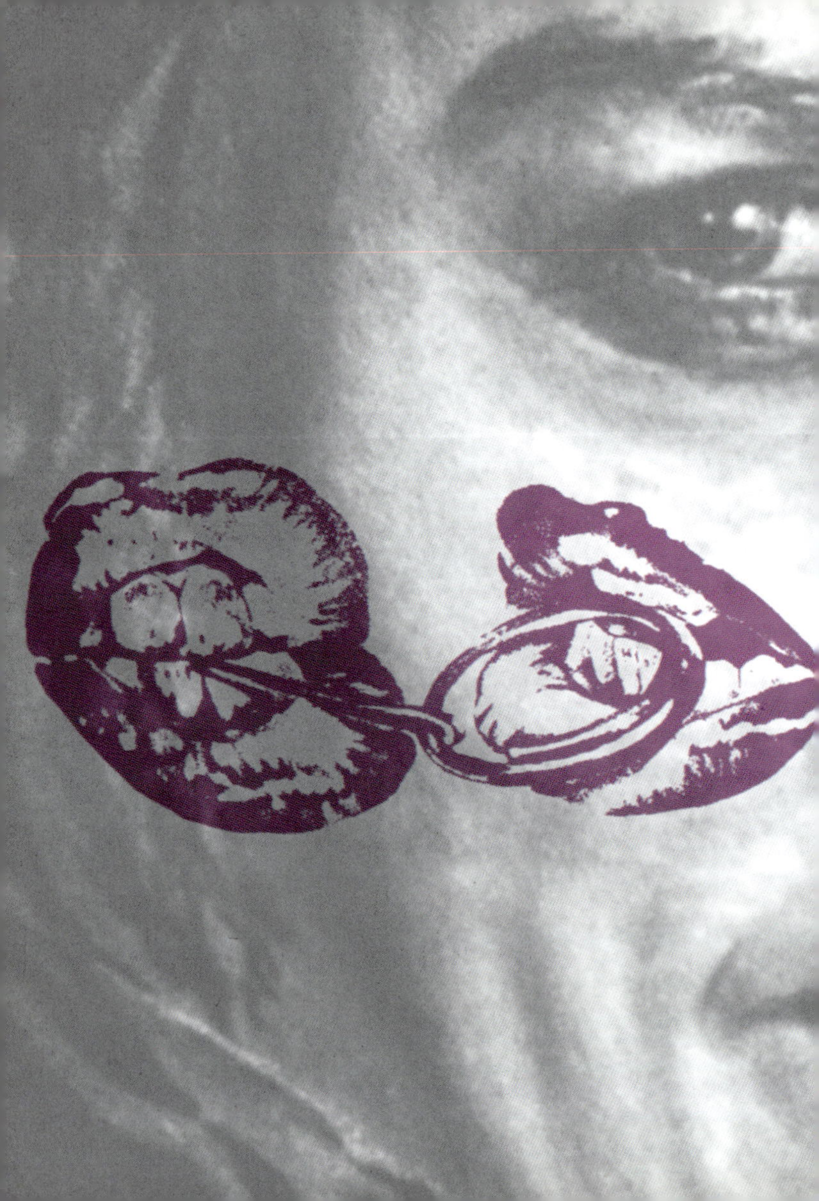

Realistic tattoos

Tatouages réalistes

Realistische Tätowierungen

Realistische tatoeages

Broadly speaking, realism tries to capture an image as close and faithful to reality as possible. As in the universe of pictorial art, realistic tattoo requires the great skill of the artist who performs it: the mastery of the technique is what distinguishes a good illustration from another. Today, realistic tattooing is usually carried out to portray idols, loved ones and even pets. Generally, the drawing is done by copying the image from a photograph.

Dans les grandes lignes, le réalisme tente de représenter une image de la façon la plus proche et la plus fidèle possible à la réalité. Comme dans l'univers de l'art de la peinture, le tatouage réaliste demande une grande habileté de l'artiste le réalisant : c'est la maîtrise de la technique qui différenciera une bonne illustration d'une autre ne l'étant pas.
Actuellement, le tatouage réaliste est généralement demandé pour représenter des idoles, des êtres chers et y compris des animaux familiers. Le dessin est généralement réalisé en copiant l'image d'une photographie.

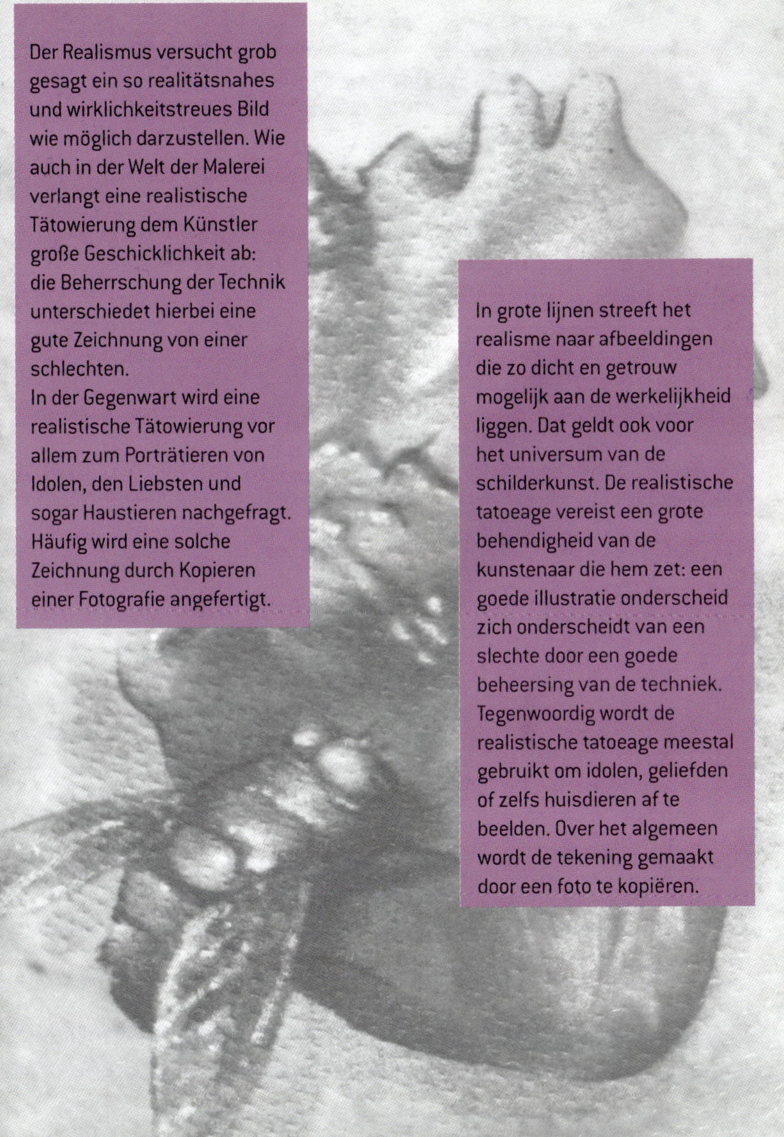

Der Realismus versucht grob gesagt ein so realitätsnahes und wirklichkeitstreues Bild wie möglich darzustellen. Wie auch in der Welt der Malerei verlangt eine realistische Tätowierung dem Künstler große Geschicklichkeit ab: die Beherrschung der Technik unterschiedet hierbei eine gute Zeichnung von einer schlechten.
In der Gegenwart wird eine realistische Tätowierung vor allem zum Porträtieren von Idolen, den Liebsten und sogar Haustieren nachgefragt. Häufig wird eine solche Zeichnung durch Kopieren einer Fotografie angefertigt.

In grote lijnen streeft het realisme naar afbeeldingen die zo dicht en getrouw mogelijk aan de werkelijkheid liggen. Dat geldt ook voor het universum van de schilderkunst. De realistische tatoeage vereist een grote behendigheid van de kunstenaar die hem zet: een goede illustratie onderscheid zich onderscheidt van een slechte door een goede beheersing van de techniek. Tegenwoordig wordt de realistische tatoeage meestal gebruikt om idolen, geliefden of zelfs huisdieren af te beelden. Over het algemeen wordt de tekening gemaakt door een foto te kopiëren.

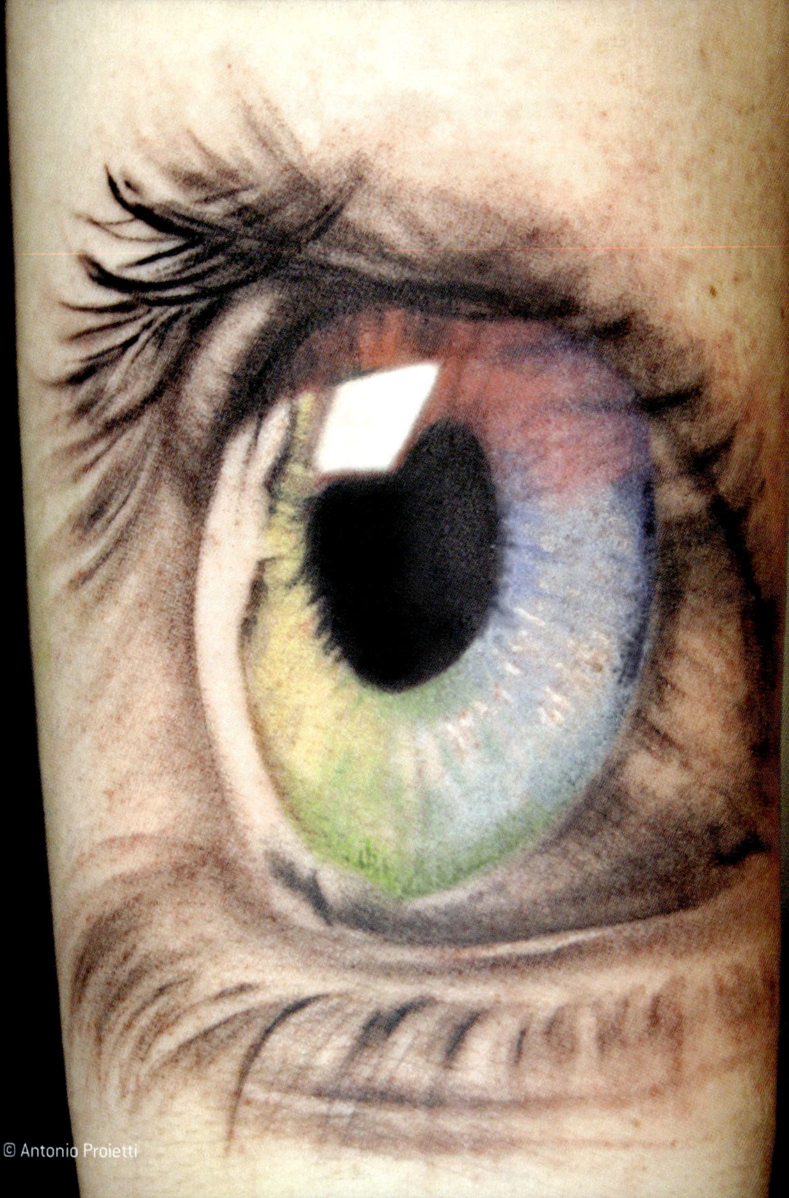

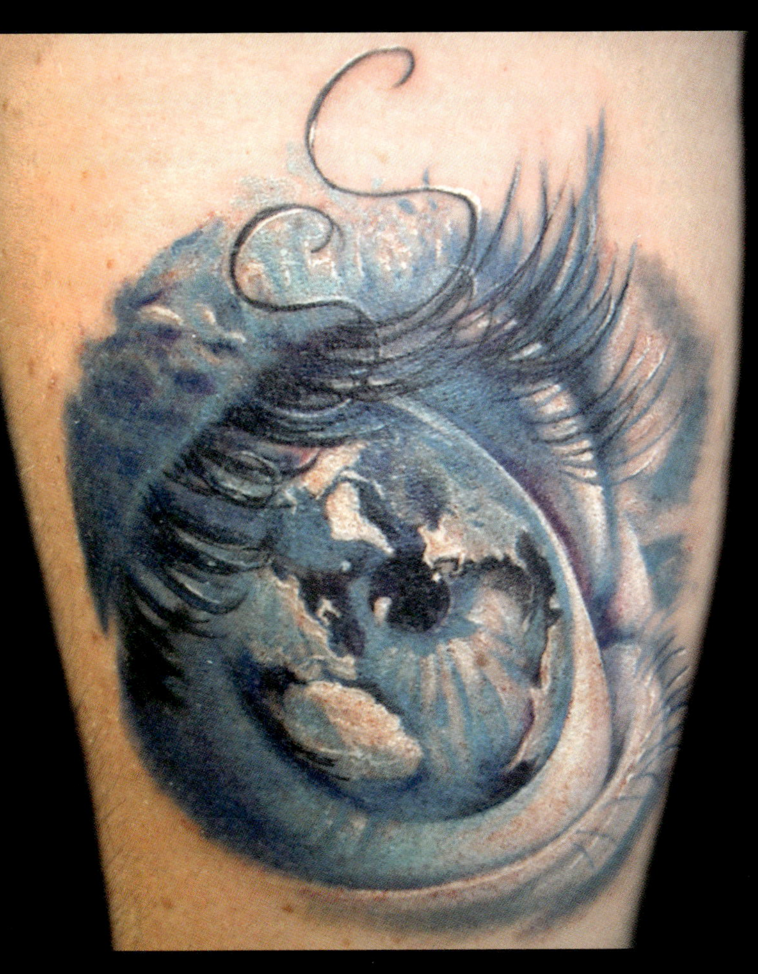

© Antonio Proietti

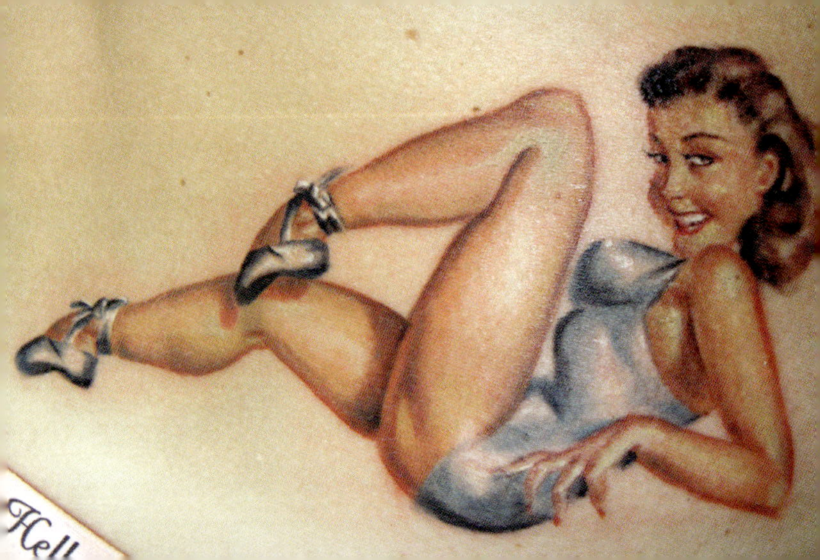
Hell

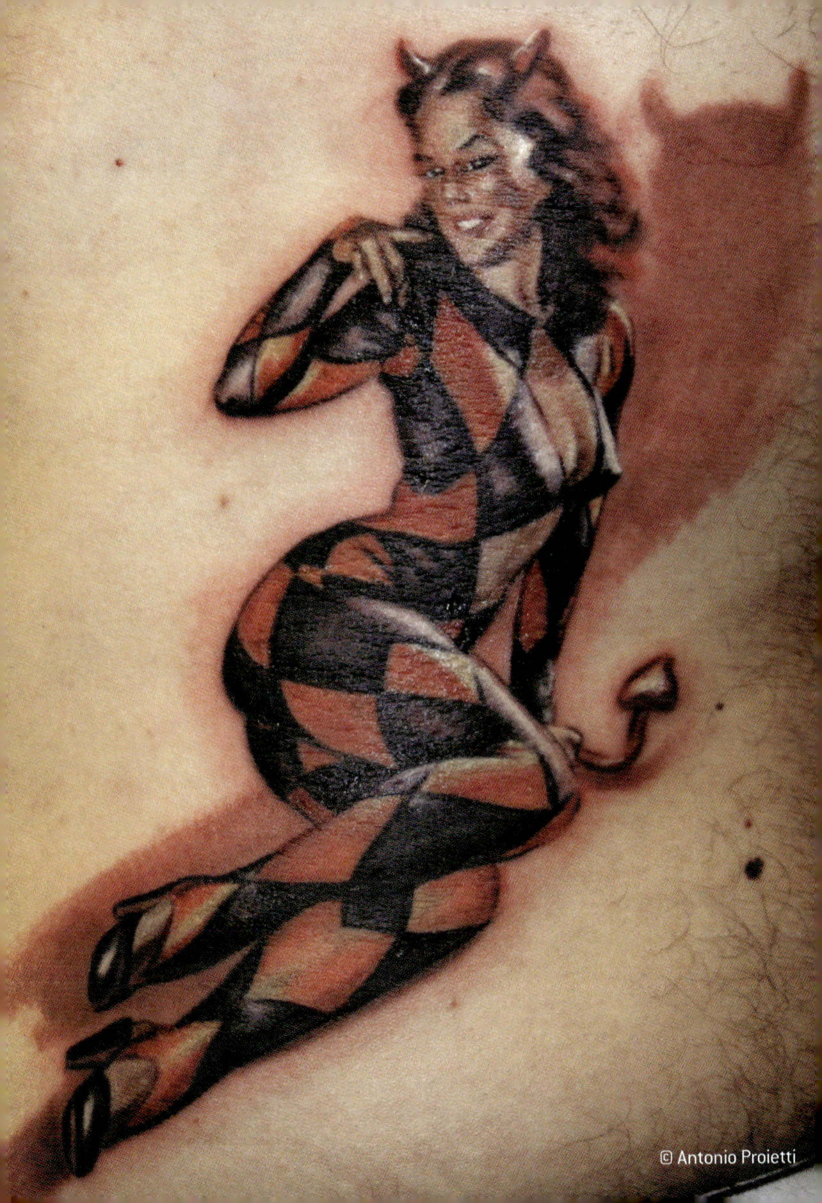
© Antonio Proietti

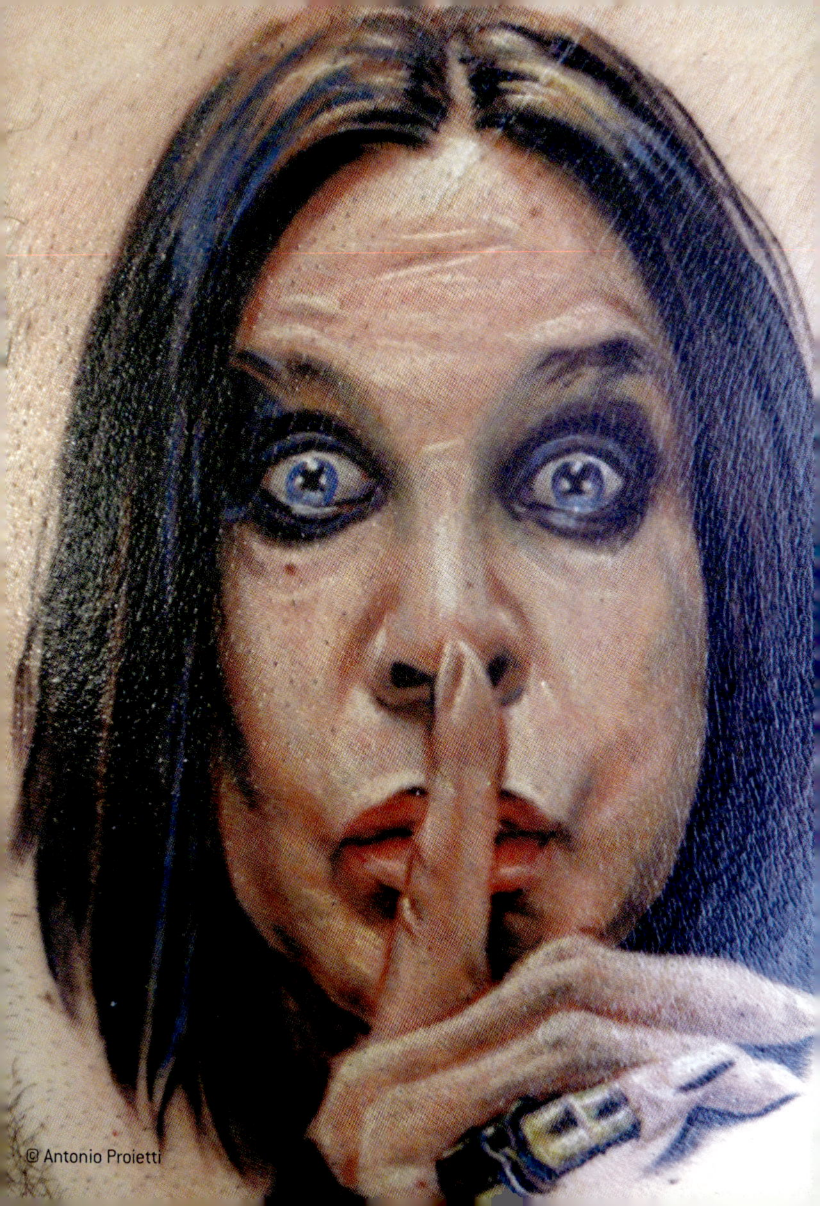
© Antonio Proietti

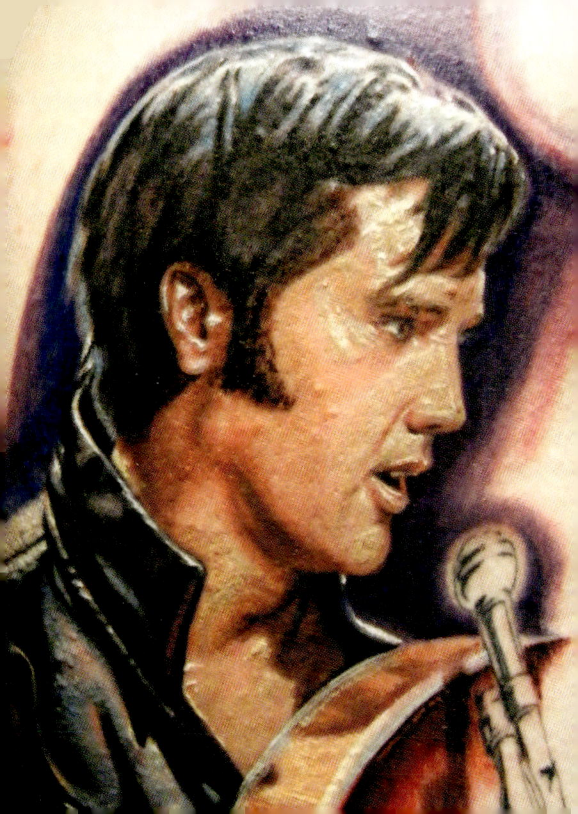

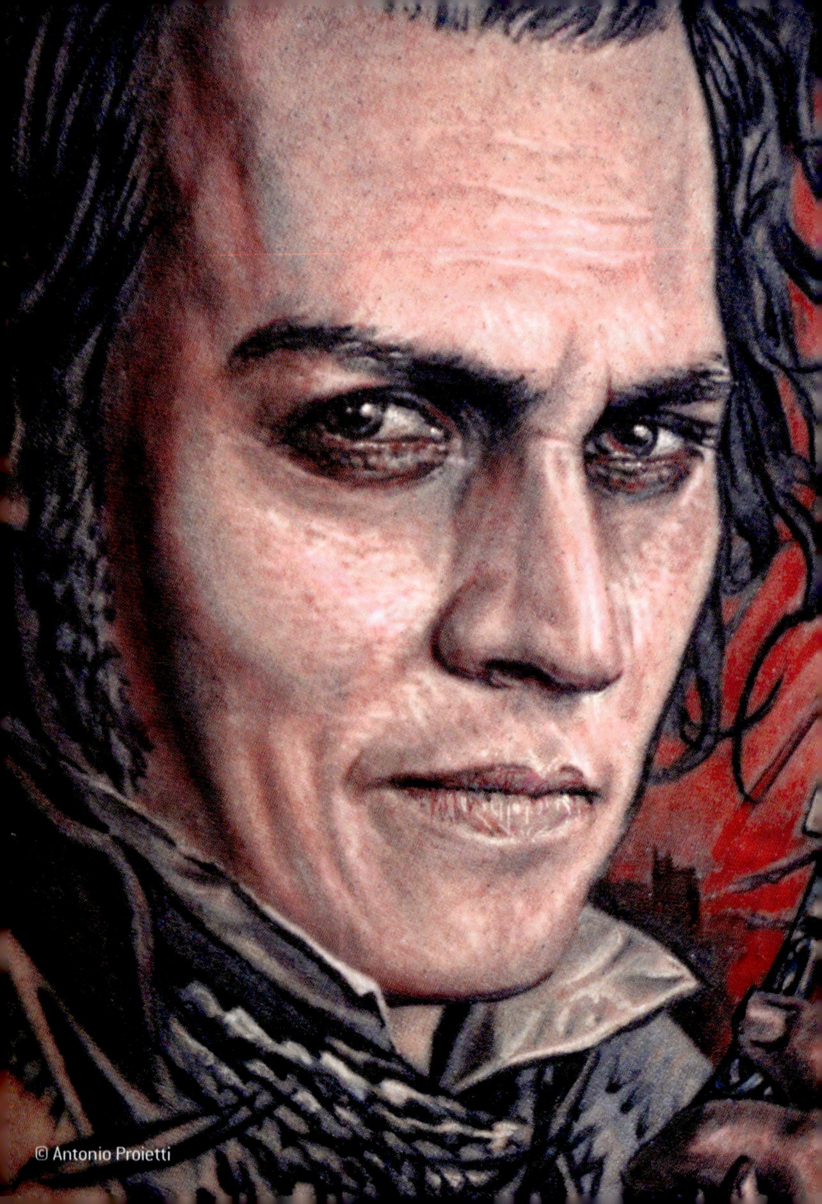
© Antonio Proietti

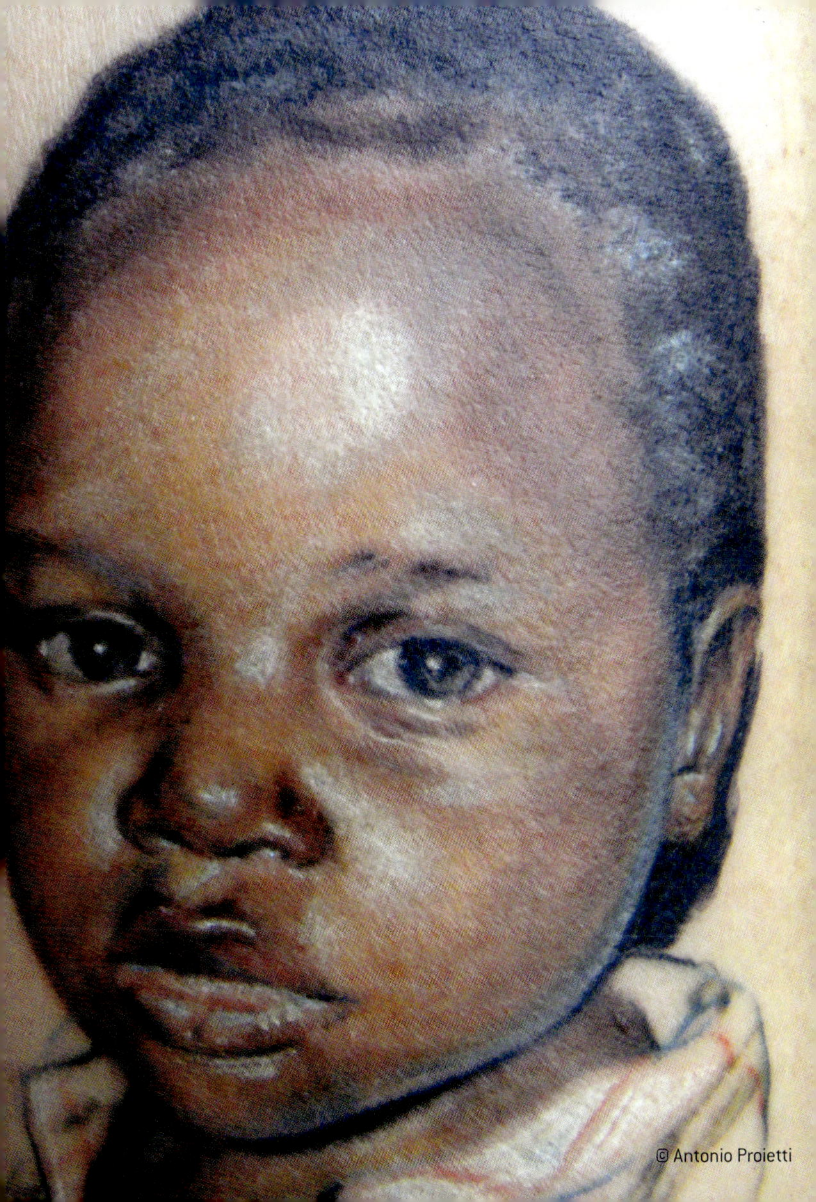
© Antonio Proietti

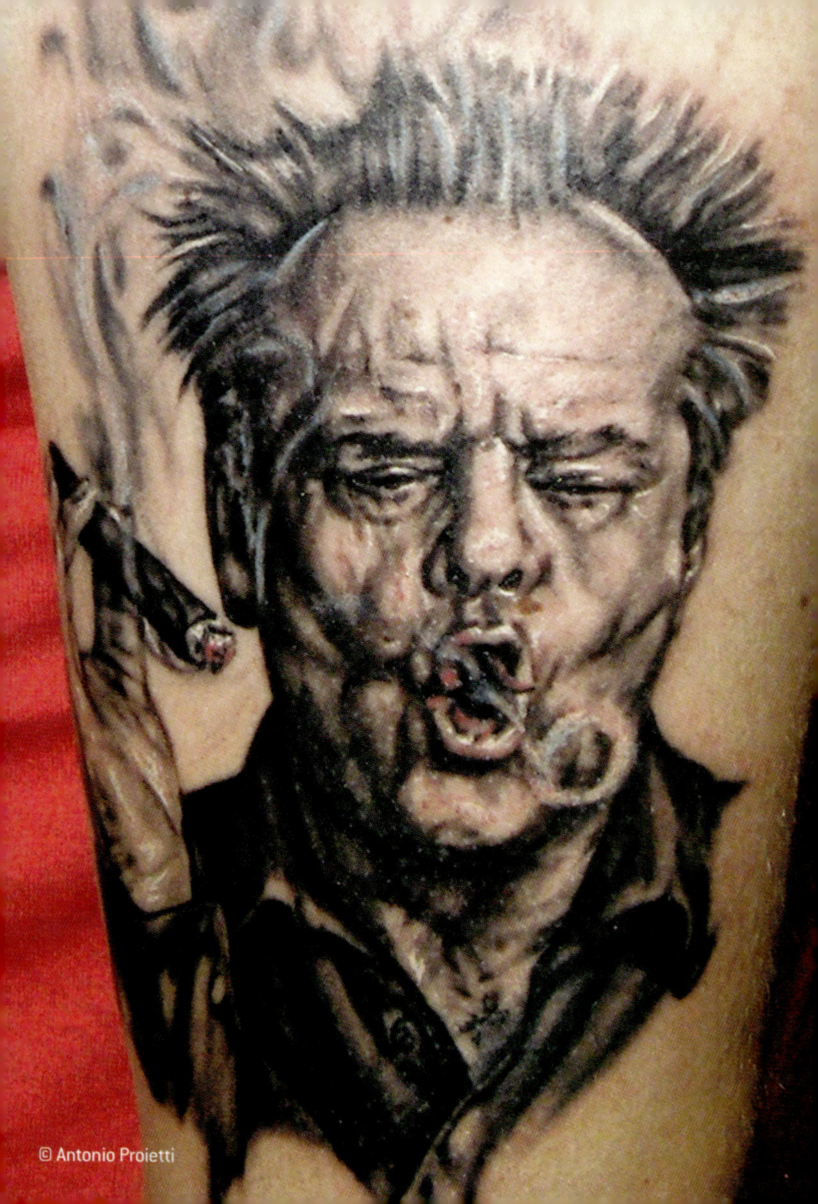
© Antonio Proietti

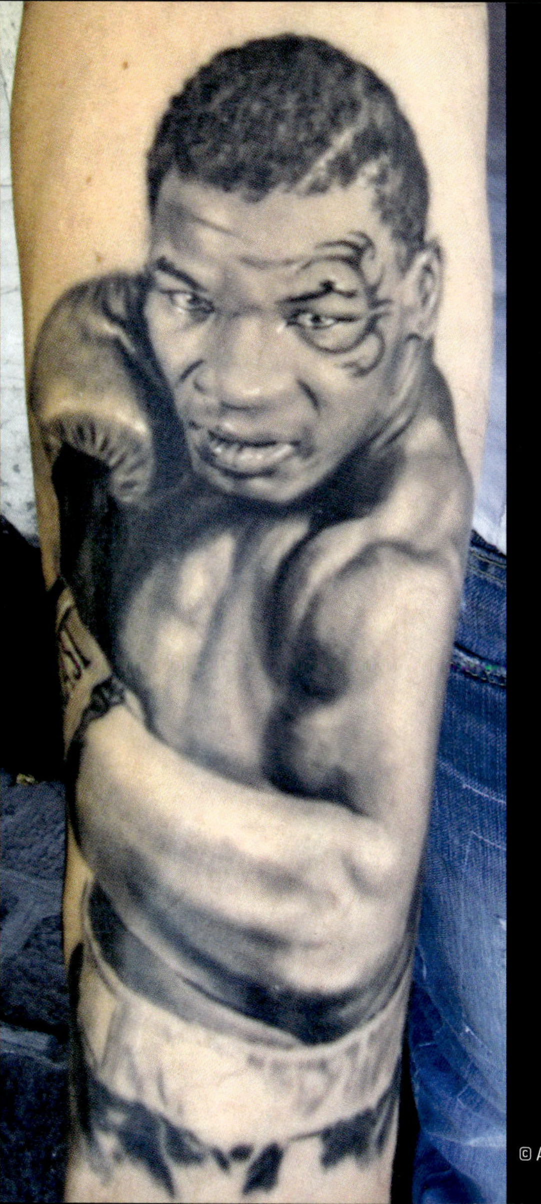
© Ant

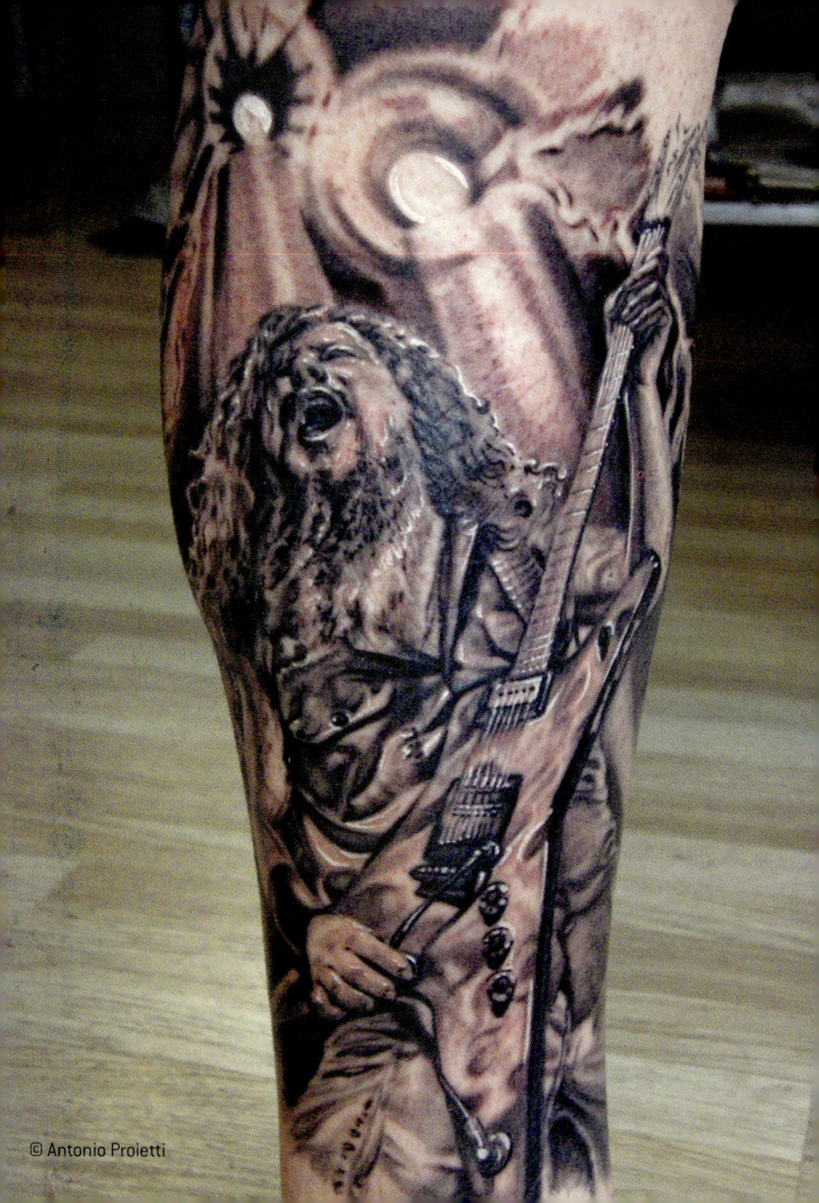

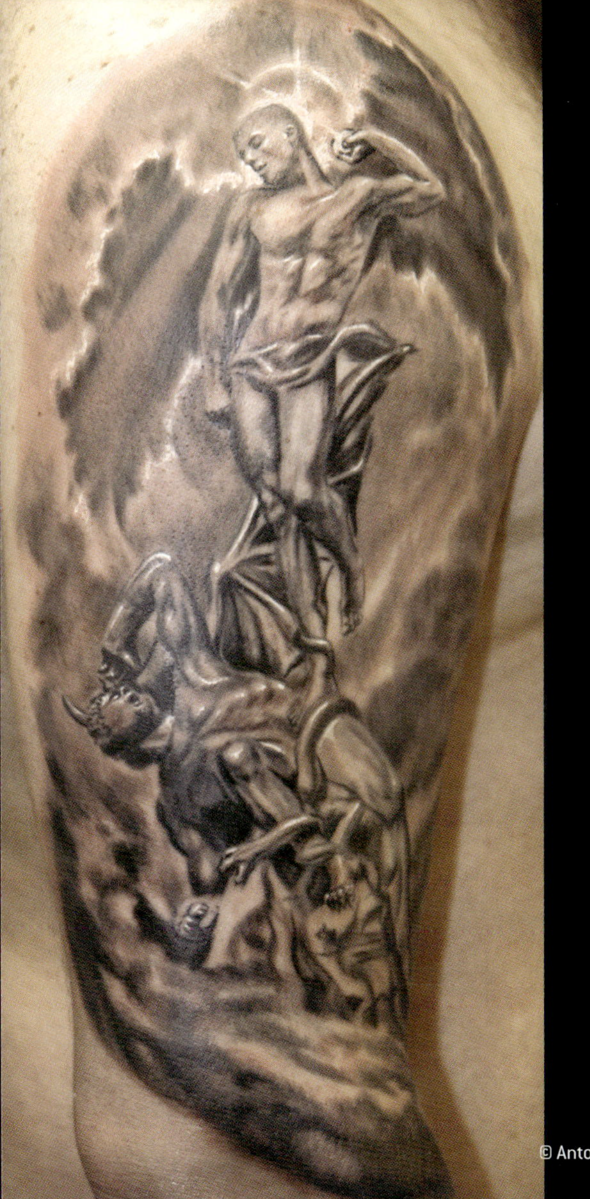
© Antonio

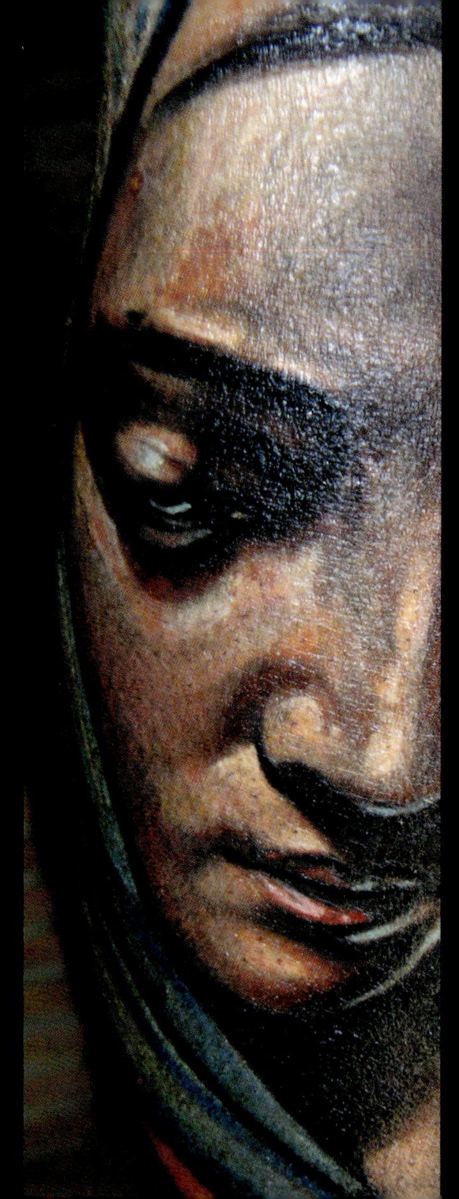

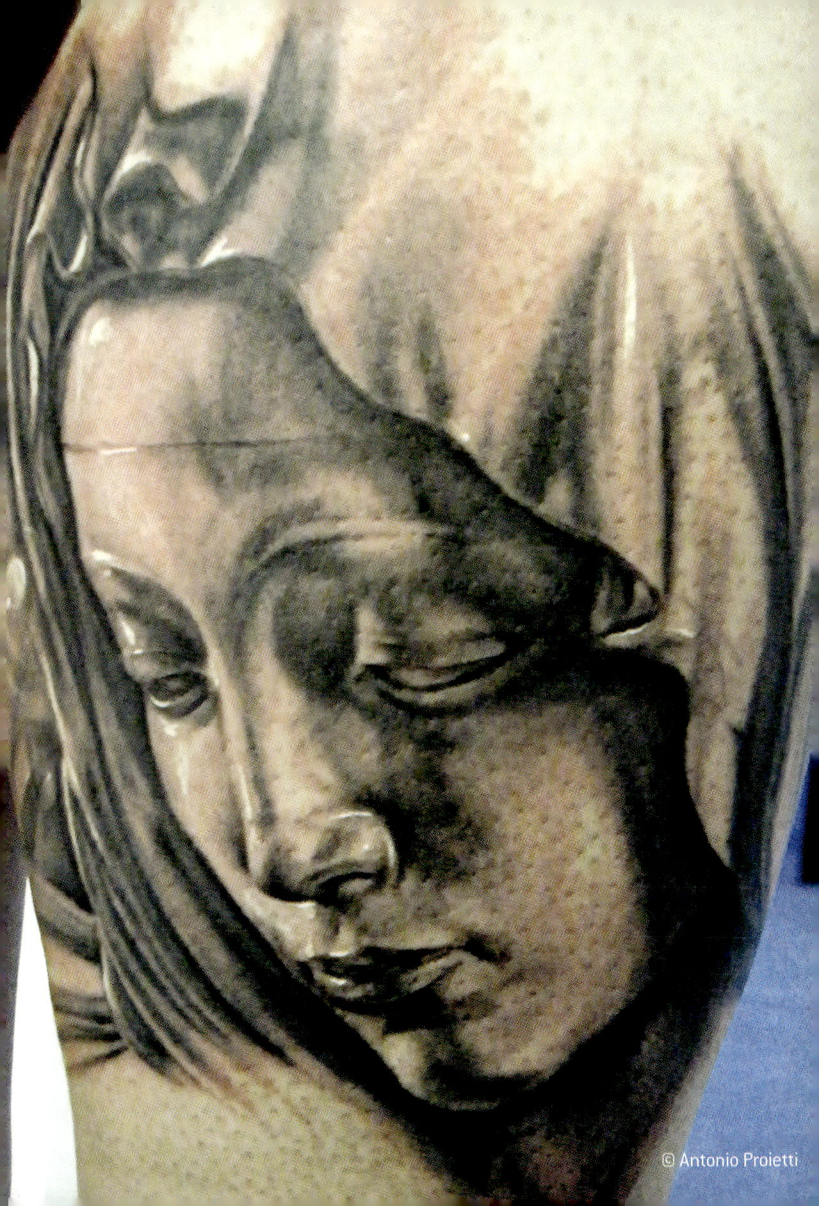
© Antonio Proietti

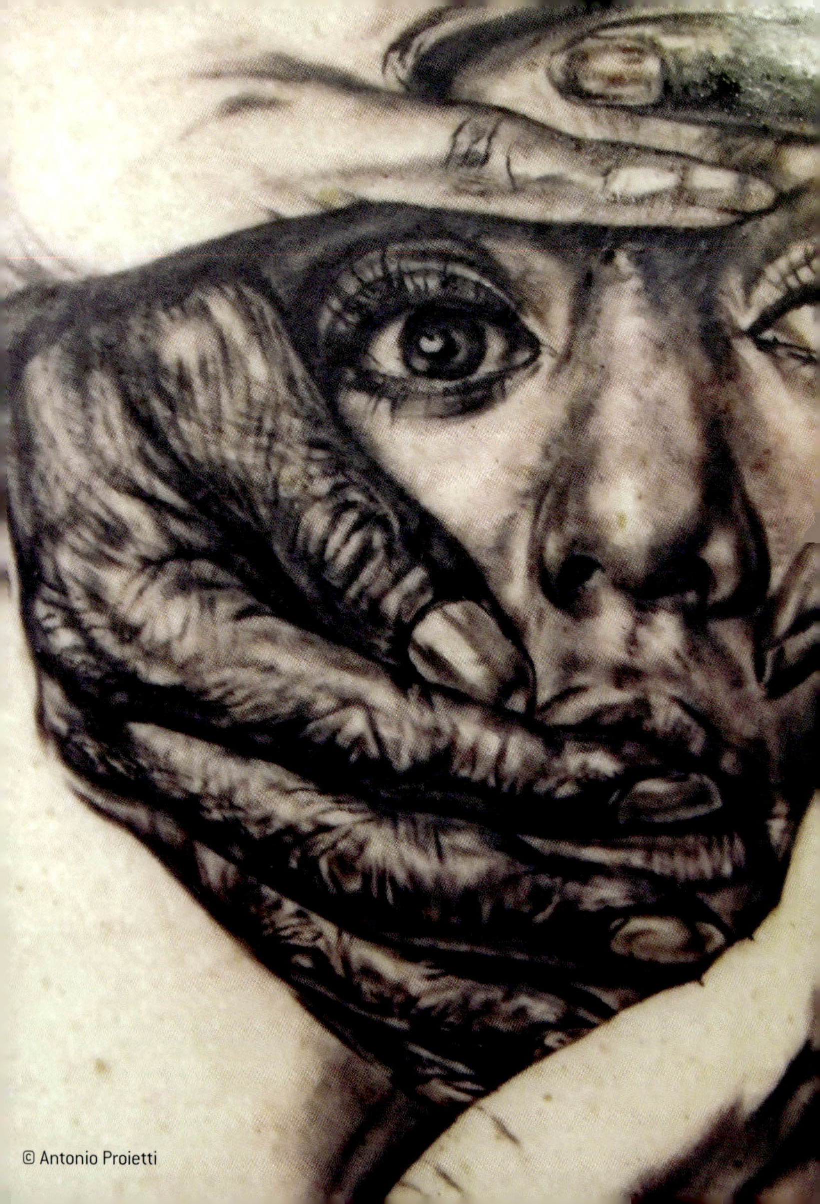

© Antonio Proietti

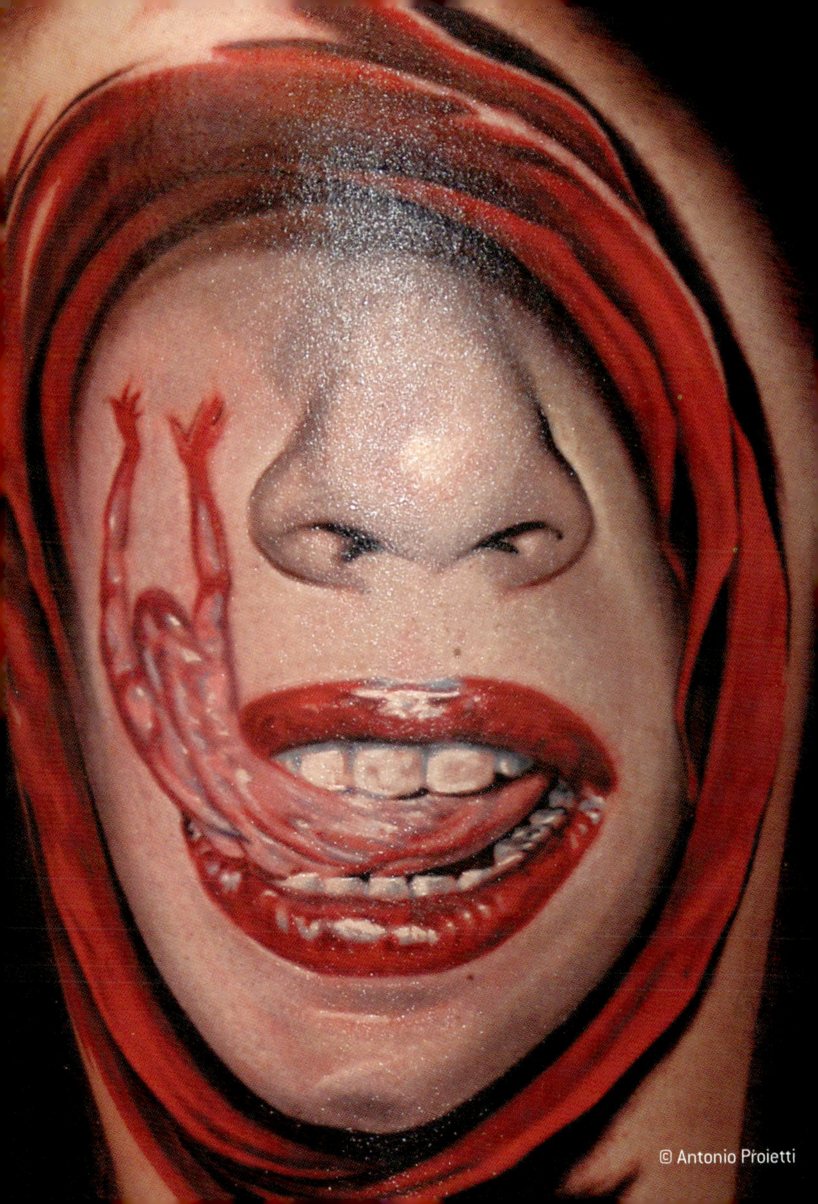

© Antonio Proietti

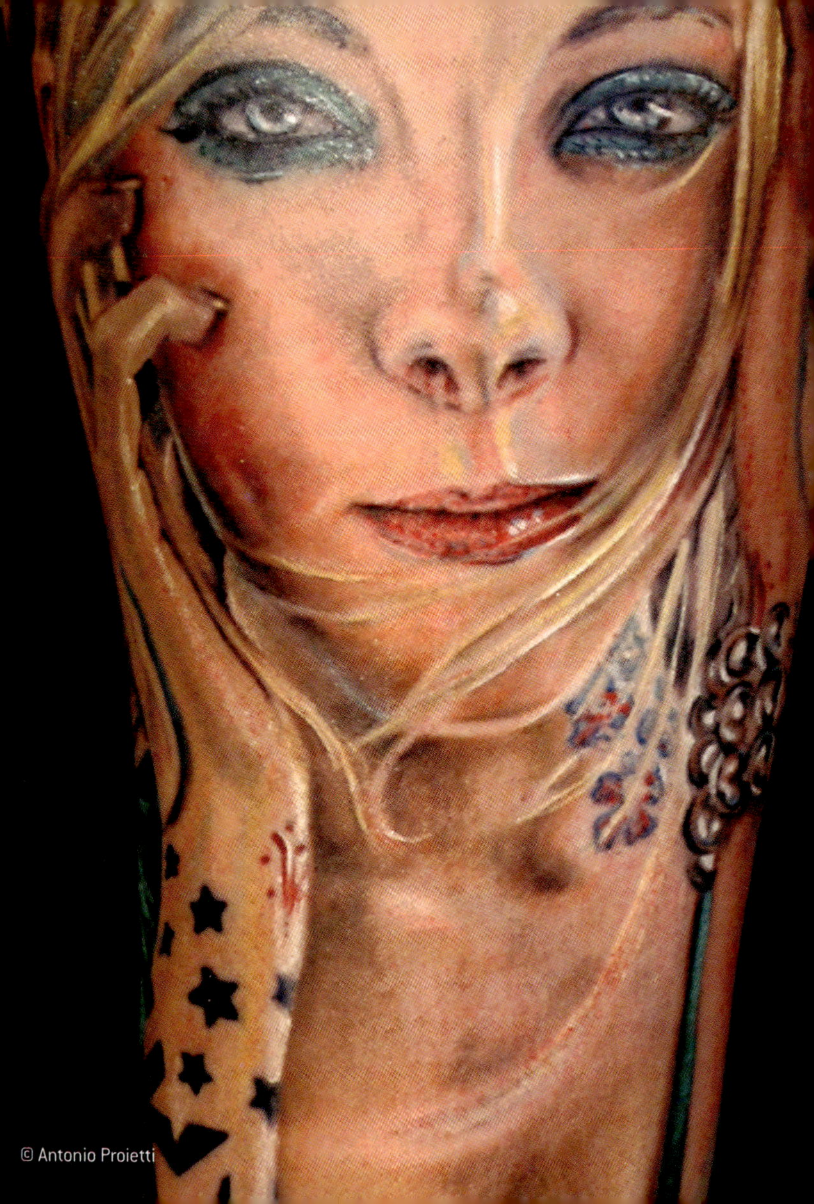
© Antonio Proietti

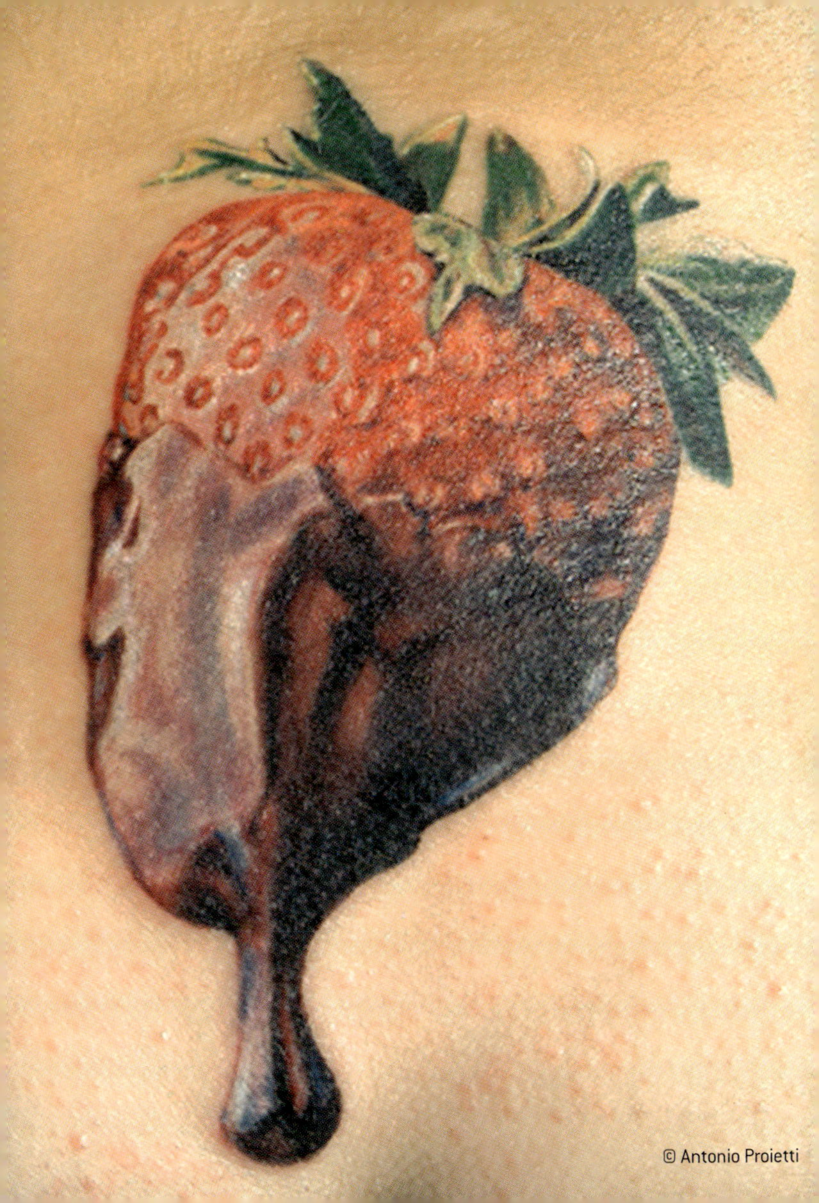
© Antonio Proietti

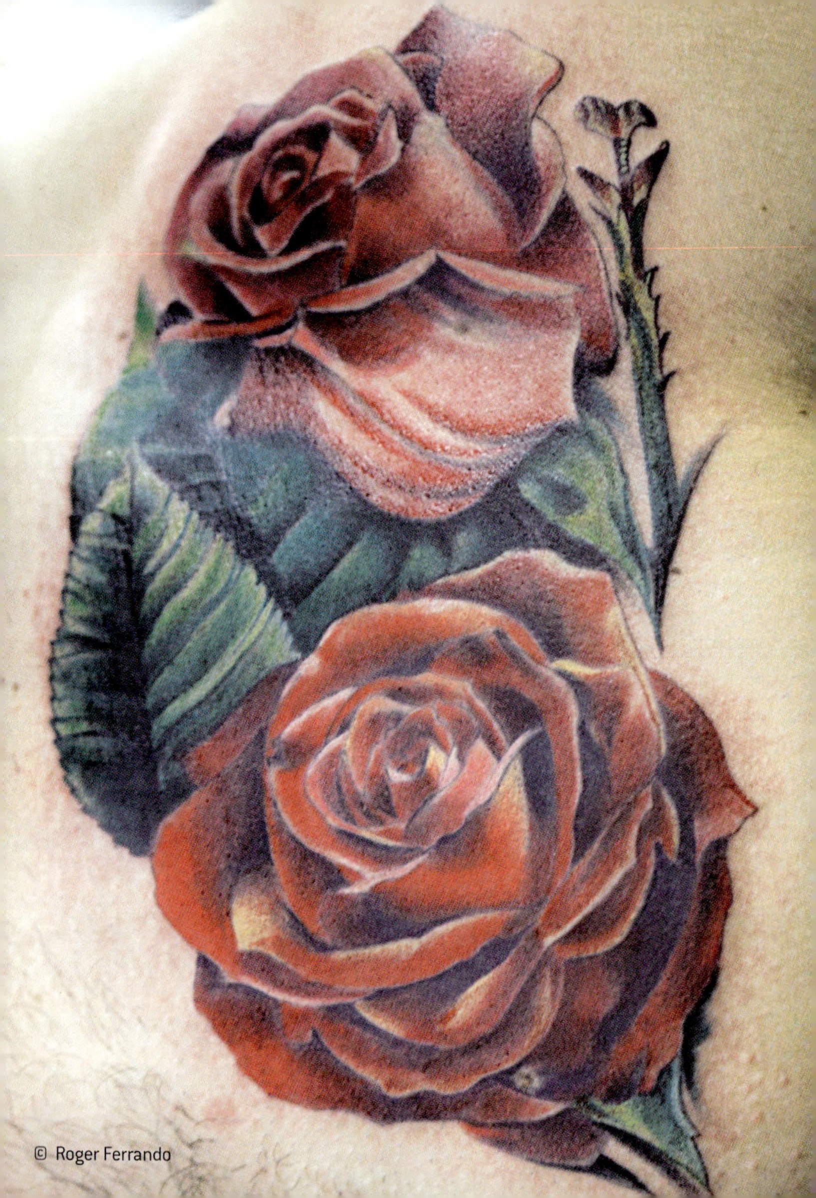

© Roger Ferrando

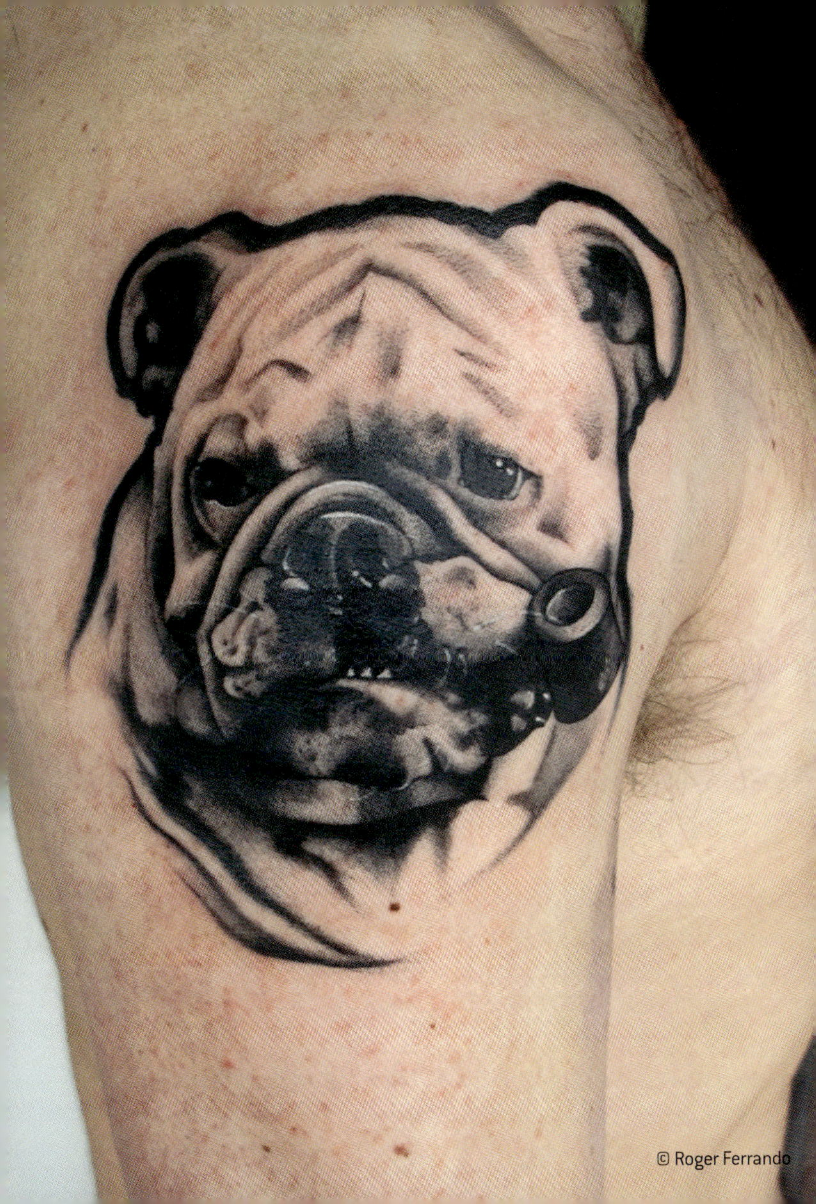

© Roger Ferrando

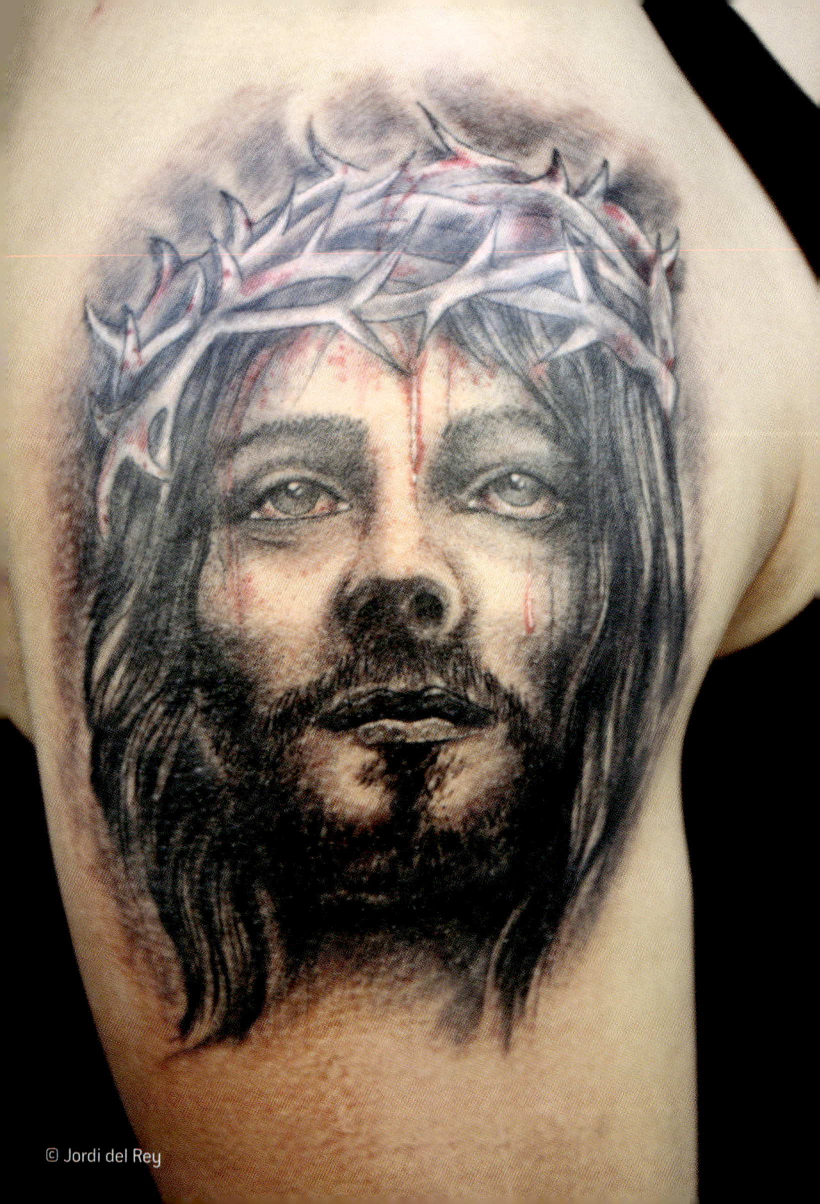
© Jordi del Rey

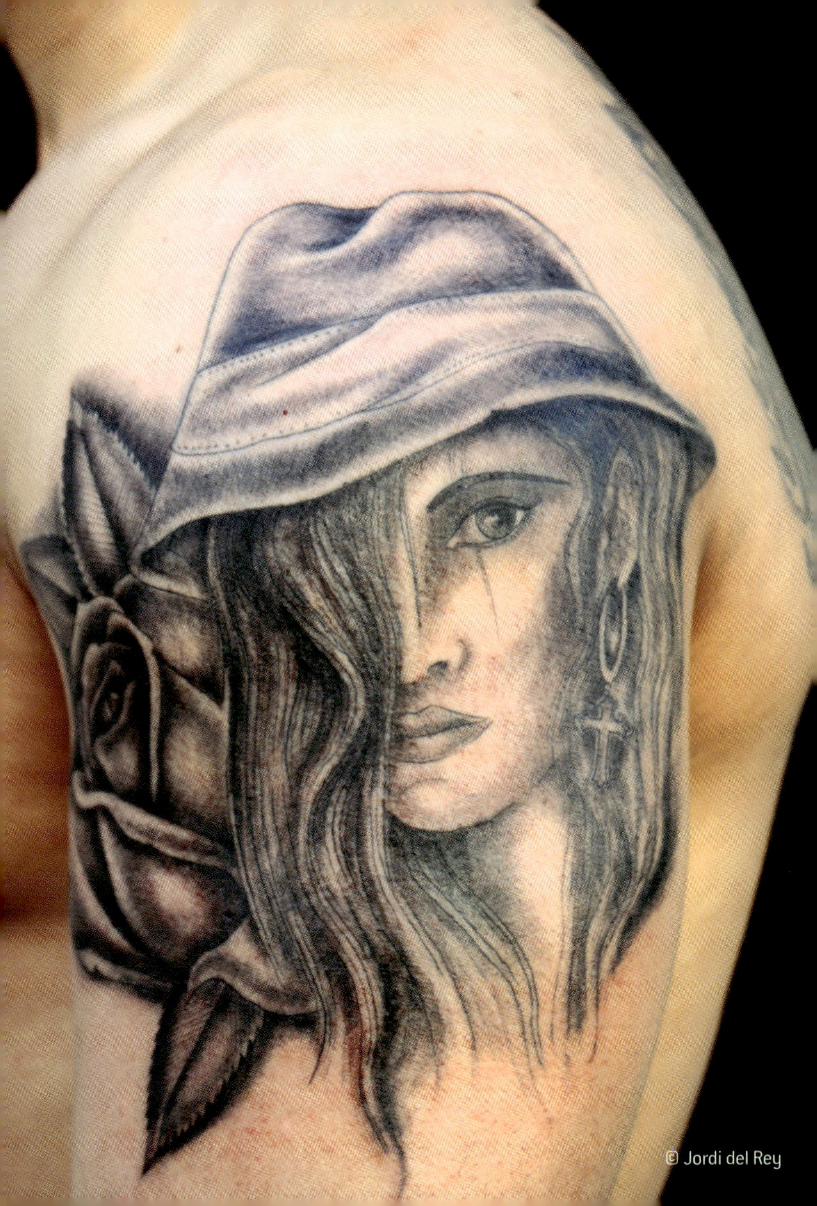
© Jordi del Rey

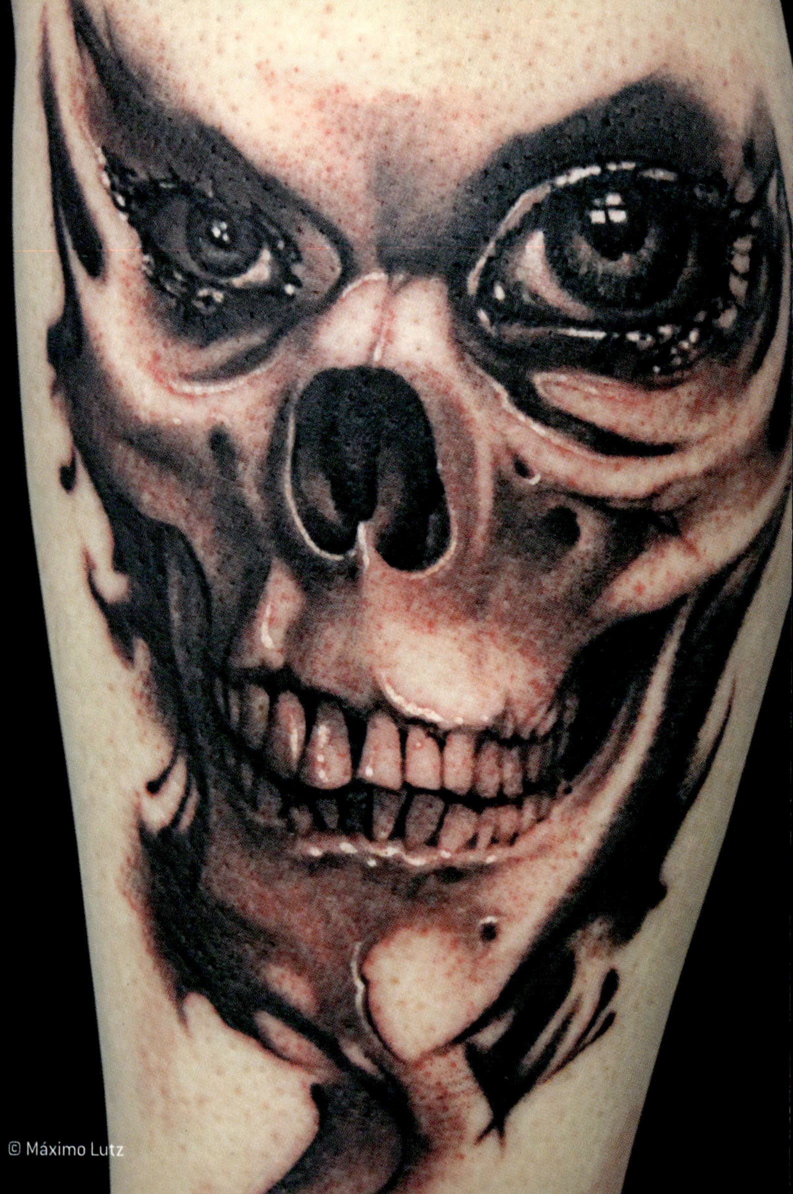

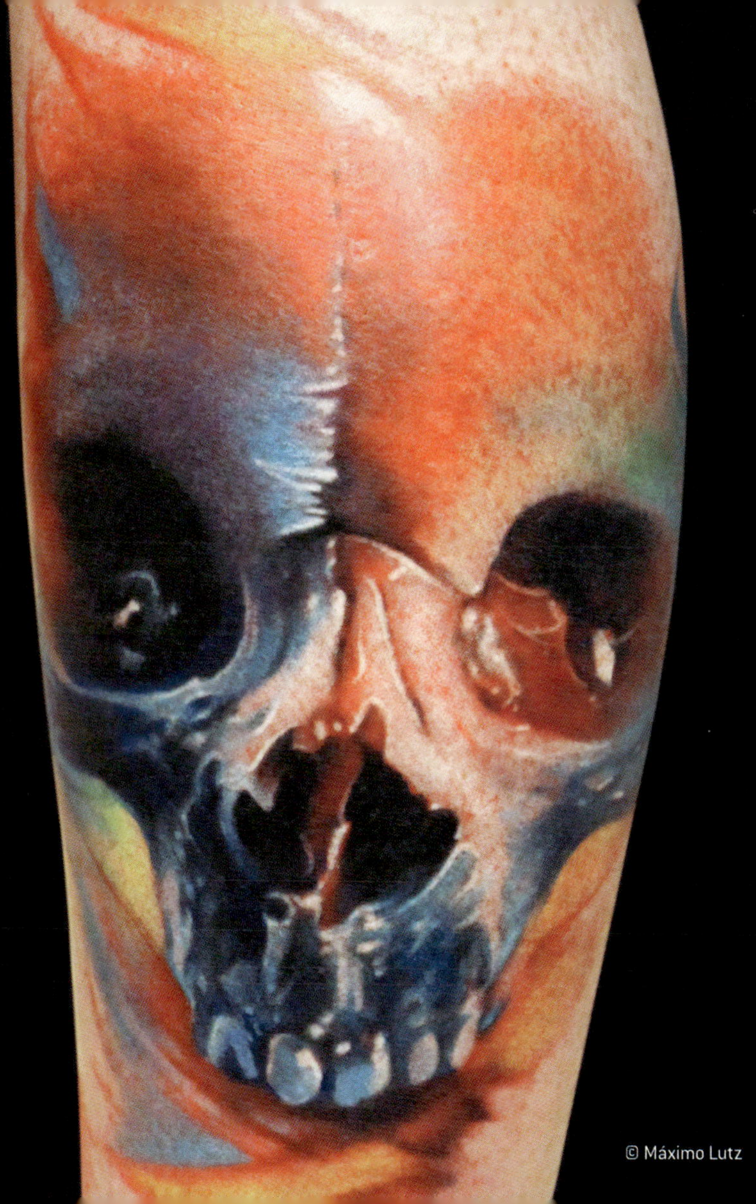

© Máximo Lutz

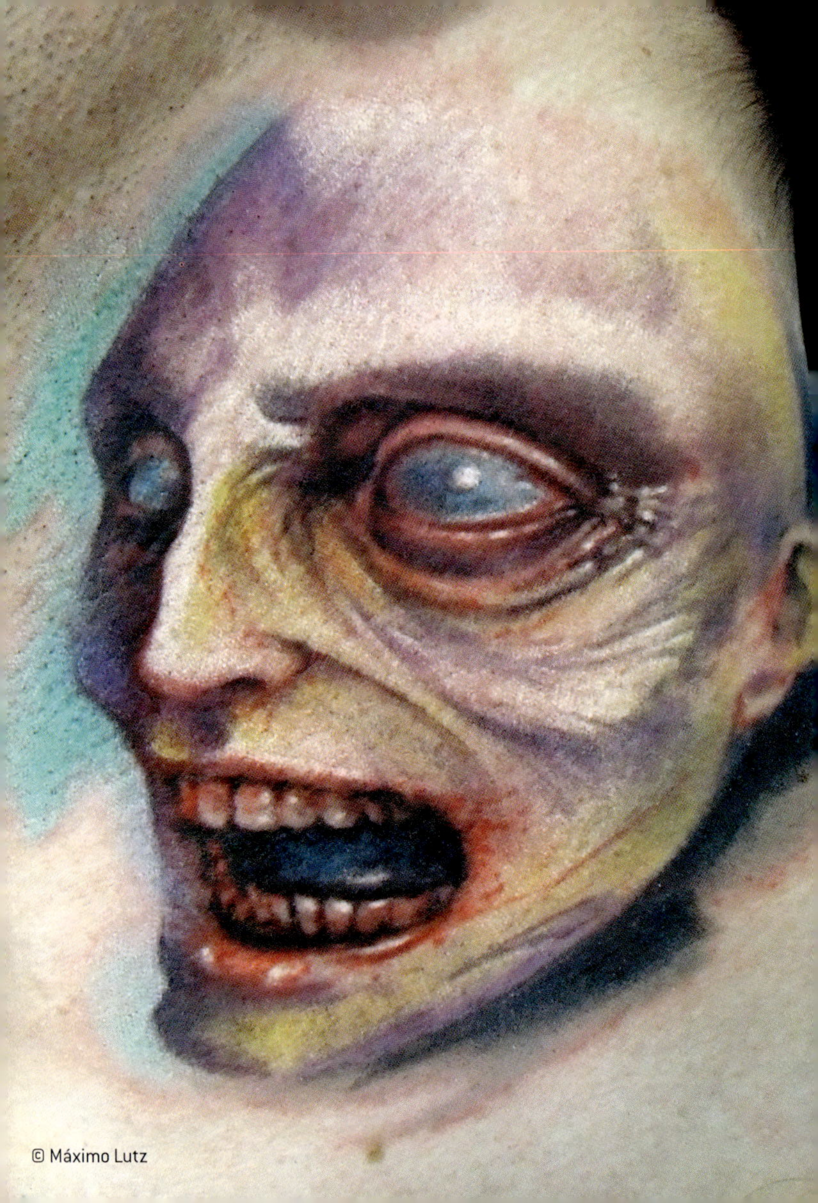

© Máximo Lutz

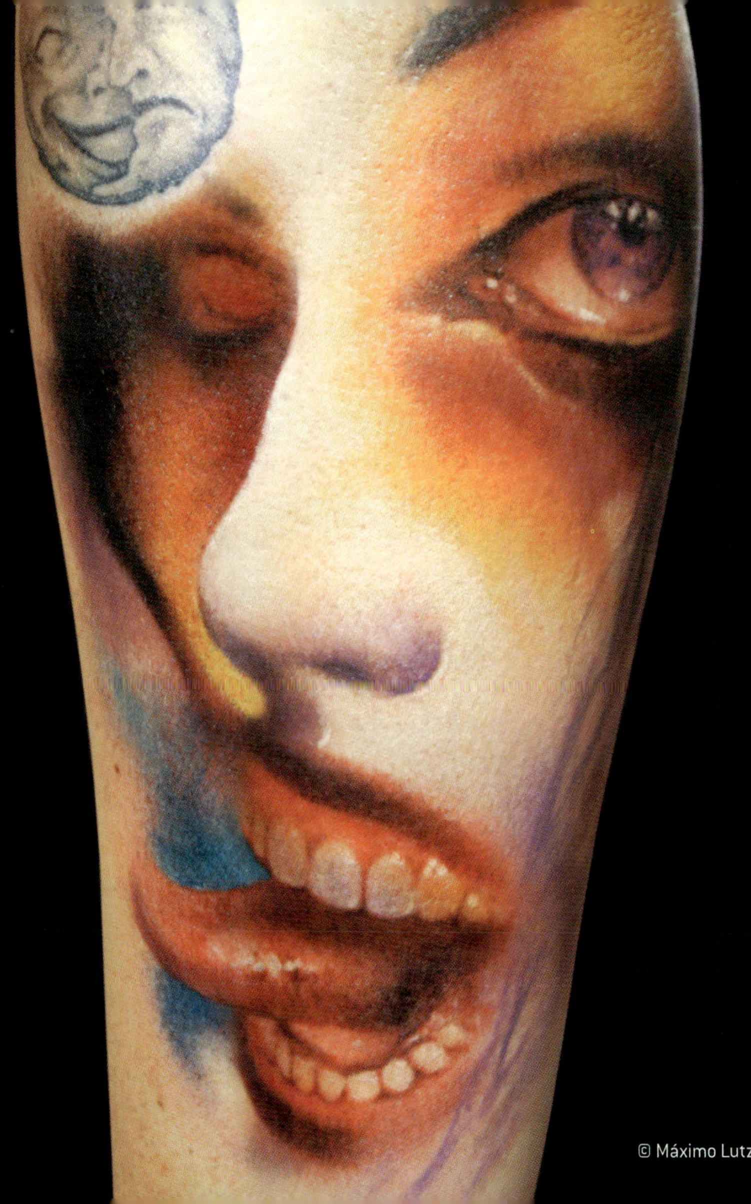
© Máximo Lutz

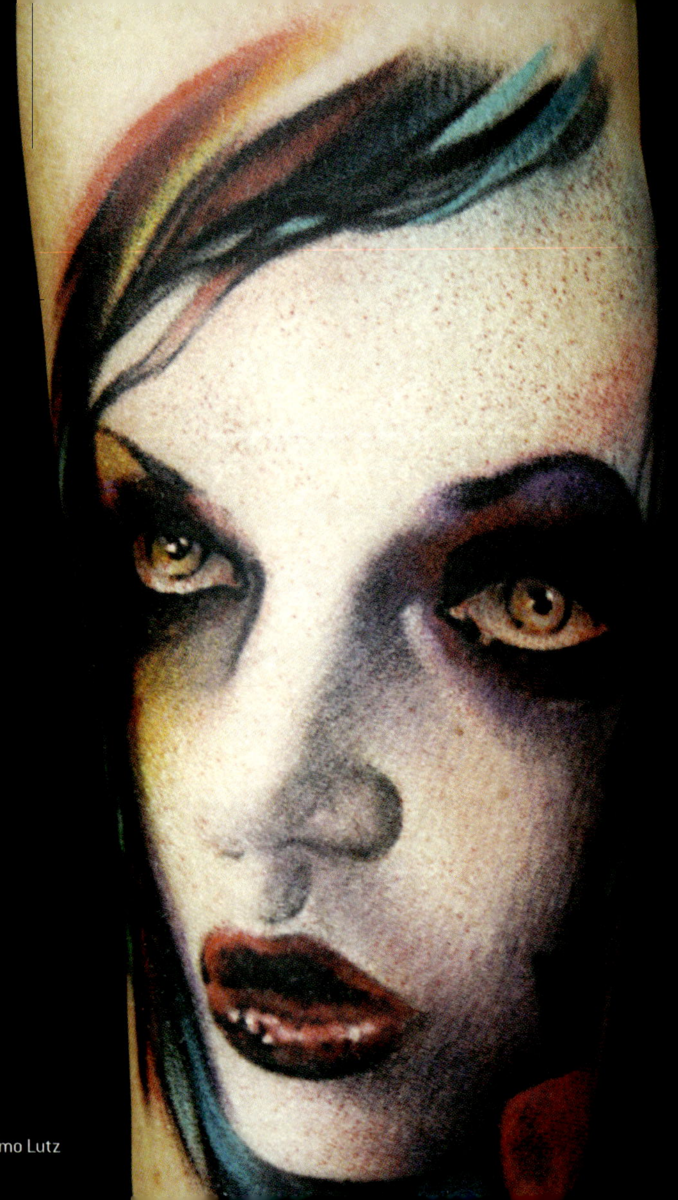

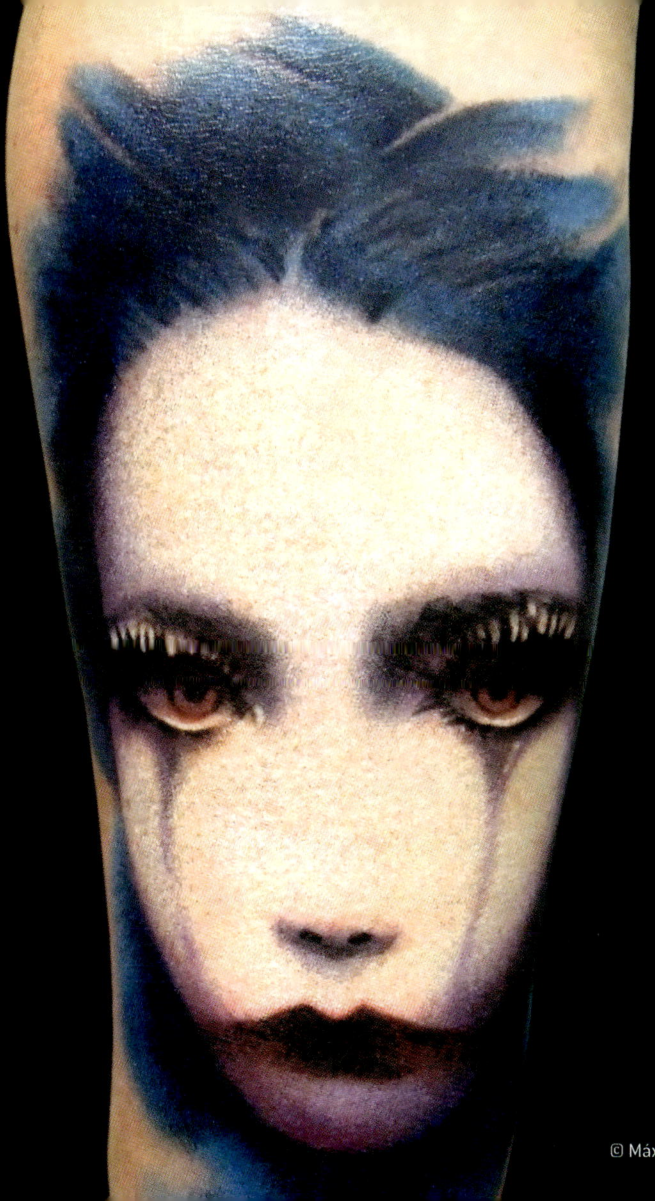
© Máximo Lutz

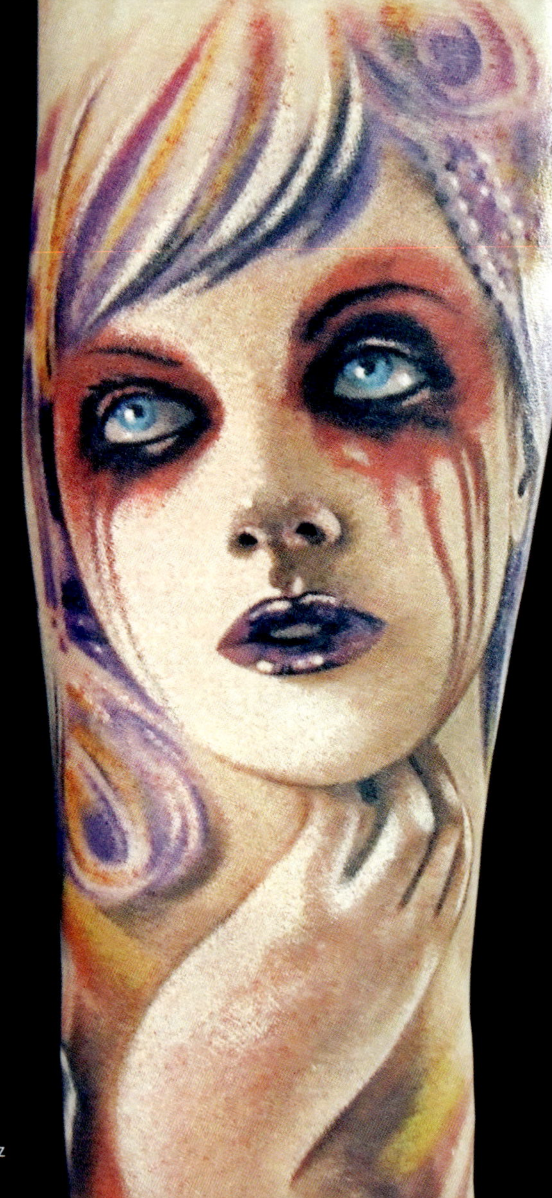

Máximo Lutz

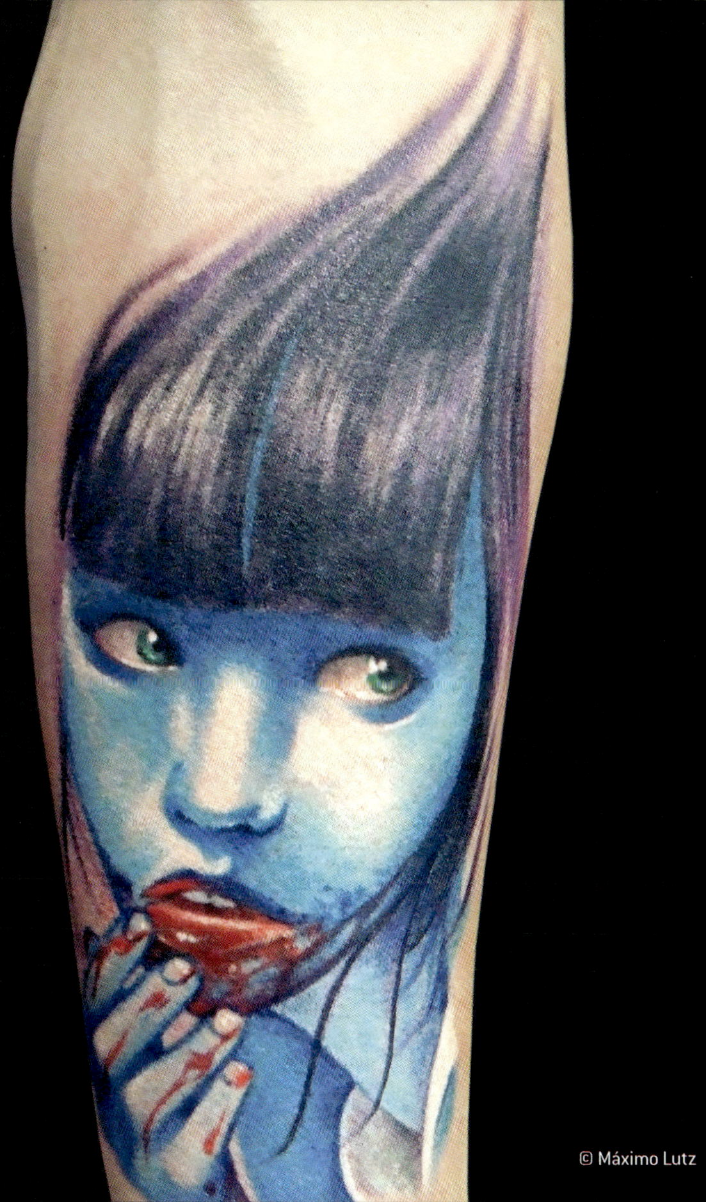
© Máximo Lutz

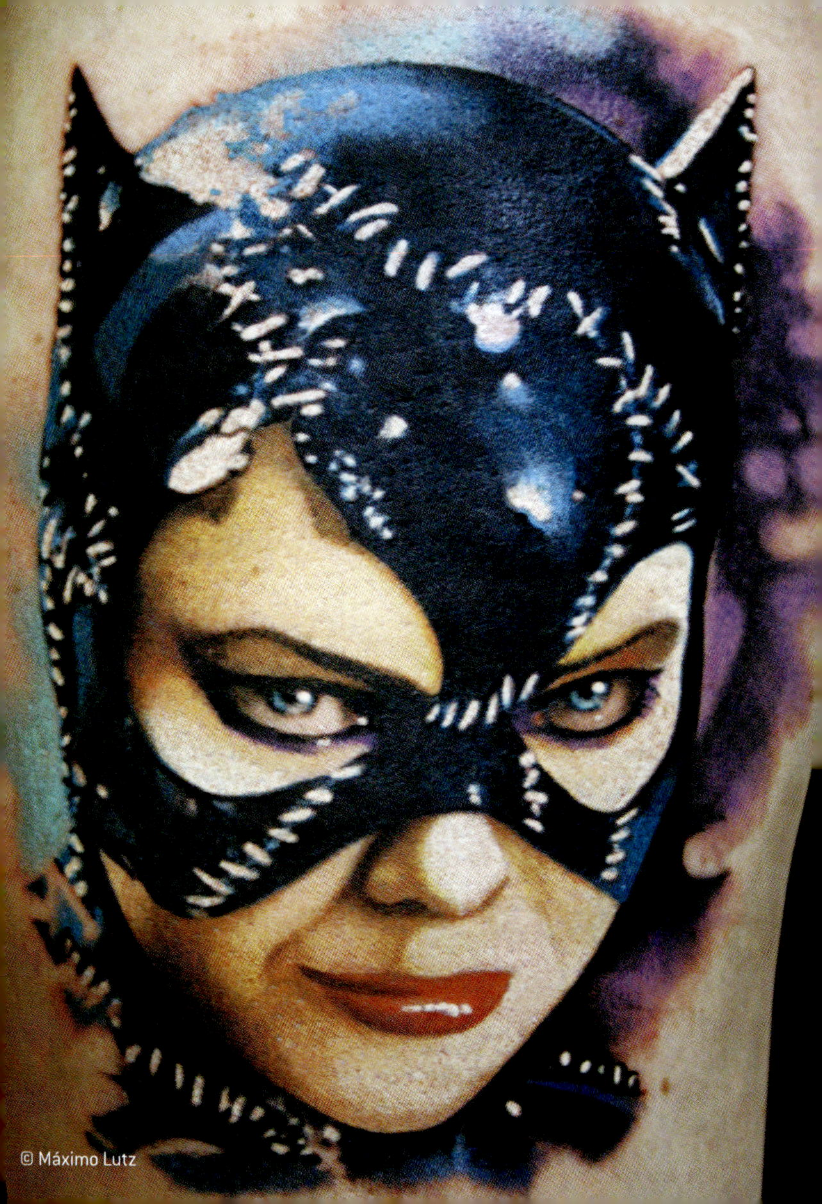

© Máximo Lutz

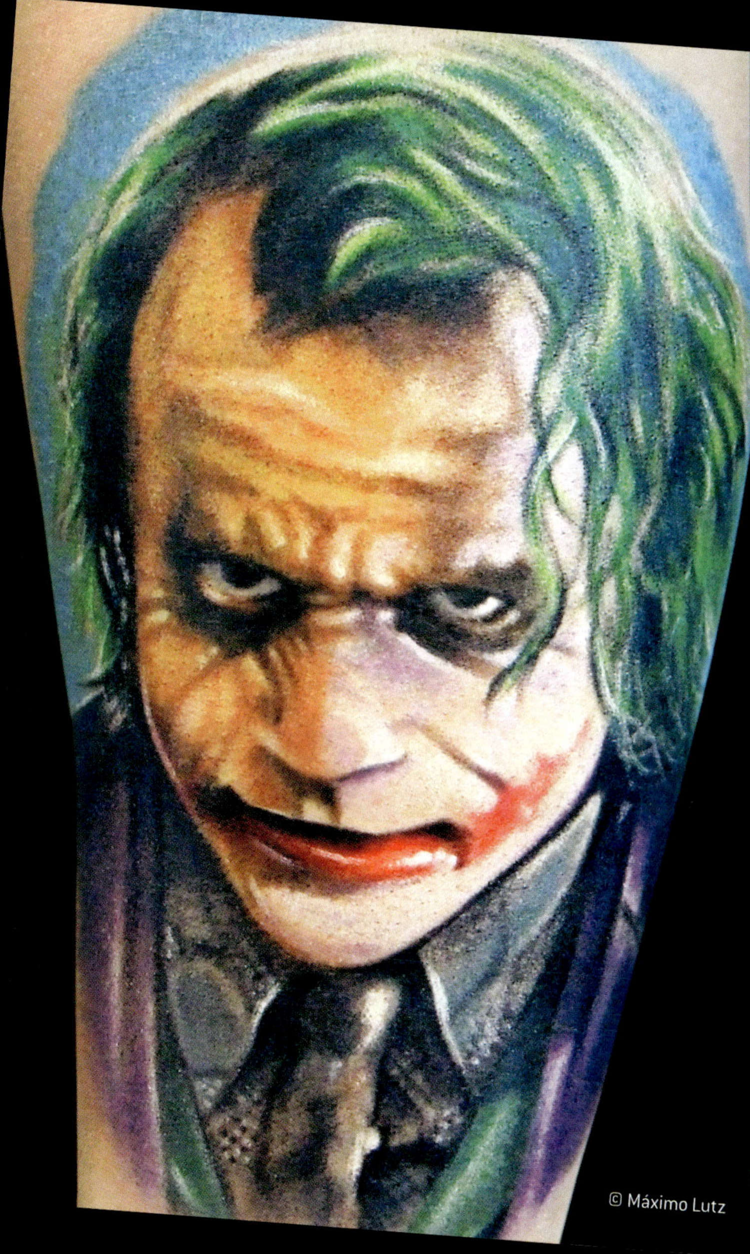
© Máximo Lutz

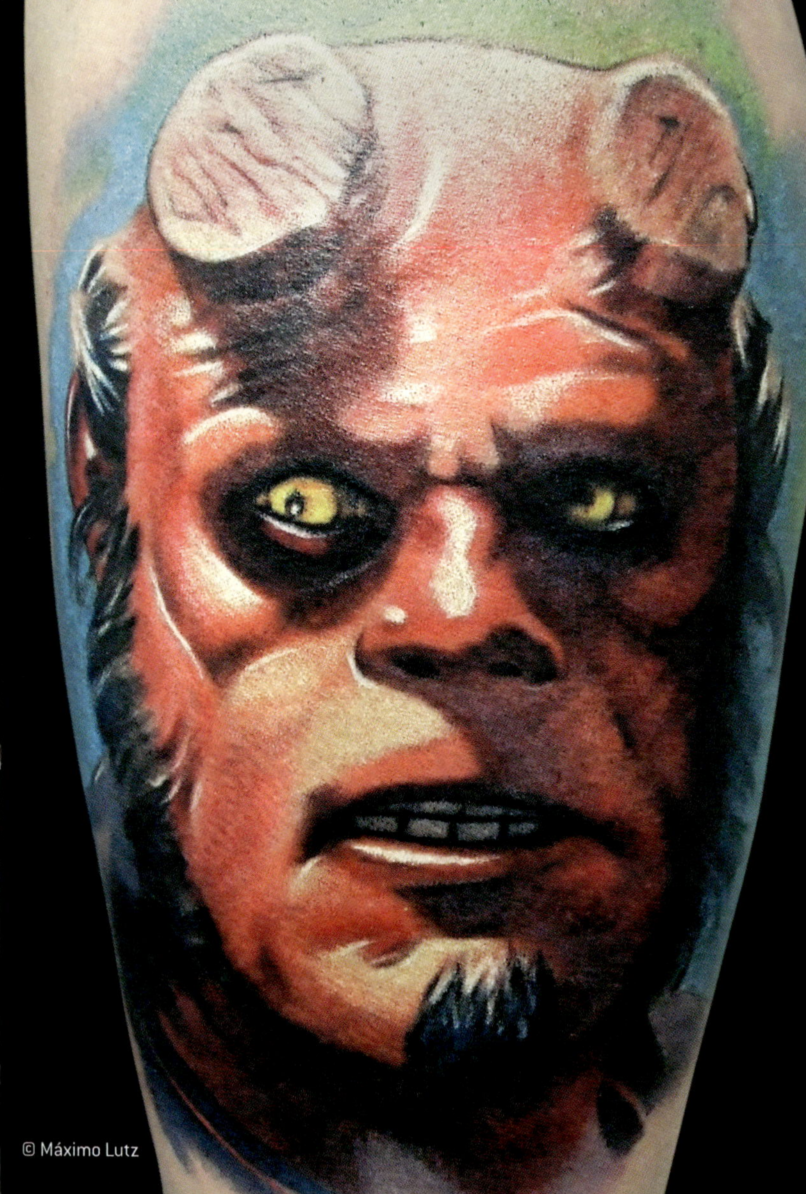
© Máximo Lutz

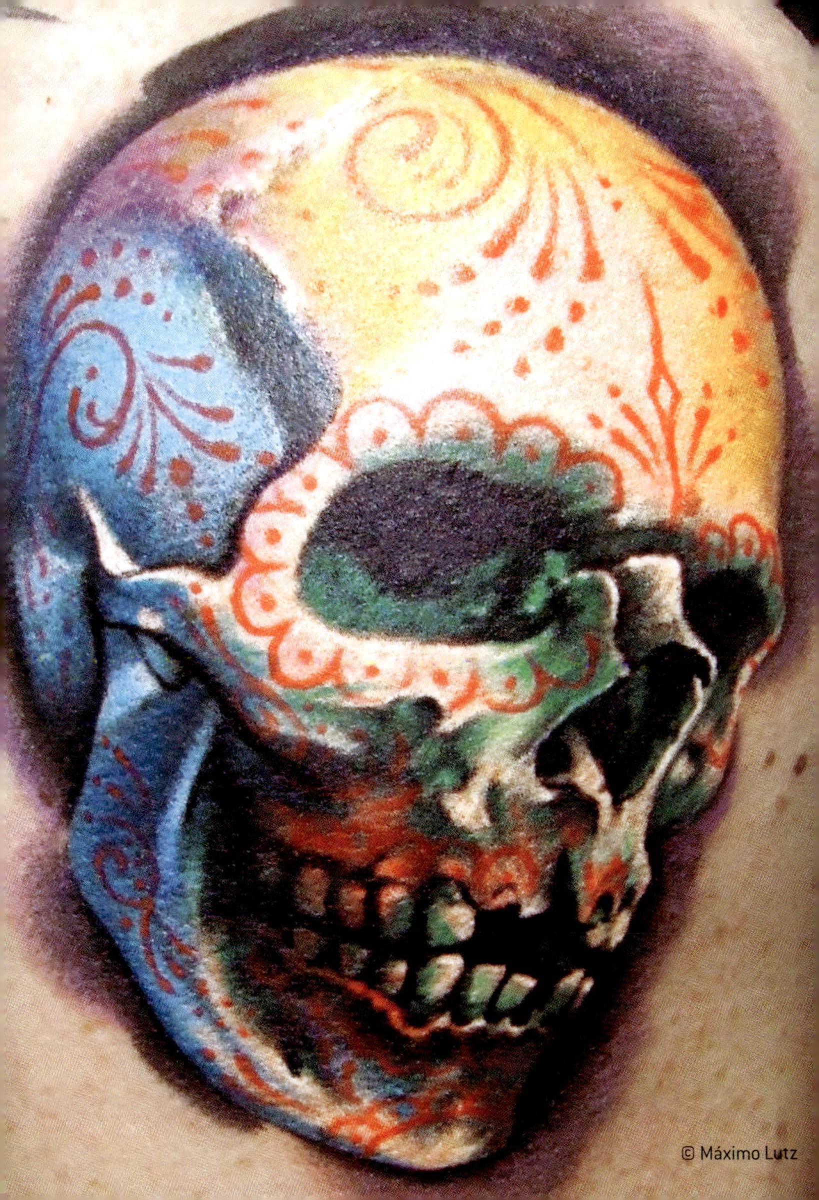
© Máximo Lutz

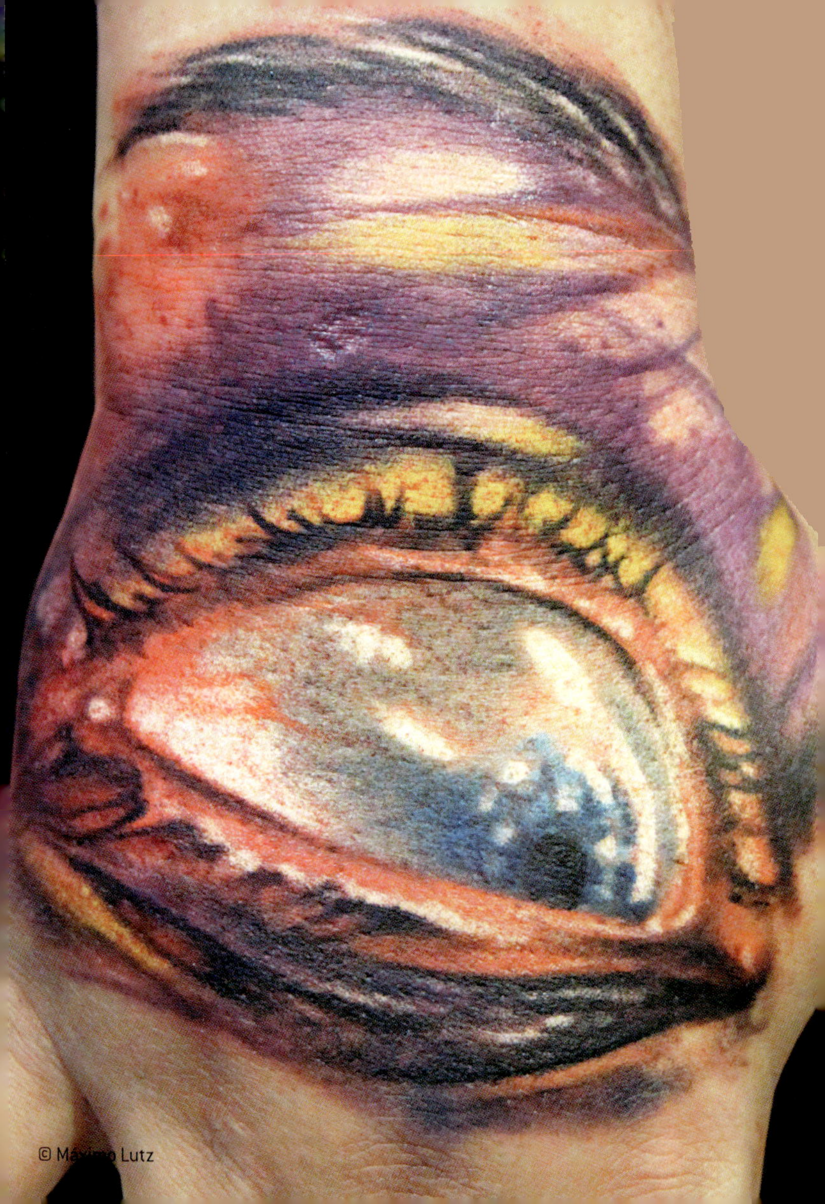
© Máximo Lutz

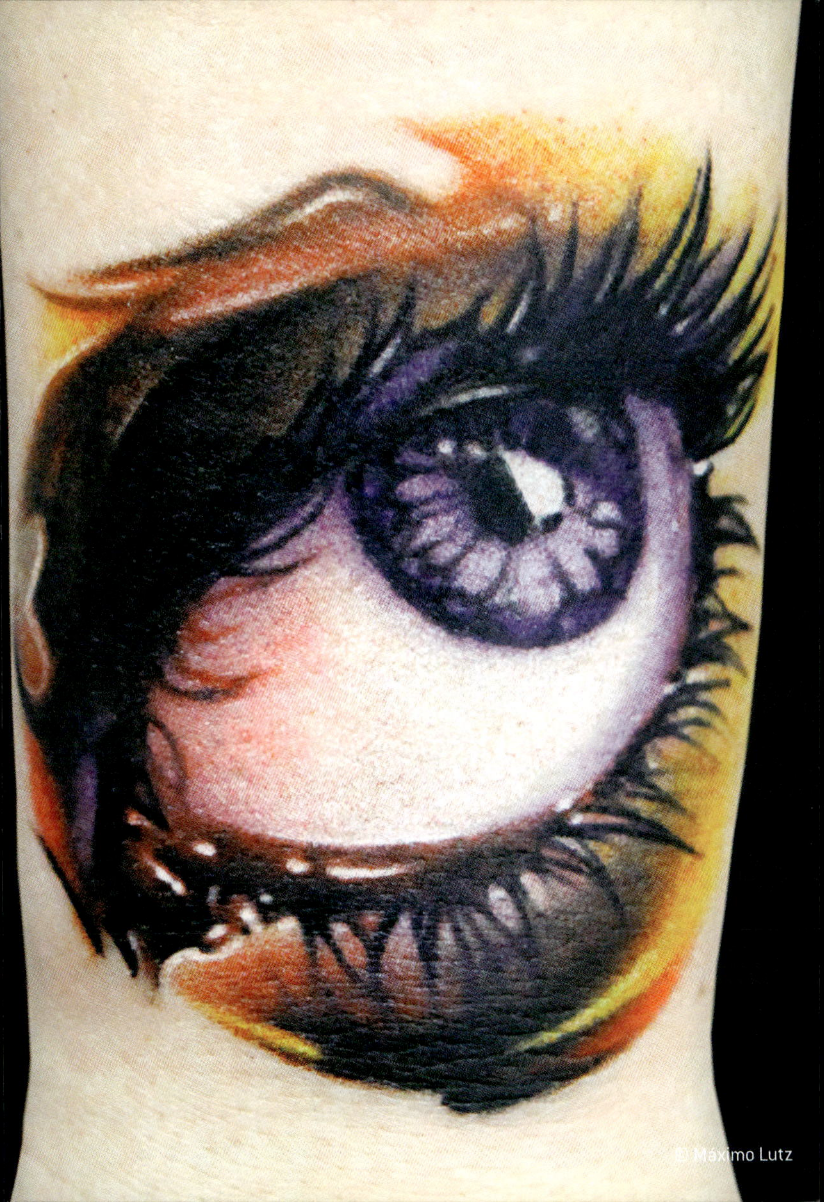
© Máximo Lutz

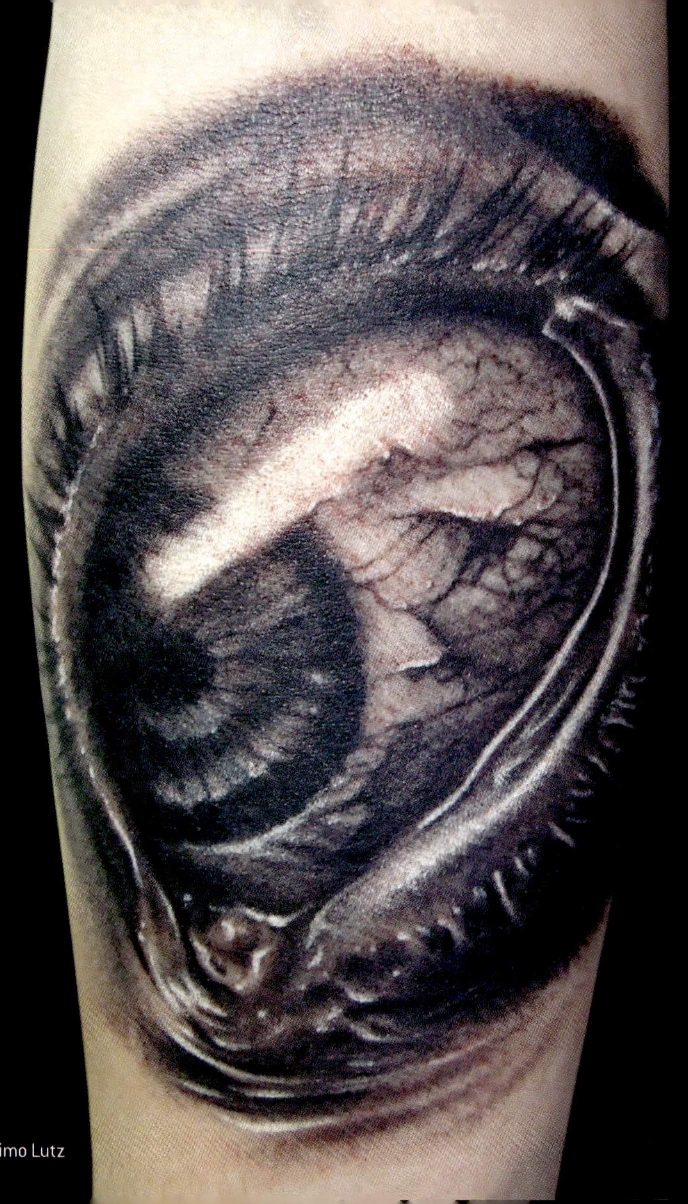

© Máximo Lutz

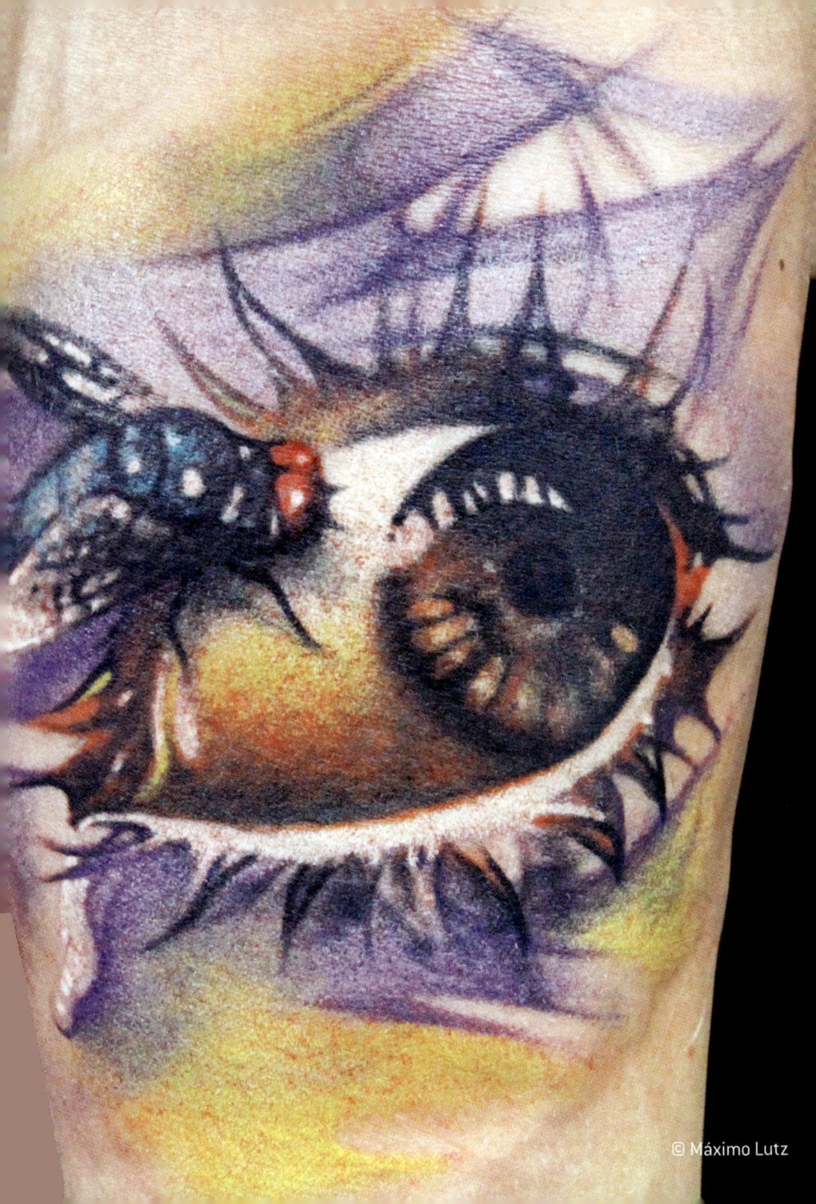
© Máximo Lutz

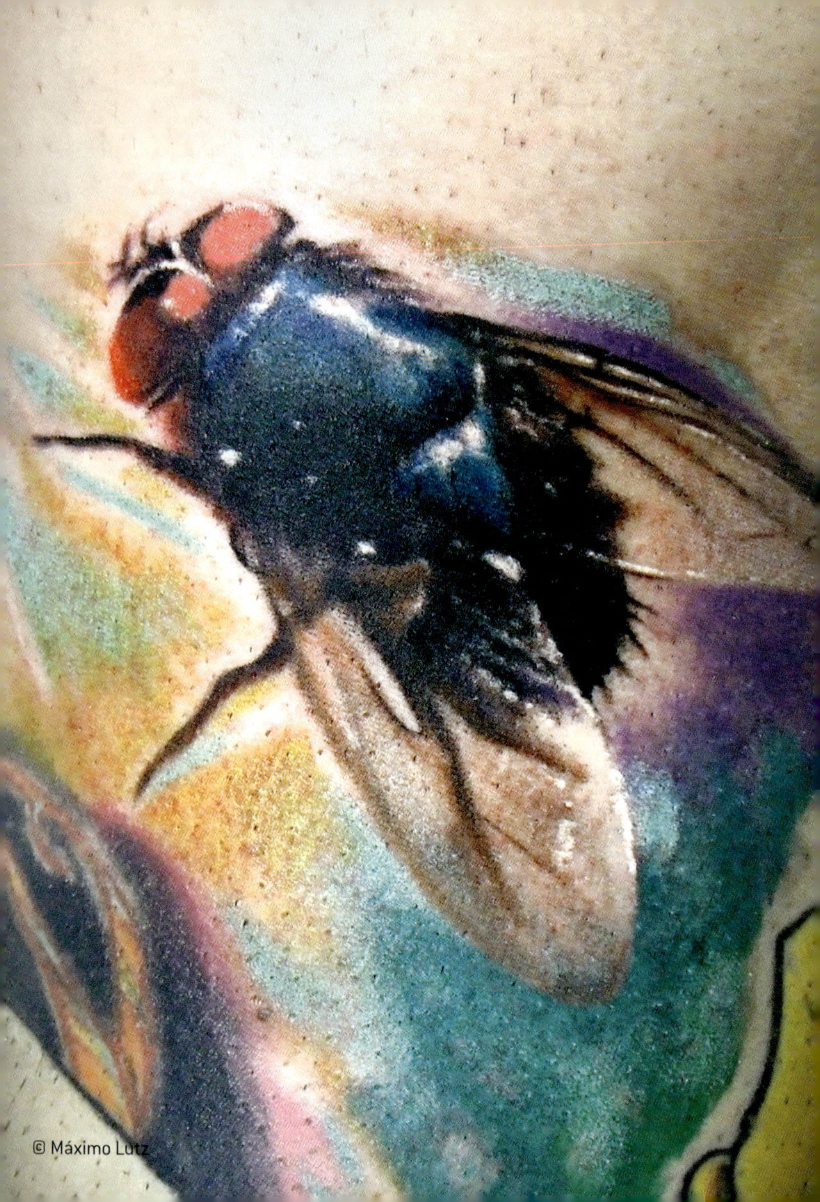
© Máximo Lutz

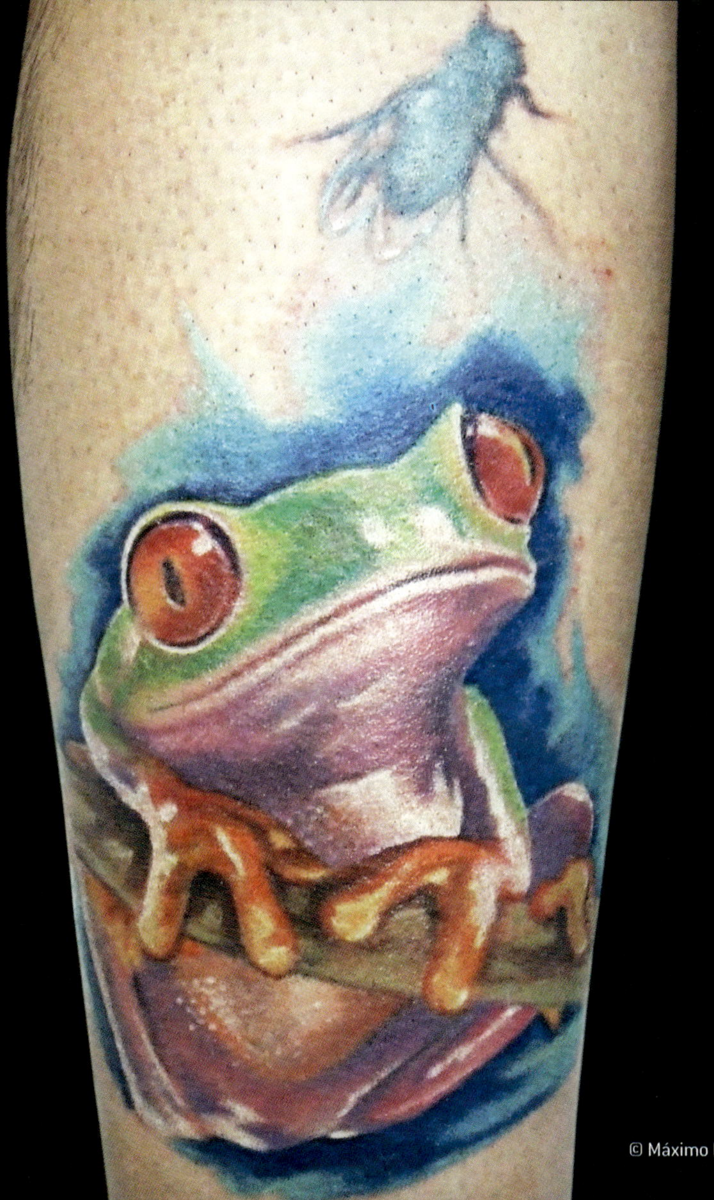

© Máximo Lutz

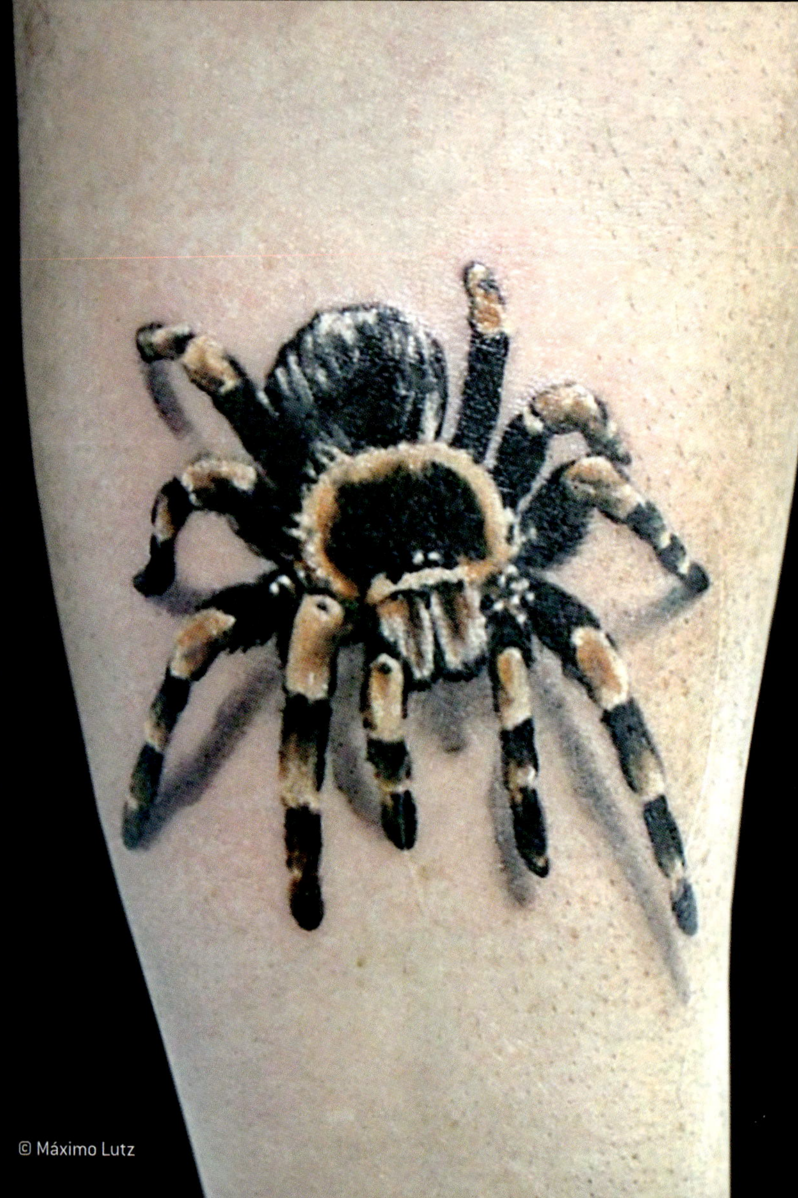

© Máximo Lutz

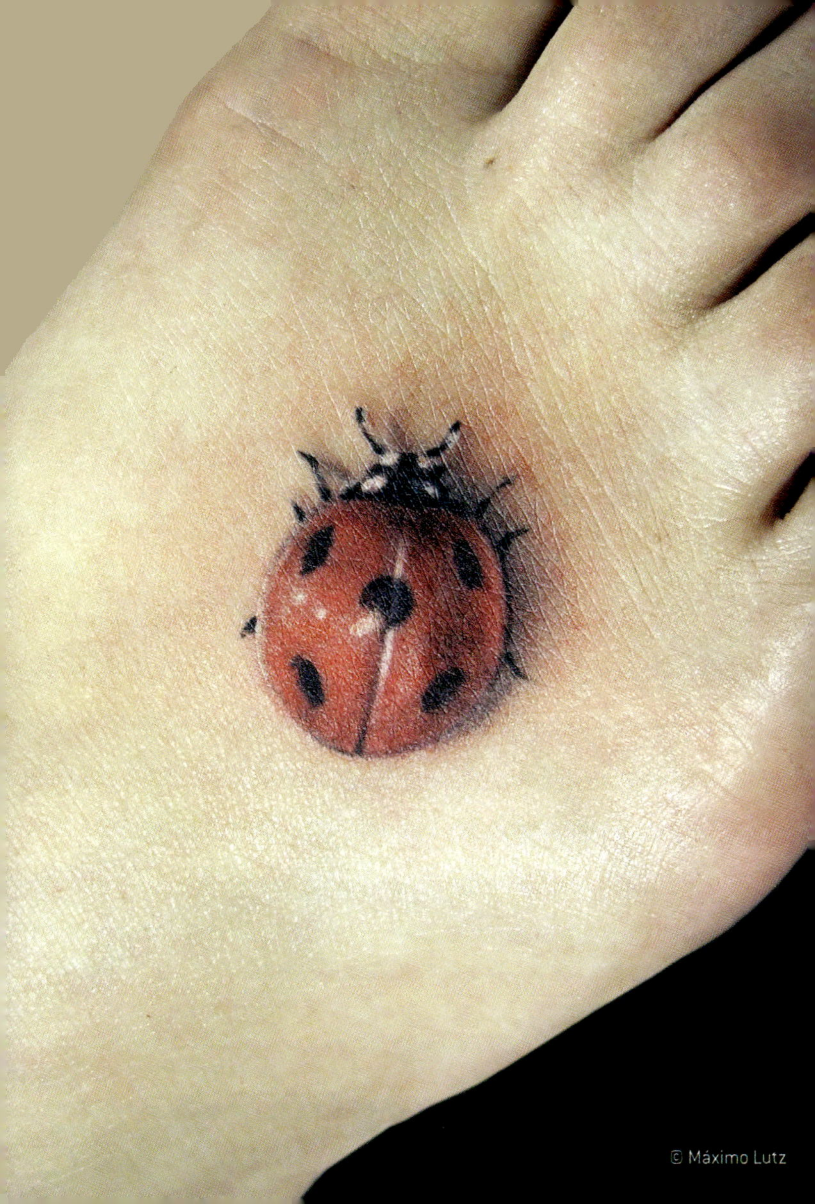

© Máximo Lutz

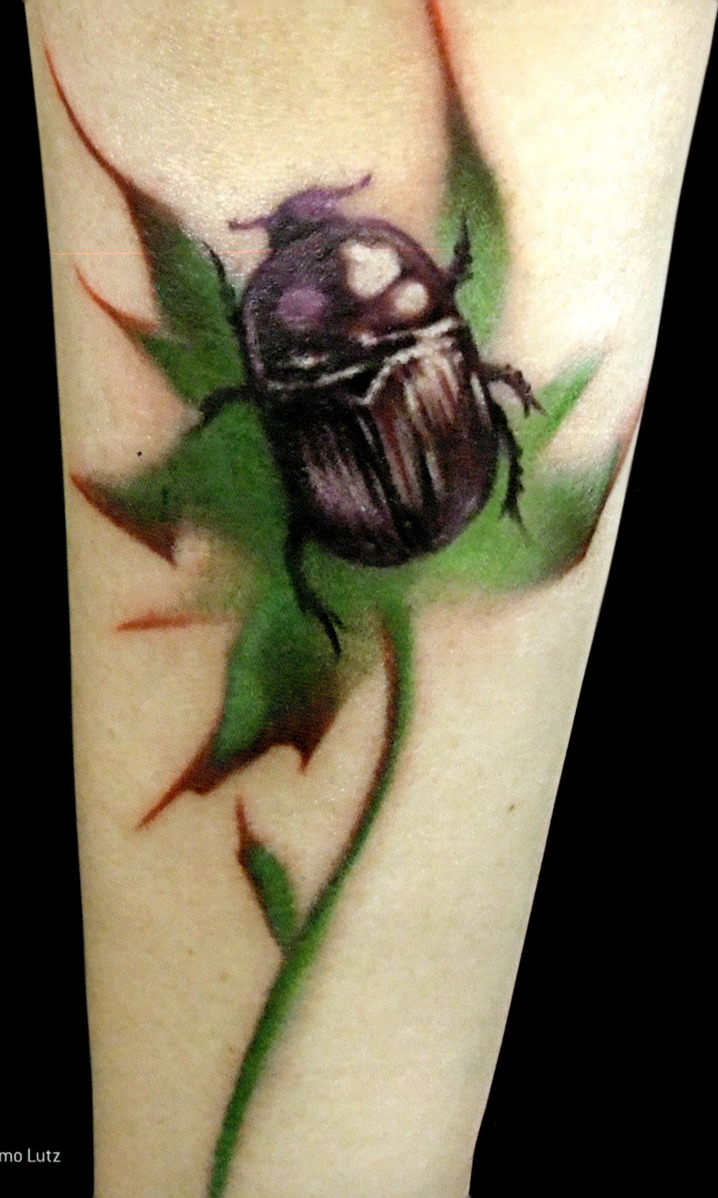

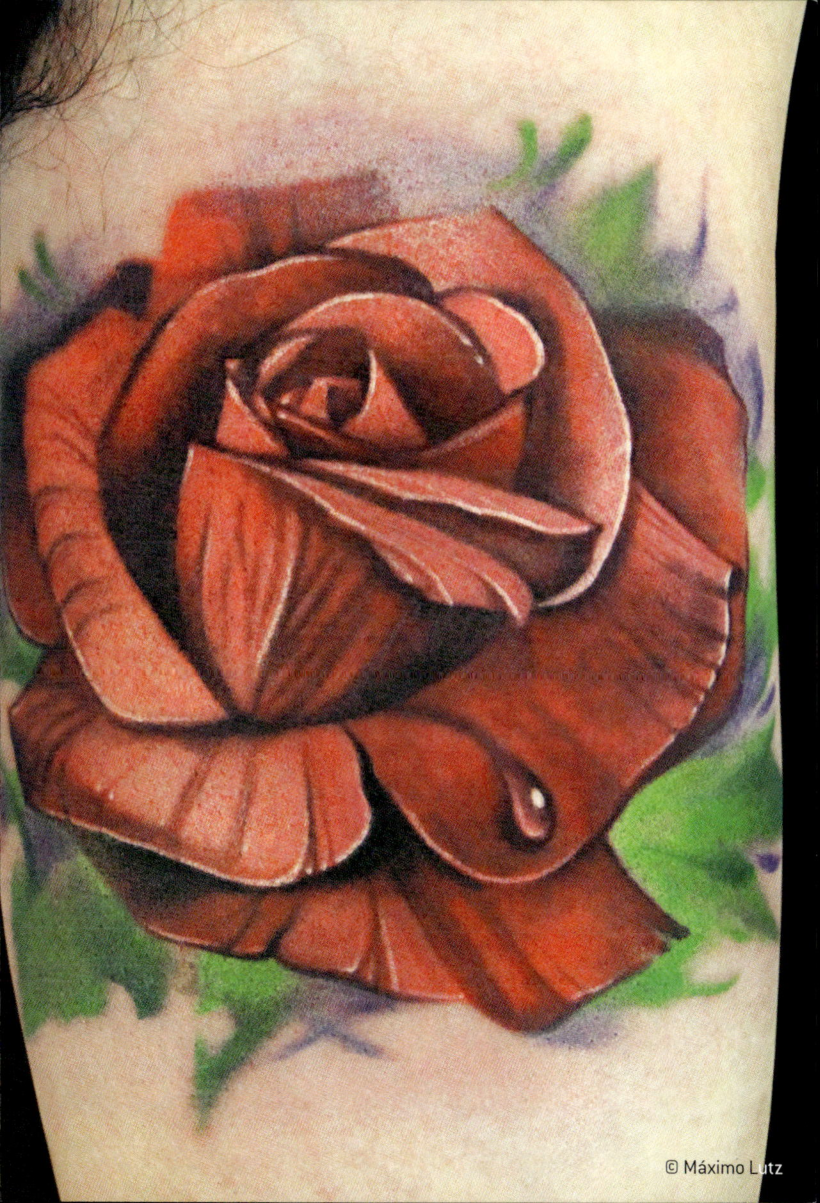

© Máximo Lutz

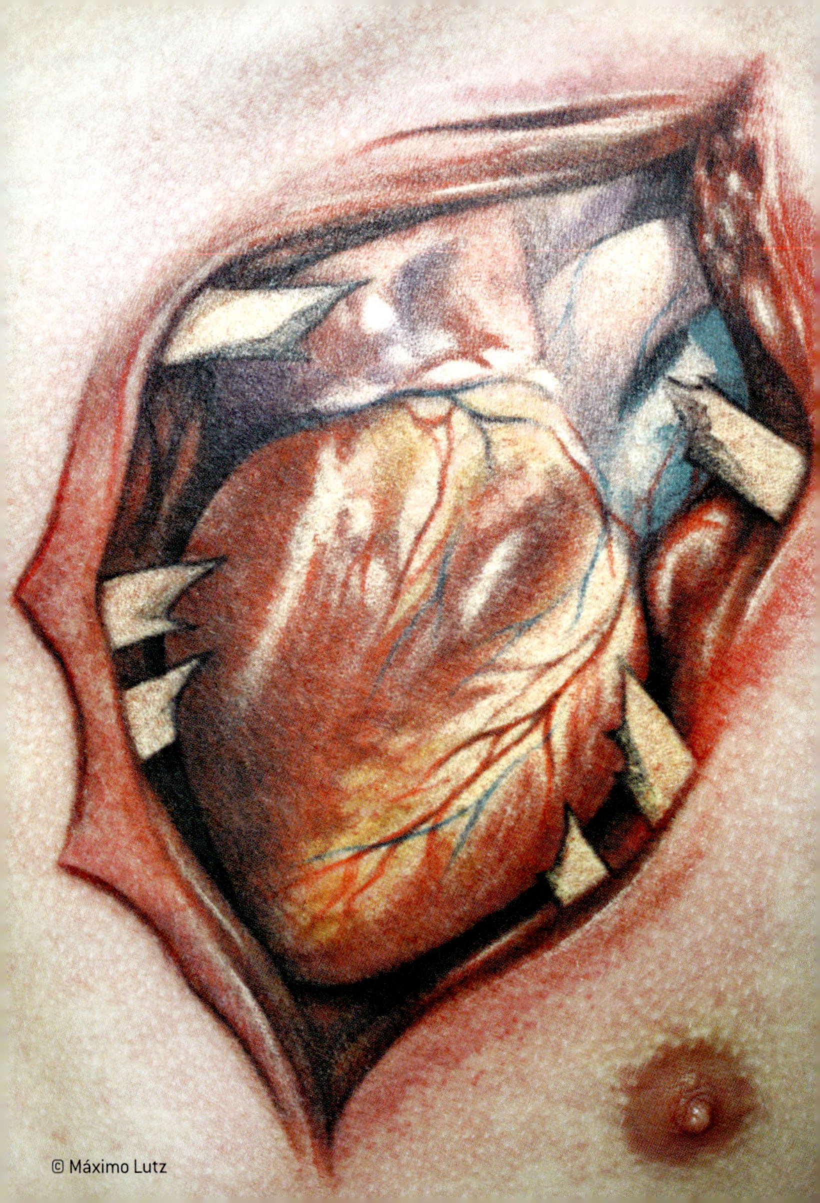
© Máximo Lutz

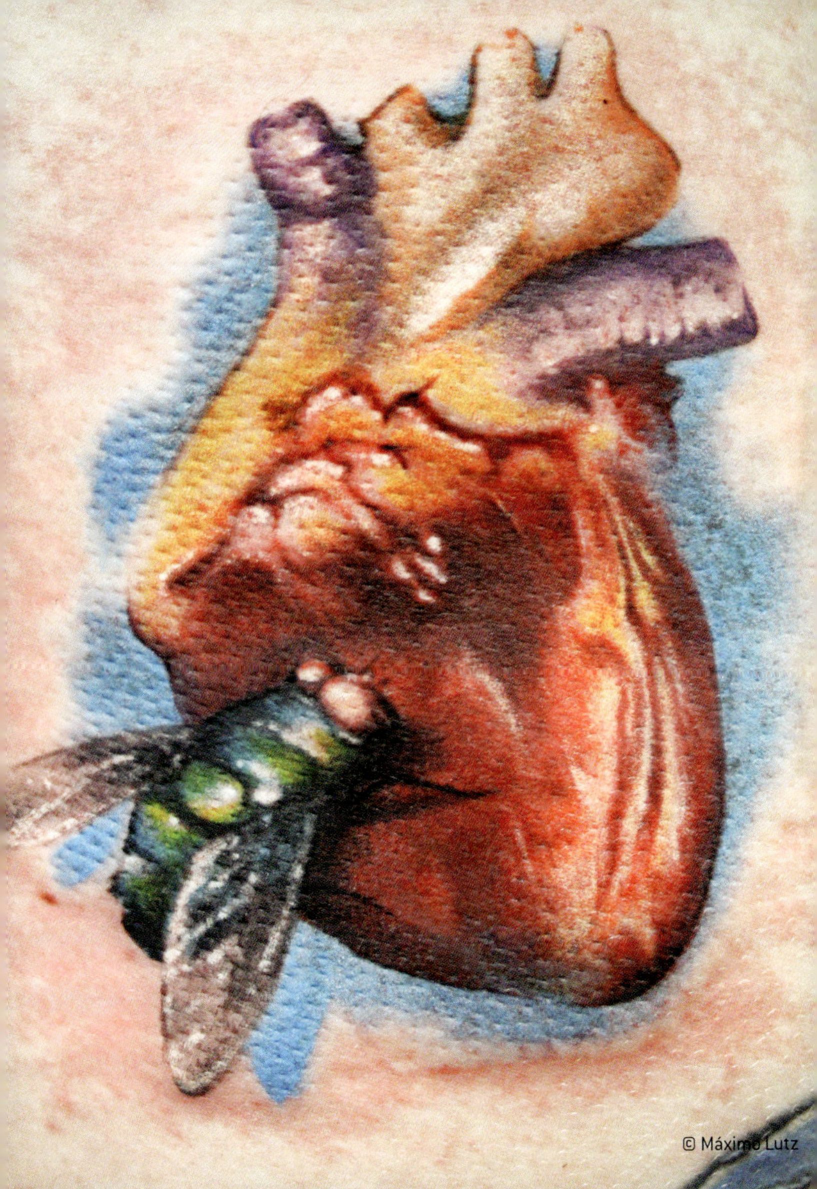

© Máximo Lutz

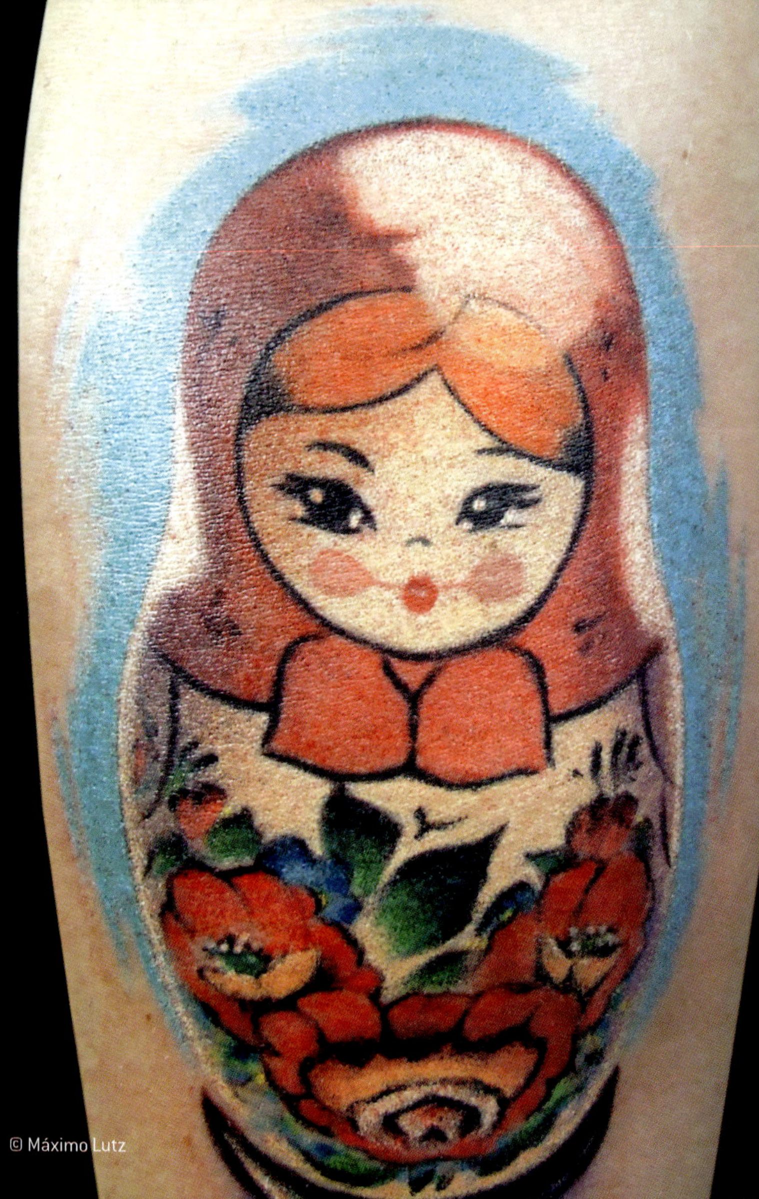

© Máximo Lutz

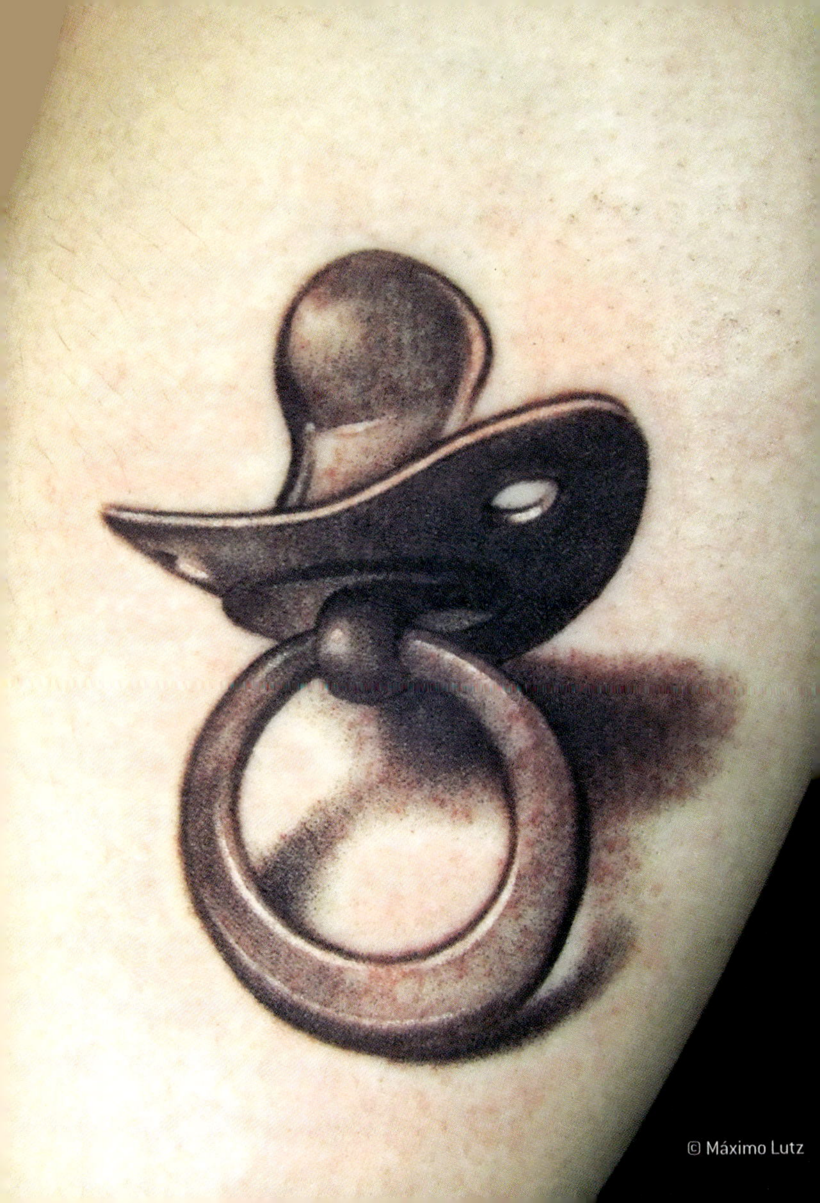

© Máximo Lutz

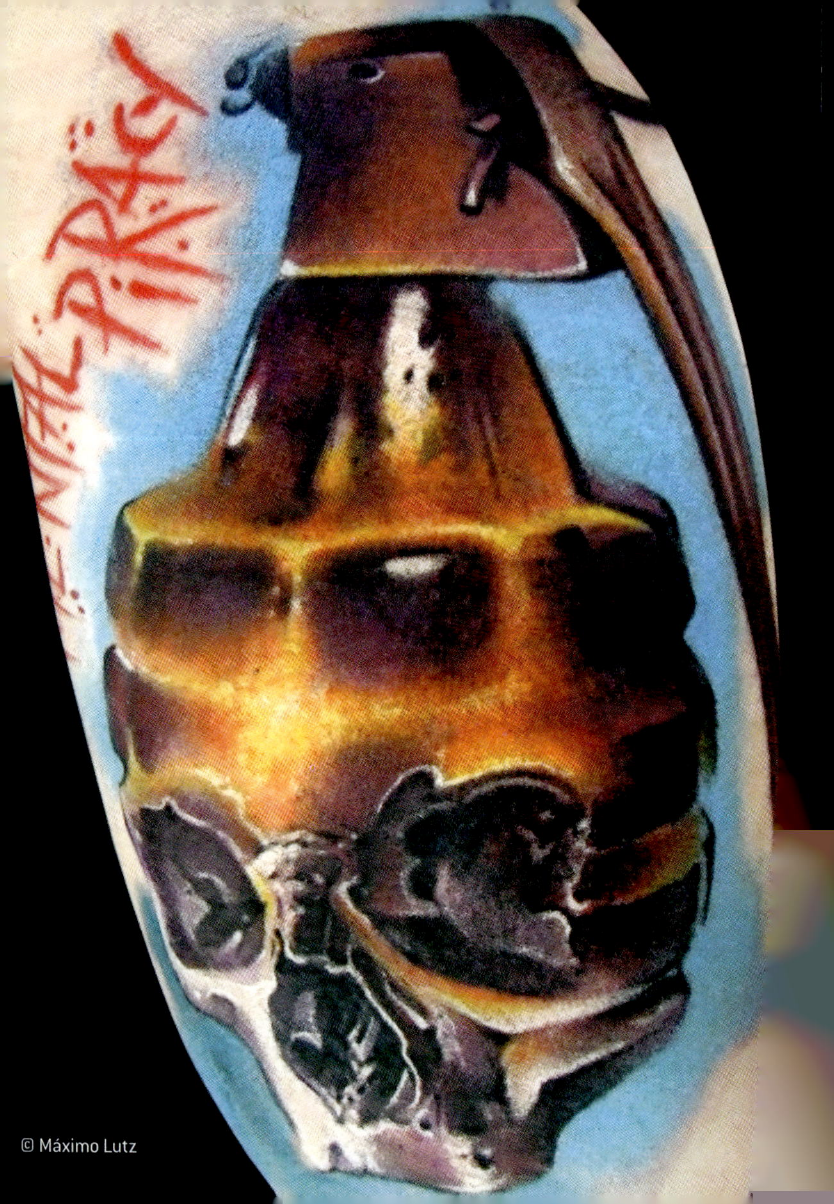

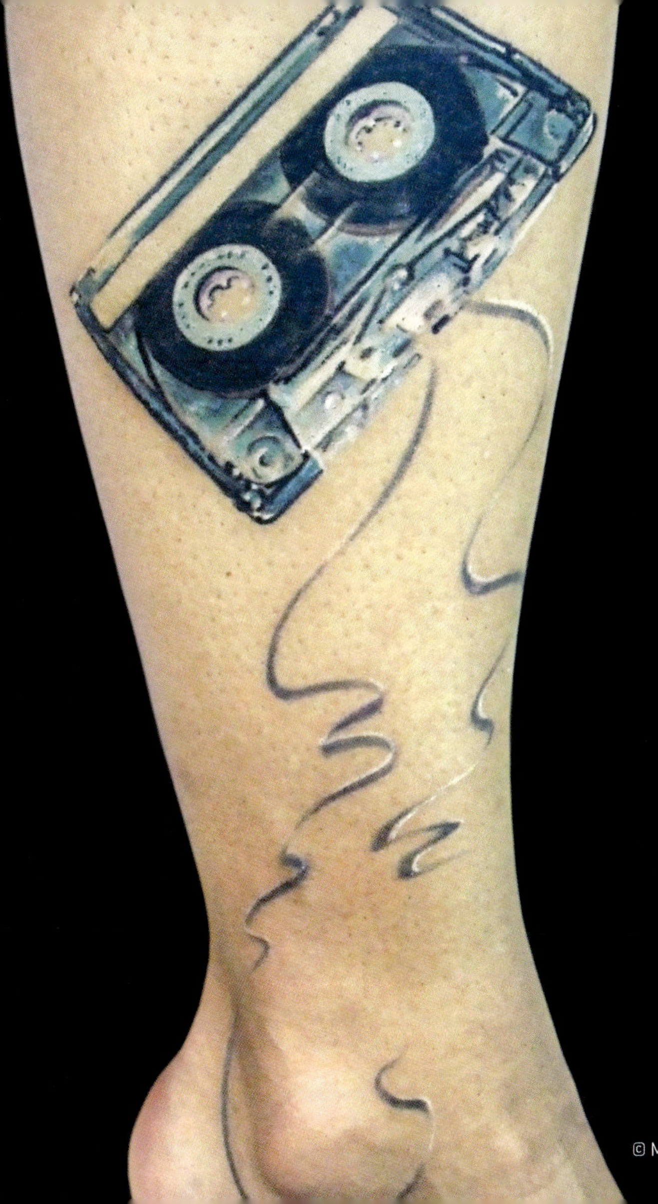

© Máximo Lutz

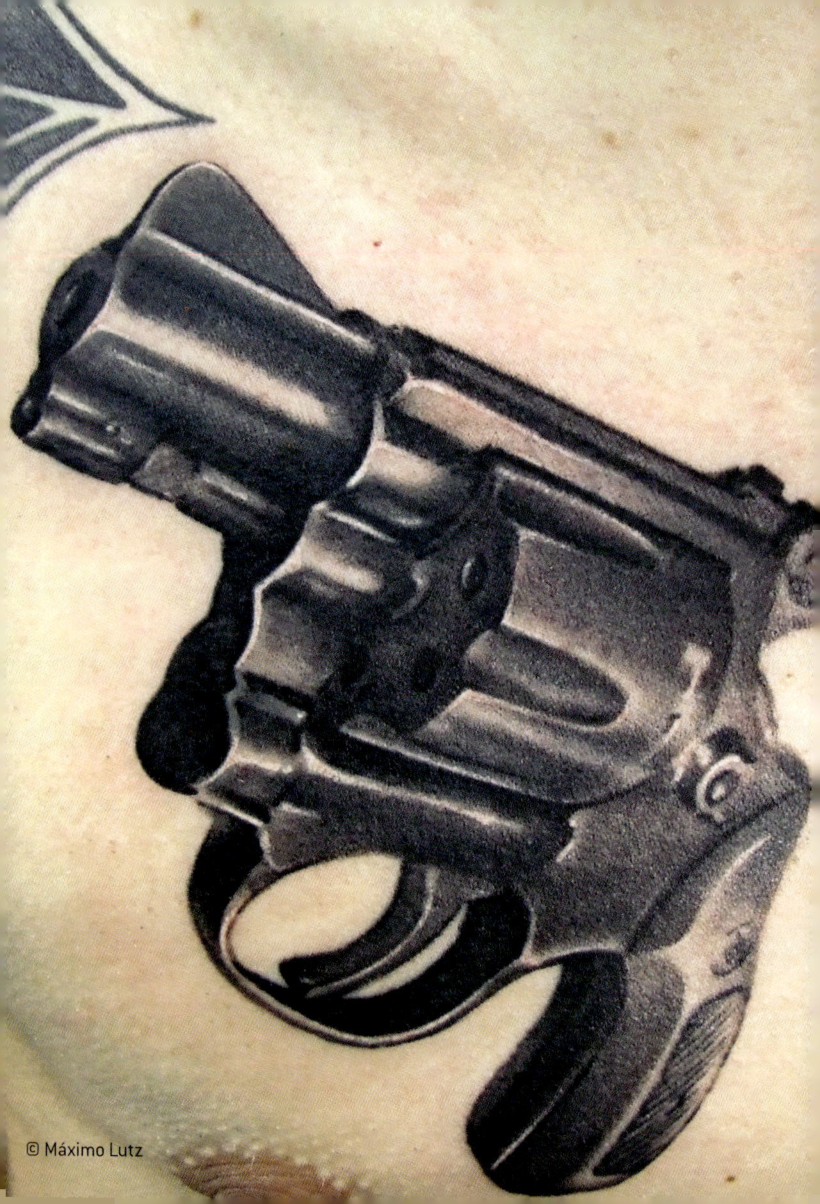
© Máximo Lutz

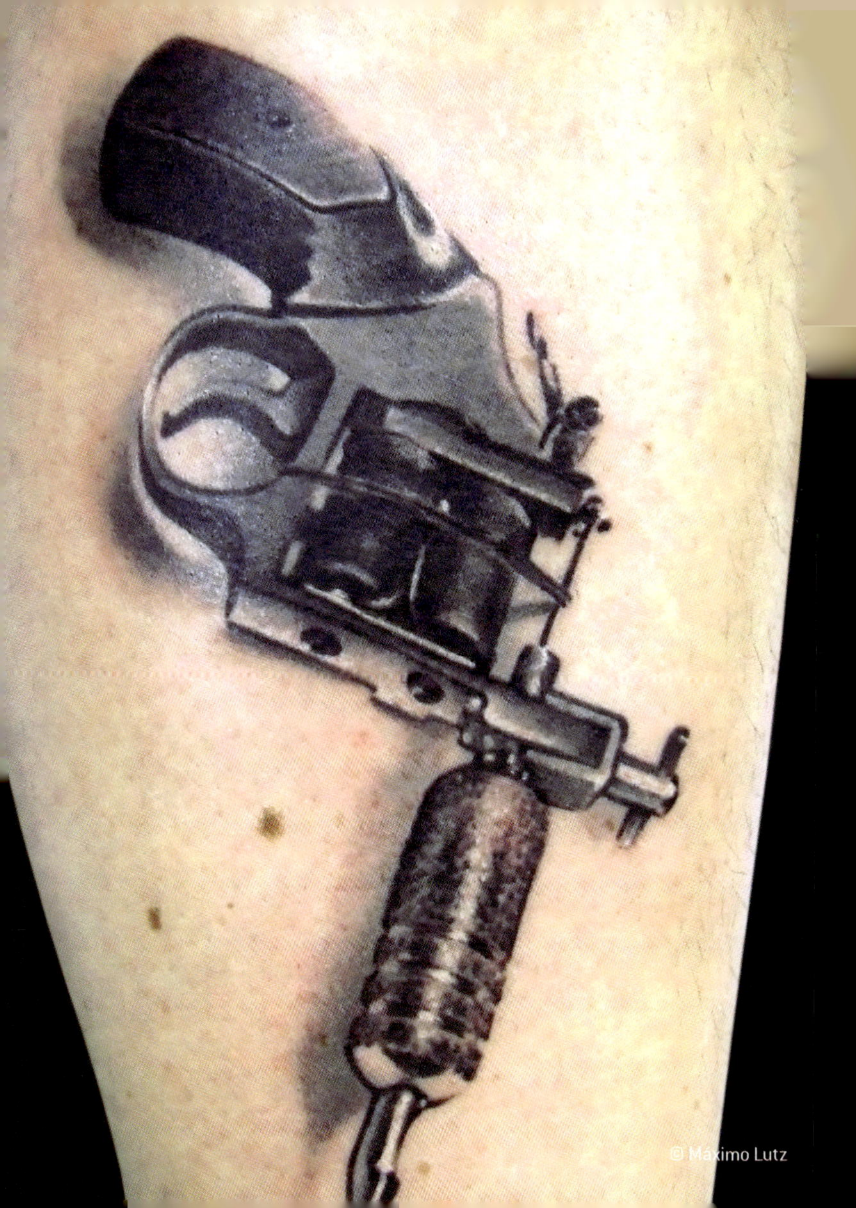
© Máximo Lutz

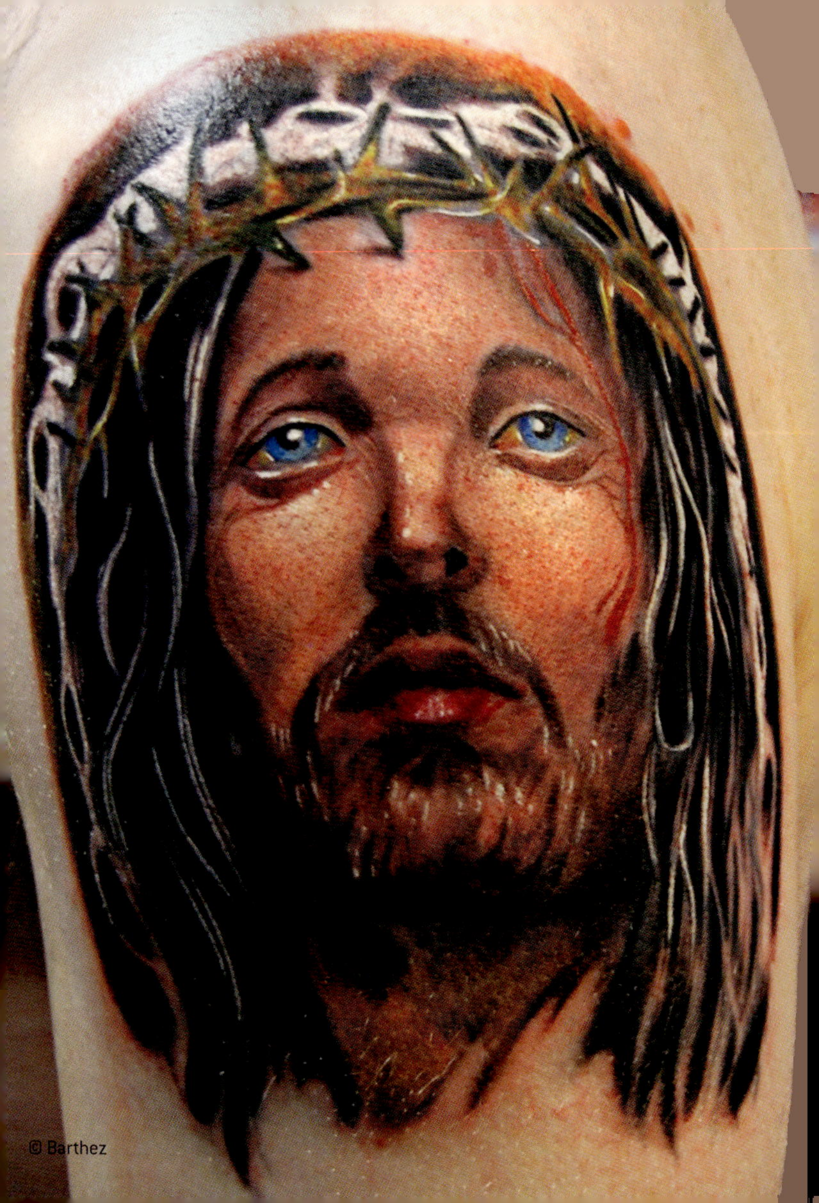
© Barthez

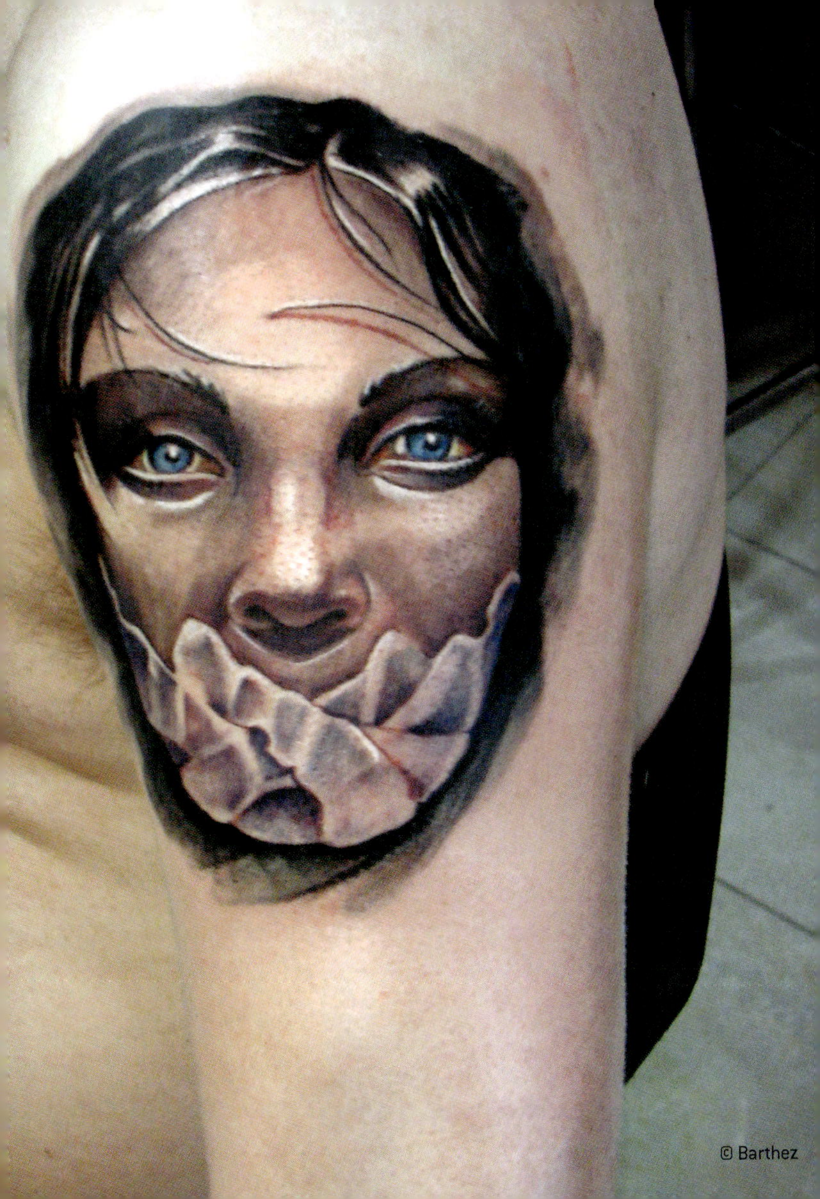
© Barthez

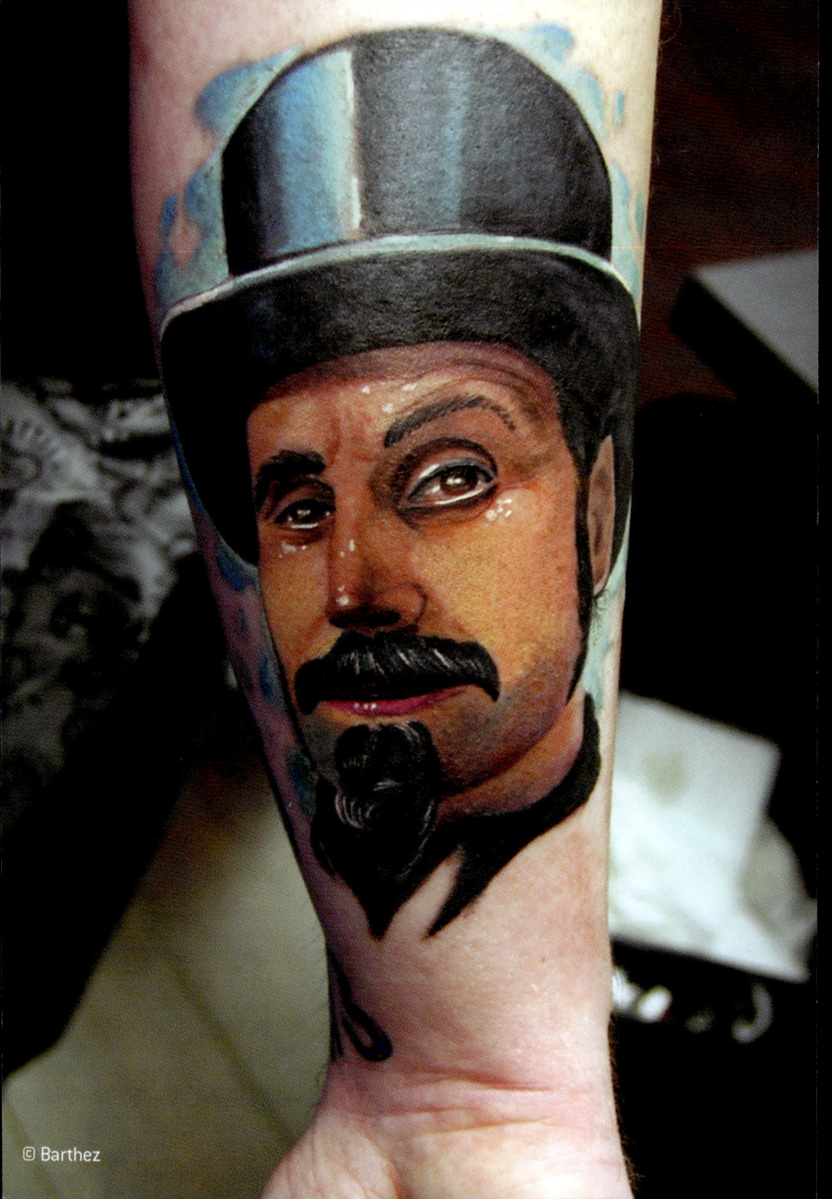
© Barthez

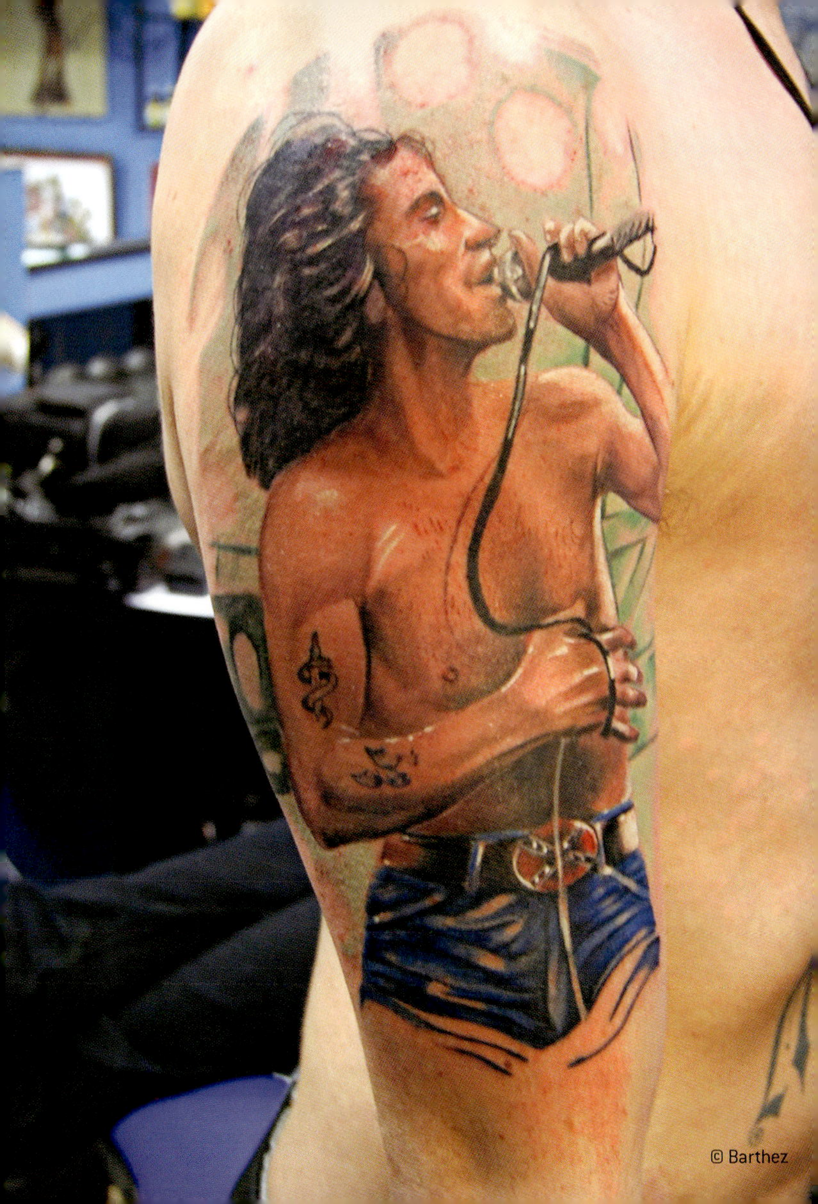
© Barthez

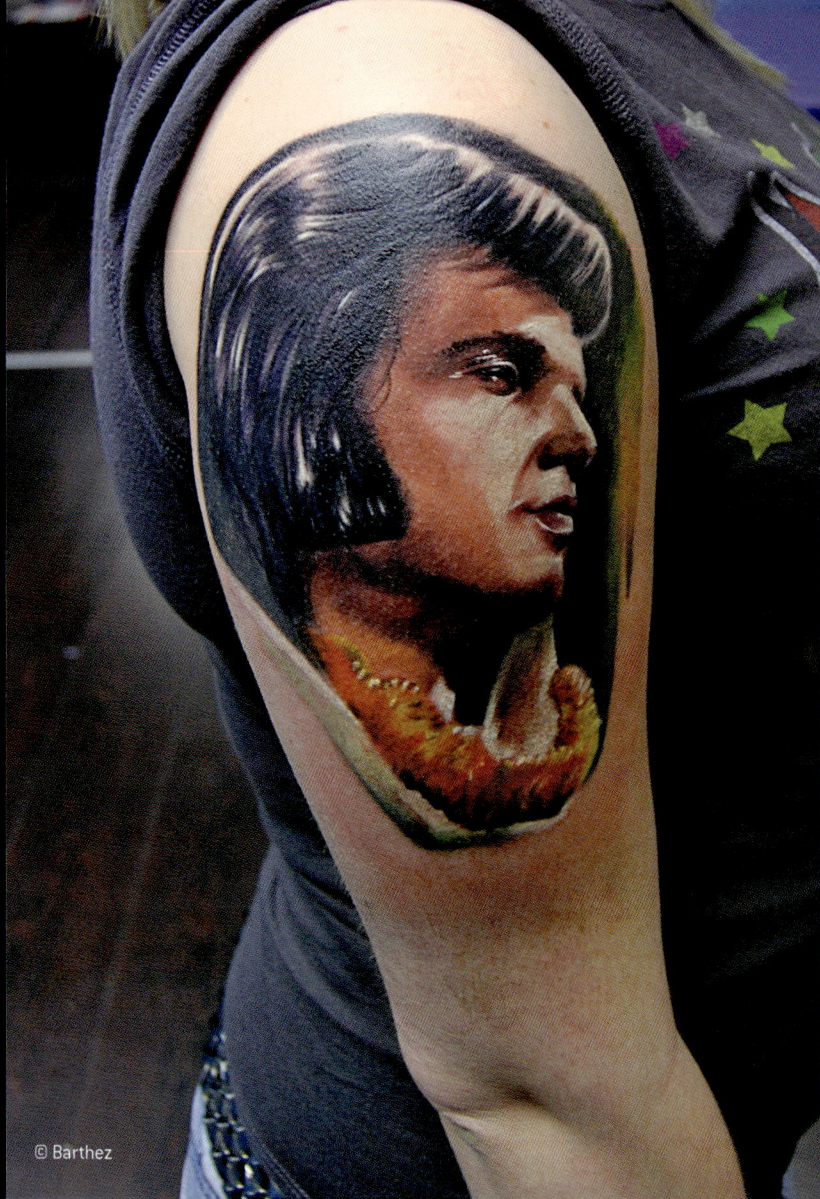
© Barthez

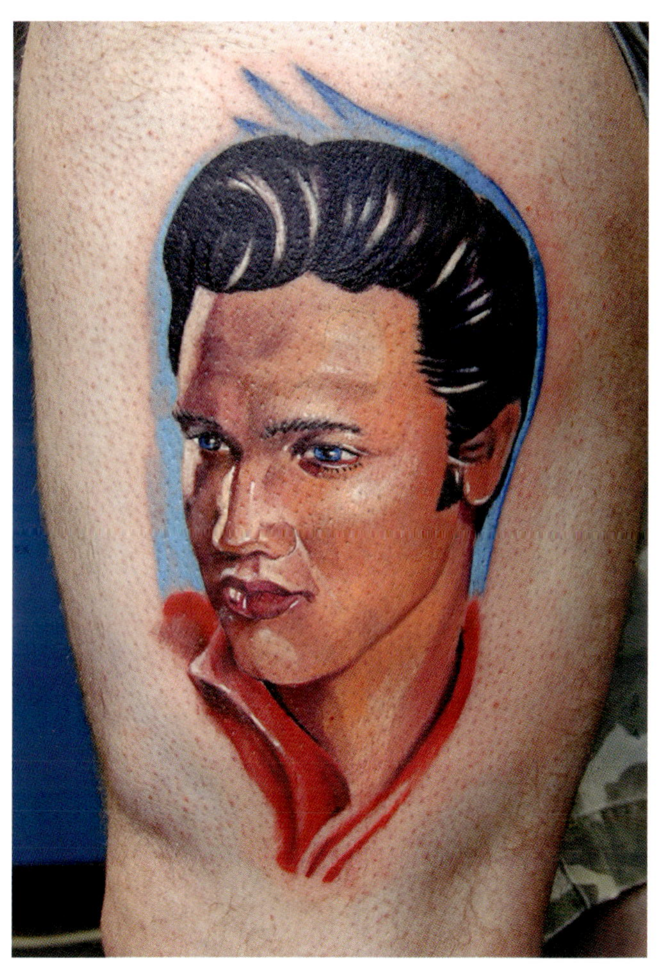

© Barthez

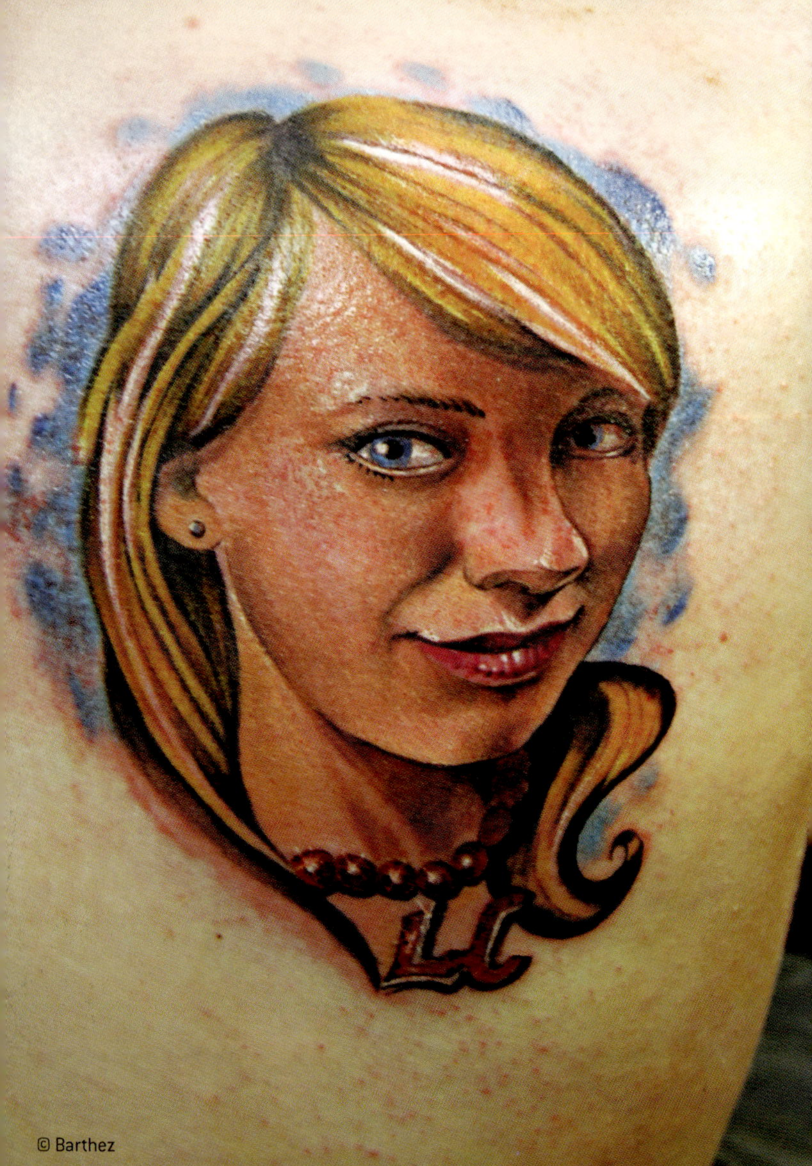

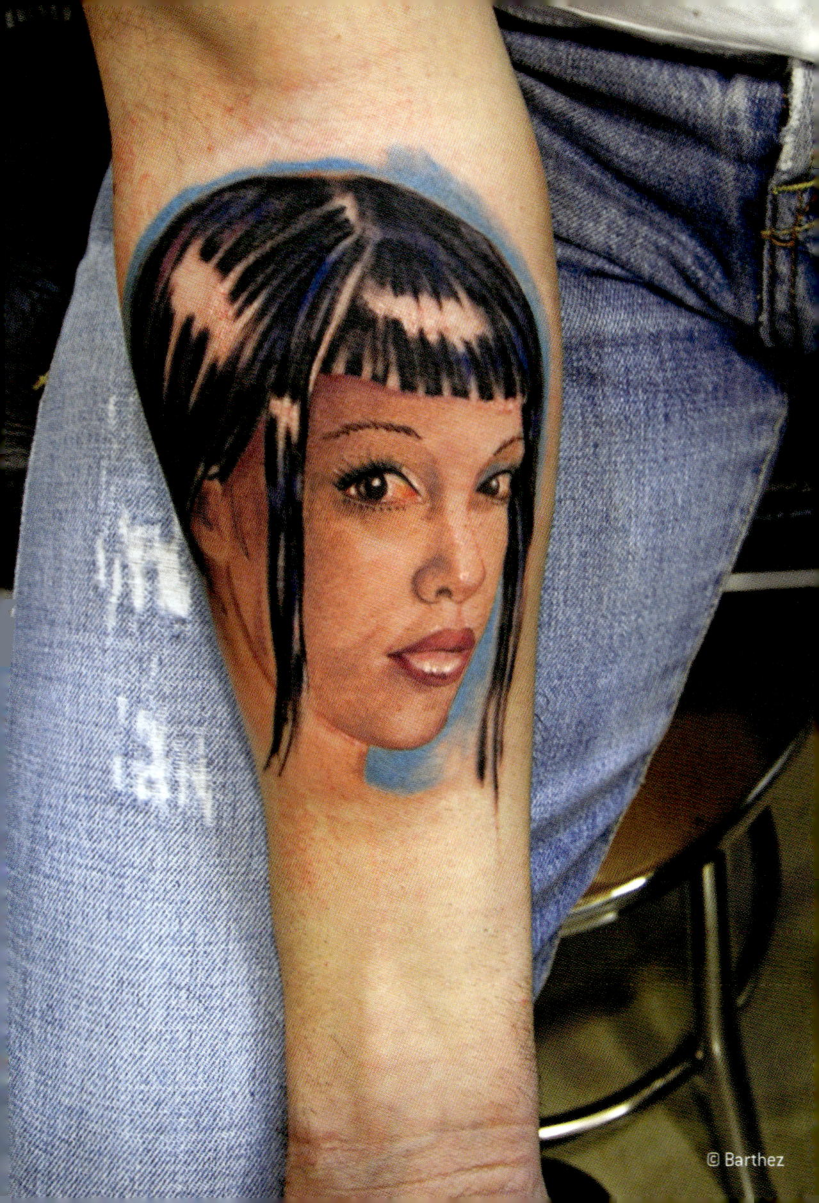
© Barthez

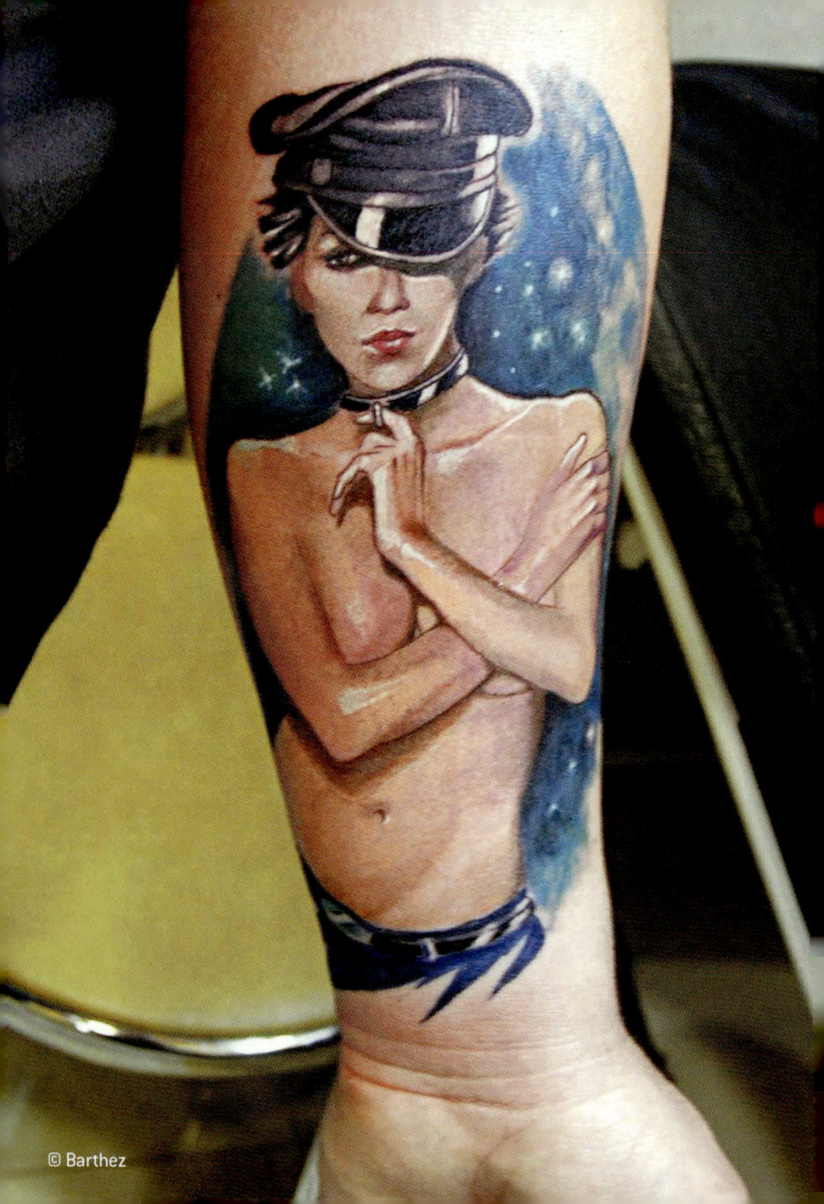
© Barthez

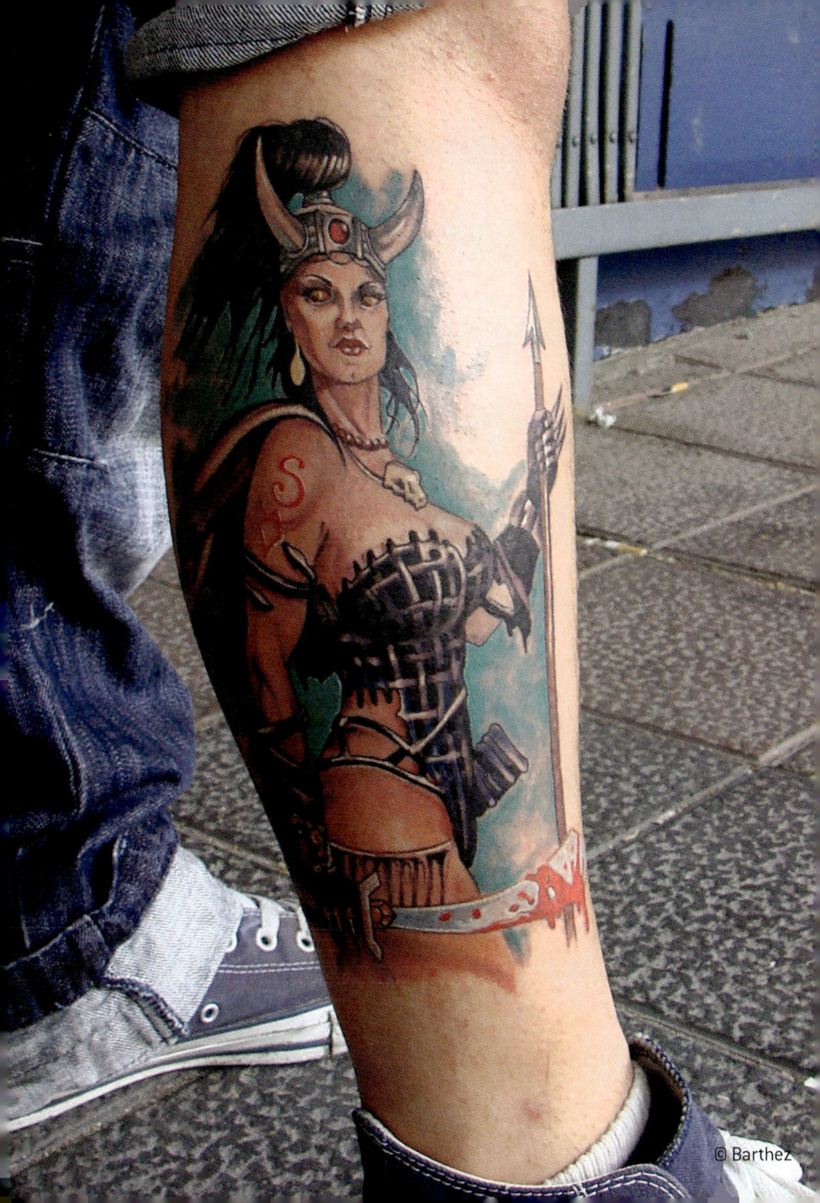
© Barthez

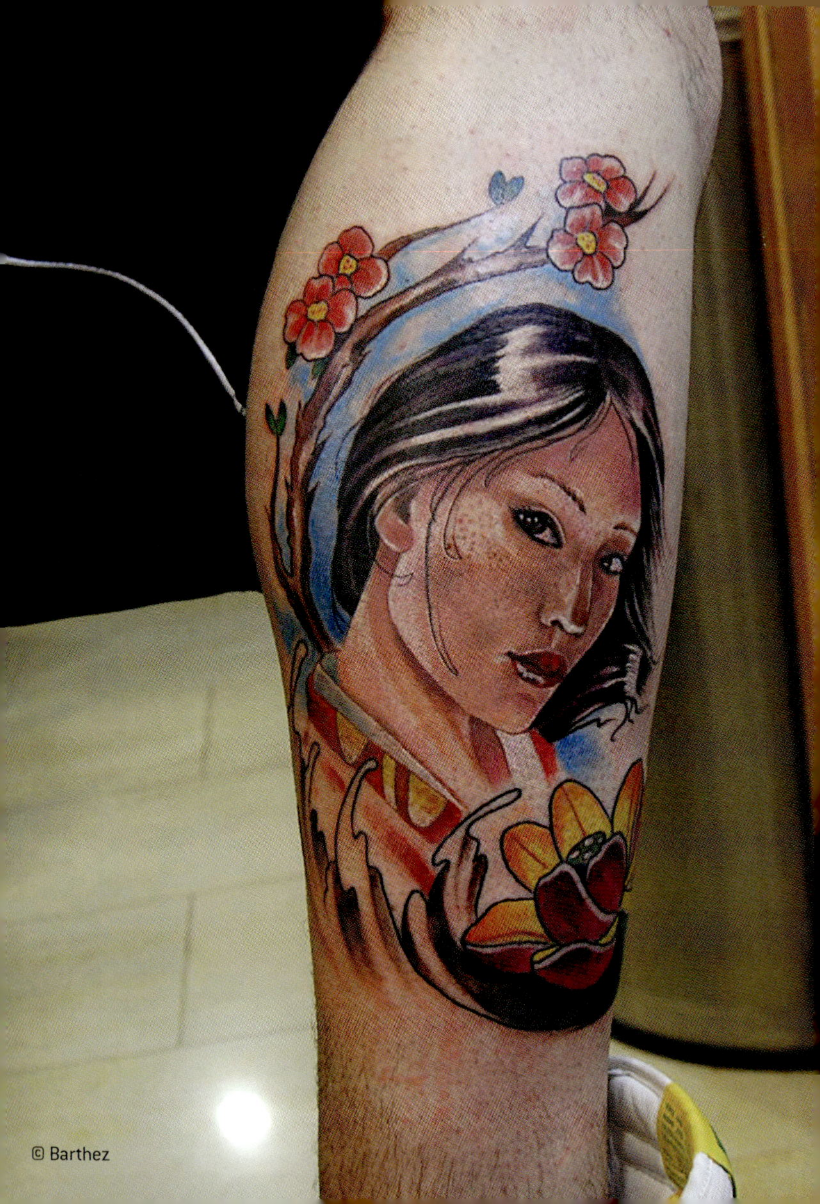
© Barthez

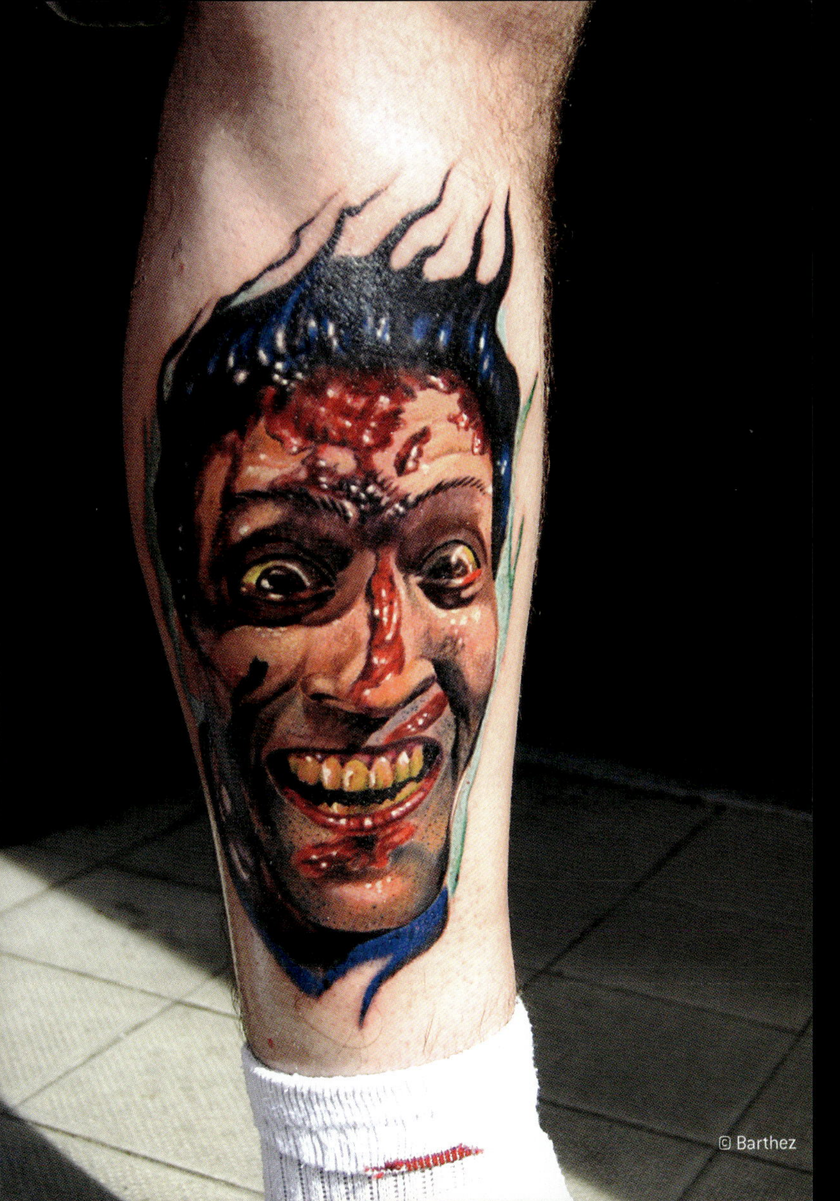
© Barthez

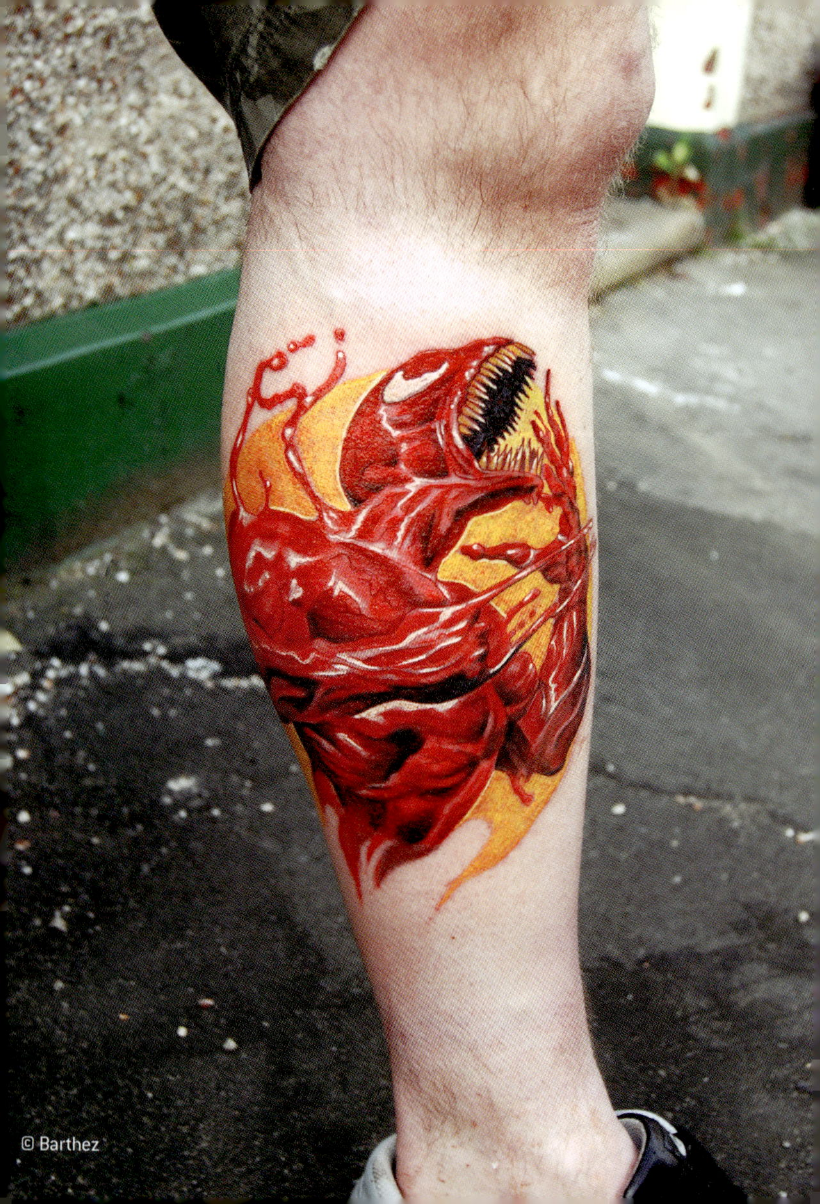
© Barthez

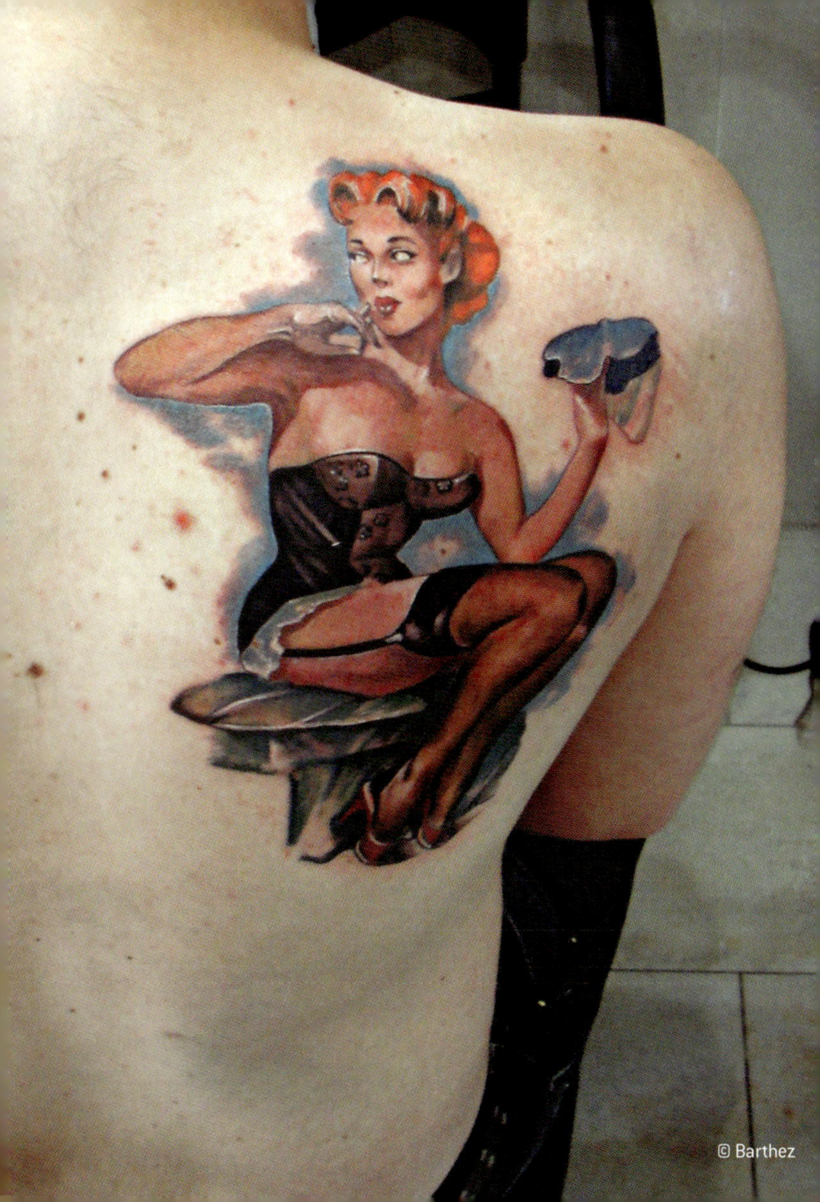
© Barthez

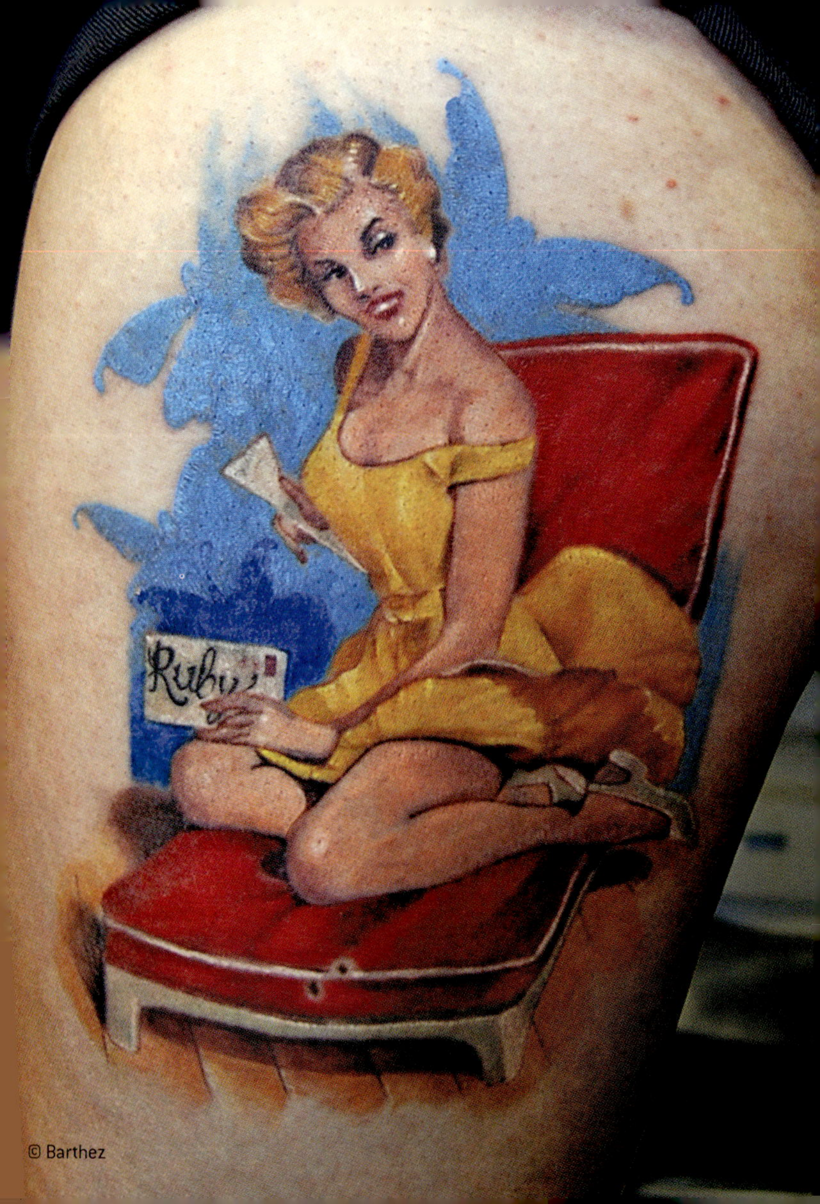

Ruby
© Barthez

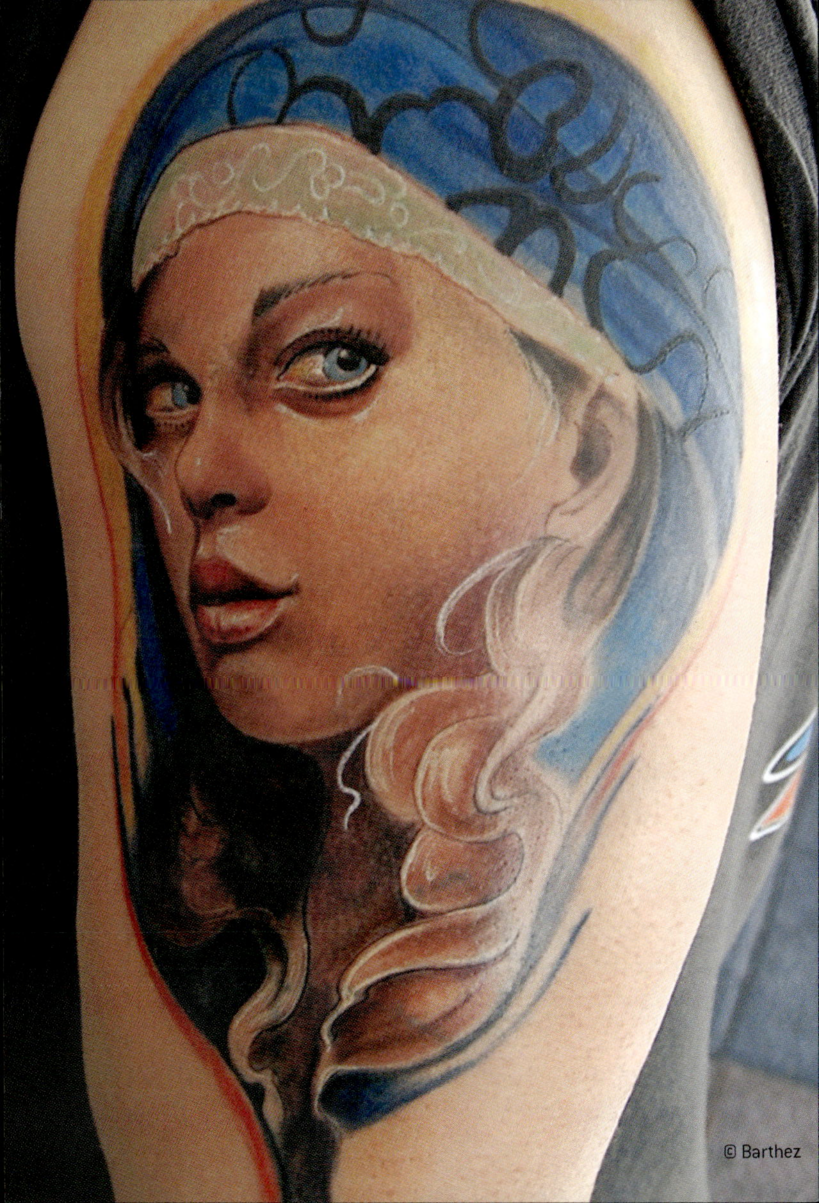

© Barthez

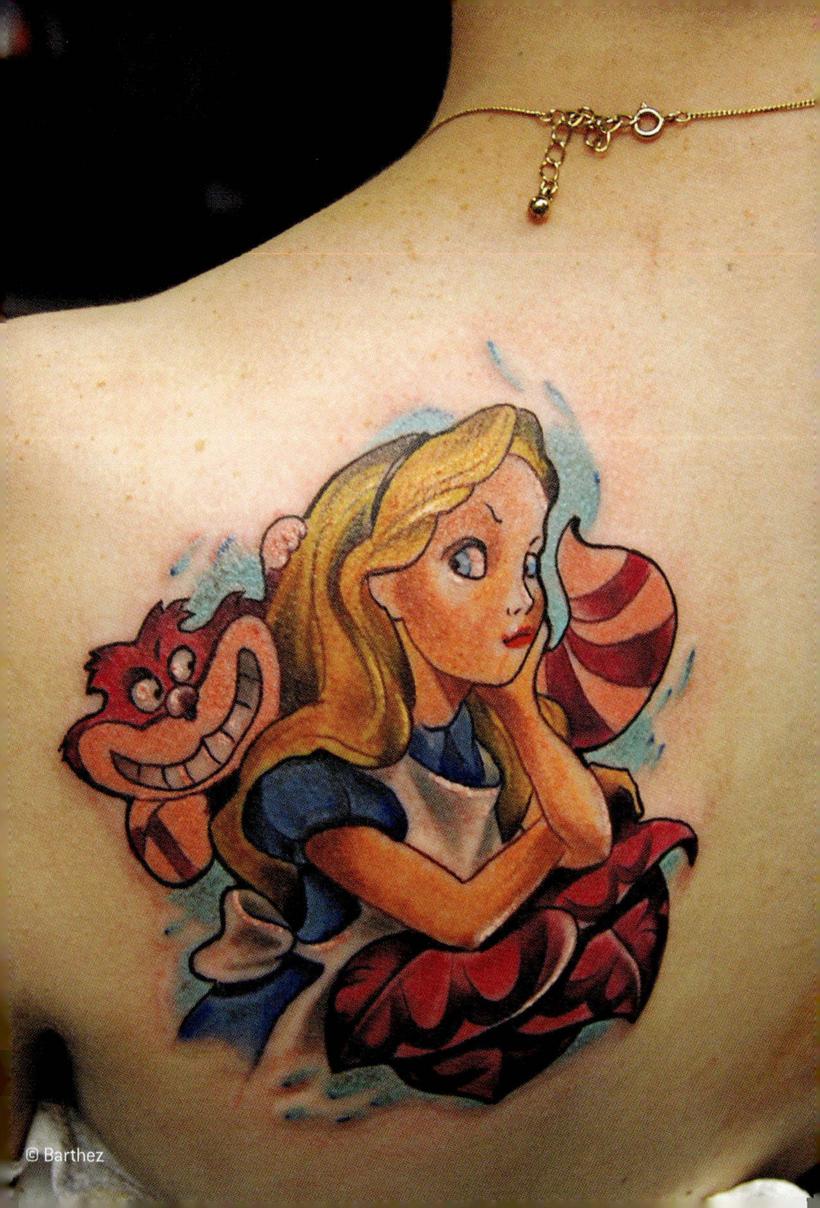
© Barthez

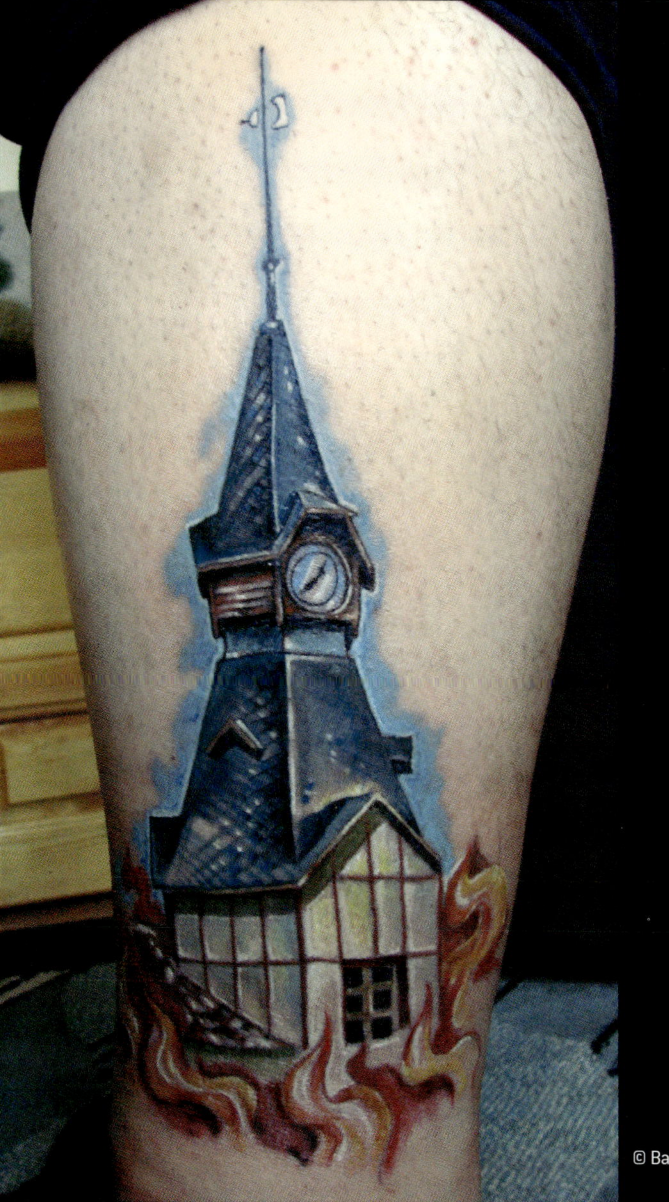
© Barth

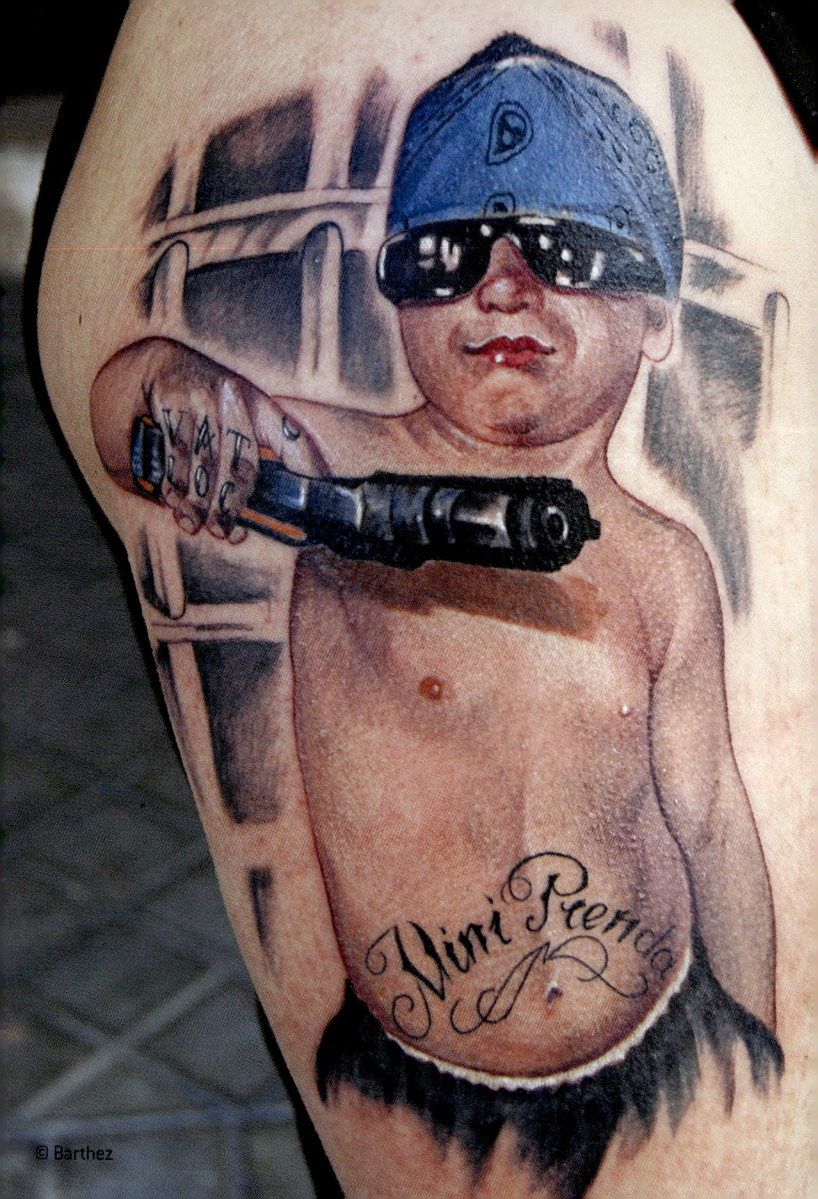

VATO LOCO
Mini Prenda

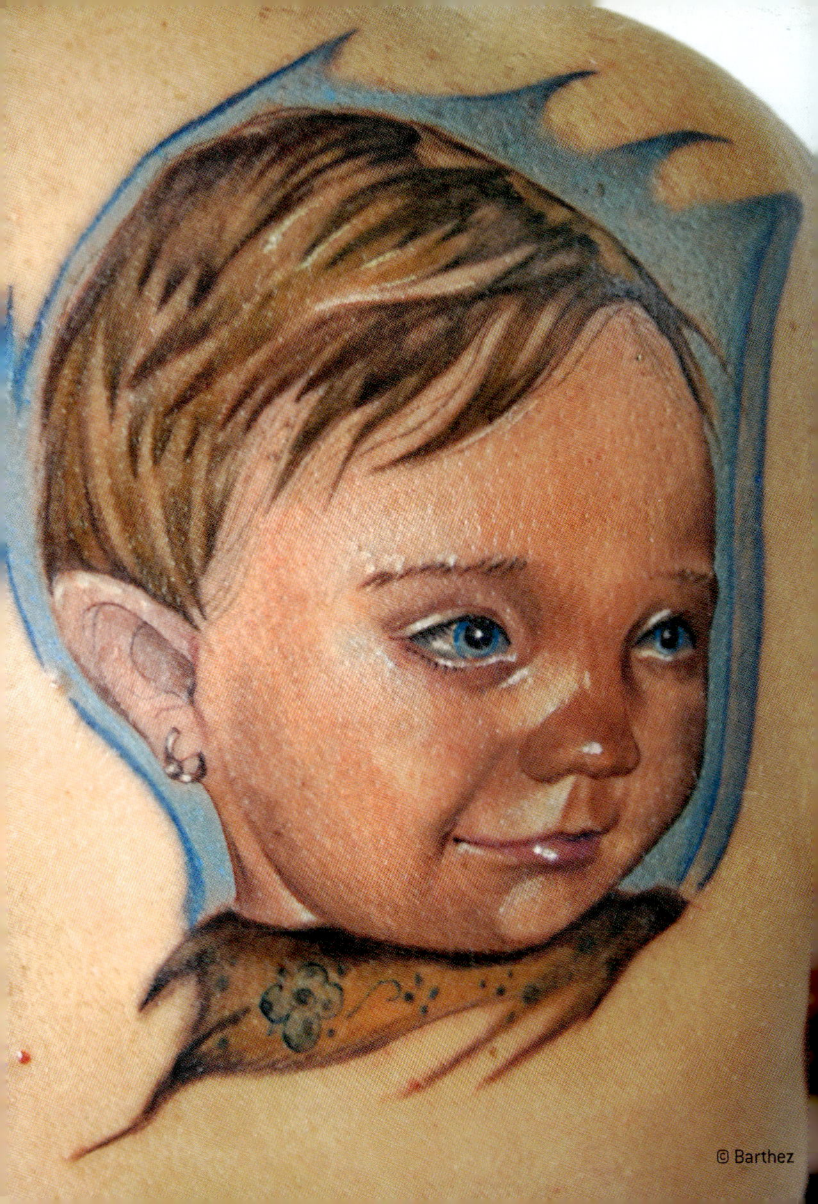
© Barthez

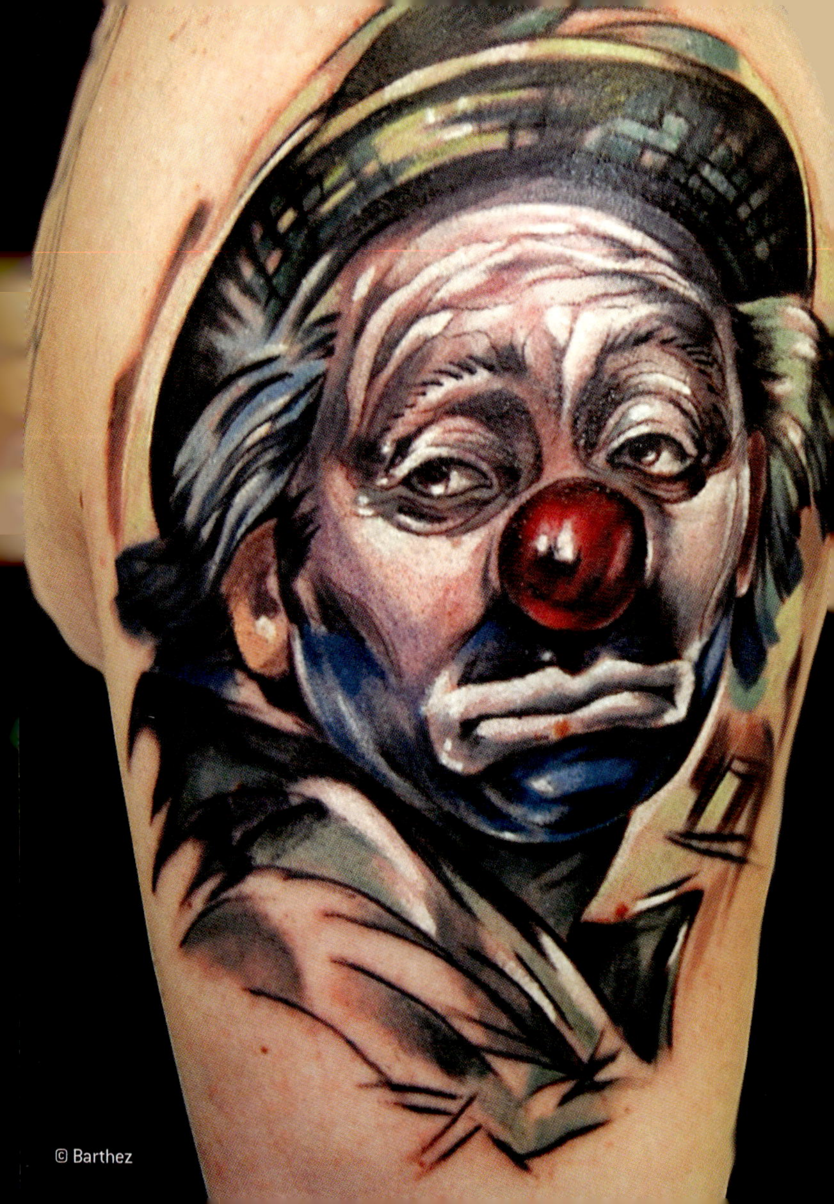
© Barthez

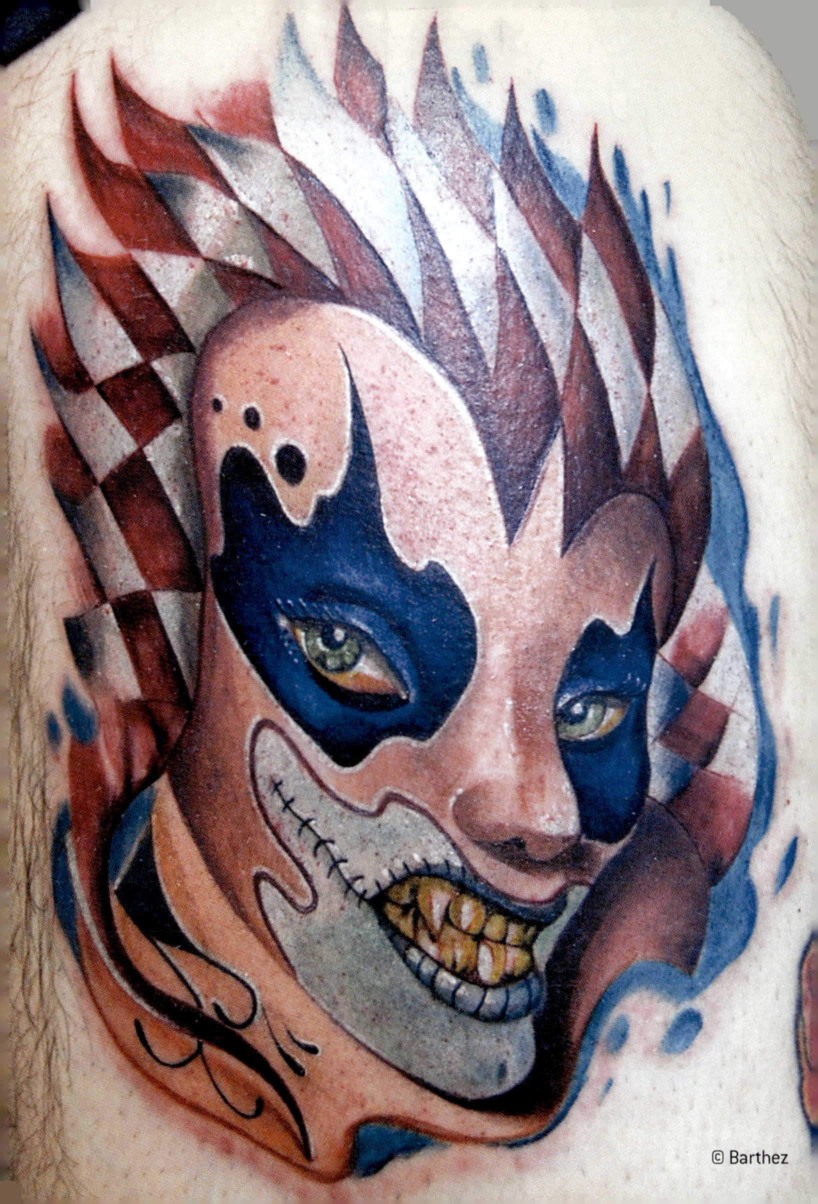

© Barthez

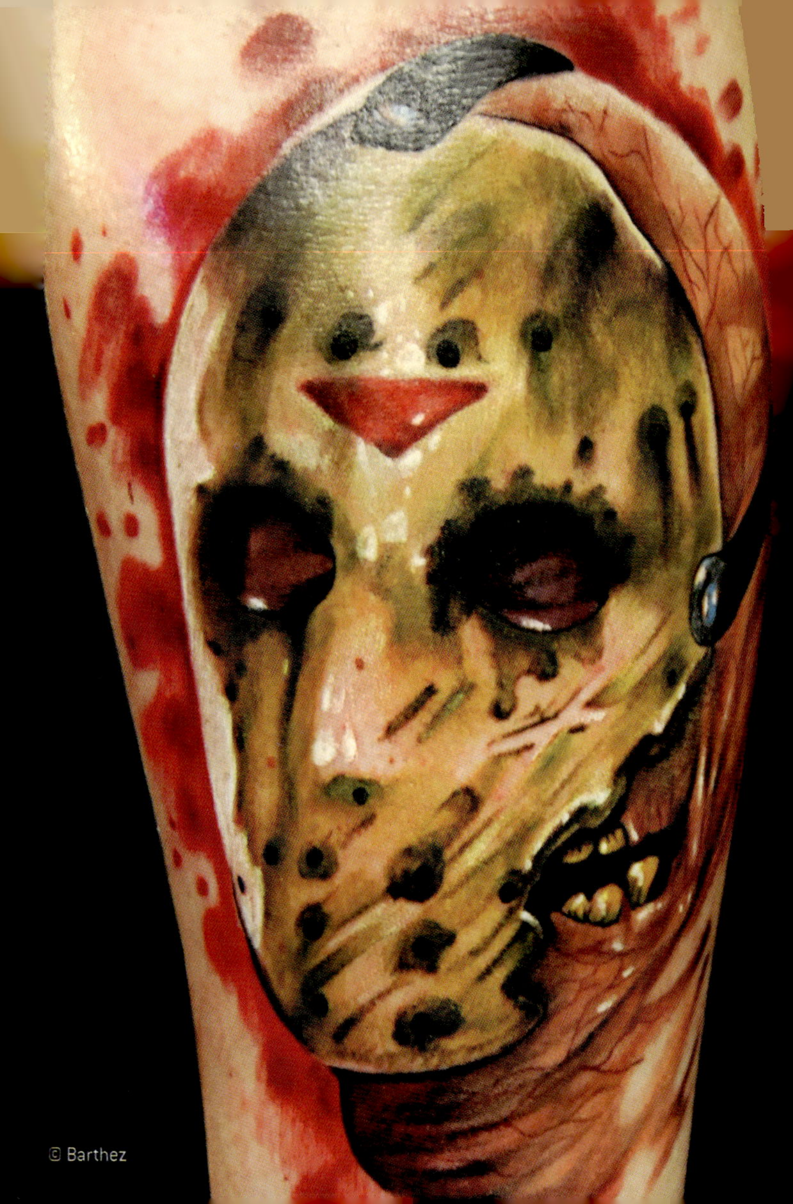

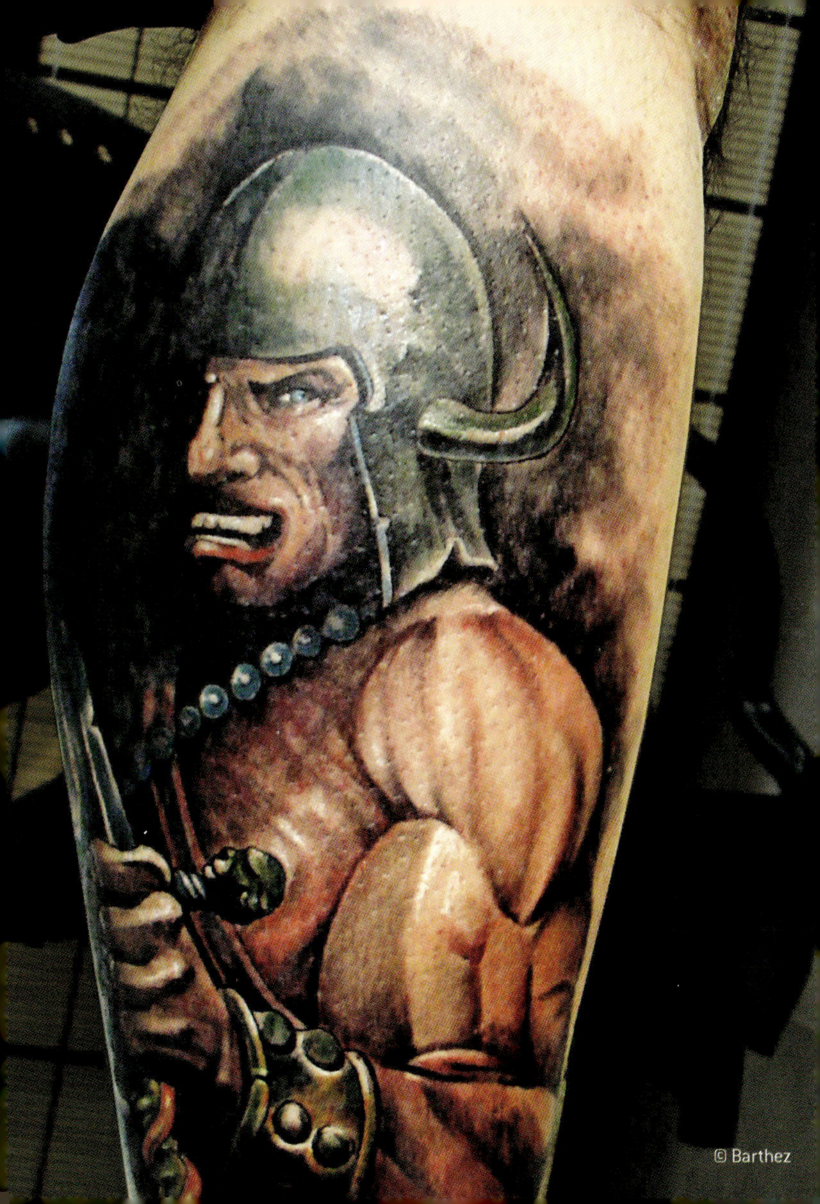
© Barthez

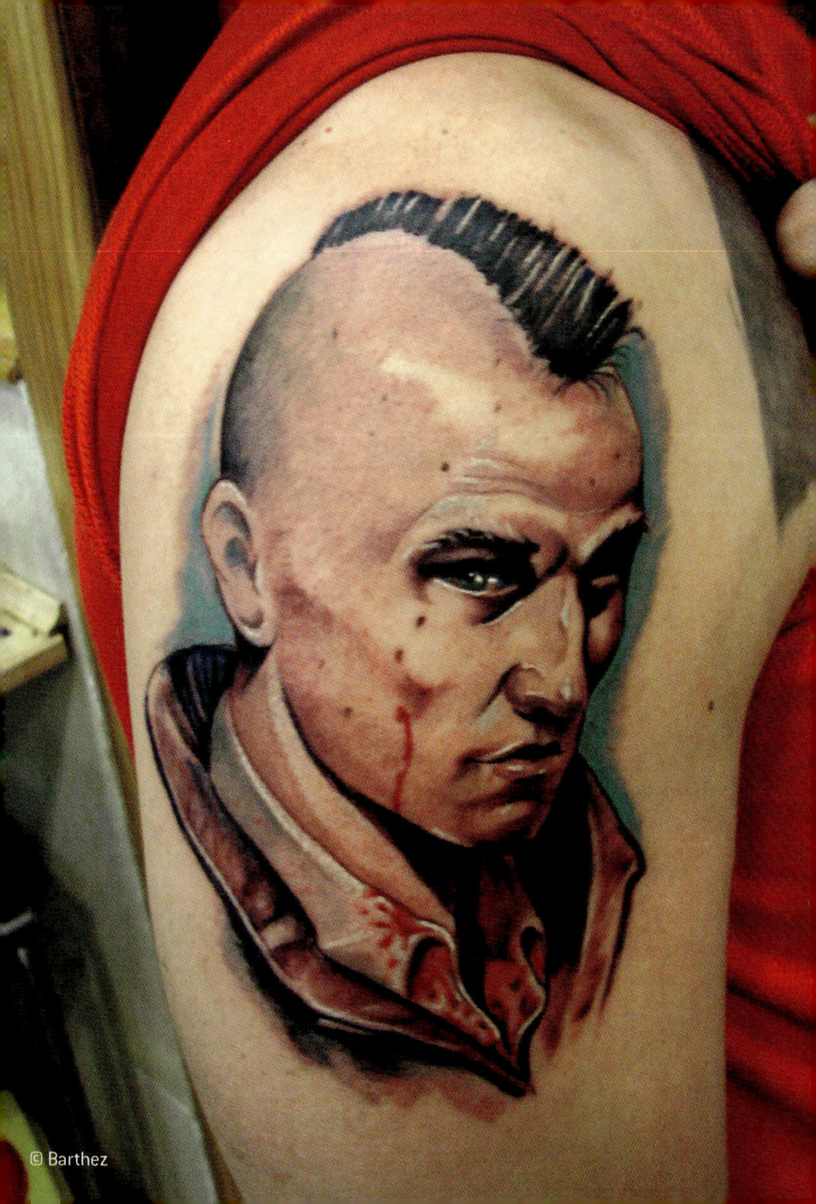
© Barthez

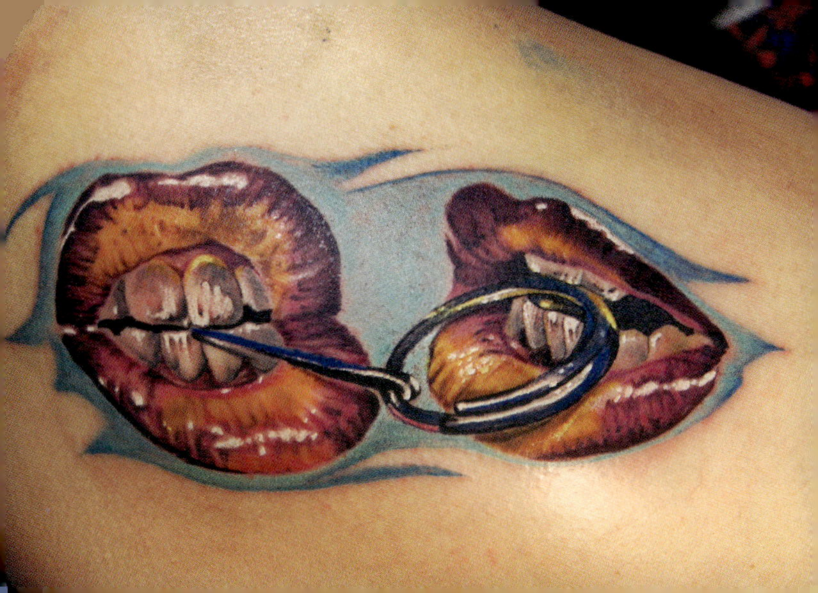

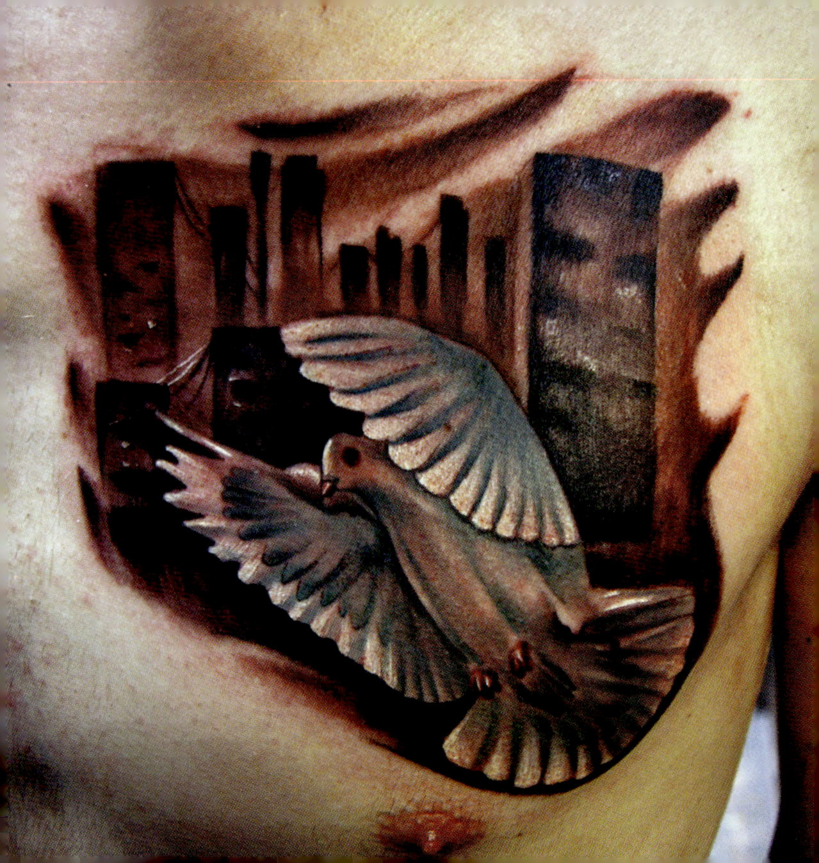

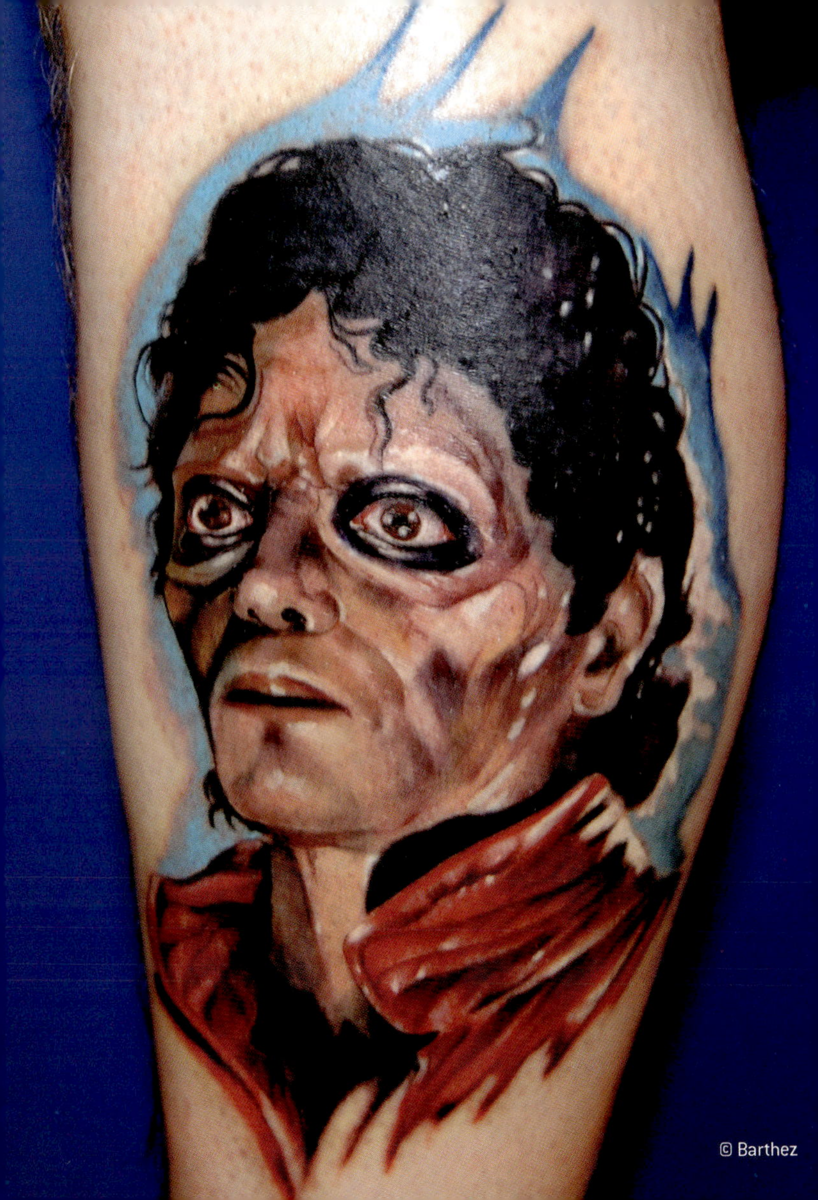
© Barthez

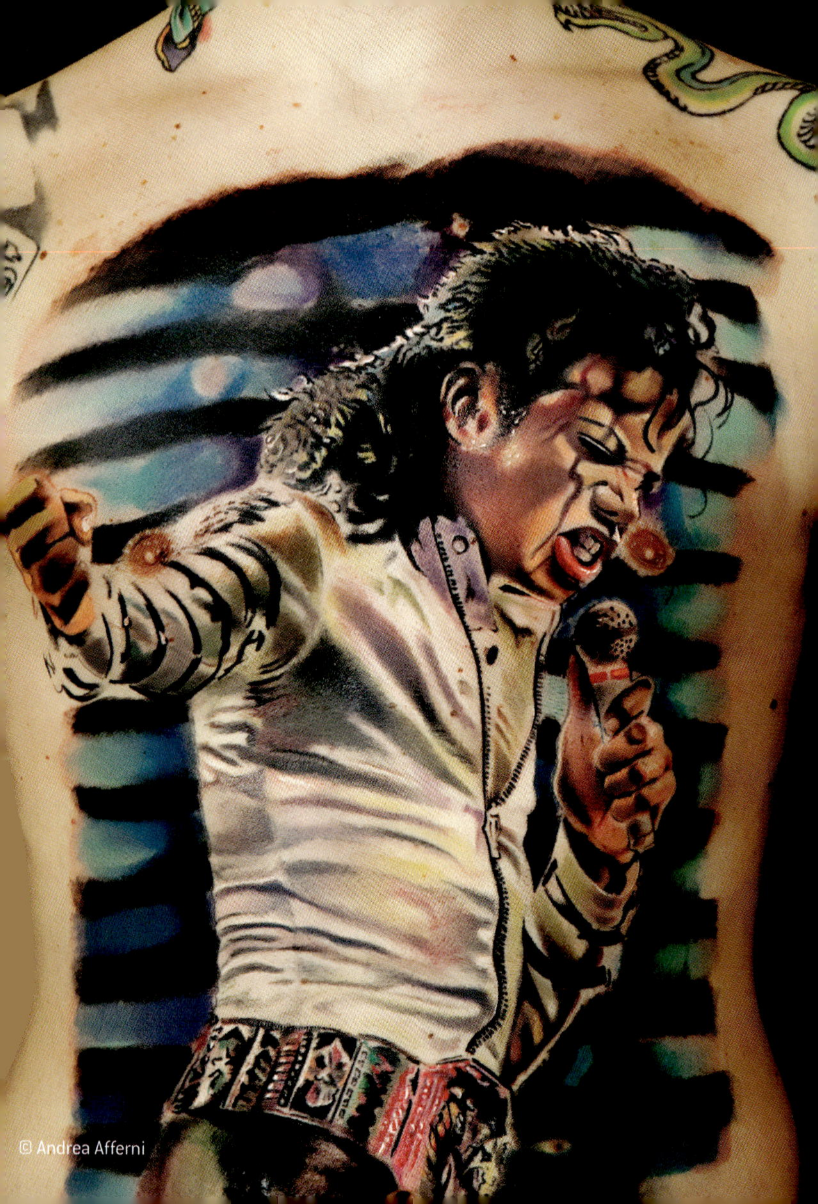
© Andrea Afferni

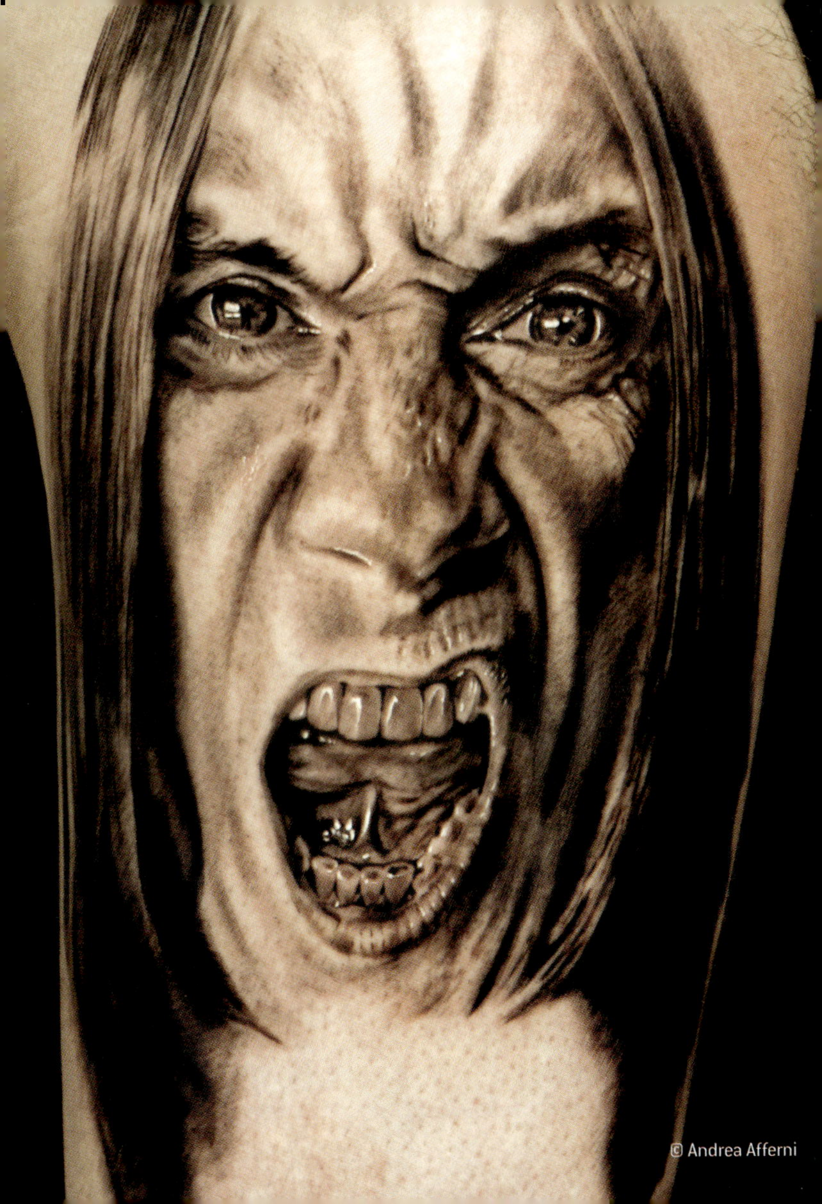

© Andrea Afferni

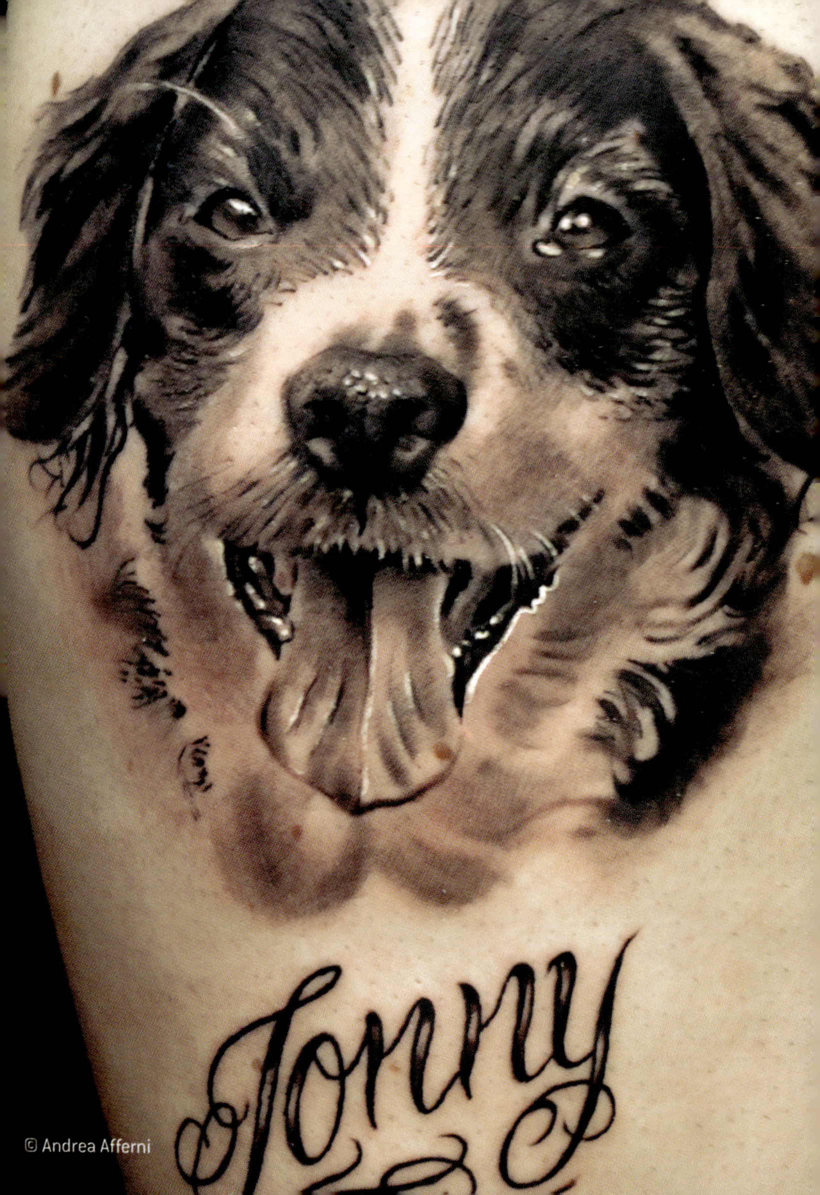

Jonny
© Andrea Afferni

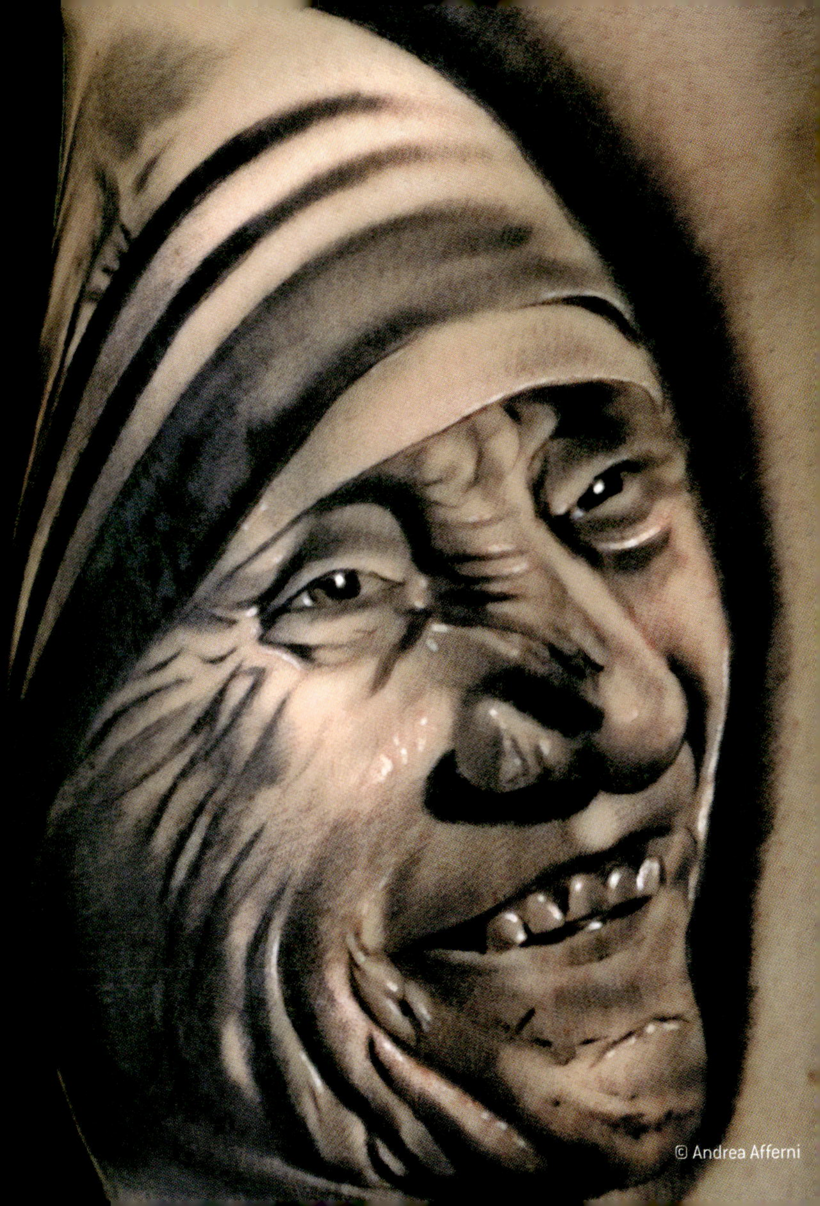
© Andrea Afferni

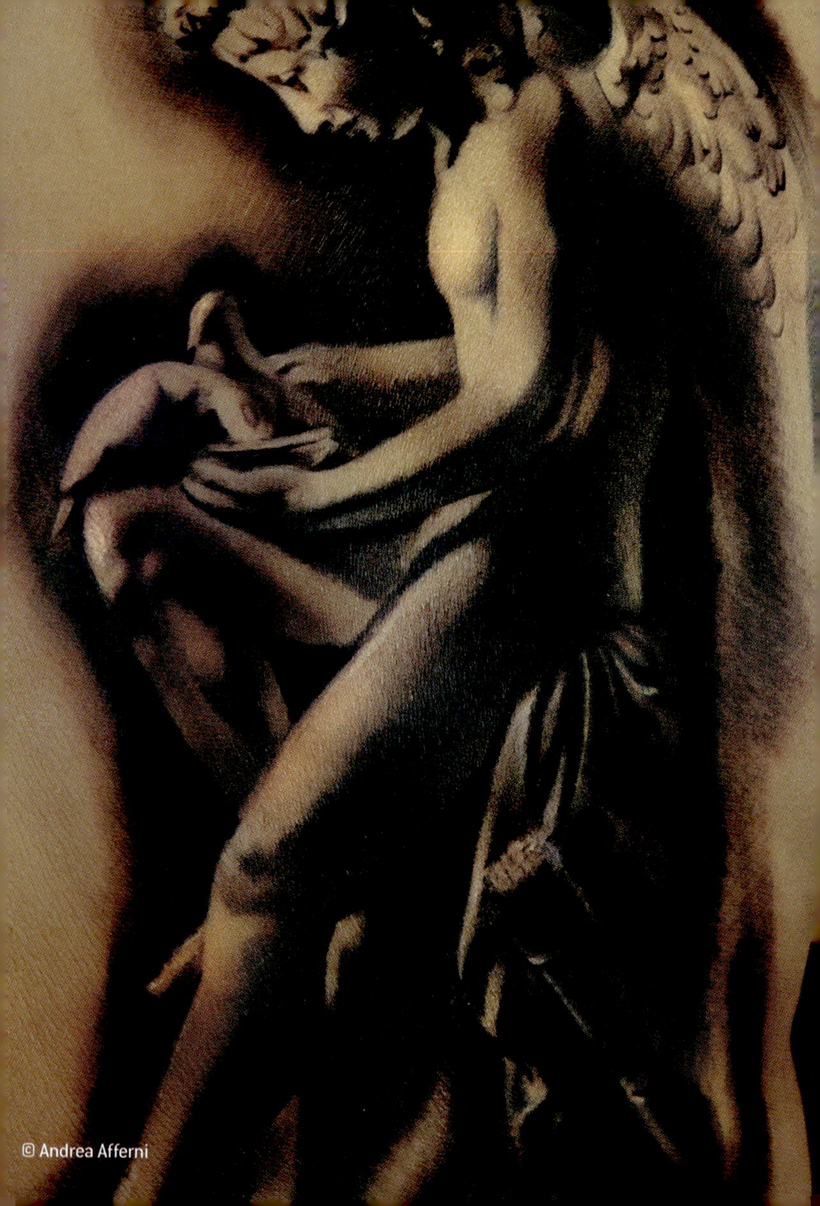
© Andrea Afferni

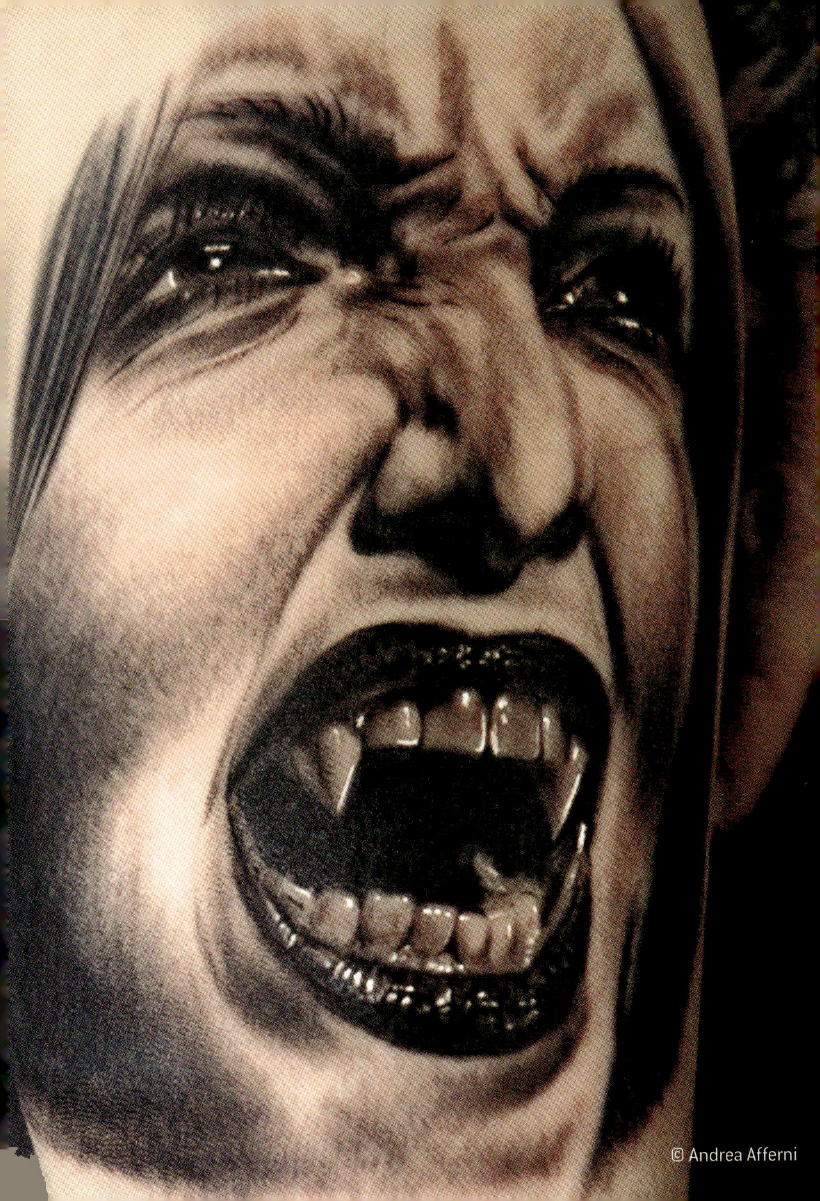
© Andrea Afferni

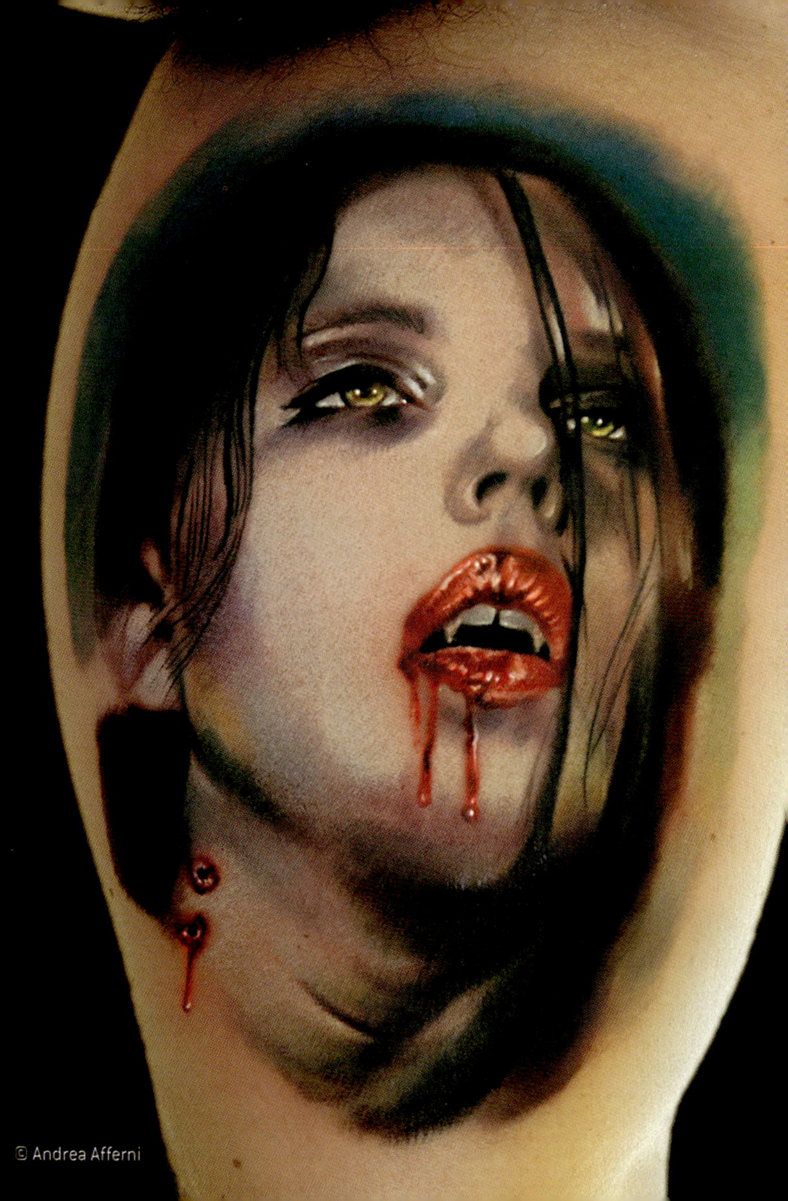
© Andrea Afferni

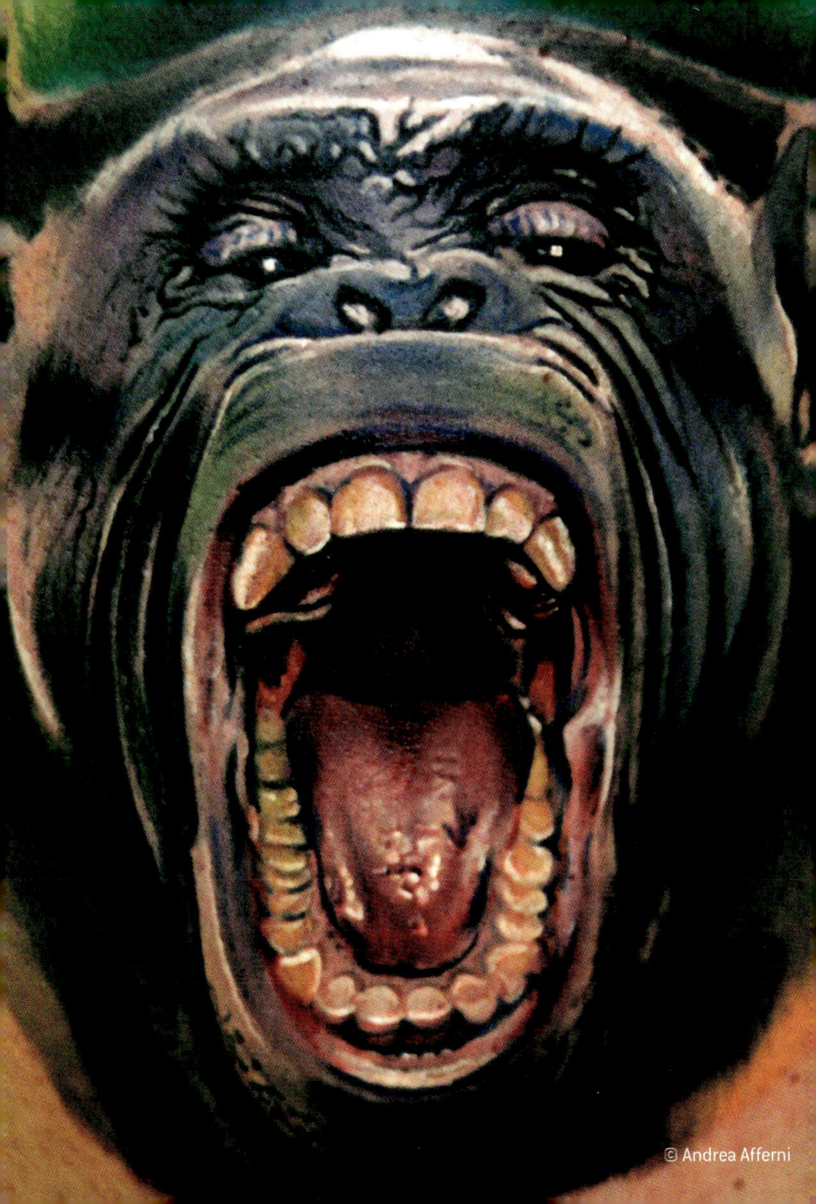
© Andrea Afferni

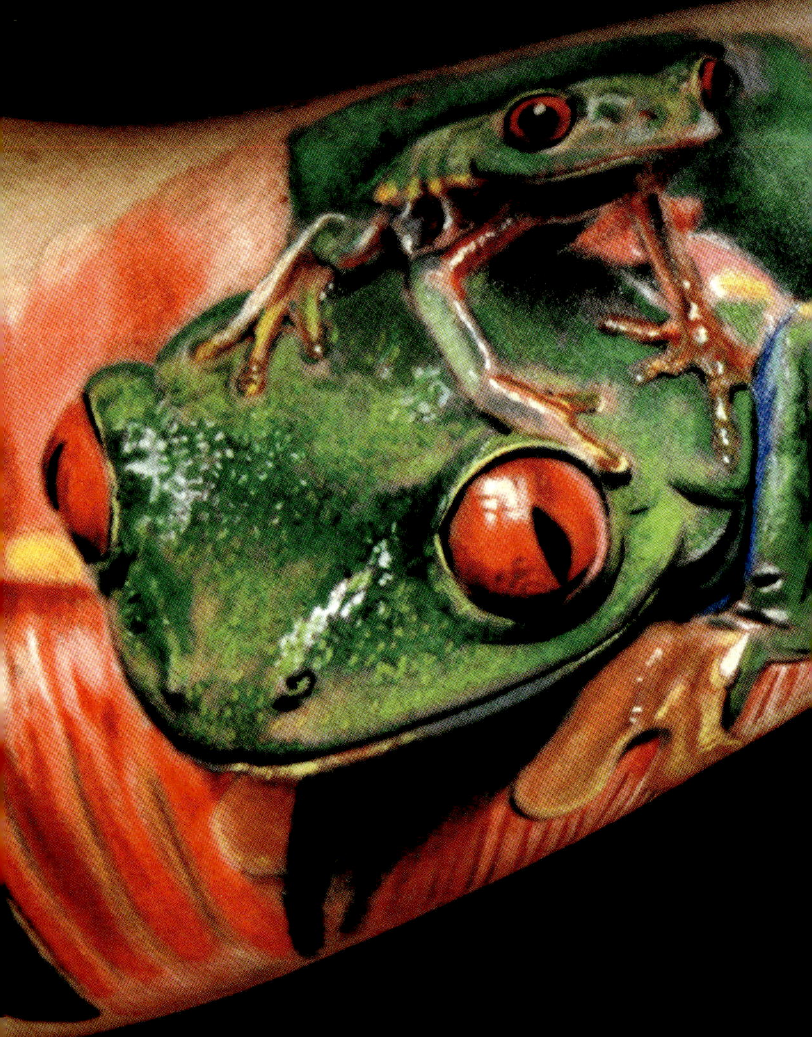

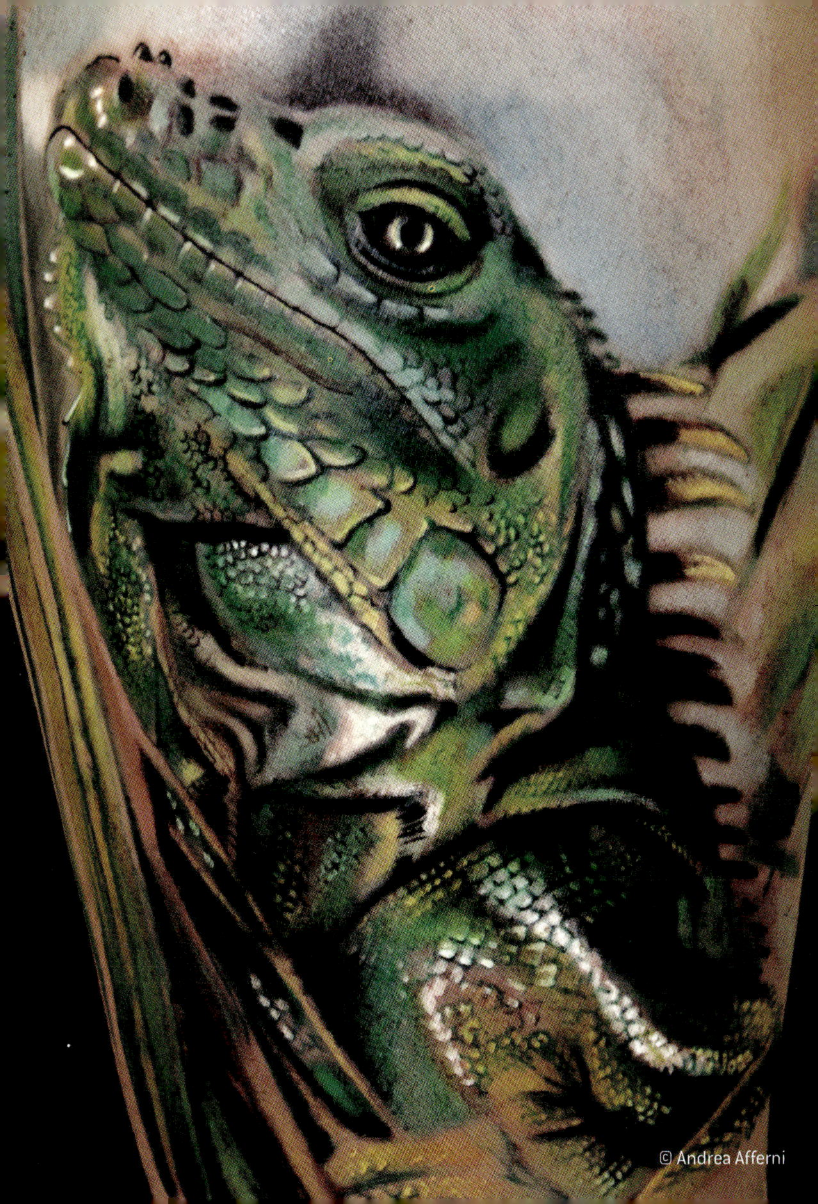
© Andrea Afferni

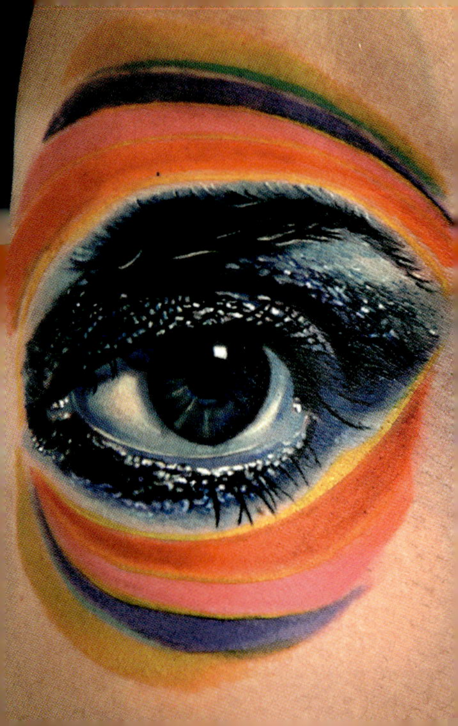

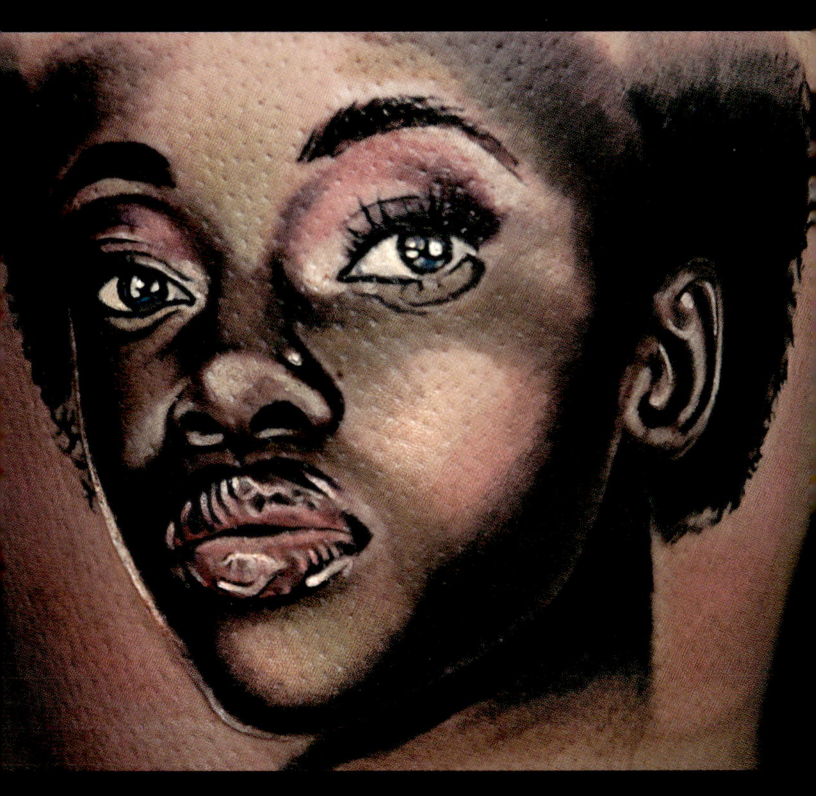

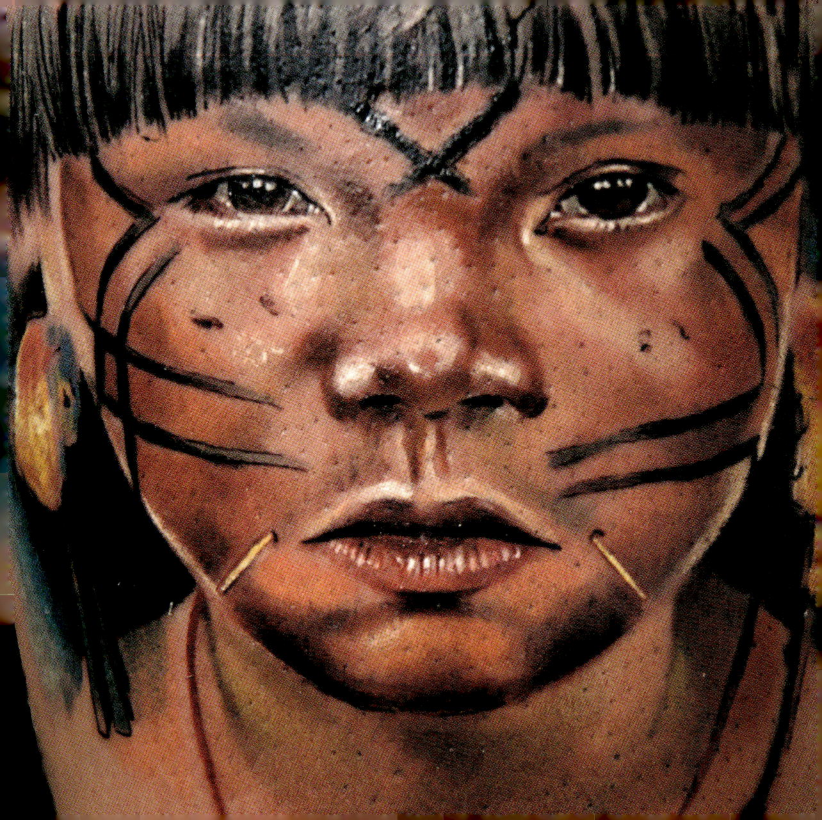

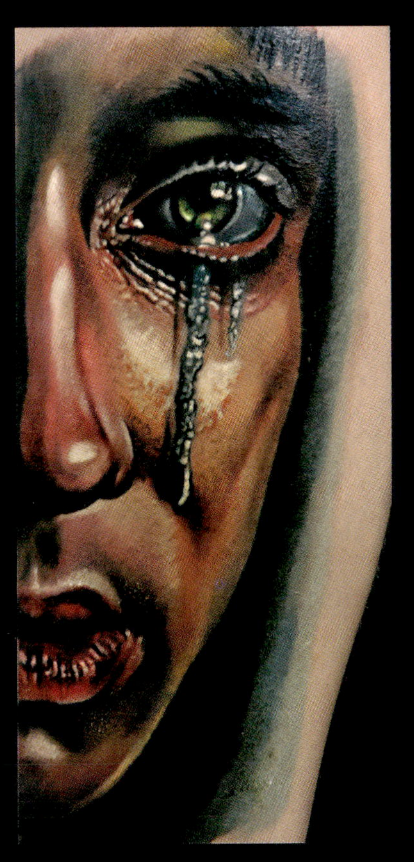

© Andrea Afferni

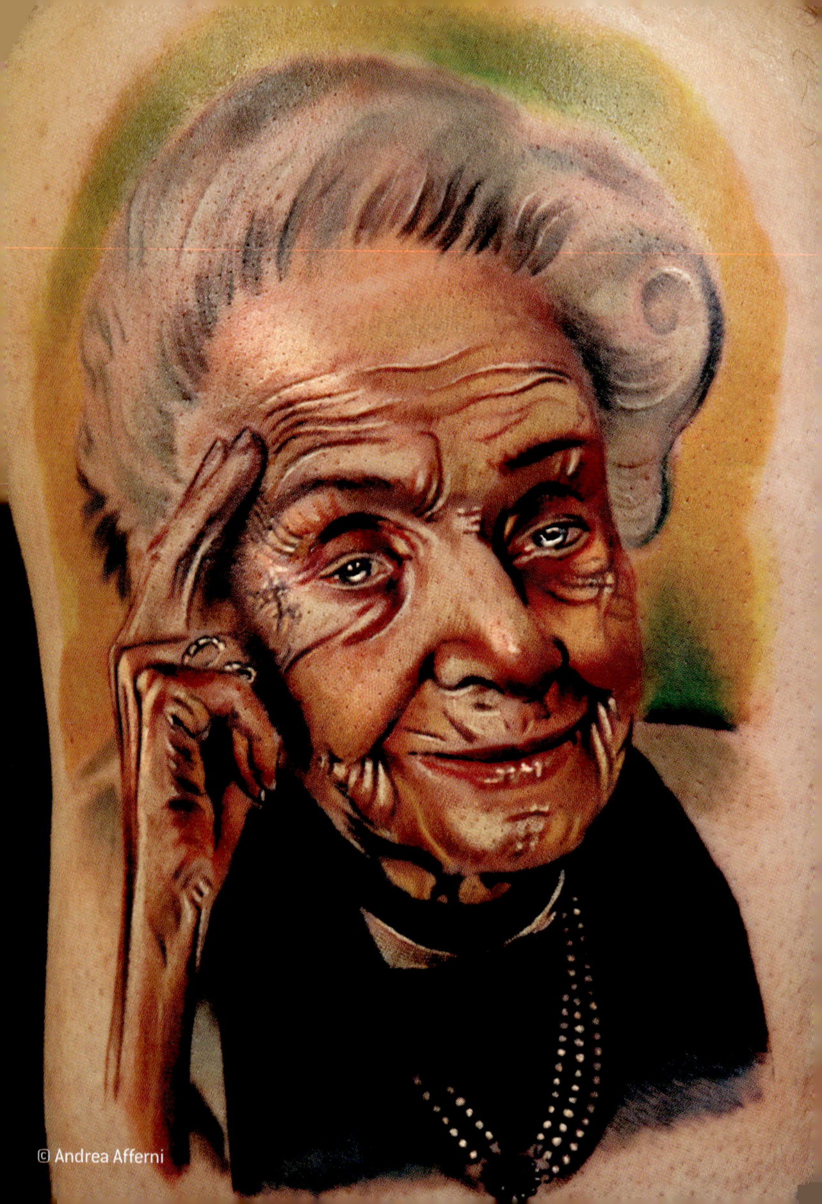

© Andrea Afferni

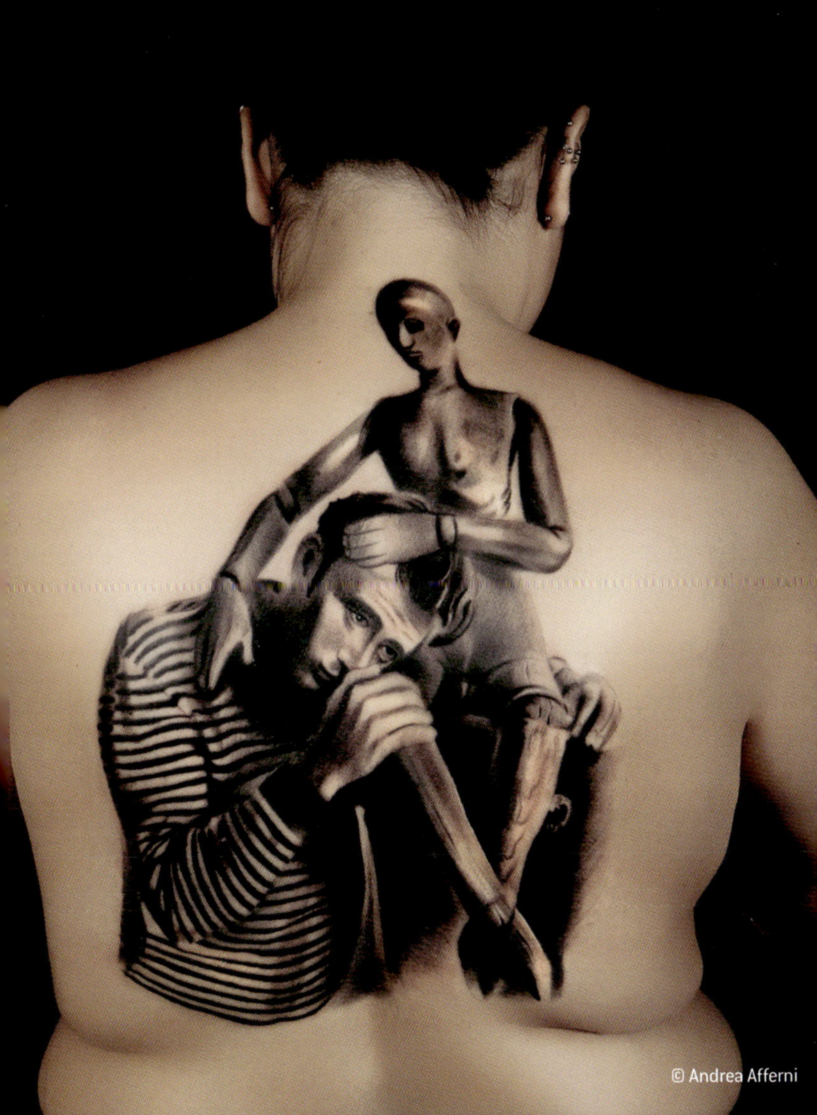
© Andrea Afferni

Tattoo artists

Artistes du tatouage

Künstler des Tattoo

Tatoeage-artiesten

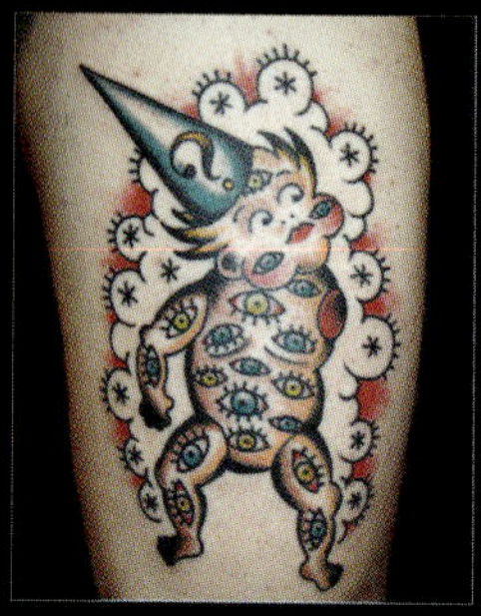

Adam Shrewsbury
apshrewsbury.com

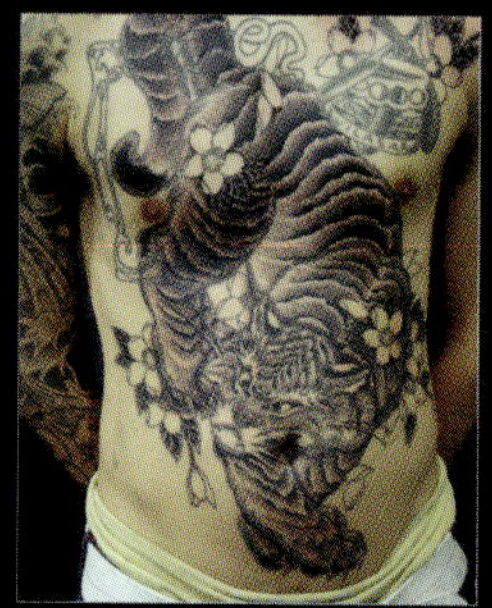

Agustín Cavalieri
www.agustincavalieri.com

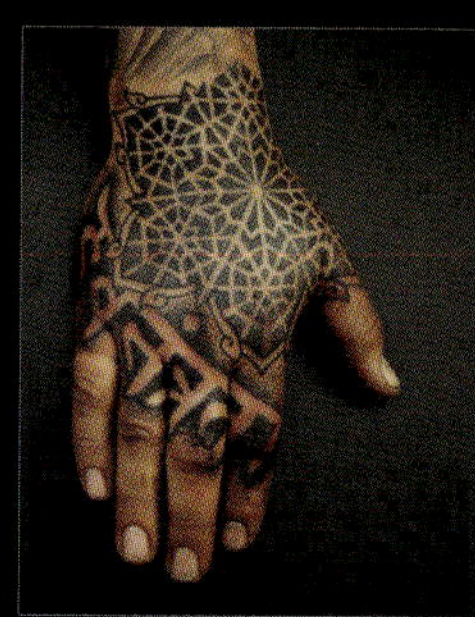

Amos
Macaroni Crew Tattoo, Varese
www.myspace.com
/amosblackink

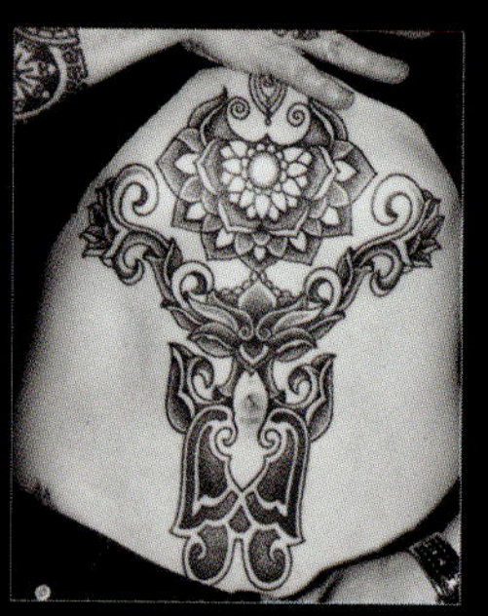

Calypso Tattoo
www.myspace.com
/calypsotattoo

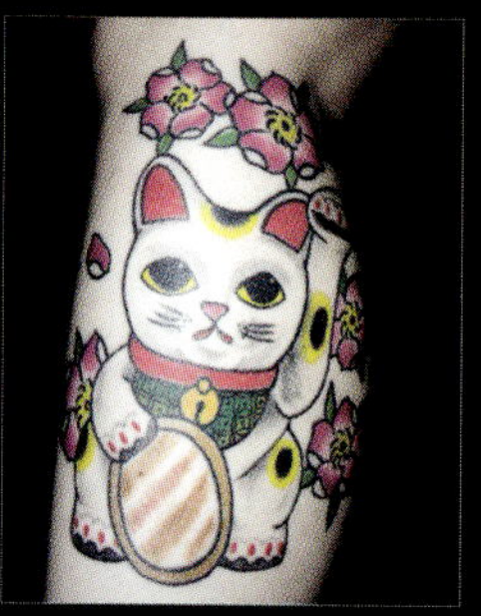

Chío
www.myspace.com
/chiopqd

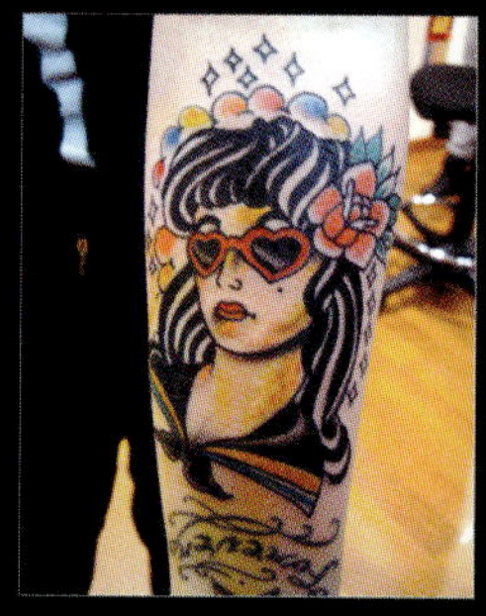

Daniel Anibal
www.myspace.com
/dannylove17

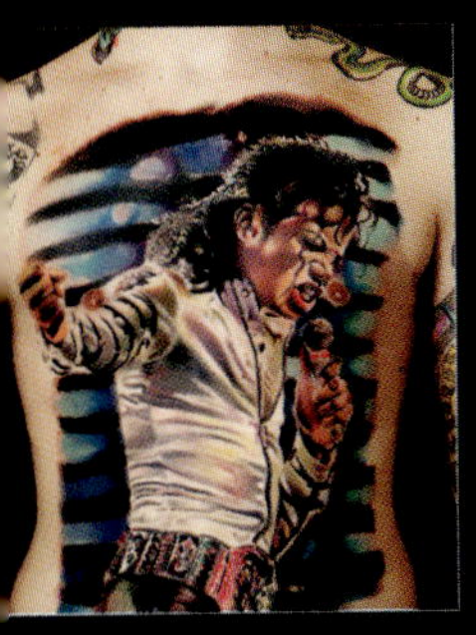

Andrea Afferni
www.afferniandrea.com

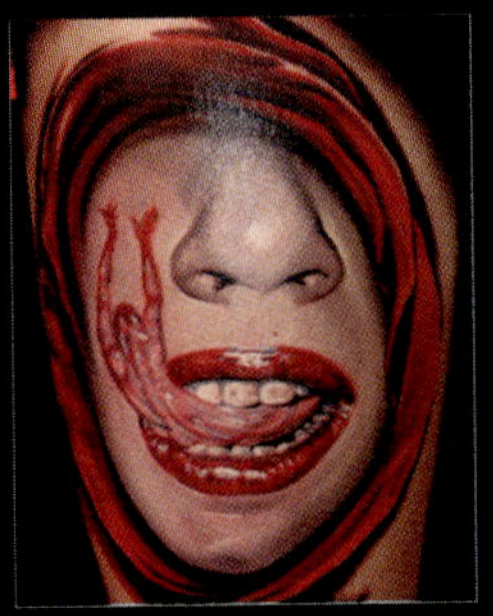

Antonio Proietti
Angel's Vision
www.myspace.com
/antonioproietti

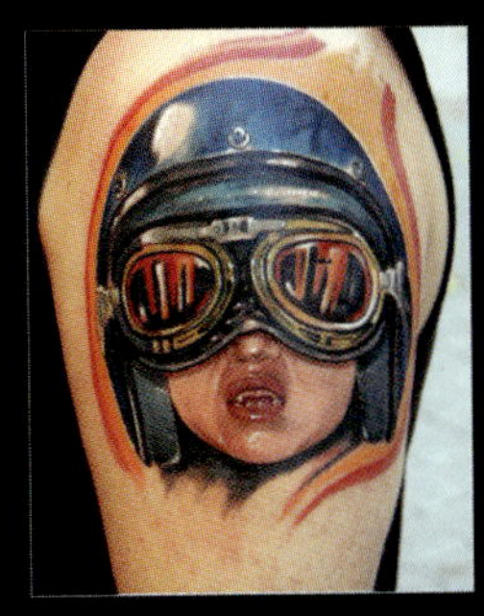

Barthez
www.myspace.com
/bartheztattoos

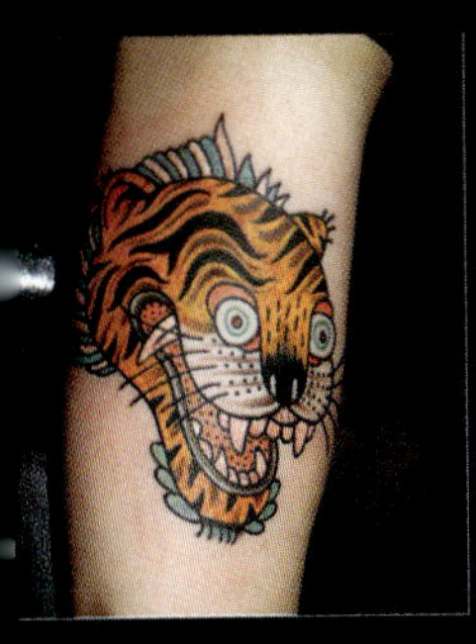

Deno
www.myspace.com
/denotattoo

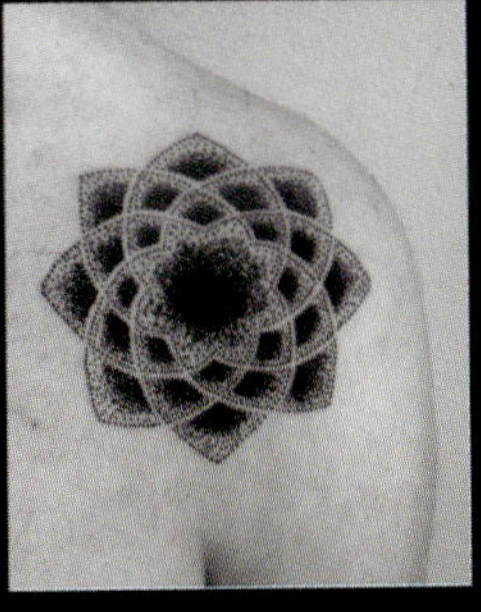

Fernando "Fefe" Hindenlang
www.myspace.com
/fefeeljefe

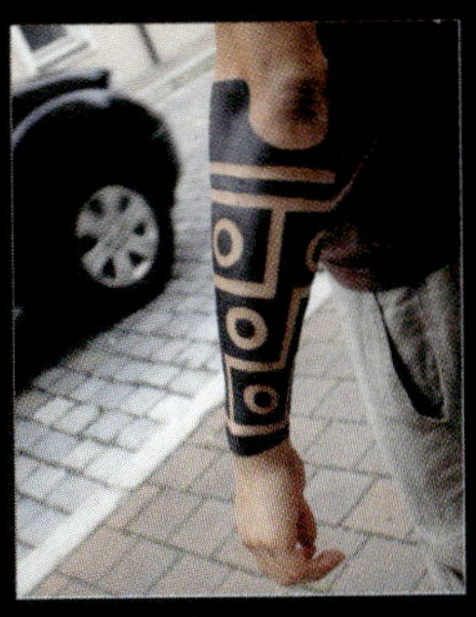

Gerhard Wiesbeck
www.myspace.com
/162872966

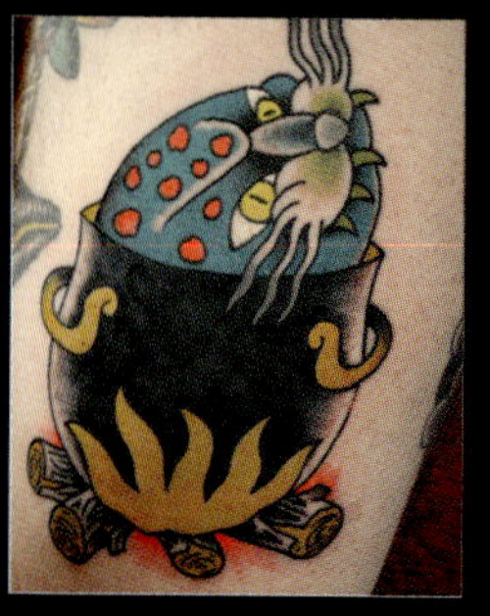

Gore
www.myspace.com
/goreart

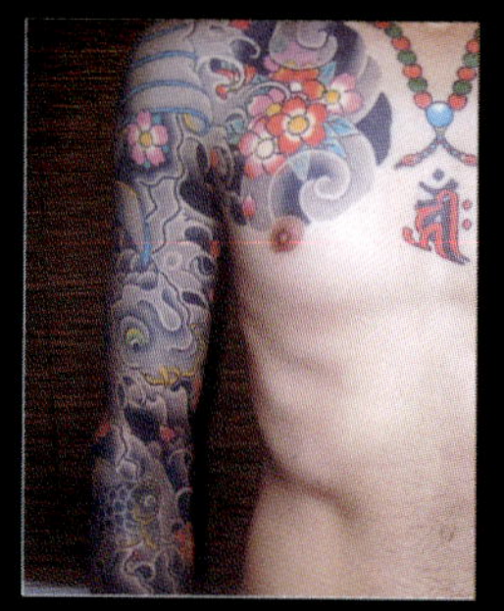

Horimomo
www.myspace.com
/1004196575

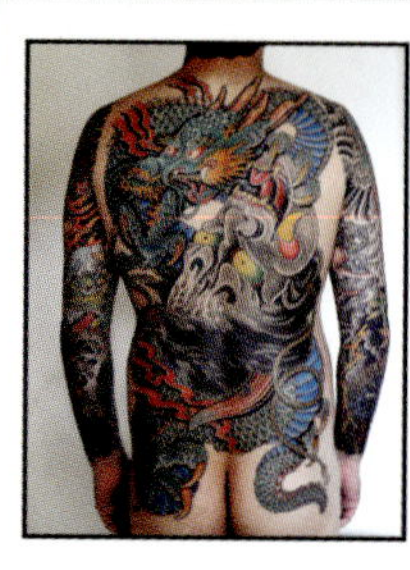

Javi Castaño
www.myspace.com
/javicastano

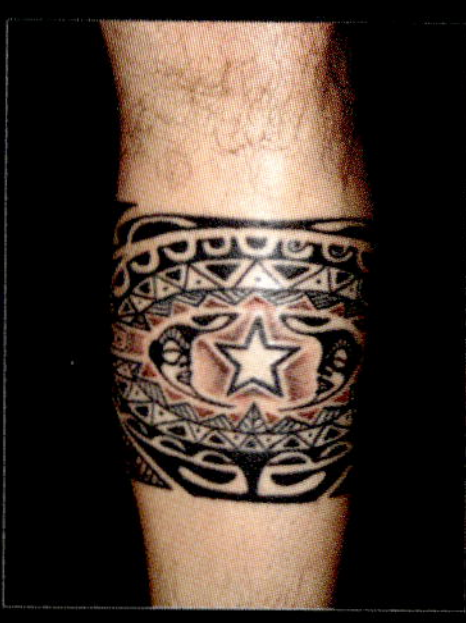

Juanky Tattoo
www.juankytattoo.com

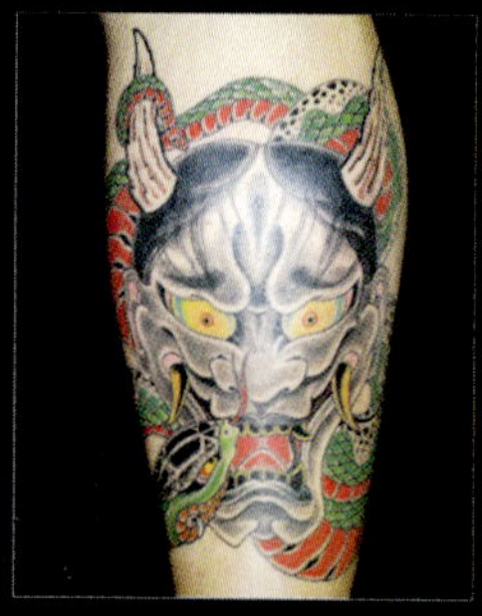

Leonardo Denegri
www.myspace.com
/leodenegri

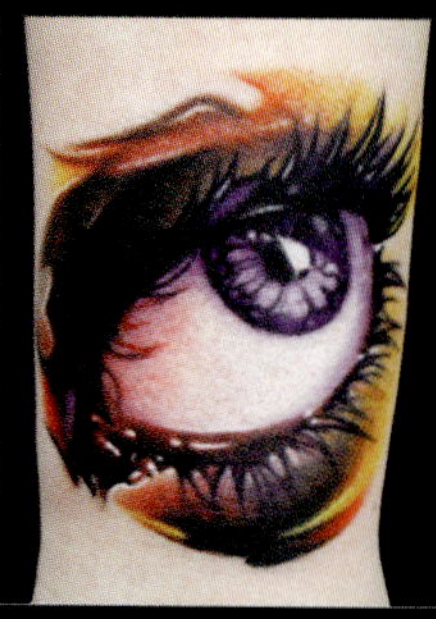

Máximo Lutz
Blood & Tears Tattoo
www.myspace.com
/maximolutztattoo

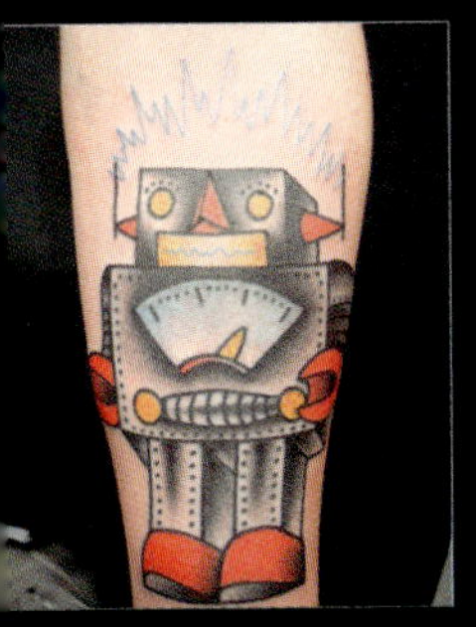

Javi Rodriguez
www.myspace.com
javilin88

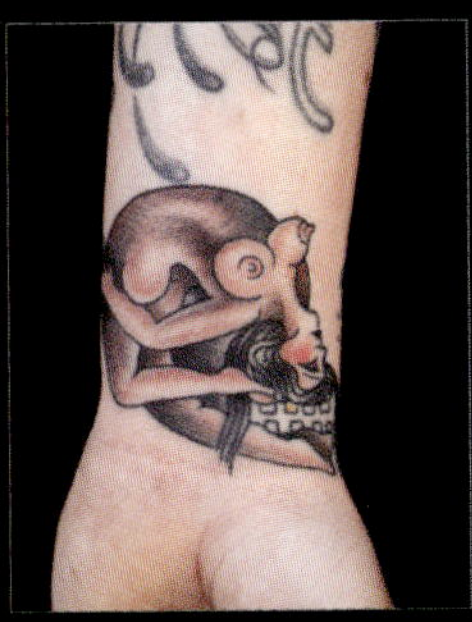

Jordi del Rey
www.myspace.com/
jordidelrey

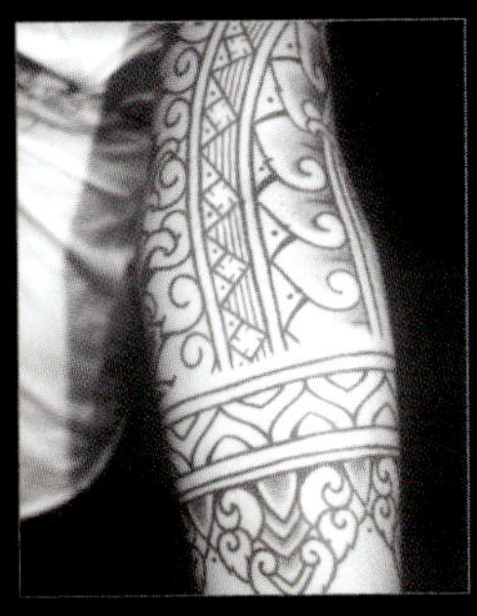

Jorge Terán
www.myspace.com
/tattoosbyteran

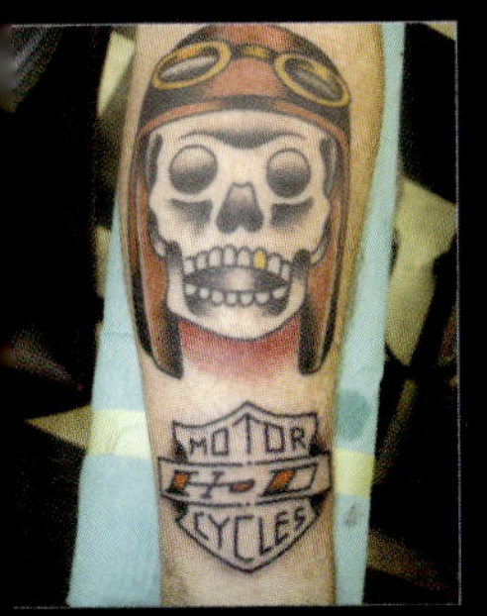

Michael Aul
www.myspace.com
457608

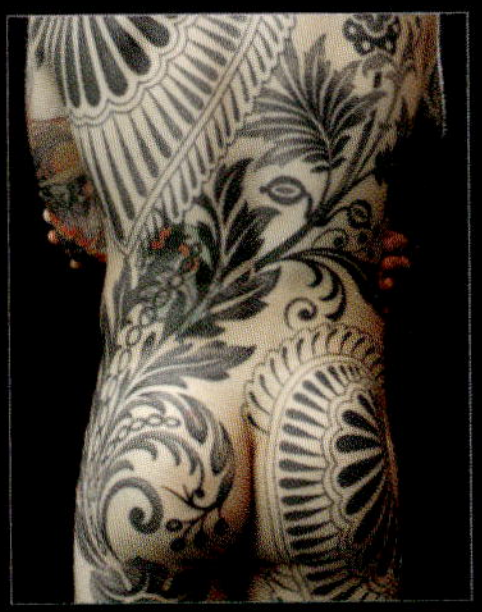

Nazareno Tubaro
www.tattoosbynaza.com

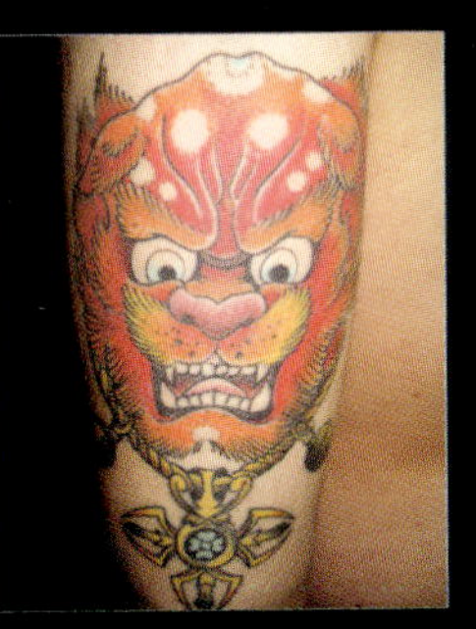

Néco
www.myspace.com
/_neco_

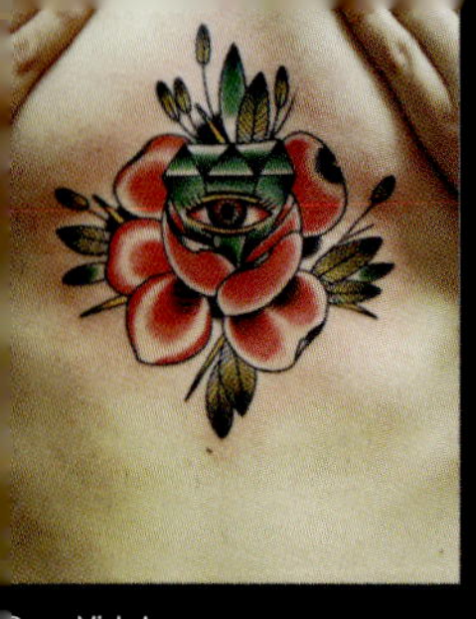

Pera Vidal
www.myspace.com
/stresstattoo

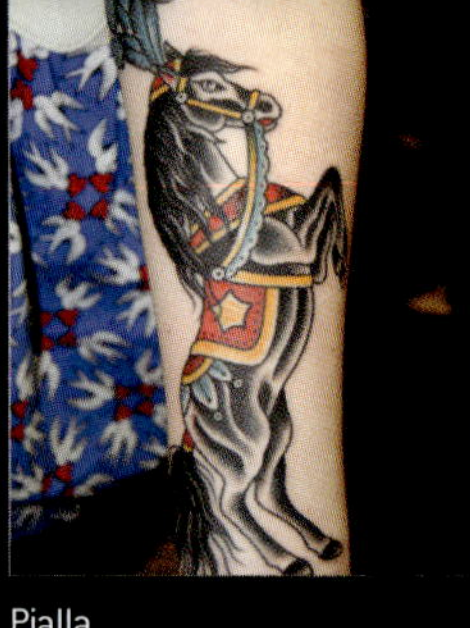

Pialla
www.myspace.com
/pialla

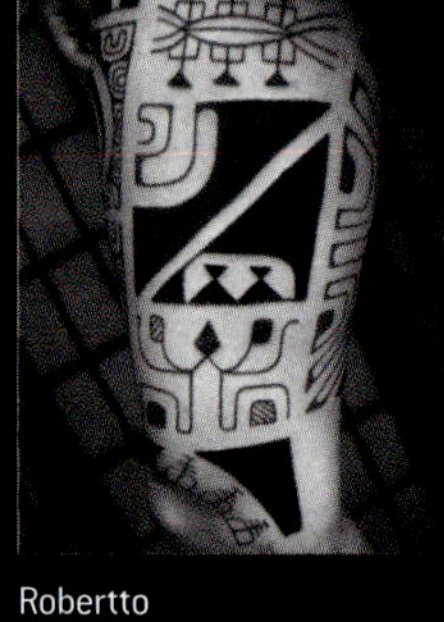

Robertto
Original Tattoo Studio
www.myspace.com
/originaltattoostudio

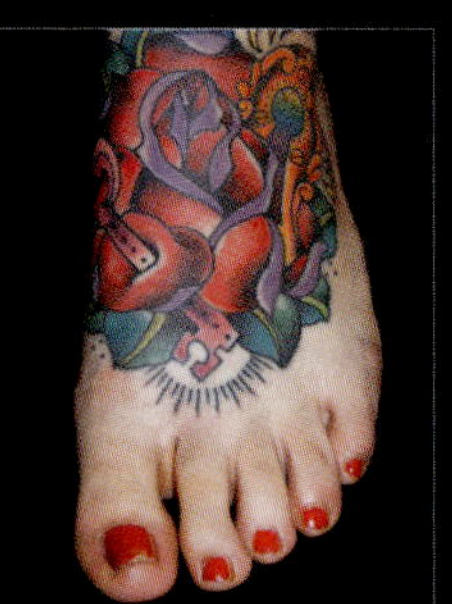

Soledad Aznar
www.stademonia.com

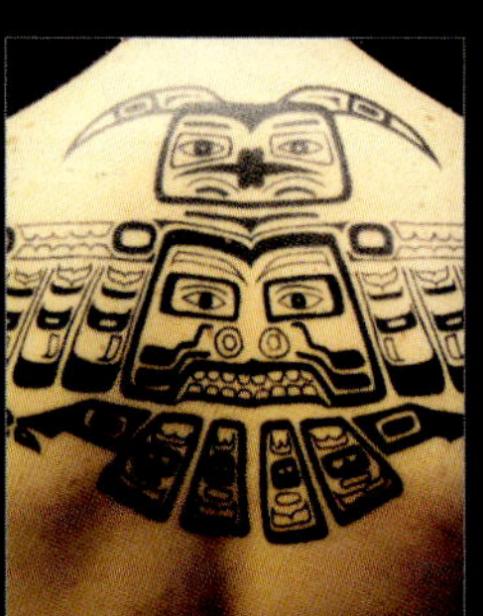

Xavi
Budatattoo
budatattoo.com

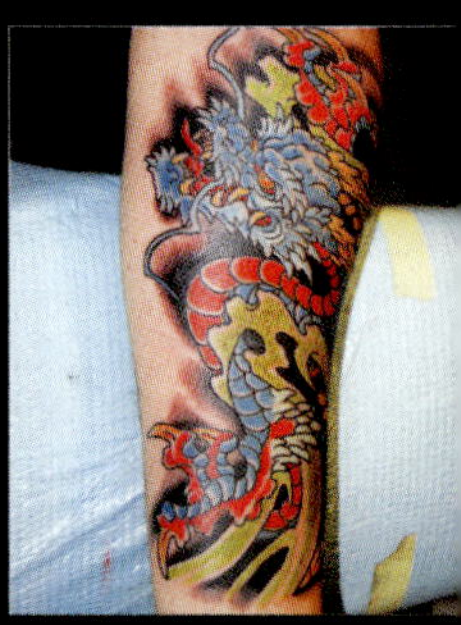

Zach Johnson
www.myspace.com
/zachjohnsontattoo

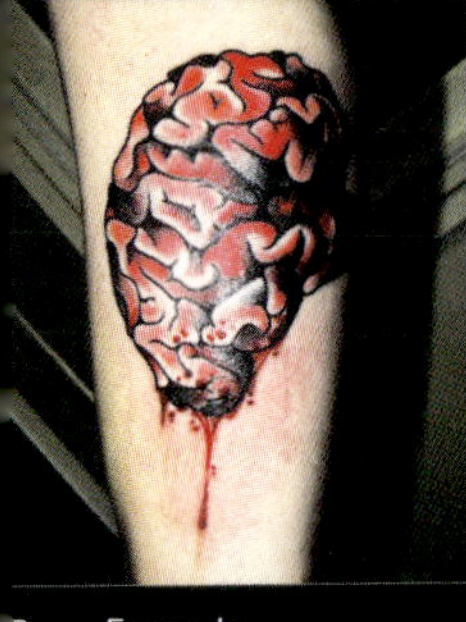

Roger Ferrando
www.myspace.com
/lunatictattoo

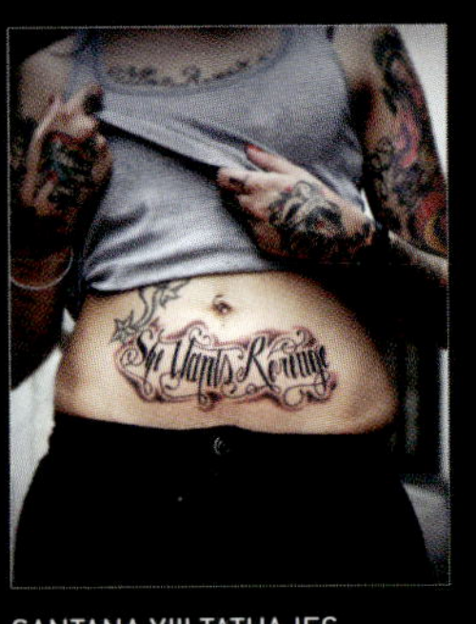

SANTANA XIII TATUAJES
"NACIDO Y CRIADO EN EL SUR"
http://www.flickr.com
/santanatrece

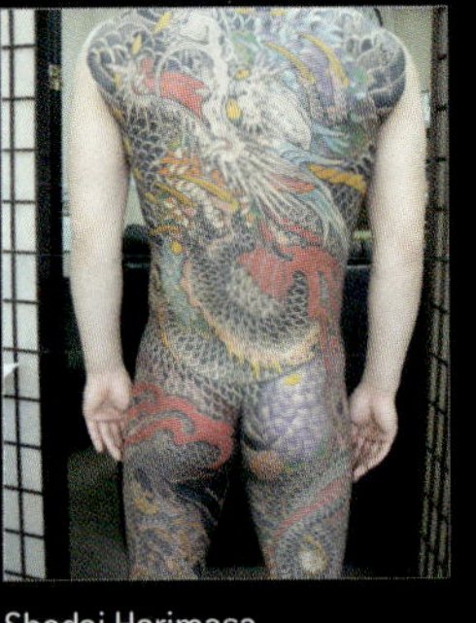

Shodai Horimasa
www.myspace.com
/horimasa